The Longman Anthology of British Literature
Fourth Edition

David Damrosch and Kevin J. H. Dettmar

General Editors

VOLUME 1A

THE MIDDLE AGES
Christopher Baswell *and* Anne Howland Schotter

Longman

New York   San Francisco   Boston
London   Toronto   Sydney   Tokyo   Singapore   Madrid
Mexico City   Munich   Paris   Cape Town   Hong Kong   Montreal

Editor-in-Chief: *Joseph Terry*
Associate Development Editor: *Erin Reilly*
Executive Marketing Manager: *Joyce Nilsen*
Senior Supplements Editor: *Donna Campion*
Production Manager: *Ellen MacElree*
Project Coordination, Text Design, and Page Makeup: GGS Higher Education Resources, a
　Division of PreMedia Global, Inc.
Cover Design Manager: *Nancy Danahy*
On the Cover: Anne, Duchess of Bedford, Kneeling Before the Virgin Mary and Saint Anne,
　from The Bedford Hours *early 15th century. By permission of the British Library.*
Photo Researcher: *Julie Tesser*
Senior Manufacturing Buyer: *Dennis J. Para*
Printer and Binder: *Quebecor-World/Taunton*
Cover Printer: *Lehigh-Phoenix Color/Hagerstown*

For permission to use copyrighted material, grateful acknowledgment is made to the copyright
holders on pages 621–622, which are hereby made part of this copyright page.

Library of Congress Cataloging-in-Publication Data
The Longman anthology of British literature / David Damrosch and Kevin J.H. Dettmar,
general editors.—4th ed.
　　p. cm.
　Includes bibliographical references and index.
　ISBN–13: 978–0–205–65524–3 (v. 1 : alk. paper)
　ISBN–10: 0–205–65524–6 (v. 1 : alk. paper)
　ISBN–13: 978–0–205–65519–9 (v. 2 : alk. paper)
　ISBN–10: 0–205–65519–X (v. 2 : alk. paper)　1. English literature. 2. Great Britain—Literary
collections.　I. Damrosch, David.　II. Dettmar, Kevin J. H., 1958–
PR1109.L69 2010
820.8—dc22

　　　　　　　　　　　　　　　　　　　　　　　　　　　　　　　　2009020241

Copyright © 2010, 2006, 2003, 1999 by Pearson Education, Inc.

ISBN-10 Single Volume Edition, Volume 1: 0-205-65524-6
ISBN-13 Single Volume Edition, Volume 1: 978-0-205-65524-3

ISBN-10 Volume 1A, The Middle Ages: 0-205-65530-0
ISBN-13 Volume 1A, The Middle Ages: 978-0-205-65530-4

ISBN-10 Volume 1B, The Early Modern Period: 0-205-65532-7
ISBN-13 Volume 1B, The Early Modern Period: 978-0-205-65532-8

ISBN-10 Volume 1C, The Restoration and the 18th Century: 0-205-65527-0
ISBN-13 Volume 1C, The Restoration and the 18th Century: 978-0-205-65527-4

Longman
is an imprint of

1 2 3 4 5 6 7 8 9 0—QWT—12 11 10 09

www.pearsonhighered.com

CONTENTS

The Middle Ages

ADDITIONAL RESOURCES

CULTURAL EDITIONS

Longman Cultural Editions present major texts along with a generous selection of contextual material that reveal the conversations and controversies of its historical moment. Taken together, our new edition and the Longman Cultural Editions offer an unparalleled set of materials for the enjoyment and study of British literary culture from its earliest beginnings to the present. One Longman Cultural Edition is available at no additional cost when packaged with the anthology. Contact your local Pearson Publisher's Representative for packaging details. Some titles of interest for Volume One include the following works:

Beowulf, Anonymous. Translated by Alan Sullivan and Timothy Murphy & ed. Anderson
ISBN-10: 0-321-10720-9 | ISBN-13: 978-0-321-10720-6

Julius Caesar. Shakespeare. ed. Arnold.
ISBN-10: 0-321-20943-5 | ISBN-13: 978-0-321-20943-6

Henry IV, Parts One and Two. Shakespeare. ed. Levao
ISBN-10: 0-321-18274-X | ISBN-13: 978-0-321-18274-6

The Merchant of Venice, Shakespeare. ed. Danson
ISBN-10: 0-321-16419-9 | ISBN-13: 978-0-321-16419-3

Antony and Cleopatra, Shakespeare, ed. Quint
ISBN-10: 0-321-19874-3 | ISBN-13: 978-0-321-19874-7

Hamlet, Shakespeare. ed. Jordan
ISBN-10: 0-321-31729-7 | ISBN-13: 978-0-321-31729-2

King Lear, Shakespeare. ed. McEachern
ISBN-10: 0-321-10722-5 | ISBN-13: 978-0-321-10722-0

Othello and *The Tragedy of Mariam*, Shakespeare and Cary. ed. Carroll and Damrosch
ISBN-10: 0-321-09699-1 | ISBN-13: 978-0-321-09699-9

The History of the Adventures of Joseph Andrews, Fielding. ed. Potkay
ISBN-10: 0-321-20937-0 | ISBN-13: 978-0-321-20937-5

The Castle of Otranto and *The Man of Feeling*, Walpole and MacKenzie. ed. Mandell
ISBN-10: 0-321-39892-0 | ISBN-13: 978-0-321-39892-5

For a complete listing of Longman Cultural Edition titles, please visit www.pearsonhighered.com/literature.

WEB SITE FOR *THE LONGMAN ANTHOLOGY* *OF BRITISH LITERATURE*

www.myliteraturekit.com

The fourth edition makes connections beyond its covers as well as within them. The Web site we have developed for the course provides a wealth of resources:

Student Resources

- **Discussion Questions for Major Selections and Perspectives Sections.** Designed to prepare students for the kind of deeper-level analysis expected in class discussions, these compelling prompts are available for each period introduction and for major selections and Perspectives groupings.

- **Self-Grading Multiple Choice Practice Questions.** Available for each period introduction and for all major authors and Perspectives groupings, these objective practice quizzes are designed to help students review their basic understanding of the reading.

- **An Interactive Timeline.** Our interactive timeline helps students visualize the key literary, political, and cultural events of an era. Each event is accompanied by a detailed explanation, usually including references to relevant texts that can be found in the anthology, links to helpful sites, and colorful pictures and illustrations.

- **Links to Valuable British Literature Resources.** Our Online Research Guide provides a wealth of annotated links to excellent Web resources on major authors, texts, and related historical and cultural movements and events.

- **An Archive of Additional Texts.** Our new online archive contains a wealth of selections that could not fit within the bounds of the print anthology. A listing of many of these works can be found in context in our table of contents.

- **Additional Reference Materials.** The Web site also features an extensive glossary of literary and cultural terms, useful summaries of British political and religious organizations, and of money, weights, and measures. For further reading, we provide carefully selected, up-to-date bibliographies for each period and author.

Instructor's Section

- **An Online Instructor's Manual (0-205-67976-5).** The online version of our print manual uses a hyperlink format to allow instructors to jump directly to the author or selection they want to access.

- **PowerPoint Presentations.** A visually rich presentation is available for each period.

- **Sample Syllabi.** Our collection of syllabi include samples of a wide variety of approaches to both the survey-level and period-specific courses.

PREFACE

Literature has a double life. Born in one time and place and read in another, literary works are at once products of their age and independent creations, able to live on long after their original world has disappeared. The goal *The Longman Anthology of British Literature* is to present a wealth of poetry, prose, and drama from the full sweep of the literary history of Great Britain and its empire, and to do so in ways that will bring out both the works' original cultural contexts and their lasting aesthetic power. These aspects are in fact closely related: form and content, verbal music and social meanings, go hand in hand. This double life makes literature, as Aristotle said, "the most philosophical" of all the arts, intimately connected to ideas and to realities that the writer transforms into moving patterns of words. The challenge is to show these works in the contexts in which, and for which, they were written, while at the same time not trapping them within those contexts. The warm response this anthology has received from the hundreds of teachers who have adopted it in its first three editions reflects the growing consensus that we are not forced to choose between the literature's aesthetic and cultural dimensions. Our users' responses have now guided us in seeing how we can improve our anthology further, so as to be most pleasurable and stimulating to students, most useful to teachers, and most responsive to ongoing developments in literary studies. This preface can serve as a road map to this book's goals and structure.

NEW TO THIS EDITION

- **Period at a Glance features.** These informative illustrated features open each volume, providing thumbnail sketches of daily life during each period.

- **Enhanced Web site.** A new fourth edition site includes an archive of valuable texts from previous editions, detailed bibliographies, an interactive timeline, discussion questions, and Web resources for major selections and authors.

- **New major, classic texts.** In response to instructors' requests, major additions of important works frequently taught in the British Literature course have been added, including the following selections:
  - A selection from the Irish epic *The Táin Bó Cuailnge*
  - William Baldwin's *Beware the Cat* (sometimes called the first English novel)
  - Edmund Spenser's *The Faerie Queene, Book 6* and *the Cantos of Mutabilitie*
  - William Shakespeare's *Othello* and *King Lear*

- **New selections across the anthology.** We have continued to refine our contents, adding new selections to established units across the anthology, including authors such as John Skelton, Fynes Moryson, Edmund Spenser, and John Donne.

- **Penguin Classics editions of *Beowulf* translated by Michael Alexander and *Sir Gawain and the Green Knight* translated by Brian Stone.** The *Longman Anthology of British Literature* now includes authoritative Penguin Classic translations, trusted throughout the world as editions of classics texts that are both riveting and scholarly.

- **New Perspectives groupings of works in cultural context.** "Perspectives" groupings new to this edition include *The English Sonnet and Sonnet Sequences in the Sixteenth Century, Early Modern Books*, and *England, Britain, and the World*.

- **New Response pairings.** A selection from Sir Francis Bacon's *New Atlantis* is paired with Sir Thomas More's *Utopia*.

LITERATURE IN ITS TIME—AND IN OURS

When we engage with a rich literary history that extends back over a thousand years, we often encounter writers who assume their readers know all sorts of things that are little known today: historical facts, social issues, literary and cultural references. Beyond specific information, these works will have come out of a very different literary culture than our own. Even the contemporary British Isles present a cultural situation—or a mix of cultures—very different from what North American readers encounter at home, and these differences only increase as we go farther back in time. A major emphasis of this anthology is to bring the works' original cultural moment to life: not because the works simply or naively reflect that moment of origin, but because they do refract it in fascinating ways. British literature is both a major heritage for modern North America and, in many ways, a very distinct culture; reading British literature will regularly give an experience both of connection and of difference. Great writers create imaginative worlds that have their own compelling internal logic, and a prime purpose of this anthology is to help readers to understand the formal means—whether of genre, rhetoric, or style—with which these writers have created works of haunting beauty. At the same time, as Virginia Woolf says in *A Room of One's Own*, the gossamer threads of the artist's web are joined to reality "with bands of steel."

The Longman Anthology pursues a range of strategies to bring out both the beauty of these webs of words and their points of contact with reality and to bring related authors and works together in several ways:

- ☞ PERSPECTIVES: **Broad groupings that illuminate underlying issues in a variety of the major works of a period.**

- ☞ AND ITS TIME: **A focused cluster that illuminates a specific cultural moment or a debate to which an author is responding.**

- ☞ RESPONSES: **One or more texts in which later authors in the tradition respond creatively to the challenging texts of their forebears.**

These groupings provide a range of means of access to the literary culture of each period. The Perspectives sections do much more than record what major writers thought about an issue: they give a variety of views in a range of voices, to illustrate the wider culture within which the literature was being written. Theological reflections by the pioneering scientist Isaac Newton; these and many other vivid readings featured in Volume One give rhetorical as well as social contexts for the poems, plays, and stories around them. Perspectives sections typically relate to several major authors of the period, as with a section on the sixteenth-century sonnet that brings the poetry of Edmund Spenser and Sir Philip Sidney into conversation with less widely read figures like Sir Thomas Wyatt and Henry Howard, Earl of Surrey. Most of the writers included in Perspectives sections are important figures of the period who might be neglected if they were listed on their own with just a few pages each; grouping them together has proved to be useful pedagogically as well as intellectually. Perspectives sections may also include work by a major author whose primary listing appears elsewhere in the period; thus, a Perspective section on the Civil War features a selection from Milton's *Eikonoklastes*, and a section on British perceptions of other lands includes a selection from Spenser's *View of the State of Ireland*, so as to give a rounded presentation of the issue in ways that can inform the reading of those authors in their individual sections.

When we present a major work "And Its Time," we give a cluster of related materials to suggest the context within which the work was written. Thus Sir Philip Sidney's great *Apology for Poetry* is accompanied by readings showing the controversy that was raging at the time concerning the nature and value of poetry. Some of the writers in these groupings and in our Perspectives sections have not traditionally been seen as literary figures, but all have produced lively and intriguing works, from medieval clerics writing about saints and sea monsters, to a polemical seventeenth-century tract giving *The Arraignment of Lewd, Idle, Froward, and Unconstant Women,* to economic writings by William Petty—of the type parodied by Swift in his "Modest Proposal."

We also include "Responses" to significant texts in the British literary tradition, demonstrating the sometimes far-reaching influence these works have had over the decades and centuries, and sometimes across oceans and continents. *Beowulf* and John Gardner's *Grendel* are separated by the Atlantic ocean, perhaps eleven hundred or twelve hundred years—and, most notably, by their attitude toward the poem's monster. The *Morte Darthur* is reinterpreted comically by the 1970s British comedy troupe Monty Python's Flying Circus.

WHAT IS BRITISH LITERATURE?

Stepping back from the structure of the book, let us define our basic terms: What is "British" literature? What is literature itself? And just what should an anthology of this material look like at the present time? The term "British" can mean many things, some of them contradictory, some of them even offensive to people on whom the name has been imposed. If the term "British" has no ultimate essence, it does have a history. The first British were Celtic people who inhabited the British Isles and the northern coast of France (still called Brittany) before various Germanic tribes of Angles and Saxons moved onto the islands in the fifth and sixth centuries. Gradually the Angles and Saxons amalgamated into the Anglo-Saxon culture that became dominant in the southern and eastern regions of Britain and then spread outward; the old British people were pushed west, toward what became known as Cornwall,

Wales, and Ireland, which remained independent kingdoms for centuries, as did Celtic Scotland to the north. By an ironic twist of linguistic fate, the Anglo-Saxons began to appropriate the term "British" from the Britons they had displaced, and they took as a national hero the early, semimythic Welsh King Arthur. By the seventeenth century, English monarchs had extended their sway over Wales, Ireland, and Scotland, and they began to refer to their holdings as "Great Britain." Today, Great Britain includes England, Wales, Scotland, and Northern Ireland, but does not include the Republic of Ireland, which has been independent since 1922.

This anthology uses "British" in a broad sense, as a geographical term encompassing the whole of the British Isles. For all its fraught history, it seems a more satisfactory term than to speak simply of "English" literature, for two reasons. First, most speakers of English live in countries that are not the focus of this anthology (for instance, the United States and Canada); second, while the English language and its literature have long been dominant in the British Isles, other cultures in the region have always used other languages and have produced great literature in these languages. Important works by Irish, Welsh, and Scots writers appear regularly in the body of this anthology, some of them written directly in their languages and presented here in translation, and others written in an English inflected by the rhythms, habits of thought, and modes of expression characteristic of these other languages and the people who use them.

We use the term "literature" in a similarly capacious sense, to refer to a range of artistically shaped works written in a charged language, appealing to the imagination at least as much as to discursive reasoning. It is only relatively recently that creative writers have been able to make a living composing poems, plays, and novels, and only in the past hundred years or so has creating "belles lettres" or high literary art been thought of as a sharply separate sphere of activity from other sorts of writing that the same authors would regularly produce. Sometimes, early modern poets wrote sonnets to reflect and honor loves won and lost; at other times, they wrote sonnets to realize courtly ambition and material gain; and always, they wrote their sonnets with an eye to posterity, and with the goal of a poetic form of immortality ("Not marble, nor the gilded monuments / Of princes, shall outlive this pow'rful rhyme"—Shakespeare, Sonnet 55).

VARIETIES OF LITERARY EXPERIENCE

Above all, we have strived to give as full a presentation as possible to the varieties of great literature produced from the eighth to the eighteenth centuries in the British Isles, by women as well as by men, in outlying regions as well as in the metropolitan center of London, and in prose, drama, and verse alike. For these earlier periods, we include More's entire Utopia, Baldwin's Beware the Cat, and Milton's Paradise Lost, and we give major space to narrative poetry by Chaucer and Spenser, and to Swift's Gulliver's Travels, among others. Drama appears throughout the anthology, from the medieval Second Play of the Shepherds and Mankind to a range of early modern and restoration plays: Marlowe's The Tragical History of Dr. Faustus, Shakespeare's Twelfth Night, Othello, and King Lear, Jonson's The Alchemist, William Wyncherly's The Country Wife, and John Gay's The Beggar's Opera. Finally, lyric poetry appears in profusion throughout the anthology, from early lyrics by anonymous Middle English poets and the trenchantly witty Dafydd ap Gwilym to the great flowering of lyric poetry in the early modern period in the writings of Shakespeare, Sidney, and Spenser—to name just the "S's"—to the formal perfection and august rhetoric of Restoration and eighteenth-century poets like Swift, Dryden, Pope, and Johnson. Prose fiction always struggles for space in a literary anthology, but we close this volume with a selection from some of the most vital novelistic writing of the eighteenth century. We hope that this anthology will show that the great works of earlier centuries can speak to us compellingly today, their value only increased by the resistance they offer to our views of ourselves and our world. To read and reread the full sweep of this literature is to be struck anew by the degree to which the most radically new works are rooted in centuries of prior innovation.

ILLUSTRATING VISUAL CULTURE

Another important context for literary production has been a different kind of culture: the visual. This edition includes a suite of color plates in each volume, along with hundreds of black-and-white illustrations throughout the anthology, chosen to show artistic and cultural images that figured importantly for literary creation. Sometimes, a poem refers to a specific painting, or more generally emulates qualities of a school of visual art. At other times, more popular materials like frontispieces may illuminate scenes in early modern writing. In some cases, visual and literary creation have merged, as in William Hogarth's series *A Rake's Progress*, included in Volume One. Thumbnail portraits of many major authors mark the beginning of author introductions.

AIDS TO UNDERSTANDING

We have attempted to contextualize our selections in suggestive rather than exhaustive ways, trying to enhance rather than overwhelm the experience of reading the texts themselves. Thus, when difficult or archaic words need defining in poems, we use glosses in the margins, so as to disrupt the reader's eye as little as possible; footnotes are intended to be concise and informative, rather than massive or interpretive. Important literary and social terms are defined when they are used. For convenience of reference, new Period at a Glance features appear at the beginning of each period, providing a thumbnail sketch of daily life during the period. With these informative, illustrated features readers can begin to connect with the world that the anthology is illuminating. Sums of money, for instance, can be understood better when one knows what a loaf of bread cost at the time; the symbolic values attached to various articles of clothing are sometimes difficult for today's readers to decipher, without some information about contemporary apparel and its class associations. And the gradual shift of the Empire's population from rural regions to urban centers is graphically presented in charts for each period.

LOOKING—AND LISTENING—FURTHER

Beyond the boundaries of the anthology itself, we have expanded our Web site, available to all readers at www.myliteraturekit.com; this site gives a wealth of information, annotated links to related sites, and an archive of texts for further reading. For reference, there is also an extensive glossary of literary and cultural terms available there, together with useful summaries of British political and religious organization, and of money, weights, and measures. For further reading, carefully selected, up-to-date bibliographies for each period and for each author can be found in on the

Web site. A guide to our media resources can be found at the end of the table of contents.

For instructors, we have revised and expanded our popular companion volume, *Teaching British Literature*, written directly by the anthology editors, 600 pages in length, available free to everyone who adopts the anthology.

David Damrosch & Kevin J. H. Dettmar

ACKNOWLEDGMENTS

In planning and preparing the fourth edition of our anthology, the editors have been fortunate to have the support, advice, and assistance of many committed and gifted people. Our editor, Joe Terry, has been unwavering in his enthusiasm for the book and his commitment to it; he and his associates Roth Wilkofsky, Mary Ellen Curley, and Joyce Nilsen have supported us in every possible way throughout the process, ably assisted by Katy Needle, Rosie Ellis, and Annie England. Our developmental editor Erin Reilly guided us and our manuscript from start to finish with unfailing acuity and seemingly unwavering patience. Our copyeditor Stephanie Magean seamlessly integrated the work of a dozen editors. Erin Reilly, Elizabeth Bravo and Stefanie Liebman have devoted enormous energy and creativity to revising our Web site. Karyn Morrison cleared our many permissions, and Julie Tesser tracked down and cleared our many new illustrations. Finally, Nancy Wolitzer and Ellen MacElree oversaw the production with sunny good humor and kept the book successfully on track on a very challenging schedule, working closely with Doug Bell at GGS Higher Education Resources.

Our plans for the new edition have been shaped by comments and suggestions from many faculty who have used the book over the years. We are specifically grateful for the thoughtful advice of our reviewers for this edition, Jesse T. Airaudi (Baylor University), Thomas Crofts (East Tennessee State University), Lois Feuer (California State University, Dominguez Hills), Daniel P. Galvin (Clemson University), S. E. Gontarski (Florida State University), Stephen Harris (University of Massachusetts), Roxanne Kent-Drury (Northern Kentucky University), Carol A. Lowe (McLennan Community College), Darin A Merrill (Brigham Young University—Idaho), David G. Miller (Mississippi College), Crystal L. Mueller (University of Wisconsin Oshkosh), and Gary Schneider (University of Texas—Pan American).

We remain grateful as well for the guidance of the many reviewers who advised us on the creation of the first three editions, the base on which this new edition has been built. In addition to the people named above, we would like to thank Lucien Agosta (California State University, Sacramento), Anne W. Astell (Purdue University), Derek Attridge (Rutgers University), Linda Austin (Oklahoma State University), Arthur D. Barnes (Louisiana State University), Robert Barrett (University of Pennsylvania), Candice Barrington (Central Connecticut State University), Joseph Bartolomeo (University of Massachusetts, Amherst), Mary Been (Clovis Community College), Stephen Behrendt (University of Nebraska), Todd Bender (University of Wisconsin, Madison), Bruce Boehrer (Florida State University), Bruce Brandt (South Dakota State University), Joel J. Brattin (Worcester Polytechnic Institute), James Campbell (University of Central Florida), J. Douglas Canfield (University of Arizona), Paul A. Cantor (University of Virginia), George Allan Cate (University of Maryland, College Park), Philip Collington (Niagra University), Linda McFerrin

Cook (McLellan Community College), Eugene R. Cunnar (New Mexico State University), Earl Dachslager (University of Houston), Elizabeth Davis (University of California, Davis), Andrew Elfenbein (University of Minnesota), Hilary Englert (New Jersey City University), Margaret Ferguson (University of California, Davis), Sandra K. Fisher (State University of New York, Albany), Sandra C. Fowler (The University of Alabama), Allen J. Frantzen (Loyola University, Chicago), Kevin Gardner (Baylor University), Kate Gartner Frost (University of Texas), Leon Gottfried (Purdue University), Leslie Graff (University at Buffalo), Mark L. Greenberg (Drexel University), Peter Greenfield (University of Puget Sound), Natalie Grinnell (Wofford College), James Hala (Drew University), Wayne Hall (University of Cincinnati), Donna Hamilton (University of Maryland), Wendell Harris (Pennsylvania State University), Richard H. Haswell (Washington State University), Susan Sage Heinzelman (University of Texas, Austin), Standish Henning (University of Wisconsin, Madison), Noah Heringman (University of Missouri—Columbia), Jack W. Herring (Baylor University), Carrie Hintz (Queens College), Romana Huk (University of Notre Dame), Maurice Hunt (Baylor University), Mary Anne Hutchison (Utica College), Patricia Clare Ingham (Indiana University), Kim Jacobs (University of Cincinnati Clermont College), Carol Jamison (Armstrong Atlantic State University), Eric Johnson (Dakota State College), Mary Susan Johnston (Minnesota State University), Eileen A. Joy (Southern Illinois University—Edwardsville), Colleen Juarretche (University of California, Los Angeles), George Justice (University of Missouri), Roxanne Kent-Drury (Northern Kentucky University), R. B. Kershner (University of Florida), Lisa Klein (Ohio State University), Adam Komisaruk (West Virginia University), Rita S. Kranidis (Radford University), Leslie M. LaChance (University of Tennessee at Martin), John Laflin (Dakota State University), Lisa Lampert (University of California, San Diego), Dallas Liddle (Augsburg College), Paulino Lim (California State University, Long Beach), Elizabeth B. Loizeaux (University of Maryland), Ed Malone (Missouri Western State College), John J. Manning (University of Connecticut), William W. Matter (Richland College), Evan Matthews (Navarro College), Michael Mays (University of Southern Mississippi), Lawrence McCauley (College of New Jersey), Michael B. McDonald (Iowa State University), James J. McKeown Jr. (McLennan Community College), Kathryn McKinley (Florida International University), Peter E. Medine (University of Arizona), Barry Milligan (Wright State University), Celia Millward (Boston University), Charlotte Morse (Virginia Commonwealth University), Mary Morse (Rider University), Thomas C. Moser, Jr. (University of Maryland), James Najarian (Boston College), Deborah Craig Wester (Worcester State College), Jude V. Nixon (Baylor University), Richard Nordquist (Armstrong Atlantic State University), Daniel Novak (Tulane University), John Ottenhoff (Alma College), Violet O'Valle (Tarrant County Junior College, Texas), Joyce Cornette Palmer (Texas Women's University), Leslie Palmer (University of North Texas), Richard Pearce (Wheaton College), Rebecca Phillips (West Virginia University), Renée Pigeon (California State University, San Bernardino), Tadeusz Pioro (Southern Methodist University), Deborah Preston (Dekalb College), William Rankin (Abilene Christian University), Sherry Rankin (Abilene Christian University), Luke Reinsma (Seattle Pacific University), Elizabeth Robertson (University of Colorado), Deborah Rogers (University of Maine), David Rollison (College of Marin), Brian Rosenberg (Allegheny College), Charles Ross (Purdue University), Kathryn Rummel (California Polytechnic), Harry Rusche (Emory University), Laura E. Rutland (Berry College), Kenneth D. Shields

(Southern Methodist University), R. G. Siemens (Malaspina University-College), Clare A. Simmons (Ohio State University), Sally Slocum (University of Akron), Phillip Snyder (Brigham Young University), Isabel Bonnyman Stanley (East Tennessee University), Brad Sullivan (Florida Gulf Coast University), Margaret Sullivan (University of California, Los Angeles), Herbert Sussmann (Northeastern University), Mary L. Tanter (Tarleton State University), Ronald R. Thomas (Trinity College), Theresa Tinkle (University of Michigan), William A. Ulmer (University of Alabama), Jennifer A. Wagner (University of Memphis), Anne D. Wallace (University of Southern Mississippi), Brett Wallen (Cleveland Community College), Jackie Walsh (McNeese State University, Louisiana), Daniel Watkins (Duquesne University), John Watkins (University of Minnesota), Martin Wechselblatt (University of Cincinnati), Arthur Weitzman (Northeastern University), Bonnie Wheeler (Southern Methodist University), Jan Widmayer (Boise State University), Dennis L. Williams (Central Texas College), William A. Wilson (San Jose State University), Paula Woods (Baylor University), and Julia Wright (University of Waterloo).

Other colleagues brought our developing book into the classroom, teaching from portions of the work-in-progress. Our thanks go to Lisa Abney (Northwestern State University), Charles Lynn Batten (University of California, Los Angeles), Brenda Riffe Brown (College of the Mainland, Texas), John Brugaletta (California State University, Fullerton), Dan Butcher (Southeastern Louisiana University), Lynn Byrd (Southern University at New Orleans), David Cowles (Brigham Young University), Sheila Drain (John Carroll University), Lawrence Frank (University of Oklahoma), Leigh Garrison (Virginia Polytechnic Institute), David Griffin (New York University), Rita Harkness (Virginia Commonwealth University), Linda Kissler (Westmoreland County Community College, Pennsylvania), Brenda Lewis (Motlow State Community College, Tennessee), Paul Lizotte (River College), Wayne Luckman (Green River Community College, Washington), Arnold Markely (Pennsylvania State University, Delaware County), James McKusick (University of Maryland, Baltimore), Eva McManus (Ohio Northern University), Manuel Moyrao (Old Dominion University), Kate Palguta (Shawnee State University, Ohio), Paul Puccio (University of Central Florida), Sarah Polito (Cape Cod Community College), Meredith Poole (Virginia Western Community College), Tracy Seeley (University of San Francisco), Clare Simmons (Ohio State University), and Paul Yoder (University of Arkansas, Little Rock).

As if all this help weren't enough, the editors also drew directly on friends and colleagues in many ways, for advice, for information, sometimes for outright contributions to headnotes and footnotes, even (in a pinch) for aid in proofreading. In particular, we wish to thank David Ackiss, Marshall Brown, James Cain, Cathy Corder, Jeffrey Cox, Michael Coyle, Pat Denison, Tom Farrell, Andrew Fleck, Jane Freilich, Laurie Glover, Lisa Gordis, Joy Hayton, Ryan Hibbet, V. Lauryl Hicks, Nelson Hilton, Jean Howard, David Kastan, Stanislas Kemper, Andrew Krull, Ron Levao, Carol Levin, David Lipscomb, Denise MacNeil, Jackie Maslowski, Richard Matlak, Anne Mellor, James McKusick, Melanie Micir, Michael North, David Paroissien, Stephen M. Parrish, Peter Platt, Cary Plotkin, Desma Polydorou, Gina Renee, Alan Richardson, Esther Schor, Catherine Siemann, Glenn Simshaw, David Tresilian, Shasta Turner, Nicholas Watson, Michael Winckleman, Gillen Wood, and Sarah Zimmerman for all their guidance and assistance.

The pages on the Restoration and the eighteenth century are the work of many collaborators, diligent and generous. Michael F. Suarez, S. J. (Campion Hall,

Oxford) edited the Swift and Pope sections; Mary Bly (Fordham University) edited Sheridan's *School for Scandal*; Michael Caldwell (University of Chicago) edited the portions of "Reading Papers" on *The Craftsman* and the South Sea Bubble. Steven N. Zwicker (Washington University) co-wrote the period introduction, and the headnotes for the Dryden section. Bruce Redford (Boston University) crafted the footnotes for Dryden, Gay, Johnson, and Boswell. Susan Brown, Janice Cable, Christine Coch, Marnie Cox, Tara Czechowski, Susan Greenfield, Mary Nassef, Paige Reynolds, and Andrew Tumminia helped with texts, footnotes, and other matters throughout; William Pritchard gathered texts, wrote notes, and prepared the bibliography. To all, abiding thanks.

It has been a pleasure to work with all of these colleagues in the ongoing collaborative process that has produced this book and brought it to this new stage of its life and use. This book exists for its readers, whose reactions and suggestions we warmly welcome, as these will in turn reshape this book for later users in the years to come.

David Damrosch
HARVARD UNIVERSITY

Kevin J. H. Dettmar
POMONA COLLEGE

Christopher Baswell
BARNARD COLLEGE AND COLUMBIA UNIVERSITY

Clare Carroll
QUEENS COLLEGE, CITY UNIVERSITY OF NEW YORK

Andrew Hadfield
UNIVERSITY OF SUSSEX

Heather Henderson

Peter J. Manning
STATE UNIVERSITY OF NEW YORK, STONY BROOK

Anne Howland Schotter
WAGNER COLLEGE

William Chapman Sharpe
BARNARD COLLEGE

Stuart Sherman
FORDHAM UNIVERSITY

Susan J. Wolfson
PRINCETON UNIVERSITY

ABOUT THE EDITORS

David Damrosch is Professor Comparative Literature at Harvard University. He is past President of the American Comparative Literature Association, and has written widely on world literature from antiquity to the present. His books include *What is World Literature?* (2003), *The Buried Book: The Loss and Rediscovery of the Great Epic of Gilgamesh* (2007), and *How to Read World Literature* (2009). He is the founding general editor of the six-volume *The Longman Anthology of World Literature*, 2/e (2009) and the editor of *Teaching World Literature* (2009).

Kevin J. H. Dettmar is W.M. Keck Professor and Chair of the Department of English at Pomona College, and Past President of the Modernist Studies Association. He is the author of *The Illicit Joyce of Postmodernism and Is Rock Dead?*, and the editor of *Rereading the New: A Backward Glance at Modernism; Marketing Modernisms: Self-Promotion, Canonization, and Rereading; Reading Rock & Roll: Authenticity, Appropriation, Aesthetics;* the Barnes & Noble Classics edition of James Joyce's *A Portrait of the Artist as a Young Man and Dubliners;* and *The Blackwell Companion to Modernist Literature and Culture,* of *The Cambridge Companion to Bob Dylan.*

Christopher Baswell is A.W. Olin Chair of English at Barnard College, and Professor of English and Comparative Literature at Columbia University. His interests include classical literature and culture, medieval literature and culture, and contemporary poetry. He is author of *Virgil in Medieval England: Figuring the "Aeneid" from the Twelfth Century to Chaucer,* which won the 1998 Beatrice White Prize of the English Association. He has held fellowships from the NEH, the National Humanities Center, and the Institute for Advanced Study, Princeton.

Clare Carroll is Director of Renaissance Studies at The Graduate Center, City University of New York and Professor of Comparative Literature at Queens College, CUNY. Her research is in Renaissance Studies, with particular interests in early modern colonialism, epic poetry, historiography, and translation. She is the author of *The Orlando Furioso: A Stoic Comedy,* and editor of Richard Beacon's humanist dialogue on the colonization of Ireland, *Solon His Follie.* Her most recent book is *Circe's Cup: Cultural Transformations in Early Modern Ireland.* She has received Fulbright Fellowships for her research and the Queens College President's Award for Excellence in Teaching.

Andrew Hadfield is Professor of English at The University of Sussex. He is the author of a number of books, including *Shakespeare and Republicanism* (2005), which was awarded the 2006 Sixteenth-Century Society Conference Roland H. Bainton Prize for Literature; *Literature, Travel and Colonialism in the English Renaissance, 1540–1625* (1998); and Spenser's *Irish Experience: Wild Fruyt and Salvage Soyl* (1997). He has also edited a number of texts, most recently, with Matthew Dimmock, *Religions of the Book: Co-existence and Conflict, 1400–1660* (2008), and with Raymond Gillespie, *The Oxford History of the Irish Book, Vol. III: The Irish Book in English, 1550–1800* (2006). He is a regular reviewer for the TLS.

Heather Henderson is a freelance writer and former Associate Professor of English Literature at Mount Holyoke College. A specialist in Victorian literature, she is the recipient of a fellowship from the National Endowment for the Humanities. She is the author of *The Victorian Self: Autobiography and Biblical Narrative*. Her current interests include homeschooling, travel literature, and autobiography.

Peter J. Manning is Professor at Stony Brook University. He is the author of *Byron and His Fictions* and *Reading Romantics*, and of numerous essays on the British Romantic poets and prose writers. With Susan J. Wolfson, he has co-edited *Selected Poems of Byron*, and *Selected Poems of Beddoes, Hood, and Praed*. He has received fellowships from the National Endowment for the Humanities and the John Simon Guggenheim Memorial Foundation, and the Distinguished Scholar Award of the Keats-Shelley Association.

Anne Schotter is Professor of English at Wagner College. She is the co-editor of *Ineffability: Naming the Unnamable from Dante to Beckett* and author of articles on Middle English poetry, Dante, and medieval Latin poetry. Her current interests include the medieval reception of classical literature, particularly the work of Ovid. She has held fellowships from the Woodrow Wilson and Andrew W. Mellon foundations.

William Sharpe is Professor of English Literature at Barnard College. A specialist in Victorian poetry and the literature of the city, he is the author of *Unreal Cities: Urban Figuration in Wordsworth, Baudelaire, Whitman, Eliot, and Williams*. He is also co-editor of *The Passing of Arthur* and *Visions of the Modern City*. He is the recipient of Guggenheim, National Endowment of the Humanities, Fulbright, and Mellon fellowships, and recently published *New York Nocturne: The City After Dark in Literature, Painting, and Photography*.

Stuart Sherman is Associate Professor of English at Fordham University. He received the Gottschalk Prize from the American Society for Eighteenth-Century Studies for his book *Telling Time: Clocks, Diaries, and English Diurnal Form, 1660–1775*, and is currently at work on a study called "News and Plays: Evanescences of Page and Stage, 1620–1779." He has received the Quantrell Award for Undergraduate Teaching, as well as fellowships from the American Council of Learned Societies and the Chicago Humanities Institute.

Susan J. Wolfson teaches at Princeton University and is general editor of Longman Cultural Editions. She has also produced editions of Felicia Hemans, Lord Byron, Thomas L. Beddoes, William M. Praed, and Thomas Hood. She is the editor of the innovative Longman Cultural Editions of John Keats, and of Mary Shelley's *Frankenstein*, and coeditor (with Barry V. Qualls) of *Three Tales of Doubles*, and (with Claudia Johnson) of Jane Austen's *Pride and Prejudice*. She is author of *The Questioning Presence* (1986), *Formal Charges: The Shaping of Poetry in British Romanticism* (1997), and *Borderlines: The Shiftings of Gender* (2007).

The Longman Anthology of British Literature

VOLUME 1A

THE MIDDLE AGES

Laurence, Prior of Durham, depicted as a scribe, from a 12th-century manuscript.

THE MIDDLE AGES

POPULATION[1]

NATIONAL POPULATION (IN MILLIONS)[2]

	England	Scotland	Ireland
1100	around 2	—	—
1300	4.5 to 5.5[3]	0.5 to 1.0	c. 0.9
1377	2.5 to 3.0[4]	—	c. 0.5
Late Middle Ages	4.0[5]	—	—

URBAN POPULATION[6]

London	Edinburgh	Dublin
London is already a major city during the Roman occupation. After a population collapse in the early 5th century, its population grows again in the 9th century. By 1200, it is a populous city, with more than 100 parish churches.	Edinburgh is a royal burgh by 1127.	Dublin is a Viking trading center by the mid-9th century. It is conquered by the Anglo-Angevins in 1170 and became their colonial administrative center.

	London	Edinburgh	Dublin
1300	60,000–80,000	10,000	11,000
1340s	Near 90,000	—	—
1377	50,000 at the most[7]	—	—

LIFE EXPECTANCY

In the years after the Black Death, life expectancy at birth is 25–30 years. As many as 50% of babies die in their first year.

DAILY LIFE

WAGES

1300s	A master mason makes 5 pounds per year. A laborer makes 2 pounds per year at the maximum.
1316	A common knight, working as a mercenary, might make 30 pounds per year for his services; knightly income from land varies enormously.
1350s	Laborers' wages rise after the population decline caused by the Black Death. A thatcher makes 3 pence per day; his assistant makes 1 penny.
1379	A chantry priest earns about 5 pounds per year.
1380s	A thatcher make 4 pence per day; his assistant, a little over 2 pence.

Coin from the reign of Alfred the Great

1. Population estimates for the Middle Ages are highly speculative.
2. The population of today's United Kingdom is 60,943,912 (July 2008 est.).
3. England's medieval population peaked in the late 12th and 13th centuries.
4. After peaking, population then declined in 1315–1317 perhaps 10% after poor crops and famine. The Black Death first struck in the summer of 1348, then again in 1361, 1368, and 1375, causing a massive decline in population.
5. The population rose only slowly after the Black Death. For much of the Middle Ages, the population was densest in East Anglia. The Black Death had its greatest impact there.
6. The population of today's London is over 7.6 million (October 2008 est.).
7. The Black Death of 1348 and the years that followed cut London's population by more than a third. It did not rise to more than 60,000 until around 1500.

COST OF GOODS

1374   A knight's two horses costs 10 pounds. (A fine war horse could cost 80 pounds.)
One knight's total armor is worth 16 pounds.

14th century A cow costs 10 shillings (120 pence). A sheep costs between 1 and 1½ shillings; a pig 2 or 3
shillings; two chickens or a dozen eggs cost a penny.
Good wine costs 4–8 pence per gallon. Average ale costs 1 penny per gallon.
A wealthy peasant's shoes might cost 6 pence; his tunic, 3 shillings. Fine wool fabric is 5 shillings a yard.

FOOD AND DRINK

Most trade in food is local. It includes grains, dairy, fish, poultry, and meat. Wheat is the preferred grain
for bread, but the more easily grown rye and barley are used. The cheapest bread is made from a meal of
peas and beans. Oats are used for gruel and for brewing. Ale is a major part of daily nutrition. Because
it is perishable, it is locally produced, most often by women until the mid-14th century. At that point
guilds increasingly organize production and women's roles decline.[8]

As the population grows between 1200 and 1348, most people depend on grains for their nutrition.
Population pushes the edges of agricultural production,
and protein deficiency may have been widespread by the
1300s. In the smaller population that followed the Black
Death, consumption of wheat bread, barley ale, and meat
rises fast.

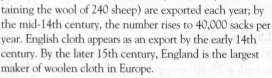

APPAREL

Most British clothing during the middle ages is made of
wool, although linen is also used for underclothing. Wool
and cloth are the main sources of England's wealth, and
high taxes on their export are key sources of royal income. In the 1270s, almost 27,000 sacks (each con-

taining the wool of 240 sheep) are exported each year; by
the mid-14th century, the number rises to 40,000 sacks per
year. English cloth appears as an export by the early 14th
century. By the later 15th century, England is the largest
maker of woolen cloth in Europe.

In military apparel, chain mail is a knight's major
protection until about 1200. Plate armor appears before
1214, and the breast plate by 1250. In 1314, at the
Battle of Bannockburn, the Earl of Gloucester dies from
the weight of his plate armor.

RULERS

BEFORE THE NORMAN CONQUEST (1066)
Alfred the Great (871–899)
Edmund I (940–946)
Ethelred the Unready (948–1016)
Edward the Confessor (1042–1066)
Harold II (1066)
HOUSE OF NORMANDY
William I, the Conqueror (1066–1087)

William the Conqueror

8. Guilds were important organizers of urban life by the late 13th century. They controlled production (leather, jewelry, etc.) and
trade (especially in food). But the craft guilds overlapped with guilds mostly devoted to social and religious activities. Religious
guilds provided burial if a member died in poverty, and hired priests to pray for the souls of deceased members. In many cities,
guilds were involved in forms of civic display, like plays and processions.

RULERS

William II, Rufus (1087–1100)

Henry I (1100–1135)

HOUSE OF BLOIS

Stephen (1135–1154)

HOUSE OF PLANTAGENET

Henry II (1154–1189)

Richard I "Coeur de Lion" (1189–1199)

John (1199–1216)

Henry III (1216–1272)

Edward I (1272–1307)

Edward II (1307–1327)

Edward III (1327–1377)

Richard II (1377–1399)

HOUSE OF LANCASTER

Henry IV (1399–1413)

Henry V (1413–1422)

Henry VI (1422–1471)

HOUSE OF YORK

Edward IV (1461–1483)

Edward V (1483)

Richard III (1483–1485)

(Clockwise from upper left) Henry II, Richard I, John, and Henry III

TIMELINE

410 Roman occupation of England ends.

597 St. Augustine of Canterbury's mission begins the conversion of England.

c. 600 King Arthur is first mentioned.

c. 650 Ruthwell Cross (page 149)

680 Abbess Hilda dies.

c. 700 *Book of Kells*

731 Bede's *Ecclesiastical History* (page 154)

c. 844–899 King Alfred is noted for learning to read in his middle years. Many of his clergy are illiterate in Latin, one reason he sponsors translation of key texts into Old English.

899 King Alfred dies.

c. 1000 The *Beowulf* manuscript appears, although the story itself is probably 200 years older (page 32).

1066 William the Conqueror crosses the English Channel and defeats King Harold to begin the Norman Conquest. Between 7,000 and 10,000 men fight on each side of the Battle of Hastings. ⊢

1075 The Investiture Controversy, a debate concerning who has the authority to "invest" or appoint bishops to their positions, results when the papacy claims sole authority to appoint bishops and to depose secular rulers who oppose this right.

1086 The Domesday Book is the first—and still astonishing—systematic public record in English history.

1086 Water mills are the main source of power during the Middle Ages. While there were fewer than 100 in the 900s, the Domesday Book records 5,624. ⊢

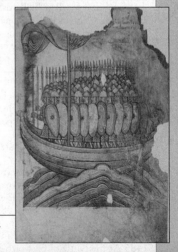

1095 Pope Urban II calls for the First Crusade.

12th century *The Táin* "Recension II" (page 111)

c. 1136 Geoffrey of Monmouth's *The History of the Kings of Britain* (page 183)

1154 The last entries in *The Peterborough Chronicle,* a series of (usually) yearly descriptions of important events throughout England that began in the late 9th century

1170 Thomas Becket is murdered in Canterbury Cathedral after quarrelling with Henry II over the right of the church or the state to try priests for criminal acts.

1170–1180 Marie de France's *Lais* (page 201)

1200 An increasingly diverse but still limited population is able to read.

1215 *The Magna Carta,* the founding document of British constitutional history, is signed by King John.

1215 The Fourth Lateran Council promulgates the doctrine of transubstantiation, an educational program based upon preaching, a set of disciplinary codes for wayward clerics, and the call for yearly confession at Easter.

1258 The Provisions of Oxford (a declaration of baronial rights) is distributed to sheriffs across England in Latin, French, and English.

1286 Mechanical clocks appear; their spread leads to the standardization of the hour.

14th century Dafydd ap Gwilym (page 566)

14th century Windmills become numerous.

1327 Edward II is deposed.

1337 The Hundred Years' War between France and England begins.

1346–1347 The largest known English army, totaling over 36,000, is assembled at the Siege of Calais.

1347 The Black Death, also known as the Bubonic Plague because of the swollen lymph nodes or "buboes" of its victims, strikes Europe. According to many authorities, up to 50% of the population of Europe and Asia is killed by the wave of infection.

1351 The Statute of Laborers sets wages to pre-Plague levels and prevents the working classes from leaving their feudal domains to seek better work and pay.

1375–1400 London literary culture flourishes—home to Geoffrey Chaucer, John Gower, and William Langland.

1378 The Great Schism begins, during which there were two lines of popes (and even a third line for a time), one in France and one in Rome.

1380 John Wyclif, often seen as a predecessor to the Protestant Reformation, is condemned as a heretic, and his followers, called "Lollards," are persecuted.

1381 The Rising of 1381 occurs. Led by Wat Tyler and encouraged by the preaching of John Ball, rebels from throughout the countryside converge upon London in response to the punitive poll tax of that year (page 468).

1399 Richard II is deposed.

1400 Roughly 30% of the population can read English; some know French and Latin. Literacy is increasingly taken for granted in the upper classes.

1400 Chaucer dies (page 312).

1415 At the Battle of Agincourt, a pivotal battle of the Hundred Years' War, Henry V of England defeats a much larger French army.

c.1420 Julian of Norwich dies (page 481).

c. 1438 Margery Kempe dies (page 529).

1453 The Hundred Years' War ends.

c. 1464–1479 *Mankind* (page 587)

1465 Charles d'Orléans dies (page 584).

1474 The first book is printed in English by William Caxton.

1485 At the Battle of Bosworth Field, Henry Tudor kills Richard III and ascends the throne as Henry VII, beginning the Tudor reign in England.

1485 William Caxton publishes *Morte Darthur* (page 279).

1492 Columbus sails.

Late 15th century Scotland enjoys a brief flowering of poetry centered in a sophisticated court society (page 573).

1517 To protest the disingenuous sale of indulgences (forgiveness of sins after death), Martin Luther posts his 95 Theses on a door at the University of Wittenberg, starting the Reformation in Germany.

The Middle Ages

At the present time, there are five languages in Britain, just as the divine law is written in five books, all devoted to seeking out and setting forth one and the same kind of wisdom, namely the knowledge of sublime truth and of true sublimity. These are the English, British, Irish, Pictish, as well as the Latin languages; through the study of the scriptures, Latin is in general use among them all.

—Bede, *Ecclesiastical History of the English People*

The Venerable Bede's famous and enormously influential *Ecclesiastical History of the English People*, written in the early 700s, reflects a double triumph. First, its very title acknowledges the dominance by Bede's day of the Anglo-Saxons, who, centuries earlier, had established themselves on an island already inhabited by Celtic Britons and by Picts. Second, the Latin of Bede's text and his own life as a monk point to the presence of ancient Mediterranean influences in the British Isles, earlier through Rome's military colonization of ancient Britain and later through the conversion of Bede's people to Roman Christianity.

In this first chapter of his first book, Bede shows a complex awareness of the several populations still active in Britain and often resisting or encroaching on Anglo-Saxon rule, and much of his *History* narrates the successive waves of invaders and missionaries who had brought their languages, governments, cultures, and beliefs to his island. This initial emphasis on peoples and languages should not be taken as early medieval multiculturalism, however: Bede's brief comparison to the single truth embodied in the five books of divine law also shows us his eagerness to draw his fragmented world into a coherent and transcendent system of Latin-based Christianity.

It is useful today, however, to think about medieval Britain, before and long after Bede, as a multilingual and multicultural setting, densely layered with influences and communities that divide, in quite different ways, along lines of geography, language, and ethnicity, as well as religion, gender, and class. These elements produced extraordinary cultures and artistic works, whose richness and diversity challenge the modern imagination. The medieval British Isles were a meeting place, but also a point of resistance, for wave after wave of cultural and political influences. Awareness of these multiple origins, moreover, persisted. In the mid-thirteenth century, Matthew Paris's map of England (Color Plate 4) reflects an alertness to the complex geography of history and settlement on his island. Six hundred years after Bede we encounter a historian like Sir Thomas Gray complaining that recent disorders were "characteristic of a medley of different races. Wherefore some people are of the opinion that the diversity of spirit among the English is the cause of their revolutions" (*Scalacronica*, c. 1363).

This complex mixture sometimes resulted from systematic conquest, as with the Romans and, three centuries after Bede, the famous Norman Conquest of 1066; sometimes it was from slower, less unified movements of ethnic groups, such as the Celts, Anglo-Saxons, the Irish in Scotland, and the Vikings. Other important influences arrived more subtly: various forms of Christianity, classical Latin literature and learning, continental French culture in the thirteenth century, and an imported Italian humanism toward the close of the British Middle Ages.

Our understanding of this long period and our very name for it also reflect a long history of multiple influences and cultural and political orders. The term "medieval" began as a condescending and monolithic label, first applied by Renaissance human-

> *The term "medieval" began as a condescending and monolithic label . . .*

ists who were eager to distinguish their revived classical scholarship from what they interpreted as a "barbarous" past. They and later readers often dismissed the Middle Ages as rigidly hierarchical, feudal, and Church-dominated. Others embraced the period for equally tendentious reasons, rosily picturing "feudal" England and Europe as a harmonious society of contented peasants, chivalrous nobles, and holy clerics. It is true that those who exercised political and religious control during the Middle Ages—the Roman church and the Anglo-Norman and then the English monarchy—sought to impose hierarchy on their world and created explicit ideologies to justify doing so. They were not unopposed, however; those who had been pushed aside continued to resist—and to contribute to Britain's multiple and dynamic literatures.

The period that we call "the Middle Ages" is vast and ungainly, spanning eight hundred years by some accounts. Scholars traditionally divide medieval English literature into the Old English period, from about 700 to 1066 (the date of the Norman Conquest), and the Middle English period, from 1066 to about 1500. Given the very different state of the English language during the two periods and given the huge impact of the Norman Conquest, this division is reasonable and is reflected in this collection under the headings "Before the Norman Conquest" and "After the Norman Conquest." There were substantial continuities, nevertheless, before and after the Conquest, especially in the Celtic areas beyond the Normans' immediate control.

THE CELTS

It is with the Celts, in fact, that the recorded history of Britain begins, and their literatures continue to the present day in Ireland and Wales. The Celts first migrated to Britain about 400 B.C.E., after spreading over most of Europe in the two preceding centuries. In England these "Brittonic" Celts absorbed some elements of Roman culture and social order during Rome's partial occupation of the island from the first to the fifth centuries C.E. After the conversion of the Roman emperor Constantine in the fourth century and the establishment of Christianity as the official imperial religion, many British Celts adopted Christianity. The language of these "British" to whom Bede refers gave rise to Welsh. The Celts maintained contact with their people on the Continent, who were already being squeezed toward what is now Brittany, in the west of France. The culture of the Brittonic Celts was thus not exclusively insular, and their myths and legends came to incorporate these cross-Channel memories, especially in the stories of King Arthur.

Celts also arrived in Ireland; and as one group, the "Goidelic" Celts, achieved linguistic and social dominance there, their language split off from that of the Britons. Some of these Irish Celts later established themselves in Argyll and the western isles of Scotland, "either by friendly treaty or by the sword," says Bede, and from them the Scottish branch of the Celtic languages developed. Bede mentions this language as the "Irish" that is spoken in Britain. The Irish converted to Christianity early but slowly, without the pressure of a Christianized colonizer. When the great Irish monasteries flourished in the sixth century, their extraordinary Latin scholarship seems to have developed alongside the traditional learning preserved by the rigorous schools of vernacular poetry, as we see in the section "Early Irish Verse" (pages 133–42). If anything, Irish monastic study was stimulated by these surviving institutions of a more poetic and priestly class. The Irish monasteries in turn became the impetus behind Irish and Anglo-Saxon missionaries who carried Christianity to the northern and eastern reaches of Europe. Both as missionaries and as scholars, insular Christians had great impact on continental Europe, especially in the eighth and ninth centuries.

By 597 when Pope Gregory the Great sent Augustine (later "of Canterbury") to expand the Christian presence in England, there was already a flourishing Christian Celtic society, especially in Ireland. Ensuing disagreements over Celtic versus Roman ways of worship were ultimately resolved in favor of the Roman liturgy and calendar, but the cultural impact of Celts on British Christianity remained enormous. The Irish *Book of Kells* (page 14), and the Lindisfarne Gospels (Color Plate 1), produced in England, are enlivened by the swirls, interlace, and stylized animals long evident in the work of pagan Celtic craftsmen on the continent. The monks who illuminated such magnificent gospel books also copied classical Latin texts, notably Virgil's *Aeneid* and works by Cicero and Seneca, thereby helping keep ancient Roman literature alive when much of continental Europe fell into near chaos during the Germanic invasions that led to the fall of Rome.

Included in this anthology are examples from the two great literatures written in Celtic languages, Irish and Welsh. Passages from the eighth-century Irish *Táin Bó Cuailnge* reveal a heroic spirit and an acceptance of the magical which can be compared with aspects of *Beowulf*. Like much Irish heroic narrative, though, the *Táin* also reveals a far more prominent and assertive role for women, some of whom retain resemblances to the goddess figures of Ireland's pagan era. Welsh literature is represented first by lyrics attributed to the early, shadowy poet Taliesin and later by the sophisticated lyrics of fourteenth-century Dafydd ap Gwilym, who draws on Latin and European traditions as well as on the rich poetic techniques of Wales.

THE GERMANIC MIGRATIONS

While Celtic culture flourished in Ireland, the British Celts and their faith suffered a series of disastrous reversals after the withdrawal of the Romans and the aggressive incursions of the pagan Angles, Saxons, and Jutes from the continent. The Picts and Scots in the north, never Romanized, had begun to harass the Britons, who responded by inviting allies from among the Germanic tribes on the continent in the mid-fifth century. These protectors soon became predators, demanding land and establishing small kingdoms of their own in roughly the eastern half of modern-day England. Uneasy and temporary treaties followed. The Britons retained a presence in the northwest, in the kingdoms of Rheged and of the Strathclyde Welsh; others were slowly pressed toward present-day Wales in the southwest.

The Angles, Saxons, and Jutes were not themselves a monolithic force, though. Divided into often warring states, they faced resistance, however diminishing, from the Britons and still had to battle the aggressive Picts and Scots, who were the original reason for their arrival. Their own culture was further changed as they converted to Christianity. The piecemeal Anglo-Saxon colonization of England in the sixth and seventh centuries and the island's conversion and later reconversion to Christianity present a complex picture, then—one that could be retold very differently depending on the perspectives of later historians. As the Angles and Saxons settled in and extended their control, the emerging "English" culture drew on new interpretations of the region's history. The most influential account of all was Bede's *Ecclesiastical History*, completed in 731. Our most reliable and eloquent source for early British history, Bede nonetheless wrote as an Anglo-Saxon. He presented his people's history from a providential perspective, seeing their role in Britain and their conversion to Christianity as a crucial part of a divine plan. King Alfred extended this world view when, in the late ninth century, he wrote of his people's struggle against the invading pagan Vikings.

Bede thus adopts an approach to history that reflects his own devout Christian faith and the disciplined religious practices of his monastic brethren in Northumberland. Nevertheless, Bede lived in a wider culture still deeply imbued with the tribal values of its Germanic and pagan past, a culture that maintained at least a nostalgic regard for the kind of individual heroic glory that rarely looks beyond this world. Even in Bede's day, most kings died young and on the battlefield. And natural disasters such as those in 664 (a plague, and the deaths of a king and an archbishop occurring on the day of an eclipse) could send the Anglo-Saxons back to pagan worship. The two worlds, one with its roots in Mediterranean Christianity and the other in Germanic paganism, overlapped and interpenetrated for generations.

The two worlds, one with its roots in Mediterranean Christianity and the other in Germanic paganism, overlapped and interpenetrated for generations.

The pagan culture that is the setting for the epic *Beowulf* still strongly resembled that of the Germanic "barbarians" described by the Roman historian Tacitus in the first century. The heroic code of the Germanic warrior bands—what Tacitus called the "*comitatus*"—valued courage in battle above all, followed by loyalty to the tribal leader and the warband. These formed the core of heroic identity. A warrior whose leader fell in battle was obliged to seek vengeance at any cost; it was an indelible shame to survive an unavenged leader. Family links were also profound, however, and a persistent tragic theme in Germanic and Anglo-Saxon heroic narrative pits the claims of vengeance against those of family loyalty.

Early warrior culture in the British Isles, as elsewhere, was fraught with violence, as fragile truces between warring tribes and clans were continually broken.

The tone of Old English poetry (as of much of Old Irish heroic narrative) is consequently somber, often suffused with a sense of doom. Even moments of high festivity are darkened by allusions to later disasters. Humor often occurs through a kind of ironic understatement: a poet may state that a warrior strode less swiftly into battle, for example, when the warrior in fact is dead. Similarly Cet, an Irish warrior, claims that if his brother were in the house, he would overcome his opponent, Conall. Conall replies, "But he is in the house," and almost casually flings the brother's head at Cet. A lighter tone is found mostly in shorter forms, such as the playful Anglo-Saxon riddles and in some Old Irish poetry.

The Angles and Saxons had come to England as military opportunists, and they in turn faced attacks and settlement from across the Channel. Their increasingly ordered political world and their thriving monastic establishments, such as Bede's monastery of Jarrow, were plundered by Vikings in swift attacks by boat as early as the end of the eighth century. Irish monastic culture faced similar depradations. This continued for a hundred years, and eventually resulted in widespread Scandinavian settlements north of the Thames, in areas called the Danelaw, and around modern-day Dublin. By the 890s Christian Viking kings reigned at York and in East Anglia, extending a history of independence from the southern kingdoms. The period of raids and looting was largely over by 900, but even King Alfred (d. 899) faced Viking incursions in Wessex and consciously depicted himself as a Christian hero holding the line against pagan invaders. Only his kingdom, in fact, resisted their attacks with complete success. Vikings also intermarried with Anglo-Saxons and expanded their influence by political means. Profiting from English dynastic disorder around the turn of the eleventh century, aristocrats in the Danelaw became brokers of royal power. From 1016 to 1035 the Danish Cnut (Canute) was king of both England and Denmark, briefly uniting the two in a maritime empire. The Scandinavian presence was not exclusively combative, however. They sent peaceful traders to the British Isles—among them Ohthere, whose tale of his voyages is included here. They also left their mark on literature and language, as in the early Middle English romance *Havelock the Dane*, which contains many words borrowed from Old Norse.

PAGAN AND CHRISTIAN: TENSION AND CONVERGENCE

Given that writing in the Roman alphabet was introduced to pre-Conquest England by churchmen, it is not surprising that most texts from the period are written in Latin on Christian subjects. Most writing even in the Old English language was also religious. In Anglo-Saxon England and in the Celtic cultures, vernacular literature tended at first to be orally composed and performed. The body of written vernacular Anglo-Saxon poetry that survives is thus very small indeed, although there are plenty of prose religious works. It is something of a miracle that *Beowulf*, which celebrates the exploits of a pagan hero, was deemed worthy of being copied by scribes who were almost certainly clerics. (In fact, almost all the

It is something of a miracle that Beowulf, *which celebrates the exploits of a pagan hero, was deemed worthy of being copied by scribes who were almost certainly clerics.*

greatest Anglo-Saxon poetry survives in only a single copy—so tenuous is our link to that past.) Yet the copying of *Beowulf* also hints at the complex interaction of the pagan and Christian traditions in Anglo-Saxon culture.

The conflict between the two traditions was characterized (and perhaps exaggerated) by Christian writers and readers as a struggle between pagan violence and Christian values of forgiveness. The old, deep-seated respect for treasure as a sign of power and achievement seemed to conflict with Christian contempt for worldly goods. In fact, however, pagan Germanic and Christian values were alike in many respects and coexisted with various degrees of mutual influence.

Old English poets explored the tensions as well as the overlap between the two sets of values in two primary poetic modes—the heroic and the elegiac. The heroic mode, of which *Beowulf* is the supreme example, celebrates the values of bravery, loyalty, vengeance, and desire for treasure. The great buckle from the Sutton Hoo ship-burial (Color Plate 2) is a surviving artifact of such treasure. The elegiac mode, by contrast, calls the value of these things into question, as at best transient and at worst a worldly distraction from spiritual life. The elegiac speaker, usually an exile, laments the loss of earthly goods—his lord, his comrades, the joys of the mead hall—and, in the case of the short poem known as *The Wanderer*, turns his thoughts to heaven. *Beowulf*, composed most likely by a Christian poet looking back at the deeds of his pagan Scandinavian ancestors, uses elements of both the heroic and the elegiac to focus on the overlap of pagan and Christian virtues. A similar, though less adversarial, interaction of a heroic code and the new religion is also encountered in medieval Irish literature, such as the examples of early Irish verse offered here.

The goals of earthly glory and heavenly salvation that concern Old English poetry are presented primarily as they affect men. Recent scholarship, however, reveals the active roles played in society by Anglo-Saxon women, particularly aristocratic ones. One of these is Aethelflaed, daughter of King Alfred, who co-ruled the kingdom of Mercia with her brother Edward at the turn of the tenth century, taking an active military role in fighting off the Danes. Better known today is Abbess Hilda, who founded and ran the great monastery at Whitby from 657 until her death in 680; five Whitby monks became bishops across England during her rule. Nevertheless, women generally take a marginal role in Old English poetry. In secular works marriages are portrayed as being arranged to strengthen military alliances, in efforts (often doomed) to heal bloody rifts between clans. Women thus function primarily as "peace weavers," a term referring occasionally to their active diplomacy in settling disputes but more often to their passive role in marriage exchanges. This latter role was fraught with danger, for if a truce were broken between the warring groups, the woman would face tragically conflicting loyalties to husband and male kin.

> *In secular works marriages are portrayed as being arranged to strengthen military alliances, in efforts (often doomed) to heal bloody rifts between clans.*

The effect of the Germanic heroic code on women is explored in two tantalizingly short poems that invest the elegiac mode with women's voices: *Wulf and Eadwacer* and *The Wife's Lament*. In both, a woman speaker laments her separation from her lord, whether husband or lover, through some shadowy events of heroic warfare. More indicative of the actual power of aristocratic and religious women in Anglo-Saxon society, perhaps, is the Old English poem *Judith*, a biblical narrative which uses heroic diction reminiscent of that in *Beowulf* to celebrate the heroine's military triumph over the pagan Holofernes.

ORAL POETRY, WRITTEN MANUSCRIPTS

For all their deep linguistic differences and territorial conflicts, the Celts and Anglo-Saxons had affinities in the heroic themes and oral settings of their greatest surviving narratives and in the echoes of a pre-Christian culture that endure there. Indeed, these can be compared to conditions of authorship in oral cultures worldwide, from Homer's Greece to parts of contemporary Africa. In a culture with little or no writing, the singer of tales has an enormously important role as the conservator of the past. In *Beowulf*, for instance, the traditional content and verbal formulas of the poetry of praise are swiftly reworked to celebrate the hero's killing of the monster Grendel:

> a fellow of the king's,
> whose head was a storehouse of the storied verse,
> whose tongue gave gold to the language
> of the treasured repertory, wrought a new lay
> made in the measure.

A poet of this kind (in Anglo-Saxon, a *scop* or "shaper") does not just enhance the great warrior's prestige by praising his hero's ancestors and accomplishments. He also recalls and performs the shared history and beliefs of the entire people, in great feats of memory that make the poet virtually the encyclopedia of his culture. A poet from the oral tradition might also become a singer of the new Christian cosmology, like the illiterate herdsman Caedmon, whom Bede describes as having been called to monastic vows by the Abbess Hilda, in honor of his Christian poems composed in the vernacular oral mode.

In Celtic areas, oral poets had even greater status. The ancient class of learned Irish poets were honored servants of noblemen and kings; they remained as a powerful if reduced presence after the establishment of Christianity. The legal status of such a poet (a *fili*) was similar to that of a bishop, and indeed the *fili* carried out some functions of spells and divination inherited from the pagan priestly class, the druids. The ongoing influence of these poets in Irish politics and culture is reflected in the body of surviving secular literature from medieval Ireland, which is considerably larger than that from Anglo-Saxon England. A comparable situation prevailed in Wales. Even in the quite late Welsh *Tale of Taliesin*, the poet Taliesin appears as a public performer before the king as well as a possessor of arcane wisdom, magic, and prophecy.

This attitude of awe toward the word as used by the oral poet was only enhanced by the arrival of Christianity, a faith that attributes creation itself to an act of divine speech. Throughout the Middle Ages and long after orally composed poetry had retreated from many centers of high culture, the power of the word also inhered in its written form, as encountered in certain prized books. Chief among these were the Bible and other books of religious story, especially by such church

Saint John, from *The Book of Kells.* Late 8th century.

fathers as Saints Augustine and Jerome, and books of the liturgy. Since these texts bore the authority of divine revelation, the manuscripts that contained them shared in their charisma.

The power of these manuscripts was both reflected and aided by their visual grandeur. Among the highest expressions of the fervor and discipline of early insular monasticism is its production of beautifully copied and exquisitely decorated books of the Bible. The extreme elaboration of their production and the great labor and expense lavished on them suggest their almost holy status. Figures depicted holding a book in the late eighth-century *Book of Kells,* or writing in the Lindisfarne Gospels, indicate this importance; a fascination with the new technology is suggested by Old English riddles whose answers are "a hand writing," "a book worm," or "a bookcase."

The cost and effort of making manuscript books and their very scarcity contributed to their aura. Parchment was produced from animal skins, stretched and scraped. The training and discipline involved in copying texts, especially sacred texts, were great. The decoration of the most ambitious manuscripts involved rare colors, gold leaf, and often supreme artistry. Thus these magnificent manuscripts could become almost magical icons: Bede, for example, tells of scrapings from Irish manuscripts which mixed with water cured the bites of poisonous snakes.

Manuscripts slowly became more widely available. By the twelfth century we hear more of manuscripts in private hands and the beginning of production outside ecclesiastical settings. By the fourteenth century merchants and private scholars were buying books from shops that resembled modern booksellers. The glamour and prestige of beautiful manuscripts remained, though, even if the sense of their magic faded to a degree. Great families would donate psalters and gospels to religious foundations, with the donor carefully represented in the decoration presenting the book to the Virgin Mary or the Christ child. Spectacular books of private devotion were at once a medium for spiritual meditation and proof of great wealth (see Color Plate 10). Stories of epic conquest like the *Aeneid* would sometimes feature their aristocratic owners' coat of arms.

THE NORMAN CONQUEST

By the time of these developments in book production, though, a gigantic change had occurred. In a single year, 1066, England witnessed the death of the Anglo-Saxon King Edward and the coronation of his disputed successor King Harold, the invasion and triumph of the foreigner William of Normandy, and his own coronation as King William. These events are recorded, from very different perspectives, in *The Anglo-Saxon Chronicle* and the Bayeux Tapestry (page 166). The Normans conquered, with relative ease, an Anglo-Saxon kingdom disordered by civil strife. The monastic movement had lost much of its earlier fervor and discipline, despite reform in the tenth century. Baronial interests had weakened severely the reign of the late King Edward "the Confessor." On an island that already perceived itself as repeatedly colonized, 1066 nonetheless represented a climactic change, experienced and registered at virtually all levels of social, religious, and cultural experience.

One sign of how great a breach had been opened in England, paradoxically, is the multifaceted effort put forth by conquerors and conquered to maintain—or invent—continuity with the pre-Conquest past. In religious institutions, in dynastic genealogies, in the intersection of history and racial myth, in the forms and records of social institutions, the generations after 1066 sought to absorb a radically changed world yet to ground their world in an increasingly mythicized Anglo-Saxon or Briton antiquity. The Normans and their dynastic successors the Angevins eagerly took up and adapted to their own preoccupations ancient Briton political myths such as that of King Arthur and his court, and the stories of such saintly Anglo-Saxon kings as Oswald and Edward the Confessor.

They promoted narratives of their ancestors, like Wace's *Roman de Rou*, the story of the Normans' founder Rollo, commissioned by Henry II. Geoffrey of Monmouth dedicated his *History of the Kings of England* partly to Henry II's uncle, Robert Duke of Gloucester. In that work Geoffrey links the Celtic myths of King Arthur and his followers to an equally ancient myth that England was founded by descendants of the survivors of Troy; he makes his combined, largely fictive but enormously appealing work available to a Norman audience by writing it in Latin. Geoffrey's story was soon retold in "romance," the French from which vernacular

The Three Living and the Three Dead, from *The De Lisle Psalter*. The transience of life, especially of worldly glory, was never far from the medieval imagination. In this image from a Psalter made in the early 14th century for Baron Robert de Lisle, three kings in elegant courtly array face three rotting corpses. While most of the Psalter is in French and Latin, this scene has a "caption" in rhymed Middle English at the top. The kings say in turn (in modernized form), "I am afeared. Lo, what I see! I think that here are devils three." The corpses reply, "I was well fair. Such shall thou be. For God's love beware by me."

texts took their name. The Angevin court also supported the "romances of antiquity," poems in French that narrate the story of Troy (the *Roman de Troie*), its background (*Roman de Thèbes*), and its aftermath (*Roman d'Eneas*), thus creating a model in the antique past for the Normans and their westward conquest of England. And the *Song of Roland*, the great crusading narrative celebrating the heroic death of Charlemagne's nephew as he protected Christendom from the Spanish Moslems, was probably written in the milieu of Henry II's court.

The Normans brought with them a new system of government, a freshly renovated Latin culture, and most important a new language. Anglo-Saxon sank into relative insignificance at the level of high culture and central government. Norman French became the language of the courts of law, of literature, and of most of the nobility. By the time English rose again to widespread cultural significance, about 250 years later, it was a hybrid that combined Romance and Germanic elements.

Latin offered a lifeline of communication at some social levels of this initially fractured society. The European clerics who arrived under the immigrant archbishops Lanfranc and Anselm brought a new and different learning, and often new and deeply unwelcome religious practices: a celibate priesthood, skepticism about local saints, and newly disciplined monasticism. Yet despite these differences and the tensions that accompanied them, clerics of European or British origin were linked by a common liturgy, a considerable body of shared reading, and most of all

Latin offered a lifeline of communication at some social levels of this initially fractured society.

a common learned language. Secular as well as religious society were coming to be based more and more on the practical use of the written word: the letter, the charter, the documentary record, and the written book. Whereas Anglo-Saxon England had been governed by the word enacted and performed—a law of oral witness and a culture of oral poets—Norman England increasingly became a land of documents and books.

SOCIAL AND RELIGIOUS ORDER

The famed Domesday Book is a first instance of many of these developments. The Domesday survey was a gigantic undertaking, carried out with a speed that still astonishes between Christmas 1085 and William the Conqueror's death in September 1087. A county-by-county survey of the lands of King William and those held by his tenants-in-chief and subtenants, Domesday also records the obligations of landholders and thus reflects a new feudal system by which, increasingly, land was held in post-Conquest England.

Under the Normans, a nobleman held land from the king as a fief, in exchange for which he owed the king certain military and judicial services, including the provision of armed knights. These knights in turn held land from their lord, to whom they also owed military service and other duties. Some of this land they might keep for their own farming and profit, and the rest they divided among serfs (who were obliged, in theory, to stay on the land to which they were born) and free peasantry. Both groups owed their knight or lord labor and either a portion of their agricultural produce or rents in cash. This system of land tenure was surely more complex and irregular in practice than in the theoretical model called feudalism. For instance, services at all levels were sometimes (and increasingly) commuted to cash payment, and while fiefs were theoretically held only by an individual for a lifetime, increasingly there were expectations that they would be inherited. Royal power gradually grew during the thirteenth and fourteenth centuries, yet the local basis of landholding and social order always acted as a counterbalance, even a block, to royal ambition.

The Domesday Book was only one piece of the multifaceted effort by which the Norman and later kings sought to extend and centralize royal power in their territories. William and his successors established a system of royal justices who traveled throughout the realm and reported ultimately to the king, and an organized royal bureaucracy began to appear. The most powerful and learned of these Anglo-Norman kings was William the Conqueror's great-grandson, Henry II, who ruled from 1154 to 1189. Under Henry, royal justice, bureaucracy, and record-keeping made great advances; the production of documents was centralized and took on more standardized forms, and copies of these documents (called "pipe rolls") began to be produced for later reference and proof.

Along with a stronger royal government, the Normans brought a clergy invigorated both by new learning and by the spirituality of recent monastic reforms. Saint Anselm, the second of the Norman archbishops of Canterbury, was a great prelate and the writer of beautiful and widely influential texts and prayers of private devotion. The Victorines and the Cistercians (inspired in part by Saint Bernard of Clairvaux) also brought a strong mystical streak to English monasticism. All these would bear fruit once again in the fourteenth century in a group of mystics writing in Latin and in English.

On the other hand, the Norman prelates, like their kings, brought an urge toward centralized order in the church and a belief that the church and its public justice (the "canon law") should be independent of secular power. This created frequent conflict with kings and aristocrats, who wanted to extend their judicial power and expected to wield considerable influence in the appointment of church officials.

The most explosive moment in this ongoing controversy occurred in the disagreements between Henry II and Thomas Becket, who was Henry's Chancellor and then Archbishop of Canterbury. Becket's increasingly public refusal to accommodate the king, either in the judicial sphere or the matter of clerical appointments, finally led to his murder by Henry's henchmen in 1170 at the altar of Canterbury Cathedral and his canonization very soon thereafter. A large body of hagiography (narratives of his martyrdom and posthumous miracles) swiftly developed, adding to an already rich tradition of writing about the lives of English saints. As Saint Thomas, Becket became a powerful focus for ecclesiastical ambition, popular devotion and pilgrimage, and religious and secular narrative. In fact, the characters of Chaucer's *Canterbury Tales* tell their stories while making a pilgrimage to his shrine.

At least in theory, feudal tenure involved an obligation of personal loyalty between lord and vassal that was symbolically enacted in the rituals of enfeoffment, in which the lord would bestow a fief on his vassal. This belief was elaborated in a large body of secular literature in the twelfth century and after. Yet feudal loyalty was always fragile and ideologically charged. Vassals regularly resisted the wills of their lord or king when their interests collided, sometimes to the extent of officially withdrawing from the feudal bond. Connected to feudal relations was the notion of a chivalric code among the knightly class (those who fought on horses, *chevaliers*), which involved not just loyalty to the lord but also honorable behavior within the class, even among enemies. Chivalric literature is thus full of stories of captured opponents being treated with the utmost politeness, as indeed happened when Henry II's son Richard was held hostage for years in Germany, awaiting ransom.

Connected to feudal relations was the notion of a chivalric code among the knightly class . . .

Similarly, although medieval theories of social order had some basis in fact, they exercised shifting influence within a much more complex social reality. For instance, medieval society was often analyzed by the model of the "three estates"— those who fought (secular aristocrats), those who prayed (the clergy), and those who worked the land (the free and servile peasantry). This model appears more or less explicitly in the poetry of William Langland and Chaucer. Such a system, though, did not allow for the gradual increase in manufacturing (weaving, pottery, metalwork, even the copying of books) or for the urban merchants who traded in such products. As society became more complex, a model of the "mystical social body" gained popularity, especially in the fourteenth century. Here a wider range of classes and jobs was compared to limbs and other body parts. Even this more flexible image was strictly hierarchical, though. Peasants and laborers were the feet, knights (on

The Murder of Thomas Becket, from Matthew Paris's *Historia Major,* mid-13th century.

the right) and merchants (on the left) were hands, and townspeople were the heart, but the head was made up of kings, princes, and prelates of the church.

CONTINENTAL AND INSULAR CULTURES

The arrival of the Normans, and especially the learned clerics who came then and after, opened England to influences from a great intellectual current that was stirring on the continent, the "renaissance of the twelfth century," which was to have a significant impact in the centuries that followed. A period of comparative political stability and economic growth made travel easier, and students and teachers were on the move, seeking new learning in Paris and the Loire valley, in northern Italy, and in Toledo with its Arab and Jewish cultures. Schools were expanding beyond the monasteries and into the precincts of urban cathedrals and other religious foundations. Along with offering traditional biblical and theological study, these schools sparked a revived interest in elegant Latin writing, Neoplatonic philosophy, and science deriving from Aristotle.

Because the Normans and Angevins ruled large territories on the Continent, movement across the Channel was frequent; by the mid-twelfth century learned English culture was urbane and international. English clerics like John of Salisbury studied at Chartres and Paris, and texts by eminent speculative and scientific writers like William of Conches and Bernard Silvestris came to England. As these foreign works entered England, education became more ambitious and widely available, and its products show growing contact with the works of classical Latin writers such as Horace, Virgil, Terence, Cicero, Seneca, and Ovid in his erotic as much as in his mythological poetry.

The renewed attention to these works went along with a revival of interest in the *trivium,* the traditional division of the arts of eloquence: grammar, rhetoric, and dialectic. The most aggressive of these was dialectic, a form of logic developed by the Greeks and then rediscovered by Christian Europe from Arab scholars who had preserved and pursued Greek learning. John of Salisbury, who promoted dialectic in his *Metalogicon*, described dialectic with metaphors of military prowess, as though it were an extension of knightly jousting. "Since dialectic is carried on between two persons," he writes, Aristotle's *Topics* "teaches the matched contestants whom it trains and provides with reasons and topics, to handle their proper weapons and engage in verbal, rather than physical conflict." Rhetoric was elaborately codified in technical manuals of poetry. Though in one sense it was merely ornamental, teaching how to flesh out a description or incident with figures of speech, rhetoric could be as coercive as dialectic, though, since it specified strategies of persuasion in a tradition deriving from ancient oratory. Rhetorical texts also instructed the student in letter-writing, increasingly important as an administrative skill and as a form of elevated composition.

> John of Salisbury, who promoted dialectic in his Metalogicon, *described dialectic with metaphors of military prowess, as though it were an extension of knightly jousting.*

The study of the *trivium* generated many Latin school texts and helped foster a high level of Latinity and a self-consciously sophisticated, classicizing literature in the second half of the twelfth century. Some school texts had great influence on vernacular literature, such as the *Poetria Nova* by Geoffrey of Vinsauf, a rhetorical handbook filled with vivid poetic examples. More intriguing is *Pamphilus,* a short Ovidian poem about a seduction, aided by Venus, which turns into a rape. It is thought to have been an exercise in *disputatio,* the oral form that dialectic assumed in the classroom. The poem was immensely popular in the next few centuries and was translated into many vernacular languages. *Pamphilus* was a conduit at once for Ovidian eroticism and for the language of debate on love. Chaucer mentions it as a model of passionate love and seems to have adapted some of its plot devices in his *Troilus and Criseyde*.

While classical Latin literature was often read with a frank interest in pagan ideas and practices, commentators also offered allegorical interpretations that drew pagan stories into the spiritual and cosmological preoccupations of medieval Christianity. Ovid's *Metamorphoses* were thus interpreted in a French poem, the *Ovide Moralisé,* that was clearly known to Chaucer, and in Latin commentaries such as the *Ovidius moralizatus* of Pierre Bersuire. For instance, Ovid describes Jupiter, in the form of a bull, carrying the Tyrian princess Europa into the sea to rape her. Bersuire interprets this as Christ taking on human flesh in order to take up the human soul he loves. Alternatively, he offers an explicitly misogynist allegory, casting Europa as young women who like to see handsome young men—bulls: "They are drawn through the stormy sea of evil temptations and are raped." Neither text is often very subtle in the extraction of Christian or moral analogies from Ovid's stories, yet both were popular and influential, if only because they also tell Ovid's tales before allegorizing them.

Allegory became a complex and fruitful area of the medieval imagination, with profound implications not only for reading, but for artistic production as well. In its simplest sense, an allegorical text takes a metaphor and extends it into narrative, often personifying a quality as a character. For instance, the enormously popular dream vision the *Roman de la Rose* by Guillaume de Lorris and Jean de Meun (which Chaucer translated into English) presents a lady's ambivalence toward courtship as the conflict between such personifications as "Reserve" and "Fair Welcome," both aspects of her own mind. When Christine de Pizan came to challenge the misogynist texts of Western tradition—the *Roman de la Rose* among them—she too chose the allegorical mode. In the *Book of the City of Ladies*, it is three virtues personified as ladies—Reason, Rectitude, and Justice—who refute the slanders of men and who encourage the poet to build a city celebrating female achievements. (The continuing influence of this text is reflected by the English translation printed in 1521.) The English morality play *Mankind* uses allegory to portray external forces, presenting its hero as tempted by the vices of the modern age, "New-Guise" (trendy behavior), "Nowadays," and "Nought." Medieval writers also employed an allegorical method known as typology, derived from biblical interpretation, in which Old Testament events are seen as literally true but also symbolically predictive of, and fulfilled by, events in the New Testament. An example of this occurs in *Piers Plowman*, which, among all its other allegorical devices, presents Abraham both as an Old Testament Patriarch, and, in his willingness to sacrifice his son, a type of Faith.

The Continent, particularly France, provided a variety of vernacular influences. French was the international language of aristocratic culture and an important literary language in England; continental French literature was crucial in the rise of courtly literature in Middle English. Many English Arthurian works, including *Sir Gawain and the Green Knight* and Sir Thomas Malory's *Morte Darthur*, are less indebted to English sources than to French romances, whether written on the Continent or in England by authors such as Marie de France and Thomas of Britain. Chaucer borrowed the conventions and imagery of the love poetry of Guillaume de Machaut and Eustache Deschamps, and even the meter of his earlier poetry derives from their French octosyllabic couplets. To a lesser extent, influences from Italy can be seen in Chaucer's use of Dante's *Divine Comedy*, and his extensive borrowing from Petrarch and Boccaccio. Such continental vernacular literatures infiltrated even the Celtic cultures, as we see in the witty mix of Welsh and European traditions in the poems of Dafydd ap Gwilym.

> *French literature was critical in the rise of courtly literature in Middle English. Many English Arthurian works . . . are less indebted to English sources than to French romances . . .*

If such writers and records reflect the higher achievements of education in England of the twelfth century and later, literacy was also diffusing in wider circles and new venues. In a society like England's that continued to produce considerable oral and public literature, indeed, the divide between literacy and illiteracy was always unstable and permeable. A secular aristocrat might have a clerk read to him or her; an urbanite could attend and absorb parts of public rituals that involved poems and orations; even a peasant would be able to pick up Latin tags from sermons or the liturgy. Thus a fourteenth-century writer like William Langland could expect his wide and mixed audience to recognize at least some of the Latin phrases he used along with English; and Chaucer could imagine a character like the Wife of

Bath who, at best semiliterate, could still quote bits of the Latin liturgy. Access to texts and the self-awareness fostered by private reading may have helped promote the social ambitions and disruptions within the mercantile and even peasant classes during the later Middle Ages.

WOMEN, COURTLINESS, AND COURTLY LOVE

Access to books also increased the self-awareness of women. Possession of books that encouraged prayer and private devotion, such as psalters and Books of Hours, appears to have facilitated early language training in the home. The many images in manuscripts of women reading—especially the Virgin Mary and her mother, Saint Anne—have interesting implications for our understanding of women's literacy and cultural roles. (See for instance the illumination from the *Bedford Hours*, Color Plate 10.) A number of aristocratic Norman and Angevin women received good educations at convents. Women in the holy life possessed at least some literacy, though this often may have been minimal indeed. Even well-educated women were more likely to read English or French than Latin, with the exception of liturgical books.

The roles of women in the society and cultural imagination of post-Conquest England are complex and contradictory. No Anglo-Norman woman held ecclesiastical prestige like the Anglo-Saxon abbess Hilda or other Anglo-Saxon holy women. Women's power seems to have declined in the long term, both in worldly affairs and in the church, as the Normans consolidated their hold on England and imposed their order on society. Nevertheless, ambitious women could have great influence, especially when they siezed upon moments of disruption. In civil strife over the succession to King Henry I, the Empress Matilda organized an army, issued royal writs, and in the end guaranteed the accession of her son Henry II. If Henry II's wife, Eleanor of Aquitaine, spent the latter decades of her husband's reign under virtual house arrest, it was largely because she had conspired with her sons to raise an army against her own husband.

Despite the limitations of their actual power, women were the focus, often the worshiped focus, of much of the best imaginative literature of the twelfth and thirteenth centuries; and women were central to the social rituals we associate with courtliness and the idea of courtly love. Despite her later imprisonment, Eleanor of Aquitaine was a crucial influence in the diffusion of courtly ideas from the continent, especially the south of France; and among the great writers of the century was Marie de France, who was probably related to Henry II. Scholars continue to debate whether the observances of "courtly love" were in fact widely practiced and whether its worship of women was empowering or restrictive: the image of the distant, adored lady implies immobility and even silence on her part. Certainly lyrics and narratives that embody courtly values are widespread, even if they often question what they celebrate; and the ideals of courtliness may have had as great an impact through these imaginative channels as through actual enactment.

> *Despite the limitations of their actual power, women were the focus, often the worshiped focus, of much of the best imaginative literature . . .*

Grotesques and a Courtly Scene, from the *Ormesby Psalter*, c. 1310–1325.

The ideas and rituals of courtliness reach back to Greek and Roman models of controlled and stylized behavior in the presence of great power. In the Middle Ages, values of discretion and modesty also may have filtered into the secular world from the rigidly disciplined setting of the monasteries. As the society of western Europe took on a certain degree of order in the eleventh and twelfth centuries, courtly attainments began to converge and even compete with simple martial prowess in the achievement of worldly power. The presence of large numbers of armed and ambitious men at the great courts provided at once an opportunity for courtly behavior and the threat of its disruption.

Whatever its historical reality, courtly love as a literary concept had an immense influence. In this it adopted the vocabulary of two distinct traditions: the veneration of the Virgin Mary and the love poetry of Ovid and his heirs. Mariolatry, which has a particularly rich tradition in England, celebrates the perfection of Mary as a woman and mother, who undid the sins of Eve and now intercedes for fallen mankind. Ovid, with his celebration of sensuality and cynical instructions for achieving the lover's desire, provided medieval Europe with a whole catalog of love psychology and erotic persuasion.

> *Whatever its historical reality, courtly love as a literary concept had an immense influence.*

The self-conscious command of fine manners, whether the proper way of hunting, dressing, addressing a superior, or wooing a lady, became a key mark of an aristocrat. Great reputations grew around courtly attainment, as in the legends that circulated about Richard I. Centuries later, the hero of *Sir Gawain and the Green Knight* is tested as much through his courtly behavior as through his martial bravery. A literature of etiquette emerged as early as the reign of Henry I in England and continued through the thirteenth century. In the court of Henry II, Daniel of Beccles wrote *Urbanus Magnus*, a verse treatise in Latin on courtesy. In this poem he offers detailed advice in many arenas of specific behavior at court: avoiding frivolity, giving brief counsel, and especially comporting oneself among the wealthy:

> Eating at the table of the rich, speak little
> Lest you be called a chatterbox among the diners.
> Be modest, make reverence your companion.

In a mildly misogynist passage, Daniel especially warns against becoming involved with the lord's wife, even if she makes an overture, as occurs in Marie de France's *Lanval*. Should this happen, Daniel offers polite evasive strategies, skills we see demonstrated in *Sir Gawain and the Green Knight*.

A Knight, early 14th century. This rubbing from a funerary brass depicts a knight as he presented himself to eternity, sheathed in chain mail and fully armed but with his hands joined in prayer. The dog at his feet is a symbol of fidelity.

ROMANCE

Courtliness was expressed both in lyric poetry and in a wide range of vernacular narratives that we now loosely call "romances"—referring both to their genre and to the romance language in which they were first written. The Arthurian tradition, featured in this anthology, is only one of many romance traditions; others include the legends of Tristan and Isolde, Alexander, and Havelock the Dane. In romances that focus on courtly love, the hero's devotion to an unapproachable lady tends to elevate his character. Although many courtly romances conclude in a happy and acceptable marriage of hero and heroine, others such as Marie's *Lanval* warn of the dangers of transgressive love to the hero and his society. To the extent that they portray women as disruptive agents of erotic desire, some romances take on elements of the misogynist tradition that persisted in clerical thought alongside the adoration of the Virgin. Near the end of *Sir Gawain and the Green Knight,* even the courtly Gawain explodes in a virulent diatribe against women.

Love was not the only subject of romance, however. Stories of love and war typically lead the protagonists into encounters with the uncanny, the marvelous, the taboo. This is not so surprising when we recall the practices of medieval Christianity that brought the believer into daily contact with such miracles as the Eucharist; even chronicles of saints' lives regularly showed the divine will breaking miraculously into everyday life. We may say today that romance looses the hero and heroine onto the landscape of the private or social subconscious; a medieval writer might have stressed that nature itself is imbued with mystery both by God and by other, more shadowy, spiritual forces.

In romances, the line between the mundane and the extraordinary is often highly permeable: an episode may move swiftly from a simple ride to a meeting with a magical lady or malevolent dwarf, as often occurs in Thomas Malory. Romance also seems to be a form of imaginative literature in which medieval society could acknowledge the transgressions of its own ordering principles: adultery, incest, unmotivated martial violence. And it often revisits areas of belief and imagination that official culture long had put aside: *Sir Gawain and the Green Knight,* for instance, features a magical knight who can survive having his head cut off and a powerful aged woman who is called a goddess. Both characters reach back, however indirectly, to pre-Christian figures encountered in early Irish and Welsh stories.

THE RETURN OF ENGLISH

The romances are another of the dense points of contact among the many languages and ethnicities of the medieval British Isles. These powerful and evocative narratives often feature figures of Celtic origin like the British King Arthur and his court who came to French- and English-language culture through the Latin *History* of Geoffrey of Monmouth. Such transmission is typical of the linguistic mix in post-Conquest England. The language of the aristocracy was French, used in government and law as well as in the nascent vernacular literature. A few conservative monasteries continued the famed *Anglo-Saxon Chronicle* in its original language after the Conquest. But increasingly English or an evolving form of Anglo-Saxon was the working language of the peasantry. Mixed-language households must have appeared as provincial Anglo-Saxon gentry began, quite quickly, to intermarry with the Normans and their descendants. The twelfth-century satirist Nigel of Canterbury (or "Wireker"), author of the *Mirror of Fools,* came from just such a mixed family.

Few writings in Middle English survive from the late twelfth century, and very little of value besides the extraordinary *Brut* of Layamon, which retranslates much of Geoffrey of Monmouth's *History* from a French version. A manuscript containing the earliest English lyric in this collection, the thirteenth-century *Cuckoo Song,* can suggest the linguistic complexity of the era: it contains lyrics in English and French, and instructions for performance in Latin.

English began to reenter the world of official discourse in the thirteenth century. Communications between the church and the laity took place increasingly in English, and by the late 1250s, Archbishop Sewal of York tended to reject papal candidates for bishoprics if they did not have good English. In 1258 King Henry III issued a proclamation in Latin, French, and English, though the circumstances were unusual. Teaching glossaries include a growing number of English words, as well as the French traditionally used to explain difficult Latin.

The fourteenth century inaugurated a distinct change in the status of English, however, as it became the language of parliament and a growing number of governmental activities. We hear of Latin being taught in the 1340s through English rather than French. In 1362 a statute tried (but failed) to switch the language of law courts from French to English, and in 1363 Parliament was opened in English. The period also witnesses tremendous activity in translating a wide range of works into English, including Chaucer's version of Boethius' *Consolation of Philosophy* and the Wycliffite translations of the Bible, completed by 1396. Finally, at the close of the century, the Rolls of Parliament record in Latin the overthrow of Richard II, but they feature Henry IV (in what was probably a self-consciously symbolic gesture) claiming the throne in a brief, grave speech in English and promising to uphold "the gude lawes and custumes of the Rewme."

The reemergence of English allowed an extraordinary flowering of vernacular literature, most notably the achievements of Chaucer, Langland, and the anonymous genius who wrote *Sir Gawain and the Green Knight.* It would be more accurate, nevertheless, to speak of the reemergence of "Englishes" in the second half of the fourteenth century. The language scholars now call Middle English divides into four quite distinct major dialects in different regions of the island. These dialects were in many ways mutually unintelligible, so that Chaucer, who was from London in the Southeast Midlands, might have been hard-pressed to understand *Sir Gawain and the Green Knight,* written in the West Midlands near Lancashire. (Certainly Chaucer was aware of dialects and mimics some northern vocabulary in his *Canterbury Tales.*) London was the center of government and commerce in this era and later the place of early book printing, which served to stabilize the language. Thus Chaucer's dialect ultimately dominated and developed into modern English. Therefore English-speaking students today can read Chaucer in the original without much difficulty, whereas Langland's *Piers Plowman* is very challenging and *Sir Gawain* may seem virtually a foreign tongue. As a result, the latter two works are offered in translation in this anthology. (For a practical guide to Chaucer's Middle English, also helpful in reading some of the lyrics and plays in this section, see pages 315–17.)

Color Plate 1 Stylized Beasts and Sacred Words. First page of the Gospel of Matthew, from the *Lindisfarne Gospels,* c. 698. This illustrated gospel book was made on the "holy island" of Lindisfarne off the coast of Northumberland, partly in honor of St. Cuthbert, who had died there 11 years earlier and whose cult was fast developing at the time. The manuscript reflects an extraordinary flowering of artistic production during these years, the meeting of world cultures that occurred in Northumbrian monastic life: Mediterranean Latin language and imagery, Celtic interlace, and Germanic animal motifs. In the 10th century an Anglo-Saxon translation was added in the margins and between the lines. *(Copyright © British Library Board. All Rights Reserved.)*

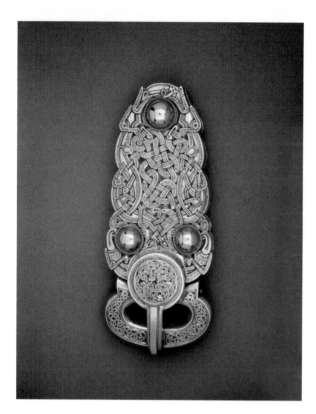

Color Plate 2   A Prince's Burial Horde.   Gold buckle, from the Sutton Hoo ship-burial, c. 625–630. Fragments of a remarkably preserved ship-burial, probably for an Anglo-Saxon king, were discovered among other burial mounds at Sutton Hoo, in Suffolk, England, in 1939. The burial mound contained numerous coins and 41 objects in gold, among them this magnificent buckle. Stylized animal heads (including two dragons in the circle at bottom) invite comparison with the powerful animal imagery in *Beowulf*. Other objects in the ship include two silver spoons inscribed "Saul" and "Paul," signs of the mixing of pagan practices and Christian influences in this era. (*Copyright © The Trustees of the British Museum.*)

Color Plate 3   Celtic Arts and Christian Ceremony.   The Ardagh Chalice, c. 9th century. This greatest surviving piece of medieval Celtic metalwork was found near the site of an ancient fort at Ardagh, in County Limerick in the southwest of Ireland. Measuring 9.5 inches across and 7 inches tall, the chalice was probably used for wine on great holidays like Easter, when laypeople took Communion. In the 7th century, the learned Irish monk Adamnan had described the chalice of the Last Supper as a silver cup with two opposite handles. The Ardagh Chalice is very similar. It is made of silver alloy, magnificently decorated with gilt and enamel. Its elaborate interlace decoration uses a wide range of Celtic motifs, including fearsomely toothed animal heads. In a band running around the entire bowl are the names of the 12 apostles, further linking its liturgical role to the Last Supper. (*National Museum of Ireland.*)

Color Plate 4 A Map of Multi-Ethnic Britain. Map of England, from Matthew Paris's *Historia Major*, mid-13th century. A monk of St. Albans, Matthew Paris wrote a monumental *History of England*, of which two illustrated copies in his own hand survive. Matthew's richly detailed map of England, including counties and major towns, illustrates the geographical knowledge of his day. It further suggests how alert he was to the ethnic divisions that still crossed his island and to the settlements and invasions, both mythic and actual, that had given rise to them. His inscription near the depiction of Hadrian's Wall, for example, informs us that the wall "once divided the English and the Picts." Recalling the claim that the original Britons were Trojan refugees, he writes about Wales (left center): "The people of this region are descended from the followers of Brutus." The story of Arthur's conception may have led Paris to identify Tintagel ("Tintaiol," lower left). Matthew also links geography and racial character, as in his comment on northern Scotland (top center): "A mountainous, woody region producing an uncivilized people." *(Copyright © British Library Board. All Rights Reserved.)*

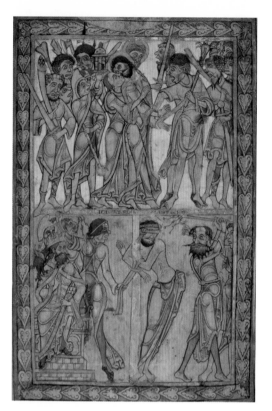

Color Plate 5 Ethnic Hostilities and the Sufferings of Christ. *Passion Scenes,* from the *Winchester Psalter,* 1150–1160. A series of full-page miniatures of crucial scenes from the Bible precedes the Psalter texts of this manuscript. The page reproduced here depicts scenes of the betrayal and flagellation of Christ. The vividly drawn images show the clinging drapery and exaggerated expressions typical of the manuscript; equally exaggerated are the African and Semitic features of some of the tormentors, associating them with peoples who were exotic or reviled in 12th-century England. Some of the original richness of color of this manuscript has been lost through damp, but also because blue pigment has been scraped off, presumably for reuse—a sign of how costly was the making of such manuscripts. (*Copyright © British Library Board. All Rights Reserved.*)

Color Plate 6 The Storytellers of the Round Table. *King Arthur and His Knights,* from a manuscript of the *Prose Lancelot,* late 13th century. This miniature appears in a manuscript of French prose Arthurian romances, which were also widely known in England. Here, King Arthur asks his knights to tell about their adventures on the quest for the Holy Grail. (*Beinecke Rare Book and Manuscript Library, Yale University.*)

Color Plate 7 Language Miracles at the Birth of Christ. *Annunciation to the Shepherds* (top) and *Nativity Scene* (bottom), from *The Holkham Bible Picture Book*, c. 1325–1330. This vividly illustrated manuscript depicts episodes from the Bible, adding events from later Christian legends. Crowded scenes are vigorous and full of gesture; they may reflect contact with liturgical drama and look forward to vernacular enactments such as the *Second Play of the Shepherds*. Short rhyming narratives above each picture mix up the major languages of early 14th-century England. At first the shepherds cannot understand the angel's Latin "*Gloria in excelsis*"; in Anglo-French they say "Glum? Glo? That means nothing. Let's go there, we'll understand better." At the scene of the Nativity, below, Middle English breaks in and "Songen alle with one stevene [voice]," though the shepherds can now sing famous Latin hymns: "*Gloria in excelsis deo*" and "*Te deum laudamus.*" Both the images and French and Middle English text mediate between the learned clerical class and the wealthy laypeople who were the manuscript's intended audience. (*Copyright © British Library Board. All Rights Reserved.*)

Color Plate 8 Symbols of Royal Power. *Richard II with His Regalia*, 1394–1395. Richard himself commissioned this splendid life-size and unusually lifelike portrait soon after the death of his beloved first wife, Anne of Bohemia. It was probably mounted at the back of the King's private pew at Westminster Abbey in London, but it also may suggest his wish to be perpetually near Anne, who was entombed nearby. At the same time, the throne, crown, orb, and scepter are all signs of Richard's sense of kingship and secular authority. (*Copyright © The Dean and Chapter of Westminster.*)

Color Plate 9 The Wife of Bath Begins Her Tale. From the Ellesmere manuscript of Chaucer's *Canterbury Tales*, 1405–1410. One of the two earliest surviving manuscripts of the *Tales*, it was owned for centuries by the Egerton family, who became Earls of Ellesmere in the nineteenth-century. The Ellesmere Chaucer was probably made in London, by then the center of book production in England. Its elaborate decoration and illustration are all the more striking, given how few Middle English texts received such treatment. The portrait of the Wife of Bath is positioned to highlight the beginning of her tale. Her red clothing, whip, and large hat follow details of her description in the *General Prologue* of the *Tales*, and her own words in the prologue to her tale. The grandeur of the treatment of text and decoration in this manuscript—clearly meant both for display and reading—reflect the speed with which Chaucer became a "canonical" author in the years after his death in 1400, and perhaps the wish of wealthy patrons to associate themselves and their interests with work. It is partly the same wish that ultimately led the American railroad tycoon Henry E. Huntington to buy the manuscript in 1917 and leave it to his library in San Marino, California. (*Copyright © The Huntington Library Art Collection & Botanical Gardens, San Marino California/Superstock, Inc.*)

Color Plate 10 The Virgin Mary Learns to Read. *Anne, Duchess of Bedford, Kneeling Before the Virgin Mary and Saint Anne,* from the *Bedford Hours,* early 15th century. A book of hours was a prayerbook used by laypeople for private devotion. The *Bedford Hours* was produced in a Paris workshop for the Duke of Bedford, a brother of Henry V, and his wife, Anne of Burgundy. Here, Saint Anne is shown teaching her daughter, the Virgin Mary, to read; another book lies open on a lectern in front of the kneeling Anne of Burgundy. *(Copyright © British Library Board. All Rights Reserved.)*

Not only are *Piers Plowman* and *Sir Gawain* written in dialects different from that of Chaucer's London, they also employ a quite distinct poetic style which descends from the alliterative meter of Old English poetry, based on repetitions of key consonants and on general patterns of stress. By contrast, the rhymed syllabic style used by poets like Chaucer developed under the influence of medieval French poetry and its many lyric forms. Fourteenth-century alliterative poetry was part of a revival that occurred in the North and West of the country, at a time when the form would have seemed old fashioned to many readers in the South. In the next two centuries, in a region even more distant from London, alliterative poetry or its echoes persisted in the Middle Scots poetry of William Dunbar, Robert Henryson, and Gavin Douglas.

POLITICS AND SOCIETY IN THE FOURTEENTH CENTURY

The fourteenth-century authors wrote in a time of enormous ferment, culturally and politically as well as linguistically. During the second half of the fourteenth century, new social and theological movements shook past certainties about the divine right of kings, the division of society among three estates, the authority of the church, and the role of women. An optimistic backward view can see in that time the struggle of the peasantry for greater freedom, the growing power of the Commons in Parliament, and the rise of a mercantile middle class. These changes often appeared far darker at the time, though, with threatening, even apocalyptic implications, as can be seen in *Piers Plowman*.

The forces of nature also cast a shadow across the century. In a time that never produced large agricultural surpluses, poor harvests led to famine in the second and third decades of the century, and an accompanying deflation drove people off the land. In 1348 the Black Death arrived in England, killing at least thirty-five percent of the population by 1350. Plague struck violently three more times before 1375, emptying whole villages. Overall, as much as half the population may have died.

> *In 1348 the Black Death arrived in England, killing at least thirty-five percent of the population by 1350.*

The kingship was already in trouble. After the consolidation of royal power under Henry II and the Angevins in the twelfth century, the regional barons began to reassert their power. In a climactic confrontation in 1215, they forced King John to sign the Magna Carta, guaranteeing (in theory at least) their traditional rights and privileges as well as due process in law and judgment by peers. In the fourteenth century the monarchy came under considerable new pressures. Edward II (1307–1327) was deposed by one of his barons, Roger de Mortimer, and with the connivance of his own queen, Isabella. His son Edward III had a long and initially brilliant reign, marked by great military triumphs in a war against France, but the conflict dragged on so long that it became known as the Hundred Years' War. Edward III's reign was marked at home by famine, deflation, and then, most horribly, plague. His later years were marked by premature senility and control by a court circle. These years were further darkened by the death of that paragon of chivalry, Edward's son and heir-apparent, Edward "The Black Prince." Edward's successor, the Black Prince's son Richard II, launched a major peace initiative in the Hundred

Years' War and became a great patron of the arts, but he was also capable of great tyranny. In 1399 like his great-grandfather, he was deposed. An ancient and largely creaky royal bureaucracy had difficulty running a growing mercantile economy, and when royal justice failed to control crime in the provinces, it was increasingly replaced by local powers.

The aristocracy too experienced pressures from the increased economic power of the urban merchants and from the peasants' efforts to exploit labor shortages and win better control over their land. The aristocrats responded with fierce, though only partly successful, efforts to limit wages and with stricter and more articulate divisions within society, even between the peerage and gentry. It is not clear, however, that fourteenth-century aristocrats perceived themselves as a threatened order. If anything, events may have pressed them toward a greater class cohesion, a more self-conscious pursuit of chivalric culture and values. The reign of Edward III saw the foundation of the royal Order of the Garter, a select group of nobles honored for their chivalric accomplishments as much as their power (the order is almost certainly evoked at the close of Sir Gawain and the Green Knight). Edward further exploited the Arthurian myth in public rituals such as tournaments and Round Tables. The ancient basis of the feudal tie, land tenure, began to give way to contract and payment in the growing, hierarchicalized retinues of the period. These were still lifelong relationships between lord and retainer, nevertheless, and contemporary historians of aristocratic sympathies like Jean Froissart idealize an ongoing community of chivalric conduct that could reach even across combating nations.

The second estate, the church, was also troubled—in part, paradoxically, because of the growing and active piety of the laity. Encouraged by the annual confession that had been required since the Fourth Lateran Council of 1215, laymen increasingly took control of their own spiritual lives. But the new emphasis on confession also led to clerical corruption. Mendicant (begging) friars, armed with manuals of penance, spread across the countryside to confess penitents in their own homes and sometimes accepted money for absolving them. Whether or not these abuses were truly widespread, they inspired much anticlerical satire—as is reflected in the works of Chaucer and Langland—and the Church's authority diminished in the process. The traditional priesthood, if better educated, was also more worldly than in the past, increasingly pulled from parish service into governmental bureaucracy; it too faced widespread literary satire. Well aware of clerical venality, the church nevertheless fearfully resisted the criticisms and innovations of "reforming clerics" like John Wyclif and his supporters among the gentry, the "Lollard knights." The church's control over religious experience was further complicated and perhaps undermined by the rise of popular mysticism, among both the clergy and the laity, which was difficult to contain within the traditional ecclesiastical hierarchy. Mystical writing by people as varied as Richard Rolle, Julian of Norwich, the anonymous author of The Cloud of Unknowing, and the emotive Margery Kempe all promulgate the notion of an individual's direct experience of the divine. Finally, and on a much broader scale, all of Christian Europe was rocked by the Great Schism of 1378, when believers faced the disconcerting spectacle of two popes ruling simultaneously.

The third estate, the commoners, was the most problematic and rapidly evolving of the three in the fourteenth century. The traditional division of medieval society into three estates had no place for the rising mercantile bourgeoisie and grouped them with the peasants who worked the land. In fact the new urban wealthy formed a class quite of their own. Patrons and consumers of culture, they also served in the royal bureaucracy under Edward III, as is illustrated by the career of Geoffrey Chaucer who came from just such a background. Yet only the wealthiest married into the landed gentry, and poor health conditions in the cities made long mercantile dynasties uncommon. Cities in anything like a modern sense were few and retained rural features. Houses often had gardens, even orchards, and pigs (and pig dung) filled the narrow, muddy streets. Only magnates built in stone; only they and ecclesiastical institutions had the luxury of space and privacy. Otherwise, cities were crowded and dirty—the suburbs especially disreputable—and venues for communicable disease.

The peasants too had a new sense of class cohesion. Events had already loosened the traditional bond of serfs to the land on which they were born, and the plagues further shifted the relative economic power of landowning and labor. As peasants found they could demand better pay, fiercely repressive laws were passed to stop them. These and other discontents, like the arrival of foreign labor and technologies, led to the Rising of 1381 (also known as the Peasants' Revolt). Led by literate peasants and renegade priests, the

Led by literate peasants and renegade priests, the rebels attacked aristocrats, foreigners, and some priests.

rebels attacked aristocrats, foreigners, and some priests. They were swiftly and violently put down, but the event was nevertheless a watershed and haunted the minds of the English.

When one leader of the revolt, the priest John Ball, cited Langland's fictional character Piers Plowman with approval, Langland reacted with dismay and revised his poem to emphasize the proper place of peasants. Even more conservative, Chaucer's friend John Gower wrote a horrified Latin allegory on the revolt, *Vox Clamantis* (*The Voice of One Crying*), where he compared the rebels to beasts. By contrast, Chaucer virtually ignored the revolt, aside from a brief comic reference in *The Nun's Priest's Tale*; it remains unclear, though, whether Chaucer's silence reflects comfortable bourgeois indifference or stems from deep anxiety and discomfort. At the same time, these disruptions introduced a period of cultural ferment, and the mercantile middle class also provided a creative force, appearing (though not without some nervous condescension) in some of Chaucer's most enduring characters like *The Canterbury Tales*' Merchant, the Wife of Bath, and the Miller.

It is both from this new middle class and from the established upper class that wider choices in the lives of women emerged in the later Middle Ages. Their social and political power had been curtailed both by clerical antifeminism and by the increasingly centralized government during the twelfth and thirteenth centuries. Starting in the fourteenth century, however, women began to regain an increased voice and presence. Among the aristocracy, Edward II's wife Isabella was an important player in events that brought about the king's deposition. And at the end of the century, Edward III's mistress Alice Perrers was widely criticized for her avarice and her influence on the aging king (for instance by William Langland who refers to her in the allegorical figure Lady Meed).

Women were also important in the spread of lay literacy among the middle class. In France, Christine de Pizan reexamined whole areas of her culture, especially ancient and biblical narrative, from a feminist perspective; her work was known and translated in England. Important autobiographical works were composed in Middle English by Julian of Norwich and Margery Kempe. Julian was an anchoress, living a cloistered religious life but able to speak to visitors such as Margery herself; Margery was an illiterate but prosperous townswoman, daughter of a mayor, who dictated to scribes her experiences of wifehood and rebellion against it, of travel to holy places, and of spiritual growth. Still, for the representation of women's voices in this period we are largely dependent on the fictional creations of men. Chaucer's famous Wife of Bath, for instance, strikes many modern readers as an articulate voice opposing women's repression and expressing their ambitions, but for all her critique of the antifeminist stereotypes of the church, she is in many ways their supreme embodiment. And in a number of Middle English lyrics, probably by men, the woman's voice may evoke scorn rather than pity as she laments her seduction and abandonment by a smooth-talking man, usually a cleric.

THE SPREAD OF BOOK CULTURE IN THE FIFTEENTH CENTURY

Geoffrey Chaucer died in 1400, a convenient date for those who like their eras to end with round numbers. Certainly literary historians have often closed off the English Middle Ages with Chaucer and left the fifteenth century as a sort of drab and undefined waiting period before the dawn of the Renaissance. Yet parts of fifteenth-century England are sites of vital and burgeoning literary culture. Book ownership spread more and more widely. Already in the late fourteenth century, Chaucer had imagined a fictional Clerk of Oxford with a solid collection of university texts despite his relative poverty. More of the urban bourgeoisie bought books and even had appealing collections assembled for them. When printing came to England in the later fifteenth century, books became even more available, though still not cheap.

Whether in manuscript or print, a swiftly growing proportion of these books was in English. The campaigns of Henry V in the second decade of the fifteenth century and his death in 1422 mark England's last great effort to reclaim the old Norman and Angevin territories on the continent. With the loss of all but a scrap of this land and the decline of French as a language of influence, these decades consolidate a notion of cultural and nationalistic Englishness. The Lancastrian kings, Henry the Fourth, Fifth, and Sixth, seem to have adopted English as the medium for official culture and patronized translators like Lydgate. Later in the period William Caxton made a great body of French and English texts available to aristocratic and middle-class readers, both by translating and by diffusing them in the new medium of print.

> *Whether in manuscript or print, a swiftly growing proportion of these books was in English.*

Ancient aristocratic narratives continued to evolve, as in Thomas Malory's retelling of the Arthurian story in his *Morte Darthur*, one of the books printed by Caxton. Malory works mostly from French prose versions but trims back much of the exploration of love and the uncanny; the result is a recharged tale of chivalric battle and familial and political intrigue. Other continental and local traditions are revived in another courtly setting by a group of Scots poets including William Dunbar and Robert Henryson.

As more and more commoners had educational and financial access to books, they also participated in a lively public literary culture in towns and cities. The fifteenth century sees the flowering of the great dramatic "mystery cycles," sets of plays on religious themes produced and in part performed by craft guilds of larger towns in the Midlands and North. Included here are two brilliant samples, the play of the *Crucifixion* from York and *The Second Play of the Shepherds* from Wakefield. Probably written by clerics, these plays are nonetheless dense with the preoccupations of contemporary working people and enriched by implicit analogies between the lives of their actors and the biblical events they portray. Lyrics and political poems continue to flourish. Sermons remain a popular and widespread form of religious instruction and literary production. And highly literary public rituals, such as Henry V's triumphal civic entries as he returned from his French campaigns, are part of Lancastrian royal propaganda.

By the time Caxton was editing and printing Malory in 1485 with an eye to sales and profit, over eight hundred years had passed since Caedmon is said to have composed his first Christian hymn under angelic direction. The idea of the poet had moved from a version of magician and priest to something more like a modern author; and the dominant model of literary transmission was shifting from listening to an oral performance to reading a book privately. Chaucer, that most bookish of poets, is a case in point. Many of his early poems refer to the pleasures of reading, not only for instruction but even as a mere pastime, often to avoid insomnia. He opens the dream vision *The Parliament of Fowls* with the poet reading a classical Latin text, Cicero's *Dream of Scipio*. Chaucer, of course, read his books and disseminated his own work in handwritten manuscript; in his humorous lyric *To His Scribe Adam* he expresses his frustration with copyists who might mistranscribe his words.

Despite such private bookishness, however, a more public and oral literary culture never disappeared from medieval Britain. Considerable interdependence between oral and literate modes of communication remained; poetry was both silently read and orally performed. In *The Canterbury Tales*, for instance, when the pilgrim Chaucer apologizes for the bawdiness of *The Miller's Tale*, he suggests that if the listener/reader does not like what he *hears*, he should simply turn the *page* and choose another tale. At the same time, literate clerics practiced what we might call learned orality, through lectures or disputations at Oxford and Cambridge or from the pulpit in a more popular setting. Langland imitates such sophisticated oral practice in the theological debates in *Piers Plowman*, and Chaucer uses the sermon form in *The Wife of Bath's Prologue*, *The Pardoner's Tale*, and *The Parson's Tale*. The popular orality of minstrel performance, harking back however distantly to the world of the Anglo-Saxon *scop* and the Irish *fili*, was also exploited with great self-consciousness by literate poets. Langland expresses harsh disapproval of those minstrels who were mere entertainers, undercutting the serious work of preachers. *Sir Gawain and the Green Knight* presents itself as an oral performance, based on a tale that the narrator has heard recited. By contrast, Chaucer gently twits minstrels in his marvelous parody of popular romance, *Sir Thopas*. Chaucer remains a learned poet whose greatest achievement, paradoxically, was the presentation of fictional oral performances—the tale-telling of the Canterbury pilgrims.

The speed with which communication technologies are changing in our own era has heightened our awareness of such changes in the past. We are now closing the era of the book and moving into the era of the endlessly malleable electronic text. In many ways the means by which we have come to receive and transmit information—television, radio, CD-ROM, Internet—mix orality and literacy in a fashion wholly new yet also intriguingly reminiscent of the later Middle Ages. In contrast to the seeming fixity of texts in the intervening centuries, contemporary literary culture may be recovering the sense of textual and cultural fluidity that brought such dynamism to literary creation in the Middle Ages.

> *. . . the means by which we have come to receive and transmit information . . . mix orality and literacy in a fashion wholly new yet also intriguingly reminiscent of the later Middle Ages.*

 For additional resources on the Middle Ages, including an interactive timeline of the period, go to *The Longman Anthology of British Literature* Web site at www.myliteraturekit .com.

BEFORE THE NORMAN CONQUEST

Beowulf

Beowulf has come down to us as if by chance, for it is preserved only in a single manuscript now in the British Library, Cotton Vitellius A.xv, which almost perished in a fire in 1731. An anonymous poem in the West Saxon dialect of Old English, it may stretch back as early as the late eighth century, although recent scholars think the version we now have was composed within one hundred years of its transcription in the late tenth century. If the later date is correct, this first "English epic" could have appealed to one of the Viking kings who ruled in northern and eastern England. This would help explain a king's burial at sea, a Viking practice, that occurs early in the poem (page 37), and the setting of most of the poem's action in Scandinavia (see map, page 33). Although it was studied by a few antiquarians during the early modern period, *Beowulf* remained virtually unknown until its first printing in 1815, and it was only in the twentieth century that it achieved a place in the canon, not just as a cultural artifact or a good adventure story but as a philosophical epic of great complexity and power.

Several features of *Beowulf* make its genre problematic: the vivid accounts of battles with monsters link it to the folktale, and the sense of sorrow for the passing of worldly things mark it as elegiac. Nevertheless, it is generally agreed to be the first postclassical European epic. Like the *Iliad* and the *Odyssey*, it is a primary epic, originating in oral tradition and recounting the legendary wars and exploits of its audience's tribal ancestors from the heroic age.

The values of Germanic tribal society are indeed central to *Beowulf*. The tribal lord was held to ideals of extraordinary martial valor. More practically, he rewarded his successful followers with treasure that symbolized their mutual obligations. A member of the lord's *comitatus*—his band of warriors—was expected to follow a rigid code of heroic behavior stressing

Peoples and places in *Beowulf*, after F. Klaeber.

bravery, loyalty, and willingness to avenge lord and comrades at any cost. He would suffer the shame of exile if he should survive his lord in battle; the speaker of *The Wanderer* (pages 172–75) may be such a man. Such values are explicitly invoked at the end of *Beowulf*, when Wiglaf, the hero's only loyal retainer, upbraids his comrades for having abandoned Beowulf to the dragon: he says that their prince wasted his war gear on them, and predicts the demise of their people, the Geats, once their ancient enemies, the Swedes, hear that Beowulf is dead.

   Beowulf offers an extraordinary double perspective, however. First, for all its acceptance of the values of the pagan heroic code, it also refers to Christian concepts that in many cases conflict with them. Although all characters in the poem—Danes, Swedes, and Geats, as well as the monsters—are pagan, the monster Grendel is described as descended from Cain and destined for hell. It is the joyous song of creation at Hrothgar's banquet, reminiscent of

Genesis 1, that inspires Grendel to renew his attacks. Furthermore, while violence in the service of revenge is presented as the proper way for Beowulf to respond to inhuman assailants such as Grendel's mother, the narrator expresses a regretful view, perhaps influenced by Christianity, of the unending chain of violence engaged in by feuding tribes. And although the Danish king Hrothgar uses wealth as a kind of social sacrament when he lavishly rewards Beowulf for his military aid, he simultaneously invokes God in a "sermon" warning him against excessive pride in his youthful strength. This rich division of emotional loyalty probably arises from a poet and audience of Christians who look back at their pagan ancestors with both pride and grief, stressing the intersection of pagan and Christian values in an effort to reconcile the two. By restricting his biblical references to events in the Old Testament, the poet shows the Germanic revenge ethic as consistent with the Old Law of retribution, and leaves implicit its conflict with the New Testament injunction to forgive one's enemies.

The style *of Beowulf* is simultaneously a challenge and a reward to the modern reader. Some of its features, such as the variation of an idea in different words—which would have been welcomed by a listening, and often illiterate, audience—can seem repetitious to a literate one. Two other stylistic features that are indebted to the poem's oral origin are highly admired today. First, like other Old English poems, *Beowulf* uses alliteration as a structural principle, beginning three of the four stressed words in a line with the same letter. The translator has sought the same effect, even when departing considerably from the original language. The poet also uses compound words, such as *mearcstapa* ("borderland-prowler") and *fifelcynnes* ("of monsterkind"), with unusual inventiveness and force. A specific type of compound used for powerful stylistic effects is the "kenning," a kind of compressed metaphor, such as "whale-road" for "ocean" or "wave-cutter" for ship. The kennings resemble the Old English riddles in their teasing, enigmatic quality.

On a larger narrative level is another stylistic feature, also traceable to the poem's oral roots: the tendency to digress into stories tangential to the action of the main plot. The poet's digressions, however, actually contribute to his artistry of broad contrasts—youth and age, joy and sorrow, good and bad kingship. For instance, Hrothgar, while urging humility and generosity on the victorious Beowulf, tells the story of the proud and parsimonious King Heremod. Similarly, when Beowulf returns home in glory to the kingdom of the Geats, the poet praises his uncle Hygelac's young Queen Hygd by contrasting her with the bad Queen Modthryth, who lost her temper and sent her suitors to death.

These episodes also return to prominent themes like nobility, heroic glory, and the distribution of treasure. Such return to key themes, as well as the poem's formulaic repetition and stylistic variation, all bear comparison to insular art of its time. As seen in the page from the *Book of Kells* illustrated on page 14, the dense repetition of lines and intertwined curves, even zoomorphic shapes (often called interlace) competes for attention with the central image of Saint John. This intricately crafted biblical image, like the royal treasure from the Sutton Hoo ship-burial (Color Plate 2), help remind us that the extraordinary artistic accomplishments of Anglo-Saxon culture went hand-in-hand with its nostalgia for heroic violence.

The poet uses digression and repetition in an especially subtle way to foreshadow dark events to come. To celebrate Beowulf's victory over Grendel, the bard at Hrothgar's hall sings of events of generations earlier, in which a feud caused the deaths of a Danish princess's brother and son. Although this story has nothing to do with the main plot of the poem, there is an implied parallel a few lines later, when, ominously, Hrothgar's queen Wealtheow hints that her husband's nephew Hrothulf should treat her young sons honorably, remembering the favors Hrothgar has shown him, and soon after, urges Beowulf also to be kind them. The original audience would have known that after Hrothgar's death, his queen will suffer a disaster like that of the princess in the song. The poet thus applies his broad principle of comparison and contrast to complex narrative situations as well as to simpler concepts such as good and

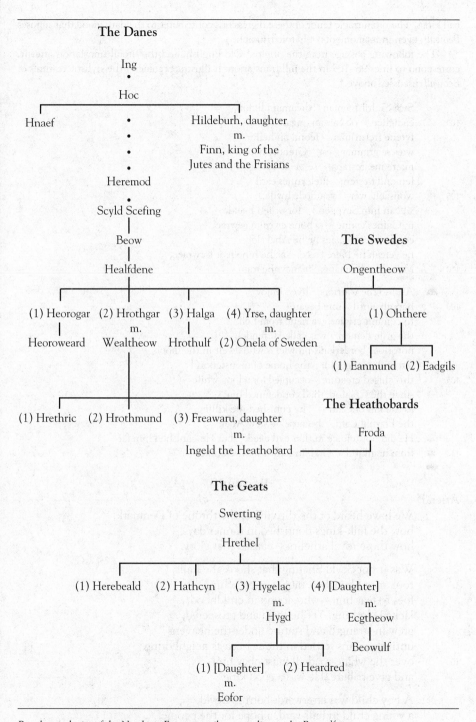

The Danes

Ing
•
Hoc

Hnaef   •   Hildeburh, daughter
         •   m.
         •   Finn, king of the
         •   Jutes and the Frisians
Heremod
•
Scyld Scefing

Beow

Healfdene

(1) Heorogar (2) Hrothgar (3) Halga (4) Yrse, daughter
                    m.   m.
Heoroweard   Wealtheow   Hrothulf (2) Onela of Sweden

(1) Hrethric (2) Hrothmund (3) Freawaru, daughter
                                   m.
                        Ingeld the Heathobard ——————

The Swedes

Ongentheow

(1) Ohthere

(1) Eanmund   (2) Eadgils

The Heathobards

Froda

The Geats

Swerting

Hrethel

(1) Herebeald (2) Hathcyn (3) Hygelac (4) [Daughter]
                                  m.   m.
                                Hygd   Ecgtheow

                                              Beowulf

(1) [Daughter]   (2) Heardred
m.
Eofor

Royal genealogies of the Northern European tribes according to the *Beowulf* text.

bad kings. The often tragic tenor of these digressions contributes to the dark mood that suffuses *Beowulf*, even in its moments of heroic triumph.

The following passage from the original Old English, and the literal translation after it, correspond to lines 98–109 in the full translation. It illustrates some of the stylistic features of *Beowulf* discussed above.*

       Swā ða drihtguman   drēamum lifdon,
100   ēadiglīce,   oð ðæt ān ongan
       fyrene fre(m)man   fēond on helle;
       wæs se grimma gæst   Grendel hāten,
       mǣre mearcstapa,   sē þe mōras hēold,
       fen ond fæsten;   fīfelcynnes eard
105   wonsǣli wer   weardode hwile,
       siþðan him Scyppend   forscrifen haefde
       in Cāines cynne—   þone cwealm gewraec
       ēce Drihten,   þaes þe hē Abel slōg;
       ne gefeah hē þǣre fǣðe,   ac hē hine feor forwraec,
110   Metod for þȳ māne   mancynne fram.

       And so the warriors   lived in joy
100   happily until   one began
       to commit crimes,   a fiend from hell
       the grim demon   was called Grendel,
       notorious borderland-prowler   who dwelt in the moors
       fen and stronghold;   the home of monsterkind
105   this cursed creature   occupied for a long while
       since the Creator   had condemned him
       as the kin of Cain—   he punished the killing,
       the Eternal Lord,   because he slew Abel;
       He did not rejoice in that evil deed,   but He banished him far
110   from mankind,   God, in return for the crime.

Beowulf[1]

Attend!

       We have heard of the thriving of the throne of Denmark,
       how the folk-kings flourished in former days,
       how those royal athelings[2] earned that glory.

       Was it not Scyld Shefing that shook the halls,
5   took mead-benches, taught encroaching
       foes to fear him—who, found in childhood,
       lacked clothing? Yet he lived and prospered,
       grew in strength and stature under the heavens
       until the clans settled in the sea-coasts neighboring
10   over the whale-road all must obey him
       and give tribute. He was a good king!

       A boy child was afterwards born to Scyld,
       a young child in hall-yard, a hope for the people,

---

*The passage is taken from *Beowulf and the Fight at Finnsburg*, 3rd ed., ed. Frederick Klaeber (Boston: D. C. Heath, 1950). The translation is by Anne Schotter.

1. This translation, which captures the alliteration of the original Old English, is by Michael Alexander.
2. Noblemen.

sent them by God; the griefs long endured
15 were not unknown to Him, the harshness of years
without a lord. Therefore the life-bestowing
Wielder of Glory granted them this blessing.
Through the northern lands the name of Beow,
the son of Scyld, sprang widely.
20 For in youth an atheling should so use his virtue,
give with a free hand while in his father's house,
that in old age, when enemies gather,
established friends shall stand by him
and serve him gladly. It is by glorious action
25 that a man comes by honor in any people.

At the hour shaped for him Scyld departed,
the hero crossed into the keeping of his Lord.
They carried him out to the edge of the sea,
his sworn arms-fellows, as he had himself desired them
30 while he wielded his words, Warden of the Scyldings,
beloved folk-founder; long had he ruled.

A boat with a ringed neck rode in the haven,
icy, out-eager, the atheling's vessel,
and there they laid out their lord and master,
35 dealer of wound gold, in the waist of the ship,
in majesty by the mast. A mound of treasures
from far countries was fetched aboard her,
and it is said that no boat was ever more bravely fitted out
with the weapons of a warrior, war accoutrement,
40 swords and body-armor; on his breast were set
treasures and trappings to travel with him
on his far faring into the flood's sway.

This hoard was not less great than the gifts he had had
from those who at the outset had adventured him
45 over seas, alone, a small child.

High over head they hoisted and fixed
a gold *signum*,[3] gave him to the flood,
let the seas take him, with sour hearts
and mourning mood. Men under heaven's
50 shifting skies, though skilled in counsel,
cannot say surely who unshipped that cargo.

Then for a long space there lodged in the stronghold
Beowulf the Dane,[4] dear king of his people,
famed among nations—his father had taken
55 leave of the land—when late was born to him
the lord Healfdene, lifelong the ruler

---

3. Banner.

4. Not to be confused with Beowulf the Geat, the hero of the poem.

and war-feared patriarch of the proud Scyldings.
He next fathered four children
that leapt into the world, this leader of armies,
60   Heorogar and Hrothgar and Halga the Good;
and Ursula,[5] I have heard, who was Onela's queen,
knew the bed's embrace of the Battle-Scylfing.

Then to Hrothgar was granted glory in battle,
mastery of the field; so friends and kinsmen
65   gladly obeyed him, and his band increased
to a great company. It came into his mind
that he would command the construction
of a huge mead-hall, a house greater
than men on earth ever had heard of,
70   and share the gifts God had bestowed on him
upon its floor with folk young and old—
apart from public land and the persons of slaves.
Far and wide (as I heard) the work was given out
in many a tribe over middle earth,
75   the making of the mead-hall. And, as men reckon,
the day of readiness dawned very soon
for this greatest of houses. Heorot he named it
whose word ruled a wide empire.
He made good his boast, gave out rings,
80   arm-bands at the banquet. Boldly the hall reared
its arched gables; unkindled the torch-flame
that turned it to ashes. The time was not yet
when the blood-feud should bring out again
sword-hatred in sworn kindred.

85   It was with pain that the powerful spirit
dwelling in darkness endured that time,
hearing daily the hall filled
with loud amusement; there was the music of the harp,
the clear song of the poet, perfect in his telling
90   of the remote first making of man's race.
He told how, long ago, the Lord formed Earth,
a plain bright to look on, locked in ocean,
exulting established the sun and the moon
as lights to illumine the land-dwellers
95   and furnished forth the face of Earth
with limbs and leaves. Life He then granted
to each kind of creature that creeps and moves.

So the company of men led a careless life,
all was well with them: until One began
100   to encompass evil, an enemy from hell.
Grendel they called this cruel spirit,

---

5. The manuscript is defective at this point. "Ursula" is a name reconstructed from Scandinavian tradition.

the fell and fen his fastness was,
the march his haunt. This unhappy being
had long lived in the land of monsters
105   since the Creator cast them out
as kindred of Cain. For that killing of Abel
the eternal Lord took vengeance.
There was no joy of that feud: far from mankind
God drove him out for his deed of shame!
110   From Cain came down all kinds misbegotten
—ogres and elves and evil shades—
as also the Giants, who joined in long
wars with God. He gave them their reward.

With the coming of night came Grendel also,
115   sought the great house and how the Ring-Danes
held their hall when the horn had gone round.
He found in Heorot the force of nobles
slept after supper, sorrow forgotten,
the condition of men. Maddening with rage,
120   he struck quickly, creature of evil:
grim and greedy, he grasped on their pallets
thirty warriors, and away he was out of there,
thrilled with his catch: he carried off homeward
his glut of slaughter, sought his own halls.
125   As the day broke, with the dawn's light
Grendel's outrage was openly to be seen:
night's table-laughter turned to morning's
lamentation. Lord Hrothgar
sat silent then, the strong man mourned,
130   glorious king, he grieved for his thanes
as they read the traces of a terrible foe,
a cursed fiend. That was too cruel a feud,
too long, too hard!
               Nor did he let them rest
but the next night brought new horrors,
135   did more murder, manslaughter and outrage
and shrank not from it: he was too set on these things.

It was not remarked then if a man looked
for sleeping-quarters quieter, less central,
among the outer buildings; now openly shown,
140   the new hall-thane's hatred was manifest
and unmistakable. Each survivor
then kept himself at safer distance.

So Grendel became ruler; against right he fought,
one against all. Empty then stood
145   the best of houses, and for no brief space;
for twelve long winters torment sat
on the Friend of the Scyldings, fierce sorrows

and woes of every kind; which was not hidden
from the sons of men, but was made known
150   in grieving songs, how Grendel warred
long on Hrothgar, the harms he did him
through wretched years of wrong, outrage
and persecution. Peace was not in his mind
towards any companion of the court of Hrothgar,
155   the feud was not abated, the blood-price was unpaid.
Nor did any counselor have cause to look for
a bright man-price[6] at the murderer's hand:
the dark death-shadow drove always against them,
old and young; abominable
160   he watched and waited for them, walked nightlong
the misty moorland. Men know not
where hell's familiars fleet on their errands!

Again and again the enemy of men
stalking unseen, struck terrible
165   and bitter blows. In the black nights
he camped in the hall, under Heorot's gold roof;
yet he could not touch the treasure-throne
against the Lord's will, whose love was unknown to him.
A great grief was it for the Guardian of the Scyldings,
170   crushing to his spirit. The council lords
sat there daily to devise some plan,
what might be best for brave-hearted
Danes to contrive against these terror-raids.
They prayed aloud, promising sometimes
175   on the altars of their idols unholy sacrifices
if the Slayer of souls would send relief
to the suffering people.
                            Such was their practice,
a heathen hope; Hell possessed
their hearts and minds: the Maker was unknown to them,
180   the Judge of all actions, the Almighty was unheard of,
they knew not how to praise the Prince of Heaven,
the Wielder of Glory.
                            Woe to him who must
in terrible trial entrust his soul
to the embrace of the burning, banished from thought
185   of change or comfort! Cheerful the man
able to look to the Lord at his death-day,
to find peace in the Father's embrace!
This season rocked the son of Healfdene[7]

---

6. *Wergild*, a cash payment to the family in compensation for
a person's death in Anglo-Saxon culture. Since it was considered an advance over violent revenge, Grendel is marked
as uncivilized for refusing to acknowledge the practice.
7. Hrothgar. An example of the poet's frequent reference
to a male character by the name of his father.

with swingeing sorrows; nor could the splendid man
190 put his cares from him. Too cruel the feud,
too strong and long-lasting, that struck that people,
a wicked affliction, the worst of nightmares!

This was heard of at his home by one of Hygelac's followers,
a good man among the Geats,[8] Grendel's raidings;
195 he was for main strength of all men foremost
that trod the earth at that time of day;
build and blood matched.
                              He bade a seaworthy
wave-cutter be fitted out for him; the warrior king
he would seek, he said, over swan's riding,
200 that lord of great name, needing men.
The wiser sought to dissuade him from voyaging
hardly or not at all, thought they held him dear;
they whetted his quest-thirst, watched omens.
The prince had already picked his men
205 from the folk's flower, the fiercest among them
that might be found. With fourteen men
he sought sound-wood; sea-wise Beowulf
led them right down to the land's edge.

Time running on, she rode the waves now,
210 hard in by headland. Harnessed warriors
stepped on her stem; setting tide churned
sea with sand, soldiers carried
bright mail-coats to the mast's foot,
war-gear well-wrought; willingly they shoved her out,
215 thorough-braced craft, on the craved voyage.

Away she went over a wavy ocean,
boat like a bird, breaking seas,
wind-whetted, white-throated,
till the curved prow had ploughed so far
220 —the sun standing right on the second day—
that they might see land loom on the skyline,
then the shimmer of cliffs, sheer fells behind,
reaching capes.
                      The crossing was at an end;
closed the wake. Weather-Geats
225 stood on strand, stepped briskly up;
a rope going ashore, ring-mail clashed,
battle-girdings. God they thanked
for the smooth going over the salt trails.

8. A Germanic tribe that lived along the southwestern coast of what is now Sweden.

The watchman saw them. From the wall where he stood,
230   posted by the Scyldings to patrol the cliffs,
he saw the polished lindens[9] pass along the gangway
and the clean equipment. Curiosity
moved him to know who these men might be.

Hrothgar's thane, when his horse had picked
235   its way down to the shore, shook his spear
fiercely at arm's length, framed the challenge:
"Strangers, you have steered this steep craft
through the sea-ways, sought our coast.
I see you are warriors; you wear that dress now.
I must ask who you are.
240   In all the years
I have lived as look-out at land's end here
—so that no foreigners with a fleet-army
might land in Denmark and do us harm—
shield-carriers have never come ashore
245   more openly. You had no assurance
of welcome here, word of leave
from Hrothgar and Hrothulf!
                              I have not in my life
set eyes on a man with more might in his frame
than this helmed lord. He's no hall-fellow
250   dressed in fine armor, or his face belies him;
he has the head of a hero.
                              I'll have your names now
and the names of your fathers; or further you shall not go
as undeclared spies in the Danish land.
Stay where you are, strangers, hear
255   what I have to say! Seas crossed,
it is best and simplest straightaway to acknowledge
where you are from, why you have come."

The captain gave him a clear answer,
leader of the troop, unlocked his word-hoard:
260   "We here are come from the country of the Geats
and are King Hygelac's hearth-companions.
My noble father was known as Edgetheow,
a front-fighter famous among nations,
who had seen many seasons when he set out at last
265   an old man from the halls; all the wiser men
in the world readily remember him.

    It is with loyal and true intention that we come
to seek your lord the son of Healfdene,
guardian of the people: guide us well therefore!
270   We have a great errand to the glorious hero,

the Shepherd of the Danes; the drift of it
shall not be kept from you. You must know if indeed
there is truth in what is told in Geatland,
that among the Scyldings some enemy,
275   an obscure assailant in the opaque night-times,
makes spectacles of spoil and slaughter
in hideous feud. To Hrothgar I would
openheartedly unfold a plan
how the old commander may overcome his foe;
280   if indeed an easing is ever to slacken
these besetting sorrows, a settlement
when chafing cares shall cool at last.
Otherwise he must miserably live out
this lamentable time, for as long as Heorot,
285   best of houses, bulks to the sky."

The mounted coastguard made reply,
unshrinking officer: "A sharp-witted man,
clear in his mind, must be skilled
to discriminate deeds and words.
290   I accept what I am told, that this troop is loyal
to the Scyldings' Protector. Pass forward with your
weapons and war-dress! I am willing to guide you,
commanding meanwhile the men under me
to guard with care this craft of yours,
295   this new-tarred boat at its berth by our strand
against every enemy until again it bear
its beloved captain over the current sea,
curve-necked keel, to the coasts of the Geat;
such a warrior shall be accorded
300   unscathed passage through the shocks of battle."

The vessel was still as they set forward,
the deep-chested ship, stayed at its mooring,
fast at its anchor. Over the cheek-pieces
boar-figures[1] shone, bristling with gold,
305   blazing and fire-hard, fierce guards
of their bearers' lives. Briskly the men went
marching together, making out at last
the ample eaves adorned with gold:
to earth's men the most glorious
310   of houses under heaven, the home of the king;
its radiance lighted the lands of the world.
The coastguard showed them the shining palace,
the resort of heroes, and how they might
rightly come to it; this captain in the wars
315   then brought his horse about, and broke silence:
"Here I must leave you. May the Lord Almighty

---

1. Boars were often depicted on Anglo-Saxon weapons and helmets.

Boar, from a bas-relief carving on Saint Nicholas Church, Ipswich, England. Although this large and vigorous boar dates from the 12th century, it retains stylistic elements of earlier Anglo-Saxon and Viking art. An ancient totem of power, boars were often depicted on early medieval weapons and helmets.

afford His grace in your undertakings
and bring you to safety. Back at the sea-shore
I resume the watch against sea-raiders."

320   There was stone paving on the path that brought
the war-band on its way. The war-coats shone
and the links of hard hand-locked iron
sang in their harness as they stepped along
in their gear of grim aspect, going to the hall.

325   Sea-wearied, they then set against the wall
their broad shields of special temper,
and bowed to bench, battle-shirts clinking,
the war-dress of warriors. The weapons of the seamen
stood in the spear-rack, stacked together,

330   an ash-wood gray-tipped. These iron-shirted men
were handsomely armed.
                 A high-mannered chieftain
then inquired after the ancestry of the warriors.
"From whence do you bring these embellished shields,
gray mail-shirts, masked helmets,

335   this stack of spears? I am spokesman here,
herald to Hrothgar; I have not seen
a body of strangers bear themselves more proudly.
It is not exile but adventure, I am thinking,
boldness of spirit, that brings you to Hrothgar."

340   The gallant Geat gave answer then,
valor-renowned, and vaunting spoke,
hard under helmet: "At Hygelac's table
we are sharers in the banquet; Beowulf is my name.

345 I shall gladly set out to the son of Healfdene,
most famous of kings, the cause of my journey,
lay it before your lord, if he will allow us kindly
to greet in person his most gracious self."

Then Wulfgar spoke; the warlike spirit
of this Wendel prince, his wisdom in judgement,
350 were known to many. "The Master of the Danes,
Lord of the Scyldings, shall learn of your request.
I shall gladly ask my honored chief,
giver of arm-bands, about your undertaking,
and soon bear the answer back again to you
355 that my gracious lord shall think good to make."

He strode rapidly to the seat of Hrothgar,
old and gray-haired among the guard of earls,
stepped forward briskly, stood before the shoulders
of the King of the Danes; a court's ways were known to him.
360 Then Wulfgar addressed his dear master:
"Men have come here from the country of the Geats,
borne from afar over the back of the sea;
these battle-companions call the man
who leads them, Beowulf. The boon they ask
365 is, my lord, that they may hold
converse with you. Do not, kind Hrothgar,
refuse them audience in the answer you vouchsafe;
accoutrement would clearly bespeak them
of earls' rank. Indeed the leader
370 who guided them here seems of great account."

The Guardian of the Scyldings gave his answer:
"I knew him when he was a child!
It was to his old father, Edgetheow, that
Hrethel the Geat gave in marriage
375 his one daughter. Well does the son
now pay this call on a proven ally!

    The seafarers used to say, I remember,
who took our gifts to the Geat people
in token of friendship—that this fighting man
380 in his hand's grasp had the strength
of thirty other men. I am thinking that
the Holy God, as a grace to us
Danes in the West, has directed him here
against Grendel's oppression. This good man shall be
385 offered treasures in return for his courage.

    Waste no time now but tell them to come in
that they may see this company seated together.
Make sure to say that they are most welcome
to the people of the Danes."
                                    Promptly Wulfgar

390   turned to the doors and told his message:
       "The Master of Battles bids me announce,
       the Lord of the North Danes, that he knows your ancestry;
       I am to tell you all, determined venturers
       over the seas, that you are sure of welcome.
395   You may go in now in your gear of battle,
       set eyes on Hrothgar, helmed as you are.
       But battle-shafts and shields of linden wood
       may here await you words' outcome."

       The prince arose, around him warriors
400   in dense escort; detailed by the chief,
       a group remained to guard the weapons.
       The Geats swung in behind their stout leader
       over Heorot's floor. The hero led on,
       hard under helmet, to the hearth, where he stopped.
405   Then Beowulf spoke; bent by smith's skill
       the meshed rings of his mail-shirt glittered.
       "Health to Hrothgar! I am Hygelac's kinsman
       and serve in his fellowship. Fame-winning deeds
       have come early to my hands. The affair of Grendel
410   has been made known to me on my native turf.
       The sailors speak of this splendid hall,
       this most stately building, standing idle
       and silent of voices, as soon as the evening light
       has hidden below the heaven's bright edge.
415   Whereupon it was urged by the ablest men
       among our people, men proved in counsel,
       that I should seek you out, most sovereign Hrothgar.
       These men knew well the weight of my hands.
       Had they not seen me come home from fights
420   where I had bound five Giants—their blood was upon me—
       cleaned out a nest of them? Had I not crushed on the wave
       sea-serpents by night in narrow struggle,
       broken the beasts? (The bane of the Geats,
       they had asked for their trouble.) And shall I not try
425   a single match with this monster Grendel,
       a trial against this troll?
                            To you I now
       put one request, Royal Scylding,
       Shield of the South Danes, one sole favor
       that you'll not deny me, dear lord of your people,
430   now that I have come thus far, Fastness of Warriors;
       that I alone may be allowed, with my loyal and determined
       crew of companions, to cleanse your hall Heorot.

          As I am informed that this unlovely one
       is careless enough to carry no weapon,
435   so that my lord Hygelac, my leader in war,
       may take joy in me, I abjure utterly

the bearing of sword or shielding yellow
board in this battle! With bare hands shall I
grapple with the fiend, fight to the death here,
440   hater and hated! He who is chosen
shall deliver himself to the Lord's judgement.

If he can contrive it, we may count upon Grendel
to eat quite fearlessly the flesh of Geats
here in this war-hall; has he not chewed
445   on the strength of this nation? There will be no need, Sir,
for you to bury my head; he will have me gladly,
if death should take me, though darkened with blood.
He will bear my bloody corpse away, bent on eating it,
make his meal alone, without misgiving,
450   bespatter his moor-lair. The disposing of my body
need occupy you no further then.
But if the fight should take me, you would forward to Hygelac
this best of battle-shirts, that my breast now wears.
The queen of war-coats, it is the bequest of Hrethel
455   and from the forge of Wayland.[2] Fate will take its course!"

Then Hrothgar spoke, the Helmet of the Scyldings:
"So it is to fight in our defence, my friend Beowulf,
and as an office of kindness that you have come to us here!
Great was the feud that your father set off
460   when his hand struck down Heatholaf in death
among the Wylfings. The Weather-Geats
did not dare to keep him then, for dread of war,
and he left them to seek out the South-Danish folk,
the glorious Scyldings, across the shock of waters.
465   I had assumed sway over the Scylding nation
and in my youth ruled this rich kingdom,
storehouse of heroes. Heorogar was then dead,
the son of Healfdene had hastened from us,
my elder brother; a better man than I!
470   I then settled the feud with fitting payment,
sent to the Wylfings over the water's back
old things of beauty; against which I'd the oath of your father.

It is a sorrow in spirit for me to say to any man
—a grief in my heart—what the hatred of Grendel
475   has brought me to in Heorot, what humiliation,
what harrowing pain. My hall-companions,
my war-band, are dwindled; Weird[3] has swept them
into the power of Grendel. Yet God could easily
check the ravages of this reckless fiend!
480   They often boasted, when the beer was drunk,
and called out over the ale-cup, my captains in battle,

2. Legendary blacksmith of the Norse gods.   3. Fate.

that they would here await, in this wassailing-place,
with deadliness of iron edges, the onset of Grendel.
When morning brought the bright daylight
485 this mead-hall was seen all stained with blood:
blood had soaked its shining floor,
it was a house of slaughter. More slender grew my
strength of dear warriors; death took them off . . .
Yet sit now to the banquet, where you may soon attend,
490 should the mood so take you, some tale of victory."

A bench was then cleared for the company of Geats
there in the beer-hall, for the whole band together.
The stout-hearted warriors went to their places,
bore their strength proudly. Prompt in his office,
495 the man who held the horn of bright mead
poured out its sweetness. The song of the poet
again rang in Heorot. The heroes laughed loud
in the great gathering of the Geats and the Danes.

Then Unferth[4] spoke, the son of Edgelaf,
500 sitting at the feet of the Father of the Scyldings,
unbound a battle-rune[5] Beowulf's undertaking,
the seaman's bold venture, vexed him much.
He could not allow that another man
should hold under heaven a higher care
505 for wonders in the world than went with his own name.
"Is this the Beowulf of Breca's swimming-match,
who strove against him on the stretched ocean,
when for pride the pair of you proved the seas
and for a trite boast entrusted your lives
510 to the deep waters, undissuadable
by effort of friend or foe whatsoever
from that swimming on the sea? A sorry contest!
Your arms embraced the ocean's streams,
you beat the wave-way, wove your hand-movements,
515 and danced on the Spear-Man. The sea boiled with whelming
waves of winter; in the water's power
you labored seven nights: and then you lost your swimming-match,
his might was the greater; morning found him
cast by the sea on the coast of the Battle-Reams.
520 He made his way back to the marches of the Brondings,
to his father-land, friend to his people,
and to the city-fastness where he had subjects, treasure
and his own stronghold. The son of Beanstan
performed to the letter what he had promised to you.
525 I see little hope then of a happier outcome
—though in other conflicts elsewhere in the world

---

4. Hrothgar's spokesman or court jester. His rude behavior
to Beowulf resembles that of other epic and romance figures
who taunt the hero before he undertakes his exploits.
5. Unleashed his hostile thought.

you may indeed have prospered—if you propose awaiting
Grendel all night, on his own ground, unarmed."

Then spoke Beowulf, son of Edgetheow:
530 "I thank my friend Unferth, who unlocks us this tale
of Breca's bragged exploit; the beer lends
eloquence to his tongue. But the truth is as I've said:
I had more sea-strength, outstaying Breca's,
and endured underwater a much worse struggle.

535   It was in early manhood that we undertook
with a pubic boast—both of us still
very young men—to venture our lives
on the open ocean; which we accordingly did.
Hard in our right hands we held each a sword
540 as we went through the sea, so to keep off
the whales from us. If he whitened the ocean,
no wider appeared the water between us.
He could not away from me; nor would I from him.
Thus stroke for stroke we stitched the ocean
545 five nights and days, drawn apart then
by cold storm on the cauldron or waters;
under lowering night the northern wind
fell on us in warspite: the waves were rough!

    The unfriendliness was then aroused of the fishes of the deep.
550 Against sea-beasts my body-armor,
hand-linked and hammered, helped me then,
this forge-knit battleshirt bright with gold,
decking my breast. Down to the bottom
I was plucked in range by this reptile-fish,
555 pinned in his grip. But I got the chance
to thrust once at the ugly creature
with my weapon's point: war took off then
the mighty monster; mine was the hand did it.
Then loathsome snouts snickered by me,
560 swarmed at my throat. I served them out
with my good sword, gave them what they asked for:
those scaly flesh-eaters sat not down
to dine on Beowulf, they browsed not on me
in that picnic they'd designed in the dingles[6] of the sea.
565 Daylight found them dispersed instead
up along the beaches where my blade had laid them
soundly asleep; since then they have never
troubled the passage of travellers over
that deep water-way. Day in the east grew,
570 God's bright beacon, and the billows sank
so that I then could see the headlands,

6. Valleys.

the windy cliffs. 'Weird saves oft
the man undoomed if he undaunted be!'—
and it was my part then to put to the sword
575   nine sea-monsters, the severest fight
by night I have heard of under heaven's vault;
a man more sorely pressed the seas never held.
I came with my life from the compass of my foes,
but tired from the struggle. The tide bore me
580   away on its currents to the coasts of Norway,
whelms of water.

            No whisper has yet reached me
of sword-ambushes survived, nor such scathing perils
in connection with your name! Never has Breca,
nor you Unferth either, in open battle-pay
585   framed such a deed of daring with your
shining swords—small as my action was.
You have killed only kindred, kept your blade
for those closest in blood; you're a clever man, Unferth,
but you'll endure hell's damnation for that.

590   It speaks for itself, my son of Edgelaf,[7]
that Grendel had never grown such a terror,
this demon had never dealt your lord
such havoc in Heorot, had your heart's intention
been so grim for battle as you give us to believe.
595   He's learnt there's in fact not the least need
excessively to respect the spite of this people,
the scathing steel-thresh of the Scylding nation.
He spares not a single sprig of your Danes
in extorting his tribute, but treats himself proud,
600   butchering and dispatching, and expects no resistance
from the spear-wielding Scyldings.
                  I'll show him Geatish

strength and stubbornness shortly enough now,
a lesson in war. He who wishes shall go then
blithe to the banquet when the breaking light
605   of another day shall dawn for men
and the sun shine glorious in the southern sky."

Great then was the hope of the gray-locked Hrothgar,
warrior, giver of rings. Great was the trust
of the Shield of the Danes, shepherd of the people,
610   attending to Beowulf's determined resolve.

There was laughter of heroes, harp-music ran,
words were warm-hearted. Wealhtheow[8] moved,
mindful of courtesies, the queen of Hrothgar,

---

7. Unferth.
8. Wealhtheow is the ideal Anglo-Saxon queen. She is a gracious hostess to her husband's guests, and later uses her diplomacy to try to safeguard the future of her sons.

glittering to greet the Geats in the hall,
615 peerless lady; but to the land's guardian
she offered first the flowing cup,
bade him be blithe at the beer-drinking,
gracious to his people; gladly the conqueror
partook of the banquet, tasted the hall-cup.
620 The Helming princess then passed about among
the old and the young men in each part of the hall,
bringing the treasure-cup, until the time came
when the flashing-armed queen, complete in all virtues,
carried out to Beowulf the brimming vessel;
625 she greeted the Geat, and gave thanks to the Lord
in words wisely chosen, her wish being granted
to meet with a man who might be counted on
for aid against these troubles. He took then the cup,
a man violent in war, at Wealhtheow's hand,
630 and framed his utterance, eager for the conflict.

Thus spoke Beowulf son of Edgetheow:
"This was my determination in taking to the ocean,
benched in the ship among my band of fellows,
that I should once and for all accomplish the wishes
635 of your adopted people, or pass to the slaughter,
viced in my foe's grip. This vow I shall accomplish,
a deed worthy of an earl; decided otherwise
here in this mead-hall to meet my ending-day!"

This speech sounded sweet to the lady,
640 the vaunt of the Geat; glittering she moved
to her lord's side, splendid folk-queen.

Then at last Heorot heard once more
words of courage, the carousing of a people
singing their victories, till the son of Healfdene
645 desired at length to leave the feast,
be away to his night's rest; aware of the monster
brooding his attack on the tall-gabled hall
from the time they had seen the sun's lightness
to the time when darkness drowns everything
650 and under its shadow-cover shapes do glide
dark beneath the clouds. The company came to its feet.

Then did the heroes, Hrothgar and Beowulf,
salute each other; success he wished him,
control of the wine-hall, and with this word left him:
655 "Never since I took up targe and sword
have I at any instance to any man beside,
thus handed over Heorot, as I here do to you.
Have and hold now the house of the Danes!
Bend your mind and your body to this task
660 and wake against the foe! There'll be no want of liberality

if you come out alive from this ordeal of courage."
Then Hrothgar departed, the Protector of the Danes
passed from the hall at the head of his troop.
The war-leader sought Wealhtheow his queen,
the companion of his bed.

665   Thus did the King of Glory,
to oppose this Grendel, appoint a hall-guard
—so the tale went abroad—who took on a special
task at the court—to cope with the monster.
The Geat prince placed all his trust
670 in his mighty strength, his Maker's favor.

He now uncased himself of his coat of mail,
unhelmed his head, handed his attendant
his embellished sword, best of weapons,
and bade him take care of these trappings of war.
675 Beowulf then made a boasting speech,
the Geat man, before mounting his bed:
"I fancy my fighting-strength, my performance in combat,
at least as greatly as Grendel does his;
and therefore I shall not cut short his life
680 with a slashing sword—too simple a business.
He has not the art to answer me in kind,
hew at my shield, shrewd though he be
at his nasty catches. No, we'll at night play
without any weapons—if unweaponed he dare
685 to face me in fight. The Father in His wisdom
shall apportion the honors then, the All-holy Lord,
to whichever side shall seem to Him fit."

Then the hero lay down, leant his head
on the bolster there; about him many
690 brave sea-warriors bowed to their hall-rest.
Not one of them thought he would thence be departing
ever to set eyes on his own country,
the home that nourished him, or its noble people;
for they had heard how many men of the Danes
695 death had dragged from that drinking-hall.
But God was to grant to the Geat people
the clue to war-success in the web of fate—
His help and support; so that they did
overcome the foe—through the force of one
700 unweaponed man. The Almighty Lord
has ruled the affairs of the race of men
thus from the beginning.
                     Gliding through the shadows came
the walker in the night; the warriors slept
whose task was to hold the horned building,
705 all except one. It was well-known to men
that the demon could not drag them to the shades

without God's willing it; yet the one man kept
unblinking watch. He awaited, heart swelling
with anger against his foe, the ordeal of battle.
710   Down off the moorlands' misting fells came
Grendel stalking; God's brand was on him.
The spoiler meant to snatch away
from the high hall some of human race.
He came on under the clouds, clearly saw at last
715   the gold-hall of men, the mead-drinking place
nailed with gold plates. That was not the first visit
he had paid to the hall of Hrothgar the Dane:
he never before and never after
harder luck nor hall-guards found.

720   Walking to the hall came this warlike creature
condemned to agony. The door gave way,
toughened with iron, at the touch of those hands.
Rage-inflamed, wreckage-bent, he ripped open
the jaws of the hall. Hastening on,
725   the foe then stepped onto the unstained floor,
angrily advanced: out of his eyes stood
an unlovely light like that of fire.
He saw then in the hall a host of young soldiers,
a company of kinsmen caught away in sleep,
730   a whole warrior-band. In his heart he laughed then,
horrible monster, his hopes swelling
to a gluttonous meal. He meant to wrench
the life from each body that lay in the place
before night was done. It was not to be;
735   he was no longer to feast on the flesh of mankind
after that night.
               Narrowly the powerful
kinsman of Hygelac kept watch how the ravager
set to work with his sudden catches;
not did the monster mean to hang back.
740   As a first step he set his hands on
a sleeping soldier, savagely tore at him,
gnashed at his bone-joints, bolted huge gobbets,
sucked at his veins, and had soon eaten
all of the dead man, even down to his
hands and feet.
745   Forward he stepped,
stretched out his hands to seize the warrior
calmly at rest there, reached out for him with his
unfriendly fingers: but the faster man
forestalling, sat up, sent back his arm.
750   The upholder of evils at once knew
he had not met, on middle earth's
extremest acres, with any man

of harder hand-grip: his heart panicked.
He was quit of the place no more quickly for that.

755 Eager to be away, he ailed for his darkness
and the company of devils; the dealings he had there
were like nothing he had come across in his lifetime.
Then Hygelac's brave kinsman called to mind
that evening's utterance, upright he stood,
760 fastened his hold till fingers were bursting.
The monster strained away: the man stepped closer.
The monster's desire was for darkness between them,
direction regardless, to get out and run
for his fen-bordered lair; he felt his grip's strength
765 crushed by his enemy. It was an ill journey
the rough marauder had made to Heorot.

The crash in the banqueting-hall came to the Danes,
the men of the guard that remained in the buildings,
with the taste of death. The deepening rage
770 of the claimants to Heorot caused it to resound.
It was indeed wonderful that the wine-supper-hall
withstood the wrestling pair, that the world's palace
fell not to the ground. But it was girt firmly,
both inside and out, by iron braces
775 of skilled manufacture. Many a figured
gold-worked wine-bench, as we heard it,
started from the floor at the struggles of that pair.
The men of the Danes had not imagined that
any of mankind by what method soever
780 might undo that intricate, antlered hall,
sunder it by strength—unless it were swallowed up in
the embraces of fire.
                       Fear entered into
the listening North Danes, as that noise rose up again
strange and strident. It shrilled terror
785 to the ears that heard it through the hall's side-wall,
the grisly plaint of God's enemy,
his song of ill-success, the sobs of the damned one
bewailing his pain. He was pinioned there
by the man of all mankind living
790 in this world's estate the strongest of his hands.

Not for anything would the earls' guardian
let his deadly guest go living:
he did not count his continued existence
of the least use to anyone. The earls ran
795 to defend the person of their famous prince;
they drew their ancestral swords to bring
what aid they could to their captain, Beowulf.
They were ignorant of this, when they entered the fight,

boldly-intentioned battle-friends,
800   to hew at Grendel, hunt his life
on every side—that no sword on earth,
not the truest steel, could touch their assailant;
for by a spell he had dispossessed all
blades of their bite on him.
                    A bitter parting
805   from life was that day destined for him;
the eldritch[9] spirit was sent off on his
far faring into the fiends' domain.

It was then that this monster, who, moved by spite
against human kind, had caused so much harm
810   —so feuding with God—found at last
that flesh and bone were to fail him in the end;
for Hygelac's great-hearted kinsman
had him by the hand; and hateful to each
was the breath of the other.
                    A breach in the giant
815   flesh-frame showed then, shoulder-muscles
sprang apart, there was a snapping of tendons,
bone-locks burst. To Beowulf the glory
of this fight was granted; Grendel's lot
to flee the slopes fen-ward with flagging heart,
820   to a den where he knew there could be no relief,
no refuge for a life at its very last stage,
whose surrender-day had dawned. The Danish hopes
in this fatal fight had found their answer.

He had cleansed Heorot. He who had come from afar,
825   deep-minded, strong-hearted, had saved the hall
from persecution. He was pleased with this night's work,
the deed he had done. Before the Danish people
the Geat captain had made good his boast,
had taken away all their unhappiness,
830   the evil menace under which they had lived,
enduring it by dire constraint,
no slight affliction. As a signal to all
the hero hung up the hand, the arm
and torn-off shoulder, the entire limb,
835   Grendel's whole grip, below the gable of the roof.

There was, as I heard it, at hall next morning
a great gathering in the gift-hall yard
to see the wonder. Along the wide highroads
the chiefs of the clans came from near and far
840   to see the foe's footprints. It may fairly be said
that his parting from life aroused no pity in any

9. Eerie, spooky.

who tracked the spoor-blood of his blind flight
for the monsters' mere-pool; with mood flagging
and strength crushed, he had staggered onwards;
845   each step evidenced his ebbing life's blood.
The tarn[1] was troubled; a terrible wave-thrash
brimmed it, bubbling; black-mingled,
the warm wound-blood welled upwards.
He had dived to his doom, he had died miserably;
850   here in his fen-lair he had laid aside
his heathen soul. Hell welcomed it.

Then the older retainers turned back on the way
journeyed with much joy; joined by the young men,
the warriors on white horses wheeled away from the Mere
855   in bold mood. Beowulf's feat
was much spoken of, and many said,
that between the seas, south or north,
over earth's stretch no other man
beneath the sky's shifting excelled Beowulf,
860   of all who wielded the sword he was worthiest to rule.
In saying this they did not slight in the least
the gracious Hrothgar, for he was a good king.
Where, as they went, their way broadened
they would match their mounts, making them leap
865   along the best stretches, the strife-eager
on their fallow horses. Or a fellow of the king's
whose head was a storehouse of the storied verse,
whose tongue gave gold to the language
of the treasured repertory, wrought a new lay
870   made in the measure. The man struck up,
found the phrase, framed rightly
the deed of Beowulf, drove the tale,
rang word-changes.
                    Of Wæls's great son,
Sigemund,[2] he spoke then, spelling out to them
875   all he had heard of that hero's strife,
his fights, strange feats, far wanderings,
the feuds and the blood spilt. Fitela alone heard
these things not well nor widely known to men,
when Sigemund chose to speak in this vein
880   to his sister's son. They were inseparable
in every fight, the firmest of allies;
their swords had between them scythed to the ground
a whole race of monsters. The reputation
that spread at his death was no slight one:
885   Sigemund it was who had slain the dragon,

1. A small lake.
2. The story of Sigemund is also told in the Old Norse
Volsunga Saga and with major variations in the Middle
High German *Niebelungenlied*. The poet's comparison of
Siegmund with Beowulf is ironic in that the order and
the outcome of Beowulf's later encounter with a dragon
will be reversed.

the keeper of the hoard; the king's son walked
under the gray rock, he risked alone
that fearful conflict; Fitela was not there.
Yet it turned out well for him, his weapon transfixed
890 the marvelous snake, struck in the cave-wall,
best of swords; the serpent was dead.
Sigemund's valor had so prevailed
that the whole ring-hoard was his to enjoy,
dispose of as he wished. Wæls's great son
895 loaded his ship with shining trophies,
stacking them by the mast; the monster shriveled away.
He was by far the most famous of adventurers
among the peoples, this protector of warriors,
for the deeds by which he had distinguished himself.

900 Heremod's[3] stature and strength had decayed then,
his daring diminished. Deeply betrayed
into the fiends' power, far among the Giants
he was done to death. Dark sorrows
drove him mad at last. A deadly grief
905 he had become to his people and the princes of his land.
Wise men among the leaders had lamented that career,
their fierce one's fall, who in former days
had looked to him for relief of their ills,
hoping that their lord's son would live and in ripeness
910 assume the kingdom, the care of his people,
the hoard and the stronghold, the storehouse of heroes,
the Scylding homeland. Whereas Hygelac's kinsman
endeared himself ever more deeply to friends
and to all mankind, evil seized Heremod.

915 The riders returning came racing their horses
along dusty-pale roads. The dawn had grown
into broadest day, and, drawn by their eagerness
to see the strange sight, there had assembled at the hall
many keen warriors. The king himself,
920 esteemed for excellence, stepped glorious
from his wife's chambers, the warden of ring-hoards,
with much company; and his queen walked
the mead-path by him, her maidens following.
Taking his stand on the steps of the hall,
925 Hrothgar beheld the hand of Grendel
below the gold gable-end; and gave speech:
"Let swift thanks be given to the Governor of All,
seeing this sight! I have suffered a thousand
spites from Grendel: but God works ever
930 miracle upon miracle, the Master of Heaven.

---

3. Heremod, an earlier Danish king, was used as an illustration of the unjust and unwise ruler. Hrothgar mentions him
again below, in line 1708.

Until yesterday I doubted whether
our afflictions would find a remedy
in my lifetime, since this loveliest of halls
stood slaughter-painted, spattered with blood.
935 For all my counselors this was a cruel sorrow,
for none of them imagined they could mount a defence
of the Scylding stronghold against such enemies—
warlocks, demons!
                But one man has,
by the Lord's power, performed the thing
940 that all our thought and arts to this day
had failed to do. She may indeed say,
whoever she be that brought into the world
this young man here—if yet she lives—
that the God of Old was gracious to her
945 in her child-bearing. Beowulf, I now take you
to my bosom as a son, O best of men,
and cherish you in my heart. Hold yourself well
in this new relation! You will lack for nothing
that lies in my gift of the goods of this world:
950 lesser offices have elicited reward,
we have honored from our hoard less heroic men,
far weaker in war. But you have well ensured
by the deeds of your hands an undying honor
for your name for ever. May the Almighty Father
955 yield you always the success that you yesternight enjoyed!"

Beowulf spoke, son of Edgetheow:
"We willingly undertook this test of courage,
risked a match with the might of the stranger,
and performed it all. I would prefer, though,
960 that you had rather seen the rest of him here,
the whole length of him, lying here dead.
I had meant to catch him, clamp him down
with a cruel lock to his last resting-place;
with may hands upon him, I would have him soon
965 in the throes of death—unless he disappeared!
But I had not a good enough grip to prevent
his getting away, when God did not wish it;
the fiend in his flight was far too violent,
my life's enemy. But he left his hand
970 behind him here, so as to have his life,
and his arm and shoulder. And all for nothing:
it bought him no respite, wretched creature.
He lives no longer, laden with sins,
to plague mankind: pain has set
975 heavy hands on him, and hasped about him
fatal fetters. He is forced to await now,
like a guilty criminal, a greater judgement,
where the Lord in His splendor shall pass sentence upon him."

The son of Edgelaf was more silent then
980 in boasting of his own battle-deeds:
the athelings gazed at what the earl's strength
had hung there—the hand, high up under the roof,
and the fingers of their foe. From the front, each one
of the socketed nails seemed steel to the eye,
985 each spur on the hand of that heathen warrior
a terrible talon. They told each other
nothing could be hard enough to harm it at all,
not the most ancient of iron swords
would bite on that bloody battle-hand.

990 Other hands were pressed then to prepare the inside
of the banqueting-hall, and briskly too.
Many were ready, both men and women,
to adorn the guest-hall. Gold-embroidered tapestries
glowed from the walls, with wonderful sights
995 for every creature that cared to look at them.
The bright building had badly started
in all its inner parts, despite its iron bands,
and the hinges were ripped off. Only the roof survived
unmarred and in one piece when the monstrous one,
1000 flecked with his crimes, had fled the place
in despair of his life.
                        But to elude death
is not easy: attempt it who will,
he shall go to the place prepared for each
of the sons of men, the soul-bearers
1005 dwelling on earth, ordained them by fate:
laid fast in that bed, the body shall sleep
when the feast is done.
                      In due season
the king himself came to the hall;
Healfdene's son would sit at the banquet.
1010 No people has gathered in greater retinue,
borne themselves better about their ring-giver.
Men known for their courage came to the benches,
rejoiced in the feast; they refreshed themselves kindly
with many a mead-cup; in their midst the brave kinsmen,
1015 father's brother and brother's son,
Hrothgar and Hrothulf. Heorot's floor was
filled with friends: falsity in those days
had no place in the dealings of the Danish people.

Then as a sign of victory the son of Healfdene
1020 bestowed on Beowulf a standard worked in gold,
a figured battle-banner, breast and head-armor;
and many admired the marvelous sword
that was borne before the hero. Beowulf drank with
the company in the hall. He had no cause to be ashamed of

1025 gifts so fine before the fighting-men!
I have not heard that many men at arms
have given four such gifts of treasure
more openly to another at the mead.
At the crown of the helmet, the head-protector,
1030 was a rim, with wire wound round it, to stop
the file-hardened blade that fights have tempered
from shattering it, when the shield-warrior
must go out against grim enemies.

The king then ordered eight war-horses
1035 with glancing bridles to be brought within walls
and onto the floor. Fretted with gold
and studded with stones was one saddle there!
This was the battle-seat of the Bulwark of the Danes,
when in the sword-play the son of Healfdene
1040 would take his part; the prowess of the king
had never failed at the front where the fighting was mortal.
The Protector of the Sons of Scyld then gave
both to Beowulf, bidding him take care
to use them well, both weapons and horses.
1045 Thus did the glorious prince, guardian of the treasure,
reward these deeds, with both war-horses and armor;
of such open-handedness no honest man
could ever speak in disparagement.

Then the lord of men also made a gift
1050 of treasure to each who had adventure with Beowulf
over the sea's paths, seated now at the benches—
an old thing of beauty. He bade compensation
to be made too, in gold, for the man whom Grendel
had horribly murdered; more would have gone
1055 had not the God overseeing us, and the resolve of a man,
stood against that weird. The Wielder guided then
the dealings of mankind, as He does even now.
A mind that seeks to understand and grasp this
is therefore best. Both bad and good,
1060 and much of both, must be borne in a lifetime
spent on this earth in these anxious days.

Then string and song sounded together
before Healfdene's Helper-in-battle:
the lute was taken up and tales recited
1065 when Hrothgar's bard was bidden to sing
a hall-song for the men on the mead-benches.[4]
It was how disaster came to the sons of Finn:

---

4. The following episode is one of the most obscure in *Beowulf*. Apparently Hnaef and Hildeburh are the children of Hoc, an earlier Danish king. Hildeburh has been sent as a "peace-weaver" to marry Finn, son of Folcwalda and king of the Jutes and the Frisians, in order to make an alliance between the two feuding tribes. Upon visiting his sister and her husband, Hnaef is ambushed and killed by Finn's men, and Hildeburh's son by Finn is also killed. Hildeburh's tragic fate foreshadows that of Hrothgar's own daughter Freawaru in her marriage to Ingeld.

first the Half-Dane champion, Hnæf of the Scyldings,
was fated to fall in the Frisian ambush.
1070 Hildeburh their lady had little cause to speak
of the good faith of the Jutes; guiltless she had suffered
in that linden-wood clash the loss of her closest ones,
her son and her brother, both born to die there,
struck down by the spear. Sorrowful princess!
1075 This decree of fate the daughter of Hoc
mourned with good reason; for when morning came
the clearness of heaven disclosed to her
the murder of those kindred who were the cause of all
her earthly bliss.   Battle had also claimed
1080 all but a few of Finn's retainers
in that place of assembly; he was unable therefore
to bring to a finish the fight with Hengest,
force out and crush the few survivors
of Hnæf's troop. The truce-terms they put to him
1085 were that he should make over a mead-hall to the Danes,
with high-seat and floor; half of it
to be held by them, half by the Jutes.
In sharing out goods, that the son of Folcwalda
should every day give honor to the Danes
1090 of Hengest's party, providing rings
and prizes from the hoard, plated with gold,
treating them identically in the drinking-hall
as when he chose to cheer his own Frisians.
On both sides they then bound themselves fast
1095 in a pact of friendship. Finn then swore
strong unexceptioned oaths to Hengest
to hold in honor, as advised by his counselors,
the battle-survivors; similarly no man
by word or deed to undo the pact,
1100 as by mischievous cunning to make complaint of it,
despite that they were serving the slayer of their prince,
since their lordless state so constrained them to do;
but that if any Frisian should fetch the feud to mind
and by taunting words awaken the bad blood,
1105 it should be for the sword's edge to settle it then.

The pyre was erected, the ruddy gold
brought from the hoard, and the best warrior
of Scylding race was ready for the burning.
Displayed on his pyre, plain to see
1110 were the bloody mail-shirt, the boars on the helmets,
iron-hard, gold-clad; and gallant men about him
all marred by their wounds; mighty men had fallen there.
Hildeburgh then ordered her own son
to be given to the funeral fire of Hnæf
1115 for the burning of his bones; bade him be laid

at his uncle's side. She sang the dirges,
bewailed her grief. The warrior went up;
the greatest of corpse-fires coiled to the sky,
roared before the mounds. There were melting heads
1120   and bursting wounds, as the blood sprang out
from weapon-bitten bodies. Blazing fire,
most insatiable of spirits, swallowed the remains
of the victims of both nations. Their valor was no more.

The warriors then scattered and went to their homes.
1125   Missing their comrades, they made for Friesland,
the home and high stronghold. But Hengest still,
as he was constrained to do, stayed with Finn
a death-darkened winter in dreams of his homeland.
He was prevented from passage of the sea
1130   in his ring-beaked boat: the boiling ocean
fought with the wind; winter locked the seas
in his icy binding; until another year
came at last to the dwellings, as it does still,
continually keeping its season,
the weather of rainbows.
1135   Now winter had fled
and earth's breast was fair, the exile strained
to leave these lodgings; yet it was less the voyage
that exercised his mind than the means of his vengeance,
the bringing about of the bitter conflict
1140   that he meditated for the men of the Jutes.
So he did not decline the accustomed remedy,
when the son of Hunlaf set across his knees
that best of blades, his battle-gleaming sword;
the Jutes were acquainted with the edges of that steel.

1145   And so, in his hall, at the hands of his enemies,
Finn received the fatal sword-thrust;
Guthlaf and Oslaf, after the sea-crossing,
proclaimed their tribulations, their treacherous entertainment,
and named the author of them; anger in the breast
1150   rose irresistible. Red was the hall then
with the lives of foemen. Finn was slain there,
the king among his troop, and the queen taken.
The Scylding crewmen carried to the ship
the hall-furnishings of Friesland's king,
1155   all they could find at Finnsburh
in gemstones and jewelwork. Journeying back,
they returned to the Danes their true-born lady,
restored her to her people.
              Thus the story was sung,
the gleeman's[5] lay. Gladness mounted,

---

5. Bard, oral poet.

1160 bench-mirth rang out, the bearers gave
wine from wonderful vessels. Then came Wealhtheow forward,
going with golden crown to where the great heroes
were sitting, uncle and nephew; their bond was sound at that time,[6]
each was true to the other. Likewise Unferth the spokesman
1165 sat at the footstool of Hrothgar. All had faith in his spirit,
accounted his courage great—though toward his kinsmen he had not been
kind at the clash of swords.
　　　　　　　　　　　The Scylding queen then spoke:
"Accept this cup, my king and lord,
giver of treasure. Let your gaiety be shown,
1170 gold-friend of warriors, and to the Geats speak
in words of friendship, for this well becomes a man.
Be gracious to these Geats, and let the gifts you have had
from near and far, not be forgotten now.

　　I hear it is your wish to hold this warrior
1175 henceforward as your son. Heorot is cleansed,
the ring-hall bright again: therefore bestow while you may
these blessings liberally, and leave to your kinsmen
the land and its people when your passing is decreed,
your meeting with fate. For may I not count
1180 on my gracious Hrothulf to guard honorably
our young ones here, if you, my lord,
should give over this world earlier than he?
I am sure that he will show to our children
answerable kindness, if he keeps in remembrance
1185 all that we have done to indulge and advance him,
the honors we bestowed on him when he was still a child."

Then she turned to the bench where her boys were sitting,
Hrethric and Hrothmund, among the heroes' sons,
young men together; where the good man sat also
1190 between the two brothers, Beowulf the Geat.
Then the cup was taken to him and he was entreated kindly
to honor their feast; ornate gold
was presented in trophy: two arm-wreaths,
with robes and rings also, and the richest collar
1195 I have ever heard of in all the world.[7]

Never under heaven have I heard of a finer
prize among heroes—since Hama carried off
the Brising necklace to his bright city,
that gold-cased jewel; he gave the slip
1200 to the machinations of Eormenric, and made his name forever.

---

6. Likely an allusion to the later usurpation of the Danish throne by Hrothgar's nephew Hrothulf.
7. The narrative here jumps ahead beyond Beowulf's return home to the Geats. His uncle, King Hygelac, will not only receive the collar from Beowulf but will die with it in battle among the Frisians. The collar thus connects different events at different times.

This gold was to be on the neck of the grandson of Swerting
on the last of his harryings, Hygelac the Geat,
as he stood before the standard astride his plunder,
defending his war-haul: Weird struck him down;

1205   in his superb pride he provoked disaster
in the Frisian feud. This fabled collar
the great war-king wore when he crossed
the foaming waters; he fell beneath his shield.
The king's person passed into Frankish hands,

1210   together with his corselet, and this collar also.
They were lesser men that looted the slain;
for when the carnage was over, the corpse-field was littered
with the people of the Geats.
                            Applause filled the hall;
then Wealhtheow spoke, and her words were attended.

1215   "Take pride in this jewel, have joy of this mantle
drawn from our treasuries, most dear Beowulf!
May fortune come with them and may you flourish in your youth!
Proclaim your strength; but in counsel to these boys
be a gentle guardian, and my gratitude will be seen.

1220   Already you have so managed that men everywhere
will hold you in honor for all time,
even to the cliffs at the world's end, washed by Ocean,
the wind's range. All the rest of your life
must be happy, prince; and prosperity I wish you too,

1225   abundance of treasure! But be to my son
a friend in deed, most favored of men.
You see how open is each earl here with his neighbor,
temperate of heart, and true to his lord.
The nobles are loyal, the lesser people dutiful;

1230   wine mellows the men to move to my bidding."

She walked back to her place. What a banquet that was!
The men drank their wine: the weird they did not know,
destined from of old, the doom that was to fall
on many of the earls there. When evening came

1235   Hrothgar departed to his private bower,[8]
the king to his couch; countless were the men
who watched over the hall, as they had often done before.
They cleared away the benches and covered the floor
with beds and bolsters: the best at the feast

1240   bent to his hall-rest, hurried to his doom.
Each by his head placed his polished shield,
the lindens of battle. On the benches aloft,
above each atheling, easily to be seen,
were the ring-stitched mail-coat, the mighty helmet

---

8. Bed chamber.

1245   steepling above the fray, and the stout spear-shaft.
       It was their habit always, at home or on campaign,
       to be ready for war, in whichever case,
       whatsoever the hour might be
       that the need came on their lord: what a nation they were!

1250   Then they sank into sleep. A savage penalty
       one paid for his night's rest! It was no new thing for that people
       since Grendel had occupied the gold-giving hall,
       working his evil, until the end came,
       death for his misdeeds. It was declared then to men,
1255   and received by every ear, that for all this time
       a survivor had been living, an avenger for their foe
       and his grim life's-leaving: Grendel's Mother herself,
       a monstrous ogress, was ailing for her loss.
       She had been doomed to dwell in the dread waters,
1260   in the chilling currents, because of that blow
       whereby Cain became the killer of his brother,
       his own father's son. He stole away, branded,
       marked for his murder, from all that men delight in,
       to inhabit the wastelands.
                              Hosts of the ill ones
1265   sprang from his begetting; as Grendel, that hateful
       accursed outcast, who encountered at Heorot
       a watchful man waiting for the fight.
       The grim one fastened his grip upon him there,
       but he remembered his mighty strength,
1270   the gift that the Lord had so largely bestowed on him,
       and, putting his faith in the favor of the Almighty
       and His aid and comfort, he overcame the foe,
       put down the hell-fiend. How humbling was that flight
       when the miserable outcast crept to his dying-place!
1275   Thus mankind's enemy. But his Mother now purposed
       to set out at last—savage in her grief—
       on that wrath-bearing visit of vengeance for her son.

       She came down to Heorot, where the heroes of the Danes
       slept about the hall. A sudden change
1280   was that for the men there when the Mother of Grendel
       found her way in among them—though the fury of her onslaught
       was less frightful than his; as the force of a woman,
       her onset in a fight, is less feared by men,
       where the bound blade, beaten out by hammers,
1285   cuts, with its sharp edges shining with blood,
       through the boars that bristle above the foes' helmets!

       Many a hard sword was snatched up in the hall
       from its rack above the benches; the broad shield was raised,
       held in the hand firm; helmet and corselet

1290   lay there unheeded when the horror was on them.
She was all eager to be out of the place
now that she was discovered, and escape with her life.
She caught a man quickly, clutched him to herself,
one of the athelings, and was away to the fen.
1295   This was the hero that Hrothgar loved better
than any on earth among his retinue,
destroyed thus as he slept; he was a strong warrior,
noted in battle. (Beowulf was not there:
separate lodging had been assigned that night,
1300   after the treasure-giving, to the Geat champion.)
Heorot was in uproar; the hand had gone with her,
blood-stained, familiar.

                 And so a fresh sorrow
came again to those dwellings. It was an evil bargain,
with both parties compelled to batter
1305   the lives of their dearest. What disturbance of spirit
for the wise king, the white-haired soldier,
hearing the news that the nearest of his thanes
was dead and gone, his dearest man!

Beowulf was soon summoned to the chamber,
1310   victory-blest man. And that valiant warrior
came with his following—it was at first light—
captain of his company, to where the king waited
to see if by some means the Swayer of All
would work a turning into this tale of sorrow.
1315   The man excellent in warfare walked across the hall
flanked by his escort—the floor-timbers boomed—
to make his addresses to the Danish lord,
the Guide of the Ingwine. He inquired of him whether
the night had been quiet, after a call so urgent.

1320   Hrothgar spoke, the Helmet of the Scyldings:
"Do not ask about our welfare! Woe has returned
to the Danish people with the death of Ashhere,
the elder brother of Yrmenlaf.
He was my closest counselor, he was keeper of my thoughts,
1325   he stood at my shoulder when we struck for our lives
at the crashing together of companies of foot,
when blows rained on boar-crests. Men of birth and merit
all should be as Ashhere was!
A bloodthirsty monster has murdered him in Heorot,
1330   a wandering demon; whither this terrible one,
glorying in her prey, glad of her meal,
has returned to, I know not. She has taken vengeance
for the previous night, when you put an end to Grendel
with forceful finger-grasp, and in a fierce manner,
1335   because he had diminished and destroyed my people
for far too long. He fell in that struggle

and forfeited his life; but now is followed by another
most powerful ravager. Revenge is her motive,
and in furthering her son's feud she has gone far enough,
1340   —or thanes may be found who will think it so;
in their breasts they will grieve for their giver of rings,
bitter at heart. For the hand is stilled
that would openly have granted your every desire.

      I have heard it said by subjects of mine
1345   who live in the country, counselors in this hall,
that they have seen such a pair
of huge wayfarers haunting the moors,
otherworldly ones; and one of them,
so far as they might make it out,
1350   was in woman's shape; but the shape of a man,
though twisted, trod also the tracks of exile
—save that he was more huge than any human being.
The country people have called him from of old
by the name of Grendel; they know of no father for him,
1355   nor whether there have been such beings before
among the monster-race.
                          Mysterious is the region
they live in—of wolf-fells, wind-picked moors
and treacherous fen-paths: a torrent of water
pours down dark cliffs and plunges into the earth,
1360   an underground flood. It is not far from here,
in terms of miles, that the Mere[9] lies,
overcast with dark, crag-rooted trees
that hang in groves horary with frost.
An uncanny sight may be seen at night there
1365   —the fire in the water! The wit of living men
is not enough to know its bottom.
The hart that roams the heath, when hounds have pressed him
long and hard, may hide in the forest
his antlered head; but the hart will die there
1370   sooner than swim and save his life;
he will sell it on the brink there, for it is not a safe place.
And the wind can stir up wicked storms there,
whipping the swirling waters up
till they climb the clouds and clog the air,
1375   making the skies weep.
                          Our sole remedy
is to turn again to you. The treacherous country
where that creature of sin is to be sought out
is strange to you as yet: seek then if you dare!
I shall reward the deed, as I did before,
1380   with wealthy gifts of wreathèd ore,

9. A small lake.

treasures from the hoard, if you return once more."
Beowulf spoke, son of Edgetheow:
"Bear your grief, wise one! It is better for a man
to avenge his friend than to refresh his sorrow.

1385 As we must all expect to leave
our life on this earth, we must earn some renown,
if we can, before death; daring is the thing
for a fighting man to be remembered by.

Let Denmark's lord arise, and we shall rapidly see then
1390 where this kinswoman of Grendel's has gone away to!
I can promise you this, that she'll not protect herself by hiding
in any fold of the field, in any forest of the mountain,
in any dingle of the sea, dive where she will!
For this day, therefore, endure all your woes
1395 with the patience that I may expect of you."

The ancient arose and offered thanks to God,
to the Lord Almighty, for what this man had spoken.
A steed with braided mane was bridled then,
a horse for Hrothgar; the hero-patriarch
1400 rode out shining; shieldbearers marched
in troop beside him. The trace of her going
on the woodland paths was plainly to be seen,
stepping onwards; straight across
the fog-bound moor she had fetched away there
1405 the lifeless body of the best man
of all who kept the courts of Hrothgar.
The sons of men then made their way
up steep screes, by scant tracks
where only one might walk, by wall-faced cliffs,
1410 through haunted fens—uninhabitable country.
Going on ahead with a handful of the
keener men to reconnoitre,
Beowulf suddenly saw where some ash-trees
hung above a hoary rock
1415 —a cheerless wood! And the water beneath it
was turbid with blood; bitter distress
was to be endured by the Danes who were there,
a grief for the earls, for every thane
of the Friends of the Scyldings, when they found there
1420 the head of Ashhere by the edge of the cliff.

The men beheld the blood on the water,
its warm upwellings. The war-horn sang
an eager battle-cry. The band of foot-soldiers,
sitting by the water, could see multitudes
1425 of strange sea-drakes swerving through the depths,
and water-snakes lay on the ledges of the cliffs,
such serpents and wild beasts as will sally out

in middle morning to make havoc
in the seas where ships sail.
                    Slithering away
1430 at the bright phrases of the battle-horn,
they were swollen with anger. An arrow from the
bow of Beowulf broke the life's thread
of one wave-thrasher; wedged in his throat
the iron dart; with difficulty then
1435 did he swim through the deep, until death took him.
They struck him as he swam, and straightaway,
with their boar-spears barbed and tanged;
gaffed and battered, he was brought to the cliff-top,
strange lurker of the waves. They looked with wonder
1440 at their grisly guest!
                    The Geat put on
the armor of a hero, unanixious for his life:
the manufacture of the mailed shirt,
figured and vast, that must venture in the deep,
made it such a bulwark to his bone-framed chest
1445 that the savage attack of an incensed enemy
could do no harm to the heart within it.
His head was encircled by a silver helmet
that was to strike down through the swirl of water,
disturb the depths. Adorned with treasure,
1450 clasped with royal bands, it was right as at first
when the weapon-smith had wonderfully made it,
so that no sword should afterward be able to cut through
the defending wild boars that faced about it.
Not least among these mighty aids
1455 was the hilted sword that Hrothgar's spokesman,
Unferth, lent him in his hour of trial.
Hrunting was its name; unique and ancient,
its edge was iron, annealed in venom
and tempered in blood; in battle it never
1460 failed any hero whose hand took it up
at his setting out on a stern adventure
for the house of foes. This was not the first time
that it had to do heroic work.

It would seem that the strapping son of Edgelaf
1465 had forgotten the speech he had spoken earlier,
eloquent with wine, for he offered the weapon now
to the better swordsman; himself he would not go
beneath the spume to display his valor
and risk his life; he lost his reputation there
1470 for nerve and action. With the other man
it was otherwise once he had armed himself for battle.

Beowulf spoke, son of Edgetheow:
"I am eager to begin, great son of Healfdene.

Remember well, then, my wise lord,
1475   provider of gold, what we agreed once before,
that if in your service it should so happen
that I am sundered from life, that you would assume the place
of a father towards me when I was gone.
Now extend your protection to the troop of my companions,
1480   my young fellows, if the fight should take me;
convey also the gifts that you have granted to me,
beloved Hrothgar, to my lord Hygelac.
For on seeing this gold, the Geat chieftain,
Hrethel's son, will perceive from its value
1485   that I had met with magnificent patronage
from a giver of jewels, and that I had joy of him.
Let Unferth have the blade that I inherited
—he is a widely-known man—this wave-patterned sword
of rare hardness. With Hrunting shall I
1490   achieve this deed—or death shall take me!'

After these words the Weather-Geat prince
dived into the Mere—he did not care
to wait for an answer—and the waves closed over
the daring man. It was a day's space almost
1495   before he could glimpse ground at the bottom.
The grim and greedy guardian of the flood,
keeping her hungry hundred-season watch,
discovered at once that one from above,
a human, had sounded the home of the monsters.
1500   She felt for the man and fastened upon him
her terrible hooks; but no harm came thereby
to the hale body within—the harness so ringed him
that she could not drive her dire fingers
through the mesh of the mail-shirt masking his limbs.

1505   When she came to the bottom she bore him to her lair,
the mere-wolf, pinioning the mail-clad prince.
Not all his courage could enable him
to draw his sword; but swarming through the water,
throngs of sea-beasts threw themselves upon him
1510   with ripping tusks to tear his battle-coat,
tormenting monsters. Then the man found
that he was in some enemy hall
where there was no water to weigh upon him
and the power of the flood could not pluck him away,
1515   sheltered by its roof: a shining light he saw,
a bright fire blazing clearly.

It was then that he saw the size of this water-hag,
damned thing of the deep. He dashed out his weapon,
not stinting the stroke, and with such strength and violence
1520   that the circled sword screamed on her head

a strident battle-song. But the stranger saw
his battle-flame refuse to bite
or hurt her at all; the edge failed
its lord in his need. It had lived through many
1525 hand-to-hand conflicts, and carved through the helmets
of fated men. This was the first time
that this rare treasure had betrayed its name.
Determined still, intent on fame,
the nephew of Hygelac renewed his courage.
1530 Furious, the warrior flung it to the ground,
spiral-patterned, precious in its clasps,
stiff and steel-edged; his own strength would suffice him,
the might of his hands. A man must act so
when he means in a fight to frame himself
1535 a long-lasting glory; it is not life he thinks of.

The Geat prince went for Grendel's mother,
seized her by the shoulder—he was not sorry to be fighting—
his mortal foe, and with mounting anger
the man hard in battle hurled her to the ground.
1540 She promptly repaid this present of his
as her ruthless hands reached out for him;
and the strongest of fighting-men stumbled in his weariness,
the firmest of foot-warriors fell to the earth.
She was down on this guest of hers and had drawn her knife,
1545 broad, burnished of edge; for her boy was to be avenged,
her only son. Overspreading his back,
the shirt of mail shielded his life then,
barred the entry to edge and point.
Edgetheow's son would have ended his venture
1550 deep under ground there, the Geat fighter,
had not the battle-shirt then brought him aid,
his war-shirt of steel. And the wise Lord,
the holy God, gave out the victory;
the Ruler of the Heavens rightly settled it
1555 as soon as the Geat regained his feet.

He saw among the armor there the sword to bring him victory,
a Giant-sword from former days: formidable were its edges,
a warrior's admiration. This wonder of its kind
was yet so enormous that no other man
1560 would be equal to bearing it in battle-play
—it was a Giant's forge that had fashioned it so well.
The Scylding champion, shaking with war-rage,
caught it by its rich hilt, and, careless of his life,
brandished its circles, and brought it down in fury
1565 to take her full and fairly across the neck,
breaking the bones; the blade sheared
through the death-doomed flesh. She fell to the ground;
the sword was gory; he was glad at the deed.

Light glowed out and illumined the chamber
1570 with a clearness such as the candle of heaven
sheds in the sky. He scoured the dwelling
in single-minded anger, the servant of Hygelac;
with his weapon high, and, holding to it firmly,
he stalked by the wall. Nor was the steel useless yet
1575 to that man of battle, for he meant soon enough
to settle with Grendel for those stealthy raids
—there had been many of them—he had made on the West-Danes;
far more often than on that first occasion
when he had killed Hrothgar's hearth-companions,
1580 slew them as they slept, and in their sleep ate up
of the folk of Denmark fifteen good men,
carrying off another of them
in foul robbery. The fierce champion
now settled this up with him: he saw where Grendel
1585 lay at rest, limp from the fight;
his life had wasted through the wound he had got
in the battle at Heorot. The body gaped open
as it now suffered the stroke after death
from the hard-swung sword; he had severed the neck.

1590 And above, the wise men who watched with Hrothgar
the depths of the pool descried soon enough
blood rising in the broken water
and marbling the surface. Seasoned warriors,
gray-headed, experienced, they spoke together,
1595 said it seemed unlikely that they would see once more
the prince returning triumphant to seek out
their famous master. Many were persuaded
the she-wolf of the deep had done away with him.
The ninth hour had come; the keen-hearted Scyldings
1600 abandoned the cliff-head; the kindly gold-giver
turned his face homeward. But the foreigners sat on,
staring at the pool with sickness at heart,
hoping they would look again on their beloved captain,
believing they would not.
                              The blood it had shed
1605 made the sword dwindle into deadly icicles;
the war-tool wasted away. It was wonderful indeed
how it melted away entirely, as the ice does in the spring
when the Father unfastens the frost's grip,
unwinds the water's ropes—He who watches over
1610 the times and the seasons; He is the true God.
The Great champion did not choose to take
any treasures from that hall, from the heaps he saw there,
other than that richly ornamented hilt,
and the head of Grendel. The engraved blade
1615 had melted and burnt away: the blood was too hot,

the fiend that had died there too deadly by far.
The survivor of his enemies' onslaught in battle
now set to swimming, and struck up through the water;
both the deep reaches and the rough wave-swirl
1620   were thoroughly cleansed, now the creature from the otherworld
drew breath no longer in this brief world's space.

Then the seamen's Helm came swimming up
strongly to land, delighting in his sea-trove,
those mighty burdens that he bore along with him.
1625   They went to meet him, a manly company,
thanking God, glad of their lord,
seeing him safe and sound once more.
Quickly the champion's corselet and helmet
were loosened from him. The lake's waters,
1630   sullied with blood, slept beneath the sky.

Then they turned away from there and retraced their steps,
pacing the familiar paths back again
as bold as kings, carefree at heart.
The carrying of the head from the cliff by the Mere
1635   was no easy task for any of them,
brave as they were. They bore it up,
four of them, on a spear, and transported back
Grendel's head to the gold-giving hall.
Warrior-like they went, and it was not long
1640   before they came, the fourteen bold Geats,
marching to the hall, and, among the company
walking across the land, their lord the tallest.
The earl of those thanes then entered boldly
—a man who had dared deeds and was adorned with their glory,
1645   a man of prowess—to present himself to Hrothgar.
Then was the head of Grendel, held up by its locks,
manhandled in where men were drinking;
it was an ugly thing for the earls and their queen,
an awesome sight; they eyed it well.

1650   Beowulf spoke, son of Edgetheow:
"Behold! What you see here, O son of Healfdene,
prince of the Scyldings, was pleasant freight for us:
—these trophies from the lake betoken victory!

      Not easily did I survive
1655   the fight under water; I performed this deed
not without a struggle. Our strife had ended
at its very beginning if God had not saved me.
Nothing could I perform in that fight with Hrunting,
it had no effect, fine weapon though it be.
1660   But the Guide of mankind granted me the sight
—He often brings aid to the friendless—

of a huge Giant-sword hanging on the wall,
ancient and shining—and I snatched up the weapon.
When the hour afforded, in that fight I slew
1665 the keepers of the hall. The coiling-patterned
blade burnt all away, as the blood sprang forth,
the hottest ever shed; the hilt I took from them.
So I avenged the violent slaughter
and outrages against the Danes; indeed it was fitting.
1670 Now, I say, you may sleep in Heorot
free from care—your company of warriors
and every man of your entire people,
both the young men and the guard. Gone is the need
to fear those fell attacks of former times
1675 on the lives of your earls, my lord of the Scyldings."

Then the golden hilt was given into the hand
of the older warrior, the white-haired leader.
A Giant had forged it. With the fall of the demons
it passed into the possession of the prince of the Danes,
1680 this work of wonder-smiths. The world was rid
of that invidious enemy of God
and his mother also, with their murders upon them;
and the hilt now belonged to the best of the kings
who ruled the earth in all the North
1685 and distributed treasure between the seas.
Hrothgar looked on that long-treasured hilt
before he spoke. The spring was cut on it
of the primal strife, with the destruction at last
of the race of Giants by the rushing Flood,
1690 a terrible end. Estranged was that race
from the Lord of Eternity: the tide of water
was the final reward that the Ruler sent them.
On clear gold labels let into the cross-piece
it was rightly told in runic letters,
1695 set down and sealed, for whose sake it was
that the sword was first forged, that finest of iron,
spiral-hilted, serpent-bladed.
                              At the speaking of the wise
son of Healfdene the hall was silent:
"One who has tendered justice and truth to his people,
1700 their shepherd from of old, surely may say this,
remembering all that's gone—that this man was born
to be the best of men. Beowulf, my friend,
your name shall resound in the nations of the earth
that are furthest away.

                              How wise you are to bear
1705 your great strength so peaceably! I shall perform my vows
agreed in our forewords. It is granted to your people

that you shall live to be a long-standing comfort
and bulwark to the heroes.

               Heremod was not so
for the honored Scyldings, the sons of Edgewela:

1710   his manhood brought not pleasure but a plague upon us,
death and destruction to the Danish tribes.
In his fits he would cut down his comrade in war
and his table-companion—until he turned away
from the feastings of men, that famous prince.

1715   This though the Almighty had exalted him in the bliss
of strength and vigor, advancing him far
above all other men. Yet inwardly his heart-hoard
grew raw and blood-thirsty; no rings did he give
to the Danes for his honor. And he dwelt an outcast,

1720   paid the penalty for his persecution of them
by a life of sorrow. Learn from this, Beowulf:
study openhandedness! It is for your ears that I relate this,
and I am old in winters.

                  It is wonderful to recount
how in his magnanimity the Almighty God

1725   deals out wisdom, dominion and lordship
among mankind. The Master of all things
will sometimes allow to the soul of a man
of well-known kindred to wander in delight:
He will grant him earth's bliss in his own homeland,

1730   the sway of the fortress-city of his people,
and will give him to rule regions of the world,
wide kingdoms: he cannot imagine,
in his unwisdom, that an end will come.
His life of bounty is not blighted by hint

1735   of age or ailment; no evil care
darkens his mind, malice nowhere
bares the sword-edge, but sweetly the world
swings to his will; worse is not looked for.
At last his part of pride within him

1740   waxes and climbs, the watchman of the soul
slumbering the while. That sleep is too deep,
tangled in its cares! Too close is the slayer
who shoots the wicked shaft from his bow!
For all his armor he is unable to protect himself:

1745   the insidious bolt buries in his chest,
the crooked counsels of the accursed one.
What he has so long enjoyed he rejects as too little;
in niggardly anger renounces his lordly
gifts of gilt torques, forgets and misprises

1750   his fore-ordained part, endowed thus by God,
the Master of Glory, with these great bounties.
And ultimately the end must come,

the frail house of flesh must crumble
and fall at its hour. Another then takes
1755 the earl's inheritance; open-handedly
he gives out its treasure, regardless of fear.

Beloved Beowulf, best of warriors,
resist this deadly taint, take what is better,
your lasting profit. Put away arrogance,
1760 noble fighter! The noon of your strength
shall last for a while now, but in a little time
sickness or a sword will strip it from you:
either enfolding flame or a flood's billow
or a knife-stab or the stoop of a spear
1765 or the ugliness of age; or your eyes' brightness
lessens and grows dim. Death shall soon
have beaten you then, O brave warrior!

So it is with myself. I swayed the Ring-Danes
for fifty years here, defending them in war
1770 with ash and with edge over the earth's breadth
against many nations; until I numbered at last
not a single adversary beneath the skies' expanse:
But what change of fortune befell me at my hearth
with the coming of Grendel; grief sprang from joy
1775 when the old enemy entered our hall!
Great was the pain that persecution
thrust upon me. Thanks be to God,
the Lord everlasting, that I have lived until this day,
seen out this age of ancient strife
1780 and set my gaze upon this gory head!
But join those who are seated, and rejoice in the feast,
O man clad in victory! We shall divide between us
many treasures when morning comes."
The Geat went most gladly to take
1785 his seat at the bench, at the bidding of the wise one.
Quite as before, the famous men,
guests of the hall, were handsomely feasted
on this new occasion. Then night's darkness
grew on the company. The guard arose,
1790 for their wise leader wished to rest,
the gray-haired Scylding. The Geat was ready enough
to go to his bed too, brave shieldsman.

The bower-thane soon brought on his way
this fight-wearied and far-born man.
1795 His courteous office was to care for all
a guest's necessities, such as at that day
the wants of a seafaring warrior might be.
The hero took his rest; the hall towered up
gilded, wide-gabled, its guest within sleeping

1800   until the black raven blithe-hearted greeted
    the heaven's gladness. Hastening, the sunlight
    shook out above the shadows. Sharp were the bold ones,
    each atheling eager to set off,
    back to his homeland: the high-mettled stranger
1805   wished to be forging far in his ship.
    That hardy man ordered Hrunting to be carried
    back to the son of Edgelaf, bade him accept again
    his well-loved sword; said that he accounted it
    formidable in the fight, a good friend in war,
1810   thanked him for the loan of it, without the least finding fault
    with the edge of that blade; ample was his spirit!

    By then the fighting-men were fairly armed-up
    and ready for the journey; the Joy of the Danes went,
    a prince, to the high seat where Hrothgar was,
1815   one hero brave in battle hailed the other.

    Beowulf then spoke, son of Edgetheow.
    "We now wish to say, seafarers who
    are come from far, how keenly we desire
    to return again to Hygelac. Here we were rightly,
1820   royally, treated; you have entertained us well.
    If I can ever on this earth earn of you,
    O lord of men, more of your love
    than I have so far done, by deeds of war,
    I shall at once be ready. If ever I hear
1825   that the neighboring tribes intend your harm,
    as those who hate you have done in the past,
    I'll bring a thousand thanes and heroes
    here to help you. As for Hygelac, I know
    that the Lord of the Geats, Guide of his flock,
1830   young though he is, will yield his support
    both in words and deeds so I may do you honor
    and bring you a grove of gray-tipped spears
    and my strength in aid when you are short of men.
    Further, when Hrethric shall have it in mind
1835   to come, as a king's son, to the courts of the Geats
    he shall find many friends there. Far countries are seen
    by a man of mark to much advantage."

    Hrothgar spoke to him in answer:
    "These words you have delivered, the Lord in His wisdom
1840   put in your heart. I have heard no man
    of the age that you are utter such wisdom.
    You are rich in strength and ripe of mind,
    you are wise in your utterance. If ever it should happen
    that spear or other spike of battle,
1845   sword or sickness, should sweep away
    the son of Hrethel; your sovereign lord,

shepherd of his people, my opinion is clear,
that the Sea-Geats will not be seeking for a better
man to be their king and keep their war-hoard,

1850   if you still have life and would like to rule
the kingdom of your kinsmen. As I come to know
your temper, dear Beowulf, the better it pleases me.
You have brought it about that both the peoples,
the Sea-Geats and the Spear-Danes,

1855   shall share out peace; the shock of war,
the old sourness, shall cease between us.
So long as I shall rule the reaches of this kingdom
we shall exchange wealth; a chief shall greet
his fellow with gifts over the gannet's bath

1860   as the ship with curved prow crosses the seas
with presents and pledges. Your people, I know,
always open-natured in the old manner,
are fast to friends and firm toward enemies."

Then the Shield of the Heroes, Healfdene's son,

1865   presented him with twelve new treasures in the hall,
bade him with these tokens betake himself
safe to his people; and soon return again.
Then that king of noble race, ruler of the Scyldings,
embraced and kissed that best of thanes,

1870   taking him by the neck; tears fell from
the gray-haired one. With the wisdom of age
he foresaw two things, the second more likely,
that they would never again greet one another,
meet thus as heroes. The man was so dear to him

1875   that he could not stop the surging in his breast;
but hidden in the heart, held fast in its strings,
a deep longing for this dearly loved man
burned against the blood.

                       Beowulf went from him,
trod the green earth, a gold-resplendent warrior

1880   rejoicing in his rings. Riding at anchor
the strayer of ocean stayed for her master.
Chiefly the talk returned as they walked
to Hrothgar's giving. He was a king
blameless in all things, until old age at last,

1885   that brings down so many, removed his proud strength.

They came then to the sea-flood, the spirited band
of warrior youth, wearing the ring-meshed
coat of mail. The coastguard saw
the heroes approaching, as he had done before.

1890   Nor was it ungraciously that he greeted the strangers
from his ridge by the cliff; but rode down to meet them:
how welcome they would be to the Weather-Geats, he said
to those shipward-bound men in their shining armor.

The wide sea-boat with its soaring prow
1895   was loaded at the beach there with battle-raiment,
with horses and arms. High rose the mast
above the lord Hrothgar's hoard of gifts.
To the boat-guard Beowulf gave
a gold-cleated sword; it gained the man
1900   much honor on the mead-benches,
that treasured heirloom. Out moved the boat then
to divide the deep water, left Denmark behind.
A special sea-dress, a sail, was hoisted
and belayed to the mast. The beams spoke.
1905   The wind did not hinder the wave-skimming ship
as it ran through the seas, but the sea-going craft
with foam at its throat, furled back the waves,
her ring-bound prow planning the waters
till they caught sight of the cliffs of the Geats
1910   and headlands they knew. The hull drove ahead,
urged by the breeze, and beached on the shore.

The harbor-guard was waiting at the water's edge;
his eye had been scouring the stretches of the flood
in a long look-out for these loved men.
1915   Now he moored the broad-ribbed boat in the sand,
held fast with hawsers, so no heft of the waves
should drive away again those darling timbers.
He had the heroes' hoard brought ashore,
their gold-plated armor. To go to their lord
1920   was now but a step, to see again Hygelac
the son of Hrethel, at his home where he dwells
himself with his hero-band, hard by the sea-wall.

That was a handsome hall there. And high within it sat
a king of great courage. His consort was young,
1925   but wise and discreet for one who has lived
so few years at court; the queen's name was Hygd,
Hareth's daughter. When she dealt out treasure
to the Geat nation, the gifts were generous,
there was nothing narrowly done.
                                    It was not so with Modthryth,[1]
1930   imperious queen, cruel to her people.
There was no one so rash among the retainers of the house
as to risk a look at her—except her lord himself—
turn his eyes on her, even by day;
or fatal bonds were fettled for him,
1935   twisted by hand: and when hands had been laid on him
he could be sure that the sword would be present,

---

1. The rash and arrogant queen Modthryth (or Thryth) is described in order to contrast her to the wise queen Hygd. The principle of broad contrast was similarly used in the earlier comparison between the unwise king Heremod and Beowulf.

and settle it quickly, its spreading inlays
proclaim its killing-power. Unqueenly ways
for a woman to follow, that one who weaves peace,
1940   though of matchless looks, should demand the life
of a well-loved man for an imagined wrong!
Hemming's son Offa put an end to that.
And the ale-drinkers then told a tale quite different:
little was the hurt or harm that she brought
1945   on her subjects then, as soon as she was given,
gold-decked, in marriage, to the mighty young champion
of valiant lineage, when she voyaged out
on the pale flood at her father's bidding
to the hall of Offa. All that followed
1950   of a life destined to adorn a throne
she employed well, and was well-loved for it,
strong in her love for that leader of heroes,
the outstanding man, as I have heard tell,
of all mankind's mighty race
1955   from sea to sea. So it was that Offa,
brave with the spear, was spoken of abroad
for his wars and his gifts; he governed with wisdom
the land of his birth. To him was born Eomer,
helper of the heroes, Hemming's kinsman,
1960   Garmund's grandson, great in combat.

The war-man himself came walking along
by the broad foreshores with his band of picked men,
trod the sea-beach. From the south blazed
the sun, the world's candle. They carried themselves forward,
1965   stepping on eagerly to the stronghold where
Ongentheow's conqueror, the earls' defender,
the warlike young king, was well-known for his
giving of neck-rings. The news of Beowulf's
return was rapidly told to Hygelac
1970   —that the shield of warriors, his own shoulder-companion,
had walked alive within the gates,
unscathed from the combat, and was coming to the hall.
The floor was quickly cleared of men
for the incoming guests, by order of the king.

1975   When he had offered greetings in grave words,
as usage obliged him, to his lord of men,
the survivor of the fight sat facing the king,
kinsman and kinsman. Carrying the mead-cup
about the hall was Hareth's daughter,
1980   lover of the people, presenting the wine-bowl
to the hand of each Geat. Hygelac then made
of his near companion in that noble hall
courteous inquiry. Curiosity burned in him
to hear the adventures of this voyage of the Geats.

1985 "What luck did you meet with, beloved Beowulf,
on your suddenly resolved seeking out
of distant strife over salt water,
battle at Heorot? Did you bring to that famous
leader Hrothgar some alleviation
1990 of those woes so widely known? Overwhelming doubts
troubled my mind, mistrusting this voyage
of my dear liegeman. Long did I beg you
never to meet with this murderous creature
but to let the South Danes themselves bring an end
1995 to their feud with Grendel. God be thanked
that safe and sound I see you here today!"

Thus spoke Beowulf, son of Edgetheow:
"It has been told aloud, my lord Hygelac,
and to many men by now, the meeting that there was
2000 between myself and Grendel, the great time
we fought in that place where he had inflicted so much
grief and outrage, age-long disgrace
on the Victor-Scyldings. I avenged all.
No kinsman of Grendel shall have cause to take pride
2005 in the sound that arose in the stretches of the night
—not the last of that alien and evil brood
on the face of the earth.
                                   First I went in
to greet Hrothgar in the hall of the ring-giving.
As soon as the glorious son of Healfdene
2010 knew my mind, he immediately
offered me a seat at his sons' bench.
What hall-joys were there! A happier company
seated over mead I've not met with in my time
beneath the heavens. A noble princess
2015 fit to be the pledge of peace between nations
would move through the young men in the hall,
stirring their spirits; bestowing a torque
often upon a warrior before she went to her seat.
Or the heroes would look on as Hrothgar's daughter
2020 bore the ale-flagon to each earl in turn.
I heard those who sat in the hall calling her
by the name of Freawaru[2] as she fetched each warrior
the nailed treasure-cup.
                                   She is betrothed to Ingeld,
this girl attired in gold, to the gracious son of Froda.
2025 The Protector of the Danes has determined this
and accounts it wisdom, the keeper of the land,
thus to end all the feud and their fatal wars

2. Freawaru's tragic fate as a "peace-weaver" married off to cement an alliance between warring tribes recalls that of Hildeburh in the earlier song of Finn.

by means of the lady. Yet when a lord is dead
it is seldom the slaying-spear sleeps for long—
2030   seldom indeed—dear though the bride may be.

The lord of the Heathobards may not like it well
at the bringing home of his bride to the hall:
nor may it please every earl in that nation
to have the pride and daring of Denmark at table
2035   —their guests resplendent in the spoil of their ancestors!
Heathobards had treasured these trenchant, ring-patterned
weapons until they could wield them no longer,
having taken part in that play of the shields
where they lost their lives and the lives of their friends.

2040   An old spear-fighter shall speak at the feast,
eyeing the hilt-ring—his heart grows fierce
as he remembers all the slaying of the man by the spear.
In his dark mood he deliberately
tries out the mettle of a man who is younger,
2045   awakens his war-taste in words such as these:
'My friend, is that not a familiar sword?
Your father carried it forth to battle,
—excellent metal—masked as for war
on his last expedition. There the Danes slew him,
2050   the keen Scyldings, and kept the field
when Withergyld was dead, when the warriors had fallen.
The son of one of his slayers now
sports the weapon here, and, spurning our hall-floor,
boasts of the killing: he carries at his side
2055   the prize that you should possess by right.'

With such biting words of rebuke and reminder
he taunts him at every turn; until the time comes
when one sleeps blood-stained from the blow of a sword:
the follower of the lady forfeits with his life
2060   for the actions of his father; the other contrives
to lose himself, and lives; the land is familiar to him.
Both sides then will break the pact
sworn by the earls; and Ingeld's vengefulness
will well up in him, overwhelming gall
2065   shall cause his wife-love to cool thereafter.
So I do not believe that this liking of the Heathobards
for alliance with the Danes is all what it seems,
or that their friendship is sound.
                                    I shall speak further
of Grendel again, O giver of treasure,
2070   that you may rightly know the result of the champions'
hand-to-hand meeting. When heaven's jewel
had glided from the world, the wrathful creature,
dire dusk-fiend, came down to seek us out

where, still whole, we held the building.
2075 The weight of the fight fell on Handscio,
the doomed blow came down on him; he died the first,
a warrior in his harness; the hero, my fellow,
was ground to death between Grendel's jaws,
our friend's body was bolted down whole.
2080 But the bloody-toothed slayer, bent on destruction,
was not going to go from that gold-giving hall
any the sooner: not empty-handed!
Proud of his might, he made proof of me,
groped out his greedy palm. A glove hung from it,
2085 uncouth and huge, clasped strangely,
and curiously contrived; it was cobbled together
all of dragons' skins, and with devilish skill.
It was inside this bag that the bold marauder
was going to put me, guiltless as I was,
2090 as the first of his catch; but he could not manage it
once I had stood up in anger against him.
Too long to repeat here how I paid back
the enemy of the people for his every crime;
but to your people, O my prince, my performance there
2095 will bring honor. He broke away,
tasted life's joys for a little while,
but his strong right hand stayed behind
in the hall of Heorot; humbled he went thence
and sank despairing in the depths of the Mere.

2100   For this deadly fight the Friend of the Scyldings
recompensed me with plated gold,
a mort of treasure, when the morrow came
and we had benched ourselves as the banqueting table.
There was music and laughter, lays were sung:
2105 the veteran of the Scyldings, versed in saga,
would himself fetch back far-off times to us;
the daring-in-battle would address the harp,
the joy-wood, delighting; or deliver a reckoning
both true and sad; or he would tell us the story
2110 of some wonderful adventure, valiant-hearted king.
Or the seasoned warrior, wrapped in age,
would again fall to fabling of his youth
and the days of his battle-strength; his breast was troubled
as his mind filled with the memories of those years.

2115   And thus we spent the space of a day there
seeking delight, until the ensuing dusk
came to mankind. Quick on its heels
the mother of Grendel moved to her revenge,
spurred on by sorrow; her son was death-taken
2120 by Geat warspite. That gruesome she

avenged her son, struck down a warrior,
and boldly enough! The breath was taken
from the ancient counselor, Ashhere, there.
Nor could the Danish people, when day came,
2125   give their death-wearied dear one to be burned,
escort him to the pyre: she had carried the body
to the mountain-torrent's depth in her monstrous embrace.
This was for Hrothgar the harshest of the blows
that since so long had fallen on the leader of the people.
2130   Distraught with care, the king then asked of me
a noble action—and in your name, Hygelac—
that I should risk my life among the rush of waters
and perform a great deed; he promised me reward.

    Far and wide it is told how I found in the surges
2135   the grim and terrible guardian of the deep.
After a hard hand-to-hand struggle
the whirlpool boiled with the blood of the mother;
I had hewn off her head in that hall underground
with a sword of huge size. I survived that fight
2140   not without difficulty; but my doom was not yet.

    The protector of warriors rewarded me
with a heap of treasure, Healfdene's son.
The ways of that king accorded to usage:
I was not to forgo the guerdon he had offered,
2145   the meed of my strength; he bestowed upon me
the treasures I would have desired, the son of Healfdene;
now, brave king, I bring them to you.
I rejoice to present them. Joy, for me, always
lies in your gift. Little family
2150   do I have in the world, Hygelac, besides yourself."

Then he bade them bring in the boar's head standard,
the battle-dwarfing helmet, the hoar war-shirt
and the lambent sword; and delivered this speech:
"Hrothgar gave me all this garb of war
2155   with one word—the wisest of princes—
that I should first relate to you whose legacy it is.
His brother Heorogar had it, he told me,
for a long while, as Lord of the Scyldings,
yet chose not to give this guardian of his breast
2160   to his own son, the spirited Heoroweard,
friend though he was to him.
                      Flourish in the use if it!"

I heard that four fast-stepping horses
followed these treasures, a team of bays
matching as apples. All these he gave him,
2165   both horses and armor—the act of a kinsman!
A kinsman knits no nets of malice

darkly for his fellow. Does he devise the end
of the man that is next to him? The nephew of Hygelac
held fast to that man hardy in battle;
2170   each thought only of the other's welfare.

Beowulf, I heard, gave Hygd the neck-ring,
the wonderful treasure work Wealhtheow had given him
—high was her breeding—and three horses also,
graceful in their gait, and with gay saddles.
2175   Her breast was made more beautiful by the jewel.

Such was the showing of the son of Edgetheow,
known for his combats and his courage in action.
His dealings were honorable: in drink he did not strike
at the slaves of his hearth; his heart was not savage.
2180   The hero guarded well the great endowment
God had bestowed on him, a strength unequalled
among mankind. He had been misprised for long,
the sons of the Geats seeing little in him
and the lord of the Weather-Geats not willing to pay him
2185   much in the way of honor on the mead-benches.
They firmly believed in his laziness
—"the atheling was idle"! But for all such humblings
time brought reversal, invested him with glory.

Then the king bold in war, keeper of the warriors,
2190   required them to bring in the bequest of Hrethel,
elaborate in gold; the Geats at that day
had no more royal treasure of the rank of sword.
This he then laid in the lap of Beowulf
and bestowed on him an estate of seven thousand hides,
2195   a chief's stool and a hall. Inherited land,
a domain by birthright, had come down to them both
in the Geat nation; the greater region
to the better-born of them—the broad kingdom.

But it fell out after, in other days,
2200   among the hurl of battle—when Hygelac lay dead
and the bills of battle had dealt death to his Heardred,
despite the shield's shelter, when the Scylfings found him
amid his conquering people, and those keen war-wolves
grimly hemmed in Hereric's nephew—
2205   that the broad kingdom came by this turn
into Beowulf's hands.
                    Half a century
he ruled it, well: until One began
—the king had grown gray in the guardianship of the land—
to put forth his power in the pitch-black night-times
2210   —the hoard-guarding Dragon of a high barrow
raised above the moor.
                    Men did not know

of the way underground to it; but one man did enter,
went right inside, reached the treasure,
the heathen hoard, and his hand fell
2215   on a golden goblet. The guardian, however,
if he had been caught sleeping by the cunning of the thief,
did not conceal this loss. It was not long till the near-
dwelling people discovered that the dragon was angry.

The causer of his pain had not purposed this;
2220   it was without relish that he had robbed the hoard;
necessity drove him. The nameless slave
of one of the warriors, wanting shelter,
on the run from a flogging, had felt his way inside,
a sin-tormented soul. When he saw what was there
2225   the intruder was seized with sudden terror;
but for all his fear, the unfortunate wretch
still took the golden treasure-cup . . .
There were heaps of hoard-things in this hall underground
which once in gone days gleamed and rang;
2230   the treasure of a race rusting derelict.

In another age an unknown man,
brows bent, had brought and hid here
the beloved hoard. The whole race
death-rapt, and of the ring of earls
2235   one left alive; living on in that place
heavy with friend-loss, the hoard-guard
waited the same weird. His wit acknowledged
that the treasures gathered and guarded over the years
were his for the briefest while.
                                              The barrow stood ready
2240   on flat ground where breakers beat at the headland,
new, near at hand, made narrow of access.
The keeper of rings carried into it
the earls' holdings, the hoard-worthy part
fraught with gold, and few words he spoke:[3]
2245   "Hold, ground, the gold of the earls!
Men could not. Cowards they were not
who took it from thee once, but war-death took them,
that stops life, struck them, spared not one
man of my people, passed on now.
2250   They have had their hall-joys. I have not with me
a man able to unsheathe this . . .
Who shall polish this plated vessel,
this treasured cup? The company is elsewhere.
    This hardened helmet healed with gold

---

3. The speech of the "last survivor" that follows resembles Old English elegies such as *The Wanderer* in its lament for the transience of the joys of heroic society.

2255   shall lose its shell. They sleep now
whose work was to burnish the battle-masks;
so with the cuirass that in the crash took
bite of iron among breaking shields:
it moulders with the man. This mail-shirt travelled far,
2260   hung from a shoulder that shouldered warriors:
it shall not jingle again.
                            There's no joy from harp-play,
glee-wood's gladness, no good hawk
swings through hall now, no swift horse
tramps at the threshold. Terrible slaughter
2265   has carried into darkness many kindreds of mankind."

So the sole survivor, in sorrowful mood,
bewailed his grief; he wandered cheerless
through days and nights until death's flood
reached to his heart.
                            The Ravager of the night,
2270   the burner who has sought out barrows from of old,
then found this hoard of undefended joy.
The smooth evil dragon swims through the gloom
enfolded in flame; the folk of that country
hold him in dread. He is doomed to seek out
2275   hoards in the ground, and guard for an age there
the heathen gold: much good does it do him!

Thus for three hundred winters this waster of peoples
guarded underground the great hoard-hall
with his enormous might; until a man awoke
2280   the anger in his breast by bearing to his master
the plated goblet as a peace-offering,
a token of new fealty. Thus the treasure was lightened
and the treasure-house was breached; the boon was granted
to the luckless slave, and his lord beheld
2285   for the first time that work of a former race of men.

The waking of the worm awoke a new feud:
he glided along the rock, glared at the sight
of a foeman's footprint: far too near his head
the intruder had stepped as he stole by him!
2290   (An undoomed man may endure affliction
and even exile lightly, for as long as the Ruler
continues to protect him.) The treasure-guard eagerly
quartered the ground to discover the man
who had done him wrong during his sleep.
2295   Seething with rage, he circled the barrow's
whole outer wall, but no hint of a man
showed in the wilderness. Yet war's prospect pleased him,
the thought of battle-action! He went back into the mound

2300 to search for the goblet, and soon saw that one
of the tribe of men had tampered with the gold
of the glorious hoard.
                              The hoard's guardian
waited until evening only with difficulty.
The barrow-keeper was bursting with rage:
his fire would cruelly requite the loss
2305 of the dear drinking-vessel.
                              At last day was gone,
to the worm's delight; he delayed no further
inside his walls, but issued forth flaming,
armed with fire.
                              That was a fearful beginning
for the people of that country; uncomfortable and swift
2310 was the end to be likewise for their lord and treasure-giver!

So the visitant began to vomit flames
and burn the bright dwellings; the blazing rose skyward
and men were afraid: the flying scourge
did not mean to leave one living thing.
2315 On every side the serpent's ravages,
the spite of the foe, sprang to the eye—
how this hostile assailant hated and injured
the men of the Geats. Before morning's light
he flew back to the hoard in its hidden chamber.
2320 He had poured out fire and flame on the people,
he had put them to the torch; he trusted now to the barrow's walls
and to his fighting strength. His faith misled him.

Beowulf was acquainted quickly enough
with the truth of the horror, for his own hall had itself
2325 been swallowed in flame, the finest of buildings,
and the gift-stool of the Geats. Grief then struck
into his ample heart with anguished keenness.
The chieftain supposed he had sorely angered
the Ruler of all, the eternal Lord,
2330 by breach of ancient law. His breast was thronged
with dark unaccustomed care-filled thoughts.
The fiery dragon's flames had blasted
all the land by the sea, and its safe stronghold,
the fortress of the people. The formidable king
2335 of the Geats now planned to punish him for this.
The champion of the fighting-men, chief of the earls,
gave orders for the making of a marvelous shield
worked all in iron; well he knew
that a linden shield would be of little service
2340 —wood against fire. For the foremost of athelings
the term of his days in this transitory world
was soon to be endured; it was the end, too, for the dragon's
long watch over the wealth of the hoard.

The distributor of rings disdained to go
2345   with a troop of men or a mighty host
to seek the far-flier. He had no fear for himself
and discounted the worm's courage and strength,
its prowess in battle. Battles in plenty
he had survived; valiant in all dangers,
2350   he had come though many clashes since his cleansing of Heorot
and his extirpation of the tribe of Grendel,
hated race.
                    That was hardly the least
of hand-to-hand combats when Hygelac was slain,
when that kindly lord of peoples, the king of the Geats,
2355   the son of Hrethel, among the hurl of battle
slaked the sword's thirst on the soil of Friesland
and the blows beat down on him!
                                        Beowulf came away
by the use of his force in a feat of swimming;
alone into the ocean he leapt, holding
2360   thirty men's mail-coats on his arm.

There was little cause for crowing among the Hetware
about their conduct of the foot-fight: they carried their lindens
forward against him; but few came back
from the wolf in war, walked home again.
2365   Solitary and wretched was the son of Edgetheow[4]
on the sweep of waters as he swam back to his people.
There Hygd offered him the hoard and the kingdom,[5]
the gift-stool and its treasure; not trusting that her son
would be able to hold the inherited seats
2370   against foreign peoples now his father was dead.
But the bereaved people could arrive at no conditions
under which the atheling[6] would accept the kingdom
or allow himself to be lord over Heardred.
Rather he fostered him among the people with friendly counsel,
2375   with kindliness and respect, until he came of age
and ruled the Geats.
                        Guests sought out Heardred,
outcasts from oversea: Ohthere's sons.

They had risen against Onela, ruler of the Scylfings,
highest of the princes who provided treasure
2380   in all the sea-coasts of the Swedish realms,
a famous lord. This led to the end
of Hygelac's son;[7] his hospitality
cost him a weapon-thrust and a wound to the life.

4. Beowulf.
5. Beowulf refuses the throne when Hygd offers it to him after Hygelac's death. Instead, he serves as her son Heardred's adviser until he is old enough to rule. Only after Heardred is killed in battle by the Swedish king Onela does Beowulf finally agree to be king of the Geats.
6. I.e., Beowulf.
7. Heardred.

Ongentheow's son, Onela, turned
2385   to seek his home again once Heardred was dead;
the gift-stool and the ruling of the Geat people
he left to Beowulf; who was a brave king,
and kept it before his mind to requite his lord's death.
In after-days he was Eadgils' friend
2390   when Eadgils was deserted, supporting his cause
across the wide water with weapons and an army,
Ohthere's son; who took his own revenge
by terror-campaigns that at last trapped Onela.

So the son of Edgetheow survived unscathed
2395   each of these combats, calamitous onslaughts,
works of prowess: until this one day
when he must wage war on the serpent.
The Lord of the Geats went with eleven companions
to set eyes on the dragon; his anger rose in him.
2400   He had by then discovered the cause of the attack
that had ravaged his people; the precious drinking-cup
had come into his hands from the hands of the informer.
He who had brought about the beginning of the feud
now made the thirteenth man in their company,
2405   a miserable captive; cowed, he must show them
the way to the place, an unwilling guide.
For he alone knew the knoll and its earth-hall,
hard by the strand and the strife of the waves,
the underground hollow heaped to the roof
2410   with intricate treasures. Attendant on the gold
was that underground ancient, eager as a wolf,
an awesome guardian; it was no easy bargain
for any mortal man to make himself its owner.

The stern war-king sat on the headland,
2415   spoke encouragement to the companions of his hearth,
the gold-friend of the Geats. Gloomy was his spirit though,
death-eager, wandering; the weird was at hand
that was to overcome the old man there,
seek his soul's hoard, and separate
2420   the life from the body; not for long now
would the atheling's life be lapped in flesh.
Beowulf spoke, son of Edgetheow:
"Many were the struggles I survived in youth
in times of danger; I do not forget them.
2425   When that open-handed lord beloved by the people
received me from my father I was seven years old:
King Hrethel kept and fostered me,
gave me treasure and table-room, true to our kinship.
All his life he had as little hatred for me,
2430   a warrior in hall, as he had for a son,
Herebeald, or Hathkin, or Hygelac my own lord.

A murderous bed was made for the eldest
by the act of a kinsman, contrary to right:
a shaft from Hathkin's horn-tipped bow
2435   shot down the man that should have become his lord;
mistaking his aim, he struck his kinsman,
his own brother, with the blood-stained arrow-head.
A sin-fraught conflict that could not be settled,
unthinkable in the heart; yet thus it was,
2440   and the atheling lost his life unavenged.

    Grief such as this a gray-headed man
might feel if he saw his son in youth
riding the gallows. Let him raise the lament then,
a song of sorrow, while his son hangs there,
2445   a sport for the raven. Remedy is there none
that an age-stricken man may afford him then.
Every morning reminds him again
that his son has gone elsewhere; another son,
an heir in his courts, he cares not to wait for,
2450   now that the first has found his deeds
have come to an end in the constriction of death.
He sorrows to see among his son's dwellings
the wasted wine-hall, the wind's home now,
bereft of all joy. The riders are sleeping,
2455   the heroes in the grave. The harp does not sound,
there is no laughter in the yard as there used to be of old.
He goes then to his couch, keens the lament
for his one son alone there; too large now seem to him
his houses and fields.
                 The Helm of the Geats
2460   sustained a like sorrow for Herebeald
surging in his heart. Hardly could he settle
the feud by imposing a price on the slayer;
no more could he offer actions to that warrior
manifesting hatred; though he held him not dear.

2465   Hard did this affliction fall upon him:
he renounced men's cheer, chose God's light.
But he left to sons his land and stronghold
at his life's faring-forth—as the fortunate man does.

    On Hrethel's death the hatred and strife
2470   of the Swedes and the Geats, the grievances between them,
broke into bitter war across the broad water.
The sons of Ongentheow were strong fighters,
active in war; they would not keep
peace on the lakes, but plotted many
2475   a treacherous ambush about Hreosnabeorgh.

    It has come to be known that my kinsmen and friends
revenged both the feud and the violent attack,

though the price that one of them paid was his life,
a hard bargain. That battle proved

2480   mortal for Hathkin, Master of the Geats.
But came the morrow, and a kinsman, as I heard,
avenged him on his slayer with the sword's edge:
in his attack on Eofor, Ongentheow's
war-mask shattered, and the Scylfing patriarch

2485   fell pale from the wound; the wielding hand
forgot not the feud, flinched not from the death-blow.

　　　I had the fortune in that battle, by my bright sword,
to make return to Hygelac for the treasures he had given me.
He had granted me land, land to enjoy

2490   and leave to my heirs. Little need was there
that Hygelac should go to the Gifthas or the Spear-Danes
or seek out ever in the Swedish kingdom
a weaker champion, and chaffer for his services.
I was always before him in the footing host,

2495   by myself in the front.
　　　　　　　　　　　　So, while I live,
I shall always do battle, while this blade lasts
that early and late has often served me
since, with my bare hands, I broke Dayraven,
the champion of the Franks, before the flower of the host.

2500   He was not to be permitted to present his Frisian lord
with the breast-armor that had adorned Hygelac,
for he was slain in the struggle, the standard-bearer,
noble in his prowess. It was not my sword
that broke his bone-cage and the beatings of his heart

2505   but my warlike hand-grasp.
　　　　　　　　　　　　Now shall hard edge,
hand and blade, do battle for the hoard!"
Beowulf made speech, spoke a last time
a word of boasting: "Battles in plenty
I ventured in youth; and I shall venture this feud

2510   and again achieve glory, the guardian of my people,
old though I am, if this evil destroyer
dares to come out of his earthen hall."

Then he addressed each of the men there
on this last occasion, courageous helm-bearers,

2515   cherished companions: "I would choose not to take
any weapon to this worm, if I well knew
of some other fashion fitting to my boast
of grappling with this monster, as with Grendel before.
But as I must expect here the hot war-breath

2520   of venom and fire, for this reason I have
my board and corselet. From the keeper of the barrow
I shall not flee one foot; but further than that
shall be worked out at the wall as our weird is given us

by the Creator of men. My mood is strong;
2525   I forgo further words against the winged fighter.

    Men in armor! Your mail-shirts protect you:
await on the barrow the one of us two
who shall be better able to bear his wounds
after this onslaught. This affair is not for you,
2530   nor is it measured to any man but myself alone
to match strength with this monstrous being,
attempt this deed. By daring will I
win this gold; war otherwise
shall take your king, terrible life's-bane!"
2535   The strong champion stood up beside his shield,
brave beneath helmet, he bore his mail-shirt
to the rocky cliff's foot, confident in his strength,
a single man; such is not the coward's way!
Then did the survivor of a score of conflicts,
2540   the battle-clashes of encountering armies,
excelling in manhood, see in the wall
a stone archway, and out of the barrow broke
a stream surging through it, a stream of fire
with waves of deadly flame; the dragon's breath
2545   meant he could not venture into the vault near the hoard
for any time at all without being burnt.

    Passion filled the prince of the Geats:
he allowed a cry to utter from his breast,
roared from his stout heart: as the horn clear in battle
2550   his voice re-echoed through the vault of gray stone.
The hoard-guard recognized a human voice,
and there was no more time for talk of friendship:
hatred stirred. Straightaway
the breath of the dragon billowed from the rock
2555   in a hissing gust; the ground boomed.

He swung up his shield, overshadowed by the mound,
the lord of the Geats against this grisly stranger.
The temper of the twisted tangle-thing was fired
to close now in battle. The brave warrior-king
2560   shook out his sword so sharp of edge,
an ancient heirloom. Each of the pair,
intending destruction, felt terror at the other:
intransigent beside his towering shield
the lord of friends, while the fleetness of the serpent
2565   wound itself together; he waited in his armor.
It came flowing forward, flaming and coiling,
rushing on its fate.
                        For the famous prince
the protection lent to his life and person
by the shield was shorter than he had shaped it to be.

2570 He must now dispute this space of time,
the first in his life when fate had not assigned him
the glory of the battle. The Geat chieftain
raised his hand, and reached down such a stroke
with his huge ancestral sword on the horribly-patterned snake
2575 that, meeting the bone, its bright edge turned
and it bit less strongly than its sorely-straitened lord
required of it then. The keeper of the barrow
after this stroke grew savage in mood,
spat death-fire; the sparks of their battle
2580 blazed into the distance.
      He boasted of no triumphs then,
the gold-friend of the Geats, for his good old sword
bared in the battle, his blade, had failed him,
as such iron should not do.
      That was no easy adventure,
when the celebrated son of Edgetheow
2585 had to pass from that place on earth
and against his will take up his dwelling
in another place; as every man must give up
the days that are lent him.
      It was not long again
to the next meeting of those merciless ones.
2590 The barrow-guard took heart: his breast heaved
with fresh out-breath: fire enclosed
the former folk-king; he felt bitter pain.

The band of picked companions did not come
to stand about him, as battle-usage asks
2595 offspring of athelings; they escaped to the wood,
saved their lives.
    Sorrow filled
the breast of one man. The bonds of kinship
nothing may remove for a man who thinks rightly.
This was Wiglaf, Weoxstan's son,
2600 well-loved shieldsman, a Scylfing prince
of the stock of Alfhere; he could see his lord
tormented by the heat through his mask of battle.
He remembered then the favors he had formerly bestowed on him,
the wealthy dwelling-place of the Waymundings,
2605 confirming him in the landrights his father had held.
He could not then hold back: hand gripped the yellow
linden-wood shield, shook out that ancient
sword that Eanmund, Ohthere's son,
had left among men.
      He met his end in battle,
2610 a friendless exile, felled by the sword
wielded by Weoxstan: who went back to his kinsmen
with the shining helm, the shirt of ring-mail
and the ancient giant-sword. All this war-harness,

eager for use, Onela then gave to him,
2615   though it had been his nephew's; nor did he speak
of the blood-feud to the killer of his brother's son.
Weoxstan kept this war-gear many years,
sword and breast-armor, till his son was able
to perform manly deeds as his father had of old.
2620   He gave him among the Geats these garments of battle
of incalculable worth; then went his life's journey
wise and full of years.
                            For the youthful warrior
this was the first occasion when he was called on to stand
at his dear lord's shoulder in the shock of battle.
2625   His courage did not crumble, nor did his kinsman's heirloom
weaken at the war-play: as the worm found
when they had got to grips with one another.

Wiglaf then spoke many words that were fitting,
addressed his companions; dark was his mood.
2630   "I remember the time, as we were taking mead
in the banqueting hall, when we bound ourselves
to the gracious lord who granted us arms,
that we would make return for these trappings of war,
these helms and hard swords, if an hour such as this
2635   should ever chance for him. He chose us himself
out of all his host for this adventure here,
expecting action; he armed me with you
because he accounted us keen under helmet,
men able with the spear—even though our lord
2640   intended to take on this task of courage
as his own share, as shepherd of the people,
and champion of mankind in the achieving of glory
and deeds of daring.
                        That day has now come
when he stands in need of the strength of good fighters,
2645   our lord and liege. Let us go to him,
help our leader for as long as it requires,
the fearsome fire-blast. I had far rather
that the flame should enfold my flesh-frame there
alongside my gold-giver—as God knows of me.
2650   To bear our shields back to our homes
would seem unfitting to me, unless first we have been able
to kill the foe and defend the life
of the prince of the Weather-Geats. I well know
that former deeds deserve not that, alone
2655   of the flower of the Geats, he should feel the pain,
sink in the struggle; sword and helmet,
corselet and mail-shirt, shall be our common gear."

He strode through the blood-smoke, bore his war-helmet
to the aid of his lord, uttered few words:

2660 "Beloved Beowulf, bear all things well!
You gave it out long ago in your youth
that, living, you would not allow your glory
ever to abate. Bold-tempered chieftain,
famed for your deeds, you must defend your life now
2665 with all your strength. I shall help you."

When these words had been spoken, the worm came on wrathful,
attacked a second time, terrible visitant,
sought out his foes in a surge of flame,
the hated men.
                    Mail-shirt did not serve
2670 the young spear-man; and shield was withered
back to the boss by the billow of fire;
but when the blazing had burnt up his own,
the youngster stepped smartly to take
the cover of his kinsman's. Then did that kingly warrior
2675 remember his deeds again and dealt out a sword-blow
with his full strength: it struck into the head
with annihilating weight. But Nailing snapped,
failed in the battle, Beowulf's sword
of ancient gray steel. It was not granted to him
2680 that an iron edge could ever lend him
help in a battle; his hand was too strong.
I have heard that any sword, however hardened by wounds,
that he bore into battle, his blow would overtax
—any weapon whatever; it was the worse for him.

2685 A third time the terrible fire-drake
remembered the feud. The foe of the people
rushed in on the champion when a chance offered:
seething with warspite, he seized his whole neck
between bitter fangs: blood covered him,
2690 Beowulf's life-blood, let in streams.
Then I heard how the earl alongside the king
in the hour of need made known the valor,
boldness and strength that were bred in him.
His hand burned as he helped his kinsman,
2695 but the brave soldier in his splendid armor
ignored the head and hit the attacker
somewhat below it, so that the sword went in,
flashing-hilted; and the fire began
to slacken in consequence.
                    The king once more
2700 took command of his wits, caught up a stabbing-knife
of the keenest battle-sharpness, that he carried in his harness:
and the Geats' Helm struck through the serpent's body.
So daring drove out life: they had downed their foe
by common action, the atheling pair,

2705 and had made an end of him. So in the hour of need
a warrior must live! For the lord this was
the last victory in the list of his deeds
and works in the world. The wound that the earth-drake
had first succeeded in inflicting on him
2710 began to burn and swell; he swiftly felt
the bane beginning to boil in his chest,
the poison within him. The prince walked across
to the side of the barrow, considering deeply;
he sat down on a ledge, looked at the giant-work,
2715 saw how the age-old earth-hall contained
stone arches anchored on pillars.
Then that excellent thane with his own hands washed
his battle-bloodied prince, bathed with water
the famous leader, his friend and lord,
2720 sated with fighting; he unfastened his helmet.

Beowulf spoke; he spoke through the pain
of his fatal wound. He well knew
that he had come to the end of his allotted days,
his earthly happiness; all the number
2725 of his days had disappeared: death was very near.
"I would now wish to give my garments in battle
to my own son, if any such
after-inheritor, an heir of my body,
had been granted to me. I have guarded this people
2730 for half a century; not a single ruler
of all the nations neighboring about
has dared to affront me with his friends in war,
or threaten terrors. What the times had in store for me
I awaited in my homeland; I held my own,
2735 sought no secret feud, swore very rarely
a wrongful oath.
               In all of these things,
sick with my life's wound, I may still rejoice:
for when my life shall leave my body
the Ruler of Men may not charge me
2740 with the slaughter of kinsmen.
                    Quickly go now,
beloved Wiglaf, and look upon the hoard
under the gray stone, now the serpent lies dead,
sleeps rawly wounded, bereft of his treasure.
Make haste, that I may gaze upon that golden inheritance,
2745 that ancient wealth; that my eyes may behold
the clear skilful jewels: more calmly then may I
on the treasure's account take my departure
of life and of the lordship I have long held."

Straightaway, as I have heard, the son of Weoxstan

2750 obeyed his wounded lord, weak from the struggle.
Following these words, he went in his ring-coat,
his broidered battle-tunic, under the barrow's roof.
Traversing the ledge to the treasure-house of jewels,
the brave young thane was thrilled by the sight
2755 of the gold gleaming on the ground where it lay,
the devices by the wall and the den of the serpent,
winger of the darkness. Drinking-cups stood there,
the unburnished vessels of a vanished race,
their ornaments awry. Old and tarnished
2760 were the rows of helmets and the heaps of arm-rings,
twisted with cunning. Treasure can easily,
gold in the ground, get the better of
one of human race, hide it who will!
High above the hoard there hung, as he also saw,
2765 a standard all woven wonderfully in gold,
the finest of finger-linkages: the effulgence it gave
allowed him to see the surface of the ground
and examine the treasures. No trace of the worm
was to be seen there, for the sword had finished him.
2770 I heard of the plundering of the hoard in the knoll,
that ancient Giant-work, by that one man;
he filled his bosom with such flagons and vessels
as he himself chose; the standard he took also,
best of banners.
                    Old Beowulf's sword,
2775 iron of edge, had already struck
the creature who had been keeper of the treasures
for so long an age, employing his fire-blast
in the hoard's defence, flinging out its heat
in the depth of the nights; he died at last, violently.

2780 The envoy made haste in his eagerness to return,
urged on by his prizes. He was pressed by anxiety
as to whether he would find his fearless man,
the lord of the Geats, alive in the open
where he had left him, lacking in strength.
2785 Carrying the treasures, he came upon his prince,
the famous king, covered in blood
and at his life's end; again he began
to sprinkle him with water, until this word's point
broke through the breast-hoard.
                                    The battle-king spoke,
2790 an aged man in sorrow; he eyed the gold.
"I wish to put in words my thanks
to the King of Glory, the Giver of All,
the Lord of Eternity, for these treasures that I gaze upon,
that I should have been able to acquire for my people
2795 before my death-day an endowment such as this.

My life's full portion I have paid out now
for this hoard of treasure; you must attend the people's
needs henceforward; no further may I stay.
Bid men of battle build me a tomb
2800   fair after fire, on the foreland by the sea
that shall stand as a reminder of me to my people,
towering high above Hronesness
so that ocean travelers shall afterwards name it
Beowulf's barrow, bending in the distance
2805   their masted ships through the mists upon the sea."

He unclasped the golden collar from his neck,
staunch-hearted prince, and passed it to the thane,
with the gold-plated helmet, harness and arm-ring;
he bade the young spear-man use them well:
2810   "You are the last man left of our kindred,
the house of the Waymundings! Weird has lured
each of my family to his fated end,
each earl through his valor; I must follow them."

This was the aged man's uttermost word
2815   from the thoughts of his breast; he embraced the pyre's
seething surges; soul left its case,
going its way to the glory of the righteous.

How wretchedly it went with the warrior then,
the younger soldier, when he saw on the ground
2820   his best-beloved at his life's end
suffering miserably! The slayer lay also
bereft of life, beaten down in ruin,
terrible earth-drake. He was unable any longer
to rule the ring-hoard, the writhing serpent,
2825   since the hammers' legacy, hard and battle-scarred,
the iron edges, had utterly destroyed him;
the far-flier lay felled along the ground
beside his store-house, still from his wounds.
He did not mount the midnight air,
2830   gliding and coiling, glorying in his hoard,
flaunting his aspect; he fell to the earth
at the powerful hand of that prince in war.
Not one of the men of might in that land,
however daring in deeds of every kind,
2835   had ever succeeded, from all I have heard,
in braving the venomous breath of that foe
or putting rude hands on the rings in that hall
if his fortune was to find the defender of the barrow
waiting and on his guard. The gaining of the hoard
2840   of beautiful treasure was Beowulf's death;
so it was that each of them attained the end
of his life's lease.

It was not long then
till they budged from the wood, the battle-shirkers,
ten of them together, those traitors and weaklings
2845 who had not dared deploy their spears
in their own lord's extreme need.
They bore their shields ashamedly,
their armor of war, to where the old man lay.
They regarded Wiglaf. Wearily he sat,
2850 a foot-soldier, at the shoulder of his lord,
trying to wake him with water; but without success.
For all his desiring it, he was unable to hold
his battle-leader's life in this world
or affect anything of the All-Wielder's;
2855 for every man's action was under the sway
of God's judgement, just as it is now.

There was a rough and a ready answer
on the young man's lips for those who had lost their nerve.
Wiglaf spoke, Weoxstan's offspring,
2860 looked at the unloved ones with little joy at heart:
"A man who would speak the truth may say with justice
that a lord of men who allowed you those treasures,
who bestowed on you the trappings that you stand there in
—as, at the ale-bench, he would often give
2865 to those who sat in hall both helmet and mail-shirt
as a lord to his thanes, and things of the most worth
that he was able to find anywhere in the world—
that he had quite thrown away and wasted cruelly
all that battle-harness when the battle came upon him.
2870 The king of our people had no cause to boast
of his companions of the guard. Yet God vouchsafed him,
the Master of Victories, that he should avenge himself
when courage was wanted, by his weapon alone.
I was little equipped to act as body-guard
2875 for him in the battle, but, above my own strength,
I began all the same to support my kinsman.
Our deadly enemy grew ever the weaker—
when I had struck him with my sword—less strongly welled
the fire from his head. Too few supporters
2880 flocked to our prince when affliction came.
Now there shall cease for your race the receiving of treasure,
the bestowal of swords, all satisfaction of ownership,
all comfort of home. Your kinsmen every one,
shall become wanderers without land-rights
2885 as soon as athelings over the world
shall hear the report of how you fled,
a deed of ill fame. Death is better
for any earl than an existence of disgrace!"

He bade that the combat's result be proclaimed in the city

2890 over the brow of the headland; there the band of earls
had sat all morning beside their shields
in heavy spirits, half expecting
that it would be the last day of their beloved man,
half hoping for his return. The rider from the headland
2895 in no way held back the news he had to tell;
as his commission was, he called out over all:
"The Lord of the Geats lies now on his slaughter-bed,
the leader of the Weathers, our loving provider,
dwells in his death-rest through the dragon's power.
2900 Stretched out beside him, stricken with the knife,
lies his deadly adversary. With the edge of the sword
he could not contrive, try as he might,
to wound the monster. Weoxstan's son
Wiglaf abides with Beowulf there,
2905 one earl waits on the other one lifeless;
in weariness of heart he watches by the heads
of friend and foe.
     The fall of the king,
when it spreads abroad and is spoken of
among the Frisians and the Franks, forebodes a time
2910 of wars for our people. The war against the Hugas
had a hard beginning when Hygelac[8] sailed
into the land of the Frisians with his fleet-army:
there it was that the Hetware hurled themselves upon him
and with their greater strength stoutly compelled
2915 that battle-clad warrior to bow before them;
he fell among the troop, distributed no arms
as lord to the guard. It has not been granted to us since
to receive mercy from the Merovingian king.

  Nor can I expect peace or fair dealing
2920 from the Swedish nation; it is no secret
that it was Ongentheow who put an end to the life
of Hrethel's son, Hathkin, by Hrefnawudu
when in their pride the people of the Geats
first made attack upon the fighting Scylfings.
2925 Quickly did the formidable father of Ohthere,
terrible veteran, return that blow,
he cut down the sea-king, recaptured his wife,
the mother of Onela and Ohthere in her youth,
now an aged woman, her ornaments stripped from her.
2930 He then drove after his deadly foes
so that they hid themselves, hard-pressed,
in the Ravenswood, and without a lord.

  With his host he besieged those whom swords had left
ailing from their wounds. All through the night

8. One of the only historical events in the poem, Hygelac's disastrous raid is mentioned by the Latin historian Gregory of Tours as occurring in 521.

2935 he promised horrors to that unhappy band,
      saying that on the morrow he would mutilate them
      with the edges of the sword, and set some on the gallows
      as sport for the birds. With break of day
      what comfort came to those care-oppressed men
2940 when they heard Hygelac's horn and trumpet
      giving voice, as that valiant one came up
      with the flower of his host, following on their tracks!

          The bloody swathe of the Swedes and the Geats
      in their slaughterous pursuit could be seen from afar
2945 —how the peoples had stirred up the strife between them.
      The earl Ongentheow took the upper ground;
      the wise champion went up to his stronghold
      in the van of his kinsmen; the veteran grieved,
      but he knew the power of the superb Hygelac,
2950 his strength in war; he was not confident
      of his resistance, that he could stand against the vikings,
      defend his hoard against the fighters from the sea,
      his children and his queen. He chose to draw back,
      old behind his earth-wall.
                              Then was the offering of the chase
2955 to the people of the Swedes; sweeping forward,
      the standards of Hygelac surged over the camp
      as Hrethel's brood broke through the rampart.
      Then was Ongentheow the ashen-haired
      brought to bay by the brightness of swords
2960 and the king of a nation must kneel as Eofor
      singly disposed. It was a desperate blow
      that Wulf Wonreding's weapon fetched him,
      and at the stroke streams of blood
      sprang forth beneath his hair. The hoary-headed Scylfing,
2965 undismayed by this deadly blow,
      gave in exchange a graver stroke
      as he came round to face him, king of the people.
      Wonred's brave son was incapable
      of the answer-blow upon the older man,
2970 for the king had cut through the casque[9] on his head,
      forced him to bend; he bowed to the earth
      marked with blood. Yet he was not marked for death;
      it was a keen wound, but he recovered from it.
      Then as his brother lay there, the brave Eofor,
2975 Hygelac's follower, fetched his broad sword,
      an ancient giant-blade, to the giant-helm of Ongentheow
      above his shield, and split it; then the shepherd of the people,
      the king, fell down, fatally wounded.

          There were many to bind up the brother's wounds;

9. Helmet.

2980 they raised him at once, now the way was open
and the battlefield had fallen to them.
One sturdy warrior then stripped the other,
took from Ongentheow his iron war-shirt,
his hilted sword and his helmet also,
2985 the old man's accoutrement, and carried it to Hygelac.
He accepted the harness with a handsome promise
of rewards among the people; a promise he kept.
For at his homecoming Hrethel's offspring
rewarded Eofor and Wulf for their assault
2990 with copious treasures. The king of the Geats
handed to each of them a hundred thousand
in lands and linked rings; there was little cause for any
on middle earth to begrudge them these glories earned in battle.
He also gave to Eofor his only daughter,
2995 a grace to his home and a guarantee of favor.

It is this feud, this fierce hostility,
this murder-lust between men, I am moved to think,
that the Swedish people will prosecute against us
when once they learn that life has fled
3000 from the lord of the Geats, guardian for so long
of hoard and kingdom, of keen shield-warriors
against every foe. Since the fall of the princes
he has taken care of our welfare, and accomplished yet more
heroic deeds.   Haste is best now,
3005 that we should go to look on the lord of the people,
then bring our ring-bestower on his road,
escort him to the pyre. More than one portion of wealth
shall melt with the hero, for there's a hoard of treasure
and gold uncounted; a grim purchase,
3010 for in the end it was with his own life
that he bought these rings: which the burning shall devour,
the fire enfold. No fellow shall wear
an arm-ring in his memory; no maiden's neck
shall be enhanced in beauty by the bearing of these rings.
3015 Bereft of gold, rather, and in wretchedness of mind
she shall tread continually the tracks of exile
now that the leader of armies has laid aside his mirth,
his sport and glad laughter. Many spears shall therefore
feel cold in the mornings to the clasping fingers
3020 and the hands that raise them. Nor shall the harper's melody
arouse them for battle; and yet the black raven,
quick on the marked men, shall have much to speak of
when he tells the eagle of his takings at the feast
where he and the wolf bared the bodies of the slain."

3025 Such was the rehearsal of the hateful tidings
by that bold messenger; amiss in neither

words nor facts. The war-band arose;
they went unhappily under Earna-ness
to look on the wonder with welling tears.
3030   They found him on the sand, his soul fled,
keeping his resting-place: rings he had given them
in former times! But the final day
had come for the champion; and the chief of the Geats,
the warrior-king, had met his wondrous death.

3035   Stranger the creature they encountered first
in the level place—the loathsome worm
stretched out opposite. Scorched by its own flames
lay the fire-drake in its fatal markings,
and it measured fifty feet as it lay.
3040   He had once been master of the midnight air,
held sweet sway there, and swooped down again
to seek his den; now death held him fast,
he had made his last use of lairs in the earth.

Standing by him there were bowls and flagons,
3045   there were platters lying there, and precious swords,
quite rusted through, as they had rested there
a thousand winters in the womb of earth.

And this gold of former men was full of power,
the huge inheritance, hedged about with a spell:
3050   no one among men was permitted to touch
that golden store of rings unless God Himself,
the true King of Victories, the Protector of mankind,
enabled one He chose to open the hoard,
whichever among men should seem meet to Him.
3055   It was plain to see then that this plan had failed
the creature who had kept these curious things hidden
wrongfully within the wall; the warden had slain
a man like few others; but the feud was straightaway
avenged and wrathfully. It is a wonder to know
3060   where the most courageous of men may come to the end
of his allotted life, and no longer dwell
a man in the mead-hall among companions!

So it was for Beowulf when he embarked on that quarrel,
sought out the barrow-guard; he himself did not know
3065   in what way his parting from the world was to come.
The great princes who had placed the treasure there
had laid on it a curse to last until Doomsday,
that the man who should plunder the place would thereby
commit a crime, and be confined with devils,
3070   tortured grievously in the trammels of hell.
But Beowulf had not looked on the legacy of these men
with too eager an eye, for all its gold.

Wiglaf spoke, Weoxstan's son:
"Many must often endure distress
3075 for the sake of one; so it is with us.
We could not urge any reason
on our beloved king, the keeper of the land,
why he should not approach the protector of the gold
but let him lie where he had long been already
3080 and abide in his den until the end of the world.
He held to his high destiny.
                              The hoard has been seen
that was acquired at such a cost; too cruel the fate
that impelled the king of the people towards it!
I myself was inside there, and saw all
3085 the wealth of the chamber once my way was open
—little courtesy was shown in allowing me to pass
beneath the earth-wall. I urgently filled
my hands with a huge heap of the treasures
stored in the cave, carried them out
3090 to my lord here. He was alive still
and commanded his wits. Much did he say
in his grief, the old man; he asked me to speak to you,
ordered that on the place of the pyre you should raise
a barrow fitting your friend's achievements;
3095 conspicuous, magnificent, as among men he was
while he could wield the wealth of his stronghold
the most honored of warriors on the wide earth.

    Let us now hasten to behold again,
and approach once more that mass of treasures,
3100 awesome under the walls; I shall guide you,
so that from near at hand you may behold sufficiently
the thick gold and the bracelets. Let a bier be made ready,
contrive it quickly, so that when we come out again
we may take up our king, carry the man
3105 beloved by us to his long abode
where he must rest in the Ruler's keeping."

Then the son of Weoxstan, worthy in battle,
had orders given to owners of homesteads
and a great many warriors, that the governors of the people
3110 from far and wide should fetch in wood
for the hero's funeral pyre.
                              "Now the flames shall grow dark
and the fire destroy the sustainer of the warriors
who often endured the iron shower
when, string-driven, the storm of arrows
3115 sang over shield-wall, and the shaft did its work,
sped by its feathers, furthered the arrow-head."

Then in his wisdom Weoxstan's son
called out from the company of the king's own thanes
seven men in all, who excelled among them,
3120   and, himself the eighth warrior, entered in beneath
that unfriendly roof. The front-stepping man
bore in his hand a blazing torch.

When the men perceived a piece of the hoard
that remained unguarded, mouldering there
3125   on the floor of the chamber, they did not choose by lot
who should remove it; undemurring,
as quickly as they could, they carried outside
the precious treasures; and they pushed the dragon,
the worm, over the cliff, let the waves take him
3130   and the flood engulf the guardian of the treasures.
Untold profusion of twisted gold
was loaded onto a wagon, and the warrior prince
borne hoary-headed to Hronesness.

The Great race then reared up for him
3135   a funeral pyre. It was not a petty mound,
but shining mail-coats and shields of war
and helmets hung upon it, as he had desired.
Then the heroes, lamenting, laid out in the middle
their great chief, their cherished lord.
3140   On top of the mound the men then kindled
the biggest of funeral-fires. Black wood-smoke
arose from the blaze, and the roaring of flames
mingled with weeping. The winds lay still
as the heat at the fire's heart consumed
3145   the house of bone. And in heavy mood
they uttered their sorrow at the slaughter of their lord.

A woman of the Geats in grief sang out
the lament for his death. Loudly she sang,
her hair bound up, the burden of her fear
3150   that evil days were destined her
—troops cut down, terror of armies,
bondage, humiliation. Heaven swallowed the smoke.

Then the Storm-Geat nation constructed for him
a stronghold on the headland, so high and broad
3155   that seafarers might see it from afar.
The beacon to that battle-reckless man
they made in ten days. What remained from the fire
they cast a wall around, of workmanship
as fine as their wisest men could frame for it.
3160   They placed in the tomb both the torques[1] and the jewels,
all the magnificence that the men had earlier
taken from the hoard in hostile mood.

1. Collars or necklaces with twisted bands.

They left the earls' wealth in the earth's keeping,
the gold in the dirt. It dwells there yet,
3165 of no more use to men than in ages before.

Then the warriors rode around the barrow,
twelve of them in all, athelings' sons.
They recited a dirge to declare their grief,
spoke of the man, mourned their king.
3170 They praised his manhood and the prowess of his hands,
they raised his name; it is right a man
should be lavish in honoring his lord and friend,
should love him in his heart when the leading-forth
from the house of flesh befalls him at last.

3175 This was the manner of the mourning of the men of the Geats,
sharers in the feast, at the fall of their lord:
they said that he was of all the world's kings
the gentlest of men, and the most gracious,
the kindest to his people, the keenest for fame.

✑

RESPONSE
John Gardner: from *Grendel*[1]
CHAPTER ONE

The old ram stands looking down over rockslides, stupidly triumphant. I blink. I stare in horror. "Scat!" I hiss. "Go back to your cave, go back to your cowshed— whatever." He cocks his head like an elderly, slow-witted king, considers the angles, decides to ignore me. I stamp. I hammer the ground with my fists. I hurl a skull-size stone at him. He will not budge. I shake my two hairy fists at the sky and I let out a howl so unspeakable that the water at my feet turns sudden ice and even I myself am left uneasy. But the ram stays; the season is upon us. And so begins the twelfth year of my idiotic war.

The pain of it! The stupidity!

"Ah, well," I sigh, and shrug, trudge back to the trees.

Do not think my brains are squeezed shut, like the ram's, by the roots of horns. Flanks atremble, eyes like stones, he stares at as much of the world as he can see and feels it surging in him, filling his chest as the melting snow fills dried-out creekbeds, tickling his gross, lopsided balls and charging his brains with the same unrest that made him suffer last year at this time, and the year before, and the year before that. (He's forgotten them all.) His hindparts shiver with the usual joyful, mindless ache

1. John Gardner was a best-selling American novelist and professor of medieval literature who died in a motorcycle acci-dent in 1982 at the age of 49. His first popular success came with the 1971 publication of *Grendel*, a rewriting of *Beowulf* from the monster's point of view. Alienated from traditional morality and the comforts of the beer hall, Grendel gorges himself gleefully on the bodies he has carried off from Hrothgar's hall, and fondly recalls the places where he "tore off sly old Athelgard's head" or ate an old woman who "tasted of urine and spleen." Though Gardner does not portray him en-tirely sympathetically, Grendel can be seen in the romantic tradition of the outsider hero, like the monster in Mary Shel-ley's *Frankenstein* or Satan in Blake's rereading of Milton's *Paradise Lost*.

While Gardner's interpretation of the monster is distinctly modern, the style of the novel reveals his background as a medievalist: he imitates the Old English of *Beowulf* in his use of alliteration and of Germanic compound words such as "falconswift," "whalecocks," and "earth-rim-rover."

to mount whatever happens near—the storm piling up black towers to the west, some rotting, docile stump, some spraddle-legged ewe. I cannot bear to look. "Why can't these creatures discover a little dignity?" I ask the sky. The sky says nothing, predictably. I make a face, uplift a defiant middle finger, and give an obscene little kick. The sky ignores me, forever unimpressed. Him too I hate, the same as I hate these brainless budding trees, these brattling birds.

Not, of course, that I fool myself with thoughts that I'm more noble. Pointless, ridiculous monster crouched in the shadows, stinking of dead men, murdered children, martyred cows. (I am neither proud nor ashamed, understand. One more dull victim, leering at seasons that never were meant to be observed.) "Ah, sad one, poor old freak!" I cry, and hug myself, and laugh, letting out salt tears, he he! till I fall down gasping and sobbing. (It's mostly fake.) The sun spins mindlessly overhead, the shadows lengthen and shorten as if by plan. Small birds, with a high-pitched yelp, lay eggs. The tender grasses peek up, innocent yellow, through the ground: the children of the dead. (It was just here, this shocking green, that once when the moon was tombed in clouds, I tore off sly old Athelgard's head. Here, where the startling tiny jaws of crocuses snap at the late-winter sun like the heads of baby watersnakes, here I killed the old woman with the irongray hair. She tasted of urine and spleen, which made me spit. Sweet mulch for yellow blooms. Such are the tiresome memories of a shadow-shooter, earth-rim-roamer, walker of the world's weird wall.) "Waaah!" I cry, with another quick, nasty face at the sky, mournfully observing the way it is, bitterly remembering the way it was, and idiotically casting tomorrow's nets. "Aargh! Yaww!" I reel, smash trees. Disfigured son of lunatics. The big-boled oaks gaze down at me yellow with morning, beneath complexity. "No offense," I say, with a terrible, sycophantish smile, and tip an imaginary hat.

It was not always like this, of course. On occasion it's been worse.

No matter, no matter.

The doe in the clearing goes stiff at sight of my horridness, then remembers her legs and is gone. It makes me cross. "Blind prejudice!" I bawl at the splintered sunlight where half a second ago she stood. I wring my fingers, put on a long face. "Ah, the unfairness of everything," I say, and shake my head. It is a matter of fact that I have never killed a deer in all my life, and never will. Cows have more meat and, locked up in pens, are easier to catch. It is true, perhaps, that I feel some trifling dislike of deer, but no more dislike than I feel for other natural things—discounting men. But deer, like rabbits and bears and even men, can make, concerning my race, no delicate distinctions. That is their happiness: they see all life without observing it. They're buried in it like crabs in mud. Except men, of course. I am not in a mood, just yet, to talk of men.

So it goes with me day by day and age by age, I tell myself. Locked in the deadly progression of moon and stars. I shake my head, muttering darkly on shaded paths, holding conversation with the only friend and comfort this world affords, my shadow. Wild pigs clatter away through brush. A baby bird falls feet-up in my path, squeaking. With a crabby laugh, I let him lie, kind heaven's merciful bounty to some sick fox. So it goes with me, age by age. (Talking, talking. Spinning a web of words, pale walls of dreams, between myself and all I see.)

The first grim stirrings of springtime come (as I knew they must, having seen the ram), and even under the ground where I live, where no light breaks but the red of my fires and nothing stirs but the flickering shadows on my wet rock walls, or scampering rats on my piles of bones, or my mother's fat, foul bulk rolling over, restless again—molested by nightmares, old memories—I am aware in my chest of tuberstir-rings in the blacksweet duff of the forest overhead. I feel my anger coming back, building up like invisible fire, and at last, when my soul can no longer resist, I go up—as mechanical as anything else—fists clenched against my lack of will, my belly growling, mindless as wind, for blood. I swim up through the firesnakes, hot dark whalecocks prowling the luminous green of the mere, and I surface with a gulp among churning waves and smoke. I crawl up onto the bank and catch my breath.

It's good at first to be out in the night, naked to the cold mechanics of the stars. Space hurls outward, falconswift, mounting like an irreversible injustice, a final dis-ease. The cold night air is reality at last: indifferent to me as a stone face carved on a high cliff wall to show that the world is abandoned. So childhood too feels good at first, before one happens to notice the terrible sameness, age after age. I lie there resting in the steaming grass, the old lake hissing and gurgling behind me, whisper-ing patterns of words my sanity resists. At last, heavy as an ice-capped mountain, I rise and work my way to the inner wall, beginning of wolfslopes, the edge of my realm. I stand in the high wind balanced, blackening the night with my stench, gaz-ing down to cliffs that fall away to cliffs, and once again I am aware of my potential: I could die. I cackle with rage and suck in breath.

"Dark chasms!" I scream from the cliff-edge, "seize me! Seize me to your foul black bowels and crush my bones!" I am terrified at the sound of my own huge voice in the darkness. I stand there shaking from head to foot, moved to the deep-sea depths of my being, like a creature thrown into audience with thunder.

At the same time, I am secretly unfooled. The uproar is only my own shriek, and chasms are, like all things vast, inanimate. They will not snatch me in a thou-sand years, unless, in a lunatic fit of religion, I jump.

I sigh, depressed, and grind my teeth. I toy with shouting some tidbit more—some terrifying, unthinkable threat, some blackly fuliginous riddling hex—but my heart's not in it. "Missed me!" I say with a coy little jerk and a leer, to keep my spir-its up. Then, with a sigh, a kind of moan, I start very carefully down the cliffs that lead to the fens and moors and Hrothgar's hall. Owls cross my path as silently as raiding ships, and at the sound of my foot, lean wolves rise, glance at me awkwardly, and, neat of step as lizards, sneak away. I used to take some pride in that—the cau-tion of owls when my shape looms in, the alarm I stir in these giant northern wolves. I was younger then. Still playing cat and mouse with the universe.

I move down through the darkness, burning with murderous lust, my brains rag-ing at the sickness I can observe in myself as objectively as might a mind ten cen-turies away. Stars, spattered out through lifeless night from end to end, like jewels scattered in a dead king's grave, tease, torment my wits toward meaningful patterns that do not exist. I can see for miles from these rock walls: thick forest suddenly still at my coming—cowering stags, wolves, hedgehogs, boars, submerged in their stifling, unmemorable fear; mute birds, pulsating, thoughtless clay in hushed old trees, thick limbs interlocked to seal drab secrets in.

I sigh, sink into the silence, and cross it like wind. Behind my back, at the world's end, my pale slightly glowing fat mother sleeps on, old, sick at heart, in our dingy underground room. Life-bloated, baffled, long-suffering hag. Guilty, she imag-ines, of some unremembered, perhaps ancestral crime. (She must have some human in her.) Not that she thinks. Not that she dissects and ponders the dusty mechanical bits of her miserable life's curse. She clutches at me in her sleep as if to crush me. I break away. "Why are we here?" I used to ask her. "Why do we stand this putrid, stinking hole?" She trembles at my words. Her fat lips shake. "Don't ask!" her wig-gling claws implore. (She never speaks.) "Don't ask!" It must be some terrible secret, I used to think. I'd give her a crafty squint. She'll tell me, in time, I thought. But she told me nothing. I waited on. That was before the old dragon, calm as winter, unveiled the truth. He was not a friend.

And so I come through trees and towns to the lights of Hrothgar's meadhall. I am no stranger here. A respected guest. Eleven years now and going on twelve I have come up this clean-mown central hill, dark shadow out of the woods below, and have knocked politely on the high oak door, bursting its hinges and sending the shock of my greeting inward like a cold blast out of a cave. "Grendel!" they squeak, and I smile like exploding spring. The old Shaper, a man I cannot help but admire, goes out the back window with his harp at a single bound, though blind as a bat. The drunkest of Hrothgar's thanes come reeling and clanking down from their wall-hung beds, all shouting their meady, outrageous boasts, their heavy swords aswirl like eagles' wings. "Woe, woe, woe!" cries Hrothgar, hoary with winters, peeking in, wide-eyed, from his bedroom in back. His wife, looking in behind him, makes a scene. The thanes in the meadhall blow out the lights and cover the wide stone fireplace with shields. I laugh, crumple over; I can't help myself. In the darkness, I alone see clear as day. While they squeal and screech and bump into each other, I silently sack up my dead and with-draw to the woods. I eat and laugh and eat until I can barely walk, my chest-hair mat-ted with dribbled blood, and then the roosters on the hill crow, and dawn comes over the roofs of the houses, and all at once I am filled with gloom again.

"This is some punishment sent us," I hear them bawling from the hill.

My head aches. Morning nails my eyes.

"Some god is angry," I hear a woman keen. "The people of Scyld and Herogar and Hrothgar are mired in sin!"

My belly rumbles, sick on their sour meat. I crawl through bloodstained leaves to the eaves of the forest, and there peek out. The dogs fall silent at the edge of my spell, and where the king's hall surmounts the town, the blind old Shaper, harp clutched tight to his fragile chest, stares futilely down, straight at me. Otherwise nothing. Pigs root dully at the posts of a wooden fence. A rumple-horned ox lies chewing in dew and shade. A few men, lean, wearing animal skins, look up at the gables of the king's hall, or at the vultures circling casually beyond. Hrothgar says nothing, hoarfrost-bearded, his features cracked and crazed. Inside, I hear the people praying—whimpering, whining, mumbling, pleading—to their numerous sticks and stones. He doesn't go in. The king has lofty theories of his own.

"Theories," I whisper to the bloodstained ground. So the dragon once spoke. ("They'd map out roads through Hell with their crackpot theories!" I recall his laugh.)

Then the groaning and praying stop, and on the side of the hill the dirge-slow shoveling begins. They throw up a mound for the funeral pyre, for whatever arms or legs or heads my haste has left behind. Meanwhile, up in the shattered hall, the builders are hammering, replacing the door for (it must be) the fiftieth or sixtieth time, industrious and witless as worker ants—except that they make small, foolish changes, adding a few more iron pegs, more iron bands, with tireless dogmatism.

Now fire. A few little lizard tongues, then healthy flames reaching up through the tangled nest of sticks. (A feeble-minded crow could have fashioned a neater nest.) A severed leg swells up and bursts, then an arm, then another, and the red fire turns on the blackening flesh and makes it sizzle, and it reaches higher, up and up into greasy smoke, turning, turning like falcons at warplay, rushing like circling wolves up into the swallowing, indifferent sky. And now, by some lunatic theory, they throw on golden rings, old swords, and braided helmets. They wail, the whole crowd, women and men, a kind of song, like a single quavering voice. The song rings up like the greasy smoke and their faces shine with sweat and something that looks like joy. The song swells, pushes through woods and sky, and they're singing now as if by some lunatic theory they had won. I shake with rage. The red sun blinds me, churns up my belly to nausea, and the heat thrown out of the bone-fire burns my skin. I cringe, clawing my flesh, and flee for home.

—•—❉—•—

The Táin Bó Cuailnge

The Táin Bó Cuailnge (The Cattle Raid of Cooley), the chief work in the "Ulster Cycle" of Irish heroic narratives, was already a famed and ancient story by the twelfth century, when an expanded version was copied into the manuscript now called the Book of Leinster. That manuscript also contains a legend about the recovery of the whole *Táin* by the poets of Ireland, who knew it only in fragments. Followers of the chief poet set out for Brittany, the story reports, where a complete copy had been carried. In the course of their journey, though, they pass the grave of Fergus mac Roich, an earlier poet and a hero in the events of the *Táin*. Alone at the grave, the chief poet's son calls up the spirit of Fergus, who recites to him the tale in its entirety.

This legend offers a window on Irish literary culture and its sense of the past at the time. The legend comes from a world of written books that could be sought out and copied; yet it also recalls the prestige and priority of an oral tradition. Further, the story evokes the aura of magic surrounding poets in medieval Ireland and the poets' own sense of themselves as spiritual and even genealogical heirs of an ancient calling which stretched back into the mythic past. Ireland had developed a deeply Christian culture yet celebrated its native secular stories and did so with a vigor that has little of the elegiac nostalgia and biblical echoes seen in *Beowulf*. The highest class of poets, the *filid* (singular *fili*), also inherited practices like divination which had been the work of other learned classes, such as the druids, in the pagan era.

If the Book of Leinster thus displays a lively but complicated connection to a rich literary past, the *Táin* itself looks backward to a still more ancient world of warring heroes, magical weapons, shape-shifters, and wondrous beasts, in which the line between mortals and gods was blurry and often crossed. The earliest version of the *Táin* stems from an oral tradition perhaps as early as the fourth century, but the society it depicts—with warriors riding in battle chariots, fighting naked, and taking the heads of conquered enemies—mirrors what we know of Celtic peoples on the Continent as early as the second century B.C.E. The Roman geographer Strabo called the "whole race . . . madly fond of war, high-spirited and quick to battle." Some of their habits persisted in Ireland but were long over by the sixth century C.E. Other social practices—such as clientship, rigid standards of hospitality, and the obligation to safeguard anyone taken under protection—continued late into the medieval period.

Four great stories converge in the *Táin*. It draws, first, on the history of the bulls Finnbennach the White Horned and Donn Cuailnge the Brown Bull of Cooley, who originated as two pig-keepers and passed through a series of animal forms before the moment of the main narrative. Second, the immediate occasion of the cattle raid emerges from a debate between Ailill, king of Connacht, and his wife, Medb.

Medb's quest to match the wealth of Ailill leads her into an armed attempt to take Donn Cuailnge from its owner on the borderlands of Ulster. To achieve this end, third, Medb and Ailill gather an army to march against Ulster. Finally, the hero Cú Chulainn single-handedly protects Ulster's borders until the men of Ulster can recover from a seasonal debility with which they have been long cursed.

The debate of Ailill and Medb introduces one of the most powerful women in medieval Irish literature, stemming partly from a pagan goddess of sovereignty. Medb and similar women reflect a persistent aspect of mythic and literary imagination in the Irish heroic narratives, although in medieval Irish law women actually had fewer rights than their Anglo-Saxon counterparts. The story acknowledges Medb's power as a wealthy woman, leader of armies, and queen, but constantly places that power in question. Indeed, several important men are openly hostile to Medb's strong will; even the bull Finnbennach is in Ailill's herds because he refused to be owned by a woman. Medb's power is explicity sexual. Far from the passive object of desire that we often meet elsewhere in the period, she uses her sexuality as an active force, often for political gain. Yet Medb is much more than a cunning body; she exploits her wealth and is willing to debate and even to battle with her own ally and husband over issues of military strategy.

The armies that gather against the Ulstermen are replete with heroic fighters and complex allegiances, and much of the *Táin*'s emotional weight lies in the passionate devotion and divided loyalties of its warriors. There is particular sadness in the plight of a group of Ulstermen, among them Fergus mac Roich, whose own king Conchobar had killed men taken under their protection; they have fled his court and placed themselves in the service of Ailill. Even more personal is the repeated clash between political fidelity and the quasi-familial link of fosterage in the story.

These issues press hard on the *Táin*'s heroic center, Cú Chulainn, the preeminent hero of the Ulster Cycle. The line between the heroic, the superhuman, and the monstrous can be fluid in the *Táin*, as it is in the curious links between Beowulf and Grendel. Cú Chulainn is of divine birth, and has performed a series of wondrous boyhood exploits, before the events of this story. Even within the *Táin*, he is persistently boyish in appearance and often distracted by activities that approach play. We witness Cú Chulainn coming into his maturity as he fights an exhausting series of border combats single-handedly and unwaveringly, and as he finally must face and defeat his foster-brother Ferdia. Despite this poignant humanity, Cú Chulainn possesses godlike strength and skill with weapons; yet his heroic rage works a physical distortion on him that is almost monstrous, eliciting comparisons with a giant or "a man from the sea-kingdom."

Geography is as important as heroism in the *Táin*. Battles, wonders, and other events repeatedly lead to the naming of a locale, so that the story virtually maps the mythic significance of place in the northern parts of Ireland. It also enfolds much of the genealogy of its legendary heroes. In style and theme, too, the *Táin* counterbalances the wonders of superhuman force by the works of human skill, with elaborate descriptions of clothing, ornament, and decorated weaponry. It narrates the physical beauty of men and women alike with an exquisite attention not found in *Beowulf*. Like much narrative that derives closely from its oral background, the *Táin* is as much the encyclopedia of a people's beliefs and values—or a commemoration of its past beliefs and their impact on current values—as it is a single story of heroic action.

These indications are imprecise but give a rough sense of how key names in the *Táin* sounded in Old Irish. The spelling -ch is slightly guttural, as in *loch* or *Bach*.

Ailill	AL-ill	Finnbennach	finn-VEN-ach
Bricriu	BRIK-roo	Láeg	loig
Cet	ket	Medb	maive
Conchobar	CON-cho-wer	Morrígu	MO-ree-ga
Cú Chulainn	coo-CHULL-in	Nemain	NE-van
Dubthach Dáel Ulad	DUV-thach	Ráth Crúachain	rawth CROO-a-chan
doil u-lad		Samain	SA-win
Emain Macha	EV-in MA-cha	Sid	sheethe
Fedelm	FETH-elm	Táin Bó Cuailnge	toin bow COO-ling-e
Ferdia	fer-DEE-a		
Findabair	FIN-a-wer		

from **The Táin**[1]
THE PILLOW TALK

One night when the royal bed had been prepared for Ailill and Medb in Crúachan Fort[2] in Connacht, they engaged in pillow-talk:

"It's true what they say, girl," said Ailill. "Well-off woman, wealthy man's wife."

"True enough," said the woman. "What makes you say it?"

"Just this," said Ailill, "that you're better off now than the day I took you."

"I was well-off before it," said Medb.

"If you were, I never heard tell of it," said Ailill, "apart from your woman's assets that your neighbor enemies kept plundering and raiding."

"Not so," said Medb, "for my father was High King of Ireland[3]—namely, Eochu Feidlech son of Finn son of Finnoman son of Finnen son of Fingall son of Roth son of Rigéon son of Blathacht son of Beothacht son of Enna Agnech son of Angus Turbech. He had six daughters: Derbriu, Ethne, Éle, Clothru, Muguin, Medb. I was the noblest and most celebrated of them all. The most generous in bestowing gifts and favors. The best at warfare, strife and combat.[4] I had fifteen hundred royal mercenaries, the sons of exiles, and as many more the sons of freeborn native men, and for every soldier of them I had ten, and for every ten I had nine more, and eight, and seven, and six, and five, and four, and three, and two, and one. And that was just my household guard.

"Then my father gave me a province of Ireland, Connacht that is ruled from Crúachan. That is why I am called Medb of Crúachan. Envoys came from Finn the King of Leinster, the son of Ross Ruad, to woo me, and from Cairbre the son of Niafer King of Tara—another son of Ross Ruad—and from Conchobar King of Ulster, son of Fachtna, and from Eochaid Bec. I turned them all down. I asked a more exacting wedding-gift than any woman ever before me—a man without meanness, jealousy and fear.

---

1. Translated by Ciaran Carson. Carson's translation uses the early, perhaps eighth century "Recension I" of the *Táin*; for some passages (such as the opening section here), absent from that recension, Carson uses "Recension II," copied in the 12th-century Book of Leinster.

2. Ráth Crúachain, the royal fortress of Connacht. Like many fortress towns in Irish legend, it was founded by a woman (Cruacha) and retained traces of its ancient role as a sacred place.

3. Early Ireland was ruled by a shifting company of petty kings, some of whom entered into dependence and service (clientship) with "high kings." The idea of a high king of all Ireland was pure legend until long after the era of the *Táin*.

4. Medb's wealth and military resources probably derive from her namesake, the goddess of sovereignty on whose assent (and sometimes sexual favors) the kingship depended.

"If he were mean, we'd be ill-matched, because I am generous in bestowing gifts and favors. And it would be a disgrace if I were more generous than him, but no disgrace if we are equal, both bestowing freely. If he were cowardly, we'd be ill-matched, for I am powerful in warfare, fight and fray. It would be a disgrace if I were more forcible than him, but no disgrace if both of us are forcible. Nor would it do for my husband to be jealous: I never had one man without another waiting in his shadow. I got the right man—yourself, Ailill, the other son of Ross Ruad of Leinster. You are not mean, you are not jealous, you are not cowardly. When we made the contract, I gave you a bride-price that befits a woman: outfits for a dozen men, a chariot worth thrice seven bondmaids, the breadth of your face in red gold, the weight of your left arm in white bronze. Whoever brings you shame or strife or trouble, you've no claim to compensation or redress, beyond what I claim, for you're a man dependent on a woman's wealth."

"Not so," said Ailill, "for I have two brothers, Cairbre who rules Tara, and Finn the King of Leinster. And I let them rule because of seniority, not because they were more generous with their largesse. I never heard of a province of Ireland that depended on a woman's assets except this one, which is why I came and assumed the throne in succession to my mother, for she is Máta Muiresc, Mágach's daughter. And what better queen for me, than the daughter of the High King of Ireland?"

"All the same," said Medb, "my wealth is greater than yours."

"You astonish me," said Ailill. "No one has more wealth, more goods and jewels than myself. I know this for a fact."

So the least valuable of their assets were brought out, to see who had more wealth and goods and jewels: their cauldrons and buckets and pots, their porringers and tubs and basins. Then their gold artefacts, their rings and their bracelets and their thumb-rings were brought out, and their outfits of purple and blue and black and green and yellow, whether plain or multi-colored, plaid, checked or striped. Their flocks of sheep were brought in from the fields and the meadows and the green lawns. They were counted and compared, and found to be equal in number and size. Among Medb's sheep was a prize ram worth one bondmaid, and among Ailill's was one to match.

From pasture and paddock and stable their horses and steeds were brought in. Among Medb's horses was a prize stallion worth one bondmaid, and Ailill had one to match. Their great herds of swine were brought in from the woods and the glens and the wastelands. They were reckoned and counted and claimed, and found to be equal in size and number. Medb had a prize boar, and Ailill had another.

Then their herds of cows and droves of cattle were brought in from the woods and the wastes of the province. They were reckoned and counted and claimed, and found to be equal in size and number. But among Ailill's cattle was a prize bull, that had been a calf of one of Medb's cows—Finnbennach his name, the White-horned.[5] Not wanting to be reckoned as a woman's asset, he had gone over to the king's herd. And to Medb it was as if she hadn't a single penny, for there was no bull to equal Finnbennach among her cattle.

Mac Roth the Messenger[6] was summoned by Medb, and Medb told Mac Roth to go and see if the match of the bull might be found in any of the provinces of Ireland.

5. A gigantic, blood-red bull with white head and feet. He and Donn Cúailnge, the Brown Bull of Cooley, are the final incarnations of two pig-keepers who fought over their supernatural powers in a series of animal and human shapes.

6. The name means "son of wheel," apt for a messenger.

"I know where to find such a bull and better," said Mac Roth, "in the province of Ulster in the district of Cúailnge, in the house of Dáire Mac Fiachna. His name is the Donn Cúailnge, the Brown Bull of Cúailnge."[7]

"Take yourself there, Mac Roth," said Medb, "and ask Dáire for a year's loan of the Donn Cúailnge, and when the year is up I'll give him back the Brown Bull and fifty heifers to boot. And you can make him another offer, Mac Roth. If the people of those borderlands begrudge the loan of the Pride of the Herd, the Donn Cúailnge, let Dáire himself bring me the bull and I'll grant him a piece of the smooth plain of Aí as big as all his lands, and a chariot worth thrice seven bondmaids, as well as the friendship of my own thighs."

Messengers set out for Dáire Mac Fiachna's house. There were nine of them in Mac Roth's band. Mac Roth was made welcome in Dáire's house, as was right and proper for a Head Messenger. Dáire asked him what had brought him on his journey, and why he had come. The Messenger told him why he had come, and of the dispute between Medb and Ailill.

"So I've come to ask for the loan of the Donn Cúailnge," he said, "to match the White-horned Bull. And when the loan is up, you'll get back the Brown Bull and fifty heifers into the bargain. And there's more on offer: if you bring the bull yourself, you'll get a piece of the smooth plain of Aí as big as all your lands, and a chariot worth thrice seven bondmaids, as well as the friendship of Medb's thighs."

Dáire was well pleased by this. He leaped up and down on his couch and the seams of the flock mattress burst beneath him.

"'Pon my soul!" he cried. "Let the Ulstermen say what they will, I'll take the Pride of the Herd, the Donn Cúailnge, to Ailill and Medb in the land of Connacht."

Mac Roth was well pleased by Dáire's response.

The messengers were attended to, and straw and fresh rushes strewn for them. They were given a feed of meat and drink, until they were well full. Two of the messengers' tongues got loose.

"It's true what they say," said one, "that the man of this house is a great man."

"Very true," said the other.

"Is there a better man in Ulster?" said the first messenger.

"There is indeed," said the second messenger. "Dáire's master, Conchobar,[8] is a better man, for if every man in Ulster bowed to him, there'd be no shame on them. Mind you, it was very great of Dáire to give us nine foot-soldiers what would have been a job for the four strong provinces of Ireland, that is, to bring the Donn Cúailnge out of Ulster."

A third messenger joined the conversation.

"What's all the talk about?" he said.

"Your man here was saying that the man of this house is a great man. Very true, says your other man. Is there a better man in Ulster? says your man here. There is indeed, says your other man. Dáire's master, Conchobar, is a better man, for if every man in Ulster bowed to him there'd be no shame on them. Mind you, it was very great of Dáire to give us nine foot-soldiers what would been for a job for the four strong provinces of Ireland, that is, to bring the Donn Cúailnge out of Ulster."

"I'd like to see the mouth that said that spout blood, for if he hadn't given willingly, we would have taken the bull anyway."

---

7. An outlying district on the east coast of Ireland, on the borders of Ulster.

8. High king of Ulster and, in some stories, Mebd's lover before her marriage to Ailill.

Just then Dáire Mac Fiachna's head butler came into their quarters with a man carrying drink and another food, and he heard what they were saying. In a fit of rage he put down the food and drink. And he didn't say, "Help yourselves," and he didn't say, "Don't help yourselves." He went straight to Dáire Mac Fiachna's quarters, and said:

"Are you the man who gave the messengers the Pride of the Herd, the Donn Cúailnge?"

"I am indeed," said Dáire.

"That's not the gesture of a king, for what they say is true, that if you hadn't given him willingly, he would have been taken anyway by the forces of Ailill and Medb, and the craftiness of Fergus Mac Róich."[9]

"By the gods I worship, nothing will leave here without my leave!"

They waited until morning. The messengers were up early and they went to Dáire's quarters.

"Tell us, your lordship, where we might find the Donn Cúailnge."

"Indeed I will not," said Dáire, "and if I were the sort of man to give foul play to any messenger or traveler or guest that comes this way, none of you would leave here alive."

"Why's that?" said Mac Roth.

"There's a very good reason why," said Dáire, "You said that whatever I didn't give willingly, it would be taken from me anyway by the forces of Ailill and Medb, and craftiness of Fergus Mac Róich."

"Come now," said Mac Roth, "you shouldn't heed what messengers say when they've a feed of your meat and drink in them. It's not as if it was Ailill's and Medb's fault."

"All the same, Mac Roth, I won't be giving up my bull."

The messengers returned to Crúachan Fort in Connacht. Medb asked them for their news, and Mac Roth broke the news—that they had not brought back the bull from Dáire.

"Why not?" said Medb.

Mac Roth told her why not.

"There's no need to iron out the knots in this one, Mac Roth," said Medb, "for it was known that if the bull were not given willingly, he would be taken by force. And taken he shall be."

THE TÁIN BEGINS

A great army was mustered in Connacht by Ailill and Medb, and a call to arms went out to the other three provinces. Ailill sent messengers to his six brothers, namely, Cet, Anlúan, Maccorb, Bascall, Én and Dóche, all sons of Mágach. Each brought three thousand men. And Ailill sent word to Cormac Conn Longas the Exile,[1] who was billeted in Connacht with his three thousand men.

Cormac's men marched to Crúachan in three divisions. The first division wore dappled cloaks. Their heads were shaved. They wore knee-length tunics. Each man was equipped with a long shield, a silver-handled sword and a broad bright spear on a slender shaft.

9. Warrior, poet, and prophet, he had been king of Ulster before Conchobar took the throne from him. Conchobar had further violated Fergus's honor by arranging the murder of men who were under his protection, after which Fergus and Ulstermen loyal to him fled into Connacht.

He became an advisor to Ailill and one of Medb's many lovers.
1. Cormac, "Leader of the Exiles," is a son of Conchobar who had fled with Fergus and entered the service of Ailill and Medb.

"Is that Cormac?" said they all.

"Not yet," said Medb.

The second division wore dun-gray cloaks and calf-length tunics with red embroidery. Their long hair hung down their backs. Each man was equipped with a bright shield, swords with guards of gold and a five-pronged spear.

"Is that Cormac?" said they all.

"Not yet," said Medb.

The third division arrived. They wore purple cloaks and hooded, ankle-length tunics with red embroidery. Their hair was cut shoulder-length. Each man was equipped with a curved, scallop-edged shield and a "palace-turret" spear. Together they lifted their feet, and together they put them down again.

"Is that Cormac?" said they all.

"That's Cormac," said Medb.

That night they pitched camp and thick smoke rose from their fires between the four fords of Aí—Moga, Bercna, Slissen and Coltna. They stayed there for a fortnight, drinking and feasting and reveling to ease the hardship of the imminent campaign. Then Medb asked her charioteer to hitch up the horses for her to go and consult her druid.[2] She arrived at the druid's place and asked him to look into the future.

"There are those today who leave behind lovers, friends and relations. And if they do not come back safe and sound, they all will curse me, because I made the call to arms. Yet I too have to go, and count myself as much as them. Find out for me if I will come back or not."

And the druid said: "Whoever comes back or not, you will come back."

The driver turned the chariot round. As they made to go back to camp a young woman appeared before them. She had yellow hair. She wore a dappled cloak with a gold pin, a hooded tunic with red embroidery and shoes with gold buckles. Her face was broad above and slender beneath, her eyebrows dark, and her black eyelashes cast a shadow halfway down her cheek. Her lips were of a Parthian red, inset with teeth like pearls. Her hair was done up in three plaits, two wound round her head and the third hanging down her back to her calf. In her hand was a weaver's beam of white bronze inlaid with gold. Her eyes had triple irises. The young woman was armed. Her chariot was drawn by two black horses.

"What is your name?" said Medb to the young woman.

"My name is Fedelm, one of the women poets of Connacht."

"Where have you come from?" said Medb.

"From learning poetry in Alba," said the young woman.

"Have you the Second Sight?" said Medb.

"I have that too," said the young woman.

"Look for us, then, and see how our expedition will fare."

The girl looked.

And Medb said: "For our army, Fedelm, what lies ahead?"

Fedelm replied: "I see it crimson, I see it red."

"That can't be right," said Medb, "for Conchobar is in Emain, laid low by the Curse, together with the rest of the Ulster warriors.[3] My spies have told me so."

2. Another archaizing touch. The Druids had been a pagan priestly class, expert in prophecy.
3. Macha, a goddess of war, had come among the Ulstermen in human guise. Conchobar forced her to race with his horses even though she was pregnant. She won but gave birth just over the finish line. She cursed the Ulstermen, in times of danger, to suffer a period of weakness like that of a woman in labor. Only women, children, and Cú Chulainn were exempt. Emain is Conchobar's capital.

And Medb said: "For our army, Fedelm, what lies ahead?"

Fedelm replied: "I see it crimson, I see it red."

"That can't be right," said Medb, "for Conchobar Mac Uthidir is in Dún Lethglaise with a third of Ulster's forces, and Fergus son of Róich Mac Echdach and his force of three thousand are here with us in exile."

And Medb said: "For our army, Fedelm, what lies ahead?"

Fedelm replied: "I see it crimson, I see it red."

"That's neither here nor there," said Medb. "Whenever a great army musters, there is bound to be trouble and strife and bloody wounds. Soldiers will boast and soldiers will quarrel before the onset of any expedition. I want the truth."

And Medb said: "For our army, Fedelm, what lies ahead?"

Fedelm replied: "I see it crimson, I see it red."

Then the young woman chanted this verse:

> I see a forceful blond man,
> on whom victories are built.
> A fierce light springs from his head,
> wounds hang on him like a belt.
>
> Seven jewels play about
> the stark pupil of each eye.
> His sharp teeth are unsheathed.
> He wears a shirt of crimson dye.
>
> His features are beautiful,
> his form pleasing to women—
> deadly handsome and youthful,
> in battle like a dragon.
>
> That same courage can be found
> in the famous Blacksmith's Hound—
> Cú Chulainn of Muirthemne.[4]
> Who this is I do not know,
> but this I know for certain—
> he stains red his every foe.
>
> I see him loom on the plain,
> a whole army to withstand,
> wielding four short, sharp, smart swords
> in each of his two deft hands.
>
> He attacks in battle-gear
> with his fierce barbed *gae bolga*,[5]
> his bone-hilted sword, his spear,
> each picked for a special use.
>
> Red-cloaked he drives through the field,
> uttering a battle-hymn.

4. The "hound of Culann," so named for a boyhood feat in which he killed the savage dog of Culann the Smith, then offered to guard his house in the dog's place. Muirthemne is a plain on the coast of County Louth.

5. The "belly spear" is one of Cú Chulainn's magical weapons, the gift of the woman warrior who trained him in arms. Once it enters the body, it opens into 30 barbs.

From his chariot he deals
death across the left wheel-rim,
the Torqued Man[6] changed terribly
from when his form first struck me.

He's taken the war-path now.
Havoc unless you pay heed
to Sualdam's son, the Hound.
He pursues you with all speed.

Acres will be dense with dead,
as he mows the battlefield,
leaving a thousand lopped heads:
these things I do not conceal.

Blood spurts from soldiers' bodies,
released by this hero's hand.
He kills on sight, scattering
Dada's followers and clan.[7]
Women wail at the corpse-mound
because of him—the Forge-Hound.

They set out the Monday after Samhain. This was their route, south-east from Crúachan Aí:[8]

> through Mag Cruinn, the Round Plain,
> through Tuaim Móna, the Mound of Turf,
> through Turloch Teóra Crích, the Vanishing
>   Lake of the Borderlands,
> through Cúl Sílinne, the Dripping Backwater,
> through Dubloch, the Black Lake,
> through Fid Dubh, the Black Wood,
> through Badbna,
> through Coltain, the Feast,
> across the Shannon,
> through Glúine Gabur, the Goat's Knees,
>
> through Mag Trega, the Plain of Spears,
> through North Tethba,
> through South Tethba,
> through Cúl, the Backwater,
> through Ochaín,
> northwards through Uata,
> southwards through Tiarthechta,
> through Ord, the Hammer,
> thorugh Slaiss, the Blows,
> through Indeoin, the Anvil . . .

* * *

Such was the route they took.

6. In his battle frenzy, Cú Chulainn undergoes a monstrous distortion, one eye swelling over his cheek, a beam of light leaping from his forehead, and blood erupting from his skull.

7. One of the three warrior races of Ireland.
8. This catalog of place-names, along with genealogies elsewhere, reflects the encyclopedic impulse in the *Táin*.

On the first stage of their march they went from Crúachan to Cúl Sílinne, the site of Loch Carrcín today. Medb told her driver to hitch up her nine chariots for her to make a circuit of the camp, to see who was keen to be on the march, and who was not so keen.

Meanwhile Ailill's tent had been pitched, and fitted with beds and blankets. Next to Ailill was Fergus Mac Róich in his tent; next to Fergus, Cormac Conn Longas; next to him, Conall Cernach; and next to him, Fiacha Mac Fir Febe, the son of Conchobar's daughter. Medb, daughter of Eochaid Fedlech, was on Ailill's other side; next to her, their daughter Finnabair; next to her was Flidais. Not to mention underlings and servants.

Medb came back from inspecting the army and said it wouldn't do for them to proceed further if the three-thousand-strong division of the Gailéoin[9] were to go as well.

"Why do you disrespect them?" said Ailill.

"I don't disrespect them," said Medb. "They are excellent soldiers. While the others were just getting round to building their huts, they had thatched theirs, and were busy cooking. While the others were beginning to eat, they had finished, and their harpers were playing for them. So it won't do for them to come. They'd take all the credit for our army's triumph."

"But they're on our side," said Ailill.

"They can't come," said Medb.

"Let them stay, then," said Ailill.

THE GATHERING OF THE ULSTERMEN[1]

While these events were taking place, Sualdam of Ráith Sualdaim in Muirthemne Plain heard how his son Cú Chulainn had been under constant attack. And he said:

"Are the heavens rent? Does the sea leave its bed? Does the earth open up? Or is this the cry of my son as he fights against the odds?"

He went to his son. But the son was not pleased to see him. True, he was badly wounded, but he knew his father would not be strong enough to fight on anyone's account.

"Go to the men of Ulster," said Cú Chulainn, "and get them to do battle with the army. If they do not, we will never be avenged."

Then his father saw that on Cú Chulainn's body there was not so much as a spot that the tip of a rush couldn't cover that wasn't pierced. Even the left hand, which was protected by his shield, had fifty wounds in it. Sualdam went to Emain Macha and cried out to the men of Ulster:

"Men murdered, women raped, cattle plundered!"

His first cry was from the side of the fort, his next from the royal rampart, and his third from the Mound of Hostages inside Emain itself.

---

9. A tribe from North Leinster.

1. In the intervening episodes the men of Ireland do suc-
ceed in seizing the Brown Bull of Cooley. The armies of
Medb and Ailill also move around a large part of central
and northern Ireland, trying to penetrate the borders of
Ulster. Cú Chulainn repeatedly prevents this, despite the
continuing debility of the Ulstermen. He first places
impassable taboo signs along their route, then stages night
raids on the armies, and finally conducts an exhausting
series of single combats, mostly at fords, which climax in a
three-day battle with his foster-brother Ferdia. In the face
of his onslaught and the gathering army of the Ulstermen
as they begin to recover, the men of Ireland retreat south-
ward into Meath, toward Connacht.

No one answered, for among the Ulster people it was not permissible to speak until Conchobar had spoken, and Conchobar would not speak until his druids had spoken. Then a druid said:

"Who rapes? Who plunders? Who murders?"

"Ailill Mac Máta murders and rapes and plunders," said Sualdam, "aided and abetted by Fergus Mac Róich. Your people have been harassed as far as Dún Sobairche. Their cattle, their women and their herds have been carried off. Cú Chulainn has kept them out of Muirthemne and Crích Rois for the three months of winter. He's held together with bent hoops of wood, and dry wisps plug his wounds. Wounds that almost finished him off."[2]

"It would be appropriate" said the druid, "for a man who so provokes the king to die."

"It would serve him right," said Conchobar.

"And serve him right," said the men of Ulster.

"What Sualdam says is true," said Conchobar. "Since the last Monday of summer to the first Monday of spring we've been raped and pillaged."

Sualdam stormed out, dissatisfied with this response. He fell on to his shield and his head was cut off by the scalloped rim. His horse brought his head on the shield back to his house in Emain, and the head kept repeating the same warning.

"Truly, that is too powerful a cry," said Conchobar, "and I swear by the sea before them and the sky above them and the earth beneath them that I will restore every cow to its byre and every woman and child to their homes after victory in battle."

Then Conchobar laid his hand on his son Finnchad Ferr Benn the Horned Man, so called because he wore silver horns. And he said:

"Arise, Finnchad! Go to Dedad in his inlet, to Leamain, to Fallach, to Illann Mac Fergusa, to Gabar, to Dorlunsa, to Imchlár, to Feidlimid Cilair Cétaig, to Fáeladán, to Rochaid Mac Faithemain at Rigdonn, to Lugaid, to Lugda, to Cathbath in his inlet, to the three Cairpres . . ."[3]

* * *

It was not difficult for Finnchad to deliver that summons, for all the chieftains in Conchobar's province had been waiting for the word from Conchobar. From east and north and west of Emain they came, and entered Emain to hear the news that Conchobar had risen from his sick-bed. Then they struck out southwards from Emain in search of the enemy. The first stage of their march brought them to Iraird Cuillenn.

"Why are you waiting here?" said Conchobar.

"We're waiting for your sons," said the Ulster army. "They've gone to Tara with three thousand men to contact Erc, the Freckled Calf, son of Coirpre Nia Fer and Fedelm Noíchride. We won't leave this spot until they return to join us."

"Well, I'll not wait," said Conchobar, "for the men of Ireland to find out that I've risen from my sick-bed, recovered from the Curse."

So Conchobar and Celtchar set off with three fifties of chariots, and brought back eight score enemy heads from the ford of Airthir Mide in East Meath. Hence its name now, Áth Féne, Warrior Ford. These were the heads of men who had been watching there for Conchobar's army. They also brought back eight score women

2. Near collapse, Cú Chulainn is tied down with wooden hoops lest he return to battle and injure himself mortally.

3. A catalog of Ulster warriors follows.

who had been held captive. When Conchobar and Celtchar brought the heads to the camp Celtchar said to Conchobar:

> ramparts awash   with blood   the king
> of slaughter   beyond compare   sundered
> body parts   the ground   surrendered
> to a hundred   streams   thirty four-horsed chariots
> steeds harnessed to   a hundred cruelties
> no want of leaders   two hundred druids
> a steadfast man   at Conchobar's back   prepare
> for battle   warriors   arise
> the battle   will erupt   at Gáirech and Ilgáirech

The same night Dubthach the Beetle of Ulster had a vision where he saw the army assembled at Gáirech and Ilgáirech. He spoke these words in his sleep:

> bewildering morning   bewildering times
> disordered armies   kings cast down
> necks broken   in the bloody sand
> three armies wiped out   by the Ulster army
> Conchobar at the heart   their women huddled
> herds driven   dawn after morning
> heroes cut down   hounds torn apart
> horses mangled   in the bloody mire
> as tribe   tramples tribe

This disturbed their sleep. The Nemain[4] deranged the army. A hundred men fell dead. When everything was silent they heard Cormac Con Longes—or it might have been Ailill Mac Máta—chanting to the west of the camp:

> great the truce   the truce at Cuillenn
> great the plot   the plot at Delind
> great the cavalcade   the cavalcade at Assal
> great the torment   the torment at Tuath Bressi

While these visions were happening the men of Connacht, advised by Ailill and Medb and Fergus, decided to send scouts to see if the men of Ulster had reached the plain.

"Go, Mac Roth," said Ailill, "and find out if their men have arrived on the plain of Meath. As it is, I've taken all their goods and cattle. If they want a fight, they can have one. But if they haven't reached the plain, we'll be off."

Mac Roth went out to scan the plain. He returned to Ailill and Medb and reported that when he first looked into the distance from Sliab Fúait he had seen all the beasts of the forest leaving their home and pouring out on to the plain.

"Then I took a second look," said Mac Roth, "and saw a thick mist filling the glens and valleys, so that the hills appeared like islands in a lake. I saw sparks of fire coming through the mist, sparks of every shade and color in the world. Then there was a flash of lightning, and a great rumble of thunder, and a wind that nearly took the hair from my head and threw me on my back, though there's hardly a breeze today."

"What is this, Fergus?" said Ailill. "What can it mean?"

---

4. Panic, one of a group of war goddesses and wife of the war god, Net.

"I can tell you exactly what it means," said Fergus. "It's the men of Ulster, risen from their sick-beds. It was they who entered the forest. The vast number of their warriors and the violence of their passage shook the forest and caused the beasts of the forest to flee before them on to the plain. The thick mist that you saw was the breath of those powerful men filling the low ground so that the high ground appeared like islands in a lake. The lightning and the sparks of fire and the many colors that you saw, Mac Roth," said Fergus, "those were the eyes of the warriors flashing in their heads like sparks of fire. The thunder and the rumble and the clamor that you heard, that was the whirring of their swords and their ivory-hilted blades, their weapons rattling, chariots clattering, hoof-beats hammering, the shouts and roars and cries of chariot-fighters, warriors and soldiers, the ferocious rage and fury of heroes as they storm towards the battle. They're so fired up, they think they'll never get there."

"We'll be waiting for them," said Ailill. "We have warriors to take them on."

"You'll need them," said Fergus, "for no one—not in Ireland, nor the western world from Greece and Scythia westwards to the Orkney Islands and the Pillars of Hercules, as far as Breogan's Tower and the Isles of Gades—can withstand the men of Ulster in their battle-fury."

Mac Roth set off again to gauge the advance of the Ulstermen and went as far as their camp at Slane in Meath. He reported back to Ailill and Medb and Fergus, giving them a detailed account of what he had seen.

"A great company came to the hill at Slane in Meath," said Mac Roth, "proud and powerful and battle-hungry. I'd put their numbers at about three thousand. Without further ado they stripped down and dug a mound of sods as a throne for their leader. He was a most impressive, regal figure as he led that company, slim, tall and handsome, with finely cut blond hair falling down in waves and curls between his shoulder-blades. He wore a pleated shirt of royal purple and a red-embroidered white hooded tunic. A dazzling brooch of red gold was pinned to the breast of his mantle. His gray eyes had a calm gaze. His face was ruddy-cheeked, with a broad brow and a fine jaw. He had a forked beard of golden curls. Slung across his shoulders was a sword with a gold pommel and a bright shield inlaid with animal designs. He held a slender-shafted spear with a blued steel head. His retinue was the finest of any prince on earth, a fearsome and formidable body of men, magnificently equipped, whose bearing spoke of triumph, rage, implacable resolve and dignity.

"Another company came up," said Mac Roth, "almost as impressive as the first in terms of numbers, bearing, dress and fierce resolve. A handsome young hero led that company. He wore a bordered knee-length tunic and a green cloak fastened at the shoulder with a gold brooch. He had a head of curly yellow hair. An ivory-hilted sword hung at his left side, and he carried a deadly scallop-edged shield. In his hand was a spear like a palace torch-standard, with three silver rings around it that ran freely up and down the shaft from grip to tip and back again. The company took up a position to the left of the first company, with knee to ground and shield-rim held to chin. I detected a stammer in the speech of the great stern warrior who led that company.

"Another company came up," said Mac Roth. "I'd put their numbers at above three thousand. A brave, handsome, broad-faced man was at their head. He had wavy brown hair and a long, forked, wispy beard. He wore a white knee-length hooded tunic and dark-gray fringed cloak pinned at the breast with a leaf-shaped brooch of white bronze. He carried a shield inlaid with animal designs in many colors. At his waist hung a sword with a domed silver pommel, and he held a five-pronged spear in his hand. He sat down facing the leader of the first company."

"Who were they, Fergus?" said Ailill.

"I know them well," said Fergus. "Conchobar, king of a province of Ireland, is the one who was seated on the mound of sods. Seancha Mac Ailill, the most eloquent man in Ulster, is the one who sat facing him. And Cúscraid Menn Macha the Stammerer, Conchobar's son, is the one who sat by his father's side. As for those three rings around his spear, they only run up and down like that before a victory. And as for the companies assembled there, these are men you can count on to do great damage in any battle, said Fergus.

"They'll find men to answer them here," said Medb.

"I swear by the gods my people swear by," said Fergus, "that the army has not been raised in Ireland that could withstand the men of Ulster."

"Another company came up," said Mac Roth, "more than three thousand of them, led by a big strong warrior, swarthy, fiery-faced and fearsome, with a glib of brown hair plastered to his forehead. He carried a curved scallop-edged shield. He held a five-pronged spear and a forked javelin besides. A bloodstained sword was slung on his back. He wore a white knee-length tunic, and a purple cloak pinned at the shoulder with a gold brooch."

"Who was that, Fergus?" said Ailill.

"A man built for battle," said Fergus, "first to the fray, the doom of enemies: Eoghan Mac Durthacht, King of Fernmag."

"Another powerful and imperious company came to the hill at Slane in Meath," said Mac Roth, "harbingers of dread and terror, their cloaks thrown back behind them, marching resolutely towards the hill with a fearsome clattering of arms. Their leader was a grim-looking fellow with a thick-set, grizzled head and big yellow eyes. He was wrapped in a yellow cloak with a white border. A deadly scalloped-edged shield hung by his side. In one hand he held a long, broad-bladed spear; in the other he held its match, the blade stained with the blood of his enemies. A long, lethal sword was slung across his shoulders."

"Who was that, Fergus?" said Ailill.

"A warrior who never turns his back on battle: Láegaire Buadach the Victorious, son of Connad son of Ilech from Impail in the north," said Fergus.

"Another great company came to the hill at Slane in Meath," said Mac Roth, "headed by a fine-looking, barrel-chested, thick-necked warrior. He had ruddy cheeks, a shock of black curls and flashing gray eyes. He wore a cloak of brown shaggy wool pinned with a bright silver brooch. He carried a black shield with a bronze boss. A spear with a needle's-eye head glittered in his hand. The ivory pommel of his sword sat proud against his red-embroidered braided tunic."

"Who was that, Fergus?" said Ailill.

"The instigator of many battles. A tidal wave that overwhelms little streams. A man of three cries. The vicious doom of enemies," said Fergus. "Munremar Mac Gerrcinn the Thick-Necked, from Moduirn in the north."

"Another great company came to the hill at Slane in Meath," said Mac Roth, "a most impressive company, their cohorts well drilled and splendidly kitted out. They marched imperiously up to the hill. The clatter of their arms as they advanced shook everyone. They were led by a majestic warrior, superlative among men for his hair and eyes and grim demeanor, for dress and build and clarity of voice, for dignity and grandeur and gracefulness, for range and style of fighting skills, for equipment, application and discernment, for honor and nobility of lineage."

"You have him in a nutshell," said Fergus. "That brilliant figure is Feidlimid the Handsome, the raging warrior, the overwhelming wave, the irresistible force, who comes home in triumph after slaughtering his enemies abroad: Feidlimid Cilair Cétaig."

"Another company came to the hill at Slane in Meath," said Mac Roth, "at least three thousand strong, led by a big, stalwart warrior, sallow-complexioned, with a head of black curls and a haughty stare in his gray eyes. A great, rugged bull of a man. He wore a white hooded tunic and a gray cloak with a silver pin at the shoulder. A sword hung at his hip, and he carried a red shield with a hammered silver boss. The spear in his hand had a broad blade and triple rivets."

"Who was that, Fergus?" said Ailill.

"A furious flame, bold in battle, a man who wins wars: Connad Mac Morna from Callann," said Fergus.

"Another company came to the hill at Slane in Meath," said Mac Roth, "a veritable army of them. As for the leader of that vast force, seldom will you find a warrior so poised and stylishly equipped. His auburn hair was neatly trimmed, his handsome, well-proportioned face aglow. Finely shaped red lips, pearl-white teeth, a firm, clear voice: every aspect of him was superlative. Draped over his red-embroidered hooded tunic was a purple cloak with an inlaid gold brooch. At his left side hung a silver-bossed shield inlaid with animal designs in many colors. In one hand he held a spear with a head of blued steel: in the other hand he held a deadly sharp dagger. A gold-hilted golden sword was slung on his back."

"Who was that, Fergus?" said Ailill.

"Someone well known to us," said Fergus. "A men equal to an army, tenacious as a bloodhound, a deciding factor in any combat: Rochad Mac Faithemain from Brig Dumae, your son-in-law, who took your daughter Finnabair."

"Another company came to the hill at Slane in Meath," said Mac Roth, "led by a feisty-looking, dark-haired warrior with brawny lags and bulging thighs. Each of his four limbs was as thick as a man. He was every inch a man, and more," said Mac Roth. "He had a scarred, purple face and haughty, bloodshot eyes: a formidable, bustling man, alert and dangerous, his entourage equipped and kitted out in admirable fashion; a proud, aggressive man, whose scorn and anger drives him into battle against overwhelming odds to beat his enemies, who ventures unprotected into hostile territory—no wonder his company marched so boldly to the hill at Slane in Meath."

"A brave warlike man indeed," said Fergus, "hot-blooded, tough, vehement and dignified, a force to be reckoned with in any army: my own foster-brother, Fergus Mac Leiti, King of Líne, battle-spearhead of the north of Ireland."

"Another great imposing company came to the hill at Slane in Meath," said Mac Roth. "They were wonderfully equipped. At their head was a fine, tall figure of a man with brilliant hair and eyes and skin, magnificently proportioned. He held himself with immense aplomb. He wore five gold chains, a green cloak pinned at the shoulder with a gold brooch, and a white hooded tunic. In his hand was a spear like the turret of a palace. A gold-hilted sword was slung on his back."

"Fearsome and formidable indeed the same conquering hero," said Fergus. "That was Amargin son of Eiccet Salach the smith, from Buais in the north."[5]

* * *

5. Mac Roth goes on to describe eight further companies and their leaders, and Fergus identifies each in turn as heroic Ulstermen.

"Another company came to the hill at Slane in Meath," said Mac Roth, "count-less numbers of heroes wearing strange outfits, very different to the other companies. With all their gear and weapons and equipment they made a marvelous spectacle as they advanced. They were an army in themselves. At their head was a bright-faced, freckled, perfectly formed little boy. He held a gold-studded, gold-rimmed shield with a white boss and a shimmering, keen-bladed light javelin. He wore a red-embroidered white hooded tunic and a purple fringed cloak held at the breast with a silver pin. A gold-hilted sword sat proud against his garments."

Fergus paused before he spoke.

"I don't know," said Fergus, "of any boy among the Ulster people who would fit that description. These must be the men of Tara, and this must be the fine and noble Erc, son of Coirpre Niad Fer and Conchobar's daughter. There's no love lost between Coirpre and Conchobar, and the boy must have come to his grandfather's aid without the permission of his father. Because of that young lad," said Fergus, "you will lose the battle. He will plunge fearlessly into the heart of the fray, and the warriors of Ulster will raise a great shout as they rush forward, cutting down your army before them to rescue their beloved little calf. They will all feel the ties that bind them when they see the boy under attack. Then will be heard the whirr of Conchobar's sword, like the growl of a bloodhound, as he comes to save the boy. Conchobar will cast up three ramparts of dead men around the battlefield in the search for his grandson. And, moved by the ties that bind them, the warriors of Ulster will descend on your vast army."

"I have been overlong," said Mac Roth, "in describing everything I saw. But I thought I should let you know what was going on."

"You have certainly done that," said Fergus.

"However," said Mac Roth, "Conall Cernach did not come with his great com-pany. Nor did Conchobar's three sons, with their three divisions. Nor did Cú Chulainn come, for he was wounded fighting against the odds. But many hundreds and thousands converged on the Ulster camp. Many heroes, champions and warriors came racing on their horses to that great meeting. And many more companies were still arriving as I left. Wherever I cast my eye," said Mac Roth, "on any hill or height from Fer Diad's Ford to Slane in Meath, all I could see was men and horses."

"What you saw was a people coming together," said Fergus.

* * *

The Final Battle

Conchobar came with his forces and camped beside the others. He asked Ailill for a truce until sunrise. Ailill consented on behalf of the men of Ireland and the Ulster exiles, and Conchobar consented on behalf of the men of Ulster. The men of Ireland pitched their tents, and before the sun had set there was hardly a bare piece of ground between them and the Ulstermen. In the twilight between the two camps the Morrígan[6] spoke:

> ravens gnaw   men's necks   blood gushes
> fierce fray   hacked flesh   battle-drunk
> men's sides   blade-struck   war-torn
> raking fingers   battle-brave   men of Crúachan

6. Great Queen or Queen of Demons, the major goddess of war, a shape-shifter and sower of discord.

> ruination   bodies crushed   underfoot
> long live Ulster   woe to Ireland
> woe to Ulster   long live Ireland

These last words—"woe to Ulster"—she conveyed to the ears of the men of Ireland,[7] to make them think the war was as good as won. That night Nét's consorts, Nemain and the Badb, began howling at the men of Ireland, and a hundred warriors dropped dead of fright. It was not the most peaceful of nights for them.

On the eve of the battle Ailill Mac Mata chanted:

"Rise up, Traighthrén, powerful of foot. Summon for me the three Conaires from Sliab Mis, the three Lussens from Lúachair, the three Niad Chorb from Tilach Loiscthe, the three Dóelfers from Dell, the three Dámaltachs from Dergderc, the three Bodars from the Buas, the three Baeths from the river Buaidnech, the three Búageltachs from Mag mBreg, the three Suibnes from the river Suir, the three Eochaids from Ane, the three Malleths from Loch Erne, the three Abatruads from Loch Ríb, the three Mac Amras from Ess Rúaid, the three Fiachas from Fid Nemain, the three Maines from Mureisc, the three Muredachs from Mairg, the three Loegaires from Lecc Derg, the three Brodonns from the river Barrow, the three Brúchnechs from Cenn Abrat, the three Descertachs from Druim Fornacht, the three Finns from Finnabair, the three Conalls from Collamair, the three Carbres from Cliu, the three Maines from Mossa, the three Scáthglans from Scaire, the three Echtaths from Erce, the three Trénfers from Taite, the three Fintans from Femen, the three Rótanachs from Raigne, the three Sárchorachs from Suide Lagen, the three Etarscéls from Étarbán, the three Aeds from Aidne, the three Guaires from Gabal."

These Triads, as they were known, had survived Cú Chulainn's attacks on the Irish army.

Meanwhile Cú Chulainn was close by at Fedain Collna. His supporters would bring him food by night, and talk things over with him by day. He killed no one north of Fer Diad's Ford.

"Some cattle have strayed from the western camp to the eastern camp," his charioteer said to Cú Chulainn, "and look, a party of young fellows have gone out to round them up. What's more, a party of our own young fellows have gone after the cattle too."[8]

"The two lots of young fellows will clash," said Cú Chulainn, "and they'll be joined by others who will give no quarter. The cattle will stray all the more."

It happened as Cú Chulainn said it would.

"How are the Ulster boys fighting?" said Cú Chulainn.

"Like men," said the charioteer.

"The same boys would be proud to die for their herd," said Cú Chulainn. "And now?"

"The beardless youngsters have joined them now," said the charioteer.

"Is there any ray of sunlight yet?" said Cú Chulainn.

"Not a glimmer," said the charioteer.

"If only I was fit to go and help them," said Cú Chulainn.

"Now the real fighting begins," said the charioteer as the sun came up. "The higher echelons are going into battle, except the kings, for they are asleep."

---

7. The allies of Mebd and Ailill from outside Connacht, who now begin to withdraw their allegiance.
8. Probably the boy troops who train in mock battles around Conchobar's capital. Cú Chulainn, when still a boy and untutored in the ways of the court, had first challenged and then joined them. Because of their age they are untouched by the debility of the Ulstermen and rush into battle before their elders.

As the sun came up, Fachtna spoke (or maybe it was Conchobar, chanting in his sleep):

> Arise   brave kings of Macha   generous people
> sharpen swords   wage war   dig in
> strike shields   arms weary   bellowing herds
> of men   in rightful strife   battle ranks
> their reign   brought down   by fighting men
> as enemies   ambush   killing all day
> imbibing   deep draughts   of blood
> the hearts   of queens   swelling
> with grief   and blood   soaks
> the trampled grass   whereon   they stand
> and fall   arise   kings of Macha

"Who chanted that?" said they all.
"Conchobar Mac Nessa," said some.
"Fachtna," said others.
"Sleep on, sleep on, but still keep watch!"
And Láegaire Buadach the Victorious said:

> Beware   kings of Macha
> ready swords   to guard   what cattle
> you have plundered   drive   the Connachtmen
> from Uisnech Hill   body   torque-twisted
> sinews blazing   he will strike   the world
> on the plain of Gáirech

"Who chanted that?" said they all.
"Láegaire Buadach, son of Connad Buide son of Illiach. Sleep on, sleep on, but still keep watch!"
"Wait a little longer," said Conchobar, "till the sun has risen well above the hills and glens of Ireland."
When Cú Chulainn saw the western kings putting on their crowns and rallying their troops, he told his charioteer to rouse up the men of Ulster.
The charioteer spoke—or maybe it was the poet Amargin Mac Eicit:

> Arise   brave kings of Macha
> generous people   the Badb   lusts after
> Impail cattle   heart's blood   pouring forth
> as men pour in   to battle   brave deeds
> heads skewed   in flight   bogged down
> in blood   and battle-weariness   for there is
> no one   like Cú Chulainn   to enforce
> the will of Macha   all for   Cúailnge cattle
> arise   kings of Macha

"I've roused them up," said the charioteer. "They've charged into battle stark naked, wearing nothing but their weapons. Any man whose tent door was facing east, he's gone westward through his tent for a shortcut."
"Speedy help in time of need," said Cú Chulainn.
After a while, he said:
"Take a look for us, comrade Láeg, and tell us how the men of Ulster are fighting."

"Bravely," said the charioteer. "If Conall Cernach's charioteer En and myself were to drive from one wing of the battle to the other, not a wheel nor a hoof would touch ground, so closely do they fight."

"This has the makings of a great encounter," said Cú Chulainn. "Whatever happens in the battle, be sure to let me know about it."

"I'll do my level best," said the charioteer.

"Right now the western warriors have broken through the eastern battle-line," he said.

"And now the eastern warriors have broken through the western battle-line."

"If only I were fit," said Cú Chulainn, "you'd see me breaking through along with the rest."

The Irish Triads began to advance towards the battle at Gáirech and Ilgáirech. Accompanying them were the nine chariot-fighters from Iruath, each preceded by three foot-soldiers keeping pace with the chariots. Medb was keeping them in reserve to take Ailill out of harm's way if they were beaten, or to kill Chochobar if they won.

Then the charioteer told Cú Chulainn that Ailill and Medb were pressurizing Fergus to go into battle, saying that it was only right that he should do so, after all that they had done for him during his exile.

"If only I had my own sword," said Fergus, "the soldiers' heads I'd cut off would bounce off their shields like hailstones into the mud churned up by the king's horses as they plough through the battlefield."[9]

And he swore his oath:

"I swear by the god my people swear by, that I'd strike jaws from necks, necks from shoulders, shoulders from elbows, elbows from forearms, forearms from fists, fists from fingers, fingers from nails; crowns from skulls, skulls from trunks, trunks from thighs, thighs from calves, calves from feet, feet from toes, and toes from nails. Heads would fly from necks like bees buzzing to and fro on a fine day."

Then Ailill said to his charioteer:

"Bring me the sword that violates flesh. I swear the oath of my people that if it has lost any of its bloom since the day I gave it to you on that wet hill-slope in Ulster, all of Ireland will not save you from me.

The sword was brought to Fergus and Ailill said:

take your sword   though once   you struck out
at Ireland   one of her sons   a mighty hero
will fight at Gáirech   if this be   the truth
for the sake of   your honor   wreak not
your wrath   on us but on   Ulster's chariot-warriors
at dawn   at Gáirech   the field sodden
with the deep   red morning

Fergus said:

well met   Harshblade   Léte's sword[1]
the Badb's swift messenger   of doom
and horror   no longer concealed   come
avenge   and sever   sinews

9. Ailill's charioteer had taken the sword when he spotted Fergus having sex with Medb, and Fergus was reduced to carrying a wooden sword.
1. Léte was Fergus's father.

> topple heads   this sword   no longer
> in a king's keeping   the story   to be told
> again   I take   my kingly stance
> before the men   of Ireland

"A pity indeed, were you to fall in the thick of battle," said Fergus to Ailill.

Fergus seized his weapons and went towards the fighting. Wielding his sword in both hands, he took out a hundred men. Medb also seized her weapons and plunged into the fray. Three times she cleared all before her until she was repelled by a thicket of spears.

"I'd like to know," said Conchobar to his companions, "who it is that's taking the battle to us in the north. Hold the line here and I'll go and seek him out."

"We'll stick to this spot," said the warriors, "and unless the ground opens up under us, or the heavens fall on us, we'll not give an inch."

Then Conchobar went to meet Fergus. He raised his shield against him—the shield Óchaín, the Dazzling Ear, with its four gold spikes and four gold plates. Fergus dealt it three blows, but the rim of the shield did not even touch Conchobar's head.

"Who is the Ulsterman that holds this shield?" said Fergus.

"A better man than you," said Conchobar. "One who drove you into exile to dwell among the wolves and foxes; one who by dint of his deeds will repel you before all the men of Ireland."

With that, Fergus raised his sword in a two-handed grip, intending to deal Conchobar a vengeful blow. As the point of his sword touched the ground on the backswing, Cormac Mac Loinges gripped his arm with his two hands and said:

> reckless   careful
> comrade Fergus   too considered
> ill considered   comrade Fergus
> friend   becoming foe
> behold   your enemies
> the friends   you forsook
> as you prepare   to strike
> these wicked blows   comrade Fergus

"What then should I do?" said Fergus.

"Strike out at those three hills yonder. Turn your hand. Strike anywhere. Be as reckless as you like. But remember that the honor of Ulster has never been compromised, and never will be, unless by you today."

"Come away from here, Conchobar," said Cormac to his father. "This man will no longer vent his rage on Ulstermen."

Fergus turned round and in a single onslaught cut down a hundred Ulstermen with his sword. He came up against Conall Cernach.

"You're very fierce," said Conall, "against your own kith and kin, and all for the sake of a whore's backside."

"What then should I do?" said Fergus.

"Strike out at those hills yonder, and anything on top of them," said Conall.

Fergus struck the hills and with three blows sheared off the tops of the Máela Midi, the Flat-topped Hills of Meath.

Cú Chulainn, heard the blows which Fergus dealt the hills, just as he heard those struck on Conchobar's shield.

"Who strikes those tremendous blows in the distance?" said Cú Chulainn,

> the heart swells with blood
> rage sunders the world
> quick, undo the hoops

Láeg answered:

"Those blows were struck by the bold and dauntless Fergus Mac Róich. A man who is a byword for much blood and slaughter. His sword was hidden in the chariot-shaft in the event of Conchobar's horse-soldiers joining the war."

And Cú Chulainn said:

> quick, undo the hoops
> men covered in blood
> swords to be wielded
> lives to be cut short

Then the dry wisps which had plugged his wounds soared up into the air like skylarks and the hoops around him sprang asunder and bits of them landed as far away as Mag Tuag—the Plain of the Hoops—in Connacht. They flew away from him in all directions. The blood in his wounds began to boil. He knocked together the heads of the two women who had been watching over him so that each was spattered with gray from the other's brains. These were two handmaidens sent by Medb to make a show of sorrow over him, so that his wounds would open afresh, and to tell him that Ulster had been beaten and Fergus killed in battle because Cú Chulainn was not fit to join the fight. Then the Torque seized him. The twenty-seven leather corsets he would wear going into battle, lashed to his body with ropes and thongs, were now brought to him. He took up his chariot on his back—frame, wheels and all—and walked the battle-field in search of Fergus.

"Over here, comrade Fergus," said Cú Chulainn.

Three times he called him. Three times there was no answer.

"I swear by the god of the Ulstermen," said Cú Chulainn, "that I'll thrash you like flax in a pond! I'll rear up on you like a tail over a cat! I'll spank you the way a fond mother spanks her wee boy!"

"Who's the Irishman who speaks to me like that?" said Fergus.

"Cú Chulainn, son of Sualdam and Conchobar's sister," said Cú Chulainn, "Now yield to me."

"I did promise that once," said Fergus.

"Then give what's due," said Cú Chulainn.

"All right, so," said Fergus. "You yielded to me once, and now look at you, all full of holes."

So Fergus left the field and took his three thousand men with him. The Gailéoin and the men of Munster left too. Nine divisions of three thousand—those of Medb and Ailill and their seven sons—were left in the battle. It was noon when Cú Chulainn joined the fray. By the time the sun had brushed the tops of the trees, he had scattered the last of their companies, and all that remained of his chariot was a handful of ribs from the frame and handful of spokes from the wheels.

Medb covered the retreat of the men of Ireland. She sent the Donn Cúailnge on to Crúachan along with fifty of his heifers and eight of her messengers, so that the Bull would arrive there, as she had sworn.

Then Medb got her gush of blood.

"Fergus," she said, "cover the retreat of the men of Ireland, for I must relieve myself."

"By god," said Fergus, "you picked a bad time to go."

"I can't help it," said Medb. "I'll die if I don't go."

So Fergus covered the retreat. Medb relieved herself, and it made three great trenches, each big enough for a cavalcade. Hence the place is known as Fúal Medba, Medb's Piss-pot.

Cú Chulainn came upon Medb as she was doing what she had to.

"I'm at your mercy," said Medb.

"If I were to strike, and kill you," said Cú Chulainn, "I'd be within my rights."

But he spared her, because usually he did not kill women. He escorted them west until they crossed the ford of Áth Luain.[2] He struck three blows with his sword at the nearby hills, which are now known as Máelana Átha Luain, the Flat-topped Hills of Athlone: this was his response to the Flat-topped Hills of Meath.

Now that they had lost the battle, Medb said to Fergus:

"The pot was stirred, Fergus, and today a mess was made."

"That's usually what happens," said Fergus, "when a mare leads a herd of horses—all their energy gets pissed away, following the rump of a skittish female."

The Donn Cúailnge was brought to Connacht. When he saw this strange and beautiful new land he let three great bellows out of him. Finnbennach, the White-horned Bull, heard him. On account of Finnbennach no male beast on the Plain of Aí dared raise a sound louder than a moo. He threw up his head and proceeded to Crúachan to seek out the Brown Bull. Everyone who had escaped the battle now had nothing better to do than to watch the two bulls fighting.

The men of Ireland debated as to who should referee the contest of the two bulls. They agreed it should be Bricriu Mac Carbada the Venom-tongued. A year before the events narrated in the Táin, Bricriu had gone from one province to the other to negotiate some deal or other with Fergus. Fergus took him into his employ until such times as his possessions would arrive. They were playing chess when they had a difference of opinion, and Bricriu insulted Fergus rather badly. Fergus struck him on the head with the chessman he had been holding and broke a bone in his skull. So Bricriu had lain recuperating while the men of Ireland went forth on the Táin. The day they returned, he got up from his sick-bed. They chose Bricriu because he did not discriminate between friend and foe. They brought him to the gap between the bulls to referee the contest.

When the two bulls saw each other they pawed the ground and hurled the earth over their shoulders. Their eyes blazed in their heads like great fiery orbs and their cheeks and their nostrils swelled like forge bellows. They charged towards each other and Bricriu got caught in between. He was flattened, trampled and killed. Such was the death of Bricriu.

The Brown Bull got his hoof stuck on his opponent's horn. For a day and a night he made no attempt to withdraw the hoof, until Fergus gave off to him and took a stick to his hide.

"It would be a poor show," said Fergus, "for this feisty old calf to be brought all this way only to disgrace his fine breeding. Especially since so many died on his account."

2. Modern Athlone, on the river Shannon at the border of Connacht.

When the Brown Bull heard this he pulled away his hoof and broke his leg. The other bull's horn flew off and stuck in the side of a nearby mountain. Hence the name Sliab nAdarca, Horn Mountain.

The bulls fought for a long time. Night fell upon the men of Ireland and they could do nothing but listen to the bulls roaring and bellowing in the darkness. All next day the Donn Cúailnge drove Finnbennach before him and at nightfall they plunged into the lake at Crúachan. He emerged with Finnbennach's loins and shoulderblade and liver on his horns. The army went to kill him but Fergus stopped them, saying he should be let roam. So the Bull headed for his homeland. He stopped on the way to drink at Finnleithe, where he left Finnbennach's shoulderblade. Hence the name Finnleithe, White Shoulder. He drank again at Áth Luain, and left Finnbennach's loins there. Hence the name Áth Luain, the Ford of the Loins. At Iraird Cuillenn he let a great bellow out of him that was heard all over the province. He drank again at Tromma, where Finnbennach's liver fell from his horns. Hence the name Tromma, Liver. He went then to Éten Tairb, where he rested his brow against the hill. Hence the name Éten Tairb, the Bull's Brow, in Muirthemne Plain. Then he went by the Midluachair Road to Cuib, where he used to dwell with the dry cows of Dáire, and he tore up the ground there. Hence the name Gort mBúraig, Trench Field. Then he went on and fell dead at the ridge between Ulster and Uí Echach. That place is now called Druim Tairb, Bull Ridge.

Ailill and Medb made a peace with the Ulstermen and Cú Chulainn. For seven years after that no one was killed in battle between them. The men of Connacht went back to their own country, and the men of Ulster returned in triumph to Emain Macha.

Early Irish Verse

Although copied by clerics in a world of written manuscripts, *The Táin Bó Cuailnge* looks backward to an age of oral tales about legendary heroes and heroines, many of them still closely linked to the native gods and goddesses of pre-Christian Ireland. The following samples of Irish verse from the ninth and tenth centuries suggest some of the complex but enormously fruitful interactions of those native Irish traditions and the new Christian culture.

Ireland began to be Christianized from the mid-fifth century, but Christianity came to Ireland more by genuine and gradual conversion than by the point of a sword. The learned monks and hermits, well established by the ninth and tenth centuries, encountered far more disruption from the raids of Vikings, beginning in 795 B.C.E., than from surviving Irish pre-Christian cultures. Instead, the ancient native dynasties of learned poets, genealogists, and diviners interacted with the new learning of Latin Christianity. Indeed, Saint Columba (c. 521–597) was partly educated by the *fili* Gemmán, the chief poet of Leinster. (*Fili*, plural *filid*, was the highest class of poet in medieval Ireland.) One of Columba's few returns to Ireland after founding his monastery on the isle of Iona was to defend the native poets from clerical forces that wanted them suppressed. In fact we know that many monks were also vernacular poets; and conversely, secular *filid* wrote praise poems to clerics, most famously to Saint Columba himself. Their cultural prestige and preservation of ancient learning continued, even as their religious and quasi-magical activity dwindled. All this led to a rich and persistent convergence (not without competition) of native and Christian elements in medieval Irish culture.

The figure addressed in *To Crinog*, for instance, is at once a wise crone—a traditional figure of initiation—and a book of Christian wisdom, perhaps a Latin primer. Irish myths report instruction in craft or battle by a wise woman, with whom the apprentice also enjoys physical intimacy (as a youthful Cú Chulainn had with the woman warrior Scáthach), although in this poem Crinog's teaching is explicitly chaste. Monks also began using the resources of Irish poetry to record religious study—the Word, to which their faith was so attached—and the making of written books. *Pangur the Cat* explores the solitary pleasures of the monk or hermit, and the challenge of textual interpretation, in contrast with the more heroic mold of many saints' lives or contemporary heroic tales: "Fame comes second to the peace/Of study. . . ." *Writing in the Wood* is a poem of labor, but undertaken in a holiday spirit, away from the monastic scriptorium where books were usually copied.

Other voices look to the legendary past with open regret. *A Grave Marked with Ogam* evokes a disastrous battle in which the speaker, now quite alone, fought on the losing side. *Findabair Remembers Fróech* is a yearning lament for a lost lover. It is quite unconnected to monasticism, but a similar history of passions that efface the present also informs the powerful monologue *The Old Woman of Beare*; there the contrast also involves the shift from a lost world of secular heroes to declining mortality in a convent. Her name, and the memories she has of past generations and eras, may link the Old Woman of Beare to a mythic figure of sovereignty, rejuvenated by each man to whom she gives her body and her powers. At the same time, she is a voice of wise lament on the passing of greater times (not unlike many moments in *Beowulf*); she is a rich concubine who has lost her beauty and become a nun; and—in a land where women's powers were usually quite limited—she is a woman who has gone her own way and made choices that now leave her poor, unprotected, and rueful, but not regretful. *The Old Woman of Beare* records the unresolved dialogue between the era of heroic legend and the era of Christ, between joys mortal and immortal: "for Mary's Son / too soon redeems."

The Voyage of Máel Dúin shows us, perhaps most clearly of all, how native secular genres and attitudes persisted, but were revised, under the influence of Christianity. Both in structure and detail, the *Voyage* echoes the *immrana*, native tales of wondrous voyages to otherworldly islands, places both of terror and sybaritic pleasures. Máel Dúin and his companions visit many such islands, but they also pause at the island homes of four Christian hermits, themselves not without magical qualities. Máel Dúin's own genealogy mirrors this meeting of traditions; he is the illegitimate child of a nun and a great warrior. His father has been killed by raiders, he learns, and his voyage is a quest to find them and take obligatory vengeance in the heroic style. The fourth hermit he meets, though, convinces Máel Dúin to forgive his father's murderers and return home in peace. At the levels of genre, genealogy, and narrative, then, the *Voyage* enacts at once a preservation and revision of native traditions under Christian influence.

To Crinog[1]

Crinog, melodious is your song.
Though young no more you are still bashful.
We two grew up together in Niall's[2] northern land,
When we used to sleep together in tranquil slumber.

---

1. Translated by Kuno Meyer.   2. Legendary Irish king, whose dynasty ruled Ulster and other areas.

5   That was my age when you slept with me.
    O peerless lady of pleasant wisdom:
    A pure-hearted youth, lovely without a flaw,
    A gentle boy of seven sweet years.

    We lived in the great world of Banva[3]
10 Without sullying soul or body,
    My flashing eyes full of love for you,
    Like a poor innocent untempted by evil.

    Your just counsel is ever ready,
    Wherever we are to seek it:
15 To love your penetrating wisdom is better
    Than glib discourse with a king.

    Since then you have slept with four men after me,
    Without folly or falling away:
    I know, I hear it on all sides,
20 You are pure, without sin from man.

    At last, after weary wanderings,
    You have come to me again,
    Darkness of age has settled on your face:
    Sinless your life draws near its end.

25 You are still dear to me, faultless one,
    You shall have welcome from me without stint:
    You will not let us be drowned in torment;
    We will earnestly practice devotion with you.

    The lasting world is full of your fame.
30 Far and wide you have wandered on every track:
    If every day we followed your ways,
    We should come safe into the presence of dread God.

    You leave an example and a bequest
    To every one in this world,
35 You have taught us by your life:
    Earnest prayer to God is no fallacy.

    Then may God grant us peace and happiness!
    May the countenance of the King
    Shine brightly on us
40 When we leave behind us our withered bodies.

Pangur the Cat[1]

    Myself and Pangur, cat and sage
    Go each about our business;
    I harass my beloved page,
    He his mouse.

---

3. An early name for Ireland   1. Translated by Eavan Boland.

5   Fame comes second to the peace
       Of study, a still day.
       Unenvious, Pangur's choice
       Is child's play.

       Neither bored, both hone
10   At home a separate skill,
       Moving, after hours alone,
       To the kill.

       On my cell wall here,
       His sight fixes. Burning.
15   Searching. My old eyes peer
       At new learning.

       His delight when his claws
       Close on his prey
       Equals mine, when sudden clues
20   Light my way.

       So we find by degrees
       Peace in solitude,
       Both of us—solitaries—
       Have each the trade

25   He loves. Pangur, never idle
       Day or night
       Hunts mice. I hunt each riddle
       From dark to light.

Writing in the Wood[1]

       Overwatched by woodland wall
            merles make melody full well;
       above my book—lined, lettered—
            birds twittered a soothing spell.

5   Cuckoos call clear—fairest phrase—
            cloaked in grays, from leafy leas.
       Lord's love, what blessings show' ring!
            Good to write 'neath tow' ring trees.

The Viking Terror[1]

       Bitter is the wind to-night,
       It tosses the ocean's white hair:
       To-night I fear not the fierce warriors of Norway
       Coursing on the Irish Sea.

---

1. Translated by Ruth P. M. Lehmann. This translation
aims to reproduce much of the complex internal rhyme
and end-rhyme, assonance, and alliteration of the original; it takes minor liberties with the literal sense.

1. Translated by Kuno Meyer.

The Old Woman of Beare[1]

The ebbing that has come on me
is not the ebbing of the sea.
What knows the sea of grief or pain?—
Happy tide will flood again.

5   I am the hag of Bui and Beare[2]—
the richest cloth I used to wear.
Now with meanness and with thrift
I even lack a change of shift.

It is wealth
10   and not men that you love.
In the time that we lived
it was men that we loved.

Those whom we loved, the plains
we ride today bear their names;
15   gaily they feasted with laughter
nor boasted thereafter.

To-day they gather in the tax
but, come to handing out, are lax;
the very little they bestow
20   be sure that everyone will know.

Chariots there were, and we
had horses bred for victory.
Such things came in a great wave;
pray for the dead kings who gave.

25   Bitterly does my body race
seeking its destined place;
now let God's Son come and take
that which he gave of his grace.

These arms, these scrawny things you see,
30   scarce merit now their little joy
when lifted up in blessing
    over sweet student boy.

These arms you see,
    these bony scrawny things,
35   had once more loving craft
    embracing kings.

When Maytime comes
    the girls out there are glad,

1. Translated by James Carney. The speaker's name, "caillech," "veiled one," can mean old woman, hag, widow, and nun. The hag figure has resonance with teachers of crafts and wisdom, as well as early mythic female figures of sovereignty and initiation, rejuvenated when they are embraced by a chosen hero.
2. A peninsula in Munster, in the far southwest of Ireland, or a tiny island off its coast. "Bui" may be the small nearby island of Dursey.

and I, old hag, old bones,
40   alone am sad.

No wedding wether killed for me,
an end to all coquetry;
a pitiful veil I wear
on thin and faded hair.

45   Well do I wear
plain veil on faded hair;
many colors I wore
and we feasting before.

Were it not for Feven's plain[3]
50   I'd envy nothing old;
I have a shroud of aged skin,
     Feven's crop is gold.

Ronan's city there in Bregon[4]
and in Feven the royal standing stone,
55   why are their cheeks not weathered,
     only mine alone?

Winter comes and the sea will rise
     crying out with welcoming wave;
but no welcome for me from nobleman's son
60   or from son of a slave.

What they do now, I know, I know:
     to and fro they row and race;
but they who once sailed Alma's ford[5]
     rest in a cold place.

65   It's more than a day
     since I sailed youth's sea,
beauty's years not devoured
     and sap flowing free.

It's more than a day, God's truth,
70   that I'm lacking in youth;
I wrap myself up in the sun—
I know Old Age, I see him come.

There was a summer of youth
     nor was autumn the worst of the year,
75   but winter is doom
     and its first days are here.

God be thanked, I had joy in my youth.
     I swear that it's true,

---

3. In inland Munster; connected with power and wealth.   5. An unidentified site.
4. Probably an 8th-century king who ruled in the area of
Feven.

if I hadn't leapt the wall
    this old cloak still were not new.

The Lord on the world's broad back
    threw a lovely cloak of green;
first fleecy, then it's bare,
    and again the fleece is seen.

All beauty is doomed.
    God! Can it be right
to kneel in a dark prayer-house
    after feasting by candlelight?

I sat with kings drinking wine and mead
    for many a day,
and now, a crew of shriveled hags,
    we toast in whey.

Be this my feast, these cups of whey;
    and let me always count as good
the vexing things that come of Christ
    who stayed God's ire with flesh and blood.

The mind is not so clear,
    there's mottling of age on my cloak,
gray hairs sprouting through skin,
    I am like a stricken oak.

For deposit on heaven
    of right eye bereft,
I conclude the purchase
    with loss of the left.

Great wave of flood
    and wave of ebb and lack!
What flooding tide brings in
    the ebbing tide takes back.

Great wave of flood
    and wave of ebbing sea,
the two of them I know
    for both have washed on me.

Great wave of flood
    brings no step to silent cellar floor;
a hand fell on all the company
    that feasted there before.

The Son of Mary knew right well
    he'd walk that floor one day;
grasping I was, but never sent
    man hungry on his way.

Pity Man!—
    If only like the elements he could

come out of ebbing in the very way
    that he comes out of flood.

125   Christ left with me on loan
        flood tide of youth, and now it seems
there's ebb and misery, for Mary's Son
    too soon redeems.

Blessed the island in the great sea
130   with happy ebb and happy flood.
For me, for me alone, no hope:
    the ebbing is for good.

Findabair Remembers Fróech[1]

This, thereafter, is what Findabair used to say,
seeing anything beautiful:
it would be more beautiful for her
to see Fróech crossing the dark water,
5   body for shining whiteness,
hair for loveliness,
face for shapeliness,
eye for blue-grayness,
a well-born youth
10   without fault or blemish,
face broad above, narrow below,
and he straight and perfect,
the red branch with its berries
between throat and white face.
15   This is what Findabair used to say:
She had never seen
anything a half
or a third as beautiful as he.

A Grave Marked with Ogam[1]

Ogam in stone on grave stead,
    where men sometimes tread on course;
king's son of Ireland cut low,
    hit by spear's throw hurled from horse.

5   Cairpre let a quick cast fly
        from high on horseback, stout steed;

1. Translated by James Carney. Findabair (FIN-a-wer) was a daughter of Medb and Ailill (central characters in the Táin). She falls in love with the famously handsome warrior Fróech (Froich, guttural -ch) but her parents resist their marriage. When Fróech is killed by Cú Chulainn, Findabair ultimately dies of heartbreak.
1. Translated by Ruth P. M. Lehmann. This translation again aims to reproduce much of the rhyme, assonance, and alliteration of the original; it takes minor liberties with the literal sense. Ogam is the earliest Irish alphabet, used before the Latin alphabet was applied to Irish. It is a system of long lines marked with short dashes, cross-hatches, and small figures. Most often found in inscriptions or associated with secret messages and divination, it is too awkward an alphabet for writing longer texts.

ere he wearied his hand struck,
    cut down Oscar, cruel deed.[2]

10   Oscar hurled a hard throw, crude,
    like a lion, rude his rage;
killed Con's kin, Cairpre proud,
    ere they bowed on battle stage.

Tall, keen, cruel were the lads
    who found their death in the strife,
15   just before their weapons met;
    more were left in death than life.

I myself was in the fight
    on right, south of Gabair green;
twice fifty warriors I killed,
20   my skilled hand slew them, clear, clean.

I'd play for pirates in bale,
    the while the trail I must tread,
in holy holt boar I'd fell,
    or would snatch the snell bird's egg.

25   That ogam there in the stone,
    around which the slain fall prone,
if Finn the fighter could come,
    long would he think on ogam.

from The Voyage of Máel Dúin[1]

They went to an island with a high enclosure of the color of a swan
In which they found a noble pavilion, a dwelling of brightness.
Silver brooches, gold-hilted swords, large necklets,
Beautiful beds, excellent food, golden rows.
5   Strengthening delicate food in the midst of the house, sound savory liquor;
With fierce greediness upon a high pillar a seemly very quick cat.
It leapt then over the pillars, a speedy feat;
Not very big was the guardian of the meat, it was not repulsive.
One of the three foster brothers of the powerful chief, it was a
    courageous action,
10   Takes with him—it was a proud ounce-weight—a golden necklet.[2]
The fiery claw of the mysterious cat rent his body,
The guilty body of the unfortunate man was burnt ash.
The large necklet was brought back, it created friendship again,
The ashes of the unfortunate man were cast into the ocean.

* * *

2. Characters from the "Finn Cycle," a group of tales even more popular than the Ulster Cycle and its central epic the *Táin.* Oscar is Finn's grandson and the cycle's greatest warrior. He and Cairpre, high king of Ireland, kill one another at the Battle of Gabair (GAV-*ar*), which ends the power of Finn's people.

1. Verse redaction of chs. 11, 19, and 34, translated by H. P. A. Oskamp. Máel Dúin (*Moil Doon*), the illegitimate son of a nun and a warrior, is brought up by a queen. Learning at the same time of his father's death, he sets out on a sea journey to find and take vengeance on his father's killers. Máel Dúin and his companions came upon a series of islands, each with its marvel or danger.

2. Máel Dúin's foster brothers had swum to his boat as it departed, violating a druid's prohibition; none return from the journey.

Then they saw in a small island a psalm-singing old man;
Excellent was his dignified noble appearance, holy were his words.
Hair of his noble head—delightful the bright covering—a garment
    with whiteness,
A brilliant large mantle; bright-covered coloring covering was around him.
5   The excellent chief said to him: "Whence were you sent?"
"I shall not hide from you what you ask: from Ireland.
My pilgrimage brought me without any penance
In the body of a boat over the swift sea; I did not regret it.
My prowed boat came apart under me on the very violent sea;
10   A bitter, twisting, active, big-waved course put me ashore.
I cut a sod from the gray-green surface of my fatherland;
To the place in which I am a breeze brought me: small is the fame.
The star-strong King established under me out of the miraculous sod
A delightful island with the color of a seagull over the dark sea.
15   A foot was added to the island every year—
It is a victorious achievement—and a tree above the sea's crest.
A clear well came to me—everlasting food—
By the grace of angels, sound beautiful food—a holy gathering.
You will all reach your countries, a fruitful company along the ocean's track,
20   Though it will be a long journey; all except one man."[3]
By the grace of the angels to each single man of them
Came a complete half-loaf and a noble morsel of fish as provision.

* * *

Then they went to an island full of flocks, a famed halting-place,
A victorious achievement; they found there an Irish falcon.
Then they rowed after it, swift to encounter,
Over the crest of the waves to an island in which was their enemy.
5   They made peace there with the swift Máel Dúin, in the presence of
    every swift man;
After true pledging they went to their country, a prosperous journey.
Many remarkable things, many marvels, many mysteries
Was their pleasant story, as swift Máel Dúin told.
A long life and peace while I am in the famous world,
10   May I have cheerful company with virtue from my King of Kings.
When I die may I then reach heaven past the fierce, violent host of demons
In the Kingdom of angels, a famous affair, a very high dwelling.

+⊷ ⋈⊹⊠ ⊷+

Judith

The Old English poem *Judith*, concerning the legendary beheader of the Assyrian general
Holofernes, has been seen most often as a heroic poem, like *Beowulf*, which it immediately follows in the same unique manuscript. It expresses the same fierce love of battle, and uses the
same heroic poetic conventions—archaic diction, formulas, and themes. *Judith* achieves ironic

---

3. One of the three foster brothers still remains with the voyagers at this point. A later hermit prophesies, "though you
will meet your enemies, you will not slay them."

effects, however, by placing these conventions in unexpected contexts—for instance, calling Holofernes a "brave man" as he hides behind a net to spy on his retainers. Similarly, it presents his raucous feast as an antifeast—a symbol of misrule rather than of social harmony—and his henchmen as a parody of the traditional band of loyal retainers, as they flee in terror to save their lives.

In addition to *Beowulf*, *Judith* has affinities with Old English poems based on the Old Testament, like *Exodus* and *Daniel*, whose heroes devote their military zeal to the glory of God. Like them, it assumes the timeless perspective of Christian salvation history, so that the apparent anachronisms of Judith's praying to the Trinity or Christ's abhorring Holofernes are entirely appropriate. Based on the Book of Judith in the Latin Bible, which the Anglo-Saxons considered canonical, this poem, like many others in Old English, exists only in fragmentary form. The original audience would have known that Holofernes had entered Judea to besiege the Hebrew city of Bethulia. At the point where the Old English poem begins, the "wickedly promiscuous" general, after his drunken feast, orders the beautiful Hebrew maiden Judith to be brought to his bed. Finding him stretched out in a drunken stupor, she first prays for help and then decapitates him. She thereupon returns to her camp, brandishing the head and exhorting the Hebrews to battle with a stirring speech, which inspires them to victory over the leaderless Assyrians.

The poem does not simply express the timeless Christian theme of the struggle of God's people against the pagans, but also comments on the immediate social and historical context of its time. It seems to reflect the resistance of the Christian Anglo-Saxons against the pagan Danes during the ninth-century invasions, perhaps exaggerating the Assyrians' drunkenness in order to comment on the notorious Danish drinking habits. Furthermore, Holofernes' plan to rape Judith may evoke the rape of Anglo-Saxon women by Danish soldiers in the presence of their husbands and fathers.

Judith's identity as a woman warrior also puts the poem in the social context of the time. The poem's emphasis on her power, in contrast to the biblical source's emphasis on God's power to operate through the hand of a mere woman, reflects the relatively strong role of aristocratic women in England before the Norman Conquest. (Other Old English poems that reflect this strength include *Juliana*, a typical saint's legend whose heroine is martyred while resisting a Roman general's advances, and *Elene*, whose heroine—Constantine's mother Saint Helen—was believed to have discovered the true cross.) Finally, Judith's heroic action has been seen as an inversion of the rape which Holofernes himself intends to commit upon her, as, seeing him unconscious on his bed, she "took the heathen man by the hair, dragged him ignominiously towards her with her hands, and carefully laid out the debauched and odious man."

Judith[1]

. . . She was suspicious of gifts in this wide world. So she readily met with a helping hand from the glorious Prince when she had most need of the supreme Judge's support and that he, the Prime Mover, should protect her against this supreme danger. The illustrious Father in the skies granted her request in this because she always had firm faith in the Almighty.

I have heard, then, that Holofernes cordially issued invitations to a banquet and had dishes splendidly prepared with all sorts of wonderful things, and to it this lord over men summoned all the most senior functionaries. With great alacrity those shield-wielders complied and came wending to the puissant prince, the nation's chief

1. Prose translation by S. A. J. Bradley.

person. That was on the fourth day after Judith, shrewd of purpose, the woman of elfin beauty first visited him.

So they went and settled down to the feasting, insolent men to the wine-drinking, all those brash armored warriors, his confederates in evil. Deep bowls were borne continually along the benches there and brimming goblets and pitchers as well to the hall-guests. They drank it down as doomed men, those celebrated shield-wielders—though the great man, the awesome lord over evils, did not foresee it. Then Holofernes, the bountiful lord of his men, grew merry with tippling. He laughed and bawled and roared and made a racket so that the children of men could hear from far away how the stern-minded man bellowed and yelled, insolent and flown with mead, and frequently exhorted the guests on the benches to enjoy themselves well. So the whole day long the villain, the stern-minded dispenser of treasure, plied his retainers with wine until they lay unconscious, the whole of his retinue drunk as though they had been struck dead, drained of every faculty.

Thus the men's elder commanded the hall-guests to be ministered to until the dark night closed in on the children of men. Then, being wickedly promiscuous, he commanded the blessed virgin, decked with bracelets and adorned with rings, to be fetched in a hurry to his bed. The attendants promptly did as their master, the ruler of armored warriors, required them. They went upon the instant to the guest-hall where they found the astute Judith, and then the shield-wielding warriors speedily conducted the noble virgin to the lofty pavilion where the great man always rested of a night, Holofernes, abhorrent to the Savior.

There was an elegant all-golden fly-net there, hung about the commandant's bed so that the debauched hero of his soldiers could spy through on every one of the sons of men who came in there, but no one of humankind on him, unless, brave man, he summoned one of his evilly renowned soldiers to go nearer to him for a confidential talk.

Hastily, then, they brought the shrewd lady to bed. Then they went, stout-hearted heroes, to inform their master that the holy woman had been brought to his pavilion. The man of mark, lord over cities, then grew jovial of mood: he meant to defile the noble lady with filth and with pollution. To that heaven's Judge, Shepherd of the celestial multitude, would not consent but rather he, the Lord, Ruler of the hosts, prevented him from the act.

So this species of fiend, licentious, debauched, went with a crowd of his men to seek his bed—where he was to lose his life, swiftly, within the one night: he had then come to his violent end upon earth, such as he had previously deserved, the stern-minded prince over men, while he lived in this world under the roof of the skies.

Then the great man collapsed in the midst of his bed, so drunk with wine that he was oblivious in mind of any of his designs. The soldiers stepped out of his quarters with great alacrity, wine-glutted men who had put the perjurer, the odious persecutor, to bed for the last time.

Then the glorious handmaid of the Savior was sorely preoccupied as to how she might most easily deprive the monster of his life before the sordid fellow, full of corruption, awoke. Then the ringletted girl, the Maker's maiden, grasped a sharp sword, hardy in the storms of battle, and drew it from its sheath with her right hand. Then she called by name upon the Guardian of heaven, the Savior of all the world's inhabitants, and spoke these words:

"God of beginnings, Spirit of comfort, Son of the universal Ruler, I desire to entreat you for your grace upon me in my need, Majesty of the Trinity. My heart is now sorely anguished and my mind troubled and much afflicted with anxieties. Give me, Lord of heaven, victory and true faith so that with this sword I may hew down this dispenser of violent death. Grant me my safe deliverance, stern-minded Prince over men. Never have I had greater need of your grace. Avenge now, mighty Lord, illustrious Dispenser of glory, that which is so bitter to my mind, so burning in my breast."

Then the supreme Judge at once inspired her with courage—as he does every single man dwelling here who looks to him for help with resolve and with true faith. So hope was abundantly renewed in the holy woman's heart. She then took the heathen man firmly by his hair, dragged him ignominiously towards her with her hands and carefully laid out the debauched and odious man so as she could most easily manage the wretch efficiently. Then the ringletted woman struck the malignant-minded enemy with the gleaming sword so that she sliced through half his neck, so that he lay unconscious, drunk and mutilated.

He was not then yet dead, not quite lifeless. In earnest then the courageous woman struck the heathen dog a second time so that his head flew off on to the floor. His foul carcass lay behind, dead; his spirit departed elsewhere beneath the deep ground and was there prostrated and chained in torment ever after, coiled about by snakes, trussed up in tortures and cruelly prisoned in hellfire after his going hence. Never would he have cause to hope, engulfed in darkness, that he might get out of that snake-infested prison, but there he shall remain forever to eternity henceforth without end in that murky abode, deprived of the joys of hope.

Judith then had won outstanding glory in the struggle according as God the Lord of heaven, who gave her the victory, granted her. Then the clever woman swiftly put the harrier's head, all bloody, into the bag in which her attendant, a pale-cheeked woman, one proved excellent in her ways, had brought food there for them both; and then Judith put it, all gory, into her hands for her discreet servant to carry home. From there the two women then proceeded onwards, emboldened by courage, until they had escaped, brave, triumphant virgins, from among the army, so that they could clearly see the walls of the beautiful city, Bethulia, shining. Then the ring-adorned women hurried forward on their way until, cheered at heart, they had reached the rampart gate.

There were soldiers, vigilant men, sitting and keeping watch in the fortress just as Judith the artful-minded virgin had enjoined the despondent folk when she set out on her mission, courageous lady. Now she had returned, their darling, to her people, and quickly then the shrewd woman summoned one of the men to come out from the spacious city to meet her and speedily to let them in through the gate of the rampart; and to the victorious people she spoke these words:

"I can tell you something worthy of thanksgiving: that you need no longer grieve in spirit. The ordaining Lord, the Glory of kings, is gracious to you. It has been revealed abroad through the world that dazzling and glorious success is impending for you and triumph is granted you over those injuries which you long have suffered."

Then the citizens were merry when they heard how the saintly woman spoke across the high rampart. The army was in ecstasies and the people rushed towards the fortress gate, men and women together, in flocks and droves; in throngs and troops they surged forward and ran towards the handmaid of the Lord, both old and young in their thousands. The heart of each person in that city of mead-halls was exhilarated when they realized that Judith had returned home; and then with humility they hastily let her in.

Then the clever woman ornamented with gold directed her attentive servant-girl to unwrap the harrier's head and to display the bloody object to the citizens as proof of how she had fared in the struggle. The noble lady then spoke to the whole populace:

"Victorious heroes, leaders of the people; here you may openly gaze upon the head of that most odious heathen warrior, the dead Holofernes, who perpetrated upon us the utmost number of violent killings of men and painful miseries, and who intended to add to it even further, but God did not grant him longer life so that he might plague us with afflictions. I took his life, with God's help. Now I want to urge each man among these citizens, each shield-wielding soldier, that you immediately get yourselves ready for battle. Once the God of beginnings, the steadfastly gracious King, has sent the radiant light from the east, go forth bearing shields, bucklers in front of your breasts and mail-coats and shining helmets into the ravagers' midst; cut down the commanders, the doomed leaders, with gleaming swords. Your enemies are sentenced to death and you shall have honor and glory in the fight according as the mighty Lord has signified to you by my hand."

Then an army of brave and keen men was quickly got ready for the battle. Renowned nobles and their companions advanced; they carried victory-banners; beneath their helms the heroes issued forth straight into battle from out of the holy city upon the very dawning of the day. Shields clattered, loudly resonated. At that, the lean wolf in the wood rejoiced, and that bird greedy for carrion, the black raven. Both knew that the men of that nation meant to procure them their fill among those doomed to die; but in their wake flew the eagle, eager for food, speckled-winged; the dark-feathered, hook-beaked bird sang a battle-chant.

On marched the soldiers, warriors to the warfare, protected by their shields, hollowed linden bucklers, they who a while previously had been suffering the abuse of aliens, the blasphemy of heathens. This was strictly repaid to all the Assyrians in the spear-fight once the Israelites under their battle-ensigns had reached the camp. Firmly entrenched, they vigorously let fly from the curved bow showers of darts, arrows, the serpents of battle. Loudly the fierce fighting-men roared and sent spears into their cruel enemies' midst. The heroes, the in-dwellers of the land, were enraged against the odious race. Stern of mood they advanced; hardened of heart they roughly roused their drink-stupefied enemies of old. With their hands, retainers unsheathed from scabbards bright-ornamented swords, proved of edge, and set about the Assyrian warriors in earnest, intending to smite them. Of that army they spared not one of the men alive, neither the lowly nor the mighty, whom they could overpower.

Thus in the hour of morn those comrades in arms the whole time harried the aliens until those who were their adversaries, the chief sentries of the army, acknowledged that the Hebrew people were showing them very intensive sword-play. They went to inform the most senior officers of this by word of mouth and they roused those warriors and fearfully announced to them in their drunken stupor the dreadful news, the terror of the morning, the frightful sword-encounter.

Then, I have heard, those death-doomed heroes quickly shook off their sleep and thronged in flocks, demoralized men, to the pavilion of the debauched Holofernes. They meant to give their lord warning of battle at once, before the terror and the force of the Hebrews descended upon him; all supposed that the men's leader and that beautiful woman were together in the handsome tent, the noble Judith and the lecher, fearsome and ferocious. Yet there was not one of the nobles who dared awaken the warrior to inquire how it had turned out for the soldier with the holy virgin, the woman of the Lord.

The might of the Hebrews, their army, was drawing closer; vehemently they fought with tough and bloody weapons and violently they indemnified with gleaming swords their former quarrels and old insults: in that day's work the Assyrians' repute was withered, their arrogance abased. The men stood around their lord's tent, extremely agitated and growing gloomier in spirit. Then all together they began to cough and loudly make noises and, having no success, to chew the grist with their teeth, suffering agonies. The time of their glory, good fortune and valorous doings was at an end. The nobles thought to awaken their lord and friend; they succeeded not at all.

Then one of the soldiers belatedly and tardily grew so bold that he ventured pluckily into the pavilion as necessity compelled him. Then he found his lord lying pallid on the bed, deprived of his spirit, dispossessed of life. Straightway then he fell chilled to the ground, and distraught in mind he began to tear his hair and his clothing alike and he uttered these words to the soldiers who were waiting there miserably outside:

"Here is made manifest our own perdition, and here it is imminently signalled that the time is drawn near, along with its tribulations, when we must perish and be destroyed together in the strife. Here, hacked by the sword, decapitated, lies our lord."

Then distraught in mind they threw down their weapons; demoralized they went scurrying away in flight. The nation magnified in strength attacked them in the rear until the greatest part of the army lay on the field of victory levelled by battle, hacked by swords, as a treat for the wolves and a joy to the carrion-greedy birds. Those who survived fled from the linden spears of their foes. In their wake advanced the troop of Hebrews, honored with the victory and glorified in the judgment: the Lord God, the almighty Lord, had come handsomely to their aid. Swiftly then with their gleaming swords those valiant heroes made an inroad through the thick of their foes; they hacked at targes and sheared through the shield-wall. The Hebrew spear-throwers were wrought up to the fray; the soldiers lusted mightily after a spear-contest on that occasion. There in the dust fell the main part of the muster-roll of the Assyrian nobility, of that odious race. Few survivors reached their native land.

The soldiers of royal renown turned back in retirement amidst carnage and reeking corpses. That was the opportunity for the land's in-dwellers to seize from those most odious foes, their old dead enemies, bloodied booty, resplendent accoutrements, shield and broad sword, burnished helmets, costly treasures. The guardians of their homeland had honorably conquered their enemies on the battlefield and destroyed with swords their old persecutors. In their trail lay dead those who of living peoples had been most inimical to their existence.

Then the whole nation, most famous of races, proud, curled-locked, for the duration of one month were carrying and conveying into the beautiful city, Bethulia, helmets and hip-swords, gray mail-coats, and men's battle-dress ornamented with gold, more glorious treasures than any man among ingenious men can tell. All that the people splendidly gained, brave beneath their banners in the fray, through the shrewd advice of Judith, the courageous woman. As a reward the celebrated spearmen brought back for her from the expedition the sword and the bloodied helmet of Holofernes as well as his huge mail-coat adorned with red gold; and everything the ruthless lord of the warriors owned of riches or personal wealth, of rings and of beautiful treasures, they gave it to that beautiful and resourceful lady.

For all this Judith gave glory to the Lord of hosts who granted her esteem and renown in the realm of earth and likewise too a reward in heaven, the prize of victory in the glory of the sky because she always had true faith in the Almighty. Certainly at the end she did not doubt the reward for which she long had yearned.

For this be glory into eternity to the dear Lord who created the wind and the clouds, the skies and the spacious plains and likewise the cruel seas and the joys of heaven, through his peculiar mercy.

⊷ ⊠◆⊠ ⊶

The Dream of the Rood

The Dream of the Rood is a remarkable tenth-century poem, a mystical dream vision whose narrator tells of his dream that the rood—Christ's cross—appeared to him and told the story of its unwilling role in the crucifixion. The poem is an excellent illustration of how the conventions of Old English heroic poems like *Beowulf* were adapted to the doctrines of Christianity. Christ's Passion is converted into a heroic sacrifice as the cross reports that it watched him—the young hero—strip himself naked, as if preparing for battle, and bravely ascend it. In the same vein, the cross presents itself as a thane (retainer) forced into disloyalty, as it watches—and participates in—the crucifixion, unable to avenge its beloved Lord.

In addition to heroic poetry, *The Dream of the Rood* recalls Old English genres such as the riddle and the elegy. In riddle fashion, the cross asks, "What am I?"—that started as a tree, became an instrument of torture, and am now a beacon of victory, resplendent with jewels. In the manner of elegies like *The Wanderer,* the speaker, stained with sin, presents himself as a lonely exile whose companions have left him and gone to heaven. After his vision, he resolves to seek the fellowship of his heavenly Lord and his former companions, which he pictures as taking place in a celestial mead hall: "the home of joy and happiness, / where the people of God are seated at the feast / in eternal bliss."

One of the most striking poetic effects of *The Dream of the Rood* is its focus on the Incarnation, God's taking on human flesh. The poet often juxtaposes references to Christ's humanity and divinity in the same line, thereby achieving a powerful effect of paradox, as when he tells of the approach of "the young warrior, God Almighty." It is noteworthy that the aspect of Christ's humanity which the poet stresses is the heroism rather than the pathos which was to become so prominent in later medieval poetry and art. This heroism provides a context for a cryptic passage at the end of the poem, where the dreamer refers to Christ's "journey" to bring "those who before suffered burning" victoriously to heaven. In *The Harrowing of Hell* (based on the apocryphal Gospel of Nicodemus), Christ heroically freed the virtuous Old Testament patriarchs from damnation and led them to eternal bliss.

The fame of *The Dream of the Rood* appears to have been widespread in its own time. Our knowledge of it comes from three sources: the huge stone Ruthwell Cross in southern Scotland built in the eighth century (on which a short version is inscribed in runic letters); the silver Brussels Cross, made in England in the tenth century; and the manuscript found in Vercelli in northern Italy, also written in the tenth century—the only complete version of the poem. These varied locations are a testament to the wide influence of Anglo-Saxon scholars, not only in the British Isles but on the Continent as well.

The Dream of the Rood[1]

> Listen! I will describe the best of dreams
> which I dreamed in the middle of the night
> when, far and wide, all men slept.
> It seemed that I saw a wondrous tree
> 5   soaring into the air, surrounded by light,
> the brightest of crosses; that emblem was entirely
> cased in gold; beautiful jewels
> were strewn around its foot, just as five
> studded the cross-beam. All the angels of God,

---

1. Translated by Kevin Crossley-Holland.

The Ruthwell Cross, north side, top section, 7th–8th century. Preserved in a church in southern Scotland, this 18-foot stone cross is carved with many Christian scenes, including this depiction of Saint John the Baptist, bearded and holding the Lamb of God. The Latin inscription beneath the saint is written in runes—the traditional Germanic alphabet, used for ritualistic purposes. Runic inscriptions elsewhere on the cross reproduce portions of *The Dream of the Rood* in Old English. Still other inscriptions are in Latin and employ the Roman alphabet. Thus, like *The Dream of the Rood* itself, whose Christlike hero resembles a Germanic warrior, the Ruthwell Cross illustrates the fusion of Mediterranean and Germanic traditions in Anglo-Saxon Christian culture.

10   fair creations, guarded it. That was no cross
of a criminal, but holy spirits and men on earth
watched over it there—the whole glorious universe.

Wondrous was the tree of victory, and I was stained
by sin, stricken by guilt. I saw this glorious tree
15   joyfully gleaming, adorned with garments,
decked in gold; the tree of the Ruler
was rightly adorned with rich stones;
yet through that gold I could see the agony
once suffered by wretches, for it had bled
20   down the right hand side. Then I was afflicted,
frightened at this sight; I saw that sign often change
its clothing and hue, at times dewy with moisture,
stained by flowing blood, at times adorned with treasure.
Yet I lay there for a long while

25 and gazed sadly at the Savior's cross
until I heard it utter words;
the finest of trees began to speak:
"I remember the morning a long time ago
that I was felled at the edge of the forest
30 and severed from my roots. Strong enemies seized me,
bade me hold up their felons on high,
made me a spectacle. Men shifted me
on their shoulders and set me on a hill.
Many enemies fastened me there. I saw the Lord of Mankind
35 hasten with such courage to climb upon me.
I dared not bow or break there
against my Lord's wish, when I saw the surface
of the earth tremble. I could have felled
all my foes, yet I stood firm.
40 Then the young warrior, God Almighty,
stripped Himself, firm and unflinching. He climbed
upon the cross, brave before many, to redeem mankind.
I quivered when the hero clasped me,
yet I dared not bow to the ground,
45 fall to the earth. I had to stand firm.
A rood was I raised up; I bore aloft the mighty King,
the Lord of Heaven. I dared not stoop.
They drove dark nails into me; dire wounds are there to see,
the gaping gashes of malice; I dared not injure them.
50 They insulted us both together; I was drenched in the blood
that streamed from the Man's side after He set His spirit free.

"On that hill I endured many grievous trials;
I saw the God of Hosts stretched
on the rack; darkness covered the corpse
55 of the Ruler with clouds, His shining radiance.
Shadows swept across the land, dark shapes
under the clouds. All creation wept,
wailed for the death of the King; Christ was on the cross.
Yet men hurried eagerly to the Prince
60 from afar; I witnessed all that too.
I was oppressed with sorrow, yet humbly bowed to the hands of men,
and willingly. There they lifted Him from His heavy torment,
they took Almighty God away. The warriors left me standing there,
stained with blood; sorely was I wounded by the sharpness of spear-shafts.
65 They laid Him down, limb-weary; they stood at the corpse's head,
they beheld there the Lord of Heaven; and there He rested for a while,
worn-out after battle. And then they began to build a sepulchre;
under his slayers' eyes, they carved it from the gleaming stone,
and laid therein the Lord of Victories. Then, sorrowful at dusk,
70 they sang a dirge before they went, weary,
from their glorious Prince; He rested in the grave alone.
But we still stood there, weeping blood,

long after the song of the warriors
had soared to heaven; the corpse grew cold,
75   the fair human house of the soul. Then our enemies
began to fell us; that was a terrible fate.
They buried us in a deep pit; but friends
and followers of the Lord found me there
and girded me with gold and shimmering silver.

80   "Now, my loved man, you have heard
how I endured bitter anguish
at the hands of evil men. Now the time is come
when men far and wide in this world,
and all this bright creation, bow before me;
85   they pray to this sign. On me the Son of God
suffered for a time; wherefore I now stand on high,
glorious under heaven; and I can heal
all those who stand in awe of me.
Long ago I became the worst of tortures,
90   hated by men, until I opened
to them the true way of life.
Lo! The Lord of Heaven, the Prince of Glory,
honored me over any other tree
just as He, Almighty God, for the sake of mankind
95   honored Mary, His own mother,
before all other women in the world.
Now I command you, my loved man,
to describe your vision to all men;
tell them with words this is the tree of glory
100   on which the Son of God suffered once
for the many sins committed by mankind,
and for Adam's wickedness long ago.
He sipped the drink of death. Yet the Lord rose
with His great strength to deliver man.
105   Then He ascended into heaven. The Lord Himself,
Almighty God, with His host of angels,
will come to the middle-world again
on Domesday to reckon with each man.
Then He who has the power of judgment
110   will judge each man just as he deserves
for the way in which he lived this fleeting life.
No-one then will be unafraid
as to what words the Lord will utter.
Before the assembly, He will ask where that man is
115   who, in God's name, would undergo the pangs of death,
just as He did formerly upon the cross.
Then men will be fearful and give
scant thought to what they say to Christ.
But no-one need be numbed by fear
120   who has carried the best of all signs in his breast;

each soul that has longings to live with the Lord
must search for a kingdom far beyond the frontiers of this world."

Then I prayed to the cross, eager
and light-hearted, although I was alone
125   with my own poor company. My soul
longed for a journey, great yearnings
always tugged at me. Now my hope in this life
is that I can turn to that tree of victory
alone and more often than any other man
130   and honor it fully. These longings master
my heart and mind, and my help comes
from holy cross itself. I have not many friends
of influence on earth; they have journeyed on
from the joys of this world to find the King of Glory,
135   they live in heaven with the High Father,
dwell in splendor. Now I look day by day
for that time when the cross of the Lord,
which once I saw in a dream here on earth,
will fetch me away from this fleeting life
140   and lift me to the home of joy and happiness
where the people of God are seated at the feast
in eternal bliss, and set me down
where I may live in glory unending and share
the joy of the saints. May the Lord be a friend to me,
145   He who suffered once for the sins of men
here on earth on the gallows-tree.
He has redeemed us; He has given life to us,
and a home in heaven.   Hope was renewed,
blessed and blissful, for those who before suffered burning.
150   On that journey the Son was victorious,
strong and successful. When He, Almighty Ruler,
returned with a thronging host of spirits
to God's kingdom, to joy among the angels
and all the saints who lived already
155   in heaven in glory, then their King,
Almighty God, entered His own country.

⇒⊢ PERSPECTIVES ⊣⇐
Ethnic and Religious Encounters

In the centuries of their insurgency and the consolidation of their influence in Britain, the Angles and Saxons negotiated a series of encounters that left them, and England, profoundly transformed. They arrived from the distant coasts of northwest continental Europe as self-conscious foreigners, divided into large tribal groups and often warring among themselves. They were pagans and masters of a great but essentially oral culture. By the end of their dominance, in 1066, they were long-Christianized and increasingly had come to perceive themselves as a single people. Moreover, their conversion involved a new commitment to the practical uses of writing and the talismanic power of the written book, as well as a heightened sense of the conflicting claims and uses of their ancient vernacular and of Latin. They now experienced England as their native place and registered their ancestral geography on the Continent as an area of nostalgic exploration or, equally, the source of hostile invasion.

All this was the work of centuries. It was not an unconscious or "natural" development, however. The passages in this section, in their different ways, offer key moments in the lengthy and complex process by which the Germanic newcomers encountered other peoples, religions, textual cultures, and geographies.

The initial contact between the Germanic invaders and the prior inhabitants of England—Britons, the "Irish" of the northwest, and the Picts—was based on military service which turned into military aggression. Relatively soon, though, and even as their territorial ambitions continued, the Angles and Saxons developed other contacts, especially with the Britons. The British were already Christian, and the Angles and Saxons first came to Christianity through British models if not by British hands. Later, the Anglo-Saxons themselves would face invasion by Vikings, who ultimately settled north of the Humber in the "Danelaw." Much of Asser's *Life of King Alfred* documents Alfred's struggle against Viking raiders.

Though he celebrated Alfred's West Saxon kingship and culture, Asser was himself a Welshman. His presence at Alfred's court is a sign of how Latin learning had declined in the disordered era of Viking incursions; Alfred was obliged to turn to other peoples to restore education in his own realm. The Norwegian trader Ohthere, too, came to Alfred's court even while the King was fending off Viking raiders. Ohthere seems to have sparked lively interest in his own people and their social order, as well as in his visits to what the Anglo-Saxons knew was their ancestral home.

Christianization was also a slow, complex, and incomplete process of acculturation. Bede recounts a number of moments when the differing responses to a single event register the encounters of pagan and Christian, literate and illiterate, and Latin and Germanic traditions. The conversion of King Edwin, for instance, involved not just the King fulfilling a promise made in a vision but also his nobles learning to imagine a new spiritual geography which went far beyond the brief joys of their warrior cohort. In the story of Imma, the magical loosing of a prisoner's chains is seen by some as the effect of an ancient pagan "loosing spell," but by Imma (and Bede's Christian readers) as the effect of masses said for his soul.

Language and literacy equally figure in the conversion of the Angles and Saxons and in the slow emergence of the idea of an "English" people. Imma is freed by the uncanny (and somewhat misdirected) power of the Latin mass. The high level of Bede's own Latin suggests how that language was becoming a cohesive force, at least among clerics. Yet in one of his tenderest stories, Bede tells about the illiterate Caedmon who learned, by divine intervention, to tell biblical stories in vernacular poetry. Bede admits that his Latin version of *Caedmon's Hymn* is inadequte, which suggests that Anglo-Saxon could assume its own place in the operations of the sacred. And Asser celebrates Alfred's childhood love of Saxon poems, laments Alfred's illiteracy, yet tells how the illiterate prince competed for the gift of a book he valued almost as a talisman. Alfred's acquisition of literacy and of Latin is part of his rise to successful kingship, and he caps his own reign with the series of translations that bring crucial texts of Latin Christianity into an Anglo-Saxon that Alfred now seems to see as a unifying national tongue.

Finally, even as some Anglo-Saxons aspire to nationhood, they do so by nostalgic memories of their foreign past, as seen in the information they draw from the Norwegian visitor Ohthere. At the same time, though, they mark themselves off from this geography and see themselves as the sinning victims of invasions that will end their power, just as their own successful invasions had punished and subdued the earlier Britons. This is repeatedly made explicit in *The Anglo-Saxon Chronicle*'s report of the twin battles fought by King Harold against Norwegian aggressors in the North and then against the triumphant Normans in the South. Their sense of nationhood and of being folded into processes of Christian history is clearest as the Chronicler witnesses the close of Anglo-Saxon dominance.

⊛   For additional resources on medieval ethnic and religious encounters, go to *The Longman Anthology of British Literature* Web site at www.myliteraturekit.com.

Bede
672–735

Bede was born on lands belonging to the abbey of Wearmouth-Jarrow. He entered that monastery at the age of seven and never traveled more than seventy-five miles away. Bede is the most enduring product of the golden age of Northumbrian monasticism. In the generations just preceding his, a series of learned abbots had brought Roman liturgical practices and monastic habits to Wearmouth-Jarrow, as well as establishing there the best library in England. Out of this settled life and disciplined religious culture Bede created a diverse body of writings that are learned both in scholarly research and in the purity of their Latin. They include biblical commentaries, school texts from spelling to metrics, treatises on the liturgical calendar, hymns, and lives of saints.

Bede's *An Ecclesiastical History of the English People*, completed in 731, marks the apex of his achievement. Given the localism of his life, Bede's grasp of English history is extraordinary, not just in terms of his eager pursuit of information, but equally in his balanced and complex sense of the broad movement of history. Bede registers a persistent concern about his sources and their reliability. He prefers written and especially documentary evidence, but he will use oral reports if they come from several sources and are close enough to the original event.

The *Ecclesiastical History* suggests the contours of a national history, even a providential history, in the arrival of the Angles and Saxons, and in the island's uneven conversion to Christianity. Despite his frequent stories of battles among the Germanic peoples in Britain, Bede speaks of the English people emphatically in the singular. Nevertheless, Bede is delicately aware of the historical layering brought about by colonization and the ongoing resistance of earlier inhabitants. Further, he is always alert to profoundly transformative influences, aside from ethnicity, that color his time: the process of conversion to Christianity, and the variable coexistence of Christian and pagan instincts in individual minds; the interplay of oral and written culture; the status in religious and official life of Latin and the Anglo-Saxon vernaculars.

from An Ecclesiastical History of the English People[1]
[THE CONVERSION OF KING EDWIN][2]

King Edwin hesitated to accept the word of God which Paulinus[3] preached but, as we have said, used to sit alone for hours at a time, earnestly debating within himself what he ought to do and what religion he should follow. One day Paulinus came to him and, placing his right hand on the king's head, asked him if he recognized this sign. The king began to tremble and would have thrown himself at the bishop's feet but Paulinus raised him up and said in a voice that seemed familiar, "First you have escaped with God's help from the hands of the foes you feared; secondly you have acquired by His gift the kingdom you desired; now, in the third place, remember your own promise; do not delay in fulfilling it but receive the faith and keep the commandments of Him who rescued you from your earthly foes and raised you to the honor of an earthly kingdom. If from henceforth you are willing to follow His will which is made known to you through me, He will also rescue you from the everlasting torments of the wicked and make you a partaker with Him of His eternal kingdom in heaven."

When the king had heard his words, he answered that he was both willing and bound to accept the faith which Paulinus taught. He said, however, that he would confer about this with his loyal chief men and his counselors so that, if they agreed with him, they might all be consecrated together in the waters of life. Paulinus agreed and the king did as he had said. A meeting of his council was held and each one was asked in turn what he thought of this doctrine hitherto unknown to them and this new worship of God which was being proclaimed.

Coifi, the chief of the priests, answered at once, "Notice carefully, King, this doctrine which is now being expounded to us. I frankly admit that, for my part, I have found that the religion which we have hitherto held has no virtue nor profit in it. None of your followers has devoted himself more earnestly than I have to the worship of our gods, but nevertheless there are many who receive greater benefits and greater honor from you than I do and are more successful in all their undertakings. If the gods had any power they would have helped me more readily, seeing that I have always served them with greater zeal. So it follows that if, on examination, these new doctrines which have now been explained to us are found to be better and more effectual, let us accept them at once without any delay."

Another of the king's chief men agreed with this advice and with these wise words and then added, "This is how the present life of man on earth, King, appears to me in comparison with that time which is unknown to us. You are sitting feasting with your ealdormen and thegns[4] in winter time; the fire is burning on the hearth in the middle of the hall and all inside is warm, while outside the wintry storms of rain and snow are raging; and a sparrow flies swiftly through the hall. It enters in at one door and quickly flies out through the other. For the few moments it is inside, the storm and wintry tempest cannot touch it, but after the briefest moment of calm, it

---

1. Edited and translated by Bertram Colgrave and R. A. B. Mynors.

2. From bk. 2, chs. 12–14. Edwin became king of Northumbria in 616, aided by Raedwald, king of the East Angles. Exiled at Raedwald's court, Edwin had a vision wherein he promised a shadowy visitor he would convert if he achieved the crown. The visitor laid his right hand on Edwin's head as a sign to remember that promise when the gesture was repeated.

3. Later archbishop of York, Paulinus had been sent to Northumbria from Kent with Edwin's Christian wife after Edwin had promised tolerance of Christian worship.

4. Ealdorman: the highest Anglo-Saxon rank below king; thegn: a noble warrior still serving within the king's household.

flits from your sight, out of the wintry storm and into it again. So this life of man appears but for a moment; what follows or indeed what went before, we know not at all. If this new doctrine brings us more certain information, it seems right that we should accept it."[5] Other elders and counselors of the king continued in the same manner, being divinely prompted to do so.

Coifi added that he would like to listen still more carefully to what Paulinus himself had to say about God. The king ordered Paulinus to speak, and when he had said his say, Coifi exclaimed, "For a long time now I have realized that our religion is worthless; for the more diligently I sought the truth in our cult, the less I found it. Now I confess openly that the truth shines out clearly in this teaching which can bestow on us the gift of life, salvation, and eternal happiness. Therefore I advise your Majesty that we should promptly abandon and commit to the flames the temples and the altars which we have held sacred without reaping any benefit." Why need I say more? The king publicly accepted the gospel which Paulinus preached, renounced idolatry, and confessed his faith in Christ. When he asked the high priest of their religion which of them should be the first to profane the altars and the shrines of the idols, together with their precincts, Coifi answered, "I will; for through the wisdom the true God has given me no one can more suitably destroy those things which I once foolishly worshiped, and so set an example to all." And at once, casting aside his vain superstitions, he asked the king to provide him with arms and a stallion; and mounting it he set out to destroy the idols. Now a high priest of their religion was not allowed to carry arms or to ride except on a mare. So, girded with a sword, he took a spear in his hand and mounting the king's stallion he set off to where the idols were. The common people who saw him thought he was mad. But as soon as he approached the shrine, without any hesitation he profaned it by casting the spear which he held into it; and greatly rejoicing in the knowledge of the worship of the true God, he ordered his companions to destroy and set fire to the shrine and all the enclosures. The place where the idols once stood is still shown, not far from York, to the east, over the river Derwent. Today it is called Goodmanham, the place where the high priest, through the inspiration of the true God, profaned and destroyed the altars which he himself had consecrated.[6]

So King Edwin, with all the nobles of his race and a vast number of the common people, received the faith and regeneration by holy baptism in the eleventh year of his reign, that is in the year of our Lord 627 and about 180 years after the coming of the English to Britain. He was baptized at York on Easter Day, 12 April, in the church of Saint Peter the Apostle, which he had hastily built of wood while he was a catechumen and under instruction before he received baptism. He established an episcopal see for Paulinus, his instructor and bishop, in the same city.

[THE STORY OF IMMA][7]

In this battle in which King Aelfwine[8] was killed, a remarkable incident is known to have happened which in my opinion should certainly not be passed over in silence, since the story may lead to the salvation of many. During the battle one of the king's retainers, a young man named Imma, was struck down among others; he lay all that

---

5. This famous simile is put in the mouth of a lay noble-man, not the pagan priest Coifi whose argument for conversion was based on disappointed self-interest.
6. This detail is typical of Bede's liking for textual or archaeological authentication.

7. Bk. 4, ch. 22.
8. A battle in 679, between King Ecgfrith of Northumbria and Aethelred king of the Mercians caused the death of this under-king and brother of Ecgfrith.

day and the following night as though dead, among the bodies of the slain, but at last he recovered consciousness, sat up, and bandaged his wounds as best he could; then, having rested for a short time, he rose and set out to find friends to take care of him. But as he was doing so, he was found and captured by men of the enemy army and taken to their lord, who was a *gesith*[9] of King Aethelred. On being asked who he was, he was afraid to admit that he was a thegn; but he answered instead that he was a poor peasant and married; and he declared that he had come to the army in company with other peasants to bring food to the soldiers. The *gesith* took him and had his wounds attended to. But when Imma began to get better, he ordered him to be bound at night to prevent his escape. However, it proved impossible to bind him, for no sooner had those who chained him gone, than his fetters were loosed.

Now he had a brother whose name was Tunna, a priest and abbot of a monastery in a city which is still called *Tunnacaestir* after him. When Tunna heard that his brother had perished in the fight, he went to see if he could find his body; having found another very like him in all respects, he concluded that it must be his brother's body. So he carried it to the monastery, buried it with honor, and took care to offer many masses for the absolution of his soul. It was on account of these celebrations that, as I have said, no one could bind Imma because his fetters were at once loosed. Meanwhile the *gesith* who kept him captive grew amazed and asked him why he could not be bound and whether he had about him any loosing spells such as are described in stories. But Imma answered that he knew nothing of such arts. "However," said he, "I have a brother in my country who is a priest and I know he believes me to be dead and offers frequent masses on my behalf; so if I had now been in another world, my soul would have been loosed from its punishment by his inter-cessions." When he had been a prisoner with the *gesith* for some time, those who watched him closely realized by his appearance, his bearing, and his speech that he was not of common stock as he had said, but of noble family. Then the *gesith* called him aside and asked him very earnestly to declare his origin, promising that no harm should come to him, provided that he told him plainly who he was. The prisoner did so, revealing that he had been one of the king's thegns. The *gesith* answered, "I real-ized by every one of your answers that you were not a peasant, and now you ought to die because all my brothers and kinsmen were killed in the battle: but I will not kill you for I do not intend to break my promise."

As soon as Imma had recovered, the *gesith* sold him to a Frisian in London; but he could neither be bound on his way there nor by the Frisian. So after his enemies had put every kind of bond on him and as his new master realized that he could not be bound, he gave him leave to ransom himself if he could. Now the bonds were most frequently loosed from about nine in the morning, the time when masses were usually said. So having sworn that he would either return or send his master the money for his ransom, he went to King Hlothhere of Kent, who was the son of Queen Aethelthryth's sister already mentioned, because he had once been one of Aethelthryth's thegns; he asked for and received the money from him for his ransom and sent it to his master as he had promised.[1]

He afterwards returned to his own country, where he met his brother and gave him a full account of all his troubles and the comfort that had come to him in those

---

9. A nobleman, serving a king but having his own house-hold of retainers and servants.
1. Imma had been thegn to Aethelthryth, wife of King

Ecgfrith, before he entered Aelfwine's service. He now turns to her nephew, implicitly invoking obligations of kinship, for help with his ransom.

adversities; and from what his brother told him, he realized that his bonds had generally been loosed at the time when masses were being celebrated on his behalf; so he perceived that the other comforts and blessings which he had experienced during his time of danger had been bestowed by heaven, through the intercession of his brother and the offering up of the saving Victim. Many who heard about this from Imma were inspired to greater faith and devotion, to prayer and almsgiving and to the offering up of sacrifices to God in the holy oblation, for the deliverance of their kinsfolk who had departed from the world; for they realized that the saving sacrifice availed for the everlasting redemption of both body and soul.

This story was told me by some of those who heard it from the very man to whom these things happened; therefore since I had so clear an account of the incident, I thought that it should undoubtedly be inserted into this *History*.

[CAEDMON'S HYMN][2]

In the monastery of this abbess[3] there was a certain brother who was specially marked out by the grace of God, so that he used to compose godly and religious songs; thus, whatever he learned from the holy Scriptures by means of interpreters, he quickly turned into extremely delightful and moving poetry, in English, which was his own tongue. By his songs the minds of many were often inspired to despise the world and to long for the heavenly life. It is true that after him other Englishmen attempted to compose religious poems, but none could compare with him. For he did not learn the art of poetry from men nor through a man but he received the gift of song freely by the grace of God. Hence he could never compose any foolish or trivial poem but only those which were concerned with devotion and so were fitting for his devout tongue to utter. He had lived in the secular habit until he was well advanced in years and had never learned any songs.[4] Hence sometimes at a feast, when for the sake of providing entertainment, it had been decided that they should all sing in turn, when he saw the harp approaching him, he would rise up in the middle of the feasting, go out, and return home.

On one such occasion when he did so, he left the place of feasting and went to the cattle byre, as it was his turn to take charge of them that night. In due time he stretched himself out and went to sleep, whereupon he dreamed that someone stood by him, saluted him, and called him by name: "Caedmon," he said, "sing me something." Caedmon answered, "I cannot sing; that is why I left the feast and came here because I could not sing." Once again the speaker said, "Nevertheless you must sing to me." "What must I sing?" said Caedmon. "Sing," he said, "about the beginning of created things." Thereupon Caedmon began to sing verses which he had never heard before in praise of God the Creator, of which this is the general sense: "Now we must praise the Maker of the heavenly kingdom, the power of the Creator and his counsel, the deeds of the Father of glory and how He, since he is the eternal God, was the Author of all marvels and first created the heavens as a roof for the children of men and then, the almighty Guardian of the human race, created the earth." This is the sense but not the order of the words which he sang as he slept. For it is not possible to translate verse, however well composed, literally from one

---

2. Bk. 4, ch. 24.
3. Hild, an aristocratic woman famed for her piety, who had founded and ruled the abbey of Whitby.
4. Monks, who devoted their lives to prayer and the celebration of the liturgy, needed to be literate in Latin. Caedmon was one of the lay brothers, who performed menial tasks and were often uneducated.

language to another without some loss of beauty and dignity. When he awoke, he remembered all that he had sung while asleep and soon added more verses in the same manner, praising God in fitting style.

In the morning he went to the reeve[5] who was his master, telling him of the gift he had received, and the reeve took him to the abbess. He was then bidden to describe his dream in the presence of a number of the more learned men and also to recite his song so that they might all examine him and decide upon the nature and origin of the gift of which he spoke; and it seemed clear to all of them that the Lord had granted him heavenly grace. They then read to him a passage of sacred history or doctrine, bidding him make a song out of it, if he could, in metrical form. He undertook the task and went away; on returning next morning he repeated the passage he had been given, which he had put into excellent verse. The abbess, who recognized the grace of God which the man had received, instructed him to renounce his secular habit and to take monastic vows. She and all her people received him into the community of the brothers and ordered that he should be instructed in the whole course of sacred history. He learned all he could by listening to them and then, memorizing it and ruminating over it, like some clean animal chewing the cud, he turned it into the most melodious verse: and it sounded so sweet as he recited it that his teachers became in turn his audience. He sang about the creation of the world, the origin of the human race, and the whole history of Genesis, of the departure of Israel from Egypt and the entry into the promised land and of many other of the stories taken from the sacred Scriptures: of the incarnation, passion, and resurrection of the Lord, of His ascension into heaven, of the coming of the Holy Spirit and the teaching of the apostles. He also made songs about the terrors of future judgment, the horrors of the pains of hell, and the joys of the heavenly kingdom. In addition he composed many other songs about the divine mercies and judgments, in all of which he sought to turn his hearers away from delight in sin and arouse in them the love and practice of good works. He was a most religious man, humbly submitting himself to the discipline of the Rule; and he opposed all those who wished to act otherwise with a flaming and fervent zeal. It was for this reason that his life had a beautiful ending.

When the hour of his departure drew near he was afflicted, fourteen days before, by bodily weakness, yet so slight that he was able to walk about and talk the whole time. There was close by a building to which they used to take those who were infirm or who seemed to be at the point of death. On the night on which he was to die, as evening fell, he asked his attendant to prepare a place in this building where he could rest. The attendant did as Caedmon said though he wondered why he asked, for he did not seem to be by any means at the point of death. They had settled down in the house and were talking and joking cheerfully with each of those who were already there and it was past midnight, when he asked whether they had the Eucharist in the house. They answered, "What need have you of the Eucharist? You are not likely to die, since you are talking as cheerfully with us as if you were in perfect health." "Nevertheless," he repeated, "bring me the Eucharist." When he had taken it in his hand he asked if they were all charitably disposed towards him and had no complaint nor any quarrel nor grudge against him. They answered that they were all in charity with him and without the slightest feeling of anger; then they asked him in turn whether he was charitably disposed towards them. He

5. Person responsible for running the monastery's estates.

answered at once, "My sons, I am in charity with all the servants of God." So, fortifying himself with the heavenly viaticum, he prepared for his entrance into the next life. Thereupon he asked them how near it was to the time when the brothers had to awake to sing their nightly praises to God. They answered, "It will not be long." And he answered, "Good, let us wait until then." And so, signing himself with the sign of the holy cross, he laid his head on the pillow, fell asleep for a little while, and so ended his life quietly. Thus it came about that, as he had served the Lord with a simple and pure mind and with quiet devotion, so he departed into His presence and left the world by a quiet death; and his tongue which had uttered so many good words in praise of the Creator also uttered its last words in His praise, as he signed himself with the sign of the cross and commended his spirit into God's hands; and from what has been said, it would seem that he had foreknowledge of his death.

Bishop Asser
?–c. 909

When Bede died in 735, he left an island that was very unstable in its political geography but apparently ever more stable and accomplished in its religion and learning. By the end of the century, that world was shattered. In 793 Vikings sacked the monastery of Lindisfarne, not far from Wearmouth-Jarrow. Waves of raiders and then settlers followed. Monastic communities fled inland, and some shifted for generations before resettling finally. However sporadic and temporary may have been the worldly impact of these Viking raiders, however quickly they became peaceful settlers, they had a disastrous effect on the kind of disciplined learning witnessed by the life of Bede. By the time of Asser, Latin learning in most of England was fragmented and in decline, though not so bad as it suits Alfred to claim. Asser, a Welsh monk and later bishop of Sherborne, was summoned to Wessex by King Alfred as part of a project to revive learning and extend its audience beyond those who read Latin. Alfred accomplished this, in part, by looking to men like Asser, from areas such as Wales which had preserved some traditions of classical learning.

Asser's worshipful and disorganized but lively *Life of King Alfred* was written in Latin during the king's life, about 893. It depicts the origins of the king's scholarly ambitions, interwoven with the struggles by which Alfred established and extended his rule and resisted renewed Viking incursions. Asser thus offers a double narrative of texts and conquests which make one another possible and worthy. The diffusion of learning and revival of religious discipline become enmeshed in a logic that also includes Alfred's ambitions to rule all the Anglo-Saxons.

from The Life of King Alfred[1]
[ALFRED'S BOYHOOD]

Now he was greatly cherished above all his brothers by the united and ardent love of his father and mother, and indeed of all people; and he was ever brought up entirely at the royal court. As he passed through his infancy and boyhood he surpassed all his brothers in beauty, and was more pleasing in his appearance, in his speech, and in his manners. From his earliest childhood the noble character of his mind gave him a desire for all things useful in this present life, and, above all, a longing for wisdom; but, alas! the culpable negligence of his relations, and of those who had care of him,

---

1. Translated by L. C. Jane.

allowed him to remain ignorant of letters until his twelfth year, or even to a later age. Albeit, day and night did he listen attentively to the Saxon poems, which he often heard others repeating, and his retentive mind enabled him to remember them.

An ardent hunter, he toiled persistently at every form of that art, and not in vain. For in his skill and success at this pursuit he surpassed all, as in all other gifts of God. And this skill we have ourselves seen on many occasions.

Now it chanced on a certain day that his mother showed to him and to his brothers a book of Saxon poetry, which she had in her hand, and said, "I will give this book to that one among you who shall the most quickly learn it." Then, moved at these words, or rather by the inspiration of God, and being carried away by the beauty of the initial letter in that book, anticipating his brothers who surpassed him in years but not in grace, he answered his mother, and said, "Will you of a truth give that book to one of us? To him who shall soonest understand it and repeat it to you?" And at this she smiled and was pleased, and affirmed it, saying, "I will give it to him." Then forthwith he took the book from her hand and went to his master, and read it; and when he had read it he brought it back to his mother and repeated it to her.

After this he learnt the Daily Course, that is, the services for each hour, and then some psalms and many prayers. These were collected in one book, which, as we have ourselves seen, he constantly carried about with him everywhere in the fold of his cloak, for the sake of prayer amid all the passing events of this present life. But, alas! the art of reading which he most earnestly desired he did not acquire in accordance with his wish, because, as he was wont himself to say, in those days there were no men really skilled in reading in the whole realm of the West Saxons.

With many complaints, and with heartfelt regrets, he used to declare that among all the difficulties and trials of this life this was the greatest. For at the time when he was of an age to learn, and had leisure and ability for it, he had no masters; but when he was older, and indeed to a certain extent had anxious masters and writers, he could not read. For he was occupied day and night without ceasing both with illnesses unknown to all the physicians of that island, and with the cares of the royal office both at home and abroad, and with the assaults of the heathen by land and sea.[2] None the less, amid the difficulties of this life, from his infancy to the present day, he has not in the past faltered in his earnest pursuit of knowledge, nor does he even now cease to long for it, nor, as I think, will he ever do so until the end of his life.

[ALFRED'S KINGSHIP]

Yet amid the wars and many hindrances of this present life, and amid the assaults of the pagans, and his daily illness, the king ceased not from the governance of the kingdom and from the pursuit of every form of hunting. Nor did he omit to instruct also his goldsmiths and all his artificers, his falconers and his huntsmen and the keepers of his dogs; nor to make according to new designs of his own articles of goldsmiths' work, more venerable and more precious than had been the wont of all his predecessors. He was constant in the reading of books in the Saxon tongue, and more especially in committing to memory the Saxon poems, and in commanding others to do so. And he by himself labored most zealously with all his might.

---

2. Alfred's patient suffering in illness is one of several patterns by which Asser implies analogies with the lives of saints.

Moreover he heard the divine offices daily, the Mass, and certain psalms and prayers. He observed the services of the hours by day and by night, and oftentimes was he wont, as we have said, without the knowledge of his men, to go in the night-time to the churches for the sake of prayer. He was zealous in the giving of alms, and generous towards his own people and to those who came from all nations. He was especially and wonderfully kindly towards all men, and merry. And to the searching out of things not known did he apply himself with all his heart.

Moreover many Franks, Frisians and Gauls, pagans, Britons, Scots and Armoricans, of their own free will, submitted them to his rule, both nobles and persons of low degree. All these he ruled, according to his excellent goodness, as he did his own people, and loved them and honored them, and enriched them with money and with power.

He was eager and anxious to hear the Holy Scripture read to him by his own folk, but he would also as readily pray with strangers, if by any chance one had come from any place. Moreover he loved with wonderful affection his bishops and all the clergy, his ealdormen and nobles, his servants and all his household. And cherishing their sons, who were brought up in the royal household, with no less love than he bore towards his own children, he ceased not day and night, among other things, himself to teach them all virtue and to make them well acquainted with letters.

But it was as though he found no comfort in all these things. For, as if he suffered no other care from within or without, in anxious sorrow, day and night, he would make complaint to the Lord and to all who were joined to him in close affection, lamenting with many sighs for that Almighty God had not made him skilled in divine wisdom and in the liberal arts.

⊷ ⊠◊⊠ ⊷

King Alfred
849–899

Alfred, king of the West Saxons, had ambitions to be king of all England, at least south of the Humber. He spent much of his reign in a series of campaigns against Viking raiders. After a decisive victory at the battle of Edington in 878, Alfred negotiated a peace that included the departure of the Danes from Wessex and the baptism of their king Guthrum. In the later years of his reign, starting about 890, he embarked on a quite different, but ultimately more influential, campaign of conquest and Christian conversion, through the series of Anglo-Saxon translations from Latin produced by his own hand and under his patronage. Pope Gregory the Great's *Pastoral Care* (c. 591), a handbook for bishops, was the first. This effort assuredly had charitable and scholarly motivations, but it also takes on interesting national overtones when it assumes that Anglo-Saxon is one language and known by all, and even more when it is linked to earlier translations and the westward movement of ancient power.

Preface to Saint Gregory's *Pastoral Care*[1]

King Alfred bids greet Bishop Waerferth[2] with his words lovingly and with friendship; and I let it be known to thee that it has very often come into my mind what wise men there formerly were throughout England, both of sacred and secular orders;

---

1. Translated by Kevin Crossley-Holland.
2. Waerferth, bishop of Worcester, had earlier translated

Gregory's *Dialogues* for Alfred and perhaps inspired the king's more ambitious program.

and what happy times there were then throughout England; and how the kings who had power over the nation in those days obeyed God and His ministers; how they preserved peace, morality, and order at home, and at the same time enlarged their territory abroad; and how they prospered both with war and with wisdom; and also how zealous the sacred orders were both in teaching and learning, and in all the services they owed to God; and how foreigners came to this land in search of wisdom and instruction, and how we should now have to get them from abroad if we were to have them. So general was its decay in England that there were very few on this side of the Humber who could understand their rituals in English, or translate a letter from Latin into English; and I believe that there were not many beyond the Humber. There were so few of them that I cannot remember a single one south of the Thames when I came to the throne. Thanks be to Almighty God that we have any teachers among us now. And therefore I command thee to do as I believe thou art willing, to disengage thyself from worldly matters as often as thou canst, that thou mayest apply the wisdom which God has given thee wherever thou canst. Consider what punishments would come upon us on account of this world, if we neither loved it [wisdom] ourselves nor suffered other men to obtain it: we should love the name only of Christian, and very few the virtues. When I considered all this, I remembered also that I saw, before it had been all ravaged and burned, how the churches throughout the whole of England stood filled with treasures and books; and there was also a great multitude of God's servants, but they had very little knowledge of the books, for they could not understand anything of them, because they were not written in their own language. As if they had said: "Our forefathers, who formerly held these places, loved wisdom, and through it they obtained wealth and bequeathed it to us. In this we can still see their tracks, but we cannot follow them, and therefore we have lost both the wealth and the wisdom, because we would not incline our hearts after their example." When I remembered all this, I wondered extremely that the good and wise men who were formerly all over England, and had perfectly learned all the books, had not wished to translate them into their own language. But again I soon answered myself and said: "They did not think that men would ever be so careless, and that learning would so decay; through that desire they abstained from it, since they wished that the wisdom in this land might increase with our knowledge of languages." Then I remembered how the law was first known in Hebrew, and again, when the Greeks had learned it, they translated the whole of it into their own language, and all other books besides. And again the Romans, when they had learned them, translated the whole of them by learned interpreters into their own language. And also all other Christian nations translated a part of them into their own language.[3] Therefore it seems better to me, if you think so, for us also to translate some books which are most needful for all men to know into the language which we can all understand, and for you to do as we very easily can if we have tranquility enough, that is, that all the youth now in England of free men, who are rich enough to be able to devote themselves to it, be set to learn as long as they are not fit for any other occupation, until they are able to read English writing well: and let those be afterwards taught more in the Latin language who are to continue in learning, and be promoted to a higher rank. When I remembered how the knowledge

---

3. An early statement of the widespread medieval idea of the persistent westward movement of learning, *translatio studii*, in parallel with the westward movement of power, *translatio imperii*. If Alfred will now revive learning in England, he may imply, should he not also consolidate power?

of Latin had formerly decayed throughout England, and yet many could read English writing, I began, among other various and manifold troubles of this kingdom, to translate into English the book which is called in Latin *Pastoralis*, and in English *Shepherd's Book*, sometimes word by word, and sometimes according to the sense, as I had learned it from Plegmund my archbishop, and Asser my bishop, and Grimbald my mass-priest, and John my mass-priest. And when I had learned it as I could best understand it, and as I could most clearly interpret it, I translated it into English; and I will send a copy to every bishopric in my kingdom; and in each there is a book-mark worth fifty mancuses.[4] And I command in God's name that no man take the book-mark from the book, or the book from the monastery. It is uncertain how long there may be such learned bishops as now, thanks be to God, there are nearly everywhere; therefore I wish them always to remain in their places unless the bishop wish to take them with him, or they be lent out anywhere, or any one be making a copy from them.

━━ ✥ ━━

Ohthere's Journeys

Along with religious and speculative works like *Pastoral Care* and Boethius's *Consolation of Philosophy*, Alfred also sponsored the translation of histories, both Bede's *Ecclesiastical History of the English People* and the early fifth-century *Seven Books of History against the Pagans*, of Paulus Orosius. In the latter, Orosius's opening survey of geography is expanded to include lands north of the Alps, and the translator inserts the following account of two northern voyages by the Norwegian trader Ohthere, who later came to Alfred's court.

Ohthere describes two journeys, one made largely for curiosity (but also for walrus tusks) and the other mostly for trade. In the first, he heads north along the west coast of Norway, around the north edge of modern Sweden and Finland, and into the White Sea—a little-known area, inhabited only by hunters and fishermen. In the second he goes to the main trading town of his nation, Sciringes-heal (on the south coast of modern Norway), and then to a large town and trading center, Hedeby (modern Schleswig in northern Germany). Along with keen details of fauna and almost anthropological observation of local tribes, Ohthere notes the great exports of his area: furs, amber, and ivory—some of which he has brought to King Alfred. Throughout the passage, an implicit, curious interlocutor mediates between the interests (and ignorance) of the English audience and the foreign traveler.

Ohthere's Journeys[1]

Ohthere told his lord, King Alfred,[2] that he lived the furthest north of all Norwegians. He said that he lived in the north of Norway on the coast of the Atlantic. He also said that the land extends very far north beyond that point, but it is all uninhabited, except for a few places here and there where the *Finnas*[3] have their camps, hunting in winter, and in summer fishing in the sea.

He told how he once wished to find out how far the land extended due north, or whether anyone lived to the north of the unpopulated area. He went due north along the coast, keeping the uninhabited land to starboard and the open sea to port

---

4. Gold coins.
1. Translated by Christine E. Fell.
2. As a foreign visitor, Ohthere would need the official protection of the king, who is thus "his lord."

3. The *Finnas* (modern Lapps) are a nomadic people who give tribute to the Norwegians. They herd deer, hunt, and fish. They are not the peoples we now call Finns, whom Ohthere called *Beormas* and *Cwenas*.

continuously for three days. He was then as far north as the whale hunters go at their furthest. He then continued due north as far as he could reach in the second three days. There the land turned due east, or the sea penetrated the land he did not know which—but he knew that he waited there for a west-northwest wind, and then sailed east along the coast as far as he could sail in four days. There he had to wait for a due northern wind, because there the land turned due south, or the sea penetrated the land he did not know which. Then from there he sailed due south along the coast as far as he could sail in five days. A great river went up into the land there. They turned up into the river, not daring to sail beyond it without permission, since the land on the far side of the river was fully settled. He had not previously come across any settled district since he left his own home, but had, the whole way, land to starboard that was uninhabited apart from fishers and bird-catchers and hunters, and they were all *Finnas*. To port he always had the open sea. The *Beormas* had extensive settlements in their country but the Norwegians did not dare to venture there. But the land of the *Terfinnas* was totally uninhabited except where hunters made camp, or fishermen or bird-catchers.

The *Beormas* told him many stories both about their own country and about the lands which surrounded them, but he did not know how much of it was true because he had not seen it for himself. It seemed to him that the *Finnas* and the *Beormas* spoke almost the same language. His main reason for going there, apart from exploring the land, was for the walruses, because they have very fine ivory in their tusks—they brought some of these tusks to the king—and their hide is very good for ship-ropes. This whale [i.e., walrus] is much smaller than other whales; it is no more than seven ells long. The best whale-hunting is in his own country; those are forty-eight ells long, the biggest fifty ells long; of these he said that he, one of six, killed sixty in two days.

He was a very rich man in those possessions which their riches consist of, that is in wild deer. He had still, when he came to see the king, six hundred unsold tame deer. These deer they call "reindeer." Six of these were decoy-reindeer. These are very valuable among the *Finnas* because they use them to catch the wild reindeer. He was among the chief men in that country, but he had not more than twenty cattle, twenty sheep and twenty pigs, and the little that he plowed he plowed with horses. Their wealth, however, is mostly in the tribute which the *Finnas* pay them. That tribute consists of the skins of beasts, the feathers of birds, whale-bone, and ship-ropes made from whale-hide and sealskin. Each pays according to his rank. The highest in rank has to pay fifteen marten skins, five reindeer skins, one bear skin and ten measures of feathers, and a jacket of bearskin or otterskin and two ship-ropes. Each of these must be sixty ells long, one made from whale-hide the other from seal.

He said that the land of the Norwegians is very long and narrow. All of it that can be used for grazing or plowing lies along the coast and even that is in some places very rocky. Wild mountains lie to the east, above and alongside the cultivated land. In these mountains live the *Finnas*. The cultivated land is broadest in the south, and the further north it goes the narrower it becomes. In the south it is perhaps sixty miles broad or a little broader; and in the middle, thirty or broader; and to the north, he said, where it is narrowest, it might be three miles across to the mountains. The mountains beyond are in some places of a width that takes two weeks to cross, in others of a width that can be crossed in six days.

Beyond the mountains Sweden borders the southern part of the land as far as the north, and the country of the *Cwenas* borders the land in the north. Sometimes

The Death of Harold, from *The Bayeux Tapestry*, c. 1073–1088. This narrative tapestry was made within living memory of the Conquest, and the scenes depicted on it overlap much of the story as told in the *Anglo-Saxon Chronicle*. The tapestry is an extraordinary production: a roll about 20 inches high and some 230 feet long thought to have been embroidered by English women, whose needlework had international fame. In this climactic scene, at left King Harold is cut down by a mounted Norman knight; at center, Anglo-Saxon foot soldiers parry spears thrown by mounted Normans. In the marginal decoration at top, birds of prey and lions face off, emblems perhaps of the noble combatants; at the bottom, in a very different tone, lie the corpses and arms of fallen soldiers.

the *Cwenas* make raids on the Norwegians across the mountains, and sometimes the Norwegians make raids on them. There are very large fresh-water lakes throughout these mountains, and the *Cwenas* carry their boats overland onto the lakes and from there make raids on the Norwegians. They have very small, very light boats.

Ohthere said that the district where he lived is called *Halgoland*.[4] He said no-one lived to the north of him. In the south part of Norway there is a trading-town which is called *Sciringes heal*. He said that a man could scarcely sail there in a month, assuming he made camp at night, and each day had a favorable wind. He would sail by the coast the whole way. To starboard is first of all *Iraland*[5] and then those islands which are between *Iraland* and this land, and then this land until he comes to *Sciringes heal*, and Norway is on the port side the whole way. To the south of *Sciringes heal* a great sea penetrates the land; it is too wide to see across. Jutland is on the far side and after that *Sillende*.[6] This sea flows into the land for many hundred miles.

From *Sciringes heal* he said that he sailed in five days to the trading-town called Hedeby, which is situated among Wends, Saxons and Angles and belongs to the Danes. When he sailed there from *Sciringes heal* he had Denmark to port and the open sea to starboard for three days. Then two days before he arrived at Hedeby he had Jutland and *Sillende* and many islands to starboard. The Angles lived in these districts before they came to this land. On the port side he had, for two days, those islands which belong to Denmark.

4. The northernmost province of Norway, much of it within the polar circle.

5. Possibly a corruption of Iceland.
6. Probably southern Jutland, modern North Schleswig.

‍‍‍‍‍‍‍‍‍‍‍‍‍‍‍‍

The Anglo-Saxon Chronicle

The Anglo-Saxon Chronicle began to be assembled in the 890s at Winchester, in the heart of King Alfred's Wessex and at the high point of his reign. The decision to use Anglo-Saxon in this originally monastic product reflects the influence of Alfred's translation projects. The original version of the *Chronicle* was distributed to a number of monasteries, which made their own additions sometimes as late as the mid-twelfth century. If the various *Chronicles* began as a gesture of common language and shared history, though, their later entries—like the one below—increasingly record dynastic struggle and civil strife. And the *Chronicles* themselves, in their extensions after the Conquest, emblematize the fate of the Anglo-Saxon vernacular and culture: increasingly isolated, fragmentary, and recorded in a disappearing tongue.

from The Anglo-Saxon Chronicle[1]
STAMFORD BRIDGE AND HASTINGS

1066   In this year King Harold came from York to Westminster at the Easter following the Christmas that the king died,[2] and Easter was then on 16 April. Then over all England there was seen a sign in the skies such as had never been seen before. Some said it was the star "comet" which some call the long-haired star; and it first appeared on the eve of the Greater Litany, that is 24 April, and so shone all the week. And soon after this Earl Tosti came from overseas into the Isle of Wight with as large a fleet as he could muster and both money and provisions were given him.[3] And King Harold his brother assembled a naval force and a land force larger than any king had assembled before in this country, because he had been told that William the Bastard[4] meant to come here and conquer this country. This was exactly what happened afterwards. Meanwhile Earl Tosti came into the Humber with sixty ships and Earl Edwin came with a land force and drove him out, and the sailors deserted him. And he went to Scotland with twelve small vessels, and there Harold, king of Norway, met him with three hundred ships, and Tosti submitted to him and became his vassal; and they both went up the Humber until they reached York. And there Earl Edwin and Morcar his brother fought against them; but the Norwegians had the victory. Harold, king of the English, was informed that things had gone thus; and the fight was on the Vigil of Saint Matthew. Then Harold our king came upon the Norwegians by surprise and met them beyond York at Stamford Bridge with a large force of the English people; and that day there was a very fierce fight on both sides. There was killed Harold Fairhair and Earl Tosti, and the Norwegians who survived took to flight; and the English attacked them fiercely as they pursued them until some got to the ships. Some were drowned, and some burned, and some destroyed in various ways so that few survived and the English remained in command of the field. The king gave quarter to Olaf, son of the Norse king, and their bishop and the earl of Orkney and all those who survived on the ships, and they went up to our king and swore oaths that they would always keep peace and friendship with this country; and the king let them go home with twenty-four ships. These two pitched battles were fought within five nights.

---

1. Translated by Kevin Crossley-Holland.
2. Edward "the Confessor" ruled 1042–1066. Harold claims the throne through his sister Edith, Edward's widow.

3. Tosti was Harold's estranged brother, and now supported the rival claim of Harold Fairhair, king of Norway.
4. William of Normandy, "the Conqueror."

Then Count William came from Normandy to Pevensey on Michaelmas Eve, and as soon as they were able to move on they built a castle at Hastings. King Harold was informed of this and he assembled a large army and came against him at the hoary apple-tree. And William came against him by surprise before his army was drawn up in battle array. But the king nevertheless fought hard against him, with the men who were willing to support him, and there were heavy casualties on both sides. There King Harold was killed and Earl Leofwine his brother, and Earl Gyrth his brother, and many good men, and the French remained masters of the field, even as God granted it to them because of the sins of the people. Archbishop Aldred and the citizens of London wanted to have Edgar *Cild*[5] as king, as was his proper due; and Edwin and Morcar promised him that they would fight on his side; but always the more it ought to have been forward the more it got behind, and the worse it grew from day to day, exactly as everything came to be at the end. The battle took place on the festival of Calixtus the pope. And Count William went back to Hastings, and waited there to see whether submission would be made to him. But when he understood that no one meant to come to him, he went inland with all his army that was left to him, and that came to him afterwards from overseas, and ravaged all the region that he overran until he reached Berkhamstead. There he was met by Archbishop Aldred and Edgar *Cild*, and Earl Edwin and Earl Morcar, and all the chief men from London. And they submitted out of necessity after most damage had been done—and it was a great piece of folly that they had not done it earlier, since God would not make things better, because of our sins. And they gave hostages and swore oaths to him, and he promised them that he would be a gracious liege lord, and yet in the meantime they ravaged all that they overran. Then on Christmas Day, Archbishop Aldred consecrated him king at Westminster. And he promised Aldred on Christ's book and swore moreover (before Aldred would place the crown on his head) that he would rule all this people as well as the best of the kings before him, if they would be loyal to him. All the same he laid taxes on people very severely, and then went in spring overseas to Normandy, and took with him Archbishop Stigand, and Aethelnoth, abbot of Glastonbury, and Edgar *Cild* and Earl Edwin and Earl Morcar, and Earl Waltheof, and many other good men from England. And Bishop Odo and Earl William stayed behind and built castles far and wide throughout this country, and distressed the wretched folk, and always after that it grew much worse. May the end be good when God wills!

⇥ END OF PERSPECTIVES: ETHNIC AND RELIGIOUS ENCOUNTERS ⇤

→ ⇌ ←

Taliesin

The name of Taliesin resonated through Welsh literary imagination for more than a millennium, from the late sixth century until the end of the Middle Ages. Only a small cluster of about a dozen poems can be securely identified with him, all of them praise poems and elegies for contemporary kings. These must have circulated for generations in oral form. They appear in their earliest surviving manuscript, the late thirteenth-century Book of Taliesin, already

---

5. Son of Edgar the Exile, grandson and great-grandson of kings; his great-uncle King Edward had titled him "Aetheling," or "throne-worthy." He was still a minor in 1066 and would have had to rule through a regent.

embedded within a nimbus of intriguing legends and falsely attributed works that had been attached to the prestige of his name across the centuries.

Despite this central role, Taliesin was not a poet of "Wales" in anything like its modern geography. In the later sixth century when he was active, Welsh-speaking kingdoms survived in the north and west of Britain and into modern Scotland. They were embattled, pressured by the expanding Anglo-Saxon kingdoms to the east and south, by Picts in the north, and by Irish Celts in the kingdom of Dalriada to the far northwest. Among these unstable Welsh kingdoms, especially Rheged around the Solway Firth, Taliesin became an important court poet.

The warrior kings in the Welsh north, such as Taliesin's chief patrons Urien king of Rheged and his son Owain, were extolled in a poetic culture that celebrated treasure and heroic violence, yet did so in forms of considerable intricacy and language of dramatic spareness. Taliesin's poems use ambitious meters and stanzas involving internal rhyme, end rhyme, and alliteration. They do not merely glory in armed bloodshed but also explore the boasts and emotions leading up to battle; they often display a haunting visual sense of its grisly aftermath. Taliesin further celebrates the generosity and gaiety of the triumphant court: in ways reminiscent of the Anglo-Saxon *Wanderer*, one poem here registers the poet's terror at the thought of losing his patron and protector. In an elegy for Owain ap Urien, Taliesin combines all these elements, yet brackets them with a suddenly broadened and suggestively discordant perspective, a Christian plea for the needs of Owain's soul.

Urien Yrechwydd[1]

Urien of Yrechwydd   most generous of Christian men,
much do you give   to the people of your land;
as you gather   so also you scatter,
the poets of Christendom   rejoice while you stand.
5   More is the gaiety   and more is the glory
that Urien and his heirs   are for riches renowned,
and he is the chieftain,   the paramount ruler,
the far-flung refuge,   first of fighters found.
The Lloegrians[2] know it   when they count their numbers,
10   death have they suffered   and many a shame,
their homesteads a-burning,   stripped their bedding,
and many a loss   and many a blame,
and never a respite   from Urien of Rheged.
Rheged's defender,   famed lord, your land's anchor,
15   all that is told of you   has my acclaim.
Intense is your spear-play   when you hear ploy of battle,
when to battle you come   'tis a killing you can,
fire in their houses ere day   in the lord of Yrechwydd's way,
Yrechwydd the beautiful   and its generous clan.
20   The Angles are succorless.   Around the fierce king
are his fierce offspring.   Of those dead, of those living,
of those yet to come,   you head the column.
To gaze upon him   is a widespread fear;

---

1. "I-*rech*-ooeed" (guttural "ch"), or Rheged. Like many Anglo-Saxon poems, this poem uses a break (caesura) in midline. Translated by Saunders Lewis.
2. The Angles and Saxons.

Gaiety clothes him,   the ribald ruler,
25   gaiety clothes him   and riches abounding,
gold king of the Northland   and of kings king.

The Battle of Argoed Llwyfain[1]

There was a great battle Saturday morning
From when the sun rose until it grew dark.
The fourfold hosts of Fflamddwyn[2] invaded,
Goddau and Rheged gathered in arms,
5   Summoned from Argoed as far as Arfynydd[3]—
They might not delay by as much as a day.

With a great blustering din, Fflamddwyn shouted,
"Have these the hostages come? Are they ready?"[4]
To him then Owain, scourge of the eastlands,
10   "They've not come, no! they're not, nor shall they be ready."
And a whelp of Coel would indeed be afflicted
Did he have to give any man as a hostage!

And Urien, lord of Erechwydd, shouted,
"If they would meet us now for a treaty,
15   High on the hilltop let's raise our ramparts,
Carry our faces over the shield rims,
Raise up our spears, men, over our heads
And set upon Fflamddwyn in the midst of his hosts
And slaughter him, ay, and all that go with him!"

20   There was many a corpse beside Argoed Llwyfain;
From warriors ravens grew red
And with their leader a host attacked.
For a whole year I shall sing to their triumph.

The War-Band's Return[1]

Through a single year
This man has poured out
Wine, bragget, and mead,
Reward for valor.
5   A host of singers,
A swarm about spits,
Their torques round their heads,
Their places splendid.
Each went on campaign,

---

1. "Ar-goid Lloo-*ee*-vine," the Welsh "ll" rather like "tl"
pronounced quickly as a single sound. Translated by An-
thony Conran.
2. "Flom-*thoo*-een," the Flame-bearer, identity uncertain.
3. Goddau ("Go-thy") and Arfynydd ("Ar-vi-nith"),

British territories.
4. Fflamddwyn arrogantly demands hostages, guarantees
of submission, before the battle. The use of direct quota-
tion is unique among Taliesin's poems.
1. Translated by Joseph P. Clancy.

10   Eager in combat,
    His steed beneath him,
    Set to raid Manaw
    For the sake of wealth,
    Profit in plenty,
15   Eight herds alike
    Of calves and cattle,
    Milch cows and oxen,
    And each one worthy.

    I could have no joy
20   Should Urien be slain,
    So loved before he left,
    Brandishing his lance,
    And his white hair soaked,
    And a bier his fate,
25   And gory his cheek
    With the stain of blood,
    A strong, steadfast man,
    His wife made a widow,
    My faithful king,
30   My faithful trust,
    My bulwark, my chief,
    Before savage pain.

    Go, lad, to the door:
    What is that clamor?
35   Is the earth shaking?
    Is the sea in flood?
    The chant grows stronger
    From marching men!

    Were a foe in hill,
40   Urien will stab him;
    Were a foe in dale,
    Urien has pierced him;
    Were foe in mountain,
    Urien conquers him;
45   Were foe on hillside,
    Urien will wound him;
    Were foe on rampart,
    Urien will smite him:
    Foe on path, foe on peak,
50   Foe at every bend,
    Not one sneeze or two
    He permits before death.
    No famine can come,
    Plunder about him.
55   Like death his spear
    Piercing a foeman.

And until I die, old,
By death's strict demand,
I shall not be joyful
60   Unless I praise Urien.

Lament for Owain Son of Urien[1]

God, consider the soul's need
    Of Owain son of Urien!
Rheged's prince, secret in loam:
    No shallow work to praise him.

5   A straight° grave, a man much praised,   *narrow*
    His whetted spear the wings of dawn:
That lord of bright Llwyfenydd,
    Where is his peer?

Reaper of enemies; strong of grip;
10   One kind with his fathers;
Owain, to slay Fflamddwyn,
    Thought it no more than sleep.

Sleepeth the wide host of England
    With light in their eyes,
15   And those that had not fled
    Were braver than were wise.

Owain dealt them doom
    As the wolves devour sheep;
That warrior, bright of harness,
20   Gave stallions for the bard.

Though he hoarded wealth like a miser
    For his soul's sake he gave it.
God, consider the soul's need
    Of Owain son of Urien!

⊢ ⊨⧫⊨ ⊣

The Wanderer

In the Exeter Book, a manuscript copied about 975 and donated to the Bishop of Exeter, are preserved some of the greatest short poems in Old English, including a number of poems referred to as elegies—laments that contrast past happiness with present sorrow and remark on how fleeting is the former. Along with *The Wanderer*, the elegies include its companion piece *The Seafarer*; *The Ruin*; *The Husband's Message*; *The Wife's Lament*; and *Wulf and Eadwacer*. While the last two are exceptional in dealing with female experience, elegies for the most part focus on male bonds and companionship, particularly the joys of the mead hall.

1. Translated by Saunders Lewis.

Old English poetry as a whole is almost entirely devoid of interest in romantic love between men and women and focuses instead on the bond between lord and retainer; elegiac poems such as *The Wanderer* have in fact been called "the love poetry of a heroic society."

The Wanderer opens with an appeal to a Christian concept, as the third-person narrator speaks of the wanderer's request for God's mercy. The body of the poem, however—primarily a first-person account in the wanderer's voice—reflects more pagan values in its regret for the loss of earthly joys. Though the poem's structure is somewhat confusing, one can discern two major parts. In the first, the wanderer laments his personal situation: he was once a member of a warrior band, but his lord—his beloved "gold-friend"—has died, leaving him a homeless exile. He dreams that he "clasps and kisses" his lord, but he then wakes to see only the dark waves, the snow, and the sea birds.

The second part of the poem turns from personal narrative to a more general statement of the transitoriness of all earthly things. The speaker (possibly someone other than the wanderer at this point), looking at the ruin of ancient buildings, is moved to express the ancient Roman motif known as *"ubi sunt"* (Latin for "where are"): "Where has the horse gone? Where the man? Where the giver of gold? / Where is the feasting place? And where the pleasures of the hall?" In the concluding five lines, the reader is urged to seek comfort in heaven.

There has been much debate about the degrees of Christianity and paganism in this tenth-century poem. The positions range from the view that the Christian opening and closing are totally extraneous to the poem and have been tacked on by a monkish copyist, to the view that the poem is a Christian allegory about a soul exiled from his heavenly home, longing for his lord Jesus Christ. It is now generally held that the poem is authentically Christian, in a literal rather than an allegorical way, but that the values of pagan society still exert a powerful pull in it.

The Wanderer[1]

Often the wanderer pleads for pity
and mercy from the Lord; but for a long time,
sad in mind, he must dip his oars
into icy waters, the lanes of the sea;
5   he must follow the paths of exile: fate is inflexible.

Mindful of hardships, grievous slaughter,
the ruin of kinsmen, the wanderer said:
"Time and again at the day's dawning
I must mourn all my afflictions alone.
10   There is no one still living to whom I dare open
the doors of my heart. I have no doubt
that it is a noble habit for a man
to bind fast all his heart's feelings,
guard his thoughts, whatever he is thinking.
15   The weary in spirit cannot withstand fate,
a troubled mind finds no relief:
wherefore those eager for glory often
hold some ache imprisoned in their hearts.
Thus I had to bind my feelings in fetters,

1. Translated by Kevin Crossley-Holland.

20   often sad at heart, cut off from my country,
      far from my kinsmen, after, long ago,
      dark clods of earth covered my gold-friend;
      I left that place in wretchedness,
      plowed the icy waves with winter in my heart;
25   in sadness I sought far and wide
      for a treasure-giver, for a man
      who would welcome me into his mead-hall,
      give me good cheer (for I boasted no friends),
      entertain me with delights. He who has experienced it
30   knows how cruel a comrade sorrow can be
      to any man who has few loyal friends:
      for him are the ways of exile, in no wise twisted gold;
      for him is a frozen body, in no wise the fruits of the earth.
      He remembers hall-retainers and treasure
35   and how, in his youth, his gold-friend
      entertained him. Those joys have all vanished.
      A man who lacks advice for a long while
      from his loved lord understands this,
      that when sorrow and sleep together
40   hold the wretched wanderer in their grip,
      it seems that he clasps and kisses
      his lord, and lays hands and head
      upon his lord's knee as he had sometimes done
      when he enjoyed the gift-throne in earlier days.
45   Then the friendless man wakes again
      and sees the dark waves surging around him,
      the sea-birds bathing, spreading their feathers,
      frost and snow falling mingled with hail.
      "Then his wounds lie more heavy in his heart,
50   aching for his lord. His sorrow is renewed;
      the memory of kinsmen sweeps through his mind;
      joyfully he welcomes them, eagerly scans
      his comrade warriors. Then they swim away again.
      Their drifting spirits do not bring many old songs
55   to his lips. Sorrow upon sorrow attend
      the man who must send time and again
      his weary heart over the frozen waves.
      "And thus I cannot think why in the world
      my mind does not darken when I brood on the fate
60   of brave warriors, how they have suddenly
      had to leave the mead-hall, the bold followers.
      So this world dwindles day by day,
      and passes away; for a man will not be wise
      before he has weathered his share of winters
65   in the world. A wise man must be patient,
      neither too passionate nor too hasty of speech,
      neither too irresolute nor too rash in battle;

not too anxious, too content, nor too grasping,
and never too eager to boast before he knows himself.
70 When he boasts a man must bide his time
until he has no doubt in his brave heart
that he has fully made up his mind.
A wise man must fathom how eerie it will be
when all the riches of the world stand waste,
75 as now in diverse places in this middle-earth
old walls stand, tugged at by winds
and hung with hoar-frost, buildings in decay.
The wine-halls crumble, lords lie dead,
deprived of joy, all the proud followers
80 have fallen by the wall: battle carried off some,
led them on journeys; the bird carried one
over the welling waters; one the gray wolf
devoured; a warrior with downcast face
hid one in an earth-cave.
85 Thus the Maker of Men laid this world waste
until the ancient works of the giants stood idle,
hushed without the hubbub of inhabitants.
Then he who has brooded over these noble ruins,
and who deeply ponders this dark life,
90 wise in his mind, often remembers
the many slaughters of the past and speaks these words:
Where has the horse gone? Where the man? Where the giver of gold?
Where is the feasting-place? And where the pleasures of the hall?
I mourn the gleaming cup, the warrior in his corselet,
95 the glory of the prince. How that time has passed away,
darkened under the shadow of night as if it had never been.
Where the loved warriors were, there now stands a wall
of wondrous height, carved with serpent forms.
The savage ash-spears, avid for slaughter,
100 have claimed all the warriors—a glorious fate!
Storms crash against these rocky slopes,
sleet and snow fall and fetter the world,
winter howls, then darkness draws on,
the night-shadow casts gloom and brings
105 fierce hailstorms from the north to frighten men.
Nothing is ever easy in the kingdom of earth,
the world beneath the heavens is in the hands of fate.
Here possessions are fleeting, here friends are fleeting,
here man is fleeting, here kinsman is fleeting,
110 the whole world becomes a wilderness."
So spoke the wise man in his heart as he sat apart in thought.
Brave is the man who holds to his beliefs; nor shall he ever
show the sorrow in his heart before he knows how he
can hope to heal it. It is best for a man to seek
115 mercy and comfort from the Father in heaven, the safe home that awaits us all.

⊷ ⚔ ⊶

Wulf and Eadwacer *and* The Wife's Lament

Old English literature focuses largely on masculine and military concerns and lacks a concept of romantic love—what the twelfth-century French would later call "*fine amour.*" Against this backdrop *Wulf and Eadwacer* and *The Wife's Lament* stand out, first, by their use of woman's voice and second, by their treatment of the sorrows of love.

Though the exact genre of these poems is problematic, some scholars classifying them as riddles and others as religious allegories, most group them with a class of Old English poems known as elegies, with which they are preserved in the same manuscript, the Exeter Book. The elegies lament the loss of earthly goods, comradeship, and the "hall joys," often, as in *The Wanderer* and *The Seafarer*, by a speaker in exile. *The Wife's Lament* and *Wulf and Eadwacer* differ from the other elegies in that the speakers, as women, had no experience of comradeship to lose, as their main function was to be exchanged in marriage to cement relationships between feuding tribes. They are in a sense twice exiled, first from the noble brotherhood by their gender, and second from their beloved by their personal history. Furthermore, unlike the speakers in *The Wanderer* and *The Seafarer*, they do not look forward to the consolation of a heavenly kingdom imagined as a warlord with his group of retainers.

Although the two elegies in woman's voice are unique in the Old English corpus, they have analogues within the larger tradition of continental woman's song, which flourished in medieval Latin and the vernaculars from the eleventh century on. Their composition was so early—990 at the latest—that this tradition could not have influenced them, although the Roman poet Ovid's *Heroides* (verse letters of abandoned heroines to their faithless lovers) could have done so. One critic has raised the question of female authorship, on the grounds that continental nuns in the eighth century were criticized for writing romantic songs. As the critic Marilynn Desmond has suggested, perhaps Virginia Woolf's speculation that "anonymous was a woman" is true of these poems.

Though scholars agree that *Wulf and Eadwacer* is "heartrending" and "haunting," they cannot agree on the dramatic situation—each translation is an act of interpretation. The present translator, Kevin Crossley-Holland, sees the poem as involving the female speaker; her husband (Eadwacer); her lover (Wulf), from whom she is separated; and her child (a "cub"). Although what transpired before is unclear, she wistfully concludes, "men easily savage what was never secure, our song together." The dramatic setting of *The Wife's Lament* is similarly ambiguous; it is not clear whether the woman's anger is directed toward her husband or to a third person who plotted to separate them.

Wulf and Eadwacer[1]

Prey, it's as if my people have been handed prey.
They'll tear him to pieces if he comes with a troop.

O, we are apart.

Wulf is on one island, I on another,
5   a fastness that island, a fen-prison.
Fierce men roam there, on that island;
they'll tear him to pieces if he comes with a troop.

O, we are apart.

---

1. Translated by Kevin Crossley-Holland.

How I have grieved for my Wulf's wide wanderings.
10   When rain slapped the earth and I sat apart weeping,
when the bold warrior wrapped his arms about me,
I seethed with desire and yet with such hatred.
Wulf, my Wulf, my yearning for you
and your seldom coming have caused my sickness,
15   my mourning heart, not mere starvation.
Can you hear, Eadwacer? Wulf will spirit
our pitiful whelp to the woods.
Men easily savage what was never secure,
our song together.

The Wife's Lament[1]

I draw these words from my deep sadness,
my sorrowful lot. I can say that,
since I grew up, I have not suffered
such hardships as now, old or new.

5   I am tortured by the anguish of exile.
First my lord forsook his family
for the tossing waves; I fretted at dawn
as to where in the world my lord might be.
In my sorrow I set out then,
10   a friendless wanderer, to search for my man.
But that man's kinsmen laid secret plans
to part us, so that we should live
most wretchedly, far from each other
in this wide world; I was seized with longings.

15   My lord asked me to live with him here;
I had few loved ones, loyal friends
in this country; that is reason for grief.
Then I found my own husband was ill-starred,
sad at heart, pretending, plotting
20   murder behind a smiling face. How often
we swore that nothing but death should ever
divide us; that is all changed now;
our friendship is as if it had never been.
Early and late, I must undergo hardship
25   because of the feud of my own dearest loved one.
Men forced me to live in a forest grove,
under an oak tree in the earth-cave.
This cavern is age-old; I am choked with longings.
Gloomy are the valleys, too high the hills,
30   harsh strongholds overgrown with briars:
a joyless abode. The journey of my lord so often
cruelly seizes me. There are lovers on earth,

1. Translated by Kevin Crossley-Holland.

lovers alive who lie in bed,
when I pass through this earth-cave alone
35   and out under the oak tree at dawn;
there I must sit through the long summer's day
and there I mourn my miseries,
my many hardships; for I am never able
to quiet the cares of my sorrowful mind,
40   all the longings that are my life's lot.

Young men must always be serious in mind
and stout-hearted; they must hide
their heartaches, that host of constant sorrows,
behind a smiling face.
                              Whether he is master
45   of his own fate or is exiled in a far-off land—
sitting under rocky storm-cliffs, chilled
with hoar-frost, weary in mind,
surrounded by the sea in some sad place—
my husband is caught in the clutches of anguish;
over and again he recalls a happier home.
50   Grief goes side by side with those
who suffer longing for a loved one.

⊱ ❦ ⊰

Riddles

Riddles were a popular genre in Anglo-Saxon England, appealing to a taste for intellectual puzzles, which we also see in *Beowulf*, with its kennings; *The Dream of the Rood*, with its speaking cross; and *Wulf and Eadwacer*, with its cryptic dramatic situation. In the Exeter Book, one of the four major manuscripts containing Anglo-Saxon poetry (including *The Wanderer*, *The Wife's Lament*, and *Wulf and Eadwacer*) there are nearly a hundred riddles in Old English, dating from the seventh to the tenth centuries. They were in some cases modeled on collections of a hundred Latin riddles by the seventh-century Anglo-Saxon scholar Aldhelm, but they also derive in large part from indigenous folk tradition. In fact, they mark an important point of intersection between literate and oral culture in Anglo-Saxon England: though designed to be recited, they are written and sometimes focus on the technology of writing.

The three Anglo-Latin riddles of Aldhelm included here reveal an attitude of awe toward writing, conceived as an almost magical act, partly because of its novelty in a recently oral culture, but more because of its ownership by a priestly class in control of Christianity, the religion of "the Book." Aldhelm gives a sense of the tremendous effort that went into book-making—scratching treated animal skins with a quill pen or cutting into tablets made of wax, wood, and leather—and the resultant splendid object, adorned with "artful windings," cut into a "fair design." In the *Alphabet*, he makes the personified letters express their pride in the paradox of writing as voiceless speech: "We / in silence quickly bring out hoarded words." The pen in the riddle of that name speaks of its origin as a bird's feather and of its ability, despite its present earthbound state, to help lead the virtuous to heaven.

Of the Old English riddles included here, four also have to do with writing, an activity important in the daily life of priests. Old English Riddle 2 traces the making of a book by speaking as a sheep slain for its skin to make parchment, describing the "bird's feather" leaving tracks on its surface, and concluding in the person of the Bible itself, decorated with "the wondrous work of smiths," sacred and useful at the same time. Old English Riddle 5 similarly traces a tool from its origin in nature to its status as a manufactured thing. The narrator speaks of its life growing by the water (as a plant), the paradox that, though "mouthless," it should "sing / to men sitting at the mead-bench" (as a flute), and the "miracle" by which it can send a private message (as a pen).

In contrast to those Old English riddles concerned with writing, the majority deal with aspects of Anglo-Saxon secular life, with answers such as a shield, a storm, an iceberg, or a ship. The poem of this sort included here, Old English Riddle 1, explores areas of experience usually ignored by Old English epic, elegiac, and religious poetry. Beginning traditionally, "I'm a strange creature," it treats domestic activity—the storage and preparation of food—by a lower-class woman, a churl's daughter. One of several sexual riddles in the Exeter Book, it is a finely sustained *double entendre*, showing that there was indeed humor in Old English poetry.

(Following the manuscripts, Aldhelm's riddles are printed with the titles that state their solutions, while those from the Exeter Book—which offers no solutions—are followed by solutions given by modern editors).

Three Anglo-Latin Riddles by Aldhelm[1]
Alphabet

We seventeen sisters, voiceless all, declare
Six others bastards are, and not of us.
Of iron we are born, and find our death
Again by iron; or at times we come
5   From pinion of a lofty-flying bird.
Three brothers got us of an unknown mother.
To him who thirsts for instant counsel, we
In silence quickly bring out hoarded words.

Writing Tablets

Of honey-laden bees I first was born,
But in the forest grew my outer coat;
My tough backs came from shoes. An iron point
In artful windings cuts a fair design,
5   And leaves long, twisted furrows, like a plow.
From heaven unto that field is borne the seed
Or nourishment, which brings forth generous sheaves
A thousandfold. Alas, that such a crop,
A holy harvest, falls before grim war.

Pen

The shining pelican, whose yawning throat
Gulps down the waters of the sea, long since
Produced me, white as he. Through snowy fields
I keep a straight road, leaving deep-blue tracks

---

1. Translated by James Hall Pitman.

5 Upon the gleaming way, and darkening
The fair champaign with black and tortuous paths;
Yet one way through the plain suffices not,
For with a thousand bypaths runs the road,
And them who stray not from it, leads to heaven.

Five Old English Riddles[1]

1

I'm a strange creature, for I satisfy women,
a service to the neighbors! No one suffers
at my hands except for my slayer.
I grow very tall, erect in a bed,
5   I'm hairy underneath. From time to time
a good-looking girl, the doughty daughter
of some churl dares to hold me,
grips my russet skin, robs me of my head
and puts me in the pantry. At once that girl
10   with plaited hair who has confined me
remembers our meeting. Her eye moistens.

2

An enemy ended my life, took away
of my bodily strength; then he dipped me
in water and drew me out again,
and put me in the sun where I soon shed
5   all my hair. The knife's sharp edge
bit into me once my blemishes had been scraped away;
fingers folded me and the bird's feather
often moved across my brown surface,
sprinkling useful drops; it swallowed the wood-dye
10   (part of the stream) and again traveled over me
leaving black tracks. Then a man bound me,
he stretched skin over me and adorned me
with gold; thus I am enriched by the wondrous work
of smiths, wound about with shining metal.
15   Now my clasp and my red dye
and these glorious adornments bring fame far and wide
to the Protector of Men, and not to the pains of hell.
If the sons of men would make use of me
they would be the safer and more sure of victory,
20   their hearts would be bolder, their minds more at ease,
their thoughts wiser, they would have more friends,
companions and kinsmen (true and honorable,
brave and kind) who would gladly increase
their honor and prosperity, and heap

---

1. Translated by Kevin Crossley-Holland.

25   benefits upon them, holding them fast
      in love's embraces. Ask what I am called,
      of such use to men. My name is famous,
      of service to men and sacred in itself.

3

      A moth devoured words. When I heard
      of that wonder it struck me as a strange event
      that a worm should swallow the song of some man,
      a thief gorge in the darkness on fine phrases
5   and their firm foundation. The thievish stranger
      was not a whit the wiser for swallowing words.

4

      I watched four curious creatures
      traveling together; their tracks were swart,
      each imprint very black. The birds' support
      moved swiftly; it flew in the air,
5   dived under the wave. The toiling warrior
      worked without pause, pointing the paths
      to all four over the beaten gold.

5

      I sank roots first of all, stood
      near the shore, close by the dyke
      and dash of waves; few men
      saw my home in that wilderness,
5   but each dawn, each dusk,
      the tawny waves surged and swirled
      around me. Little did I think
      that I, mouthless, should ever sing
      to men sitting at the mead-bench,
10   varying my pitch. It is rather puzzling,
      a miracle to men ignorant of such arts,
      how a knife's point and a right hand
      (mind and implement moving as one)
      could cut and carve me—so that I
15   can send you a message without fear,
      and no one else can overhear
      or noise abroad the words we share.

Solutions: 1. Penis or onion; 2. Bible; 3. Book worm; 4. Pen and fingers; 5. Reed.

AFTER THE NORMAN CONQUEST

⇒ PERSPECTIVES ⇐
Arthurian Myth in the History of Britain

Almost since it first appeared, the story of King Arthur has occupied a contested zone between myth and history. Far from diminishing the Arthurian tradition, though, this ambiguity has lent it a tremendous and protean impact on the political and cultural imagination of Europe, from the Middle Ages to the present. Probably no other body of medieval legend remains today as widely known and as often revisited as the Arthurian story.

One measure of Arthur's undiminished importance is the eager debate, eight centuries old and going strong, about his historical status. Whether or not a specific "Arthur" ever existed, legends and attributes gathered around his name from a very early date, mostly in texts of Welsh background. Around 600 a Welsh poem refers briefly to Arthur's armed might, and by about 1000, the story *Culhwch and Olwen*, from the Mabinogion, assumes knowledge of Arthur as a royal warlord. Other early Welsh texts begin to give him more-than-mortal attributes, associating Arthur with such marvels as an underworld quest and a mysterious tomb. In the ninth century, the Latin *History of the Britons* by the Welshman Nennius confidently speaks of Arthur as a great leader and lists his twelve victories ending with that at Mount Badon.

Some of this at least fits with better-documented history and with less-shadowy commanders who might have been models for an Arthurian figure, even if they were not "Arthur." When the Romans withdrew in 410, the romanized Britons soon faced territorial aggression from the Saxons and Picts. In the decades after midcentury, the Britons mounted a successful defense, led in part by Aurelius Ambrosius and culminating, it appears, with the battle of Badon in roughly 500, after which Saxon incursions paused for a time. In those same years of territorial threat, some Britons had emigrated to what is now Brittany, and in the 460s or 470s a warlord named Riothamus led an army, probably from Britain, and fought successfully in Gaul in alliance with local rulers sympathetic to Rome. His name was latinized from a British title meaning "supreme king." Both Riothamus and Aurelius Ambrosius correspond to parts of the later narratives of Arthur: his role as high king, his triumphs against the Saxons, his links to Rome (both friendly and hostile), and his campaigns on the continent.

Whether the origins of Arthur's story lie in fact or in an urge among the Welsh to imagine a great leader who once restored their power against the ever-expanding Anglo-Saxons, he was clearly an established figure in Welsh oral and written literature by the ninth century. Arthur, however, also held a broader appeal for other peoples of England. The British Isles were felt to lie at the outer edge of world geography, but the story of Arthur and his ancestor Brutus served to create a Britain with other kinds of centrality. The legend of Brutus made Britain the end point of an inexorable westward movement of Trojan imperial power, the *translatio imperii*, and Arthur's forebears became linked to Roman imperial dynasties. Finally, the general movement of Arthur's continental campaigns neatly reversed the patterns of Roman and then Norman colonization.

In the later Middle Ages and after, Arthur and his court are most often encountered in works that lay little claim to historical accuracy. Rather, they exploit the very uncertainty of Arthurian narrative to explore the highest (if sometimes self-deceiving) yearnings of private emotion and social order. These Arthurian romances also probe, often in tragic terms, the limits and taboos that both define and subvert such ideals, including the mutual threats posed by private emotion and social order.

Nevertheless, the Arthurian tradition has also been pulled persistently into the realm of the real. It was presented as serious historical writing from the twelfth century through the end of the Middle Ages. Political agents have used Arthur's kingship as a model or precedent for their own aspirations, as seen in the Kennedy administration's portrayal as a version of Camelot. Even elements of the Christian church wrote their doctrines into Arthurian narrative or claimed Arthur as a patron.

The texts in this section present three illuminating moments of Arthur's emergence into history and politics. Geoffrey of Monmouth's *History of the Kings of Britain*, finished around 1138, was the fullest version yet of Arthur's origin and career. Geoffrey was the first to make Arthur such a central figure in British history, and it was largely through Geoffrey's Latin "history" that Arthur became so widespread a feature of cultural imagination in the Middle Ages and beyond. Writing at the close of the twelfth century, Gerald of Wales narrates an occasion, possibly orchestrated by Henry II, in which Arthurian tradition was slightly altered and folded into emergent Norman versions of British antiquity. The section ends with two politically charged versions of national origin, English and Scottish, proposed in 1301 as part of Edward I's efforts to influence royal succession in Scotland.

Geoffrey of Monmouth
c. 1100–1155

From the perspective of surviving British peoples in Wales and Cornwall, the Norman Conquest of 1066 was only the last among successive waves of invasion by Romans, Picts, Anglo-Saxons, and Vikings. The Celtic Britons had long been pushed into the far southwest by the time the Normans arrived, where they continued to resist colonization. The Welsh maintained a vital language, culture, and ethnic mythology, including a memory of their fellow Celts in Brittany and a divided nostalgia for the long-departed Romans. Thus a whole Celtic linguistic and political world offered an alternative to the languages and legends of the Normans, much of which derived ultimately from Mediterranean antiquity. Arthur, king of the Britons, emerged as a key figure as these peoples and cultures began to articulate the complex new forms of political and private identity precipitated by the Conquest.

No one was more important in this process than Geoffrey of Monmouth. He was prior of the Abbey of Monmouth in Wales and later was named bishop of Saint Asaph, though civil disorder prevented his taking the post. Yet he was also active in the emerging schools of Oxford, he was patronized by Norman nobles and bishops, and he wrote in Latin. Geoffrey's learning reflects this double allegiance. Well schooled in the Latin curriculum that embraced ancient Roman and Christian literature, he was also deeply versed in the oral and written culture of Wales. As a creative negotiater between Welsh and Anglo-Norman legends and languages, his influence was without parallel.

Both of Geoffrey's surviving prose works, the *Prophecies of Merlin* (finished around 1135) and the *History of the Kings of Britain* (about 1138) present themselves as translations of ancient texts from Wales or Brittany. Geoffrey also wrote a *Life of Merlin* in Latin verse. He probably synthesized a number of sources and added material of his own in his "translations." It was a pointed gesture, nevertheless, to posit a Celtic text whose authority rivaled the Latin culture and legends that had underwritten later Anglo-Saxon and then Norman power in England. Geoffrey daringly inverted the general hierarchy of Latin and vernaculars in his time; instead, he offered "British" as the ancient tongue that he wanted to make more broadly accessible for Latin-reading newcomers.

Geoffrey's central heroes are Brutus, the exiled Trojan descendant who colonized and named Britain, and Arthur, who reunified England after Saxon and Pictish attacks, and repulsed Roman efforts to re-establish power there. Geoffrey's own purposes in the *History* were complex but he was responding in part to contemporary events. The 1130s were a decade of civil strife in England, as nobles shifted their allegiances between King Stephen and the other claimant to the throne, the future Henry II. Welsh nobles took advantage of this disorder to rebel and set up their own principalities. Scholars remain divided as to whether Geoffrey was more interested in a return to strong and unified rule in Norman England, or wanted rather to encourage the Welsh princes with the story of a great predecessor who might one day return.

Geoffrey's narrative carefully presents itself as history, in a century of great historical writing. He uses the typical armature of documentary and other written records, archaeological evidence, and claims to well-founded witness. Casting the story of Arthur into this respected form allows Geoffrey to employ but also to counter the dominant master-narrative of Christian history in England, which was Bede's. Rather than a story of Anglo-Saxon arrival and conversion, Geoffrey offers a story of an earlier foundation and a prior conversion; he thus creates imaginative space for a convergence between Norman power and the culture and ambitions of people and languages at its edges. Moreover, the *History* generates an exterior (if now conveniently absent) common enemy in the imperial Romans. Geoffrey pulls in yet more ancient models by frequently echoing Virgil's *Aeneid* and its story of exile and refoundation, and by placing his story within biblical, Trojan, and Roman chronologies. And he points forward to his own time by inserting the earlier *Prophecies of Merlin* in the midst of the *History*.

The continued influence of Geoffrey's *History* on later literature is testimony to the powerful themes he folded into his story. Much that is developed in later romance explorations of the Arthurian world is already here: the tragedy of a people bravely battling its own decline; the danger and overwhelming attraction of illicit sexual desire; the ambivalent position of Mordred as cousin or nephew; the Arthurian realm brought down, ultimately, by the treachery of the king's own kin and by a transgression of the marriage bed that echoes Arthur's own conception.

The following selections from Geoffrey's *History* feature the Trojan background of Britain and the birth and early kingship of Arthur. Other texts in this section and following trace later episodes in his evolving legend: the development of Arthur's court, the celebration and tragedy of romantic desire, and the death of the king.

from History of the Kings of Britain[1]
Dedication

Whenever I have chanced to think about the history of the kings of Britain, on those occasions when I have been turning over a great many such matters in my mind, it has seemed a remarkable thing to me that, apart from such mention of them as Gildas and Bede had each made in a brilliant book on the subject, I have not been able to discover anything at all on the kings who lived here before the Incarnation of Christ, or indeed about Arthur and all the others who followed on after the Incarnation. Yet the deeds of these men were such that they deserve to be praised for all time. What is more, these deeds were handed joyfully down in oral tradition, just as if they had been committed to writing, by many peoples who had only their memory to rely on.

At a time when I was giving a good deal of attention to such matters, Walter, Archdeacon of Oxford, a man skilled in the art of public speaking and well-informed about the history of foreign countries, presented me with a certain very ancient book written in the British language.[2] This book, attractively composed to

---

1. Translated by Lewis Thorpe (1966).
2. Walter and Geoffrey were both associated with an early Oxford college, and their names appear together on

several legal documents. In two of these, Geoffrey calls himself a *magister*, a teacher at an advanced level.

form a consecutive and orderly narrative, set out all the deeds of these men, from Brutus, the first King of the Britons, down to Cadwallader, the son of Cadwallo.[3] At Walter's request I have taken the trouble to translate the book into Latin, although, indeed, I have been content with my own expressions and my own homely style and I have gathered no gaudy flowers of speech in other men's gardens. If I had adorned my page with high-flown rhetorical figures, I should have bored my readers, for they would have been forced to spend more time in discovering the meaning of my words than in following the story.

I ask you, Robert, Earl of Gloucester,[4] to do my little book this favor. Let it be so emended by your knowledge and your advice that it must no longer be considered as the product of Geoffrey of Monmouth's small talent. Rather, with the support of your wit and wisdom, let it be accepted as the work of one descended from Henry, the famous King of the English; of one whom learning has nurtured in the liberal arts and whom his innate talent in military affairs has put in charge of our soldiers, with the result that now, in our own lifetime, our island of Britain hails you with heartfelt affection, as if it had been granted a second Henry.

You too, Waleran, Count of Mellent, second pillar of our kingdom, give me your support, so that, with the guidance provided by the two of you, my work may appear all the more attractive when it is offered to its public.[5] For indeed, sprung as you are from the race of the most renowned King Charles, Mother Philosophy has taken you to her bosom, and to you she has taught the subtlety of her sciences. What is more, so that you might become famous in the military affairs of our army, she has led you to the camp of kings, and there, having surpassed your fellow-warriors in bravery, you have learned, under your father's guidance, to be a terror to your enemies and a protection to your own folk. Faithful defender as you are of those dependent on you, accept under your patronage this book which is published for your pleasure. Accept me, too, as your writer, so that, reclining in the shade of a tree which spreads so wide, and sheltered from envious and malicious enemies, I may be able in peaceful harmony to make music on the reed-pipe of a muse who really belongs to you.

[TROY, AENEAS, BRUTUS' EXILE][6]

After the Trojan war, Aeneas fled from the ruined city with his son Ascanius and came by boat to Italy. He was honorably received there by King Latinus, but Turnus, King of the Rutuli, became jealous of him and attacked him. In the battle between them Aeneas was victorious. Turnus was killed and Aeneas seized both the kingdom of Italy and the person of Lavinia, who was the daughter of Latinus.[7]

When Aeneas' last day came, Ascanius was elected King. He founded the town of Alba on the bank of the Tiber and became the father of a son called Silvius. This Silvius was involved in a secret love-affair with a certain niece of Lavinia's; he married her and made her pregnant. When this came to the knowledge of his father

3. Bede's *Ecclesiastical History of the English People* was the source most used by 12th-century historians, but it has little to say about England before the coming of the Angles and Saxons. Geoffrey offers a (perhaps fictive) source for a more ancient history of the people who preceded the Saxons.
4. An illegitimate son of King Henry I. He had a hand in the education of the future Henry II, his nephew.
5. Waleran de Beaumont, Count of Meulan (1104–1166)

moved in the same circles as the Earl of Gloucester, and was patron of the Norman Abbey of Bec, a great center of learning. Geoffrey's fulsome tone is typical of dedications to great magnates in the period.
6. From bk. 1, ch. 3.
7. This summarizes the political narrative of Virgil's *Aeneid*, a text Geoffrey knew well and echoed frequently throughout his *History*.

Ascanius, the latter ordered his soothsayers to discover the sex of the child which the girl had conceived. As soon as they had made sure of the truth of the matter, the soothsayers said that she would give birth to a boy, who would cause the death of both his father and his mother; and that after he had wandered in exile through many lands this boy would eventually rise to the highest honor.

The soothsayers were not wrong in their forecast. When the day came for her to have her child, the mother bore a son and died in childbirth. The boy was handed over to the midwife and was given the name Brutus. At last, when fifteen years had passed, the young man killed his father by an unlucky shot with an arrow, when they were out hunting together. Their beaters drove some stags into their path and Brutus, who was under the impression that he was aiming his weapon at these stags, hit his own father below the breast. As the result of this death Brutus was expelled from Italy by his relations, who were angry with him for having committed such a crime. He went in exile to certain parts of Greece; and there he discovered the descendants of Helenus, Priam's son, who were held captive in the power of Pandrasus, King of the Greeks. After the fall of Troy, Pyrrhus, the son of Achilles, had dragged this man Helenus off with him in chains, and a number of other Trojans, too. He had ordered them to be kept in slavery, so that he might take vengeance on them for the death of his father.

When Brutus realized that these people were of the same race as his ancestors, he stayed some time with them. However, he soon gained such fame for his military skill and prowess that he was esteemed by the kings and princes more than any young man in the country.

[THE NAMING OF BRITAIN][8]

[*Brutus conquers the Greek king (reversing the Greek conquest of his ancestral Troy), marries the king's daughter Ignoge, and leads the Trojan descendants off to seek a new land. They pass through continental Europe, where they do battle with the Gauls.*]

In their pursuit the Trojans continued to slaughter the Gauls, and they did not abandon the bloodshed until they had gained victory.

Although this signal triumph brought him great joy, Brutus was nevertheless filled with anxiety, for the number of his men became smaller every day, while that of the Gauls was constantly increasing. Brutus was in doubt as to whether he could oppose the Gauls any longer; and he finally chose to return to his ships in the full glory of his victory while the greater part of his comrades were still safe, and then to seek out the island which divine prophecy had promised would be his. Nothing else was done. With the approval of his men Brutus returned to his fleet. He loaded his ships with all the riches which he had acquired and then went on board. So, with the winds behind him, he sought the promised island, and came ashore at Totnes.

At this time the island of Britain was called Albion. It was uninhabited except for a few giants. It was, however, most attractive, because of the delightful situation of its various regions, its forests and the great number of its rivers, which teemed with fish; and it filled Brutus and his comrades with a great desire to live there. When they had explored the different districts, they drove the giants whom they had discovered

8. From bk. 1, chs. 15–18 and bk. 2, ch. 1.

into the caves in the mountains. With the approval of their leader they divided the land among themselves. They began to cultivate the fields and to build houses, so that in a short time you would have thought that the land had always been inhabited.

Brutus then called the island Britain from his own name, and his companions he called Britons. His intention was that his memory should be perpetuated by the derivation of the name. A little later the language of the people, which had up to then been known as Trojan or Crooked Greek, was called British, for the same reason.[9]

[BRUTUS BUILDS NEW TROY]

Once he had divided up his kingdom, Brutus decided to build a capital. In pursuit of this plan, he visited every part of the land in search of a suitable spot. He came at length to the River Thames, walked up and down its banks and so chose a site suited to his purpose. There then he built his city and called it Troia Nova. It was known by this name for long ages after, but finally by a corruption of the word it came to be called Trinovantum. * * *

When the above-named leader Brutus had built the city about which I have told you, he presented it to the citizens by right of inheritance, and gave them a code of laws by which they might live peacefully together. At that time the priest Eli was ruling in Judea and the Ark of the Covenant was captured by the Philistines. The sons of Hector reigned in Troy, for the descendants of Antenor had been driven out. In Italy reigned Aeneas Silvius, son of Aeneas and uncle of Brutus, the third of the Latin Kings.[1] * * *

In the meantime Brutus had consummated his marriage with his wife Ignoge. By her he had three sons called Locrinus, Kamber and Albanactus, all of whom were to become famous. When their father finally died, in the twenty-third year after his landing, these three sons buried him inside the walls of the town which he had founded. They divided the kingdom of Britain between them in such a way that each succeeded to Brutus in one particular district. Locrinus, who was the first-born, inherited the part of the island which was afterwards called Loegria after him. Kamber received the region which is on the further bank of the River Severn, the part which is now known as Wales but which was for a long time after his death called Kambria from his name. As a result the people of that country still call themselves Kambri today in the Welsh tongue. Albanactus, the youngest, took the region which is nowadays called Scotland in our language. He called it Albany, after his own name.

[MERLIN AND THE FIRST CONQUEST OF IRELAND][2]

[*The descendants of Brutus' three sons include Leir (Shakespeare's King Lear), the brothers Brennius and Belinus who conquer Rome, and Lud who rebuilds New Troy and names it Kaerlud after himself (whence "London"). In the reign of Lud's brother, Julius Caesar invades England; generations of Britons resist, until King Coel makes peace with the Roman legate Constantius. The latter succeeds Coel, marries Coel's daughter, and sires Constantine who becomes emperor of Rome. The Romans tire of defending Britain against invaders and withdraw from the island. Vortigern usurps the throne from the Briton line,*

---

9. With this detail, Geoffrey creates a linguistic history in which early Welsh is as ancient as classical Latin, and more purely "Trojan."

1. Medieval historians often made such parallels between biblical and secular chronologies.
2. From bk. 8, chs. 10–13.

then holds it in alliance with the Saxons Hengist and Horsa. The Saxons become aggressors, and Vortigern flees them but is overcome by the brothers Aurelius Ambrosius and Utherpendragon, who restore the Briton royal line and drive the Saxons into the north. Aurelius reigns, restoring churches and the rule of law; he wants to commemorate the Britons who died fighting off the Saxons.]

Aurelius collected carpenters and stone-masons together from every region and ordered them to use their skill to contrive some novel building which would stand forever in memory of such distinguished men. The whole band racked their brains and then confessed themselves beaten. Then Tremorinus, Archbishop of the City of the Legions,[3] went to the King and said: "If there is anyone anywhere who has the ability to execute your plan, then Merlin, the prophet of Vortigern, is the man to do it.[4] In my opinion, there is no one else in your kingdom who has greater skill, either in the foretelling of the future or in mechanical contrivances. Order Merlin to come and use his ability, so that the monument for which you are asking can be put up."

Aurelius asked many questions about Merlin; then he sent a number of messengers through the various regions of the country to find him and fetch him. They traveled through the provinces and finally located Merlin in the territory of the Gewissei, at the Galabes Springs, where he often went. They explained to him what they wanted of him and then conducted him to the King. The King received Merlin gaily and ordered him to prophesy the future, for he wanted to hear some marvels from him. "Mysteries of that sort cannot be revealed," answered Merlin, "except where there is the most urgent need for them. If I were to utter them as an entertainment, or where there was no need at all, then the spirit which controls me would forsake me in the moment of need."

He gave the same refusal to everyone present. The King had no wish to press him about the future, but he spoke to him about the monument which he was planning. "If you want to grace the burial-place of these men with some lasting monument," replied Merlin, "send for the Giants' Ring which is on Mount Killaraus in Ireland. In that place there is a stone construction which no man of this period could ever erect, unless he combined great skill and artistry. The stones are enormous and there is no one alive strong enough to move them. If they are placed in position round this site, in the way in which they are erected over there, they will stand forever."

At these words of Merlin's Aurelius burst out laughing. "How can such large stones be moved from so far-distant a country?" he asked. "It is hardly as if Britain itself is lacking in stones big enough for the job!" "Try not to laugh in a foolish way, your Majesty," answered Merlin. "What I am suggesting has nothing ludicrous about it. These stones are connected with certain secret religious rites and they have various properties which are medicinally important. Many years ago the Giants transported them from the remotest confines of Africa and set them up in Ireland at a time when they inhabited that country. Their plan was that, whenever they felt ill, baths should be prepared at the foot of the stones; for they used to pour water over

---

3. Also called Caerusk or Caerleon; Geoffrey mentions it often and may have had some connection with it.
4. Merlin, son of a Briton princess and a demonic spirit, has already appeared; he triumphed over Vortigern's

magicians and uttered a series of prophecies. Merlin's roles as a royal advisor, a prophet, and even a shape-shifter can be compared to those of poets in early Celtic cultures.

them and to run this water into baths in which their sick were cured. What is more, they mixed the water with herbal concoctions and so healed their wounds. There is not a single stone among them which hasn't some medicinal virtue."

When the Britons heard all this, they made up their minds to send for the stones and to make war on the people of Ireland if they tried to hold them back. In the end the King's brother, Utherpendragon, and fifteen thousand men, were chosen to carry out the task. Merlin, too, was co-opted, so that all the problems which had to be met could have the benefit of his knowledge and advice. They made ready their ships and they put to sea. The winds were favorable and they arrived in Ireland.

At that time there reigned in Ireland a young man of remarkable valor called Gillomanius. As soon as he heard that the Britons had landed in the country, he collected a huge army together and hurried to meet them. When he learned the reason of their coming, Gillomanius laughed out loud at those standing round him. "I am not surprised that a race of cowards has been able to devastate the island of the Britons," said he, "for the Britons are dolts and fools. Who ever heard of such folly? Surely the stones of Ireland aren't so much better than those of Britain that our realm has to be invaded for their sake! Arm yourselves, men, and defend your fatherland, for as long as life remains in my body they shall not steal from us the minutest fragment of the Ring."

When he saw that the Irish were spoiling for a fight, Uther hurriedly drew up his own line of battle and charged at them. The Britons were successful almost immediately. The Irish were either mangled or killed outright, and Gillomanius was forced to flee. Having won the day, the Britons made their way to Mount Killaraus. When they came to the stone structure, they were filled with joy and wonder. Merlin came up to them as they stood round in a group. "Try your strength, young men," said he, "and see whether skill can do more than brute strength, or strength more than skill, when it comes to dismantling these stones!"

At his bidding they all set to with every conceivable kind of mechanism and strove their hardest to take the Ring down. They rigged up hawsers and ropes and they propped up scaling-ladders, each preparing what he thought most useful, but none of these things advanced them an inch. When he saw what a mess they were making of it, Merlin burst out laughing. He placed in position all the gear which he considered necessary and dismantled the stones more easily than you could ever believe. Once he had pulled them down, he had them carried to the ships and stored on board, and they all set sail once more for Britain with joy in their hearts.

The winds were fair. They came to the shore and then set off with the stones for the spot where the heroes had been buried. The moment that this was reported to him, Aurelius dispatched messengers to all the different regions of Britain, ordering the clergy and the people to assemble and, as they gathered, to converge on Mount Ambrius, where they were with due ceremony and rejoicing to re-dedicate the burial-place which I have described. At the summons from Aurelius the bishops and abbots duly assembled with men from every rank and file under the King's command. All came together on the appointed day. Aurelius placed the crown on his head and celebrated the feast of Whitsun in right royal fashion, devoting the next three days to one long festival. * * *

Once he had settled these matters, and others of a similar nature, Aurelius ordered Merlin to erect round the burial-place the stones which he had brought from Ireland. Merlin obeyed the King's orders and put the stones up in a circle round the sepulchre, in exactly the same way as they had been arranged on Mount Killaraus in Ireland, thus proving that his artistry was worth more than any brute strength.

[UTHERPENDRAGON SIRES ARTHUR][5]

[*Vortigern's son attacks Aurelius Ambrosius and Utherpendragon. They drive him off, though Aurelius is poisoned through Saxon treachery. A miraculous star appears, which Merlin interprets as a sign of Uther's destined kingship, the coming of Arthur, and the rule of Uther's dynasty. At the same time, however, Merlin prophesies the decline of the Britons. As king, Uther fights off more Saxon incursions.*]

The next Eastertide Uther told the nobles of his kingdom to assemble in that same town of London, so that he could wear his crown and celebrate so important a feast-day with proper ceremony. They all obeyed, traveling in from their various cities and assembling on the eve of the feast. The King was thus able to celebrate the feast as he had intended and to enjoy himself in the company of his leaders. They, too, were all happy, seeing that he had received them with such affability. A great many nobles had gathered there, men worthy of taking part in such a gay festivity, together with their wives and daughters.

Among the others there was present Gorlois, Duke of Cornwall, with his wife Ygerna, who was the most beautiful woman in Britain. When the King saw her there among the other women, he was immediately filled with desire for her, with the result that he took no notice of anything else, but devoted all his attention to her. To her and to no one else he kept ordering plates of food to be passed and to her, too, he kept sending his own personal attendants with golden goblets of wine. He kept smiling at her and engaging her in sprightly conversation. When Ygerna's husband saw what was happening, he was so annoyed that he withdrew from the court without taking leave. No one present could persuade him to return, for he was afraid of losing the one object that he loved better than anything else. Uther lost his temper and ordered Gorlois to come back to court, so that he, the King, could seek satisfaction for the way in which he had been insulted. Gorlois refused to obey. The King was furious and swore an oath that he would ravage Gorlois' lands, unless the latter gave him immediate satisfaction.

Without more ado, while the bad blood remained between the two of them, the King collected a huge army together and hurried off to the Duchy of Cornwall, where he set fire to towns and castles. Gorlois' army was the smaller of the two and he did not dare to meet the King in battle. He preferred instead to garrison his castles and to bide his time until he could receive help from Ireland. As he was more worried about his wife than he was about himself, he left her in the castle of Tintagel,[6] on the seacoast, which he thought was the safest place under his control. He himself took refuge in a fortified camp called Dimilioc,[7] so that, if disaster overtook them, they should not both be endangered together. When the King heard of this, he went to the encampment where Gorlois was, besieged it and cut off every line of approach.

Finally, after a week had gone by, the King's passion for Ygerna became more than he could bear. He called to him Ulfin of Ridcaradoch, one of his soldiers and a

---

5. From bk. 8, chs. 19–24.
6. Tin-*ta*-jel, on the rocky northwestern coast of Cornwall.

7. Di-*mi*-li-oc, perhaps a site roughly five miles from Tintagel.

familiar friend, and told him what was on his mind. "I am desperately in love with Ygerna," said Uther, "and if I cannot have her I am convinced that I shall suffer a physical breakdown. You must tell me how I can satisfy my desire for her, for otherwise I shall die of the passion which is consuming me." "Who can possibly give you useful advice," answered Ulfin, "when no power on earth can enable us to come to her where she is inside the fortress of Tintagel? The castle is built high above the sea, which surrounds it on all sides, and there is no other way in except that offered by a narrow isthmus of rock. Three armed soldiers could hold it against you, even if you stood there with the whole kingdom of Britain at your side. If only the prophet Merlin would give his mind to the problem, then with his help I think you might be able to obtain what you want." The King believed Ulfin and ordered Merlin to be sent for, for he, too, had come to the siege.

Merlin was summoned immediately. When he appeared in the King's presence, he was ordered to suggest how the King could have his way with Ygerna. When Merlin saw the torment which the King was suffering because of this woman, he was amazed at the strength of his passion. "If you are to have your wish," he said, "you must make use of methods which are quite new and until now unheard-of in your day. By my drugs I know how to give you the precise appearance of Gorlois, so that you will resemble him in every respect. If you do what I say, I will make you exactly like him, and Ulfin exactly like Gorlois' companion, Jordan of Tintagel. I will change my own appearance, too, and come with you. In this way you will be able to go safely to Ygerna in her castle and be admitted."

The King agreed and listened carefully to what he had to do. In the end he handed the siege over to his subordinates, took Merlin's drugs, and was changed into the likeness of Gorlois. Ulfin was changed into Jordan and Merlin into a man called Britaelis, so that no one could tell what they had previously looked like. They then set off for Tintagel and came to the Castle in the twilight. The moment the guard was told that his leader was approaching, he opened the gates and the men were let in. Who, indeed, could possibly have suspected anything, once it was thought that Gorlois himself had come? The King spent that night with Ygerna and satisfied his desire by making love with her. He had deceived her by the disguise which he had taken. He had deceived her, too, by the lying things that he said to her, things which he planned with great skill. He said that he had come out secretly from his besieged encampment so that he might make sure that all was well with her, whom he loved so dearly, and with his castle, too. She naturally believed all that he said and refused him nothing that he asked. That night she conceived Arthur, the most famous of men, who subsequently won great renown by his outstanding bravery.

Meanwhile, when it was discovered at the siege of Dimilioc that the King was no longer present, his army, acting without his instructions, tried to breach the walls and challenge the beleaguered Duke to battle. The Duke, equally ill-advisedly, sallied forth with his men, imagining apparently that he could resist such a host of armed men with his own tiny band. As the struggle between them swayed this way and that, Gorlois was among the first to be killed. His men were scattered and the besieged camp was captured. The treasure which had been deposited there was shared out in the most inequitable way, for each man seized in his greedy fist whatever good luck and his own brute strength threw in his way.[8]

---

8. Geoffrey emphasizes the destructive potential of private greed, private ambition, and brute force, even in the rule of a strong king like Uther. This becomes a dominant theme in Geoffrey and later Arthurian narratives.

Not until the outrages which followed this daring act had finally subsided did messengers come to Ygerna to announce the death of the Duke and the end of the siege. When they saw the King sitting beside Ygerna in the likeness of their leader, they blushed red with astonishment to see that the man whom they had left behind dead in the siege had in effect arrived there safely before them. Of course, they did not know of the drugs prepared by Merlin. The King put his arms round the Duchess and laughed aloud to hear these reports. "I am not dead," he said. "Indeed, as you see, I am very much alive! However, the destruction of my camp saddens me very much and so does the slaughter of my comrades. What is more, there is great danger that the King may come this way and capture us in this castle. I will go out to meet him and make peace with him, lest even worse should befall us."

The King set out and made his way towards his own army, abandoning his disguise as Gorlois and becoming Utherpendragon once more. When he learned all that had happened, he mourned for the death of Gorlois; but he was happy, all the same, that Ygerna was freed from her marital obligations. He returned to Tintagel Castle, captured it and seized Ygerna at the same time, she being what he really wanted. From that day on they lived together as equals, united by their great love for each other; and they had a son and a daughter. The boy was called Arthur and the girl Anna.

[ANGLO-SAXON INVASION]

As the days passed and lengthened into years, the King fell ill with a malady which affected him for a long time. Meanwhile the prison warders who guarded Octa and Eosa,[9] as I have explained above, led a weary life. In the end they escaped with their prisoners to Germany and in doing so terrified the kingdom: for rumor had it that they had already stirred up Germany, and had fitted out a huge fleet in order to return to the island and destroy it. This, indeed, actually happened. They came back with an immense fleet and more men than could ever be counted. They invaded certain parts of Albany[1] and busied themselves in burning the cities there and the citizens inside them. The British army was put under the command of Loth of Lodonesia, with orders that he should keep the enemy at a distance. This man was one of the leaders, a valiant soldier, mature both in wisdom and age. As a reward for his prowess, the King had given him his daughter Anna and put him in charge of the kingdom while he himself was ill. When Loth moved forward against the enemy he was frequently driven back again by them, so that he had to take refuge inside the cities. On other occasions he routed and dispersed them, forcing them to fly either into the forests or to their ships. Between the two sides the outcome of each battle was always in doubt, it being hard to tell which of them was victorious. Their own arrogance was a handicap to the Britons, for they were unwilling to obey the orders of their leaders. This undermined their strength and they were unable to beat the enemy in the field.

Almost all the island was laid waste. When this was made known to the King, he fell into a greater rage than he could really bear in his weakened state. He told all his leaders to appear before him, so that he could rebuke them for their overweening pride and their feebleness. As soon as he saw them all assembled in his presence, he

---

9. A son and a kinsman of the Saxon Hengist; Uther had imprisoned them in London. Geoffrey closely connects the resurgence of the Saxon invaders with Uther's adultery and the disorder within his own army.
1. That is, Scotland, named for Brutus's son Albanactus.

reproached them bitterly and swore that he himself would lead them against the enemy. He ordered a litter to be built, so that he could be carried in it; for his weakness made any other form of progress impossible. Then he instructed them all to be in a state of preparedness, so that they could advance against the enemy as soon as the opportunity offered. The litter was constructed immediately, the men were made ready to start and the opportunity duly came.

They put the King in his litter and set out for Saint Albans, where the Saxons I have told you about were maltreating all the local population * * *

[Despite his illness, Uther prevails. Octa and Eosa are killed.]

Once the Saxons had been defeated, as I have explained above, they did not for that reason abandon their evil behavior. On the contrary, they went off to the northern provinces and preyed relentlessly upon the people there. King Uther was keen to pursue them, as he had proposed, but his princes dissuaded him from it, for after his victory his illness had taken an even more serious turn. As a result the enemy became bolder still in their enterprises, striving by every means in their power to take complete control of the realm. Having recourse, as usual, to treachery, they plotted to see how they could destroy the King by cunning. When every other approach failed, they made up their minds to kill him with poison. This they did: for while Uther lay ill in the town of St. Albans, they sent spies disguised as beggars, who were to discover how things stood at court. When the spies had obtained all the information that they wanted, they discovered one additional fact which they chose to use as a means of betraying Uther. Near the royal residence there was a spring of very limpid water which the King used to drink when he could not keep down any other liquids because of his illness. These evil traitors went to the spring and polluted it completely with poison, so that all the water which welled up was infected. When the King drank some of it, he died immediately. Some hundred men died after him, until the villainy was finally discovered. Then they filled the well in with earth. As soon as the death of the King was made known, the bishops of the land came with their clergy and bore his body to the monastery of Ambrius and buried it with royal honors at the side of Aurelius Ambrosius, inside the Giants' Ring.

[ARTHUR OF BRITAIN][2]

After the death of Utherpendragon, the leaders of the Britons assembled from their various provinces in the town of Silchester and there suggested to Dubricius, the Archbishop of the City of the Legions, that as their King he should crown Arthur, the son of Uther. Necessity urged them on, for as soon as the Saxons heard of the death of King Uther, they invited their own countrymen over from Germany, appointed Colgrin as their leader and began to do their utmost to exterminate the Britons. They had already over-run all that section of the island which stretches from the River Humber to the sea named Caithness.[3]

Dubricius lamented the sad state of his country. He called the other bishops to him and bestowed the crown of the kingdom upon Arthur. Arthur was a young man only fifteen years old; but he was of outstanding courage and generosity, and his

---

2. From bk. 9, chs. 1–11.   3. That is, Northumberland and Scotland.

inborn goodness gave him such grace that he was loved by almost all the people. Once he had been invested with the royal insignia, he observed the normal custom of giving gifts freely to everyone. Such a great crown of soldiers flocked to him that he came to an end of what he had to distribute. However, the man to whom open-handedness and bravery both come naturally may indeed find himself momentarily in need, but poverty will never harass him for long. In Arthur courage was closely linked with generosity, and he made up his mind to harry the Saxons, so that with their wealth he might reward the retainers who served his own household. The just-ness of his cause encouraged him, for he had a claim by rightful inheritance to the kingship of the whole island. He therefore called together all the young men whom I have just mentioned and marched on York.⁴ * * *

[*Arthur and his followers attack Colgrin and ultimately subdue the Saxons; then they repel armies of Scots, Picts, and Irish. Arthur restores Briton dynasties throughout England, marries Guinevere, and establishes a stable peace.*]

Arthur then began to increase his personal entourage by inviting very distin-guished men from far-distant kingdoms to join it. In this way he developed such a code of courtliness in his household that he inspired peoples living far away to imi-tate him. The result was that even the man of noblest birth, once he was roused to rivalry, thought nothing at all of himself unless he wore his arms and dressed in the same way as Arthur's knights. At last the fame of Arthur's generosity and bravery spread to the very ends of the earth; and the kings of countries far across the sea trembled at the thought that they might be attacked and invaded by him, and so lose control of the lands under their dominion. They were so harassed by these tor-menting anxieties that they rebuilt their towns and the towers in their towns, and then went so far as to construct castles on carefully chosen sites, so that, if invasion should bring Arthur against them, they might have a refuge in their time of need.

All this was reported to Arthur. The fact that he was dreaded by all encouraged him to conceive the idea of conquering the whole of Europe.

➤━┄ ⊠◈⊠ ┄━➤

Gerald of Wales
c. 1146–1222

Geoffrey of Monmouth's *History of the Kings of Britain* was soon retold in French, early Middle English, and Welsh, and it reappears in other languages for centuries. Contemporary histori-ans, especially those interested in pre-Saxon history, were enthusiastic about this new story. Others were skeptical. Nevertheless, Geoffrey's narrative was soon accepted widely as fact, adopted, and revised to serve the interests of the Angevin dynasty.

The discovery of Arthur's bones at Glastonbury Abbey in 1191, as reported by the prolif-ic writer Gerald of Wales, is a particularly rich instance of this habit, benefiting both the sta-tus of Henry II and the prestige of the abbey. Glastonbury faced a crisis common among Anglo-Saxon monastic foundations after the Norman Conquest. It was, in fact, probably the earliest Christian community in Britain; nonetheless, the oral tradition of its antiquity was

---

4. Geoffrey links the ancient practice of a king's largesse to his warrior band together with the claim of dynastic geneal-ogy. Arthur will again use the latter claim when he decides to invade Gaul and then march toward Rome.

weakened as the Normans took power, bringing with them a new insistence on written documentation. Glastonbury had little proof of its claims to ancient privilege, either by way of charters (and those mostly spurious) or the related prestige of holy relics. At the same time, Henry II was interested in ancient narratives that might legitimize his imperial aims.

Gerald's version of events both suggests Henry's almost wondrous wisdom in identifying the very spot of Arthur's burial and implies the existence of early written records at Glastonbury. To have Arthur as a patron, authenticated by King Henry himself, greatly substantiated the abbey's other claims. At the same time, Henry's knowledge mysteriously linked him to Arthur, and the corpse itself neatly altered Arthurian tradition, certifying Arthur's actual death and perhaps damping Welsh hopes for a messianic return.

from The Instruction of Princes[1]

The memory of Arthur, that most renowned King of the Britons, will endure forever. In his own day he was a munificent patron of the famous Abbey at Glastonbury, giving many donations to the monks and always supporting them strongly, and he is highly praised in their records. More than any other place of worship in his kingdom he loved the church of the Blessed Mary, Mother of God, in Glastonbury, and he fostered its interests with much greater loving care than that of any of the others. When he went out to fight, he had a full-length portrait of the Blessed Virgin painted on the front of his shield, so that in the heat of battle he could always gaze upon her; and whenever he was about to make contact with the enemy he would kiss her feet with great devoutness.

In our lifetime Arthur's body was discovered at Glastonbury, although the legends had always encouraged us to believe that there was something otherworldly about his ending, that he had resisted death and had been spirited away to some far-distant spot.[2] The body was hidden deep in the earth in a hollowed-out oak-bole and between two stone pyramids which had been set up long ago in the churchyard there. They carried it into the church with every mark of honor and buried it decently there in a marble tomb. It had been provided with most unusual indications which were, indeed, little short of miraculous, for beneath it—and not on top, as would be the custom nowadays—there was a stone slab, with a leaden cross attached to its underside. I have seen this cross myself and I have traced the lettering which was cut into it on the side turned towards the stone, instead of being on the outer side and immediately visible. The inscription read as follows: HERE IN THE ISLE OF AVALON LIES BURIED THE RENOWNED KING ARTHUR, WITH GUINEVERE, HIS SECOND WIFE.

There are many remarkable deductions to be made from this discovery. Arthur obviously had two wives, and the second one was buried with him. Her bones were found with those of her husband, but they were separate from his. Two-thirds of the coffin, the part towards the top end, held the husband's bones, and the other section, at his feet, contained those of his wife. A tress of woman's hair, blond, and still fresh and bright in color, was found in the coffin. One of the monks snatched it up and it immediately disintegrated into dust. There had been some indications in the Abbey records that the body would be discovered on this spot, and another clue was provided by lettering carved on the pyramids, but this had been almost completely erased by the

1. Translated by Lewis Thorpe. Gerald reports the same events again in a later text, the *Speculum Ecclesiae*.
2. In his other version (the *Speculum Ecclesiae*) Gerald is more nervously dismissive: "In their stupidity the British people maintain that he is still alive. . . . According to them, once he has recovered from his wounds this strong and all-powerful King will return to rule over the Britons in the normal way."

passage of the years. The holy monks and other religious had seen visions and revelations. However, it was Henry II, King of England, who had told the monks that, according to a story which he had heard from some old British soothsayer,[3] they would find Arthur's body buried at least sixteen feet in the ground, not in a stone coffin but in a hollowed-out oak-bole. It had been sunk as deep as that, and carefully concealed, so that it could never be discovered by the Saxons, whom Arthur had attacked relentlessly as long as he lived and whom, indeed, he had almost wiped out, but who occupied the island [of Britain] after his death. That was why the inscription, which was eventually to reveal the truth, had been cut into the inside of the cross and turned inwards towards the stone. For many a long year this inscription was to keep the secret of what the coffin contained, but eventually, when time and circumstance were both opportune, the lettering revealed what it had so long concealed.

What is now known as Glastonbury used in ancient times to be called the Isle of Avalon. It is virtually an island, for it is completely surrounded by marshlands. In Welsh it is called "Ynys Avallon," which means the Island of Apples. "Aval" is the Welsh word for apple, and this fruit used to grow there in great abundance.[4] After the Battle of Camlann,[5] a noblewoman called Morgan, who was the ruler and patroness of these parts as well as being a close blood-relation of King Arthur, carried him off to the island now known as Glastonbury, so that his wounds could be cared for. Years ago the district had also been called "Ynys Gutrin" in Welsh, that is the Island of Glass, and from these words the invading Saxons later coined the place-name "Glastingebury." The word "glass" in their language means "vitrum" in Latin, and "bury" means "castrum" [camp] or "civitas" [city].

You must know that the bones of Arthur's body which were discovered there were so big that in them the poet's words seem to be fulfilled:

All men will exclaim at the size of the bones they've exhumed.[6]

The Abbot showed me one of the shin-bones. He held it upright on the ground against the foot of the tallest man he could find, and it stretched a good three inches above the man's knee. The skull was so large and capacious that it seemed a veritable prodigy of nature, for the space between the eyebrows and the eye-sockets was as broad as the palm of a man's hand. Ten or more wounds could clearly be seen, but they had all mended except one. This was larger than the others and it had made an immense gash. Apparently it was this wound which had caused Arthur's death.

Edward I
1239–1307

Beginning in 1291, King Edward I of England revived an ancient claim to be feudal overlord of Scotland and thereby sought to control a disputed succession to its throne. By 1293 the Scottish king John Balliol had become Edward's vassal, but rebelled and was forced to abdicate in 1296. The military and diplomatic struggle (later called the "Great Cause") stretched

---

3. In the *Speculum Ecclesiae*, Gerald says that Henry learned this "from the historical accounts of the Britons and from their bards."
4. Citing and explaining words from the various British vernaculars is a widespread habit in Latin historical writ-

ing as early as Bede.
5. Arthur's last battle, fought against the rebel army of his kinsman Mordred. Arthur kills Mordred but is himself mortally wounded.
6. Virgil, *Georgics*, 1.497.

across the decade. By the turn of the fourteenth century, in an extraordinary move, both the English and Scots had turned to the court of Pope Boniface VIII for a legal decision. In pursuing Edward's claim, his agents ransacked chronicles—including Geoffrey of Monmouth's *History*—as well as ancient charters, to compile a dossier of historical and legal precedents. Despite his own bureaucratic reforms requiring documentary proof for most legal claims, Edward was ready to invoke common memory and ancient legends to support his position regarding Scotland. Knowing that such chronicle material would have no status in court, in May of 1301 Edward resorted to the letter below before Pope Boniface ruled in the matter.

The written letter was a highly developed and self-conscious genre during the Middle Ages. Letters were often meant to be public and could carry the force of law. Indeed, the form of many legal documents had developed from royal letters. Letter writing became an area for textbooks and school study, the *ars dictaminis*. Elaborate formulas of salutation and closing, and other rhetorical figures, were taught and used for important correspondence as a way of establishing the sender's learning and prestige. The papal curia employed a particularly challenging system of prose rhythm called the *cursus*, which was imitated in some royal chanceries and is found in the Latin of Edward's letter.

Letter sent to the Papal Court of Rome
Concerning the king's rights in the realm of Scotland[1]

To the most Holy Father in Christ lord Boniface, by divine providence the supreme pontiff of the Holy Roman and Universal Church, Edward, by grace of the same providence king of England, lord of Ireland, and duke of Aquitaine offers his humblest devotion to the blessed saints.[2] What follows we send to you not to be treated in the form or manner of a legal plea, but altogether extrajudicially, in order to set the mind of your Holiness at rest. The All-Highest, to whom all hearts are open, will testify how it is graven upon the tablets of our memory with an indelible mark, that our predecessors and progenitors, the kings of England, by right of lordship and dominion, possessed, from the most ancient times, the suzerainty of the realm of Scotland and its kings in temporal matters, and the things annexed thereto, and that they received from the self-same kings, and from such magnates of the realm as they so desired, liege homage and oaths of fealty. We, continuing in the possession of that very right and dominion, have received the same acknowledgments in our time, both from the king of Scotland, and from the magnates of that realm; and indeed such prerogatives of right and dominion did the kings of England enjoy over the realm of Scotland and its kings, that they have even granted to their faithful folk the realm itself, removed its kings for just causes, and constituted others to rule in their place under themselves. Beyond doubt these matters have been familiar from times long past and still are, though perchance it has been suggested otherwise to your Holiness' ears by foes of peace and sons of rebellion, whose elaborate and empty fabrications your wisdom, we trust, will treat with contempt.

Thus, in the days of Eli and of Samuel the prophet, after the destruction of the city of Troy, a certain valiant and illustrious man of the Trojan race called Brutus, landed with many noble Trojans, upon a certain island called, at that time, Albion.[3] It was

---

1. Translated by E. L. G. Stones (1965). Although sent in the name of the King, a Latin letter of such formality would have been written by notaries in his chancery. A French draft also survives, which might have been used by Edward himself.
2. A flowery opening formula was typical of formal letters

between persons of power; it also provided a place for Edward to make ambitious (and in the case of Aquitaine, highly optimistic) territorial claims.
3. Here the letter borrows closely from Geoffrey of Monmouth's foundation narrative; see page 186.

then inhabited by giants, and after he had defeated and slain them, by his might and that of his followers, he called it, after his own name, Britain, and his people Britons, and built a city which he called Trinovant, now known as London. Afterwards he divided his realm among his three sons, that is he gave to his first born, Locrine, that part of Britain now called England, to the second, Albanact, that part then known as Albany, after the name of Albanact, but now as Scotland, and to Camber, his youngest son, the part then known by his son's name as Cambria and now called Wales, the royal dignity being reserved for Locrine, the eldest. Two years after the death of Brutus there landed in Albany a certain king of the Huns, called Humber, and he slew Albanact, the brother of Locrine. Hearing this, Locrine, the king of the Britons, pursued him, and he fled and was drowned in the river which from his name is called Humber, and thus Albany reverted to Locrine. * * * Again, Arthur, king of the Britons, a prince most renowned, subjected to himself a rebellious Scotland, destroyed almost the whole nation, and afterwards installed as king of Scotland one Angusel by name. Afterwards, when King Arthur held a most famous feast at Caerleon, there were present there all the kings subject to him, and among them Angusel, king of Scotland, who manifested the service due for the realm of Scotland by bearing the sword of King Arthur before him; and in succession all the kings of Scotland have been subject to all the kings of the Britons. Succeeding kings of England enjoyed both monarchy and dominion in the island, and subsequently Edward, known as the elder, son of Alfred, king of England, had subject and subordinate to him, as lord superior, the kings of the Scots, the Cumbrians, and the Strathclyde Welsh. * * *

Since, indeed, from what has been said already, and from other evidence, it is perfectly clear and well-known that the realm of Scotland belongs to us of full right, by reason of property and of possession, and that we have not done and have not dared to do anything, as indeed we could not do, in writing or in action, by which any prejudice may be implied to our right or possession, we humbly beseech your Holiness to weigh all this with careful meditation, and to condescend to keep it all in mind when making your decision, setting no store, if you please, by the adverse assertions which come to you on this subject from our enemies, but, on the contrary, retaining our welfare and our royal rights, if it so please you, in your fatherly regard. May the Most High preserve you, to rule his Holy Church through many years of prosperity.

Kempsey, 7 May 1301, the twenty-ninth year of our reign.

RESPONSE

A Report to Edward I[1]

Sir, seeing that you have lately sent a statement to the pope concerning your right to Scotland, the Scots are making efforts to nullify that statement by certain objections which are given below. * * * They say that in that letter you ground your right on old

1. The Scots learned about Edward's letter and made their own response to the pope; this report to Edward, written in the French he would actually have used with his counselors, specifies the Scots' rebuttal. The Scots carefully assert the superior force of later charters and other legal instruments, and dismiss Edward's reliance on unauthenticated legends. In case Edward's story should carry weight with Boniface, however, they also provide a counternarrative of their own national foundation by Scota, daughter of the Pharaoh, and how she expelled British influence from her land. The English and Scots diplomats thus tell opposing prehistories that underwrite their current claims. Just as important, though, they are negotiating around an unusually articulate moment in the contest between different forms of textuality—legendary and chronicle tradition versus legal documents—in the creation of contemporary political power.

chronicles, which contain various falsehoods and lies, and are abrogated and made void by the subsequent contrary actions of your predecessors and of yourself, which vitiate all the remaining part of your letter, and therefore one should give no credence to such a document. And they say further, that with only this unworthy and feeble case to rely upon, you are striving to evade the cognizance of your true judge, and to suppress the truth, and unlawfully, by force of arms, to repel your weaker neighbors, and to prevent the pope from pursuing the examination of this case. * * *

Again, they say that the old chronicles that you use as evidence of your right could not assist you, even if they were authenticated, as is not the case, they say, because it is notorious that these same old chronicles are utterly made naught and of no avail by other subsequent documents of greater significance, by contrary agreements and actions, and by papal privileges. * * * Then, sir, in order that credence be not given to the documents, histories, and deeds described in your statement, they say that allegations like those recounted in your narrative are put out of court by the true facts, and they endeavor to demonstrate their assertion by chronicles and narratives of a contrary purport. Brutus divided between his three sons the island once called Britain, and now England, and gave to one son Loegria, to another Wales, and to the third what is now called Scotland, and made them peers, so that none of them was subject to another. Afterwards came a woman named Scota, daughter of Pharaoh of Egypt, who came via Spain and occupied Ireland, and afterwards conquered the land of Albany, which she had called, after her name, *Scotland*,[2] and one place in that land she had called after the names of her son Erk and her husband Gayl, wherefore that district was called *Ergaill* [Argyll], and they drove out the Britons, and from that time the Scots, as a new race and possessing a new name, had nothing to do with the Britons, but pursued them daily as their enemies, and were distinguished from them by different ranks and customs, and by a different language. Afterwards they joined company with the Picts, by whose strength they destroyed the Britons, and the land which is now called England, and for this reason the Britons gave tribute to the Romans, to obtain the help of the Roman emperor, whose name was Severus, against the Scots, and by his help the Britons made a wall between themselves and the Scots, having a length of 130 leagues in length from one sea to the other, and they say that by this it appears that Scotland was not at any time under the lordship of the Britons.[3] But they do not deny that King Arthur by his prowess conquered Denmark, France, Norway and also Scotland, and held them until he and Mordred were slain in battle, and from that time the realm of Scotland returned to its free status. They say that the Britons were then expelled by the Saxons, and then the Saxons by the Danes, and then the Danes by the Saxons, and that in the whole period of the Saxon kings the Scots remained free without being subject to them, and at that time, by the relics of Saint Andrew which came from Greece, they were converted to the faith five hundred years before the English became Christians, and from that time the realm of Scotland, with the king and the realm [*sic*], were under the lordship of the Roman church without any intermediary, and by it were they defended against all their enemies. * * *

=+ END OF PERSPECTIVES: ARTHURIAN MYTH IN THE HISTORY OF BRITAIN +=

2. This neatly replicates Brutus's trajectory from the eastern Mediterranean, across part of continental Europe, and thence to the British Isles.

3. The Scots artfully shift the emphasis found in Geoffrey of Monmouth. Roman colonization and Hadrian's wall become evidence of an ancient ethnic division and Scots independence both from the Britons and from the Britons' later invaders.

ARTHURIAN ROMANCE

Marie de France
fl. 2nd half of the 12th century

In a famous line from the prologue to her *Lais*, Marie de France suggested that serious readers could approach an obscure old book and "supply its significance from their own wisdom." The original French text, "*de lur sen le surplus mettre*," implies that such readers add on something that is missing. In part a gesture of respect toward the study of pagan Latin literature in a Christian setting, this statement also seems to permit Marie herself a dramatically new perspective when she encounters long-established Arthurian stories such as *Lanval*, and the related tale of Tristan and Isolt in *Chevrefoil*. Starting with a scene of war that readers of Geoffrey of Monmouth might recognize, Marie swiftly brings into play elements that had been largely absent in the historicizing stories of Arthur: bodily desire and its dangers, romantic longing, the realm of the uncanny, the power of women, the force of wealth and influence in even the noblest courts. Similarly, in *Chevrefoil* the lovers' brief, ecstatic meeting occurs as a crowd of courtiers awaits her.

Marie's specific identity remains obscure, but it is clear that she was a woman of French background writing in England in the later decades of the twelfth century, widely educated, and in touch with the royal court. She dedicates her book of *Lais* to a "noble King" who was probably Henry II, and she may have been his kinswoman. Marie's works draw into that courtly culture the languages and traditions of the English and Celtic past. She rewrote a Latin narrative about the origin of "Saint Patrick's Purgatory" and the adventure of an Irish knight there; and she retold the fables of Aesop using an English translation that she attributed to King Alfred. The *Lais*, she says, came to her through oral transmission, and she connects them with the Bretons. Indeed, the best early copy of the *Lais*, Harley manuscript 978 in the British Library, is itself a multilingual compilation that includes the early Middle English poem *The Cuckoo Song* ("Sumer is icumen in"; see page 551).

Writing a generation after Geoffrey of Monmouth and not long before Gerald of Wales, Marie brings a quite different and rather critical set of preoccupations to her Arthurian stories. She opens her tale with a realistic and admirable occasion of male power and strong kingship: Arthur's battle for territory and his reward of faithful vassals. A bleaker side of that courtly world, and perhaps of Marie's own, is also implicit, however. With a terseness and indirection typical of her *lais*, Marie shows women as property in the king's gift, knights forgotten when their wealth runs out, and the perversion of judicial process. In *Chevrefoil*, again, Isolt has only the title she gained by marriage, "the queen," never her own name.

Marvels and erotic desire dominate her tales, though, and women's power, for good or ill, is their primary motivating force. Guinevere, in a hostile portrait of adulterous aggression and vengeful dishonesty, nonetheless manages to manipulate Arthur and his legal codes when Lanval rejects her advances. The queen is countered by Lanval's supernatural mistress, who commands luxurious riches that dwarf Arthur's; she rescues Lanval by being an unimpeachable legal witness in his defense. Indeed, she arrives on her white palfrey as the moment of judgment nears, almost like a knightly champion in a trial by battle. Lanval vanishes into a timeless world of fulfilled desire and limitless wealth that has analogies in much older Celtic tradition—for instance, in *The Voyage of Máel Dúin* (page 141). This closing scene defies the reintegration of male courtly order that is typical even in the erotic romances of Marie's contemporary Chrétien de Troyes.

The realm of eroticism and women's power in *Lanval*, though, is not automatically any more virtuous or stable than the ostentatious wealth and corruptible law of the world of Arthurian men. If Lanval's mysterious lady is beautiful and generous, she also takes his knightliness from him. Lanval is last seen riding behind the lady, and not on a warhorse but on a palfrey. Guinevere swiftly reduces Arthur to a weak and temporizing king. And in her initial explosion after Lanval rejects her, Guinevere accuses him of homosexuality. For all its absurdity, the moment articulates unnerving implications of the profound bonds among men in the Arthurian world, implications that could interrupt genealogical transmission of wealth and power. Marie's Guinevere again voices fears the tradition has left unsaid.

Chevrefoil ("The Honeysuckle") involves romantic desires far more elevated than those in *Lanval*, but equally dangerous to the social order, and ultimately disastrous to the lovers. Even in this brief episode, the lovers' one intimate moment is hedged about by an anxious sense of a public and hostile world nearby, as well as a more distant royal power that crushes private love. Marie can assume her readers know the story of Tristan and Isolt and their tragic love. Tristan is sent to Ireland to fetch Isolt, the fiancée of his uncle, King Mark. On a boat returning to Cornwall, Tristan and Isolt share a love potion that had been meant to seal her marriage with Mark. The adulterous (and, from a medieval Catholic perspective, incestuous) affair that follows entangles all three in a web of desire, dependency, and family loyalty. The intense joy of the lovers' brief encounter in this episode, then, is complicated and darkened by the many echoes of other famous moments in their affair: a meeting under a tree, joint exile in a forest, and the intertwining vine and rose that later grow from their adjacent graves. And Marie's readers would have known that the reconciliation Isolt promises never, in fact, takes place. This tone of superabundant meaning—perhaps another version of the "*surplus*" mentioned above—is mirrored in the *lai* by the long message Isolt can interpret from a single word, Tristan's name carved on a piece of wood.

Marie de France may be trying less to propound a critique of the received stories of Arthur and Tristan than to recall her readers' attention to elements that tradition has left aside, as she suggests in her prologue. Some of this is no more troubling than a delightful fantasy of wealth and pleasure, outside time and without consequences. Other elements imply, with startling economy, forces that (in the hands of later romancers) tear the Arthurian world to pieces.

 For additional resources on Marie de France, go to *The Longman Anthology of British Literature* Web site at www.myliteraturekit.com.

from **LAIS**[1]

Prologue

Whoever has received knowledge
and eloquence in speech from God
should not be silent or secretive
but demonstrate it willingly.

5   When a great good is widely heard of,
then, and only then, does it bloom,
and when that good is praised by many,
it has spread its blossoms.
The custom among the ancients—

10   as Priscian[2] testifies—
was to speak quite obscurely

---

1. Translated by Robert Hanning and Joan Ferrante.
2. A famed grammarian of the late Roman empire,

Priscian remained widely influential in the study of Latin
language and literature in the 12th century.

Marie de France Writing, from an illuminated manuscript of her works. While most images of writing feature men, women were also writers and copyists as well as readers (see Color Plate 10). Here, in a late-13th-century manuscript of her poems, Marie de France is shown at her writing desk, strikingly similar in posture and detail (and in authority) to Laurence of Durham more than a century earlier (see page 2).

in the books they wrote,
so that those who were to come after
and study them
15   might gloss the letter
and supply its significance from their own wisdom.[3]
Philosophers knew this,
they understood among themselves
that the more time they spent,
20   the more subtle their minds would become
and the better they would know how to keep themselves
from whatever was to be avoided.
He who would guard himself from vice
should study and understand
25   and begin a weighty work
by which he might keep vice at a distance,
and free himself from great sorrow.
That's why I began to think
about composing some good stories
30   and translating from Latin to Romance;[4]
but that was not to bring me fame:
too many others have done it.
Then I thought of the *lais* I'd heard.[5]
I did not doubt, indeed I knew well,

3. Marie refers to the practice of supplying glosses—explanatory notes such as this one—to school texts; she also implies that later readers bring their own perspective to earlier works, a point relevant to her own free adaptation of earlier Arthurian stories.

4. That is, to French.

5. A *lai* was typically a short verse narrative, meant for oral performance with music. A particular group of these, often including Arthurian tales, was especially connected with Brittany.

35   that those who first began them
and sent them forth
composed them in order to preserve
adventures they had heard.
I have heard many told;
40   and I don't want to neglect or forget them.
To put them into word and rhyme
I've often stayed awake.

In your honor, noble King,[6]
who are so brave and courteous,
45   repository of all joys
in whose heart all goodness takes root,
I undertook to assemble these *lais*
to compose and recount them in rhyme.
In my heart I thought and determined,
50   sire, that I would present them to you.
If it pleases you to receive them,
you will give me great joy;
I shall be happy forever.
Do not think me presumptuous
55   if I dare present them to you.
Now hear how they begin.

Lanval

I shall tell you the adventure of another *lai*,
just as it happened:
it was composed about a very noble vassal;
in Breton, they call him Lanval.[1]

5   Arthur, the brave and the courtly king,
was staying at Cardoel,[2]
because the Scots and the Picts
were destroying the land.[3]
They invaded Logres°   *England*
10   and laid it waste.
At Pentecost, in summer,[4]
the king stayed there.
He gave out many rich gifts:
to counts and barons,
15   members of the Round Table—
such a company had no equal in all the world—
he distributed wives and lands,

---

6. Probably Henry II.

1. Marie seems to imply knowledge of Breton, a Celtic language related to Welsh. In other works, she shows knowledge of English as well, and excellent Latin.

2. Carlisle, in the north of England.

3. Scots and Picts were Arthur's traditional enemies.

4. "Summer" here refers to late spring. The feast of Pentecost commemorates the descent of the Holy Spirit among Christ's apostles; it is often the occasion of Arthurian stories, especially those that involve marvels.

to all but one who had served him.
That was Lanval; Arthur forgot him,
20   and none of his men favored him either.
For his valor, for his generosity,
his beauty and his bravery,
most men envied him;
some feigned the appearance of love
25   who, if something unpleasant happened to him,
would not have been at all disturbed.
He was the son of a king of high degree
but he was far from his heritage.
He was of the king's household
30   but he had spent all his wealth,
for the king gave him nothing
nor did Lanval ask.
Now Lanval was in difficulty,
depressed and very worried.
35   My lords, don't be surprised:
a strange man, without friends,
is very sad in another land,
when he doesn't know where to look for help.
The knight of whom I speak,
40   who had served the king so long,
one day mounted his horse
and went off to amuse himself.
He left the city
and came, all alone, to a field;
45   he dismounted by a running stream
but his horse trembled badly.
He removed the saddle and went off,
leaving the horse to roll around in the meadow.
He folded his cloak beneath his head
50   and lay down.
He worried about his difficulty,
he could see nothing that pleased him.
As he lay there
he looked down along the bank
55   and saw two girls approaching;
he had never seen any lovelier.
They were richly dressed,
tightly laced,
in tunics of dark purple;
60   their faces were very lovely.
The older one carried basins,
golden, well made, and fine;
I shall tell you the truth about it, without fail.
The other carried a towel.
65   They went straight
to where the knight was lying.

Lanval, who was very well bred,
got up to meet them.
They greeted him first
70   and gave him their message:
"Sir Lanval, my lady,
who is worthy and wise and beautiful,
sent us for you.
Come with us now.
75   We shall guide you there safely.
See, her pavilion is nearby!"
The knight went with them;
giving no thought to his horse
who was feeding before him in the meadow.
80   They led him up to the tent,[5]
which was quite beautiful and well placed.
Queen Semiramis,
however much more wealth,
power, or knowledge she had,
85   or the emperor Octavian[6]
could not have paid for one of the flaps.
There was a golden eagle on top of it,
whose value I could not tell,
nor could I judge the value of the cords or the poles
90   that held up the sides of the tent;
there is no king on earth who could buy it,
no matter what wealth he offered.
The girl was inside the tent:
the lily and the young rose
95   when they appear in the summer
are surpassed by her beauty.
She lay on a beautiful bed—
the bedclothes were worth a castle—
dressed only in her shift.
100   Her body was well shaped and elegant;
for the heat, she had thrown over herself,
a precious cloak of white ermine,
covered with purple alexandrine,°   *embroidery*
but her whole side was uncovered,
105   her face, her neck and her bosom;
she was whiter than the hawthorn flower.
The knight went forward
and the girl addressed him.
He sat before the bed.
110   "Lanval," she said, "sweet love,

---

5. Elaborate tents are often found in contemporary narratives of kings going out to battle.
6. Semiramis, legendary queen of Assyria and builder of Babylon, led armies of conquest; she is also a conventional figure of uncontrolled sexual desire. She is interestingly placed here as a female counterpart to Octavian (Augustus Caesar), the first Roman emperor.

because of you I have come from my land;
I came to seek you from far away.
If you are brave and courtly,
no emperor or count or king
115   will ever have known such joy or good;
for I love you more than anything."
He looked at her and saw that she was beautiful;
Love stung him with a spark
that burned and set fire to his heart.
120   He answered her in a suitable way.
"Lovely one," he said, "if it pleased you,
if such joy might be mine
that you would love me,
there is nothing you might command,
125   within my power, that I would not do,
whether foolish or wise.
I shall obey your command;
for you, I shall abandon everyone.
I want never to leave you.
130   That is what I most desire."
When the girl heard the words
of the man who could love her so,
she granted him her love and her body.
Now Lanval was on the right road!
135   Afterward, she gave him a gift:
he would never again want anything,
he would receive as he desired;
however generously he might give and spend,
she would provide what he needed.
140   Now Lanval is well cared for.
The more lavishly he spends,
the more gold and silver he will have.
"Love," she said, "I admonish you now,
I command and beg you,
145   do not let any man know about this.
I shall tell you why:
you would lose me for good
if this love were known;
you would never see me again
150   or possess my body."
He answered that he would do
exactly as she commanded.
He lay beside her on the bed;
now Lanval is well cared for.
155   He remained with her
that afternoon, until evening
and would have stayed longer, if he could,
and if his love had consented.
"Love," she said, "get up.

160   You cannot stay any longer.
       Go away now; I shall remain
       but I will tell you one thing:
       when you want to talk to me
       there is no place you can think of
165   where a man might have his mistress
       without reproach or shame,
       that I shall not be there with you
       to satisfy all your desires.
       No man but you will see me
170   or hear my words."
       When he heard her, he was very happy,
       he kissed her, and then got up.
       The girls who had brought him to the tent
       dressed him in rich clothes;
175   when he was dressed anew,
       there wasn't a more handsome youth in all the world;
       he was no fool, no boor.
       They gave him water for his hands
       and a towel to dry them,
180   and they brought him food.
       He took supper with his love;
       it was not to be refused.
       He was served with great courtesy,
       he received it with great joy.
185   There was an entremet°   *side dish*
       that vastly pleased the knight
       for he kissed his lady often
       and held her close.
       When they finished dinner,
190   his horse was brought to him.
       The horse had been well saddled;
       Lanval was very richly served.
       The knight took his leave, mounted,
       and rode toward the city,
195   often looking behind him.
       Lanval was very disturbed;
       he wondered about his adventure
       and was doubtful in his heart;
       he was amazed, not knowing what to believe;
200   he didn't expect ever to see her again.
       He came to his lodging
       and found his men well dressed.
       That night, his accommodations were rich
       but no one knew where it came from.
205   There was no knight in the city
       who really needed a place to stay
       whom he didn't invite to join him
       to be well and richly served.

	Lanval gave rich gifts,
210	Lanval released prisoners,
	Lanval dressed jongleurs,° *performers*
	Lanval offered great honors.
	There was no stranger or friend
	to whom Lanval didn't give.
215	Lanval's joy and pleasure were intense;
	in the daytime or at night,
	he could see his love often;
	she was completely at his command.
	In that same year, it seems to me,
220	after the feast of Saint John,
	about thirty knights
	were amusing themselves
	in an orchard beneath the tower
	where the queen was staying.
225	Gawain was with them
	and his cousin, the handsome Yvain;[7]
	Gawain, the noble, the brave,
	who was so loved by all, said:
	"By God, my lords, we wronged
230	our companion Lanval,
	who is so generous and courtly,
	and whose father is a rich king,
	when we didn't bring him with us."
	They immediately turned back,
235	went to his lodging
	and prevailed on Lanval to come along with them.
	At a sculpted window
	the queen was looking out;
	she had three ladies with her.
240	She saw the king's retinue,
	recognized Lanval and looked at him.
	Then she told one of her ladies
	to send for her maidens,
	the loveliest and the most refined;
245	together they went to amuse themselves
	in the orchard where the others were.
	She brought thirty or more with her;
	they descended the steps.
	The knights came to meet them,
250	because they were delighted to see them.
	The knights took them by the hand;
	their conversation was in no way vulgar.
	Lanval went off to one side,

---

7. Gawain and Yvain serve to place Marie's hero in the context of more famous Arthurian episodes. Gawain, nephew of Arthur and distinguished both for bravery and courtesy, increasingly acts as Lanval's sponsor in the rest of the *lai*.

far from the others; he was impatient
255   to hold his love,
to kiss and embrace and touch her;
he thought little of others' joys
if he could not have his pleasure.
When the queen saw him alone,
260   she went straight to the knight.
She sat beside him and spoke,
revealing her whole heart:
"Lanval, I have shown you much honor,
I have cherished you, and loved you.
265   You may have all my love;
just tell me your desire.
I promise you my affection.
You should be very happy with me."
"My lady," he said, "let me be!
270   I have no desire to love you.
I've served the king a long time;
I don't want to betray my faith to him.
Never, for you or for your love,
will I do anything to harm my lord."
275   The queen got angry;
in her wrath, she insulted him:
"Lanval," she said, "I am sure
you don't care for such pleasure;
people have often told me
280   that you have no interest in women.
You have fine-looking boys
with whom you enjoy yourself.
Base coward, lousy cripple,
my lord made a bad mistake
285   when he let you stay with him.
For all I know, he'll lose God because of it."
When Lanval heard her, he was quite disturbed;
he was not slow to answer.
He said something out of spite
290   that he would later regret.
"Lady," he said, "of that activity
I know nothing,
but I love and I am loved
by one who should have the prize
295   over all the women I know.
And I shall tell you one thing;
you might as well know all:
any one of those who serve her,
the poorest girl of all,
300   is better than you, my lady queen,
in body, face, and beauty,
in breeding and in goodness."

The queen left him
and went, weeping, to her chamber.
305   She was upset and angry
because he had insulted her.
She went to bed sick;
never, she said, would she get up
unless the king gave her satisfaction
310   for the offense against her.
The king returned from the woods,
he'd had a very good day.
He entered the queen's chambers.
When she saw him, she began to complain.
315   She fell at his feet, asked his mercy,
saying that Lanval had dishonored her;
he had asked for her love,
and because she refused him
he insulted and offended her:
320   he boasted of a love
who was so refined and noble and proud
that her chambermaid,
the poorest one who served her,
was better than the queen.
325   The king got very angry;
he swore an oath:
if Lanval could not defend himself in court
he would have him burned or hanged.
The king left her chamber
330   and called for three of his barons;
he sent them for Lanval
who was feeling great sorrow and distress.
He had come back to his dwelling,
knowing very well
335   that he'd lost his love,
he had betrayed their affair.
He was all alone in a room,
disturbed and troubled;
he called on his love, again and again,
340   but it did him no good.
He complained and sighed,
from time to time he fainted;
then he cried a hundred times for her to have mercy
and speak to her love.
345   He cursed his heart and his mouth;
it's a wonder he didn't kill himself.
No matter how much he cried and shouted,
ranted and raged,
she would not have mercy on him,
350   not even let him see her.
How will he ever contain himself?

The men the king sent
arrived and told him
to appear in court without delay:
355 the king had summoned him
because the queen had accused him.
Lanval went with his great sorrow;
they could have killed him, for all he cared.
He came before the king;
360 he was very sad, thoughtful, silent;
his face revealed great suffering.
In anger the king told him:
"Vassal, you have done me a great wrong!
This was a base undertaking,
365 to shame and disgrace me
and to insult the queen.
You have made a foolish boast:
your love is much too noble
if her maid is more beautiful,
370 more worthy, than the queen."
Lanval denied that he'd dishonored
or shamed his lord,
word for word, as the king spoke:
he had not made advances to the queen;
375 but of what he had said,
he acknowledged the truth,
about the love he had boasted of,
that now made him sad because he'd lost her.
About that he said he would do
380 whatever the court decided.
The king was very angry with him;
he sent for all his men
to determine exactly what he ought to do
so that no one could find fault with his decision.
385 They did as he commanded,
whether they liked it or not.
They assembled,
judged, and decided,
that Lanval should have his day;
390 but he must find pledges for his lord
to guarantee that he would await the judgment,
return, and be present at it.[8]
Then the court would be increased,
for now there were none but the king's household.
395 The barons came back to the king
and announced their decision.
The king demanded pledges.

8. Marie introduces judicial procedures that may have recalled those in Henry's reign: summons and accusation, setting a day for judgment, the rise of royal jurisdiction, the possibility of a champion, and trial by battle.

Lanval was alone and forlorn,
he had no relative, no friend.

400 Gawain went and pledged himself for him,
and all his companions followed.
The king addressed them: "I release him to you
on forfeit of whatever you hold from me,
lands and fiefs, each one for himself."

405 When Lanval was pledged, there was nothing else to do.
He returned to his lodging.
The knights accompanied him,
they reproached and admonished him
that he give up his great sorrow;

410 they cursed his foolish love.
Each day they went to see him,
because they wanted to know
whether he was drinking and eating;
they were afraid that he'd kill himself.

415 On the day that they had named,
the barons assembled.
The king and the queen were there
and the pledges brought Lanval back.
They were all very sad for him:

420 I think there were a hundred
who would have done all they could
to set him free without a trial
where he would be wrongly accused.
The king demanded a verdict

425 according to the charge and rebuttal.
Now it all fell to the barons.
They went to the judgment,
worried and distressed
for the noble man from another land

430 who'd gotten into such trouble in their midst.
Many wanted to condemn him
in order to satisfy their lord.
The Duke of Cornwall said:
"No one can blame us;

435 whether it makes you weep or sing
justice must be carried out.
The king spoke against his vassal
whom I have heard named Lanval;
he accused him of felony,

440 charged him with a misdeed—
a love that he had boasted of,
which made the queen angry.
No one but the king accused him:
by the faith I owe you,

445 if one were to speak the truth,
there should have been no need for defense,

except that a man owes his lord honor
in every circumstance.
He will be bound by his oath,
450   and the king will forgive us our pledges
if he can produce proof;
if his love would come forward,
if what he said,
what upset the queen, is true,
455   then he will be acquitted,
because he did not say it out of malice.
But if he cannot get his proof,
we must make it clear to him
that he will forfeit his service to the king;
460   he must take his leave."
They sent to the knight,
told and announced to him
that he should have his love come
to defend and stand surety for him.
465   He told them that he could not do it:
he would never receive help from her.
They went back to the judges,
not expecting any help from Lanval.
The king pressed them hard
470   because of the queen who was waiting.
When they were ready to give their verdict
they saw two girls approaching,
riding handsome palfreys.
They were very attractive,
475   dressed in purple taffeta,
over their bare skin.
The men looked at them with pleasure.
Gawain, taking three knights with him,
went to Lanval and told him;
480   he pointed out the two girls.
Gawain was extremely happy, and begged him
to tell if his love were one of them.
Lanval said he didn't know who they were,
where they came from or where they were going.
485   The girls proceeded
still on horseback;
they dismounted before the high table
at which Arthur, the king, sat.
They were of great beauty,
490   and spoke in a courtly manner:
"King, clear your chambers,
have them hung with silk
where my lady may dismount;
she wishes to take shelter with you."
495   He promised it willingly

and called two knights
to guide them up to the chambers.
On that subject no more was said.
The king asked his barons
500   for their judgment and decision;
he said they had angered him very much
with their long delay.
"Sire," they said, "we have decided.
Because of the ladies we have just seen
505   we have made no judgment.
Let us reconvene the trial."
Then they assembled, everyone was worried;
there was much noise and strife.
While they were in that confusion,
510   two girls in noble array,
dressed in Phrygian silks
and riding Spanish mules,
were seen coming down the street.
This gave the vassals great joy;
515   to each other they said that now
Lanval, the brave and bold, was saved.
Gawain went up to him,
bringing his companions along.
"Sire," he said, "take heart.
520   For the love of God, speak to us.
Here come two maidens,
well adorned and very beautiful;
one must certainly be your love."
Lanval answered quickly
525   that he did not recognize them,
he didn't know them or love them.
Meanwhile they'd arrived,
and dismounted before the king.
Most of those who saw them praised them
530   for their bodies, their faces, their coloring;
each was more impressive
than the queen had ever been.
The older one was courtly and wise,
she spoke her message fittingly:
535   "King, have chambers prepared for us
to lodge my lady according to her need;
she is coming here to speak with you."
He ordered them to be taken
to the others who had preceded them.
540   There was no problem with the mules.
When he had seen to the girls,
he summoned all his barons
to render their judgment;

it had already dragged out too much.
545 The queen was getting angry
because she had fasted so long.
They were about to give their judgment
when through the city came riding
a girl on horseback:
550 there was none more beautiful in the world.
She rode a white palfrey,
who carried her handsomely and smoothly:
he was well apportioned in the neck and head,
no finer beast in the world.
555 The palfrey's trappings were rich;
under heaven there was no count or king
who could have afforded them all
without selling or mortgaging lands.
She was dressed in this fashion:
560 in a white linen shift
that revealed both her sides
since the lacing was along the side.
Her body was elegant, her hips slim,
her neck whiter than snow on a branch,
565 her eyes bright, her face white,
a beautiful mouth, a well-set nose,
dark eyebrows and an elegant forehead,
her hair curly and rather blond;
golden wire does not shine
570 like her hair in the light.
Her cloak, which she had wrapped around her,
was dark purple.
On her wrist she held a sparrow hawk,
a greyhound followed her.
575 In the town, no one, small or big,
old man or child,
failed to come look.
As they watched her pass,
there was no joking about her beauty.
580 She proceeded at a slow pace.
The judges who saw her
marveled at the sight;
no one who looked at her
was not warmed with joy.
585 Those who loved the knight
came to him and told him
of the girl who was approaching,
if God pleased, to rescue him.
"Sir companion, here comes one
590 neither tawny nor dark;
this is, of all who exist,

the most beautiful woman in the world."
Lanval heard them and lifted his head;
he recognized her and sighed.
595   The blood rose to his face;
he was quick to speak.
"By my faith," he said, "that is my love.
Now I don't care if I am killed,
if only she forgives me.
600   For I am restored, now that I see her."
The lady entered the palace;
no one so beautiful had ever been there.
She dismounted before the king
so that she was well seen by all.
605   And she let her cloak fall
so they could see her better.
The king, who was well bred,
rose and went to meet her;
all the others honored her
610   and offered to serve her.
When they had looked at her well,
when they had greatly praised her beauty,
she spoke in this way,
she didn't want to wait:
615   "I have loved one of your vassals:
you see him before you—Lanval.
He has been accused in your court—
I don't want him to suffer
for what he said; you should know
620   that the queen was in the wrong.
He never made advances to her.
And for the boast that he made,
if he can be acquitted through me,
let him be set free by your barons."
625   Whatever the barons judged by law
the king promised would prevail.
To the last man they agreed
that Lanval had successfully answered the charge.
He was set free by their decision
630   and the girl departed.
The king could not detain her,
though there were enough people to serve her.
Outside the hall stood
a great stone of dark marble
635   where heavy men mounted
when they left the king's court;
Lanval climbed on it.
When the girl came through the gate
Lanval leapt, in one bound,
640   onto the palfrey, behind her.

With her he went to Avalun,[9]
so the Bretons tell us,
to a very beautiful island;
there the youth was carried off.
645   No man heard of him again,
and I have no more to tell.

Chevrefoil (The Honeysuckle)

I should like very much
to tell you the truth
about the *lai* men call *Chevrefoil*—
why it was composed and where it came from.
5   Many have told and recited it to me
and I have found it in writing,
about Tristan and the queen
and their love that was so true,
that brought them much suffering
10   and caused them to die the same day.
King Mark was annoyed,
angry at his nephew Tristan;
he exiled Tristan from his land
because of the queen whom he loved.
15   Tristan returned to his own country,
South Wales, where he was born,
he stayed a whole year;
he couldn't come back.
Afterward he began to expose himself
20   to death and destruction.
Don't be surprised at this:
for one who loves very faithfully
is sad and troubled
when he cannot satisfy his desires.
25   Tristan was sad and worried,
so he set out from his land.
He traveled straight to Cornwall,
where the queen lived,
and entered the forest all alone—
30   he didn't want anyone to see him;
he came out only in the evening
when it was time to find shelter.
He took lodging that night,
with peasants, poor people.
35   He asked them for news
of the king—what he was doing.

9. Avalon is the mysterious island to which Arthur is also carried, mortally wounded, after his final battle. Marie's contemporary Gerald of Wales expresses far older associations of Avalon with powerful women (see pages 195–96).

They told him they had heard
that the barons had been summoned by ban.[1]
They were to come to Tintagel[2]
40   where the king wanted to hold his court,
at Pentecost they would all be there,
there'd be much joy and pleasure,
and the queen would be there too.
Tristan heard and was very happy;
45   she would not be able to go there
without his seeing her pass.
The day the king set out,
Tristan also came to the woods
by the road he knew
50   their assembly must take.
He cut a hazel tree in half,
then he squared it.
When he had prepared the wood,
he wrote his name on it with his knife.
55   If the queen noticed it—
and she should be on the watch for it,
for it had happened before
and she had noticed it then—
she'd know when she saw it,
60   that the piece of wood had come from her love.
This was the message of the writing[3]
that he had sent to her:
he had been there a long time,
had waited and remained
65   to find out and to discover
how he could see her,
for he could not live without her.
With the two of them it was just
as it is with the honeysuckle
70   that attaches itself to the hazel tree:
when it has wound and attached
and worked itself around the trunk,
the two can survive together;
but if someone tries to separate them,
75   the hazel dies quickly
and the honeysuckle with it.
"Sweet love, so it is with us:
You cannot live without me, nor I without you."
The queen rode along;
80   she looked at the hillside
and saw the piece of wood; she knew what it was,

---

1. A royal summons to feudal service.
2. One of Mark's castles, on the north coast of Cornwall.
In Arthurian legend, it is the site of Arthur's conception.

3. From Tristan's name alone, or possibly a few words in code or runic letters, Isolt can elicit the entire message that follows.

she recognized all the letters.
The knights who were accompanying her,
who were riding with her,
85   she ordered to stop:
she wanted to dismount and rest.
They obeyed her command.
She went far away from her people
and called her girl
90   Brenguein,[4] who was loyal to her.
She went a short distance from the road;
and in the woods she found him
whom she loved more than any living thing.
They took great joy in each other.
95   He spoke to her as much as he desired,
she told him whatever she liked.
Then she assured him
that he would be reconciled with the king—
for it weighed on him
100   that he had sent Tristan away;
he'd done it because of the accusation.[5]
Then she departed, she left her love,
but when it came to the separation,
they began to weep.
105   Tristan went to Wales,
to wait until his uncle sent for him.
For the joy that he'd felt
from his love when he saw her,
by means of the stick he inscribed
110   as the queen had instructed,
and in order to remember the words,
Tristan, who played the harp well,
composed a new *lai* about it.
I shall name it briefly:
115   in English they call it *Goat's Leaf*
the French call it *Chevrefoil*.
I have given you the truth
about the *lai* that I have told here.

⊶ ≍✦≍ ⊷

Sir Gawain and the Green Knight

As a subject of literary romance, Arthurian tradition never had the centrality in later medieval England it had gained in France. It was only one of a wide range of popular topics like Havelok the Dane, King Horn, and the Troy story. Nevertheless Arthur and his court played

---

4. Isolt's maid, who earlier substituted herself for Isolt in the marriage bed with King Mark.

5. Envious courtiers had plotted to expose the lovers' affair to the king.

an ongoing role in English society, written into histories and emulated by aristocrats and kings. And in the later fourteenth or early fifteenth century, several very distinguished Arthurian poems appeared, such as the alliterative *Morte Arthure* and the *Awntyrs* (Adventures) *off Arthure*.

Sir Gawain and the Green Knight is the greatest of the Arthurian romances produced in England. The poem embraces the highest aspirations of the late medieval aristocratic world, both courtly and religious, even while it eloquently admits the human failings that threaten those values. A knight's troth and word, a Christian's election and covenant, the breaking point of a person's or a society's virtues, all come in for celebration and painful scrutiny during Gawain's adventure.

Like *Beowulf*, *Sir Gawain and the Green Knight* comes down to us by the thread of a single copy. Its manuscript contains a group of poems (*Sir Gawain*, *Pearl*, *Purity*, and *Patience*) that mark their anonymous author as a poet whose range approaches that of his contemporary Chaucer, and whose formal craft is in some ways more ambitious than Chaucer's.

Gawain is the work of a highly sophisticated provincial court poet (likely in the northwest Midlands), working in a form and narrative tradition that is conservative in comparison with Chaucer's. The poet uses the alliterative long line, a meter with its roots in Anglo-Saxon poetry; the unrhymed alliterative stanzas, of irregular length, each end with five shorter rhymed lines often called a "bob-and-wheel" stanza. (For a further discussion of the alliterative style, see the introduction to William Langland, page 444.) Within these traditional constraints, however, the poem achieves an apex of medieval courtly literature, as a superlatively crafted and stylized version of quest romance.

The romance never aims to detach itself from society or history, though. It opens and closes by referring to Troy, the ancient, fallen empire whose survivors were legendary founders of Britain, a connection well known through Geoffrey of Monmouth. Arthur, their ultimate heir, went on later in his myth to pursue imperial ambitions that, like those of Troy, were foiled by adulterous desire and political infidelity. *Sir Gawain* also echoes its contemporary world in the technical language of architecture, crafts, and arms. This helps draw in the kind of conservative, aristocratic court for which the poem seems to have been written, probably in Cheshire or Lancashire, a somewhat backward region whose nobles remained loyal to Richard II. Along with the pleasure it takes in fine armor and courtly ritual, the poem seems to enfold anxieties about the economic pressures of maintaining chivalric display in a period of costly new technology, inflation, and declining income from land.

By the time this poem was written, toward the close of the fourteenth century, Gawain was a famous Arthurian hero. His reputation was ambiguous, though; he was both Arthur's faithful retainer and nephew, but also a suave seducer. Which side of Gawain would dominate in this particular poem? Would he stand for a civilization of Christian chivalry or one of cynical sophistication?

The test that begins to answer this question occurs during Arthur's ritual celebrations of Christmas and the New Year, and within the civilized practices of Eucharist and secular feast. A gigantic green knight interrupts Arthur's banquet to offer a deadly game of exchanged ax-blows, to be resolved in one year's time. Although the Green Knight, with his ball of holly leaves, seems at first to come from the tradition of the Wild Man—a giant force of nature itself—he is also a sophisticated knight, gorgeously attired. He knows, too, just how to taunt a young king without quite overstepping the bounds of courtly behavior. Gawain takes up the challenge, but a still greater marvel ensues.

As the term of the agreement approaches, Gawain rides off, elaborately armed, to find the Green Knight and fulfill his obligation, even if that means his death. What Gawain encounters first, though, are temptations of character and sexuality even trickier and more crucial than they at first seem.

Sir Gawain and the Green Knight is remarkable not only for the intricacy of its plot but also for the virtuosity of its descriptions, such as the almost elegiac review of the passing seasons ("So the year in passing yields its many yesterdays"). The poem rejoices in the masterful exercise of skill as the mark of civilization. Beautifully crafted knots appear everywhere, and we encounter artisanal craft as well in narrative elements like the Green Knight's dress (a dazzling mixture of leafy green and jeweler's gold), Gawain's decorated shield and arms, and the expertise of the master of the hunt who carves up the prey of Gawain's host with ritual precision. Even Gawain's exquisite courtly manners appear as a civilizing artifice.

The ambition of the poem's own craft is equally evident in its extraordinary range of formal devices. Preeminent among these is the symbolic register of number. The poem can be seen as a single unit, circling back to the Trojan scene with which it begins. It has a double structure, too, as it shifts between the courts of Arthur and Gawain's mysterious host. In the manuscript it is divided into four parts ("fits") that respond to the seasonal description at the opening of Part 2. In the original text, the narrative proper ends by echoing the very start of the poem, at line 2525 (in the original Middle English), itself a multiple of fives that recalls the pentangle on Gawain's shield symbolizing his virtues. The final rhyming stanza, with its formula of grace and salvation, brings the line total to 2530, whose individual digits add up to ten, a number associated with the divine in medieval numerology.

This symbolic structure can seem sometimes overdetermined. A range of elements, however, invites the reader to come at the poem from other perspectives. The poem's very circularity, narrative and formal, allows it to be viewed from beginning or ending. From the front it is a poem of male accomplishment, largely celebrating *men's* courts and *men's* virtues (even men's horses). At the other end, however, it focuses on a court presided over by an old woman (later called a goddess), a court whose irruption into the Arthurian world is explained as the playing out of an old and mysterious rivalry between two queens. Male, even patriarchal from one direction, the poem seems matriarchal, almost pagan, from the other. For all its formal cohesion and celebration of craft, the poem also pulls the reader back and keeps its mysteries intact by leaving many narrative loose ends and unanswered questions.

Unresolvable ambiguities reside most clearly in the pentangle on Gawain's shield and in the "green girdle" whose true owner remains uncertain. For all their differences, both are figures that insist on repetition, end where they begin, and possess a geometry that can be traced forward or backward. Yet the static perfection of the pentangle is subtly set against the protean green girdle, which passes through so many hands, alters its shape (being untied and retied repeatedly), and connects with so many issues in the poem: mortality, women's power, Gawain's fault and the acceptance of that fault by the whole Arthurian court. The girdle becomes an image both of flaw and triumph and of all the loose ends in this early episode of the Arthurian myth.

The girdle also serves to link *Sir Gawain* to political and social issues of the poet's own time, particularly efforts to revalidate a declining system of chivalry. After the last line in the manuscript, a later medieval hand has added "Hony Soyt Qui Mal Pence" ("shamed be he who thinks ill thereof"), the motto of the royal Order of the Garter, founded by Edward III in 1349 to promote a revival of knighthood. The Arthurian myth had already been redeployed to buttress royal power when Edward III refounded a Round Table in 1344. King Arthur's wisdom at the close of Gawain's adventure lies in transforming Gawain's shame, rage, and humiliated sense of sin into an emblem at once of mortal humanity and aristocratic cohesion. This is the place—back with the king and ritually connected with the Order of the Garter—where the closed circle of the poem opens to the social, historical world of empire, court, and kingship.

Sir Gawain and the Green Knight[1]

PART 1

The siege and the assault being ceased at Troy,
The battlements broken down and burnt to brands and ashes,
The treacherous trickster whose treasons there flourished
Was famed for his falsehood, the foulest on earth.
5   Aeneas[2] the noble and his knightly kin
Then conquered kingdoms, and kept in their hand
Wellnigh all the wealth of the western lands.[3]
Royal Romulus to Rome first turned,
Set up the city in splendid pomp,
10   Then named her with his own name, which now she still has:
Ticius[4] founded Tuscany, townships raising,
Longbeard[5] in Lombardy lifted up homes,
And far over the French flood Felix Brutus
On many spacious slopes set Britain with joy
15   And grace;
        Where war and feud and wonder
        Have ruled the realm a space,
        And after, bliss and blunder
        By turns have run their race.

20   And when this Britain was built by this brave noble,[6]
Here bold men bred, in battle exulting,
Stirrers of trouble in turbulent times.
Here many a marvel, more than in other lands,
Has befallen by fortune since that far time.
25   But of all who abode here of Britain's kings,
Arthur was highest in honor, as I have heard;
So I intend to tell you of a true wonder,
Which many folk mention as a manifest marvel,
A happening eminent among Arthur's adventures.
30   Listen to my lay but a little while:
Straightway shall I speak it, in city as I heard it,
        With tongue;
        As scribes have set it duly
        In the lore of the land so long,
35   With letters linking truly
        In story bold and strong.

This king lay at Camelot[7] one Christmastide
With many mighty lords, manly liegemen,

---

1. This translation, remarkably faithful to the original alliterative meter and stanza form, is by Brian Stone.
2. Aeneas led the survivors of Troy to Italy, after a series of ambiguous omens and misadventures. In medieval tradition, he was also said to have plotted to betray his own city. The "treacherous trickster" in line 3, though, may refer to the Trojan Antenor, also said to have betrayed Troy.
3. Perhaps Europe, or just the British Isles. Many royal houses traced their ancestry to Rome and Troy.
4. Possibly Titus Tatius, ancient king of the Sabines.

5. Ancestor of the Lombards, and a nephew of Brutus.
6. According to Geoffrey of Monmouth and others, a great-grandson of Aeneas, exiled after accidentally killing his father, then, later founder of Britain.
7. Arthur's capital, probably in Wales, perhaps at Caerleon-on-Usk where Arthur had been crowned. Knights were expected to gather at his court, in celebration and homage, on the five liturgical holidays on which Arthur wore his crown: Easter, Ascension, Pentecost, All Saints' Day, and Christmas.

40 Members rightly reckoned of the Round Table,[8]
In splendid celebration, seemly and carefree.
There tussling in tournament time and again
Jousted in jollity these gentle knights,
Then in court carnival sang catches and danced;
45 For fifteen days the feasting there was full in like measure
With all the meat and merry-making men could devise,
Gladly ringing glee, glorious to hear,
A noble din by day, dancing at night!
All was happiness in the height in halls and chambers
For lords and their ladies, delectable joy.
50 With all delights on earth they housed there together,
Saving Christ's self, the most celebrated knights,
The loveliest ladies to live in all time,
And the comeliest king ever to keep court.
For this fine fellowship was in its fair prime[9]
55   Far famed,
    Stood well in heaven's will,
    Its high-souled king acclaimed:
    So hardy a host on hill
    Could not with ease be named.

60 The year being so young that yester-even saw its birth,
That day double on the dais were the diners served.
Mass sung and service ended, straight from the chapel
The King and his company came into hall.
Called on with cries from clergy and laity,
65 Noël was newly announced, named time and again.
Then lords and ladies leaped forth, largesse distributing,
Offered New Year gifts in high voices, handed them out,
Bustling and bantering about these offerings.
Ladies laughed full loudly, though losing their wealth,
70 And he that won was not woeful, you may well believe.[1]
All this merriment they made until meal time.
Then in progress to their places they passed after washing,
In authorized order, the high-ranking first;
With glorious Guinevere, gay in the midst,
75 On the princely platform[2] with its precious hangings
Of splendid silk at the sides, a state over her
Of rich tapestry of Toulouse and Turkestan
Brilliantly embroidered with the best gems
Of warranted worth that wealth at any time
80   Could buy.
    Fairest of form was this queen,

---

8. Its shape symbolized the unity of Arthur's knights but also avoided disputes over precedence.
9. Arthur is emphatically a young king here. The phrase may also recall the Golden Age, an era of uncorrupted happiness.
1. The distribution of gifts on New Year's Day displayed the king's wealth and power; it was also the occasion here of some courtly game of exchange, in which the loser perhaps gave up a kiss.
2. A medieval nobleman's hall typically had a raised dais at one end, on which the "high table" stood.

Glinting and gray of eye;
No man could say he had seen
A lovelier, but with a lie.

85   But Arthur would not eat until all were served.
He was charming and cheerful, child-like and gay,
And loving active life, little did he favor
Lying down for long or lolling on a seat,
So robust his young blood and his beating brain.
90   Still, he was stirred now by something else:
His noble announcement that he never would eat
On such a fair feast-day till informed in full
Of some unusual adventure, as yet untold,
Of some momentous marvel that he might believe,
95   About ancestors, or arms, or other high theme;
Or till a stranger should seek out a strong knight of his,
To join with him in jousting, in jeopardy to lay
Life against life, each allowing the other
The favor of Fortune, the fairer lot.
100   Such was the King's custom when he kept court,
At every fine feast among his free retinue
      In hall.
      So he throve amid the throng,
      A ruler royal and tall,
105   Still standing staunch and strong,
      And young like the year withal.

Erect stood the strong King, stately of mien,
Trifling time with talk before the topmost table.
Good Gawain was placed at Guinevere's side,
110   And Agravain of the Hard Hand sat on the other side,
Both the King's sister's sons, staunchest of knights.
Above, Bishop Baldwin began the board,
And Ywain,[3] Urien's son ate next to him.
These were disposed on the dais and with dignity served,
115   And many mighty men next, marshaled at side tables.
Then the first course came in with such cracking of trumpets,
(Whence bright bedecked blazons in banners hung)
Such din of drumming and a deal of fine piping,
Such wild warbles whelming and echoing
120   That hearts were uplifted high at the strains.[4]
Then delicacies and dainties were delivered to the guests,
Fresh food in foison, such freight of full dishes
That space was scarce at the social tables
For the several soups set before them in silver

---

3. Another nephew of Arthur. The relationship of uncle and nephew is close in many Arthurian romances, and noble youths were often sent to be raised by an uncle on the mother's side.

4. Holiday banquets were formalized, almost theatrical.

125   On the cloth.
          Each feaster made free with the fare,
          Took lightly and nothing loth;
          Twelve plates were for every pair,
          Good beer and bright wine both.

130   Of their meal I shall mention no more just now,
       For it is evident to all that ample was served;
       Now another noise, quite new, neared suddenly,
       Likely to allow the liege lord to eat;
       For barely had the blast of trump abated one minute
135   And the first course in the court been courteously served,
       When there heaved in at the hall door an awesome fellow
       Who in height outstripped all earthly men.
       From throat to thigh he was so thickset and square,
       His loins and limbs were so long and so great,
140   That he was half a giant on earth, I believe;
       Yet mainly and most of all a man he seemed,
       And the handsomest of horsemen, though huge, at that;
       For though at back and at breast his body was broad,
       His hips and haunches were elegant and small,
145   And perfectly proportioned were all parts of the man,
            As seen.
          Men gaped at the hue of him
          Ingrained in garb and mien,
          A fellow fiercely grim,
150   And all a glittering green.

       And garments of green girt the fellow about—
       A two-third length tunic, tight at the waist,
       A comely cloak on top, accomplished with lining
       Of the finest fur to be found, made of one piece,
155   Marvelous fur-trimmed material, with matching hood
       Lying back from his locks and laid on his shoulders;
       Fitly held-up hose, in hue the same green,
       That was caught at the calf, with clinking spurs beneath
       Of bright gold on bases of embroidered silk,
160   But no iron shoe armored that horseman's feet.
       And verily his vesture was all vivid green,
       So were the bars on his belt and the brilliants set
       In ravishing array on the rich accoutrements
       About himself and his saddle on silken work.
165   It would be tedious to tell a tithe of the trifles
       Embossed and embroidered, such as birds and flies,
       In gay green gauds, with gold everywhere.
       The breast-hangings of the horse, its haughty crupper,
       The enameled knobs and nails on its bridle,
170   And the stirrups that he stood on, were all stained with the same;
       So were the splendid saddle-skirts and bows
       That ever glimmered and glinted with their green stones.

The steed that he spurred on was similar in hue
    To the sight,
175   Green and huge of grain,
    Mettlesome in might
    And brusque with bit and rein—
    A steed to serve that knight!

Yes, garbed all in green was the gallant rider,
180   And the hair of his head was the same hue as his horse,
And floated finely like a fan round his shoulders;
And a great bushy beard on his breast flowing down,
With the heavy hair hanging from his head,
Was shorn below the shoulder, sheared right round,
185   So that half his arms were under the encircling hair,
Covered as by a king's cape, that closes at the neck.
The mane of that mighty horse, much like the beard,
Well crisped and combed, was copiously plaited
With twists of twining gold, twinkling in the green,
190   First a green gossamer, a golden one next.
His flowing tail and forelock followed suit,
And both were bound with bands of bright green,
Ornamented to the end with exquisite stones,
While a thong running through them threaded on high
195   Many bright golden bells, burnished and ringing.
Such a horse, such a horseman, in the whole wide world
Was never seen or observed by those assembled before,
    Not one.
    Lightning-like he seemed
200   And swift to strike and stun.
    His dreadful blows, men deemed,
    Once dealt, meant death was done.

Yet hauberk[5] and helmet had he none,
Nor plastron[6] nor plate-armor proper to combat,
205   Nor shield for shoving, nor sharp spear for lunging;
But he held a holly cluster in one hand, holly
That is greenest when groves are gaunt and bare,
And an axe in his other hand, huge and monstrous,
A hideous helmet-smasher for anyone to tell of;
210   The head of that axe was an ell-rod long.
Of green hammered gold and steel was the socket,
And the blade was burnished bright, with a broad edge,
Acutely honed for cutting, as keenest razors are.
The grim man gripped it by its great strong handle,
215   Which was wound with iron all the way to the end,
And graven in green with graceful designs.
A cord curved round it, was caught at the head,

5. A tunic of chain mail.   6. A piece of armor to protect the upper part of the chest
                                    and neck.

Then hitched to the haft at intervals in loops,
With costly tassels attached thereto in plenty
220   On bosses of bright green embroidered richly.
In he rode, and up the hall, this man,
Driving towards the high dais, dreading no danger.
He gave no one a greeting, but glared over all.
His opening utterance was, "Who and where
225   Is the governor of this gathering? Gladly would I
Behold him with my eyes and have speech with him."
        He frowned;
        Took note of every knight
        As he ramped and rode around;
230   Then stopped to study who might
        Be the noble most renowned.

The assembled folk stared, long scanning the fellow,
For all men marveled what it might mean
That a horseman and his horse should have such a color
235   As to grow green as grass, and greener yet, it seemed,
More gaudily glowing than green enamel on gold.
Those standing studied him and sidled towards him
With all the world's wonder as to what he would do.
For astonishing sights they had seen, but such a one never;
240   Therefore a phantom from Fairyland the folk there deemed him.
So even the doughty were daunted and dared not reply,
All sitting stock-still, astounded by his voice.
Throughout the high hall was a hush like death;
Suddenly as if all had slipped into sleep, their voices were
245   At rest;
        Hushed not wholly for fear,
        But some at honor's behest;
        But let him whom all revere
        Greet that gruesome guest.

250   For Arthur sensed an exploit before the high dais,
And accorded him courteous greeting, no craven he,
Saying to him, "Sir knight, you are certainly welcome.
I am head of this house: Arthur is my name.
Please deign to dismount and dwell with us
255   Till you impart your purpose, at a proper time."
"May he that sits in heaven help me," said the knight,
"But my intention was not to tarry in this turreted hall.
But as your reputation, royal sir, is raised up so high,
And your castle and cavaliers are accounted the best,
260   The mightiest of mail-clad men in mounted fighting,
The most warlike, the worthiest the world has bred,
Most valiant to vie with in virile contests,
And as chivalry is shown here, so I am assured,
At this time, I tell you, that has attracted me here.
265   By this branch that I bear, you may be certain

That I proceed in peace, no peril seeking;[7]
For had I fared forth in fighting gear,
My hauberk and helmet, both at home now,
My shield and sharp spear, all shining bright,
270   And other weapons to wield, I would have brought;
However, as I wish for no war here, I wear soft clothes.
But if you are as bold as brave men affirm,
You will gladly grant me the good sport I demand
      By right."
275   Then Arthur answer gave:
    "If you, most noble knight,
    Unarmored combat crave,
    We'll fail you not in fight."

"No, it is not combat I crave, for come to that,
280   On this bench only beardless boys are sitting.
If I were hasped in armor on a high steed,
No man among you could match me, your might being meager.
So I crave in this court a Christmas game,
For it is Yuletide and New Year, and young men abound here.
285   If any in this household is so hardy in spirit,
Of such mettlesome mind and so madly rash
As to strike a strong blow in return for another,
I shall offer to him this fine axe freely;
This axe, which is heavy enough, to handle as he please.
290   And I shall bide the first blow, as bare as I sit here.
If some intrepid man is tempted to try what I suggest,
Let him leap towards me and lay hold of this weapon,
Acquiring clear possession of it, no claim from me ensuing.
Then shall I stand up to his stroke, quite still on this floor—
295   So long as I shall have leave to launch a return blow
      Unchecked.
    Yet he shall have a year
    And a day's reprieve, I direct.
    Now hasten and let me hear
300   Who answers, to what effect."

If he had astonished them at the start, yet stiller now
Were the henchmen in hall, both high and low.
The rider wrenched himself round in his saddle
And rolled his red eyes about roughly and strangely,
305   Bending his brows, bristling and bright, on all,
His beard swaying as he strained to see who would rise.
When none came to accord with him, he coughed aloud,
Then pulled himself up proudly, and spoke as follows:
"What, is this Arthur's house, the honor of which
310   Is bruited abroad so abundantly?

7. A holly branch could symbolize peace and was used in games of the Christmas season.

Has your pride disappeared? Your prowess gone?
Your victories, your valor, your vaunts, where are they?
The revel and renown of the Round Table
Is now overwhelmed by a word from one man's voice,
315   For all flinch for fear from a fight not begun!"
Upon this, he laughed so loudly that the lord grieved.
His fair features filled with blood
     For shame.
   He raged as roaring gale;
320   His followers felt the same.
   The King, not one to quail,
   To that cavalier then came.

"By heaven," then said Arthur, "What you ask is foolish,
But as you firmly seek folly, find it you shall.
325   No good man here is aghast at your great words.
Hand me your axe now, for heaven's sake,
And I shall bestow the boon you bid us give."
He sprang towards him swiftly, seized it from his hand,
And fiercely the other fellow footed the floor.
330   Now Arthur had his axe, and holding it by the haft
Swung it about sternly, as if to strike with it.
The strong man stood before him, stretched to his full height,
Higher than any in the hall by a head and more.
Stern of face he stood there, stroking his beard,
335   Turning down his tunic in a tranquil manner,
Less unmanned and dismayed by the mighty strokes,
Than if a banqueter at the bench had brought him a drink
     Of wine.
   Then Gawain at Guinevere's side
340   Bowed and spoke his design:
   "Before all, King, confide
   This fight to me. May it be mine."

"If you would, worthy lord," said Gawain to the King,
"Bid me stir from this seat and stand beside you,
345   Allowing me without lese-majesty to leave the table,
And if my liege lady were not displeased thereby,
I should come there to counsel you before this court of nobles.
For it appears unmeet to me, as manners go,
When your hall hears uttered such a haughty request,
350   Though you gladly agree, for you to grant it yourself,
When on the benches about you many such bold men sit,
Under heaven, I hold, the highest-mettled,
There being no braver knights when battle is joined.
I am the weakest, the most wanting in wisdom, I know,
355   And my life, if lost, would be least missed, truly.
Only through your being my uncle, am I to be valued;
No bounty but your blood in my body do I know.
And since this affair is too foolish to fall to you,

And I first asked it of you, make it over to me;
360   And if I fail to speak fittingly, let this full court judge
               Without blame."
                    Then wisely they whispered of it,
                    And after, all said the same:
                    That the crowned King should be quit,
365   And Gawain given the game.

Then the King commanded the courtly knight to rise.
He directly uprose, approached courteously,
Knelt low to his liege lord, laid hold of the weapon;
And he graciously let him have it, lifted up his hand
370   And gave him God's blessing, gladly urging him
To be strong in spirit and stout of sinew.
"Cousin, take care," said the King, "To chop once,
And if you strike with success, certainly I think
You will take the return blow without trouble in time."
375   Gripping the great axe, Gawain goes to the man
Who awaits him unwavering, not quailing at all.
Then said to Sir Gawain the stout knight in green,
"Let us affirm our pact freshly, before going farther.
I beg you, bold sir, to be so good
380   As to tell me your true name, as I trust you to."
"In good faith," said the good knight, "Gawain is my name,
And whatever happens after, I offer you this blow,
And in twelve months' time I shall take the return blow
With whatever weapon you wish, and with no one else
385   Shall I strive."
                    The other with pledge replied,
                    "I'm the merriest man alive
                    It's a blow from you I must bide,
                    Sir Gawain, so may I thrive."

390   "By God," said the Green Knight, "Sir Gawain, I rejoice
That I shall have from your hand what I have asked for here.
And you have gladly gone over, in good discourse,
The covenant I requested of the King in full,
Except that you shall assent, swearing in truth,
395   To seek me yourself, in such place as you think
To find me under the firmament, and fetch your payment
For what you deal me today before this dignified gathering."
"How shall I hunt for you? How find your home?"
Said Gawain, "By God that made me, I go in ignorance;
400   Nor, knight, do I know your name or your court.
But instruct me truly thereof, and tell me your name,
And I shall wear out my wits to find my way there;
Here is my oath on it, in absolute honor!"
"That is enough this New Year, no more is needed,"
405   Said the gallant in green to Gawain the courteous,

"To tell you the truth, when I have taken the blow
After you have duly dealt it, I shall directly inform you
About my house and my home and my own name.
Then you may keep your covenant, and call on me,
410   And if I waft you no words, then well may you prosper,
Stay long in your own land and look for no further
          Trial.
          Now grip your weapon grim;
          Let us see your fighting style."
415   "Gladly," said Gawain to him,
          Stroking the steel the while.

On the ground the Green Knight graciously stood,
With head slightly slanting to expose the flesh.
His long and lovely locks he laid over his crown,
420   Baring the naked neck for the business now due.
Gawain gripped his axe and gathered it on high,
Advanced the left foot before him on the ground,
And slashed swiftly down on the exposed part,
So that the sharp blade sheared through, shattering the bones,
425   Sank deep in the sleek flesh, split it in two,
And the scintillating steel struck the ground.
The fair head fell from the neck, struck the floor,
And people spurned it as it rolled around.
Blood spurted from the body, bright against the green.
430   Yet the fellow did not fall, nor falter one whit,
But stoutly sprang forward on legs still sturdy,
Roughly reached out among the ranks of nobles,
Seized his splendid head and straightway lifted it.
Then he strode to his steed, snatched the bridle,
435   Stepped into the stirrup and swung aloft,
Holding his head in his hand by the hair.
He settled himself in the saddle as steadily
As if nothing had happened to him, though he had
          No head.
440   He twisted his trunk about,
          That gruesome body that bled;
          He caused much dread and doubt
          By the time his say was said.

For he held the head in his hand upright,
445   Pointed the face at the fairest in fame on the dais;
And it lifted its eyelids and looked glaringly,
And menacingly said with its mouth as you may now hear:
"Be prepared to perform what you promised, Gawain;
Seek faithfully till you find me, my fine fellow,
450   According to your oath in this hall in these knights' hearing.
Go to the Green Chapel without gainsaying to get
Such a stroke as you have struck. Strictly you deserve

That due redemption on the day of New Year.
As the Knight of the Green Chapel I am known to many;
455   Therefore if you ask for me, I shall be found.
So come, or else be called coward accordingly!"
Then he savagely swerved, sawing at the reins,
Rushed out at the hall door, his head in his hand,
And the flint-struck fire flew up from the hooves.
460   What place he departed to no person there knew,
Nor could any account be given of the country he had come from.
   What then?
  At the Green Knight Gawain and King
  Grinned and laughed again;
465   But plainly approved the thing
  As a marvel in the world of men.

Though honored King Arthur was at heart astounded,
He let no sign of it be seen, but said clearly
To the comely queen in courtly speech,
470   "Do not be dismayed, dear lady, today:
Such cleverness comes well at Christmastide,
Like the playing of interludes,[8] laughter and song,
As lords and ladies delight in courtly carols.
However, I am now able to eat the repast,
475   Having seen, I must say, a sight to wonder at."
He glanced at Sir Gawain, and gracefully said,
"Now sir, hang up your axe:[9] you have hewn enough."
And on the backcloth above the dais it was boldly hung
Where all men might mark it and marvel at it
480   And with truthful testimony tell the wonder of it.
Then to the table the two went together,
The King and the constant knight, and keen men served them
Double portions of each dainty with all due dignity,
All manner of meat, and minstrelsy too.
485   Daylong they delighted till darkness came
  To their shores.
  Now Gawain give a thought,
  Lest peril make you pause
  In seeking out the sport
490   That you have claimed as yours.

PART 2

Such earnest of noble action had Arthur at New Year,
For he was avid to hear exploits vaunted.
Though starved of such speeches when seated at first,
Now had they high matter indeed, their hands full of it.

8. Brief performances between the courses of the banquet. 9. A literal suggestion, but also an invitation to put
    the matter aside.

495   Gawain was glad to begin the games in hall,
      But though the end be heavy, have no wonder,
      For if men are spritely in spirit after strong drink,
      Soon the year slides past, never the same twice;
      There is no foretelling its fulfilment from the start.
500   Yes, this Yuletide passed and the year following;
      Season after season in succession went by.[1]
      After Christmas comes the crabbed Lenten time,
      Which forces on the flesh fish and food yet plainer.
      Then weather more vernal wars with the wintry world,
505   The cold ebbs and declines, the clouds lift,
      In shining showers the rain sheds warmth
      And falls upon the fair plain, where flowers appear;
      The grassy lawns and groves alike are garbed in green;
      Birds prepare to build, and brightly sing
510   The solace of the ensuing summer that soothes hill
          And dell.
         By hedgerows rank and rich
         The blossoms bloom and swell,
         And sounds of sweetest pitch
515   From lovely woodlands well.

      Then comes the season of summer with soft winds,
      When Zephyrus himself breathes on seeds and herbs.
      In paradise is the plant that springs in the open
      When the dripping dew drops from its leaves,
520   And it bears the blissful gleam of the bright sun.
      Then Harvest comes hurrying, urging it on,
      Warning it because of winter to wax ripe soon;
      He drives the dust to rise with the drought he brings,
      Forcing it to fly up from the face of the earth.
525   Wrathful winds in raging skies wrestle with the sun;
      Leaves are lashed loose from the trees and lie on the ground
      And the grass becomes gray which was green before.
      What rose from root at first now ripens and rots;
      So the year in passing yields its many yesterdays,
530   And winter returns, as the way of the world is,
          I swear;
         So came the Michaelmas moon;[2]
         With winter threatening there,
         And Gawain considered soon
535   The fell way he must fare.

      Yet he stayed in hall with Arthur till All Saints' Day,[3]
      When Arthur provided plentifully, especially for Gawain,
      A rich feast and high revelry at the Round Table.

---

1. This famous passage on the cycle of seasons draws both on Germanic conventions of the battle of Winter and Summer, and on Romance spring-time lyrics, the reverdies.

2. The harvest moon at Michaelmas, on September 29.
3. On November 1, another holiday on which Arthur presided, crowned, over his court.

The gallant lords and gay ladies grieved for Gawain,
540   Anxious on his account; but all the same
They mentioned only matters of mirthful import,
Joylessly joking for that gentle knight's sake.
For after dinner with drooping heart he addressed his uncle
And spoke plainly of his departure, putting it thus:
545   "Now, liege lord of my life, I beg my leave of you.
You know the kind of covenant it is: I care little
To tell over the trials of it, trifling as they are,
But I am bound to bear the blow and must be gone tomorrow
To seek the gallant in green, as God sees fit to guide me."
550   Then the most courtly in that company came together,[4]
Ywain and Eric and others in troops,
Sir Dodinal the Fierce, The Duke of Clarence,
Lancelot and Lionel and Lucan the Good,
Sir Bors and Sir Bedivere, both strong men,
555   And many admired knights, with Mador of the Gate.
All the company of the court came near to the King
With carking care in their hearts, to counsel the knight.
Much searing sorrow was suffered in the hall
That such a gallant man as Gawain should go in quest
560   To suffer a savage blow, and his sword no more
          Should bear.
      Said Gawain, gay of cheer,
      "Whether fate be foul or fair,
      Why falter I or fear?
565   What should man do but dare?"

He dwelt there all that day, and at dawn on the morrow
Asked for his armor. Every item was brought.
First a crimson carpet was cast over the floor
And the great pile of gilded war-gear glittered upon it.
570   The strong man stepped on it, took the steel in hand.
The doublet he dressed in was dear Turkestan stuff;
Then came the courtly cape, cut with skill,
Finely lined with fur, and fastened close.
Then they set the steel shoes on the strong man's feet,
575   Lapped his legs in steel with lovely greaves,
Complete with knee-pieces, polished bright
And connecting at the knee with gold-knobbed hinges.
Then came the cuisses, which cunningly enclosed
His thighs thick of thew, and which thongs secured.
580   Next the hauberk, interlinked with argent steel rings
Which rested on rich material, wrapped the warrior round.
He had polished armor on arms and elbows,
Glinting and gay, and gloves of metal,

---

4. The list that follows would have recalled, especially to readers of French romances, other great quests and challenges encountered by Arthur's knights. The list's order may also suggest later and more tragic episodes in the Arthurian narrative, ending with Bedivere who throws Excalibur into a mere after Arthur is mortally wounded.

And all the goodly gear to give help whatever
585   Betide;
    With surcoat richly wrought,
    Gold spurs attached in pride,
    A silken sword-belt athwart,
    And steadfast blade at his side.

590 When he was hasped in armor his harness was noble;
The least lace or loop was lustrous with gold.
So, harnessed as he was, he heard his mass
As it was offered at the high altar in worship.
Then he came to the King and his court-fellows,
595 Took leave with loving courtesy of lord and lady,
Who commended him to Christ and kissed him farewell.
By now Gringolet had been got ready, and girt with a saddle
That gleamed most gaily with many golden fringes,
Everywhere nailed newly for this noble occasion.
600 The bridle was embossed and bound with bright gold;
So were the furnishings of the fore-harness and the fine skirts.
The crupper and the caparison[5] accorded with the saddle-bows,
And all was arrayed on red with nails of richest gold,
Which glittered and glanced like gleams of the sun.
605 Then his casque, equipped with clasps of great strength
And padded inside, he seized and swiftly kissed;
It towered high on his head and was hasped at the back,
With a brilliant silk band over the burnished neck-guard,
Embroidered[6] and bossed with the best gems
610 On broad silken borders, with birds about the seams,
Such as parrots painted with periwinkles between,
And turtles and true-love-knots traced as thickly
As if many beauties in a bower had been busy seven winters
     Thereabout.
615   The circlet on his head
    Was prized more precious no doubt,
    And perfectly diamonded,
    Threw a gleaming luster out.

Then they showed him the shield of shining gules,
620 With the Pentangle[7] in pure gold depicted thereon.
He brandished it by the baldric, and about his neck
He slung it in a seemly way, and it suited him well.
And I intend to tell you, though I tarry therefore,
Why the Pentangle is proper to this prince of knights.
625 It is a symbol which Solomon conceived once
To betoken holy truth, by its intrinsic right,

5. A cloth or covering spread over the saddle or harness
of a horse, often ornamented.
6. The technical language of armor is now joined by an
equally technical description of needlework, for which
English women were famous.

7. A five-pointed star and symbol of perfection and eternity, since it can be drawn with an uninterrupted line
ending at the point of the star where it begins. Inscribed
within a circle, it was called Solomon's seal.

For it is a figure which has five points,
And each line overlaps and is locked with another;
And it is endless everywhere, and the English call it,
630   In all the land, I hear, the Endless Knot.
Therefore it goes with Sir Gawain and his gleaming armor,
For, ever faithful in five things, each in fivefold manner,
Gawain was reputed good and, like gold well refined,
He was devoid of all villainy, every virtue displaying
635   In the field.
        Thus this Pentangle new
        He carried on coat and shield,
        As a man of troth most true
        And knightly name annealed.

640   First he was found faultless in his five wits.
Next, his five fingers never failed the knight,
And all his trust on earth was in the five wounds
Which came to Christ on the Cross, as the Creed tells.
And whenever the bold man was busy on the battlefield,
645   Through all other things he thought on this,
That his prowess all depended on the five pure Joys
That the holy Queen of Heaven had of her Child.[8]
Accordingly the courteous knight had that queen's image
Etched on the inside of his armored shield,
650   So that when he beheld her, his heart did not fail.
The fifth five I find the famous man practised
Were—Liberality and Lovingkindness leading the rest;
Then his Continence and Courtesy, which were never corrupted;
And Piety, the surpassing virtue. These pure five
655   Were more firmly fixed on that fine man
Than on any other, and every multiple,
Each interlocking with another, had no end,
Being fixed to five points which never failed,
Never assembling on one side, nor sundering either,
660   With no end at any angle; nor can I find
Where the design started or proceeded to its end.
Thus on his shining shield this knot was shaped
Royally in red gold upon red gules.
That is the pure Pentangle, so people who are wise
665   Are taught.
        Now Gawain was ready and gay;
        His spear he promptly caught
        And gave them all good day
        For ever, as he thought.

670   He struck the steed with his spurs and sprang on his way
So forcefully that the fire flew up from the flinty stones.

---

8. Poems and meditations on the Virgin's joys and sorrow were widespread. Her five joys were the Annunciation, Nativity, Resurrection, Ascension, and Assumption.

All who saw that seemly sight were sick at heart,
And all said to each other softly, in the same breath,
In care for that comely knight, "By Christ, it is evil
675   That yon lord should be lost, who lives so nobly!
To find his fellow on earth in faith is not easy.
It would have been wiser to have worked more warily,
And to have dubbed the dear man a duke of the realm.
A magnificent master of men he might have been,
680   And so had a happier fate than to be utterly destroyed,
Beheaded by an unearthly being out of arrogance.
Who supposed the Prince would approve such counsel
As is giddily given in Christmas games by knights?"
Many were the watery tears that whelmed from weeping eyes,
685   When on quest that worthy knight went from the court
       That day.
     He faltered not nor feared,
     But quickly went his way;
     His road was rough and weird,
690   Or so the stories say.

Now the gallant Sir Gawain in God's name goes
Riding through the realm of Britain,[9] no rapture in his mind.
Often the long night he lay alone and companionless,
And did not find in front of him food of his choice;
695   He had no comrade but his courser in the country woods and hills,
No traveler to talk to on the track but God,
Till he was nearly nigh to Northern Wales.
The isles of Anglesey he kept always on his left,
And fared across the fords by the foreshore
700   Over at Holy Head to the other side
Into the wilderness of Wirral, where few dwelled
To whom God or good-hearted man gave his love.
And always as he went, he asked whomever he met
If they knew or had knowledge of a knight in green,
705   Or could guide him to the ground where a green chapel stood.
And there was none but said him nay, for never in their lives
Had they set eyes on someone of such a hue
       As green.
     His way was wild and strange
710   By dreary hill and dean.
     His mood would many times change
     Before that fane was seen.

He rode far from his friends, a forsaken man,
Scaling many cliffs in country unknown.
715   At every bank or beach where the brave man crossed water,
He found a foe in front of him, except by a freak of chance,

9. "Logres," identified with England in Geoffrey of Monmouth, elsewhere a vaguer term for Arthur's kingdom. Here, Gawain is heading northward through Wales, then along the coast of the Irish Sea and into the forest of Wirral in Cheshire—a wild area and resort of outlaws in the 14th century.

And so foul and fierce a one that he was forced to fight.
So many marvels did the man meet in the mountains,
It would be too tedious to tell a tenth of them.
720 He had death-struggles with dragons, did battle with wolves,
Warred with wild men who dwelt among the crags;
Battled with bulls and bears and boars at other times,
And ogres that panted after him on the high fells.
Had he not been doughty in endurance and dutiful to God,
725 Doubtless he would have been done to death time and again.
Yet the warring little worried him; worse was the winter,
When the cold clear water cascaded from the clouds
And froze before it could fall to the fallow earth.
Half-slain by the sleet, he slept in his armor
730 Night after night among the naked rocks,
Where the cold streams splashed from the steep crests
Or hung high over his head in hard icicles.
So in peril and pain, in parlous plight,
This knight covered the country till Christmas Eve
735   Alone;
      And he that eventide
      To Mary made his moan,
      And begged her be his guide
      Till some shelter should be shown.

740 Merrily in the morning by a mountain he rode
Into a wondrously wild wooded cleft,
With high hills on each side overpeering a forest
Of huge hoary oaks, a hundred together.
The hazel and the hawthorn were intertwined
745 With rough ragged moss trailing everywhere,
And on the bleak branches birds in misery
Piteously piped away, pinched with cold.
The gallant knight on Gringolet galloped under them
Through many a swamp and marsh, a man all alone,
750 Fearing lest he should fail, through adverse fortune,
To see the service of him who that same night
Was born of a bright maiden to banish our strife.
And so sighing he said, "I beseech thee Lord,
And thee Mary, mildest mother so dear,
755 That in some haven with due honor I may hear Mass
And Matins[1] tomorrow morning: meekly I ask it,
And promptly thereto I pray my Pater and Ave
      And Creed."[2]
      He crossed himself and cried
760   For his sins, and said, "Christ speed
      My cause, his cross my guide!"
      So prayed he, spurring his steed.

---

1. First of the canonical hours of prayer and praise in monastic tradition, observed between midnight and dawn.

2. The Paternoster ("Our Father . . ."), Ave Maria ("Hail Mary . . ."), and Creed (the articles of the Catholic faith).

Thrice the sign of the Savior on himself he had made,
When in the wood he was aware of a dwelling with a moat
765　On a promontory above a plateau, penned in by the boughs
And tremendous trunks of trees, and trenched about;
The comeliest castle that ever a knight owned,
It was pitched on a plain, with a park all round,
Impregnably palisaded with pointed stakes,
770　And containing many trees in its two-mile circumference.
The courteous knight contemplated the castle from one side
As it shimmered and shone through the shining oaks.
Then humbly he took off his helmet and offered thanks
To Jesus and Saint Julian,[3] gentle patrons both,
775　Who had given him grace and gratified his wish.
"Now grant it be good lodging!" the gallant knight said.
Then he goaded Gringolet with his golden heels,
And mostly by chance emerged on the main highway,
Which brought the brave man to the bridge's end
780　　　　With one cast.
　　　　The drawbridge vertical,
　　　　The gates shut firm and fast,
　　　　The well-provided wall—
　　　　It blenched at never a blast.

785　The knight, still on his steed, stayed on the bank
Of the deep double ditch that drove round the place.
The wall went into the water wonderfully deep,
And then to a huge height upwards it reared
In hard hewn stone, up to the cornice;
790　Built under the battlements in the best style, courses jutted
And turrets protruded between, constructed
With loopholes in plenty with locking shutters.
No better barbican had ever been beheld by that knight.[4]
And inside he could see a splendid high hall
795　With towers and turrets on top, all tipped with crenellations,
And pretty pinnacles placed along its length,
With carved copes, cunningly worked.
Many chalk-white chimneys the chevalier saw
On the tops of towers twinkling whitely,
800　So many painted pinnacles sprinkled everywhere,
Congregated in clusters among the crenellations,
That it appeared like a prospect of paper patterning.[5]
To the gallant knight on Gringolet it seemed good enough
If he could ever gain entrance to the inner court,
805　And harbor in that house while Holy Day lasted,
　　　　Well cheered.
　　　　He hailed, and at a height

---

3. Patron saint of hospitality.
4. The poet again revels in technical vocabulary, here architectural; this is a fashionable (if exaggerated) building of the 14th century.
5. Models in cut paper sometimes decorated elaborate feasts such as that at the beginning of the poem.

A civil porter appeared,
Who welcomed the wandering knight,
810   And his inquiry heard.

"Good sir," said Gawain, "Will you give my message
To the high lord of this house, that I ask for lodging."
"Yes, by Saint Peter,"[6] replied the porter, "and I think
You may lodge here as long as you like, sir knight."
815   Then away he went eagerly, and swiftly returned
With a host of well-wishers to welcome the knight.
They let down the drawbridge and in a dignified way
Came out and did honor to him, kneeling
Courteously on the cold ground to accord him worthy welcome.
820   They prayed him to pass the portcullis, now pulled up high,
And he readily bid them rise and rode over the bridge.
Servants held his saddle while he stepped down,
And his steed was stabled by sturdy men in plenty.
Strong knights and squires descended then
825   To bring the bold warrier blithely into hall.
When he took off his helmet, many hurried forward
To receive it and to serve this stately man,
And his bright sword and buckler were both taken as well.
Then graciously he greeted each gallant knight,
830   And many proud men pressed forward to pay their respects.
Garbed in his fine garments, he was guided to the hall,
Where a fine fire was burning fiercely on the hearth.
Then the prince of those people appeared from his chamber
To meet in mannerly style the man in his hall.
835   "You are welcome to dwell here as you wish," he said,
"Treat everything as your own, and have what you please
        In this place."
        "I yield my best thanks yet:
        May Christ make good your grace!"
840   Said Gawain and, gladly met,
        They clasped in close embrace.

Gawain gazed at the gallant who had greeted him well
And it seemed to him the stronghold possessed a brave lord,
A powerful man in his prime, of stupendous size.
845   Broad and bright was his beard, all beaver-hued;
Strong and sturdy he stood on his stalwart legs;
His face was fierce as fire, free was his speech,
And he seemed in good sooth a suitable man
To be prince of a people with companions of mettle.
850   This prince led him to an apartment and expressly commanded
That a man be commissioned to minister to Gawain;
And at his bidding a band of men bent to serve

6. Swearing by St. Peter, keeper of the keys to heaven.

Brought him to a beautiful room where the bedding was noble.
The bed-curtains, of brilliant silk with bright gold hems,
855 Had skilfully-sewn coverlets with comely facings,
And the fairest fur on the fringes was worked.
With ruddy gold rings on the cords ran the curtains;
Toulouse and Turkestan tapestries on the wall
And fine carpets underfoot, on the floor, were fittingly matched.
860 There amid merry talk the man was disrobed,
And stripped of his battle-sark and his splendid clothes.
Retainers readily brought him rich robes
Of the choicest kind to choose from and change into.
In a trice when he took one, and was attired in it,
865 And it sat on him in style, with spreading skirts,
It certainly seemed to those assembled as if spring
In all its hues were evident before them;
His lithe limbs below the garment were gleaming with beauty.
Jesus never made, men judged, more gentle and handsome
870 　　A knight:
　　From wherever in the world he were,
　　At sight it seemed he might
　　Be a prince without a peer
　　In field where fell men fight.

875 At the chimneyed hearth where charcoal burned, a chair was placed
For Sir Gawain in gracious style, gorgeously decked
With cushions on quilted work, both cunningly wrought;
And then on that man a magnificent mantle was thrown,
A gleaming garment gorgeously embroidered,
880 Fairly lined with fur, the finest skins
Of ermine on earth, and his hood of the same.
In that splendid seat he sat in dignity,
And warmth came to him at once, bringing well-being.
In a trice on fine trestles a table was put up,[7]
885 Then covered with a cloth shining clean and white,
And set with silver spoons, salt-cellars and overlays.
The worthy knight washed willingly, and went to his meat.
In seemly enough style servants brought him
Several fine soups, seasoned lavishly
890 Twice-fold, as is fitting, and fish of all kinds—
Some baked in bread, some browned on coals,
Some seethed, some stewed and savored with spice,
But always subtly sauced, and so the man liked it.
The gentle knight generously judged it a feast,
895 And often said so, while the servers spurred him on thus
　　As he ate:
　　"This present penance do;

---

7. A castle's great hall had many uses; tables were set up for dining and then put aside or hung.

It soon shall be offset."[8]
The knight rejoiced anew,
900   For the wine his spirits whet.

Then in seemly style they searchingly inquired,
Putting to the prince private questions,
So that he courteously conceded he came of that court
Where high-souled Arthur held sway alone,
905   Ruler most royal of the Round Table;
And that Sir Gawain himself now sat in the house,
Having come that Christmas, by course of fortune.
Loudly laughed the lord when he learned what knight
He had in his house; such happiness it brought
910   That all the men within the moat made merry,
And promptly appeared in the presence of Gawain,
To whose person are proper all prowess and worth,
And pure and perfect manners, and praises unceasing.
His reputation rates first in the ranks of men.
915   Each knight neared his neighbor and softly said,
"Now we shall see displayed the seemliest manners
And the faultless figures of virtuous discourse.
Without asking we may hear how to hold conversation
Since we have seized upon this scion of good breeding.
920   God has given us of his grace good measure
In granting us such a guest as Gawain is,
When, contented at Christ's birth, the courtiers shall sit
        And sing.
    This noble knight will prove
925   What manners the mighty bring;
    His converse of courtly love
    Shall spur our studying."[9]

When the fine man had finished his food and risen,
It was nigh and near to the night's mid-hour.
930   Priests to their prayers paced their way
And rang the bells royally, as rightly they should,
To honor that high feast with evensong.
The lord inclines to prayer, the lady too;
Into her private pew she prettily walks;
935   Gawain advances gaily and goes there quickly,
But the lord gripped his gown and guided him to his seat,
Acknowledged him by name and benevolently said
In the whole world he was the most welcome of men.
Gawain spoke his gratitude, they gravely embraced,
940   And sat in serious mood the whole service through.
Then the lady had a longing to look on the knight;

---

8. An exchange courtesies. Gawain has politely praised the many fish dishes; his hosts demur, remind him that Christmas Eve is a day of fasting, and promise him better meals later.

9. Though Gawain is engaged on a serious quest, his reputation as a graceful courtier and master in the arts of love has preceded him.

With her bevy of beauties she abandoned her pew.
Most beautiful of body and bright of complexion,
Most winsome in ways of all women alive,
945   She seemed to Sir Gawain, excelling Guinevere.
To squire that splendid dame, he strode through the chancel.
Another lady led her by the left hand,
A matron, much older, past middle age,
Who was highly honored by an escort of squires.
950   Most unlike to look on those ladies were,
For if the one was winsome, then withered was the other.
Hues rich and rubious were arrayed on the one,
Rough wrinkles on the other rutted the cheeks.
Kerchiefed with clear pearls clustering was the one,
955   Her breast and bright throat bare to the sight,
Shining like sheen of snow shed on the hills;
The other was swathed with a wimple wound to the throat
And choking her swarthy chin in chalk-white veils.
On her forehead were folded enveloping silks,
960   Trellised about with trefoils and tiny rings.
Nothing was bare on that beldame but the black brows,
The two eyes, protruding nose and stark lips,
And those were a sorry sight and exceedingly bleary:
A grand lady, God knows, of greatness in the world
965   Well tried!
        Her body was stumpy and squat,
        Her buttocks bulging and wide;
        More pleasure a man could plot
        With the sweet one at her side.

970   When Gawain had gazed on that gracious-looking creature
He gained leave of the lord to go along with the ladies.
He saluted the senior, sweeping a low bow,
But briefly embraced the beautiful one,
Kissing her in courtly style and complimenting her.
975   They craved his acquaintance and he quickly requested
To be their faithful follower, if they would so favor him.
They took him between them, and talking, they led him
To a high room. By the hearth they asked first
For spices, which unstintingly men sped to bring,
980   And always with heart-warming, heady wine.
In lovingkindness the lord leaped up repeatedly
And many times reminded them that mirth should flow;
Elaborately lifted up his hood, looped it on a spear,
And offered it as a mark of honor to whoever should prove able
985   To make the most mirth that merry Yuletide.
"And I shall essay, I swear, to strive with the best
Before this garment goes from me, by my good friends' help."
So with his mirth the mighty lord made things merry
To gladden Sir Gawain with games in hall

Courtly Women Hunting, from the *Taymouth Hours*, 14th century. Women in courtly dress dismember a stag, usually the work of aristocratic men.

990
       That night;
       Until, the time being spent,
       The lord demanded light.
       Gawain took his leave and went
       To rest in rare delight.

995   On that morning when men call to mind the birth
       Of our dear Lord born to die for our destiny,
       Joy waxes in dwellings the world over for his sake:
       And so it befell there on the feast day with fine fare.
       Both at main meals and minor repasts strong men served
1000   Rare dishes with fine dressings to the dais company.
       Highest, in the place of honor, the ancient crone sat,
       And the lord, so I believe, politely next.
       Together sat Gawain and the gay lady
       In mid-table, where the meal was mannerly served first;
1005   And after throughout the hall, as was held best,
       Each gallant by degree was graciously served.
       There was meat and merry-making and much delight,
       To such an extent that it would try me to tell of it,
       Even if perhaps I made the effort to describe it.
1010   But yet I know the knight and the nobly pretty one

Found such solace and satisfaction seated together,
In the discreet confidences of their courtly dalliance,
Their irreproachably pure and polished repartee,
That with princes' sport their play of wit surpassingly
1015   Compares.
     Pipes and side-drums sound,
     Trumpets entune their airs;
     Each soul its solace found,
     And the two were enthralled with theirs.

1020 That day they made much merriment, and on the morrow again,
And thickly the joys thronged on the third day after;
But gentle was the jubilation on St John's Day,[1]
The final one for feasting, so the folk there thought.
As there were guests geared to go in the gray dawn
1025 They watched the night out with wine in wonderful style,
Leaping night-long in their lordly dances.
At last when it was late those who lived far off,
Each one, bid farewell before wending their ways.
Gawain also said goodbye, but the good host grasped him,
1030 Led him to the hearth of his own chamber,
And held him back hard, heartily thanking him
For the fine favor he had manifested to him
In honoring his house that high feast-tide,
Brightening his abode with his brilliant company:
1035 "As long as I live, sir, I believe I shall thrive
Now Gawain has been my guest at God's own feast."
"Great thanks, sir," said Gawain. "In good faith, yours,
All yours is the honor, may the High King requite it!
I stand at your service, knight, to satisfy your will
1040 As good use engages me, in great things and small,
     By right."
     The lord then bid his best
     Longer to delay the knight,
     But Gawain, replying, pressed
1045   His departure in all despite.

Then with courteous inquiry the castellan asked
What fierce exploit had sent him forth, at that festive season,
From the King's court at Camelot, so quickly and alone,
Before the holy time was over in the homes of men.
1050 "You may in truth well demand," admitted the knight.
"A high and urgent errand hastened me from thence,
For I myself am summoned to seek out a place
To find which I know not where in the world to look.
For all the land in Logres—may our Lord help me!
1055 I would not fail to find it on the feast of New Year.

---

1. December 27, traditionally given over to drinking and celebration.

So this is my suit, sir, which I beseech of you here,
That you tell me in truth if tale ever reached you
Of the Green Chapel, or what ground or glebe it stands on,
Or of the knight who holds it, whose hue is green.
1060   For at that place I am pledged, by the pact between us,
To meet that man, if I remain alive.
From now until the New Year is not a great time,
And if God will grant it me, more gladly would I see him
Than gain any good possession, by God's son!
1065   I must wend my way, with your good will, therefore;
I am reduced to three days in which to do my business,
And I think it fitter to fall dead than fail in my errand."
Then the lord said laughingly, "You may linger a while,
For I shall tell you where your tryst is by your term's end.
1070   Give yourself no more grief for the Green Chapel's whereabouts.
For you may lie back in your bed, brave man, at ease
Till full morning on the First, and then fare forth
To the meeting place at mid-morning to manage how you may
          Out there.
1075   Leave not till New Year's Day,
          Then get up and go with cheer;
          You shall be shown the way;
          It is hardly two miles from here."

Then Gawain was glad and gleefully exclaimed,
1080   "Now above all, most heartily do I offer you thanks!
For my goal is now gained, and by grace of yours
I shall dwell here and do what you deem good for me."
So the lord seized Sir Gawain, seated him beside himself,
And to enliven their delight, he had the ladies fetched,
1085   And much gentle merriment they long made together.
The lord, as one like to take leave of his senses
And not aware of what he was doing, spoke warmly and merrily.
Then he spoke to Sir Gawain, saying out loud,
"You have determined to do the deed I ask:
1090   Will you hold to your undertaking here and now?"
"Yes, sir, in good sooth," said the true knight,
"While I stay in your stronghold, I shall stand at your command."
"Since you have spurred," the lord said, "from afar,
Then watched awake with me, you are not well supplied
1095   With either sustenance or sleep, for certain, I know;
So you shall lie long in your room, late and at ease
Tomorrow till the time of mass, and then take your meal
When you will, with my wife beside you
To comfort you with her company till I come back to court.
1100   You stay,
          And I shall get up at dawn.
          I will to the hunt away."

When Gawain's agreement was sworn
He bowed, as brave knights may.

1105 "Moreover," said the man, "Let us make a bargain
That whatever I win in the woods be yours,
And any achievement you chance on here, you exchange for it.
Sweet sir, truly swear to such a bartering,
Whether fair fortune or foul befall from it."
1110 "By God," said the good Gawain, "I agree to that,
And I am happy that you have an eye to sport."
Then the prince of that people said, "What pledge of wine
Is brought to seal the bargain?" And they burst out laughing.
They took drink and toyed in trifling talk,
1115 These lords and ladies, as long as they liked,
And then with French refinement and many fair words
They stood, softly speaking, to say goodnight,
Kissing as they parted company in courtly style.
With lithe liege servants in plenty and lambent torches,
1120 Each brave man was brought to his bed at last,
       Full soft.
     Before they fared to bed
     They rehearsed their bargain oft.
     That people's prince, men said,
1125 Could fly his wit aloft.

PART 3

In the faint light before dawn folk were stirring;
Guests who had to go gave orders to their grooms,
Who busied themselves briskly with the beasts, saddling,
Trimming their tackle and tying on their luggage.
1130 Arrayed for riding in the richest style,
Guests leaped on their mounts lightly, laid hold of their bridles,
And each rider rode out on his own chosen way.
The beloved lord of the land was not the last up,
Being arrayed for riding with his retinue in force.
1135 He ate a sop hastily when he had heard mass,
And hurried with horn to the hunting field;
Before the sun's first rays fell on the earth,
On their high steeds were he and his knights.[2]
Then these cunning hunters came to couple their hounds,
1140 Cast open the kennel doors and called them out,
And blew on their bugles three bold notes.
The hounds broke out barking, baying fiercely,
And when they went chasing, they were whipped back.

---

2. The hunts that follow, for all their violent energy, are as ritualized in their procedure as the earlier feasts and games. The poet delights in describing still another quite technical area of knightly lore. A number of contemporary treatises on the hunt survive.

There were a hundred choice huntsmen there, whose fame
1145   Resounds.
To their stations keepers strode;
Huntsmen unleashed hounds:
The forest overflowed
With the strident bugle sounds.

1150   At the first cry wild creatures quivered with dread.
The deer in distraction darted down to the dales
Or up to the high ground, but eagerly they were
Driven back by the beaters, who bellowed lustily.
They let the harts with high-branching heads have their freedom,
1155   And the brave bucks, too, with their broad antlers,
For the noble prince had expressly prohibited
Meddling with male deer in the months of close season.
But the hinds were held back with a "Hey" and a "Whoa!"
And does driven with much din to the deep valleys.
1160   Lo! the arrows' slanting flight as they were loosed!
A shaft flew forth at every forest turning,
The broad head biting on the brown flank.
They screamed as the blood streamed out, sank dead on the sward,
Always harried by hounds hard on their heels,
1165   And the hurrying hunters' high horn notes.
Like the rending of ramped hills roared the din.
If one of the wild beasts slipped away from the archers
It was dragged down and met death at the dog-bases
After being hunted from the high ground and harried to the water,
1170   So skilled were the hunt-servants at stations lower down,
So gigantic the greyhounds that grabbed them in a flash,
Seizing them savagely, as swift, I swear,
As sight.
The lord, in humor high
1175   Would spur, then stop and alight.
In bliss the day went by
Till dark drew on, and night.

Thus by the forest borders the brave lord sported,
And the good man Gawain, on his gay bed lying,
1180   Lay hidden till the light of day gleamed on the walls,
Covered with fair canopy, the curtains closed,
And as in slumber he slept on, there slipped into his mind
A slight, suspicious sound, and the door stealthily opened.
He raised up his head out of the bedclothes,
1185   Caught up the corner of the curtain a little
And watched warily towards it, to see what it was.
It was the lady, loveliest to look upon,
Who secretly and silently secured the door,
Then bore towards his bed: the brave knight, embarrassed,
1190   Lay flat with fine adroitness and feigned sleep.
Silently she stepped on, stole to his bed,

Caught up the curtain, crept within,
And seated herself softly on the side of the bed.
There she watched a long while, waiting for him to wake.
1195 Slyly close this long while lay the knight,
Considering in his soul this circumstance,
Its sense and likely sequel, for it seemed marvelous.
"Still, it would be more circumspect," he said to himself,
"To speak and discover her desire in due course."
1200 So he stirred and stretched himself, twisting towards her,
Opened his eyes and acted as if astounded;
And, to seem the safer by such service, crossed himself
       In dread.
          With chin and cheek so fair,
1205   White ranged with rosy red,
          With laughing lips, and air
          Of love, she lightly said:

"Good morning, Sir Gawain," the gay one murmured,
"How unsafely you sleep, that one may slip in here!
1210 Now you are taken in a trice. Unless a truce come between us,
I shall bind you to your bed—of that be sure."
The lady uttered laughingly those playful words.
"Good morning, gay lady," Gawain blithely greeted her.
"Do with me as you will: that well pleases me.
1215 For I surrender speedily and sue for grace,
Which, to my mind, since I must, is much the best course."
And thus he repaid her with repartee and ready laughter.
"But if, lovely lady, your leave were forthcoming,
And you were pleased to free your prisoner and pray him to rise,
1220 I would abandon my bed for a better habiliment,
And have more happiness in our honey talk."
"Nay, verily, fine sir," urged the voice of that sweet one,
"You shall not budge from your bed. I have a better idea.
I shall hold you fast here on this other side as well
1225 And so chat on with the chevalier my chains have caught.
For I know well, my knight, that your name is Sir Gawain,
Whom all the world worships, wherever he ride;
For lords and their ladies, and all living folk,
Hold your honor in high esteem, and your courtesy.
1230 And now—here you are truly, and we are utterly alone;
My lord and his liegemen are a long way off;
Others still bide in their beds, my bower-maidens too;
Shut fast and firmly with a fine hasp is the door;
And since I have in this house him who pleases all,
1235 As long as my time lasts I shall lingering in talk take
       My fill.
          My young body is yours,
          Do with it what you will;
          My strong necessities force
1240   Me to be your servant still."

"In good truth," said Gawain, "that is a gain indeed,
Though I am hardly the hero of whom you speak.
To be held in such honor as you here suggest,
I am altogether unworthy, I own it freely.
1245   By God, I should be glad, if you granted it right
For me to essay by speech or some other service,
To pleasure such a perfect lady—pure joy it would be."
"In good truth, Sir Gawain," the gay lady replied,
"If I slighted or set at naught your spotless fame
1250   And your all-pleasing prowess, it would show poor breeding.
But there is no lack of ladies who would love, noble one,
To hold you in their arms, as I have you here,
And linger in the luxury of your delightful discourse,
Which would perfectly pleasure them and appease their woes—
1255   Rather than have riches or the red gold they own.
But as I love that Lord, the Celestial Ruler,
I have wholly in my hand what all desire
        Through his grace."
     Not loth was she to allure,
1260   This lady fair of face;
        But the knight with speeches pure
        Answered in each case.

"Madam," said the merry man, "May Mary requite you!
For in good faith I have found in you free-hearted generosity.
1265   Certain men for their deeds receive esteem from others,
But for myself, I do not deserve the respect they show me;
Your honorable mind makes you utter only what is good.
"Now by Mary," said the noble lady, "Not so it seems to me,
For were I worth the whole of womankind,
1270   And all the wealth in the world were in my hand,
And if bargaining I were to bid to bring myself a lord—
With your noble qualities, knight, made known to me now,
Your good looks, gracious manner and great courtesy,
All of which I have heard of before, but here prove true—
1275   No lord that is living could be allowed to excel you."
"Indeed, dear lady, you did better," said the knight,
"But I am proud of the precious price you put on me,
And solemnly as your servant say you are my sovereign.
May Christ requite it you: I have become your knight."
1280   Then of many matters they talked till mid-morning and after,
And all the time she behaved as if she adored him;
But Sir Gawain was on guard in a gracious manner.
Though she was the winsomest woman the warrior had known,
He was less love-laden because of the loss he must
1285   Now face—
        His destruction by the stroke,
        For come it must was the case.
        The lady of leaving then spoke;
        He assented with speedy grace.

1290 Then she gave him goodbye, glinting with laughter,
 And standing up, astounded him with these strong words:
 "May He who prospers every speech for this pleasure reward you!
 I cannot bring myself to believe that you could be Gawain."
 "How so?" said the knight, speaking urgently,
1295 For he feared he had failed to observe the forms of courtesy.
 But the beauteous one blessed him and brought out this argument:
 "Such a great man as Gawain is granted to be,
 The very vessel of virtue and fine courtesy,
 Could scarcely have stayed such a sojourn with a lady
1300 Without craving a kiss out of courtesy,
 Touched by some trifling hint at the tail-end of a speech."
 "So be it, as you say," then said Gawain,
 "I shall kiss at your command, as becomes a knight
 Who fears to offend you; no further plea is needed."
1305 Whereupon she approached him, and penned him in her arms,
 Leaned over him lovingly and gave the lord a kiss.
 Then they commended each other to Christ in comely style,
 And without more words she went out by the door.
 He made ready to rise with rapid haste,
1310 Summoned his servant, selected his garb,
 And walked down, when he was dressed, debonairly to mass.
 Then he went to the well-served meal which awaited him,
 And made merry sport till the moon rose
   At night.
1315 Never was baron bold
  So taken by ladies bright,
  That young one and the old:
  They throve all three in delight.

 And still at his sport spurred the castellan,
1320 Hunting the barren hinds in holt and on heath.
 So many had he slain, by the setting of the sun,
 Of does and other deer, that it was downright wonderful.
 Then at the finish the folk flocked in eagerly,
 And quickly collected the killed deer in a heap.
1325 Those highest in rank came up with hosts of attendants,
 Picked out what appeared to be the plumpest beasts
 And, according to custom, had them cut open with finesse.
 Some who ceremoniously assessed them there
 Found two fingers' breadth of fat on the worst.
1330 Then they slit open the slot, seized the first stomach,
 Scraped it with a keen knife and tied up the tripes.
 Next they hacked off all the legs, the hide was stripped,
 The belly broken open and the bowels removed
 Carefully, lest they loosen the ligature of the knot.
1335 Then they gripped the gullet, disengaged deftly
 The wezand[3] from the windpipe and whipped out the guts.

---

3. The esophagus.

Then their sharp knives shore through the shoulder-bones,
Which they slid out of a small hole, leaving the sides intact.
Then they cleft the chest clean through, cutting it in two.
1340　Then again at the gullet a man began to work
And straight away rived it, right to the fork,
Flicked out the shoulder-fillets, and faithfully then
He rapidly ripped free the rib-fillets.
Similarly, as is seemly, the spine was cleared
1345　All the way to the haunch, which hung from it;
And they heaved up the whole haunch and hewed it off;
And that is called, according to its kind, the numbles,[4]
　　　I find.
　　　At the thigh-forks then they strain
1350　　And free the folds behind,
　　　Hurrying to hack all in twain,
　　　The backbone to unbind.

Then they hewed off the head and also the neck,
And after sundered the sides swiftly from the chine,
1355　And into the foliage they flung the fee of the raven.[5]
Then each fellow, for his fee, as it fell to him to have,
Skewered through the stout flanks beside the ribs,
And then by the hocks of the haunches they hung up their booty.
On one of the finest fells they fed their hounds,
1360　And let them have the lights,[6] the liver and the tripes,
With bread well imbrued with blood mixed with them.
Boldly they blew the kill amid the baying of hounds.
Then off they went homewards, holding their meat,
Stalwartly sounding many stout horn-calls.
1365　As dark was descending, they were drawing near
To the comely castle where quietly our knight stayed.
　　　Fires roared,
　　　And blithely hearts were beating
　　　As into hall came the lord.
1370　　When Gawain gave him greeting,
　　　Joy abounded at the board.

Then the master commanded everyone to meet in the hall,
Called the ladies to come down with their company of maidens.
Before all the folk on the floor, he bid men
1375　Fetch the venison and place it before him.
Then gaily and in good humor to Gawain he called,
Told over the tally of the sturdy beasts,
And showed him the fine fat flesh flayed from the ribs.
"How does the sport please you? Do you praise me for it?
1380　Am I thoroughly thanked for thriving as a huntsman?"
"Certainly," said the other, "Such splendid spoils

---

4. Internal organs such as the heart, liver, lungs.
5. The gristle at the end of the breastbone was left for the

ravens, still another of the prescribed rituals of the hunt.
6. Lungs.

Have I not seen for seven years in the season of winter."
"And I give you all, Gawain," said the good man then,
"For according to our covenant you may claim it as your own."
1385 "Certes, that is so, and I say the same to you,"
Said Gawain, "For my true gains in this great house,
I am not loth to allow, must belong to you."
And he put his arms round his handsome neck, hugging him,
And kissed him in the comeliest way he could think of.
1390 "Accept my takings, sir, for I received no more;
Gladly would I grant them, however great they were."
"And therefore I thank you," the thane said, "Good!
Yours may be the better gift, if you would break it to me
Where your wisdom won you wealth of that kind."
1395 "No such clause in our contract! Request nothing else!"
Said the other, "You have your due: ask more,
     None should."
   They laughed in blithe assent
   With worthy words and good;
1400   Then to supper they swiftly went,
   To fresh delicious food.

And sitting afterwards by the hearth of an audience chamber,
Where retainers repeatedly brought them rare wines,
In their jolly jesting they jointly agreed
1405 On a settlement similar to the preceding one;
To exchange the chance achievements of the morrow,
No matter how novel they were, at night when they met.
They accorded on this compact, the whole court observing,
And the bumper was brought forth in banter to seal it.
1410 And at last they lovingly took leave of each other,
Each man hastening thereafter to his bed.
The cock having crowed and called only thrice,
The lord leaped from bed, and his liegemen too,
So that mass and a meal were meetly dealt with,
1415 And by first light the folk to the forest were bound
    For the chase.
   Proudly the hunt with horns
   Soon drove through a desert place:
   Uncoupled through the thorns
1420   The great hounds pressed apace.

By a quagmire they quickly scented quarry and gave tongue,
And the chief huntsman urged on the first hounds up,
Spurring them on with a splendid spate of words.
The hounds, hearing it, hurried there at once,
1425 Fell on the trial furiously, forty together,
And made such echoing uproar, all howling at once,
That the rocky banks round about rang with the din.
Hunters inspirited them with sound of speech and horn.
Then together in a group, across the ground they surged

1430   At speed between a pool and a spiteful crag.
    On a stony knoll by a steep cliff at the side of a bog,
    Where rugged rocks had roughly tumbled down,
    They careered on the quest, the cry following,
    Then surrounded the crag and the rocky knoll as well,
1435   Certain their prey skulked inside their ring,
    For the baying of the bloodhounds meant the beast was there.
    Then they beat upon the bushes and bade him come out,
    And he swung out savagely aslant the line of men,
    A baneful boar of unbelievable size,
1440   A solitary long since sundered from the herd,
    Being old and brawny, the biggest of them all,
    And grim and ghastly when he grunted: great was the grief
    When he thrust through the hounds, hurling three to earth,
    And sped on scot-free, swift and unscathed.
1445   They hallooed, yelled, "Look out!" cried, "Hey, we have him!"
    And blew horns boldly, to bring the bloodhounds together;
    Many were the merry cries from men and dogs
    As they hurried clamoring after their quarry to kill him on
        The track.
1450   Many times he turns at bay
        And tears the dogs which attack.
        He hurts the hounds, and they
        Moan in a piteous pack.

    Then men shoved forward, shaped to shoot at him,
1455   Loosed arrows at him, hitting him often,
    But the points, for all their power, could not pierce his flanks,
    Nor would the barbs bite on his bristling brow.
    Though the smooth-shaven shaft shattered in pieces,
    Wherever it hit, the head rebounded.
1460   But when the boar was battered by blows unceasing,
    Goaded and driven demented, he dashed at the men,
    Striking them savagely as he assailed them in rushes,
    So that some lacking stomach stood back in fear.
    But the lord on a lithe horse lunged after him,
1465   Blew on his bugle like a bold knight in battle,
    Rallied the hounds as he rode through the rank thickets,
    Pursuing this savage boar till the sun set.
    And so they disported themselves this day
    While our lovable lord lay in his bed.
1470   At home the gracious Gawain in gorgeous clothes
        Reclined:
        The gay one did not forget
        To come with welcome kind,
        And early him beset
1475   To make him change his mind.

    She came to the curtain and cast her eye
    On Sir Gawain, who at once gave her gracious welcome,

And she answered him eagerly, with ardent words,
Sat at his side softly, and with a spurt of laughter
1480 And a loving look, delivered these words:
"It seems to me strange, if, sir, you are Gawain,
A person so powerfully disposed to good,
Yet nevertheless know nothing of noble conventions,
And when made aware of them, wave them away!
1485 Quickly you have cast off what I schooled you in yesterday
By the truest of all tokens of talk I know of."
"What?" said the wondering knight, "I am not aware of one.
But if it be true what you tell, I am entirely to blame."
"I counseled you then about kissing," the comely one said;
1490 "When a favor is conferred, it must be forthwith accepted:
That is becoming for a courtly knight who keeps the rules."
"Sweet one, unsay that speech," said the brave man,
"For I dared not do that lest I be denied.
If I were forward and were refused, the fault would be mine."
1495 "But none," said the noblewoman, "could deny you, by my faith!
You are strong enough to constrain with your strength if you wish,
If any were so ill-bred as to offer you resistance."
"Yes, good guidance you give me, by God," replied Gawain,
"But threateners are ill thought of and do not thrive in my country,
1500 Nor do gifts thrive when given without good will.
I am here at your behest, to offer a kiss to when you like;
You may do it whenever you deem fit, or desist,
        In this place."
        The beautiful lady bent
1505   And fairly kissed his face;
        Much speech the two then spent
        On love, its grief and grace.

"I would know of you, knight," the noble lady said,
"If it did not anger you, what argument you use,
1510 Being so hale and hearty as you are at this time,
So generous a gentleman as you are justly famed to be;
Since the choicest thing in Chivalry, the chief thing praised,
Is the loyal sport of love, the very lore of arms?[7]
For the tale of the contentions of true knights
1515 Is told by the title and text of their feats,
How lords for their true loves put their lives at hazard,
Endured dreadful trials for their dear loves' sakes,
And with valor avenged and made void their woes,
Bringing home abundant bliss by their virtues.
1520 You are the gentlest and most just of your generation;
Everywhere your honor and high fame are known;
Yet I have sat at your side two separate times here
Without hearing you utter in any way

---

7. The lady compares Gawain's behavior to descriptions of courtly love in romances; the poem is mirrored within itself.

A single syllable of the saga of love.
1525   Being so polished and punctilious a pledge-fulfiller,
You ought to be eager to lay open to a young thing
Your discoveries in the craft of courtly love.
What! Are you ignorant, with all your renown?
Or do you deem me too dull to drink in your dalliance?
1530   For shame!
I sit here unchaperoned, and stay
To acquire some courtly game;
So while my lord is away,
Teach me your true wit's fame."

1535   "In good faith," said Gawain, "may God requite you!
It gives me great happiness, and is good sport to me,
That so fine a fair one as you should find her way here
And take pains with so poor a man, make pastime with her knight,
With any kind of clemency—it comforts me greatly.
1540   But for me to take on the travail of interpreting true love
And construing the subjects of the stories of arms
To you who, I hold, have more skill
In that art, by half, than a hundred of such
As I am or ever shall be on the earth I inhabit,
1545   Would in faith be a manifold folly, noble lady.
To please you I would press with all the power in my soul,
For I am highly beholden to you, and evermore shall be
True servant to your bounteous self, so save me God!"
So that stately lady tempted him and tried him with questions
1550   To win him to wickedness, whatever else she thought.
But he defended himself so firmly that no fault appeared,
Nor was there any evil apparent on either side,
But bliss;
For long they laughed and played
1555   Till she gave him a gracious kiss.
A fond farewell she bade,
And went her way on this.

Sir Gawain bestirred himself and went to mass:
Then dinner was dressed and with due honor served.
1560   All day long the lord and the ladies disported,
But the castellan coursed across the country time and again,
Hunted his hapless boar as it hurtled over the hills,
Then bit the backs of his best hounds asunder
Standing at bay, till the bowmen obliged him to break free
1565   Out into the open for all he could do,
So fast the arrows flew when the folk there concentrated.
Even the strongest he sometimes made start back,
But in time he became so tired he could tear away no more,
And with the speed he still possessed, he spurted to a hole
1570   On a rise by a rock with a running stream beside.
He got the bank at his back, and began to abrade the ground.

The froth was foaming foully at his mouth,
And he whetted his white tusks; a weary time it was
For the bold men about, who were bound to harass him
1575 From a distance, for none dared to draw near him
    For dread.
      He had hurt so many men
      That it entered no one's head
      To be torn by his tusks again,
1580   And he raging and seeing red.

Till the castellan came himself, encouraging his horse,
And saw the boar at bay with his band of men around.
He alighted in lively fashion, left his courser,
Drew and brandished his bright sword and boldly strode forward,
1585 Striding at speed through the stream to where the savage beast was.
The wild thing was aware of the weapon and its wielder,
And so bridled with its bristles in a burst of fierce snorts
That all were anxious for the lord, lest he have the worst of it.
Straight away the savage brute sprang at the man,
1590 And baron and boar were both in a heap
In the swirling water: the worst went to the beast,
For the man had marked him well at the moment of impact,
Had put the point precisely at the pit of his chest,
And drove it in to the hilt, so that the heart was shattered,
1595 And the spent beast sank snarling and was swept downstream,
    Teeth bare.
      A hundred hounds and more
      Attack and seize and tear;
      Men tug him to the shore
1600   And the dogs destroy him there.

Bugles blew the triumph, horns blared loud.
There was hallooing in high pride by all present;
Braches bayed at the beast, as bidden by their masters,
The chief huntsmen in charge of that chase so hard.
1605 Then one who was wise in wood-crafts
Started in style to slash open the boar.
First he hewed off the head and hoisted it on high,
Then rent him roughly along the ridge of his back,
Brought out the bowels and broiled them on coals
1610 For blending with bread as the braches' reward.
Then he broke out the brawn from the bright broad flanks,
Took out the offal, as is fit,
Attached the two halves entirely together,
And on a strong stake stoutly hung them.
1615 Then home they hurried with the huge beast,
With the boar's head borne before the baron himself,
Who had destroyed him in the stream by the strength of his arm,
    Above all:
      It seemed to him an age

1620   Till he greeted Gawain in hall.
        To reap his rightful wage
        The latter came at his call.

        The lord exclaimed loudly, laughing merrily
        When he saw Sir Gawain, and spoke joyously.
1625   The sweet ladies were sent for, and the servants assembled.
        Then he showed them the shields, and surely described
        The large size and length, and the malignity
        Of the fierce boar's fighting when he fled in the woods;
        So that Gawain congratulated him on his great deed,
1630   Commended it as a merit he had manifested well,
        For a beast with so much brawn, the bold man said,
        A boar of such breadth, he had not before seen.
        When they handled the huge head the upright man praised it,
        Expressed horror thereat for the ear of the lord.
1635   "Now Gawain," said the good man, "this game is your own
        By our contracted treaty, in truth, you know."
        "It is so," said the knight, "and as certainly
        I shall give you all my gains as guerdon, in faith."
        He clasped the castellan's neck and kissed him kindly,
1640   And then served him a second time in the same style.
        "In all our transactions since I came to sojourn," asserted Gawain,
        "Up to tonight, as of now, there's nothing that
            I owe."
            "By Saint Giles,"[8] the castellan quipped,
1645   "You're the finest fellow I know:
            Your wealth will have us whipped
            If your trade continues so!"

        Then the trestles and tables were trimly set out,
        Complete with cloths, and clearly flaming cressets
1650   And waxen torches were placed in the wall-brackets
        By retainers, who then tended the entire hall-gathering.
        Much gladness and glee then gushed forth there
        By the fire on the floor: and in multifarious ways
        They sang noble songs at supper and afterwards,
1655   A concert of Christmas carols and new dance songs,
        With the most mannerly mirth a man could tell of,
        And our courteous knight kept constant company with the lady.
        In a bewitchingly well-mannered way she made up to him,
        Secretly soliciting the stalwart knight
1660   So that he was astounded, and upset in himself.
        But his upbringing forbade him to rebuff her utterly,
        So he behaved towards her honorably, whatever aspersions might
            Be cast.
            They reveled in the hall
1665   As long as their pleasure might last

8. St. Giles, a hermit and patron saint of woodlands.

And then at the castellan's call
To the chamber hearth they passed.

There they drank and discoursed and decided to enjoy
Similar solace and sport on New Year's Eve.
1670 But the princely knight asked permission to depart in the morning,
For his appointed time was approaching, and perforce he must go.
But the lord would not let him and implored him to linger,
Saying, "I swear to you, as a staunch true knight,
You shall gain the Green Chapel to give your dues,
1675 My lord, in the light of New Year, long before sunrise.
Therefore remain in your room and rest in comfort,
While I fare hunting in the forest; in fulfilment of our oath
Exchanging what we achieve when the chase is over.
For twice I have tested you, and twice found you true.
1680 Now 'Third time, throw best!' Think of that tomorrow!
Let us make merry while we may, set our minds on joy,
For hard fate can hit man whenever it likes."
This was graciously granted and Gawain stayed.
Blithely drink was brought, then to bed with lights
1685   They pressed.
        All night Sir Gawain sleeps
        Softly and still at rest;
        But the lord his custom keeps
        And is early up and dressed.

1690 After mass, he and his men made a small meal.
Merry was the morning; he demanded his horse.
The men were ready mounted before the main gate,
A host of knightly horsemen to follow after him.
Wonderfully fair was the forest-land, for the frost remained,
1695 And the rising sun shone ruddily on the ragged clouds,
In its beauty brushing their blackness off the heavens.
The huntsmen unleashed the hounds by a holt-side,
And the rocks and surrounding bushes rang with their horn-calls.
Some found and followed the fox's tracks,
1700 And wove various ways in their wily fashion.
A small hound cried the scent, the senior huntsman called
His fellow foxhounds to him and, feverishly sniffing,
The rout of dogs rushed forward on the right path.
The fox hurried fast, for they found him soon
1705 And, seeing him distinctly, pursued him at speed,
Unmistakably giving tongue with tumultuous din.
Deviously in difficult country he doubled on his tracks,
Swerved and wheeled away, often waited listening,
Till at last by a little ditch he leaped a quickset hedge,
1710 And stole out stealthily at the side of a valley,
Considering his stratagem had given the slip to the hounds.
But he stumbled on a tracking-dogs' tryst-place unawares,
And there in a cleft three hounds threatened him at once,

                    All gray.
1715   He swiftly started back,
            And, full of deep dismay,
            He dashed on a different track;
            To the woods he went away.

         Then came the lively delight of listening to hounds
1720   When they had all met in a muster, mingling together,
         For, catching sight of him, they cried such curses on him
         That the clustering cliffs seemed to be crashing down.
         Here he was hallooed when the hunters met him,
         There savagely snarled at by intercepting hounds;
1725   Then he was called thief and threatened often;
         With the tracking dogs on his tail, no tarrying was possible.
         When out in the open he was often run at,
         So he often swerved in again, that artful Reynard.
         Yes, he led the lord and his liegemen a dance
1730   In this manner among the mountains till mid-afternoon,
         While harmoniously at home the honored knight slept
         Between the comely curtains in the cold morning.
         But the lady's longing to woo would not let her sleep,
         Nor would she impair the purpose pitched in her heart,
1735   But rose up rapidly and ran to him
         In a ravishing robe that reached to the ground,
         Trimmed with finest fur from pure pelts;
         Not coifed as to custom, but with costly jewels
         Strung in scores on her splendid hairnet.
1740   Her fine-featured face and fair throat were unveiled,
         Her breast was bare and her back as well.
         She came in by the chamber door and closed it after her,
         Cast open a casement and called on the knight,
         And briskly thus rebuked him with bountiful words
1745   Of good cheer.
             "Ah sir! What, sound asleep?
             The morning's crisp and clear,"
             He had been drowsing deep,
             But now he had to hear.

1750   The noble sighed ceaselessly in unsettled slumber
         As threatening thoughts thronged in the dawn light
         About destiny, which the day after would deal him his fate
         At the Green Chapel where Gawain was to greet his man,
         And be bound to bear his buffet unresisting.
1755   But having recovered consciousness in comely fashion,
         He heaved himself out of dreams and answered hurriedly.
         The lovely lady advanced, laughing adorably,
         Swooped over his splendid face and sweetly kissed him.
         He welcomed her worthily with noble cheer
1760   And, gazing on her gay and glorious attire,
         Her features so faultless and fine of complexion,

He felt a flush of rapture suffuse his heart.
Sweet and genial smiling slid them into joy
Till bliss burst forth between them, beaming gay
1765   And bright;
        With joy the two contended
        In talk of true delight,
        And peril would have impended
        Had Mary not minded her knight.

1770 For that peerless princess pressed him so hotly,
So invited him to the very verge, that he felt forced
Either to allow her love or blackguardly rebuff her.
He was concerned for his courtesy, lest he be called caitiff,
But more especially for his evil plight if he should plunge into sin,
1775 And dishonor the owner of the house treacherously.
"God shield me! That shall not happen, for sure," said the knight.
So with laughing love-talk he deflected gently
The downright declarations that dropped from her lips.
Said the beauty to the bold man, "Blame will be yours
1780 If you love not the living body lying close to you
More than all wooers in the world who are wounded in heart;
Unless you have a lover more beloved, who delights you more,
A maiden to whom you are committed, so immutably bound
That you do not seek to sever from her—which I see is so.
1785 Tell me the truth of it, I entreat you now;
By all the loves there are, do not hide the truth
        With guile."
        Then gently, "By Saint John,"
        Said the knight with a smile,
1790   "I owe my oath to none,
        Nor wish to yet a while."

"Those words," said the fair woman, "are the worst there could be,
But I am truly answered, to my utter anguish.
Give me now a gracious kiss, and I shall go from here
1795 As a maid that loves much, mourning on this earth."
Then, sighing, she stooped, and seemlily kissed him,
And, severing herself from him, stood up and said,
"At this adieu, my dear one, do me this pleasure:
Give me something as gift, your glove if no more,
1800 To mitigate my mourning when I remember you."
"Now certainly, for your sake," said the knight,
"I wish I had here the handsomest thing I own,
For you have deserved, forsooth, superabundantly
And rightfully, a richer reward than I could give.
1805 But as tokens of true love, trifles mean little.
It is not to your honor to have at this time
A mere glove as Gawain's gift to treasure.
For I am here on an errand in unknown regions,
And have no bondsmen, no baggages with dear-bought things in them.

1810   This afflicts me now, fair lady, for your sake.
        Man must do as he must; neither lament it
                Nor repine."
            "No, highly honored one,"
            Replied that lady fine,
1815   "Though gift you give me none,
            You must have something of mine."

        She proffered him a rich ring wrought in red gold,
        With a sparkling stone set conspicuously in it,
        Which beamed as brilliantly as the bright sun;
1820   You may well believe its worth was wonderfully great.
        But the courteous man declined it and quickly said,
        "Before God, gracious lady, no giving just now!
        Not having anything to offer, I shall accept nothing."
        She offered it him urgently and he refused again,
1825   Fast affirming his refusal on his faith as a knight.
        Put out by this repulse, she presently said,
        "If you reject my ring as too rich in value,
        Doubtless you would be less deeply indebted to me
        If I gave you my girdle, a less gainful gift."
1830   She swiftly slipped off the cincture of her gown
        Which went round her waist under the wonderful mantle,
        A girdle of green silk with a golden hem,
        Embroidered only at the edges, with hand-stitched ornament.
        And she pleaded with the prince in a pleasant manner
1835   To take it notwithstanding its trifling worth;
        But he told her that he could touch no treasure at all,
        Not gold nor any gift, till God gave him grace
        To pursue to success the search he was bound on.
        "And therefore I beg you not to be displeased:
1840   Press no more your purpose, for I promise it never
                Can be.
            I owe you a hundredfold
            For grace you have granted me;
            And ever through hot and cold
1845   I shall stay your devotee."

        "Do you say no to this silk?" then said the beauty,
        "Because it is simple in itself? And so it seems.
        Lo! It is little indeed, and so less worth your esteem.
        But one who was aware of the worth twined in it
1850   Would appraise its properties as more precious perhaps,
        For the man that binds his body with this belt of green,
        As long as he laps it closely about him,
        No hero under heaven can hack him to pieces,
        For he cannot be killed by any cunning on earth."
1855   Then the prince pondered, and it appeared to him
        A precious gem to protect him in the peril appointed him
        When he gained the Green Chapel to be given checkmate:

It would be a splendid stratagem to escape being slain.
Then he allowed her to solicit him and let her speak.
1860   She pressed the belt upon him with potent words
And having got his agreement, she gave it him gladly,
Beseeching him for her sake to conceal it always,
And hide it from her husband with all diligence.
That never should another know of it, the noble swore
1865   Outright.
        Then often his thanks gave he
        With all his heart and might,
        And thrice by then had she
        Kissed the constant knight.

1870   Then with a word of farewell she went away,
For she could not force further satisfaction from him.
Directly she withdrew, Sir Gawain dressed himself,
Rose and arrayed himself in rich garments,
But laid aside the love-lace the lady had given him,
1875   Secreted it carefully where he could discover it later.
Then he went his way at once to the chapel,
Privily approached a priest and prayed him there
To listen to his life's sins and enlighten him
On how he might have salvation in the hereafter.
1880   Then, confessing his faults, he fairly shrove himself,
Begging mercy for both major and minor sins.
He asked the holy man for absolution
And was absolved with certainty and sent out so pure
That Doomsday could have been declared the day after.
1885   Then he made merrier among the noble ladies,
With comely caroling and all kinds of pleasure,
Than ever he had done, with ecstasy, till came
        Dark night.
        Such honor he did to all,
1890   They said, "Never has this knight
        Since coming into hall
        Expressed such pure delight,"

Now long may he linger there, love sheltering him!
The prince was still on the plain, pleasuring in the chase,
1895   Having finished off the fox he had followed so far.
As he leaped over a hedge looking out for the quarry,
Where he heard the hounds that were harrying the fox,
Reynard came running through a rough thicket
With the pack all pell-mell, panting at his heels.
1900   The lord, aware of the wild beast, waited craftily,
Then drew his dazzling sword and drove at the fox.
The beast baulked at the blade to break sideways,
But a dog bounded at him before he could,
And right in front of the horse's feet they fell on him,
1905   All worrying their wily prey with a wild uproar.

The lord quickly alighted and lifted him up,
Wrenched him beyond reach of the ravening fangs,
Held him high over his head and hallooed lustily,
While the angry hounds in hordes bayed at him.
1910 Thither hurried the huntsmen with horns in plenty,
Sounding the rally splendidly till they saw their lord.
When the company of his court had come up to the kill,
All who bore bugles blew at once,
And the others without horns hallooed loudly.
1915 The requiem that was raised for Reynard's soul
And the commotion made it the merriest meet ever,
    Men said.
      The hounds must have their fee:
      They pat them on the head,
1920   Then hold the fox; and he
      Is reft of his skin of red.

Then they set off for home, it being almost night,
Blowing their big horns bravely as they went.
At last the lord alighted at his beloved castle
1925 And found upon the floor a fire, and beside it
The good Sir Gawain in a glad humor
By reason of the rich friendship he had reaped from the ladies.
He wore a turquoise tunic extending to the ground;
His softly-furred surcoat suited him well,
1930 And his hood of the same hue hung from his shoulder.
All trimmed with ermine were hood and surcoat.
Meeting the master in the middle of the floor,
Gawain went forward gladly and greeted him thus:
"Forthwith, I shall be the first to fulfil the contract
1935 We settled so suitably without sparing the wine."
Then he clasped the castellan and kissed him thrice
As sweetly and steadily as a strong knight could.
"By Christ!" quoth the other, "You will carve yourself a fortune
By traffic in this trade when the terms suit you!"
1940 "Do not chop logic about the exchange," chipped in Gawain,
"As I have properly paid over the profit I made."
"Marry," said the other man, "Mine is inferior,
For I have hunted all day and have only taken
This ill-favored fox's skin, may the Fiend take it!
1945 And that is a poor price to pay for such precious things
As you have pressed upon me here, three pure kisses
    So good."
      "Enough!" acknowledged Gawain,
      "I thank you, by the Rood."
1950   And how the fox was slain
      The lord told him as they stood.

With mirth and minstrelsy, and meals when they liked,

They made as merry then as ever men could;
With the laughter of ladies and delightful jesting,
1955 Gawain and his good host were very gay together,
Save when excess or sottishness seemed likely.
Master and men made many a witty sally,
Until presently, at the appointed parting-time,
The brave men were bidden to bed at last.
1960 Then of his host the hero humbly took leave,
The first to bid farewell, fairly thanking him:[9]
"May the High King requite you for your courtesy at this feast,
And the wonderful week of my dwelling here!
I would offer to be one of your own men if you liked,
1965 But that I must move on tomorrow, as you know,
If you will give me the guide you granted me.
To show me the Green Chapel where my share of doom
Will be dealt on New Year's Day, as God deems for me."
"With all my heart !" said the host. "In good faith,
1970 All that I ever promised you, I shall perform."
He assigned him a servant to set him on his way,
And lead him in the hills without any delay,
Faring through forest and thicket by the most straightforward route
         They might.
1975   With every honor due
         Gawain then thanked the knight,
         And having bid him adieu,
         Took leave of the ladies bright.

So he spoke to them sadly, sorrowing as he kissed,
1980 And urged on them heartily his endless thanks,
And they gave to Sir Gawain words of grace in return,
Commending him to Christ with cries of chill sadness.
Then from the whole household he honorably took his leave,
Making all the men that he met amends
1985 For their several services and solicitous care,
For they had been busily attendant, bustling about him;
And every soul was as sad to say farewell
As if they had always had the hero in their house.
Then the lords led him with lights to his chamber,
1990 And blithely brought him to bed to rest.
If he slept—I dare not assert it—less soundly than usual,
There was much on his mind for the morrow, if he meant to give
         It thought.
         Let him lie there still,
1995   He almost has what he sought;
         So tarry a while until
         The process I report.

9. Gawain's highly stylized leave-taking is typical of courtly romance and again emphasizes his command of fine manners.

PART 4

Now the New Year neared, the night passed,
Daylight fought darkness as the Deity ordained.
2000   But wild was the weather the world awoke to;
Bitterly the clouds cast down cold on the earth,
Inflicting on the flesh flails from the north.
Bleakly the snow blustered, and beasts were frozen;
The whistling wind wailed from the heights,
2005   Driving great drifts deep in the dales.
Keenly the lord listened as he lay in his bed;
Though his lids were closed, he was sleeping little.
Every cock that crew recalled to him his tryst.
Before the day had dawned, he had dressed himself,
2010   For the light from a lamp illuminated his chamber.
He summoned his servant, who swiftly answered,
Commanded that his mail-coat and mount's saddle he brought.
The man fared forth and fetched him his armor,
And set Sir Gawain's array in splendid style.
2015   First he clad him in his clothes to counter the cold,
Then in his other armor which had been well kept;
His breast- and belly-armor had been burnished bright,
And the rusty rings of his rich mail-coat rolled clean,
And all being as fresh as at first, he was fain to give thanks
2020   Indeed.
         Each wiped and polished piece
         He donned with due heed.
         The gayest from here to Greece,
         The strong man sent for his steed.

2025   While he was putting on apparel of the most princely kind—
His surcoat, with its symbol of spotless deeds
Environed on velvet with virtuous gems,
Was embellished and bound with embroidered seams,
And finely fur-lined with the fairest skins—
2030   He did not leave the lace belt, the lady's gift:
For his own good, Gawain did not forget that!
When he had strapped the sword on his swelling hips,
The knight lapped his loins with his love-token twice,
Quickly wrapped it with relish round his waist.
2035   The green silken girdle suited the gallant well,
Backed by the royal red cloth that richly showed.
But Gawain wore the girdle not for its great value,
Nor through pride in the pendants, in spite of their polish,
Nor for the gleaming gold which glinted on the ends,
2040   But to save himself when of necessity he must
Stand an evil stroke, not resisting it with knife
         Or sword.
         When ready and robed aright,

Out came the comely lord;
2045   To the men of name and might
His thanks in plenty poured.

Then was Gringolet got ready, that great huge horse.
Having been assiduously stabled in seemly quarters,
The fiery steed was fit and fretting for a gallop.
2050   Sir Gawain stepped to him and, inspecting his coat,
Said earnestly to himself, asserting with truth,
"Here in this castle is a company whose conduct is honorable.
The man who maintains them, may he have joy!
The delightful lady, love befall her while she lives!
2055   Thus for charity they cherish a chance guest
Honorably and open-handedly; may He on high,
The King of Heaven, requite you and your company too!
And if I could live any longer in lands on earth,
Some rich recompense, if I could, I should readily give you."
2060   Then he stepped into the stirrup and swung aloft.
His man showed him his shield; on his shoulder he put it,
And gave the spur to Gringolet with his gold-spiked heels.
The horse sprang forward from the paving, pausing no more
To prance.
2065   His man was mounted and fit,
Laden with spear and lance.
"This castle to Christ I commit:
May He its fortune enhance!"

The drawbridge was let down and the broad double gates
2070   Were unbarred and borne open on both sides.
Passing over the planks, the prince blessed himself
And praised the kneeling porter, who proffered him "Good day,"
Praying God to grant that Gawain would be saved.
And Gawain went on his way with the one man
2075   To put him on the right path for that perilous place
Where the sad assault must be received by him.
By bluffs where boughs were bare they passed,
Climbed by cliffs where the cold clung:
Under the high clouds, ugly mists
2080   Merged damply with the moors and melted on the mountains;
Each hill had a hat, a huge mantle of mist.
Brooks burst forth above them, boiling over their banks
And showering down sharply in shimmering cascades.
Wonderfully wild was their way through the woods;
2085   Till soon the sun in the sway of that season
Brought day.
They were on a lofty hill
Where snow beside them lay,
When the servant stopped still
2090   And told his master to stay.

"For I have guided you to this ground, Sir Gawain, at this time,
And now you are not far from the noted place
Which you have searched for and sought with such special zeal.
But I must say to you, forsooth, since I know you,
2095   And you are a lord whom I love with no little regard:
Take my governance as guide, and it shall go better for you,
For the place is perilous that you are pressing towards.
In that wilderness dwells the worst man in the world,
For he is valiant and fierce and fond of fighting,
2100   And mightier than any man that may be on earth,
And his body is bigger than the best four
In Arthur's house, or Hector,[1] or any other.
At the Green Chapel he gains his great adventures.
No man passes that place, however proud in arms,
2105   Without being dealt a death-blow by his dreadful hand.
For he is an immoderate man, to mercy a stranger;
For whether churl or chaplain by the chapel rides,
Monk or mass-priest or man of other kind,
He thinks it as convenient to kill him as keep alive himself.
2110   Therefore I say, as certainly as you sit in your saddle,
If you come there you'll be killed, I caution you, knight,
Take my troth for it, though you had twenty lives
    And more.
    He has lived here since long ago
2115   And filled the field with gore.
    You cannot counter his blow,
    It strikes so sudden and sore.

"Therefore, good Sir Gawain, leave the grim man alone!
Ride by another route, to some region remote!
2120   Go in the name of God, and Christ grace your fortune!
And I shall go home again and undertake
To swear solemnly by God and his saints as well
(By my halidom,[2] so help me God, and every other oath)
Stoutly to keep your secret, not saying to a soul
2125   That ever you tried to turn tail from any man I knew."
"Great thanks," replied Gawain, somewhat galled, and said,
"It is worthy of you to wish for my well-being, man,
And I believe you would loyally lock it in your heart.
But however quiet you kept it, if I quit this place,
2130   Fled from the fellow in the fashion you propose,
I should become a cowardly knight with no excuse whatever,
For I will go to the Green Chapel, to get what Fate sends,
And have whatever words I wish with that worthy,
Whether weal or woe is what Fate
2135   Demands.
    Fierce though that fellow be,

1. Chief hero among the defenders of Troy and, like   heroic valor; or perhaps Arthur's knight Hector de Maris.
Arthur, one of the "Nine Worthies" celebrated for their   2. By my holy relics.

Clutching his club where he stands,
Our Lord can certainly see
That his own are in safe hands."

2140 "By Mary!" said the other man, "If you mean what you say,
You are determined to take all your trouble on yourself.
If you wish to lose your life, I'll no longer hinder you.
Here's your lance for your hand, your helmet for your head.
Ride down this rough track round yonder cliff
2145 Till you arrive in a rugged ravine at the bottom,
Then look about on the flat, on your left hand,
And you will view there in the vale that very chapel,
And the grim gallant who guards it always.
Now, noble Gawain, good-bye in God's name.
2150 For all the gold on God's earth I would not go with you,
Nor foot it an inch further through this forest as your fellow."
Whereupon he wrenched at his reins, that rider in the woods,
Hit the horse with his heels as hard as he could,
Sent him leaping along, and left the knight there
2155   Alone.
        "By God!" said Gawain, "I swear
        I will not weep or groan:
        Being given to God's good care,
        My trust in Him shall be shown."

2160 Then he gave the spur to Gringolet and galloped down the path,
Thrust through a thicket there by a bank,
And rode down the rough slope right into the ravine.
Then he searched about, but it seemed savage and wild,
And no sign did he see of any sort of building;
2165 But on both sides banks, beetling and steep,
And great crooked crags, cruelly jagged;
The bristling barbs of rock seemed to brush the sky.
Then he held in his horse, halted there,
Scanned on every side in search of the chapel.
2170 He saw no such thing anywhere, which seemed remarkable,
Save, hard by in the open, a hillock of sorts,
A smooth-surfaced barrow[3] on a slope beside a stream
Which flowed forth fast there in its course,
Foaming and frothing as if feverishly boiling.
2175 The knight, urging his horse, pressed onwards to the mound,
Dismounted manfully and made fast to a lime-tree
The reins, hooking them round a rough branch;
Then he went to the barrow, which he walked round, inspecting,
Wondering what in the world it might be.
2180 It had a hole in each end and on either side,
And was overgrown with grass in great patches.

---

3. Perhaps a burial mound, which seems to link the moment to ancient, probably pagan inhabitants.

All hollow it was within, only an old cavern
Or the crevice of an ancient crag: he could not explain it
    Aright.
2185   "O God, is the Chapel Green
    This mound?" said the noble knight.
    "At such might Satan be seen
    Saying matins at midnight."

"Now certainly the place is deserted," said Gawain,
2190   "It is a hideous oratory, all overgrown,
And well graced for the gallant garbed in green
To deal out his devotions in the Devil's fashion.
Now I feel in my five wits, it is the Fiend himself
That has tricked me into this tryst, to destroy me here.
2195   This is a chapel of mischance—checkmate to it!
It is the most evil holy place I ever entered."
With his high helmet on his head, and holding his lance,
He roamed up to the roof of that rough dwelling.
Then from that height he heard, from a hard rock
2200   On the bank beyond the brook, a barbarous noise.
What! It clattered amid the cliffs fit to cleave them apart,
As if a great scythe were being ground on a grindstone there.
What! It whirred and it whetted like water in a mill.
What! It made a rushing, ringing din, rueful to hear.
2205   "By God!" then said Gawain, "that is going on,
I suppose, as a salute to myself, to greet me
    Hard by.
    God's will be warranted:
    'Alas!' is a craven cry.
2210   No din shall make me dread
    Although today I die."

Then the courteous knight called out clamorously,
"Who holds sway here and has an assignation with me?
For the good knight Gawain is on the ground here.
2215   If anyone there wants anything, wend your way hither fast,
And further your needs either now, or not at all."
"Bide there!" said one on the bank above his head,
"And you shall swiftly receive what I once swore to give you."
Yet for a time he continued his tumult of scraping,
2220   Turning away as he whetted, before he would descend.
Then he thrust himself round a thick crag through a hole,
Whirling round a wedge of rock with a frightful weapon,
A Danish axe[4] duly honed for dealing the blow,
With a broad biting edge, bow-bent along the handle,
2225   Ground on a grindstone, a great four-foot blade—
No less, by that love-lace gleaming so brightly!
And the gallant in green was garbed as at first,

---

4. A long-bladed ax, associated with Viking raiders.

His looks and limbs the same, his locks and beard;
Save that steadily on his feet he strode on the ground,
2230 Setting the handle to the stony earth and stalking beside it.
He would not wade through the water when he came to it,
But vaulted over on his axe, then with huge strides
Advanced violently and fiercely along the field's width
          On the snow.
2235   Sir Gawain went to greet
The knight, not bowing low.
The man said, "Sir so sweet,
You honor the trysts you owe."

"Gawain," said the green knight, "may God guard you!
2240 You are welcome to my dwelling, I warrant you,
And you have timed your travel here as a true man ought.
You know plainly the pact we pledged between us:
This time a twelvemonth ago you took your portion,
And now at this New Year I should nimbly requite you.
2245 And we are on our own here in this valley
With no seconds to sunder us, spar as we will.
Take your helmet off your head, and have your payment here.
And offer no more argument or action than I did
When you whipped off my head with one stroke."
2250 "No," said Gawain, "by God who gave me a soul,
The grievous gash to come I grudge you not at all;
Strike but the one stroke and I shall stand still
And offer you no hindrance; you may act freely,
          I swear."
2255   Head bent, Sir Gawain bowed,
And showed the bright flesh bare.
He behaved as if uncowed,
Being loth to display his care.

Then the gallant in green quickly got ready,
2260 Heaved his horrid weapon on high to hit Gawain,
With all the brute force in his body bearing it aloft,
Swinging savagely enough to strike him dead.
Had it driven down as direly as he aimed,
The daring dauntless man would have died from the blow.
2265 But Gawain glanced up at the grim axe beside him
As it came shooting through the shivering air to shatter him,
And his shoulders shrank slightly from the sharp edge.
The other suddenly stayed the descending axe,
And then reproved the prince with many proud words:
2270 "You are not Gawain," said the gallant, "whose greatness is such
That by hill or hollow no army ever frightened him;
For now you flinch for fear before you feel harm.
I never did know that knight to be a coward.
I neither flinched nor fled when you let fly your blow,
2275 Nor offered any quibble in the house of King Arthur.

My head flew to my feet, but flee I did not.
Yet you quail cravenly though unscathed so far.
So I am bound to be called the better man
       Therefore."
2280   Said Gawain, "Not again
      Shall I flinch as I did before;
      But if my head pitch to the plain,
      It's off for evermore.

"But be brisk, man, by your faith, and bring me to the point;
2285 Deal me my destiny and do it out of hand,
For I shall stand your stroke, not starting at all
Till your axe has hit me. Here is my oath on it."
"Have at you then!" said the other, heaving up his axe,
Behaving as angrily as if he were mad.
2290 He menaced him mightily, but made no contact,
Smartly withholding his hand without hurting him.
Gawain waited unswerving, with not a wavering limb,
But stood still as a stone or the stump of a tree
Gripping the rocky ground with a hundred grappling roots.
2295 Then again the green knight began to gird:
"So now you have a whole heart I must hit you.
May the high knighthood which Arthur conferred
Preserve you and save your neck, if so it avail you!"
Then said Gawain, storming with sudden rage,
2300 "Thrash on, you thrustful fellow, you threaten too much.
It seems your spirit is struck with self-dread."
"Forsooth," the other said, "You speak so fiercely
I will no longer lengthen matters by delaying your business,
      I vow."
2305   He stood astride to smite,
      Lips pouting, puckered brow.
      No wonder he lacked delight
      Who expected no help now.

Up went the axe at once and hurtled down straight
2310 At the naked neck with its knife-like edge.
Though it swung down savagely, slight was the wound,
A mere snick on the side, so that the skin was broken.
Through the fair fat to the flesh fell the blade,
And over his shoulders the shimmering blood shot to the ground.
2315 When Sir Gawain saw his gore glinting on the snow,
He leapt feet close together a spear's length away,
Hurriedly heaved his helmet on to his head,
And shrugging his shoulders, shot his shield to the front,[5]
Swung out his bright sword and said fiercely,
2320 (For never had the knight since being nursed by his mother

---

5. Gawain, who has displayed so much courtly refinement and religious emotion, now shows himself a practiced fighter, swiftly pulling his armor into place.

Been so buoyantly happy, so blithe in this world)
"Cease your blows, sir, strike me no more.
I have sustained a stroke here unresistingly,
And if you offer any more I shall earnestly reply.
2325   Resisting, rest assured, with the most rancorous
        Despite.
      The single stroke is wrought
      To which we pledged our plight
      In high King Arthur's court:
2330   Enough now, therefore, knight!"

The bold man stood back and bent over his axe,
Putting the haft to earth, and leaning on the head.
He gazed at Sir Gawain on the ground before him,
Considering the spirited and stout way he stood,
2335   Audacious in arms; his heart warmed to him.
Then he gave utterance gladly in his great voice,
With resounding speech saying to the knight,
"Bold man, do not be so bloodily resolute.
No one here has offered you evil discourteously,
2340   Contrary to the covenant made at the King's court.
I promised a stroke, which you received: consider yourself paid.
I cancel all other obligations of whatever kind.
If I had been more active, perhaps I could
Have made you suffer by striking a savager stroke.
2345   First in foolery I made a feint at striking,
Not rending you with a riving cut—and right I was,
On account of the first night's covenant we accorded;
For you truthfully kept your trust in troth with me,
Giving me your gains, as a good man should.
2350   The further feinted blow was for the following day,
When you kissed my comely wife, and the kisses came to me:
For those two things, harmlessly I thrust twice at you
        Feinted blows.
      Truth for truth's the word;
2355   No need for dread, God knows.
      From your failure at the third
      The tap you took arose.

"For that braided belt you wear belongs to me.
I am well aware that my own wife gave it you.
2360   Your conduct and your kissings are completely known to me,
And the wooing by my wife—my work set it on.
I instructed her to try you, and you truly seem
To be the most perfect paladin ever to pace the earth.
As the pearl to the white pea in precious worth,
2365   So in good faith is Gawain to other gay knights.
But here your faith failed you, you flagged somewhat, sir,
Yet it was not for a well-wrought thing, nor for wooing either,
But for love of your life, which is less blameworthy."

The other strong man stood considering this a while,
2370 So filled with fury that his flesh trembled,
And the blood from his breast burst forth in his face
As he shrank for shame at what the chevalier spoke of.
The first words the fair knight could frame were:
"Curses on both cowardice and covetousness!
2375 Their vice and villainy are virtue's undoing."
Then he took the knot, with a twist twitched it loose,
And fiercely flung the fair girdle to the knight.
"Lo! There is the false thing, foul fortune befall it!
I was craven about our encounter, and cowardice taught me
2380 To accord with covetousness and corrupt my nature
And the liberality and loyalty belonging to chivalry.
Now I am faulty and false and found fearful always.
In the train of treachery and untruth go woe
        And shame.
2385   I acknowledge, knight, how ill
    I behaved, and take the blame.
    Award what penance you will:
    Henceforth I'll shun ill-fame."

Then the other lord laughed and politely said,
2390 "In my view you have made amends for your misdemeanor;
You have confessed your faults fully with fair acknowledgement,
And plainly done penance at the point of my axe.
You are absolved of your sin and as stainless now
As if you had never fallen in fault since first you were born.
2395 As for the gold-hemmed girdle, I give it you, sir,
Seeing it is as green as my gown. Sir Gawain, you may
Think about this trial when you throng in company
With paragons of princes, for it is a perfect token,
At knightly gatherings, of the great adventure at the Green Chapel.
2400 You shall come back to my castle this cold New Year,
And we shall revel away the rest of this rich feast;
        Let us go."
    Thus urging him, the lord
    Said, "You and my wife, I know
2405   We shall bring to clear accord,
    Though she was your fierce foe."

"No, forsooth," said the knight, seizing his helmet,
And doffing it with dignity as he delivered this thanks,
"My stay has sufficed me. Still, luck go with you!
2410 May He who bestows all good, honor you with it!
And commend me to the courteous lady, your comely wife;
Indeed, my due regards to both dear ladies,
Who with their wanton wiles have thus waylaid their knight.
But it is no marvel for a foolish man to be maddened thus
2415 And saddled with sorrow by the sleights of women.
For here on earth was Adam taken in by one,

And Solomon by many such, and Samson likewise;
Delilah dealt him his doom; and David, later still,
Was blinded by Bathsheba, and badly suffered for it.[6]
2420 Since these were troubled by their tricks, it would be true joy
To love them but not believe them, if a lord could,
For these were the finest of former times, most favored by fortune
Of all under the heavenly kingdom whose hearts were
     Abused;
2425   These four all fell to schemes
    Of women whom they used.
    If I am snared, it seems
    I ought to be excused.

"But your girdle," said Gawain, "God requite you for it!
2430 Not for the glorious gold shall I gladly wear it,
Nor for the stuff nor the silk nor the swaying pendants,
Nor for its worth, fine workmanship or wonderful honor;
But as a sign of my sin I shall see it often,
Remembering with remorse, when I am mounted in glory,
2435 The fault and faintheartedness of the perverse flesh,
How it tends to attract tarnishing sin.
So when pride shall prick me for my prowess in arms,
One look at this love-lace will make lowly my heart.
But one demand I make of you, may it not incommode you:
2440 Since you are master of the demesne I have remained in a while,
Make known, by your knighthood—and now may He above,
Who sits on high and holds up heaven, requite you!—
How you pronounce your true name; and no more requests."
"Truly," the other told him, "I shall tell you my title.
2445 Bertilak of the High Desert I am called here in this land.
Through the might of Morgan the Fay,[7] who remains in my house,
Through the wiles of her witchcraft, a lore well learned—
Many of the magical arts of Merlin she acquired,
For she lavished fervent love long ago
2450 On that susceptible sage: certainly your knights know
     Of their fame.
    So 'Morgan the Goddess'
    She accordingly became;
    The proudest she can oppress
2455   And to her purpose tame—

"She sent me forth in this form to your famous hall
To put to the proof the great pride of the house,
The reputation for high renown of the Round Table;

---

6. Gawain suddenly erupts in a brief but fierce diatribe, including this list of treacherous Biblical women, often mentioned in contemporary antifeminist texts.
7. Morgan is Arthur's half-sister and ruler of the mysterious Avalon; she learned magical arts from Merlin. Her presence can bode good or ill. In some stories she holds a deep grudge against Guinevere, yet she carries off the wounded Arthur after his final battle, perhaps to heal him. The earlier Celtic Morrigan, possibly related, is queen of demons, sower of discord, and goddess of war.

She bewitched me in this weird way to bewilder your wits,
2460   And to grieve Guinevere and goad her to death
With ghastly fear of that ghost's ghoulish speaking
With his head in his hand before the high table.
That is the aged beldame who is at home:
She is indeed your own aunt, Arthur's half-sister,
2465   Daughter of the Duchess of Tintagel who in due course,
By Uther, was mother of Arthur, who now holds sway.[8]
Therefore I beg you, bold sir, come back to your aunt,
Make merry in my house, for my men love you,
And by my faith, brave sir, I bear you as much good will
2470   As I grant any man under God, for your great honesty."
But Gawain firmly refused with a final negative.
They clasped and kissed, commending each other
To the Prince of Paradise, and parted on the cold ground
        Right there.
2475   Gawain on steed serene
        Spurred to court with courage fair,
        And the gallant garbed in green
        To wherever he would elsewhere.

Now Gawain goes riding on Gringolet
2480   In lonely lands, his life saved by grace.
Often he stayed at a house, and often in the open,
And often overcame hazards in the valleys,
Which at this time I do not intend to tell you about.
The hurt he had had in his neck was healed,
2485   And the glittering girdle that girt him round
Obliquely, like a baldric,[9] was bound by his side
And laced under the left arm with a lasting knot,
In token that he was taken in a tarnishing sin;
And so he came to court, quite unscathed.
2490   When the great became aware of Gawain's arrival
There was general jubilation at the joyful news.
The King kissed the knight, and the Queen likewise,
And so did many a staunch noble who sought to salute him.
They all asked him about his expedition,
2495   And he truthfully told them of his tribulations—
What chanced at the chapel, the good cheer of the knight,
The lady's love-making, and lastly, the girdle.
He displayed the scar of the snick on his neck
Where the bold man's blow had hit, his bad faith to
2500   Proclaim;
        He groaned at his disgrace,
        Unfolding his ill-fame,

---

8. The poem now recalls an earlier transgression of guest-host obligations, when Uther began to lust for Ygerne while her husband, Gorlois, was at his court; he later killed Gorlois and married Ygerne.
9. A belt for a sword or bugle, worn over one shoulder and across the chest.

> And blood suffused his face
> When he showed his mark of shame.

2505   "Look, my lord," said Gawain, the lace in his hand.
      "This belt confirms the blame I bear on my neck,
      My bane and debasement, the burden I bear
      For being caught by cowardice and covetousness.
      This is the figure of the faithlessness found in me,
2510   Which I must needs wear while I live.
      For man can conceal sin but not dissever from it,
      So when it is once fixed, it will never be worked loose."
      First the King, then all the court, comforted the knight,
      And all the lords and ladies belonging to the Table
2515   Laughed at it loudly, and concluded amiably
      That each brave man of the brotherhood should bear a baldric,
      A band, obliquely about him, of bright green,
      Of the same hue as Sir Gawain's and for his sake wear it.
      So it ranked as renown to the Round Table,
2520   And an everlasting honor to him who had it,
      As is rendered in Romance's rarest book.
      Thus in the days of Arthur this exploit was achieved,
      To which the books of Brutus bear witness;
      After the bold baron, Brutus, came here,
2525   The siege and the assault being ceased at Troy
         Before.
         Such exploits, I'll be sworn,
         Have happened here of yore.
         Now Christ with his crown of thorn
2530   Bring us his bliss evermore!   AMEN

         HONY SOYT QUI MAL PENCE[1]

Sir Thomas Malory
c. 1410–1471

The full identity of Sir Thomas Malory shimmers just beyond our grasp. In several of his colophons—those closing formulas to texts—the author of the *Morte Darthur* says he is "a knyght presoner, sir Thomas Malleorré," and prays that "God sende hym good delyveraunce sone and hastely." Scholars have traced a number of such names in the era, among whom two seem particularly likely: Sir Thomas Malory of Newbold Revell, and Thomas Malory of Papworth. The former Thomas Malory had a scabrous criminal record and was long kept prisoner awaiting trial, while the latter had links to a rich collection of Arthurian books.

---

1. "Shamed be he who thinks ill thereof," the motto of the Order of the Garter, a chivalric order founded by Edward III about 1350. While the green girdle does not resemble the blue garter, this motto at the end of the poem serves to connect it with contemporary efforts to celebrate traditional knighthood.

Another colophon provides the more useful information that "the hoole book of kyng Arthur and of his noble knyghtes of the Rounde Table" was completed in the ninth year of King Edward IV, that is 1469 or 1470. So whichever Malory wrote the *Morte Darthur*, he was certainly working in the unsettled years of the Wars of the Roses, in which the great ducal families of York and Lancaster battled for control of the English throne. As one family gained dominance, adherents of the other were often jailed on flimsy charges. The spectacle of a nation threatening to crumble into clan warfare provides much of the thematic weight of the *Morte Darthur*, while the declining chivalric order of the later fifteenth century underlies Malory's increasingly elegiac tone.

Whether he gained his remarkable knowledge of French and English Arthurian tradition in or out of jail, Malory infused his version of these stories with a darkening perspective very much his own. Malory sensed the high aspirations, especially the bonds of honor and fellowship in battle, that held together Arthur's realm. Yet he was also bleakly aware of how tenuous those bonds were and how easily undone by tragically competing pressures. These include the centuries-old Arthurian preoccupation with transgressive love, but Malory is more concerned with the conflicting claims of loyalty to clan or king, the urge to avenge the death of a fellow knight, and the resulting alienation even among the best of knights. Still more unnerving, agents of a virtually unmotivated or unexplained malice have ever more impact as the *Morte Darthur* progresses.

For all his initial energy and control, Malory's Arthur is increasingly a king forced to suppress knightly grievances, to deplore religious quest, even to overlook the adultery of his wife and his greatest knight, all in the interest of his fading hopes for chivalric honor and unity. Arthur's commitment to courtesy finally undoes his honor in the eyes of his own knights. As the Round Table is broken (an image Malory uses repeatedly) Arthur is put in the agonizing position of acting as judge in his wife's trial, making war on his early companion Lancelot, and finally engaging in single combat with his own treacherous son Mordred.

Malory would have found many of these themes in his sources. Twelfth-century Arthurian romances in French verse had explored the elevation and danger of courtly eroticism, and the theme was extended in the enormous French prose versions of the thirteenth century that Malory had read in great detail. In these prose romances, too, religious and chivalric themes converged around the story of the Grail. Malory also knew the *Morte Arthur* poems of fourteenth-century England, with their emphases on conquest, treachery, and the military details of Arthur's final battles.

Malory regularly acknowledges these sources, but his powers of synthesis and the stamp of his style make his *Morte Darthur* unique. While he occasionally writes a complex, reflective sentence, Malory's prose is typically composed of simple, idiomatic narrative statements, and speeches so brief as to be almost gnomic. On hearing of his brother's death, Gawain faints, then rises and says only "Alas!" Yet the grief of his cry resonates across the closing episodes of the work. Malory's imagery is similarly resonant. He tends to strip it of the explanations that had become frequent in the French prose works, and he concentrates its impact by an almost obsessive repetition. The later episodes of the work become almost an incantation of breakage and dispersal, blood and wounds, each image cluster reaching alternately toward religious experience or secular destruction.

These versions of chivalric ambition, sacred or secular, do not divide easily in the *Morte Darthur*. The saintly Galahad and the scheming Mordred may represent extremes of contrary ambition, but Malory is more preoccupied by the sadly mixed motives of Lancelot or Arthur himself. In three late episodes offered below, the reader is drawn into the perspective of lesser knights like Bors and Bedivere, who witness great moments while affecting them only marginally. They bring back to the world of lesser men stories of uncanny experience and oversee their conversion from verbal rumor to written form, whether in books or on tombs. Much of Malory's power and his continuing appeal come from his unresolved doubleness of perspective. Whether by way of his characters or his style, resonant and mysterious elements emerge from a narrative of gritty realism.

 For additional resources on Malory, go to *The Longman Anthology of British Literature* Web site at www.myliteraturekit.com.

from Morte Darthur
from Caxton's Prologue[1]

After that I had accomplysshed and fynysshed dyuers hystoryes as wel of° contemplacyon as of other hystoryal and worldly actes of grete conquerours and prynces, and also certeyn bookes of en- saumples° and doctryne, many noble and dyuers gentylmen of thys royame° of Englond camen and demaunded me many and oftymes, wherefore that I haue not do made and enprynte the noble hystorye of the Sayntgreal° and of the moost renomed° Crysten kyng, fyrst and chyef of the thre best Crysten[2] and worthy, Kyng Arthur, whyche ought moost to be remembred emonge vs Englysshemen tofore° al other Crysten kynges. * * *
    To whome I answerd that dyuers men holde oppynyon that there was no suche Arthur, and that alle suche bookes as been maad of hym ben° but fayned and fables, bycause that somme cronycles make of hym no mencyon ne° remember hym noothynge ne of his knyghtes.
    Wherto they answerd, and one in specyal sayd, that in hym that shold say or thynke that there was neuer suche a kyng callyd Arthur myght wel be aretted° grete folye and blyndenesse; for he sayd that there were many euydences of the contrarye. Fyrst ye may see his sepulture° in the monasterye of Glastyngburye. And also in Polycronycon,[3] * * * where his body was buryed and after founden and translated into the sayd monasterye. Ye shal se also in th'ystory of Bochas, in his book De Casu Principum,[4] parte of his noble actes and also of his falle; also Galfrydus in his Brutysshe book[5] recounteth his lyf. And in dyuers places of Englond many remembraunces ben yet of hym and shall remayne perpetuelly, and also of his knyghtes. Fyrst in the Abbey of Westmestre at Saynt Edwardes Shryne remayneth the prynte of his seal in reed waxe

both about

moral tales
realm

Holy Grail / famed

before

are
nor

presumed

tomb

1. The first English printer, William Caxton exerted a major literary influence through his translations of French works and his pioneering editions of English writ- ers, including Chaucer and Gower. In 1485 he published a version of *Le Morte Darthur*, probably based on a revi- sion by Malory himself but different from the text edited by Eugene Vinaver (1947, 1975) and used here. Caxton's *Prologue* is interesting in its own right as an early response to Malory, even as Caxton takes the opportunity to pro- mote interest in his book. To give a sense of early printed

English, the passages from Caxton's *Prologue* are pre- sented in unaltered spelling.
2. Arthur appears in the traditional list of "nine wor- thies," three heroes each from pagan, Jewish, and Christ- ian narratives.
3. The *Polychronicon*, a universal history by the monk Ranulph Higden (d. 1364).
4. Boccaccio's *On the Fall of Princes*.
5. Geoffrey of Monmouth, *History of the Kings of Britain*, whose later versions were often called simply *Brut*.

closed in beryll, in which is wryton, PATRICIUS ARTHURUS BRITAN-
NIE GALLIE GERMANIE DACIE IMPERATOR.[6] Item° in the Castel of   *also*
Douer ye may see Gauwayns skulle and Cradoks mantel; at
Wynchester, the Round Table; in other places, Launcelottes
swerde, and many other thynges.

Thenne, al these thynges consydered, there can no man res-
onably gaynsaye but there was a kyng of thys lande named
Arthur. * * *

Thenne al these thynges forsayd aledged, I coude not wel
denye but that there was suche a noble kynge named Arthur, and
reputed one of the ix worthy, and fyrst and chyef of the Cristen
men. And many noble volumes be made of hym and of his noble
knyghtes in Frensshe, which I haue seen and redde beyonde the
see, which been not had in our maternal tongue. But in Walsshe ben
many, and also in Frensshe, and somme in Englysshe, but nowher
nygh alle. Wherfore suche as haue late ben drawen oute bryefly°   *abridged*
into Englysshe, I haue, after the symple connyng° that God hath   *wit*
sente to me, vnder the fauour and correctyon of al noble lordes
and gentylmen, enprysed° to enprynte a book of the noble hysto-   *undertaken*
ryes of the sayd Kynge Arthur and of certeyn of his knyghtes,
after a copye vnto me delyuerd, whyche copye Syr Thomas
Malorye dyd take oute of certeyn bookes of Frensshe and reduced
it into Englysshe. And I, accordyng to my copye, haue doon sette
it in enprynte, to the entente° that noble men may see and lerne   *with the aim*
the noble actes of chyualrye, the ientyl° and vertuous dedes that   *noble*
somme knyghtes used in tho° dayes, by whyche they came to ho-   *those*
nour, and how they that were vycious were punysshed and ofte
put to shame and rebuke. Humbly bysechyng al noble lordes and
ladyes, wyth al other estates° of what estate or degree they been   *ranks*
of, that shal see and rede in this sayd book and werke, that they
take the good and honest actes in their remembraunce and to
folowe the same, wherin they shalle fynde many ioyous and
playsaunt hystoryes and noble and renomed actes of humanyte,
gentylness, and chyualryes. For herein may be seen noble chyualrye, curtosye, humanyte, frendlynesse, hardynesse, loue, frend-
shyp, cowardyse, murdre, hate, vertue, and synne. Doo after the
good and leue the euyl, and it shal brynge you to good fame and
renommee.°   *renown*

And for to passe the tyme thys book shal be plesaunte to rede
in, but for to gyue fayth and byleue that al is trewe that is con-
teyned herin, ye be at your lyberte. But al is wryton for our doctryne and for to beware that we falle not to vyce ne synne, but
t'excersyse° and folowe vertu, by whyche we may come and at-   *to practice*
teyne to good fame and renomme in thys lyf, and after thys shorte
and transytorye lyf to come vnto euerlastyng blysse in heuen, the
whyche He graunte vs that reygneth in heuen, the Blessyd
Trynyte. Amen.

---

6. The Noble Arthur, Emperor of Britain, Gaul, Germany, Dacia.

The Miracle of Galahad[1]

Now saith the tale that Sir Galahad rode many journeys in vain, and at last he came to the abbey where King Mordrains was. And when he heard that, he thought he would abide to see him.

And so upon the morn, when he had heard mass, Sir Galahad came unto King Mordrains. And anon the king saw him, which had lain blind of long time, and then he dressed him against° him and said, [*rose to meet*]

"Sir Galahad, the servant of Jesu Christ and very° knight, whose [*true*] coming I have abiden° long, now embrace me and let me rest on thy [*awaited*] breast, so that I may rest° between thine arms! For thou art a clean vir- [*die*] gin above all knights, as the flower of the lily in whom virginity is sig- nified. And thou art the rose which is the flower of all good virtue, and in colour of fire.[2] For the fire of the Holy Ghost is taken so in thee that my flesh, which was all dead of oldness, is become again young."

When Galahad heard these words, then he embraced him and all his body. Then said he,° [*Mordrains*]

"Fair Lord Jesu Christ, now I have my will! Now I require Thee, in this point° that I am in, that Thou come and visit me." [*state*]

And anon Our Lord heard his prayer, and therewith the soul departed from the body. And then Sir Galahad put him in the earth as a king ought to be, and so departed and came into a perilous for- est where he found the well which boiled with great waves, as the tale telleth tofore.° [*earlier*]

And as soon as Sir Galahad set his hand thereto it ceased, so that it brent° no more, and anon the heat departed away. And cause why it [*burned*] brent, it was a sign of lechery that was that time much used. But that heat might not abide his pure virginity. And so this was taken in the country for a miracle, and so ever after was it called Galahad's Well.

So by adventure he came unto the country of Gore, and into the abbey where Sir Lancelot had been toforehand and found the tomb of King Bagdemagus; but he was founder thereof.[3] For there was the tomb of Joseph of Arimathea's son and the tomb of Simeon, where Lancelot had failed.[4] Then he looked into a croft° under the [*crypt*] minster,° and there he saw a tomb which brent full marvellously. [*church*] Then asked he the brethren what it was.

"Sir," said they, "a marvellous adventure that may not be brought to an end but by him that passeth of bounty and of knight- hood all them of the Round Table."

1. From *The Holy Grail*, in *King Arthur and His Knights*, ed. Eugène Vinaver (1975). Earlier in the text, Lancelot's saintly son Galahad had come to the Round Table and precipitated a brief apparition of the Holy Grail (the cup or dish with which Christ had celebrated the Last Supper). One hundred fifty of Arthur's knights then took a vow to seek a fuller vision of the Grail, but in the mysterious ad- ventures that followed, many died or despaired. Malory's attention now narrows to Lancelot and his partial vision of the Grail, and the continuing quest of Galahad, Perceval, and Bors. The blind King Mordrains is one of several maimed or aged kings cured by Galahad's presence.

2. Galahad's physical and spiritual purity are shown in a number of earlier episodes.

3. Gore, the mysterious realm of Bagdemagus, who had been gravely wounded when he presumed to take a shield intended for Galahad. Words may be missing from the fi- nal phrase.

4. In Arthurian tradition, Joseph of Arimathea was keeper of the Grail and used it to catch Christ's blood at the Crucifixion. His son Joseph was the first Christian bishop and carried both the faith and the Grail to Eng- land. Galahad is the last of their lineage. Lancelot's fail- ure refers to an episode in the French source that Malory never tells, either inadvertently or because he assumed that many readers would know the story.

"I would," said Sir Galahad, "that ye would bring me thereto."

"Gladly," said they, and so led him till° a cave. And he went *to*
down upon greses° and came unto the tomb. And so the flaming *steps*
failed, and the fire staunched° which many a day had been great. *was quenched*

Then came there a voice which said,

"Much are ye beholden to thank God which hath given you a
good hour,° that ye may draw out the souls of earthly pain and to *good luck*
put them into the joys of Paradise. Sir, I am of your kindred, which
hath dwelled in this heat this three hundred winter and four-and-
fifty to be purged of the sin that I did against Arimathea Joseph."

Then Sir Galahad took the body in his arms and bare it into the
minster. And that night lay Sir Galahad in the abbey; and on the morn
he gave him his service and put him in the earth before the high altar.

So departed he from thence, and commended the brethren to
God, and so he rode five days till that he came to the Maimed King.
And ever followed Perceval the five days asking where he had been,
and so one told him how the adventures of Logres were achieved.[5]
So on a day it befell that he came out of a great forest, and there
they met at traverse with Sir Bors[6] which rode alone. It is no need
to ask if they were glad! And so he salewed them, and they yielded
to him° honour and good adventure, and everych told other how *wished him*
they had sped. Then said Sir Bors,

"It is more than a year and a half that I ne lay° ten times where *have not slept*
men dwelled, but in wild forests and in mountains. But God was
ever my comfort."

Then rode they a great while till they came to the castle of
Corbenic. And when they were entered within, King Pelles knew
them. So there was great joy, for he wist well by their coming that
they had fulfilled the Sankgreall.[7]

Then Eliazar, King Pelles' son, brought tofore them the broken
sword wherewith Joseph was stricken through the thigh.[8] Then Bors
set his hand thereto to essay if he might have sowded° it again; but *joined*
it would not be. Then he took it to Perceval, but he had no more
power thereto than he.

"Now have ye it again," said Sir Perceval unto Sir Galahad, "for
an° it be ever achieved by any bodily man, ye must do it." *if*

And then he took the pieces and set them together, and seemed
to them as it had never be broken, and as well as it was first forged.
And when they within espied that the adventure of the sword was
achieved, then they gave the sword to Sir Bors, for it might no better
be set,° for he was so good a knight and a worthy man. *used*

And a little before even the sword[9] arose, great and marvellous,
and was full of great heat, that many men fell for dread. And anon
alight a voice among them and said, "They that ought not to sit at

---

5. Perceval has followed Galahad's movements. Malory
reduces a five-year period in his source to five days and
omits the two knights' meeting.
6. Sir Bors has also been wandering in search of the Grail.
7. Pelles is the maimed king and keeper of Corbenic, the

Grail Castle. The past tense looks forward to events not
yet achieved.
8. This sword had wounded Joseph of Arimathea; joining
its broken halves is part of the Grail quest.
9. Malory misconstrues a phrase meaning "a wind."

the table of Our Lord Jesu Christ, avoid° hence! For now there shall
very° knights be fed."

So they went thence, all save King Pelles and Eliazar, his son,
which were holy men, and a maid which was his niece. And so
there abode these three knights and these three; else were no more.
And anon they saw knights all armed come in at the hall door, and
did off their helms and their arms, and said unto Sir Galahad,

"Sir, we have hied° right much for to be with you at this table
where the holy meat shall be departed."°

Then said he, "Ye be welcome! But of whence be ye?"

So three of them said they were of Gaul, and other three said
they were of Ireland, and other three said they were of Denmark.

And so as they sat thus, there came out a bed of tree°
of° a chamber, which four gentlewomen brought; and in the bed
lay a good man sick, and had a crown of gold upon his head. And
there, in the midst of the palace, they set him down and went
again. Then he lift up his head and said,

"Sir Galahad, good knight, ye be right welcome, for much have
I desired your coming! For in such pain and in such anguish as I
have no man else° might have suffered long. But now I trust to God
the term is come that my pain shall be allayed, and so I shall pass
out of this world, so as it was promised me long ago."

And therewith a voice said, "There be two among you that be
not in the quest of the Sankgreall, and therefore departeth!"

Then King Pelles and his son departed. And therewithal be-
seemed them° that there came an old man and four angels from
heaven, clothed in likeness of a bishop, and had a cross in his hand.
And these four angels bare him up in a chair and set him down before
the table of silver whereupon the Sankgreall was. And it seemed that
he had in midst of his forehead letters which said: "See ye here Joseph,
the first bishop of Christendom, the same which Our Lord succoured[1]
in the city of Sarras in the spiritual palace." Then the knights marvelled, for that bishop was dead more than three hundred year tofore.

"Ah, knights," said he, "marvel not, for I was sometime an
earthly man."

So with that they heard the chamber door open, and there they
saw angels; and two bare candles of wax, and the third bare a towel,[2]
and the fourth a spear which bled marvellously, that the drops fell
within a box which he held with his other hand. And anon they set
the candles upon the table, and the third the towel upon the vessel,
and the fourth the holy spear even° upright upon the vessel.

And then the bishop made semblaunt as though he would
have gone to the sacring° of a mass, and then he took an
ubblie° which was made in likeness of bread. And at the lifting
up there came a figure in likeness of a child, and the visage was as
red and as bright as any fire, and smote himself° into the bread,
that all they saw it that the bread was formed of a fleshly man.

withdraw
true

hastened
distributed

wood
from

no other man

it seemed

straight

consecration
wafer

impressed itself

1. Joseph of Arimathea was blessed by Christ.   2. In the French source, a veil of samite.

And then he put it into the holy vessel again, and then he did that longed° to a priest to do mass.

And then he went to Sir Galahad and kissed him and bade him go and kiss his fellows. And so he did anon.

"Now," said he, "the servants of Jesu Christ, ye shall be fed afore this table with sweet meats that never knights yet tasted."

And when he had said he vanished away. And they set them at the table in great dread and made their prayers. Then looked they and saw a Man come out of the holy vessel that had all the signs of the Passion of Jesu Christ, bleeding all openly, and said,

"My knights and my servants and my true children which be come out of deadly life into the spiritual life, I will no longer cover me from you, but ye shall see now a part of my secrets and of my hid things. Now holdeth and receiveth the high order and meat which ye have so much desired."

Then took He himself the holy vessel and came to Sir Galahad. And he kneeled down and received his Saviour. And after him so received all his fellows, and they thought it so sweet that it was marvellous to tell. Then said He to Sir Galahad,

"Son, wotest thou what I hold betwixt my hands?"

"Nay," said he, "but if ye tell me."

"This is," said He, "the holy dish wherein I ate the lamb on Easter Day, and now hast thou seen that thou most desired to see. But yet hast thou not seen it so openly as thou shalt see it in the city of Sarras, in the spiritual palace. Therefore thou must go hence and bear with thee this holy vessel, for this night it shall depart from the realm of Logres, and it shall nevermore be seen here. And knowest thou wherefore? For he° is not served nother worshipped to his right° by them of this land, for they be turned to evil living, and therefore I shall disinherit them of the honour which I have done them. And therefore go ye three to-morn unto the sea, where ye shall find your ship ready, and with you take the sword with the strange girdles,° and no more with you but Sir Perceval and Sir Bors. Also I will that ye take with you of this blood of this spear for to anoint the Maimed King, both his legs and his body, and he shall have his heal."

"Sir," said Galahad, "why shall not these other fellows go with us?"

"For this cause: for right as I depart° my apostles one here and another there, so I will that ye depart. And two of you shall die in my service, and one of you shall come again and tell tidings."

Then gave He them His blessing and vanished away.

And Sir Galahad went anon to the spear which lay upon the table and touched the blood with his fingers, and came after to the maimed knight and anointed his legs and his body. And therwith he clothed him anon, and start upon his feet out of his bed as an whole man, and thanked God that He had healed him. And anon he left the world and yielded himself to a place of religion of white monks,[3] and was a full holy man.

what was right

it / properly

belts

separate

3. The white monks were Cistercians, whose spirituality had some role in Malory's French sources.

And that same night, about midnight, came a voice among them which said,

"My sons, and not my chief sons,[4] my friends, and not mine enemies, go ye hence where ye hope best to do, and as I bade you do."

"Ah, thanked be Thou, Lord, that Thou wilt whightsauf° to *vouchsafe* call us Thy sons! Now may we well prove that we have not lost our pains."

And anon in all haste they took their harness and departed; but the three knights of Gaul (one of them hight Claudine, King Claudas' son, and the other two were great gentlemen) then prayed° *asked* Sir Galahad to everych of them, that an° they come to King *if* Arthur's court, "to salew my lord Sir Lancelot, my father and them all of the Round Table"; and prayed them, an they came on that party,° not to forget it. *to that region*

Right so departed Sir Galahad, and Sir Perceval and Sir Bors with him, and so they rode three days. And then they came to a rivage° and found the ship whereof the tale speaketh of tofore. And *shore* when they came to the board° they found in the midst of the bed *on board* the table of silver which they had left with the Maimed King, and the Sankgreall which was covered with red samite.° Then were they *silk* glad to have such things in their fellowship; and so they entered and made great reverence thereto, and Sir Galahad fell on his knees and prayed long time to Our Lord, that at what time he asked he might pass out of this world. And so long he prayed till a voice said,

"Sir Galahad, thou shalt have thy request, and when thou asketh the death of thy body thou shalt have it, and then shalt thou have the life of thy soul."

Then Sir Perceval heard him a little, and prayed him of° fel- *for the sake of* lowship that was between them wherefore he asked such things.

"Sir, that shall I tell you," said Sir Galahad. "This other day, when we saw a part of the adventures of the Sankgreall, I was in such a joy of heart that I trow° never man was that was earthly. *believe* And therefore I wot° well, when my body is dead, my soul shall be *know* in great joy to see the Blessed Trinity every day, and the majesty of Our Lord, Jesu Christ."

And so long were they in the ship that they said to Galahad,

"Sir, in this bed ye ought to lie, for so saith the letters."° *writings*

And so he laid him down, and slept a great while. And when he awaked he looked tofore him and saw the city of Sarras. And as they would have landed they saw the ship wherein Sir Perceval had put his sister in.

"Truly," said Sir Perceval, "in the name of God, well hath my sister holden us covenant."[5]

Then they took out of the ship the table of silver, and he took it to Sir Perceval and to Sir Bors to go tofore, and Sir Galahad came behind, and right so they went into the city. And at the gate of the

---

4. A confusing phrase, perhaps in error for "stepsons."
5. Kept her promise to us. In an earlier episode Perceval's sister died after giving a basin of her blood to heal a leper woman.

city they saw an old man crooked, and anon Sir Galahad called him and bade him help "to bear this heavy thing."

"Truly," said the old man, "it is ten year ago that I might not go but with crutches."

"Care thou not," said Galahad, "and arise up and show thy good will!"

And so he essayed, and found himself as whole as ever he was. Then ran he to the table and took one part against° Galahad.   *beside*

Anon arose there a great noise in the city that a cripple was made whole by knights marvellous that entered into the city. Then anon after the three knights went to the water and brought up into the palace Sir Perceval's sister, and buried her as richly as them ought a king's daughter.

And when the king of that country knew that and saw that fellowship (whose name was Estorause), he asked them of whence they were, and what thing it was that they had brought upon the table of silver. And they told him the truth of the Sankgreall, and the power which God hath set there.

Then this king was a tyrant, and was come of the line of paynims,° and took them and put them in prison in a deep hole. But as   *pagans* soon as they were there Our Lord sent them the Sankgreall, through whose grace they were alway fulfilled° while that they were in   *fed* prison.

So at the year's end it befell that this king lay sick and felt that he should die. Then he sent for the three knights, and they came afore him, and he cried them mercy of that he had done to them, and they forgave it him goodly, and he died anon.

When the king was dead all the city stood dismayed and wist°   *knew* not who might be their king. Right so as they were in council there came a voice among them, and made them choose the youngest knight of three to be their king, "for he shall well maintain you and all yours."

So they made Sir Galahad king by all the assent of the whole city, and else they would have slain him. And when he was come to behold his land he let make° above the table of silver a chest of gold   *had made* and of precious stones that covered the holy vessel, and every day early the three knights would come before it and make their prayers.

Now at the year's end, and the self Sunday after that Sir Galahad had borne the crown of gold, he arose up early and his fellows, and came to the palace, and saw tofore them the holy vessel and a man kneeling on his knees in likeness of a bishop that had about him a great fellowship of angels, as it had been Jesu Christ himself. And then he arose and began a mass of Our Lady. And so he came to the sacring, and anon made an end. He called Sir Galahad unto him and said,

"Come forth, the servant of Jesu Christ, and thou shalt see that thou hast much desired to see."

And then he began to tremble right hard when the deadly°   *mortal* flesh began to behold the spiritual things. Then he held up his hands toward heaven and said,

"Lord, I thank Thee, for now I see that that hath been my desire many a day. Now, my Blessed Lord, I would not live in this wretched world no longer, if it might please Thee, Lord."

And therewith the good man took Our Lord's Body[6] betwixt his hands, proffered it to Sir Galahad, and he received it right gladly and meekly.

"Now wotest thou what I am?" said the good man.

"Nay, Sir," said Sir Galahad.

"I am Joseph, the son of Joseph of Arimathea, which Our Lord hath sent to thee to bear thee fellowship. And wotest thou wherefore He hath sent me more than any other? For thou hast resembled me in two things: that thou hast seen, that is the marvels of the Sankgreall, and for thou hast been a clean maiden° as I have been and am."   *chaste virgin*

And when he had said these words Sir Galahad went to Sir Perceval and kissed him and commended him to God. And so he went to Sir Bors and kissed him and commended him to God, and said,

"My fair lord, salew me° unto my lord Sir Lancelot, my father,   *give my greeting* and as soon as ye see him bid him remember of this world unstable."

And therewith he kneeled down tofore the table and made his prayers. And so suddenly departed his soul to Jesu Christ, and a great multitude of angels bare it up to heaven, even in the sight of his two fellows.

Also these two knights saw come from heaven an hand, but they saw not the body, and so it came right to the vessel, and took it, and the spear, and so bare it up to heaven. And sithen° was there   *since then* never man so hardy to say that he had seen the Sankgreall.

So when Sir Perceval and Sir Bors saw Sir Galahad dead they made as much sorrow as ever did men. And if they had not been good men they might lightly° have fallen in despair. And so people   *easily* of the country and city, they were right heavy. But so he was buried, and soon as he was buried Sir Perceval yielded him to an hermitage out of the city and took religious clothing. And Sir Bors was alway with him, but he changed never his secular clothing, for that he purposed him to go again into the realm of Logres.

Thus a year and two months lived Sir Perceval in the hermitage a full holy life, and then passed out of the world. Then Sir Bors let bury him by[7] his sister and by Sir Galahad in the spiritualities.°   *consecrated ground*

So when Bors saw that he was in so far° countries as in the   *remote* parts of Babylon, he departed from the city of Sarras and armed him and came to the sea, and entered into a ship. And so it befell him, by good adventure, he came unto the realm of Logres, and so he rode a pace° till he came to Camelot where the king was.   *swiftly*

And then was there made great joy of him in all the court, for they weened all he had been lost forasmuch as he had been so long out of the country. And when they had eaten, the king made great clerks to come before him, for cause they should chronicle of° the   *record* high adventures of the good knights. So when Sir Bors had told him

---

6. The wafer of the Eucharist.   7. Had him buried next to.

of the high adventures of the Sankgreall such as had befallen him
and his three fellows, which were Sir Lancelot, Perceval, Sir
Galahad and himself, then Sir Lancelot told the adventures of the
Sankgreall that he had seen. All this was made in great books and
put up in almeries° at Salisbury.   *libraries*

And anon Sir Bors said to Sir Lancelot,

"Sir Galahad, your own son, salewed you by me, and after you my
lord King Arthur and all the whole court, and so did Sir Perceval. For I
buried them with both mine own hands in the city of Sarras. Also, Sir
Lancelot, Sir Galahad prayed you to remember of this unsiker° world,   *uncertain*
as ye behight him° when ye were together more than half a year."   *promised*

"This is true," said Sir Lancelot; "now I trust to God his prayer
shall avail me."

Then Sir Lancelot took Sir Bors in his arms and said,

"Cousin, ye are right welcome to me! For all that ever I may do
for you and for yours, ye shall find my poor body ready at all times
while the spirit is in it, and that I promise you faithfully, and never
to fail. And wit ye well, gentle cousin Sir Bors, ye and I shall never
depart in sunder while our lives may last."

"Sir," said he, "as ye will, so will I."

THUS ENDETH THE TALE OF THE SANKGREAL THAT WAS BRIEFLY
DRAWN OUT OF FRENCH, WHICH IS A TALE CHRONICLED FOR ONE OF
THE TRUEST AND OF THE HOLIEST THAT IS IN THIS WORLD, BY SIR
THOMAS MALEORRÉ, KNIGHT.
O BLESSED JESU HELP HIM THROUGH HIS MIGHT! AMEN.

The Poisoned Apple[1]

So after the quest of the Sankgreall was fulfilled, and all knights
that were left on live were come home again unto the Table Round,
as *The Book of the Sankgreall* maketh mention, then was there great
joy in the court, and in especial King Arthur and Queen Guinevere
made great joy of the remnant that were come home. And passing
glad was the king and the queen of Sir Lancelot and of Sir Bors, for
they had been passing long away in the quest of the Sankgreall.

Then, as the book saith, Sir Lancelot began to resort unto Queen
Guinevere again and forgat the promise and the perfection° that he   *of perfection*
made in the quest; for, as the book saith, had not Sir Lancelot been in
his privy° thoughts and in his mind so set inwardly to the queen as he   *secret*
was in seeming outward to God, there had no knight passed him in
the quest of the Sankgreall. But ever his thoughts privily were on the
queen, and so they loved together more hotter than they did to fore-
hand, and had many such privy draughts° together that many in the   *meetings*
court spake of it, and in especial Sir Agravain, Sir Gawain's brother,
for he was ever open-mouthed.

So it befell that Sir Lancelot had many resorts of° ladies and   *entreaties from*
damsels which daily resorted unto him, that besought him to be

1. From the section titled *The Book of Sir Launcelot and Queen Guinevere*, in *King Arthur and His Knights*, ed. Eugène
Vinaver (1975).

their champion. In all such matters of right Sir Lancelot applied him daily to do for the pleasure of Our Lord Jesu Christ, and ever as much as he might he withdrew him from the company of Queen Guinevere for to eschew the slander and noise.° Wherefore the queen waxed wroth with Sir Lancelot.

rumor

So on a day she called him unto her chamber and said thus:

"Sir Lancelot, I see and feel daily that your love beginneth to slake,° for ye have no joy to be in my presence, but ever ye are out of this court, and quarrels and matters ye have nowadays for ladies, maidens and gentlewomen, more than ever ye were wont to have beforehand."

cool

"Ah, madam," said Sir Lancelot, "in this ye must hold me excused for divers causes. One is, I was but late in the quest of the Sankgreall, and I thank God of His great mercy, and never of my deserving, that I saw in that my quest as much as ever saw any sinful man living, and so was it told me. And if that I had not had my privy thoughts to return to your love again as I do, I had° seen as great mysteries as ever saw my son, Sir Galahad, Perceval, other Sir Bors. And therefore, madam, I was but late in that quest, and wit you well, madam, it may not be yet lightly forgotten, the high service in whom I did my diligent labour.

should have

"Also, madam, wit you well that there be many men speaketh of our love in this court, and have you and me greatly in await,° as this Sir Agravain and Sir Mordred.[2] And, madam, wit you well I dread them more for your sake than for any fear I have of them myself, for I may happen to escape and rid myself in a great need where, madam, ye must abide all that will be said unto you. And then, if that ye fall in any distress throughout° wilful folly, then is there none other help but by me and my blood.°

suspicion

through

kinsmen

"And wit you well, madam, the boldness of you and me will bring us to shame and slander; and that were me loath to see you dishonoured. And that is the cause I take upon me more for to do for damsels and maidens than ever I did toforn:° that men should understand my joy and my delight is my pleasure to have ado for damsels and maidens."

before

All this while the queen stood still and let Sir Lancelot say what he would; and when he had all said she brast out of weeping, and so she sobbed and wept a great while. And when she might speak she said,

"Sir Lancelot, now I well understand that thou art a false, recreant° knight and a common lecher, and lovest and holdest other ladies, and of me thou hast disdain and scorn. For wit thou well, now I understand thy falsehood I shall never love thee more, and look thou be never so hardy° to come in my sight. And right here I discharge thee this court, that thou never come within it, and I forfend° thee my fellowship, and upon pain° of thy head that thou see me nevermore!"

cowardly

bold

forbid /
at the risk

2. Mordred was Arthur's illegitimate son, by an incestuous encounter with his half-sister Morgause (or in some versions, Morgan le Fay).

Right so Sir Lancelot departed with great heaviness that un-
neth° he might sustain himself for great dole-making.   *scarcely*

Then he called Sir Bors, Ector de Maris and Sir Lionel, and
told them how the queen had forfended him the court, and so he
was in will to depart into his own country.

"Fair sir," said Bors de Ganis, "ye shall not depart out of this land
by mine advice, for ye must remember you what ye are, and renowned
the most noblest knight of the world, and many great matters ye have
in hand. And women in their hastiness will do oftentimes that after
them sore repenteth. And therefore, by mine advice, ye shall take
your horse and ride to the good hermit here beside Windsor, that
sometime was a good knight; his name is Sir Brastias. And there shall
ye abide till that I send you word of better tidings."

"Brother," said Sir Lancelot, "wit you well I am full loath to de-
part out of this realm, but the queen hath defended° me so highly,°   *dismissed / angrily*
that meseemeth she will never be my good lady as she hath been."

"Say ye never so," said Sir Bors, "for many times or° this time   *before*
she hath been wroth with you, and after that she was the first that
repented it."

"Ye say well," said Sir Lancelot, "for now will I do by your
counsel and take mine horse and mine harness and ride to the hermit Sir Brastias, and there will I repose me till I hear some manner
of tidings from you. But, fair brother, in that° ye can get me the love   *so far as*
of my lady, Queen Guinevere."

"Sir," said Sir Bors, "ye need not to move° me of such matters,   *persuade*
for well ye wot I will do what I may to please you."

And then Sir Lancelot departed suddenly, and no creature wist
where he was become° but Sir Bors. So when Sir Lancelot was de-   *had gone*
parted the queen outward made no manner of sorrow in showing to
none of his blood nor to none other, but wit ye well, inwardly, as
the book saith, she took great thought;° but she bare it out with a   *grief*
proud countenance, as though she felt no thought nother danger.°   *fear*

So the queen let make° a privy dinner in London unto the   *had made*
knights of the Round Table, and all was for to show outward that
she had as great joy in all other knights of the Round Table as she
had in Sir Lancelot. So there was all only at that dinner Sir Gawain
and his brethren, that is for to say Sir Agravain, Sir Gaheris, Sir
Gareth and Sir Mordred, also there was Sir Bors de Ganis, Sir
Blamore de Ganis, Sir Bleoberis de Ganis, Sir Galihad, Sir Eliodin,
Sir Ector de Maris, Sir Lionel, Sir Palomides, Sir Safir, his
brother, Sir La Cote Male Tayle, Sir Persaunt, Sir Ironside, Sir
Braundiles, Sir Kay le Seneschal, Sir Mador de la Porte, Sir Patrise,
a knight of Ireland, Sir Aliduke, Sir Ascamore, and Sir Pinel le
Savage, which was cousin to Sir Lamorak de Galis, the good knight
that Sir Gawain and his brethren slew by treason.[3]

And so these four-and-twenty knights should dine with the
queen in a privy place by themselves, and there was made a great

---

3. This catalog draws together most of the Round Table knights who survived the Grail quest.

feast of all manner of dainties. But Sir Gawain had a custom that he used daily at meat and at supper, that he loved well all manner of fruit, and in especial apples and pears. And therefore whosomever dined other° feasted Sir Gawain would commonly purvey for° good fruit for him. And so did the queen; for to please Sir Gawain she let purvey for him all manner of fruit. For Sir Gawain was a passing hot° knight of nature, and this Sir Pinel hated Sir Gawain because of his kinsman Sir Lamorak's death, and therefore, for pure envy and hate, Sir Pinel enpoisoned certain apples for to enpoison Sir Gawain. *or* / *provide*

hot-tempered

So this was well yet unto° the end of meat, and so it befell by misfortune a good knight Sir Patrise, which was cousin unto Sir Mador de la Porte, took an apple, for he was enchafed° with heat of wine. And it mishapped him to take a poisoned apple. And when he had eaten it he swall° sore till he brast,° and there Sir Patrise fell down suddenly° dead among them. *toward*

inflamed

swelled / *burst*
instantly

Then every knight leap from the board ashamed, and araged for° wrath out of their wits, for they wist not what to say; considering Queen Guinevere made the feast and dinner they had all suspicion unto her. *enraged with*

"My lady the queen!" said Sir Gawain. "Madam, wit you that this dinner was made for me and my fellows, for all folks that knoweth my condition understand that I love well fruit. And now I see well I had near been slain. Therefore, madam, I dread me lest ye will be shamed."

Then the queen stood still and was so sore abashed that she wist not what to say.

"This shall not so be ended," said Sir Mador de la Porte, "for here have I lost a full noble knight of my blood, and therefore upon this shame and despite° I will be revenged to the utterance!"° *wrong* / *utmost*

And there openly Sir Mador appealed° the queen of the death of his cousin Sir Patrise. *accused*

Then stood they all still, that° none would speak a word against him, for they all had great suspicion unto the queen because she let make that dinner. And the queen was so abashed that she could none otherways do but wept so heartily that she fell on a swough. So with this noise and cry came to them King Arthur, and when he wist of the trouble he was a passing heavy° man. And ever Sir Mador stood still before the king, and appealed the queen of treason. (For the custom was such at that time that all manner of shameful death was called treason.) *for*

sad

"Fair lords," said King Arthur, "me repenteth of this trouble, but the case is so I may not have ado° in this matter, for I must be a rightful judge. And that repenteth me that I may not do battle[4] for my wife, for, as I deem, this deed came never by her.° And therefore I suppose she shall not be all disdained° but that some good knight shall put his body in jeopardy for my queen rather than she should *intervene*

by her doing
dishonored

4. Malory refers to a procedure in law, archaic in his day, wherein an armed champion could vindicate a person's innocence in a "trial by battle."

be brent° in a wrong quarrel.° And therefore, Sir Mador, be not so   *burned / unjustly*
hasty; for, perdy,° it may happen she shall not be all friendless. And   *by God*
therefore desire thou thy day of battle, and she shall purvey her of°   *find herself*
some good knight that shall answer you, other else it were to me
great shame and to all my court."

"My gracious lord," said Sir Mador, "ye must hold me excused,
for though ye be our king, in that degree° ye are but a knight as we   *rank*
are, and ye are sworn unto knighthood as well as we be. And therefore I beseech you that ye be not displeased, for there is none of all
these four-and-twenty knights that were bidden to this dinner but
all they have great suspicion unto the queen. What say ye all, my
lords?" said Sir Mador.

Then they answered by and by and said they could not excuse
the queen for why she made the dinner, and other it must come by
her other by her servants.

"Alas," said the queen, "I made this dinner for a good intent and
never for none evil, so Almighty Jesu help me in my right,° as I was   *just cause*
never purposed to do such evil deeds, and that I report me unto God."[5]

"My lord the king," said Sir Mador, "I require you as ye be a
righteous king, give me my day that I may have justice."

"Well," said the king, "this day fifteen days look thou be ready
armed on horseback in the meadow beside Winchester. And if it so
fall° that there be any knight to encounter against you, there may   *happens*
you do your best, and God speed the right. And if so befall that
there be no knight ready at that day, then must my queen be brent,
and there she shall be ready to have her judgment."

"I am answered," said Sir Mador.

And every knight yode° where him liked.   *went*

So when the king and the queen were together the king asked
the queen how this case° befell. Then the queen said,   *misfortune*

"Sir, as Jesu be my help!" She wist not how nother° in what   *nor*
manner.

"Where is Sir Lancelot?" said King Arthur. "An° he were here   *if*
he would not grudge to do battle for you."

"Sir," said the queen, "I wot not where he is, but his brother
and his kinsmen deem that he be not within this realm."

"That me repenteth," said King Arthur, "for an he were here he
would soon stint° this strife. Well, then I will counsel you," said the   *stop*
king, "that ye go unto Sir Bors, and pray him for to do battle for you
for Sir Lancelot's sake, and upon my life he will not refuse you. For
well I see," said the king, "that none of the four-and-twenty knights
that were at your dinner where Sir Patrise was slain that will do battle for you, nother none of them will say well of you, and that shall
be great slander to you in this court."

"Alas," said the queen, "an I may not do withall,[6] but now I
miss Sir Lancelot, for an he were here he would soon put me in my
heart's ease."

---

5. I appeal to God to confirm.   6. If I cannot help it.

"What aileth you," said the king, "that ye cannot keep Sir Lancelot upon your side? For wit you well," said the king, "who hath Sir Lancelot upon his party° hath the most man of worship in this world upon his side. Now go your way," said the king unto the queen, "and require Sir Bors to do battle for you for Sir Lancelot's sake."

faction

So the queen departed from the king and sent for Sir Bors into the chamber. And when he came she besought him of succour.

"Madam," said he, "what would ye that I did? For I may not with my worship° have ado in this matter, because I was at the same dinner, for dread of any of those knights would have you in suspicion. Also Madam," said Sir Bors, "now miss ye Sir Lancelot, for he would not a failed you in your right nother in your wrong, for when ye have been in right great dangers he hath succoured you. And now ye have driven him out of this country, by whom ye and all we were daily worshipped° by. Therefore, madam, I marvel how ye dare for shame to require me to do anything for you, insomuch ye have enchased out of your court by whom° we were upborne and honoured."

with honor

honored

the man by whom

"Alas, fair knight," said the queen, "I put me wholly in your grace, and all that is amiss I will amend as ye will counsel me." And therewith she kneeled down upon both her knees, and besought Sir Bors to have mercy upon her, "other else I shall have a shameful death, and thereto I never offended."°

did wrong

Right so came King Arthur and found the queen kneeling. And then Sir Bors took her up, and said,

"Madam, ye do me great dishonour."

"Ah, gentle knight," said the king, "have mercy upon my queen, courteous knight, for I am now in certain she is untruly defamed! And therefore, courteous knight," the king said, "promise her to do battle for her, I require you for the love ye owe unto Sir Lancelot."

"My lord," said Sir Bors, "ye require me the greatest thing that any man may require me. And wit you well, if I grant to do battle for the queen I shall wrath° many of my fellowship of the Table Round. But as for that," said Sir Bors, "I will grant° for my lord Sir Lancelot's sake, and for your sake: I will at that day be the queen's champion unless that there come by adventures a better knight than I am to do battle for her."

enrage
consent

"Will ye promise me this," said the king, "by your faith?"

"Yea sir," said Sir Bors, "of that I shall not fail you, nother her; but if there come a better knight than I am, then shall he have the battle."

Then was the king and the queen passing glad, and so departed, and thanked him heartily.

Then Sir Bors departed secretly upon a day, and rode unto Sir Lancelot thereas he was with Sir Brastias, and told him of all this adventure.

"Ah Jesu," Sir Lancelot said, "this is come happily as I would have it. And therefore I pray you make you ready to do battle, but look that ye tarry till ye see me come as long as ye may. For I am sure Sir Mador is an hot knight when he is enchafed for the more ye suffer him the hastier he will be to battle."

"Sir," said Sir Bors, "let me deal with him. Doubt ye not ye shall have all your will."

So departed Sir Bors from him and came to the court again. Then it was noised° in all the court that Sir Bors should do battle for the queen, wherefore many knights were displeased with him that he would take upon him to do battle in the queen's quarrel; for there were but few knights in all the court but they deemed the queen was in the wrong and that she had done that treason. So Sir Bors answered thus to his fellows of the Table Round.

rumored

"Wit you well, my fair lords, it were shame to us all an we suffered to see the most noble queen of the world to be shamed openly, considering her lord and our lord is the man of most worship christened, and he hath ever worshipped° us all in all places."

honored

Many answered him again: "As for our most noble King Arthur, we love him and honour him as well as ye do, but as for Queen Guinevere we love her not, because she is a destroyer of good knights."

"Fair lords," said Sir Bors, "meseemeth ye say not as ye should say, for never yet in my days knew I never ne° heard say that ever she was a destroyer of good knights, but at all times as far as ever I could know, she was a maintainer of good knights; and ever she hath been large° and free of her goods to all good knights, and the most bounteous lady of her gifts and her good grace that ever I saw other heard speak of. And therefore it were shame to us all and to our most noble king's wife whom we serve an we suffered her to be shamefully slain. And wit ye well," said Sir Bors, "I will not suffer it, for I dare say so much, for the queen is not guilty of Sir Patrise's death: for she owed° him never none evil will nother none of the four-and-twenty knights that were at that dinner, for I dare say for good love she bade us to dinner, and not for no mal engine.° And that, I doubt not, shall be proved hereafter, for howsomever the game goeth, there was treason among us."

nor

generous

felt towards

evil intent

Then some said to Bors, "We may well believe your words." And so some were well pleased and some were not.

So the day came on fast until the even that° the battle should be. Then the queen sent for Sir Bors and asked him how he was disposed.°

evening before

resolved

"Truly, madam," said he, "I am disposed in like wise as I promised you, that is to say I shall not fail you unless there by adventure come a better knight than I am to do battle for you. Then, madam, I am of° you discharged° of my promise."

by / released

"Will ye," said the queen, "that I tell my lord the king thus?"

"Do as it pleaseth you, madam."

Then the queen yode° unto the king and told the answer of Sir Bors.

went

"Well, have ye no doubt," said the king, "of Sir Bors, for I call him now that is living° one of the noblest knights of the world, and most perfectest man."

of those now alive

And thus it passed on till the morn, and so the king and the queen and all manner of knights that were there at that time drew° them unto the meadow beside Winchester where the battle should

gathered

be. And so when the king was come with the queen and many knights of the Table Round, so the queen was then put in the constable's award,° and a great fire made about an iron stake, that an Sir Mador de le Porte had the better, she should there be brent; for such custom was used in those days: for favour, love, nother affinity° there should be none other but righteous judgment, as well upon a king as upon a knight, and as well upon a queen as upon another° poor lady.

So this meanwhile came in Sir Mador de la Porte, and took his oath before the king, how that the queen did this treason until° his cousin Sir Patrise, "and unto mine oath I will prove it with my body, hand for hand, who that will say the contrary."

Right so came in Sir Bors de Ganis and said that as for Queen Guinevere, "she is in the right, and that will I make good that she is not culpable of this treason that is put upon her."

"Then make thee ready," said Sir Mador, "and we shall prove whether thou be in the right or I."

"Sir Mador," said Sir Bors, "wit you well, I know you for a good knight. Notforthen° I shall not fear you so greatly but I trust to God I shall be able to withstand your malice. But thus much have I promised my lord Arthur and my lady the queen, that I shall do battle for her in this cause to the utterest, unless that there come a better knight than I am and discharge° me."

"Is that all?" said Sir Mador. "Other come thou off and do battle with me, other else say nay!"

"Take your horse," said Sir Bors, "and, as I suppose, I shall not tarry long but ye shall be answered."

Then either departed to their tents and made them ready to horseback° as they thought best. And anon Sir Mador came into the field with his shield on his shoulder and his spear in his hand, and so rode about the place crying unto King Arthur,

"Bid your champion come forth an he dare!"

Then was Sir Bors ashamed, and took his horse and came to the lists'° end. And then was he ware° where came from a wood there fast by a knight all armed upon a white horse with a strange shield of strange arms, and he came driving all that° his horse might run. And so he came to Sir Bors and said thus:

"Fair knight, I pray you be not displeased, for here must a better knight than ye are have this battle. Therefore I pray you withdraw you, for wit you well I have had this day a right great journey and this battle ought to be mine. And so I promised you when I spake with you last, and with all my heart I thank you of your good will."

Then Sir Bors rode unto King Arthur and told him how there was a knight come that would have the battle to fight for the queen.

"What knight is he?" said the king.

"I wot not," said Sir Bors, "but such covenant he made with me to be here this day. Now, my lord," said Sir Bors, "here I am discharged."

Then the king called to that knight, and asked him if he would fight for the queen. Then he answered and said,

Margin glosses (right column):

custody

kinship

any

toward

nevertheless

release

to mount

jousting field's / noticed
as fast as

"Sir, therefore come I hither. And therefore, sir king, tarry° me
no longer, for anon as I have finished this battle I must depart
hence, for I have to do many battles elsewhere. For wit you well,"
said the knight, "this is dishonour to you and to all knights of the
Round Table to see and know so noble a lady and so courteous as
Queen Guinevere is, thus to be rebuked and shamed amongst you."

delay

Then they all marvelled what knight that might be that so took
the battle upon him, for there was not one that knew him but if it
were Sir Bors. Then said Sir Mador de la Porte unto the king:

"Now let me wit with whom I shall have ado."

And then they rode to the lists' end, and there they couched°
their spears and ran together with all their mights. And anon Sir
Mador's spear brake all to pieces, but the other's spear held and bare
Sir Mador's horse and all backwards to the earth a great fall. But
mightily and deliverly he avoided his horse from him and put his
shield before him and drew his sword and bade the other knight
alight and do battle with him on foot.

lowered

Then that knight descended down from his horse and put his
shield before him and drew his sword. And so they came eagerly unto
battle, and either gave other many sad° strokes, tracing and traversing
and foining° together with their swords as it were wild boars, thus
fighting nigh an hour; for this Sir Mador was a strong knight, and
mightily proved in many strong battles. But at the last this knight
smote Sir Mador grovelling upon the earth, and the knight stepped
near him to have pulled Sir Mador flatling° upon the ground; and
therewith Sir Mador arose, and in his rising he smote that knight
through the thick of the thighs, that the blood brast out fiercely.

grievous

thrusting

at full length

And when he felt himself so wounded and saw his blood, he let
him arise upon his feet, and then he gave him such a buffet upon
the helm that he fell to the earth flatling. And therewith he strode
to him to have pulled off his helm off his head. And so Sir Mador
prayed that knight to save his life. And so he yielded him as overcome, and released the queen of his quarrel.°

accusation

"I will not grant thee thy life," said the knight, "only that° thou
freely release the queen forever, and that no mention be made upon
Sir Patrise's tomb that ever Queen Guinevere consented to that
treason."

unless

"All this shall be done," said Sir Mador, "I clearly discharge my
quarrel forever."

Then the knights parters° of the lists took up Sir Mador and led
him till his tent. And the other knight went straight to the stairfoot
where sat King Arthur. And by that time was the queen came to the
king, and either kissed other heartily.

stewards

And when the king saw that knight he stooped down to him and
thanked him, and in like wise did the queen. And the king prayed
him put off his helmet and to repose him and to take a sop of wine.

And then he put off his helm to drink, and then every knight
knew him that it was Sir Lancelot. And anon as the king wist that,
he took the queen in his hand and yode unto Sir Lancelot and said,

"Sir, gramercy of your great travail° that ye have had this day *labor*
for me and for my queen."

"My lord," said Sir Lancelot, "wit you well I ought of right ever
to be in your quarrel,° and my lady the queen's quarrel, to do battle; *on your side*
for ye are the man that gave me the high Order of Knighthood, and
that day my lady, your queen, did me worship.° And else I had been *honor*
shamed, for that same day that ye made me knight through my
hastiness I lost my sword, and my lady, your queen, found it, and
lapped° it in her train, and gave me my sword when I had need *wrapped*
thereto; and else had I been shamed among all knights. And therefore, my lord Arthur, I promised her at that day ever to be her
knight in right other in wrong."

"Gramercy," said the king, "for this journey. And wit you well,"
said the king, "I shall acquit° your goodness." *reward*

And evermore the queen beheld Sir Lancelot and wept so tenderly that she sank almost to the ground for sorrow, that he had
done to her so great kindness where she showed him great unkindness. Then the knights of his blood drew unto him, and there either
of them made great joy of other. And so came all the knights of the
Table Round that were there at that time and welcomed him.

And then Sir Mador was healed of his leechcraft,° and Sir *by surgery*
Lancelot was healed of his play.° And so there was made great joy *wound*
and many mirths there was made in that court.

And so it befell that the Damsel of the Lake that hight Ninive,
which wedded the good knight Sir Pelleas, and so she came to the
court, for ever she did great goodness unto King Arthur and to all
his knights through her sorcery and enchantments. And so when
she heard how the queen was grieved° for the death of Sir Patrise, *blamed*
then she told it openly that she was never guilty, and there she disclosed by whom it was done, and named him Sir Pinel, and for what
cause he did it. There it was openly known and disclosed, and so the
queen was excused. And this knight Sir Pinel fled into his country,
and was openly known that he enpoisoned the apples at that feast
to that intent to have destroyed Sir Gawain, because Sir Gawain
and his breathren destroyed Sir Lamorak de Galis which Sir Pinel
was cousin unto.

Then was Sir Patrise buried in the church of Westminster in a
tomb, and thereupon was written: "Here lieth Sir Patrise of Ireland,
slain by Sir Pinel le Savage, that enpoisoned apples to have slain Sir
Gawain, and by misfortune Sir Patrise ate one of the apples, and
then suddenly he brast." Also there was written upon the tomb that
Queen Guinevere was appealed° of treason of° the death of Sir *accused / for*
Patrise by Sir Mador de la Porte, and there was made the mention
how Sir Lancelot fought with him for Queen Guinevere and overcame him in plain battle. All this was written upon the tomb of Sir
Patrise in excusing of the queen.

And then Sir Mador sued daily and long to have the queen's
good grace, and so by the means of Sir Lancelot he caused him to
stand in the queen's good grace, and all was forgiven.

[*In intervening episodes, Agravain and Mordred, nursing long-held grudges, connive to expose the adultery of Lancelot and Guinevere. Their brother, Gawain, reluctantly joins their plot. Mordred traps Lancelot at night in Guinevere's chamber, and in escaping Lancelot kills Agravain. Rescuing Guinevere as she is about to be burned at the stake, Lancelot kills another of Gawain's brothers, Gareth, thereby earning Gawain's implacable enmity. Arthur must now make war on Lancelot and, pressed by Gawain, repeats his siege even after Guinevere is returned to him. Arthur thus besieges Lancelot in his French domain, leaving Mordred as regent.*]

The Day of Destiny[1]

As Sir Mordred was ruler of all England, he let make° letters as *commissioned* though that they had come from beyond the sea, and the letters specified that King Arthur was slain in battle with Sir Lancelot. Wherefore Sir Mordred made a parliament, and called the lords together, and there he made them to choose him king. And so was he crowned at Canterbury, and held a feast there fifteen days.

And afterward he drew him unto Winchester, and there he took Queen Guinevere, and said plainly that he would wed her (which was his uncle's wife and his father's wife). And so he made ready for the feast, and a day prefixed that they should be wedded; wherefore Queen Guinevere was passing heavy,° but spake fair, and *sad* agreed to Sir Mordred's will.

And anon she desired of Sir Mordred to go to London to buy all manner things that longed to the bridal. And because of her fair speech Sir Mordred trusted her and gave her leave; and so when she came to London she took the Tower of London and suddenly in all haste possible she stuffed it with all manner of victual, and well garnished° it with men, and so kept it. *garrisoned*

And when Sir Mordred wist this he was passing wroth out of measure. And short tale to make, he laid a mighty siege about the Tower and made many assaults, and threw engines° unto them, and *siege machines* shot great guns. But all might not prevail, for Queen Guinevere would never, for fair speech neither for foul, never to trust unto Sir Mordred to come in his hands again.

Then came the Bishop of Canterbury, which was a noble clerk and an holy man, and thus he said unto Sir Mordred:

"Sir, what will ye do? Will you first displease God and sithen° *then* shame yourself and all knighthood? For is not King Arthur your uncle, and no farther but your mother's brother, and upon her he himself begat you, upon his own sister? Therefore how may you wed your own father's wife? And therefore, sir," said the Bishop, "leave this opinion,° other else I shall curse you with book, bell and *intention* candle."

"Do thou thy worst," said Sir Mordred, "and I defy thee!"

---

1. From the section titled *The Most Piteous Tale of the Morte Arthur Saunz Guerdon*, in *King Arthur and His Knights*, ed. Eugène Vinaver (1975).

"Sir," said the Bishop, "and wit you well I shall not fear me to do that me ought to do. And also ye noise° that my lord Arthur is slain, and that is not so, and therefore ye will make a foul work in this land!"   *spread rumors*

"Peace, thou false priest!" said Sir Mordred, "for an thou chafe° me any more, I shall strike off thy head."   *anger*

So the Bishop departed, and did the cursing in the most orgulust° wise that might be done. And then Sir Mordred sought the Bishop of Canterbury for to have slain him. Then the Bishop fled, and took part of his goods with him, and went nigh unto Glastonbury. And there he was a priest-hermit in a chapel, and lived in poverty and in holy prayers; for well he understood that mischievous war was at hand.   *defiant*

Then Sir Mordred sought upon Queen Guinevere by letters and sonds,° and by fair means and foul means, to have her to come out of the Tower of London; but all this availed nought, for she answered him shortly, openly and privily,[2] that she had liefer° slay herself than be married with him.   *messengers*   *rather*

Then came there word unto Sir Mordred that King Arthur had araised the siege from Sir Lancelot and was coming homeward with a great host to be avenged upon Sir Mordred; wherefore Sir Mordred made write writs° unto all the barony of this land, and much people drew unto him. For then was the common voice among them that with King Arthur was never other life but war and strife, and with Sir Mordred was great joy and bliss. Thus was King Arthur depraved° and evil said of; and many there were that King Arthur had brought up of nought, and given them lands, that might not then say him a good word.   *summonses*   *disparaged*

Lo ye Englishmen, see ye not what a mischief° here was? For he that was the most kind and noblest knight of the world, and most loved the fellowship of noble knights, and by him they all were upholden, and yet might not these Englishmen hold them content with him. Lo thus was the old custom and the usages of this land, and men say that we of this land have not yet lost that custom. Alas! this is a great default of us Englishmen, for there may no thing us please no term.°   *evil*   *length of time*

And so fared the people at that time: they were better pleased with Sir Mordred than they were with the noble King Arthur, and much people drew unto Sir Mordred and said they would abide with him for better and for worse. And so Sir Mordred drew with a great host to Dover, for there he heard say that King Arthur would arrive, and so he thought to beat his own father from his own lands. And the most party of all England held with Sir Mordred, for the people were so new-fangle.°   *fond of new things*

And so as Sir Mordred was at Dover with his host, so came King Arthur with a great navy of ships and galleys and carracks, and there was Sir Mordred ready awaiting upon his landing, to let° his own father to land° upon the land that he was king over.   *stop*   *from landing*

2. At once, publicly and privately.

Then there was launching of great boats and small, and full of noble men of arms; and there was much slaughter of gentle knights, and many a full bold baron was laid full low, on both parties. But King Arthur was so courageous that there might no manner of knight let him to land, and his knights fiercely followed him. And so they landed maugre° Sir Mordred's head° and all his power, and put Sir Mordred aback, that he fled and all his people.

against / will

So when this battle was done King Arthur let search his people³ that were hurt and dead. And then was noble Sir Gawain found in a great boat, lying more than half dead. When King Arthur knew that he was laid so low he went unto him and so found him. And there the king made great sorrow out of measure, and took Sir Gawain in his arms, and thrice he there swooned. And then when he was waked, King Arthur said,

"Alas! Sir Gawain, my sister son, here now thou liest, the man in the world that I loved most. And now is my joy gone! For now, my nephew, Sir Gawain, I will discover me unto° you, that in your person and in Sir Lancelot I most had my joy and my affiance.° And now have I lost my joy of you both, wherefore all mine earthly joy is gone from me!"

disclose

trust

"Ah, mine uncle," said Sir Gawain, "now I will that ye wit that my death-days be come! And all I may wite° mine own hastiness° and my wilfulness, for through my wilfulness I was causer of mine own death; for I was this day hurt and smitten upon mine old wound that Sir Lancelot gave me, and I feel myself that I must needs be dead by the hour of noon. And through me and my pride ye have all this shame and disease,° for had that noble knight, Sir Lancelot, been with you, as he was and would have been, this unhappy war had never been begun; for he, through his noble knighthood and his noble blood, held all your cankered° enemies in subjection and danger.° And now," said Sir Gawain, "ye shall miss Sir Lancelot. But alas that I would not accord° with him! And therefore, fair uncle, I pray you that I may have paper, pen and ink, that I may write unto Sir Lancelot a letter written with mine own hand."

blame / rashness

sorrow

malignant
control
make peace

So when paper, pen and ink was brought, then Sir Gawain was set up weakly° by King Arthur, for he was shriven a little afore. And then he took his pen and wrote thus, as the French book maketh mention:

gently

"Unto thee, Sir Lancelot, flower of all noble knights that ever I heard of or saw by my days, I, Sir Gawain, King Lot's son of Orkney, and sister's son unto the noble King Arthur, send thee greeting, letting thee to have knowledge that the tenth day of May I was smitten upon the old wound that thou gave me afore the city of Benwick, and through that wound I am come to my death-day. And I will that all the world wit that I, Sir Gawain, knight of the Table Round, sought my death, and not through thy deserving, but mine own seeking. Wherefore I beseech thee, Sir Lancelot, to return again unto this realm and see my tomb and pray some prayer more

---

3. Had his people searched for.

other less for my soul. And this same day that I wrote the same cedle° I was hurt to the death, which wound was first given of thine hand, Sir Lancelot; for of a more nobler man might I not be slain.   *letter*

"Also, Sir Lancelot, for all the love that ever was betwixt us, make no tarrying, but come over the sea in all the goodly haste that ye may, with your noble knights, and rescue that noble king that made thee knight, for he is full straitly bestead with° a false traitor which is my half-brother, Sir Mordred. For he hath crowned himself king and would have wedded my lady, Queen Guinevere; and so had he done, had she not kept the Tower of London with strong hand. And so the tenth day of May last past my lord King Arthur and we all landed upon them at Dover, and there he put that false traitor, Sir Mordred, to flight. And so it misfortuned me to be smitten upon the stroke that ye gave me of old.   *hard-pressed by*

"And the date of this letter was written but two hours and a half before my death, written with mine own hand and subscribed with part of my heart blood. And therefore I require thee, most famous knight of the world, that thou wilt see my tomb."

And then he wept and King Arthur both, and swooned. And when they were awaked both, the king made Sir Gawain to receive his sacrament, and then Sir Gawain prayed the king for to send for Sir Lancelot and to cherish him above all other knights.

And so at the hour of noon Sir Gawain yielded up the ghost. And then the king let inter him° in a chapel within Dover Castle. And there yet all men may see the skull of him, and the same wound is seen that Sir Lancelot gave in battle.   *had him buried*

Then was it told the king that Sir Mordred had pight a new field upon Barham Down.[4] And so upon the morn King Arthur rode thither to him, and there was a great battle betwixt them, and much people were slain on both parties. But at the last King Arthur's party stood best, and Sir Mordred and his party fled unto Canterbury.

And there the king let search all the downs for his knights that were slain and interred them; and salved them with soft salves° that full sore were wounded. Then much people drew unto King Arthur, and then they said that Sir Mordred warred upon King Arthur with wrong.   *ointments*

And anon King Arthur drew him with his host down by the seaside westward, toward Salisbury. And there was a day assigned betwixt King Arthur and Sir Mordred, that they should meet upon a down beside Salisbury, and not far from the seaside. And this day was assigned on Monday after Trinity Sunday, whereof King Arthur was passing glad that he might be avenged upon Sir Mordred.

Then Sir Mordred araised much people about London, for they of Kent, Sussex and Surrey, Essex, Suffolk and Norfolk held the most party with Sir Mordred. And many a full noble knight drew unto him and also to the king; but they that loved Sir Lancelot drew unto Sir Mordred.

4. Set up a new battleground at Barham Down (southeast of Canterbury).

So upon Trinity Sunday at night King Arthur dreamed a wonderful dream, and in his dream him seemed that he saw upon a chaf-
flet° a chair, and the chair was fast to a wheel, and thereupon sat   *platform*
King Arthur in the richest cloth of gold that might be made. And
the king thought there was under him, far from him, an hideous
deep black water, and therein was all manner of serpents and
worms° and wild beasts, foul and horrible. And suddenly the king   *dragons*
thought that the wheel turned up-so-down, and he fell among the
serpents, and every beast took him by a limb. And then the king
cried as he lay in his bed, "Help! help!"

And then knights, squires and yeomen awaked the king, and
then he was so amazed that he wist not where he was. And then so
he awaked until it was nigh day, and then he fell on slumbering
again, not sleeping nor thoroughly waking. So° the king seemed   *to*
verily that there came Sir Gawain unto him with a number of fair
ladies with him. So when King Arthur saw him he said,

"Welcome, my sister's son, I weened° ye had been dead. And now   *thought*
I see thee on live, much am I beholden unto Almighty Jesu. Ah, fair
nephew, what been these ladies that hither be come with you?"

"Sir," said Sir Gawain, "all these be ladies for whom I have
foughten for, when I was man living. And all these are those that I
did battle for in righteous quarrels, and God hath given them that
grace at their great prayer, because I did battle for them for their
right, that they should bring me hither unto you. Thus much hath
given me leave God for to warn you of your death: for an ye fight as
to-morn with Sir Mordred, as ye both have assigned, doubt ye not
ye shall be slain, and the most party of your people on both parties.
And for the great grace and goodness that Almighty Jesu hath unto
you, and for pity of you and many more other good men there shall
be slain, God hath sent me to you of His especial grace to give you
warning that in no wise ye do battle as to-morn, but that ye take a
treatise for a month-day.[5] And proffer you largely,° so that to-morn   *generously*
ye put in a delay. For within a month shall come Sir Lancelot with
all his noble knights, and rescue you worshipfully, and slay Sir
Mordred and all that ever will hold with him."

Then Sir Gawain and all the ladies vanished, and anon the king
called upon his knights, squires, and yeomen, and charged° them   *ordered*
mightly to fetch his noble lords and wise bishops unto him. And when
they were come the king told them of his avision: that Sir Gawain had
told him and warned him that an he fought on the morn he should be
slain. Then the king commanded Sir Lucan the Butler and his brother
Sir Bedivere the Bold, with two bishops with them, and charged them
in any wise to take a treatise for a month-day with Sir Mordred:

"And spare not, proffer him lands and goods as much as you
think reasonable."

So then they departed and came to Sir Mordred where he had
a grim° host of an hundred thousand. And there they entreated   *fierce*

5. Make a compact for a month from today.

Sir Mordred long time, and at the last Sir Mordred was agreed for
to have Cornwall and Kent by° King Arthur's days;° and after that
all England, after the days of King Arthur. Then were they conde-
scended° that King Arthur and Sir Mordred should meet betwixt
both their hosts, and every each of them should bring fourteen persons. And so they came with this word unto Arthur. Then said he,
 "I am glad that this is done," and so he went into the field.
 And when King Arthur should depart he warned all his host
that an they see any sword drawn, "look ye come on fiercely and
slay that traitor, Sir Mordred, for I in no wise trust him." In like
wise Sir Mordred warned his host that "an ye see any manner of
sword drawn look that ye come on fiercely and so slay all that ever
before you standeth, for in no wise I will not trust for this treatise."
And in the same wise said Sir Mordred unto his host: "for I know
well my father will be avenged upon me."
 And so they met as their pointment was, and were agreed and
accorded thoroughly. And wine was fette,° and they drank together.
Right so came out an adder of a little heath-bush, and it stang a
knight in the foot. And so when the knight felt him so stung, he
looked down and saw the adder; and anon he drew his sword to slay
the adder, and thought none other harm. And when the host on
both parties saw that sword drawn, then they blew beams,° trumpets, and horns, and shouted grimly, and so both hosts dressed them
together.° And King Arthur took his horse and said, "Alas, this unhappy day!" And so rode to his party, and Sir Mordred in like wise.
 And never since was there seen a more dolefuller battle in no
Christian land, for there was but rushing and riding, foining° and
striking, and many a grim word was there spoken of either to other,
and many a deadly stroke. But ever King Arthur rode throughout
the battle° of Sir Mordred many times and did full nobly, as a noble
king should do, and at all times he fainted never. And Sir Mordred
did his devour° that day and put himself in great peril.
 And thus they fought all the long day, and never stinted° till
the noble knights were laid to the cold earth. And ever they fought
still till it was near night, and by then was there an hundred thousand laid dead upon the earth. Then was King Arthur wood wroth°
out of measure, when he saw his people so slain from him.
 And so he looked about him and could see no mo° of all his
host, and good knights left no mo on live but two knights: the tone°
was Sir Lucan de Butler and his brother, Sir Bedivere; and yet they
were full sore wounded.
 "Jesu mercy!" said the king, "where are all my noble knights become? Alas, that ever I should see this doleful day! For now," said
King Arthur, "I am come to mine end. But would to God," said he,
"that I wist now where were that traitor Sir Mordred that hath
caused all this mischief."°
 Then King Arthur looked about and was ware where stood
Sir Mordred leaning upon his sword among a great heap of dead
men.

during / lifetime

agreed

fetched

bugles

*confronted each
other*

thrusting

battle formation

utmost effort
ceased

wild with rage

more
one

evil

"Now, give me my spear," said King Arthur unto Sir Lucan, "for yonder I have espied the traitor that all this woe hath wrought."

"Sir, let him be," said Sir Lucan, "for he is unhappy.° And if ye pass this unhappy day ye shall be right well revenged. And, good lord, remember ye of your night's dream and what the spirit of Sir Gawain told you to-night, and yet God of His great goodness hath preserved you hitherto. And for God's sake, my lord, leave off this, for, blessed be God, ye have won the field: for yet we been here three on live, and with Sir Mordred is not one of live. And therefore if ye leave off now, this wicked day of Destiny is past!"   *unlucky*

"Now tide° me death, tide me life," said the king, "now I see him yonder alone, he shall never escape mine hands! For at a better avail° shall I never have him."   *befall*   *advantage*

"God speed you well!" said Sir Bedivere.

Then the king gat his spear in both his hands, and ran toward Sir Mordred, crying and saying,

"Traitor, now is thy death-day come!"

And when Sir Mordred saw King Arthur he ran until° him with his sword drawn in his hand, and there King Arthur smote Sir Mordred under the shield with a foin° of his spear throughout the body more than a fathom. And when Sir Mordred felt that he had his death wound he thrust himself with the might that he had up to the burr° of King Arthur's spear, and right so he smote his father, King Arthur, with his sword holding in both his hands, upon the side of the head, that the sword pierced the helmet and the tay° of the brain. And therewith Mordred dashed down stark dead to the earth.   *toward*   *thrust*   *hand guard*   *lining*

And noble King Arthur fell in a swough to the earth, and there he swooned oftentimes, and Sir Lucan and Sir Bedivere oftentimes hove° him up. And so weakly° betwixt them they led him to a little chapel not far from the sea, and when the king was there, him thought him reasonably eased.   *lifted / gently*

Then heard they people cry in the field.

"Now go thou, Sir Lucan," said the king, "and do me to wit° what betokens that noise in the field."   *let me know*

So Sir Lucan departed, for he was grievously wounded in many places; and so as he rode he saw and harkened by the moonlight how that pillers° and robbers were come into the field to pille and to rob many a full noble knight of brooches and bees° and of many a good ring and many a rich jewel. And who that were not dead all out, there they slew them for their harness° and their riches.   *plunderers*   *bracelets*   *armor*

When Sir Lucan understood his work he came to the king as soon as he might, and told him all what he had heard and seen.

"Therefore by my rede,"° said Sir Lucan, "it is best that we bring you to some town."   *advice*

"I would it were so," said the king, "but I may not stand, my head works° so. . . . Ah, Sir Lancelot!" said King Arthur, "this day have I sore missed thee! And alas, that ever I was against thee! For now have I my death, whereof Sir Gawain me warned in my dream."   *aches*

Then Sir Lucan took up the king the tone party° and Sir   *on one side*
Bedivere the other party, and in the lifting up the king swooned,
and in the lifting Sir Lucan fell in a swoon, that part of his guts fell
out of his body; and therewith the noble knight his heart brast. And
when the king awoke he beheld Sir Lucan, how he lay foaming at
the mouth and part of his guts lay at his feet.

"Alas," said the king, "this is to me a full heavy sight, to see this
noble duke so die for my sake, for he would have holpen° me that had   *helped*
more need of help than I! Alas, that he would not complain him, for
his heart was so set to help me. Now Jesu have mercy upon his soul!"

Then Sir Bedivere wept for the death of his brother.

"Now leave this mourning and weeping, gentle knight," said
the king, "for all this will not avail° me. For wit thou well an I   *aid*
might live myself, the death of Sir Lucan would grieve me evermore. But my time passeth on fast," said the king. "Therefore," said
King Arthur unto Sir Bedivere, "take thou here Excalibur, my good
sword, and go with it to yonder water's side; and when thou comest
there, I charge thee throw my sword in that water, and come again
and tell me what thou seest there."

"My lord," said Sir Bedivere, "your commandment shall be
done, and lightly° bring you word again."   *I will quickly*

So Sir Bedivere departed. And by the way he beheld that noble
sword, and the pomell° and the haft° was all precious stones. And   *hand guard /*
handle
then he said to himself, "If I throw this rich sword in the water,
thereof shall never come good, but harm and loss." And then Sir
Bedivere hid Excalibur under a tree, and so soon as he might he
came again unto the king and said he had been at the water and
thrown the sword into the water.

"What saw thou there?" said the king.

"Sir," he said, "I saw nothing but waves and winds."

"That is untruly said of thee," said the king. "And therefore go
thou lightly again, and do my commandment as thou art to me lief°   *beloved*
and dear: spare not but throw it in."

Then Sir Bedivere returned again and took the sword in his
hand; and yet him thought sin and shame to throw away that noble
sword. And so eft° he hid the sword and returned again and told the   *again*
king that he had been at the water and done his commandment.

"What sawest thou there?" said the king.

"Sir," he said, "I saw nothing but waters wap° and waves wan."°   *dark / lapping*

"Ah, traitor unto me and untrue," said King Arthur, "now hast
thou betrayed me twice! Who would ween° that thou who has been   *believe*
to me so lief and dear, and also named so noble a knight, that thou
would betray me for the riches of this sword? But now go again
lightly; for thy long tarrying putteth me in great jeopardy of my life,
for I have taken cold. And but if° thou do now as I bid thee, if ever   *unless*
I may see thee, I shall slay thee mine own hands, for thou wouldest
for my rich sword see me dead."

Then Sir Bedivere departed and went to the sword and
lightly took it up, and so he went unto the water's side. And

there he bound the girdle about the hilt, and threw the sword as far into the water as he might. And there came an arm and an hand above the water, and took it and cleight° it, and shook it   *clutched* thrice and brandished, and then vanished with the sword into the water.

So Sir Bedivere came again to the king and told him what he saw.

"Alas!" said the king, "help me hence, for I dread me I have tarried over long."

Then Sir Bedivere took the king upon his back and so went with him to the water's side. And when they were there, even fast by° the bank hoved° a little barge with many fair ladies in it, and   *next to / floated* among them all was a queen, and all they had black hoods. And all they wept and shrieked when they saw King Arthur.

"Now put me into that barge," said the king.

And so he did softly, and there received him three ladies with great mourning. And so they set him down, and in one of their laps King Arthur laid his head. And then the queen said,

"Ah, my dear brother!⁶ Why have you tarried so long from me? Alas, this wound on your head hath caught overmuch cold!"

And anon they rowed fromward° the land, and Sir Bedivere be-   *away from* held all those ladies go fromward him. Then Sir Bedivere cried and said,

"Ah, my lord Arthur, what shall become of me, now ye go from me and leave me here alone among mine enemies?"

"Comfort thyself," said the king, "and do as well as thou mayst, for in me is no trust for to trust in. For I must into the vale of Avalon to heal me of my grievous wound. And if thou hear nevermore of me, pray for my soul!"

But ever the queen and ladies wept and shrieked, that it was pity to hear. And as soon as Sir Bedivere had lost sight of the barge he wept and wailed, and so took° the forest and went all   *went into* that night.

And in the morning he was ware, betwixt two holts hoar,° of   *gray woods* a chapel and an hermitage. Then was Sir Bedivere fain,° and   *glad* thither he went, and when he came into the chapel he saw where lay an hermit grovelling° on all fours, fast thereby a tomb was   *face down /* new graven.° When the hermit saw Sir Bedivere he knew him   *freshly dug* well, for he was but little tofore Bishop of Canterbury, that Sir Mordred fleamed.°   *put to flight*

"Sir," said Sir Bedivere, "what man is there here interred that you pray so fast° for?"   *intently*

"Fair son," said the hermit, "I wot not verily but by deeming.°   *guessing* But this same night, at midnight, here came a number of ladies and brought here a dead corse and prayed me to inter him. And here they offered an hundred tapers, and gave me a thousand besants."°   *gold coins*

---

6. The queen is thus revealed as Morgan le Fay, in whose story magical healing powers mixed with inveterate hostility to Guinevere and sometimes to Arthur himself.

"Alas," said Sir Bedivere, "that was my lord King Arthur, which lieth here graven° in this chapel."   *buried*

Then Sir Bedivere swooned, and when he awoke he prayed the hermit that he might abide with him still, there to live with fasting and prayers:

"For from hence will I never go," said Sir Bedivere, "by my will, but all the days of my life here to pray for my lord Arthur."

"Sir, ye are welcome to me," said the hermit, "for I know you better than ye ween that I do: for ye are Sir Bedivere the Bold, and the full noble duke Sir Lucan de Butler was your brother."

Then Sir Bedivere told the hermit all as you have heard tofore, and so he beleft° with the hermit that was beforehand Bishop of   *remained*
Canterbury. And there Sir Bedivere put upon him poor clothes, and served the hermit full lowly in fasting and in prayers.

Thus of Arthur I find no more written in books that been authorised, neither more of the very certainty of his death heard I never read, but thus was he led away in a ship wherein were three queens; that one was King Arthur's sister, Queen Morgan le Fay, the tother was the Queen of North Galis, and the third was the Queen of the Waste Lands.

Now more of the death of King Arthur could I never find, but that these ladies brought him to his grave, and such one was interred there which the hermit bare witness that sometime° Bishop   *was once*
of Canterbury. But yet the hermit knew not in certain that he was verily the body of King Arthur; for this tale Sir Bedivere, a knight of the Table Round, made it to be written.

Yet some men say in many parts of England that King Arthur is not dead, but had° by the will of our Lord Jesu into another place;   *was carried*
and men say that he shall come again, and he shall win the Holy Cross. Yet I will not say that it shall be so, but rather I would say: here in this world he changed his life. And many men say that there is written upon the tomb this:

HIC IACET ARTHURUS REX QUONDAM REXQUE FUTURUS[7]

And thus leave I here Sir Bedivere with the hermit that dwelled that time in a chapel beside Glastonbury, and there was his hermitage. And so they lived in prayers and fastings and great abstinence.

And when Queen Guinevere understood that King Arthur was dead and all the noble knights, Sir Mordred and all the remnant, then she stole away with five ladies with her, and so she went to Amesbury. And there she let make herself° a nun, and   *became*
weared white clothes and black, and great penance she took upon her, as ever did sinful woman in this land. And never creature could make her merry, but ever she lived in fasting, prayers and alms-deeds, that all manner of people marvelled how virtuously she was changed.

7. Here lies Arthur, once and future king.

RESPONSES

Marion Zimmer Bradley: from The Mists of Avalon
PROLOGUE [1]

MORGAINE SPEAKS . . .

In my time I have been called many things: sister, lover, priestess, wise-woman, queen. Now in truth I have come to be wise-woman, and a time may come when these things may need to be known. But in sober truth, I think it is the Christians who will tell the last tale. For ever the world of Fairy drifts further from the world in which the Christ holds sway. I have no quarrel with the Christ, only with his priests, who call the Great Goddess a demon and deny that she ever held power in this world. At best, they say that her power was of Satan. Or else they clothe her in the blue robe of the Lady of Nazareth—who indeed had power in her way, too—and say that she was ever virgin. But what can a virgin know of the sorrows and travail of mankind?

And now, when the world has changed, and Arthur—my brother, my lover, king who was and king who shall be—lies dead (the common folk say sleeping) in the Holy Isle of Avalon, the tale should be told as it was before the priests of the White Christ came to cover it all with their saints and legends.

For, as I say, the world itself has changed. There was a time when a traveller, if he had the will and knew only a few of the secrets, could send his barge out into the Summer Sea and arrive not at Glastonbury of the monks, but at the Holy Isle of Avalon; for at that time the gates between the worlds drifted within the mists, and were open, one to another, as the traveller thought and willed. For this is the great secret, which was known to all educated men in our day: that by what men think, we create the world around us, daily new.

And now the priests, thinking that this infringes upon the power of their God, who created the world once and for all to be unchanging, have closed those doors (which were never doors, except in the minds of men), and the pathway leads only to the priests' Isle, which they have safeguarded with the sound of their church bells, driving away all thoughts of another world lying in the darkness. Indeed, they say that world, if it indeed exists, is the property of Satan, and the doorway to Hell, if not Hell itself.

I do not know what their God may or may not have created. In spite of the tales that are told, I never knew much about their priests and never wore the black of one of their slave-nuns. If those at Arthur's court at Camelot chose to think me so when I came there (since I always wore the dark robes of the Great Mother in her guise as wise-woman), I did not undeceive them. And indeed, toward the end of Arthur's reign it would have been dangerous to do so, and I bowed my head to expediency as my great mistress would never have done: Viviane, Lady of the Lake, once Arthur's greatest friend, save for myself, and then his darkest enemy—again, save for myself.

But the strife is over; I could greet Arthur at last, when he lay dying, not as my enemy and the enemy of my Goddess, but only as my brother, and as a dying man in need of the

---

1. The continuing appeal of the Arthurian tradition is reflected in its many retellings since the Middle Ages, and especially its revival in the nineteenth and twentieth centuries. Each era has been able to find a setting for its own fears and aspirations in the ambitions, accomplishments, and final tragedies of Arthur's court. Working in the first wave of the women's movement, Marion Zimmer Bradley (1930–1999) was a hugely productive writer of science fiction and fantasy literature. She created her most popular work, The Mists of Avalon (1982), by returning to these ancient legends, and reimagining the great events of Arthur's career in the perspectives and voices of Arthurian women, especially Morgan le Fay and Guinevere. Medieval Arthurian legends often include bonds among men that verge on the erotic, an idea Bradley makes explicit in her version of Lancelot; she also imagines lesbian attraction among the legends' women. What she shares with her predecessors, as in the Prologue included here, is a strongly elegiac tone for worlds inevitably passing. The world Bradley's Morgaine most laments is a somewhat vaguely imagined Celtic matriarchy, perhaps as laden with fantasy as were the medieval regrets for a lost, idealized chivalry.

Mother's aid, where all men come at last. Even the priests know this, with their ever-virgin Mary in her blue robe; for she too becomes the World Mother in the hour of death.

And so Arthur lay at last with his head in my lap, seeing in me neither sister nor lover nor foe, but only wise-woman, priestess, Lady of the Lake; and so rested upon the breast of the Great Mother from whom he came to birth and to whom at last, as all men, he must go. And perhaps, as I guided the barge which bore him away, not this time to the Isle of the Priests, but to the true Holy Isle in the dark world behind our own, that Island of Avalon where, now, few but I could go, he repented the enmity that had come between us.

AS I TELL THIS TALE I will speak at times of things which befell when I was too young to understand them, or of things which befell when I was not by; and my hearer will draw away, perhaps, and say: This is her magic. But I have always held the gift of the Sight, and of looking within the minds of men and women; and in all this time I have been close to all of them. And so, at times, all that they thought was known to me in one way or another. And so I will tell this tale.

For one day the priests too will tell it, as it was known to them. Perhaps between the two, some glimmering of the truth may be seen.

For this is the thing the priests do not know, with their One God and One Truth: that there is no such thing as a true tale. Truth has many faces and the truth is like to the old road to Avalon; it depends on your own will, and your own thoughts, whither the road will take you, and whether, at the end, you arrive in the Holy Isle of Eternity or among the priests with their bells and their death and their Satan and Hell and damnation . . . but perhaps I am unjust even to them. Even the Lady of the Lake, who hated a priest's robe as she would have hated a poisonous viper, and with good cause too, chid me once for speaking evil of their God.

"For all the Gods are one God," she said to me then, as she had said many times before, and as I have said to my own novices many times, and as every priestess who comes after me will say again, "and all the Goddesses are one Goddess, and there is only one Initiator. And to every man his own truth, and the God within."

And so, perhaps, the truth winds somewhere between the road to Glastonbury, Isle of the Priests, and the road to Avalon, lost forever in the mists of the Summer Sea.

But this is my truth; I who am Morgaine tell you these things, Morgaine who was in later days called Morgan le Fay.

Graham Chapman, John Cleese, Terry Gilliam, Eric Idle, Terry Jones, and Michael Palin: scene from *Monty Python and the Holy Grail*[1]

ARTHUR AND THE PEASANTS

[Exterior. Day.]

ARTHUR and PATSY riding. They stop and look. We see a castle in the distance, and before it a PEASANT is working away on his knees trying to dig the earth with his bare hands and a twig. ARTHUR and PATSY ride up, and stop before the PEASANT.

1. If Marion Zimmer Bradley honors a lost Arthurian past of powerful women, the Pythons hilariously skewer every sentimental Arthurian piety they can put their hands on. First released in 1975, their film *Monty Python and the Holy Grail* elaborates the skit comedy they had developed in the Monty Python's Flying Circus series on the BBC. In a loosely strung series of episodes, many recognizable from Malory and Tennyson, the movie deflates notions of the divine right of kings, chivalric bravery (the knights don't even have horses, only the sound effect of coconut halves), elevated love, and Camelot itself ("it is a silly place"). In the brilliant episode here, King Arthur's airy rhetoric of his elevation to the throne meets up with a band of dismissive Marxists whose own self-importance is equally parodied. All the Pythons are credited for the screenplay and all appear in the film, some in multiple roles: John Cleese, Graham Chapman, Terry Gilliam, Eric Idle, Terry Jones, and Michael Palin.

ARTHUR: Old woman!

DENNIS [*turning*]: Man.

ARTHUR: Man. I'm sorry. Old man, what knight lives in that castle?

DENNIS: I'm thirty-seven.

ARTHUR: What?

DENNIS: I'm only thirty-seven . . . I'm not *old*.

ARTHUR: Well—I can't just say: "Hey, Man!"

DENNIS: You could say: "Dennis."

ARTHUR: I didn't know you were called Dennis.

DENNIS: You didn't bother to find out, did you?

ARTHUR: I've said I'm sorry about the old woman, but from behind you looked . . .

DENNIS: What I object to is that you automatically treat me as an inferior . . .

ARTHUR: Well . . . I *am* King.

DENNIS: Oh, very nice. King, eh! I expect you've got a palace and fine clothes and courtiers and plenty of food. And how d'you get that? By exploiting the workers! By hanging on to outdated imperialistic dogma, which perpetuates the social and economic differences in our society! If there's *ever* going to be any progress . . .

   [*An* OLD WOMAN *appears.*]

OLD WOMAN: Dennis! There's some lovely filth down here . . . Oh! How d'you do?

ARTHUR: How d'you do, good lady . . . I am Arthur, King of the Britons . . . can you tell me who lives in that castle?

OLD WOMAN: King of the *who*?

ARTHUR: The Britons.

OLD WOMAN: Who are the Britons?

ARTHUR: All of us . . . we are all Britons.

   [DENNIS *winks at the* OLD WOMAN.]

ARTHUR: . . . And I am your King . . .

OLD WOMAN: Ooooh! I didn't know we had a king. I thought we were an autonomous collective . . .

DENNIS: You're fooling yourself. We're living in a dictatorship, a self-perpetuating autocracy in which the working classes . . .

OLD WOMAN: There you are, bringing class into it again . . .

DENNIS: That's what it's all about . . . If only—

ARTHUR: Please, please, good people, I am in haste. What knight lives in that castle?

OLD WOMAN: No one lives there.

ARTHUR: Well, who is your lord?

OLD WOMAN: We don't have a lord.

ARTHUR: What?

DENNIS: I told you, we're an anarcho-syndicalist commune, we take it in turns to act as a sort of executive officer for the week.

ARTHUR: Yes . . .

DENNIS: . . . But all the decisions of that officer . . .

ARTHUR: Yes, I see.

DENNIS: . . . must be approved at a bi-weekly meeting by a simple majority in the case of purely internal affairs.

ARTHUR: Be quiet.

DENNIS: . . . But a two-thirds majority . . .

ARTHUR: Be quiet! I order you to shut up.

OLD WOMAN: Order, eh? Who does he think he is?

Still of Arthur and his servant Patsy from *Monty Python and the Holy Grail*, the 1975 film directed by Terry Gilliam and Terry Jones and written and performed by the British comic troupe Monty Python's Flying Circus.

ARTHUR: I am your King.

OLD WOMAN: Well, I didn't vote for you.

ARTHUR: You don't vote for kings.

OLD WOMAN: Well, how did you become King, then?

ARTHUR: The Lady of the Lake, her arm clad in purest shimmering samite, held Excalibur aloft from the bosom of the waters to signify that by Divine Providence . . . I, Arthur, was to carry Excalibur . . . that is why I am your King.

DENNIS: Look, strange women lying on their backs in ponds handing over swords . . . that's no basis for a system of government. Supreme executive power derives from a mandate from the masses not from some farcical aquatic ceremony.

ARTHUR: Be quiet!

DENNIS: You can't expect to wield supreme executive power just because some watery tart threw a sword at you.

ARTHUR: Shut up!

DENNIS: I mean, if I went round saying I was an emperor because some moistened bint[2] had lobbed a scimitar at *me*, people would put me away.

ARTHUR [*grabbing him by the collar*]: Shut up, will you. Shut up!

DENNIS: Ah! *Now* ... we see the violence inherent in the system.

ARTHUR: Shut up!

　　[PEOPLE (*i.e. other* PEASANTS) *are appearing and watching.*]

DENNIS [*calling*]: Come and see the violence inherent in the system. Help, help, I'm being repressed!

2. Derogatory slang for a woman.

ARTHUR [*aware that people are now coming out and watching*]: Bloody peasant! [*Pushes*
   DENNIS *over into the mud and prepares to ride off.*]
DENNIS: Oooooh! Did you hear that! What a give-away.
ARTHUR: Come on, Patsy.
   [*They ride off.*]
DENNIS [*in background as we pull out*]: Did you see him repressing me, then? That's
   what I've been on about . . .

∽◈∾

⊷ ⩺◆⩹ ⊶

Geoffrey Chaucer
c. 1340–1400

On Easter weekend 1300, the Italian poet Dante Alighieri had a vision in which he descended to hell, climbed painfully through purgatory, and then attained a transcendent experience of paradise. He tells his tale in his visionary, passionately judgmental *Divine Comedy*.
One hundred years later, on 25 October 1400, Geoffrey Chaucer—the least judgmental of
poets—died quietly in his house at the outskirts of London. By a nice accident of history,
these two great writers bracket the last great century of the Middle Ages.

Of Chaucer's own life our information is abundant but often frustrating. Many documents
record the important and sensitive posts he held in government, but there are only faint hints of
his career as a poet. During his lifetime, he was frequently in France and made at least two trips to
Italy, which proved crucial for his own growth as a writer and indeed for the history of English literature. He also served under three kings: the aging Edward III, his brilliant and sometimes tyran-
nical grandson Richard II, and—at the very end of his life—Richard's usurper Henry IV.

Chaucer was born into a rising mercantile family, part of the growing bourgeois class that
brought so much wealth to England even while it disrupted medieval theories of social order.
Chaucer's family fit nowhere easily in the old model of the three estates: those who pray (the
clergy), those who fight (the aristocracy), and those who work the land (the peasants). Yet
like many of their class, they aspired to a role among the aristocracy, and in fact Chaucer's
parents succeeded in holding minor court positions. Chaucer himself became a major player
in the cultural and bureaucratic life of the court, and Thomas Chaucer (who was very probably his son) was ultimately knighted.

Geoffrey was superbly but typically educated. He probably went to one of London's fine
grammar schools, and as a young man he very likely followed a gentlemanly study of law at one of
the Inns of Court. He shows signs of knowing and appreciating the topics debated in the university life of his time. His poems reflect a vast reading in classical Latin, French, and Italian (of
which he was among the earliest English readers). *The Parliament of Fowls*, for instance, reveals
the influence not only of French court poetry but also of Dante's *Divine Comedy*; and the frame-
story structure of *The Canterbury Tales* may have been inspired by Boccaccio's *Decameron*.

By 1366 Chaucer had married Philippa de Roet, a minor Flemish noblewoman, and a
considerable step up the social hierarchy. Her sister later became the mistress and ultimately
the wife of Chaucer's great patron, John of Gaunt. Thus, when Gaunt's son Henry Boling-
broke seized the throne from Richard II, the elderly Geoffrey Chaucer found himself a distant
in-law of his king. Chaucer had been associated with Richard II and suffered reverses when
Richard's power was restricted by the magnates. But he was enough of a cultural figure that
Henry IV continued (perhaps with some prompting) the old man's royal annuities. Whatever
Western literature owes to Chaucer (and its debts are profound), in his own life his writing
made a place in the world for him and his heirs.

Despite his lifelong productivity as a writer, and despite the slightly obtuse narrative voice he consistently uses, Geoffrey Chaucer was a canny and ambitious player in the world of his time. He was a soldier, courtier, diplomat, and government official in a wide range of jobs. These included controller of the customs on wool and other animal products, a lucrative post, and later controller of the Petty Custom that taxed wine and other goods. Chaucer's frequent work overseas extended his contacts with French and Italian literature. He was ward of estates for several minors, a job that also benefited the guardian. Chaucer began to accumulate property in Kent, where he served as justice of the peace (an important judicial post) and then Member of Parliament in the mid-1380s.

Despite the comfortable worldly progress suggested by such activities, these were troubled years in the nation and in Chaucer's private life. Chaucer's personal fortunes were affected by the frequent struggles between King Richard and his magnates over control of the government. From another direction there exploded the Rising of 1381 (see pages 468–80), rocking all of English society. The year before that, Chaucer had been accused of *raptus* by Cecilia Chaumpaigne, daughter of a baker in London. A great deal of nervous scholarship has been exercised over this case, but it becomes increasingly clear that in legal language *raptus* meant some form of rape. The case was settled, and there are signs of efforts to hush it up at quite high levels of government. The somewhat bland and bumbling quality of Chaucer's narrative persona would probably have seemed more artificially constructed and more ironic to Chaucer's contemporaries than it does at first glance today.

Chaucer was a Janus-faced poet, truly innovative at the levels of language and theme yet deeply involved with literary and intellectual styles that stretched back to Latin antiquity and twelfth- and thirteenth-century France. His early poems—the dream visions such as *The Parliament of Fowls* and the tragic romance *Troilus and Criseyde*—derive from essentially medieval genres and continental traditions: the French poets Deschamps and Machaut and the Italians Dante, Boccaccio, and Petrarch. Yet in his reliance on the English vernacular, Chaucer was in a vanguard generation along with the *Gawain* poet and William Langland. English was indeed gaining importance in other parts of this world, such as in Parliament, some areas of education, and in the "Wycliffite" translations of the Bible. Chaucer's own exclusive use of English was particularly ambitious, though, for a poet whose patronage came from the court of the francophile Richard II.

The major work of Chaucer's maturity, *The Canterbury Tales*, founds an indisputably English tradition. While he still uses the craft and allusions he learned from his continental masters, he also experiments with the subject matter of everyday English life and the vocabularies of the newly valorized English vernacular. Moreover, starting with traditional forms and largely traditional models of society and the cosmos, Chaucer found spaces for new and sometimes disruptive perspectives, especially those of women and the rising mercantile class into which he had been born. Though always a court poet, Chaucer increasingly wrote in ways that reflected both the richness and the uncertainties of his entire social world. The *Tales* include a Knight who could have stepped from a twelfth-century heroic poem; yet they also offer the spectacle of the Knight's caste being aped, almost parodied, and virtually shouted down by a sword-carrying peasant, the Miller. And the entire notion of old writings as sources of authoritative wisdom is powerfully challenged by the illiterate or only minimally literate Wife of Bath.

The Canterbury Tales also differ from the work of many of Chaucer's continental predecessors in their deep hesitation to cast straightforward judgment, either socially or spiritually. Here we may return to Chaucer's connection with Dante. His *Divine Comedy* presented mortal life as a pilgrimage and an overt test in stable dogma, a journey along a dangerous road toward certain damnation or the reward of the heavenly Jerusalem. *The Canterbury Tales* are literally about a pilgrimage, and Chaucer presents the road as beautiful and fascinating in its own right. The greatness of the poem lies in its exploration of the variousness of the journey and that journey's reflection of a world pressured by spiritual and moral fractures. In depicting a mixed company of English men and women traveling England's most famous pilgrimage route and telling one

Portrait of Geoffrey the Canterbury Pilgrim, from the Ellesmere manuscript of *The Canterbury Tales*, early 15th century. This carefully produced and beautifully decorated manuscript reflects the speed with which Chaucer's works took on wide cultural prestige and were enshrined in luxury books for a wealthy, probably aristocratic audience.

another stories, Chaucer suggests not only the spiritual meaning of humankind's earthly pilgrimage, but also its overflowing beauties and attractions as well as the evils and temptations that lie along the way. The vision of the serious future, the day of judgment, is constantly attended in *The Canterbury Tales* by the troubling yet hilarious and distracting present.

Unlike Dante, however, Chaucer almost never takes it upon himself to judge, at least not openly. He records his characters with dizzying immediacy, but he never tells his reader quite what to think of them, leaving the gaps for us as readers to fill. He does end the *Tales* with a kind of sermon, the Parson's long prose treatise on the Christian vices and virtues. That coda by no means erases the humor and seriousness, sentiment and ribaldry, high spiritual love and unmasked carnal desire, profound religious belief and squalid clerical corruption that have been encountered along the way. Indeed, Chaucer's genius is to transmute the disorder of his world almost into an aesthetic of plenitude: "foyson" in Middle English. His poem overflows constantly with rich detail, from exquisite visions to squabbling pilgrims. His language overflows with its multiple vocabularies, Anglo-Saxon, Latin, and French. And finally, the tales themselves are notable for the range of genres used by the pilgrims: the Miller's bawdy fabliau, the Wife of Bath's romance, the Franklin's story of courtly love and clerkly magic, the Nun's Priest's beast fable, the Pardoner's hypocritical cautionary tale, as well as the Parson's sermon. *The Canterbury Tales* are an anthology embracing almost every important literary type of Chaucer's day.

None of this celebratory richness, however, fully masks the unresolved social and spiritual tensions that underlie the *Tales*. The notion of spiritual pilgrimage is deeply challenged by the very density of characterization and worldly detail that so enlivens the work. And the model of a competitive game, which provides the fictional pretext for the tales themselves, is only one version of what the critic Peggy Knapp has called Chaucer's "social contest" in the work as a whole. The traditional estates such as knight and peasant openly clash during the pilgrimage, and the estate of the clergy is more widely represented by its corrupt than by its virtuous members. Women, merchants, common landowners, and others from outside the traditional three estates bulk large in the tales. And their stories cast doubt upon such fundamental religious institutions as penance and such social institutions as marriage. For all their pleasures, *The Canterbury Tales* have survived, in part, because they are so riven by challenge and doubt.

 For additional resources on Chaucer, including the *Parliament of Fowles* and the *The Franklin's Tale*, go to *The Longman Anthology of British Literature* Web site at www.myliteraturekit.com.

CHAUCER'S MIDDLE ENGLISH

Grammar

The English of Chaucer's London, and particularly the English of government bureaucracy, became the source for the more standardized vernacular that emerged in the era of print at the close of the Middle Ages. As a result, Chaucer's English is easier to understand today than the dialect of many of his great contemporaries such as the *Gawain* poet, who worked far to the north. The text that follows preserves Chaucer's language, with some spellings slightly modernized and regularized by its editor, E. Talbot Donaldson. To help beginners, we include David Wright's fine translation of the General Prologue on facing pages with the original text.

The marginal glosses in the readings are intended to help the nonspecialist reader through Chaucer's language without elaborate prior study. It will be helpful, though, to explain a few key differences from Modern English.

Nouns: The possessive is sometimes formed without a final -*s*.

Pronouns: Readers will recognize the archaic *thou, thine, thee* of second-person singular, and *ye* of the plural. Occasional confusion can arise from the form *hir*, which can mean "her" or "their." *Hem* is Chaucer's spelling for "them," and *tho* for "those." Chaucer uses *who* to mean "whoever."

Adverbs: Formed, as today, with -*ly*, but also with -*liche*. Sometimes an adverb is unchanged from its adjective form: *fairly, fairliche, faire* can all be adverbs.

Verbs: Second-person singular is formed with -*est* (*thou lovest*, past tense *thou lovedest*); third-person singular often with -*eth* (*he loveth*); plurals often with -*n* (*we loven*); and infinitive with -*n* (*loven*).

Strong verbs/impersonal verbs: Middle English has many "strong verbs," which form the past and perfect by changing a vowel in their stem; these are usually recognizable by analogy with surviving forms in Modern English (*go, went, gone; sing, sang, sung;* etc.). Middle English also often uses "impersonal verbs" (*liketh*, "it pleases"; *as me thinketh*, "as I think"), in which case sometimes no obvious subject noun or pronoun occurs.

Pronunciation

A few guidelines will help approximate the sound of Chaucer's English and the richness of his versification. For fuller discussion, consult sources listed in the bibliography.

Pronounce all consonants: *knight* is "k/neecht" with a guttural *ch*, not "nite"; *gnaw* is "g/naw." Middle English consonants preserve many of the sounds of the language's Germanic roots: guttural *gh*; sounded *l* and *w* in words like *folk* or *write*. (Exceptions occur in some words that derive from French, like *honour* whose *h* is silent.)

Final -*e* was sounded in early Middle English. Such pronunciation was becoming archaic by Chaucer's time, but was available to aid meter in the stylized context of poetry.

The distinction between short and long vowels was greater in Middle English than today. Middle English short vowels have mostly remained short in Modern English, with some shift in pronunciation: short *a* sounds like the *o* in *hot*, short *o* like a quick version of the *aw* in *law*, short *u* like the *u* in *full*.

Long vowels in Middle English (here usually indicated by doubling, when vowel length is unclear by analogy to modern spelling) are close to long vowels in modern Romance languages. The chart shows some differences in Middle English long vowels.

Middle English	pronounced as in	Modern English
a (as in *name*)		*father*
open e (*deel*)		*swear, bread*
close e (*sweet*)		*fame*
i (*whit*)		*feet*
open o (*holy*)		*law*
close o (*roote*)		*note*
u (as in *town, aboute*)		*root*
u (*vertu*)		*few*

Open and close long vowels are a challenge for modern readers. Generally, open long *e* in Middle English (*deel*) has become Modern English spelling with *ea* (*deal*); close long *e* (*sweet*) has become Modern English spelling with *ee* (*sweet*). Open long *o* in Middle English has come to be pronounced as in *note*; close long *o* in Middle English has come to be pronounced *root*. This latter case illustrates the idea of "vowel shift" across the centuries, in which some long vowels have moved forward in the throat and palate.

Versification

All of Chaucer's poetry presented here is in a loosely iambic pentameter line, which Chaucer was greatly responsible for bringing into prominence in England. He is a fluid versifier, though, and often shifts stress, producing metrical effects that have come to be called trochees and spondees. Final -*e* is often pronounced within lines to provide an unstressed syllable and is typically pronounced at the end of each line. Yet final -*e* may also elide with a following word that begins with a vowel. The following lines from *The Nun's Priest's Tale* have a proposed scansion, but the reader will see that alternate scansions are possible at several places.

> "Avoi," quod she, "fy on you, hertelees!
> Allas," quod she, "for by that God above,
> Now han ye lost myn herte and al my love!
> I can nat love a coward, by my faith.
> For certes, what so any womman saith,
> We alle desiren, if it mighte be,
> To han housbondes hardy, wise, and free,
> And secree, and no nigard, ne no fool,
> Ne him that is agast of every tool,
> Ne noon avauntour. By that God above,
> How dorste ye sayn for shame unto youre love
> That any thing mighte make you aferd?
> Have ye no mannes herte and han a beerd?

from THE CANTERBURY TALES

THE GENERAL PROLOGUE   The twenty-nine "sondry folke" of the Canterbury company gather at the Tabard Inn, ostensibly with the pious intent of making a pilgrimage to England's holiest shrine, the tomb of Saint Thomas Becket at

Canterbury. From the start in the raffish and worldly London suburb of Southwark, though, the pilgrims' attentions and energy veer wildly between the sacred and the profane. The mild story-telling competition proposed by the Host also slides swiftly into a contest among social classes. Set in Chaucer's own time and place, *The Canterbury Tales* reflect both the dynamism and the uncertainties of a society still nostalgic for archaic models of church and state, yet riven by such crises as plague, economic disruption, and the new claims of peasants and mercantile bourgeoisie—claims expressed and repressed most violently in the recent Rising, or "Peasants' Revolt," of 1381.

Chaucer's *Prologue* has roots in the genre known as "estates satire." Such writings criticized the failure of the members of the three traditional "estates" of medieval society—the aristocracy, the clergy, and the peasants—to fulfill their ordained function of fighting, praying, and working the land, respectively. From the beginning the pilgrims' portraits are couched in language fraught with class connotations. The Knight, the idealized (if archaic) representative of the aristocracy, is called *gentil* (that is, "noble, aristocratic") and is said never to have uttered any *vileynye*—speech characteristic of peasants or *villeyns*. Many of the pilgrims in the other two estates display aristocratic manners, among the clergy notably the Prioress, with her "cheere of court," and the Monk, who lives like a country gentleman, hunting with greyhounds and a stable full of fine horses. Both pilgrims contrast with the ideal of their estate, the Parson, who, though "*povre*" is "rich" in holy works.

The commons are traditionally the last of the "three estates," yet they bulk largest in the Canterbury company and fit least well in that model of social order. There are old-fashioned laborers on the pilgrimage, but many more characters from the emerging and disruptive world of small industry and commerce. They are commoners, but have ambitions that lead them both to envy and to mock the powers held by their aristocratic and clerical companions.

Among the group that traditionally comprised the commons, the peasants, Chaucer singles out one ideal, the Plowman, who is, significantly, the Parson's brother. He is characterized as a diligent *swynkere* (worker), in implicit contrast to the lazy peasants castigated in estates satire. Most of the rest of the commons, however, such as the Miller and the Cook, are presented as "churlish," and their tales have a coarse vigor that Chaucer clearly relishes even as he disassociates himself from their vulgarity.

In theory, women were treated as a separate category, defined by their sexual nature and marital role rather than by their class. Nevertheless, the Prioress and the Wife of Bath are both satirized as much for their social ambition as for the failings of their gender. The Prioress prides herself on her courtesy, and the commoner Wife of Bath aspires to the same social recognition as the guildsmen's upwardly mobile wives. Her portrait is complex, however, for she is simultaneously satirized and admired for challenging the expected roles of women at the time, with her economic independence (as a rich widow and a cloth-maker) and her resultant freedom to travel. The narrator's suggestion that she goes on many pilgrimages in order to find a sixth husband bears out the stereotype of unbridled female sexuality familiar from estates satire, as her fondness of talking and laughing bears out the stereotype of female garrulousness.

Chaucer's satire is pointed but also exceptionally subtle, largely because of the irony achieved through his use of the narrator, seemingly naive and a little dense. His deadpan narration leaves the readers themselves to supply the judgment.

from THE CANTERBURY TALES

The General Prologue[1]

	Whan that April with his showres soote°	*sweet*
	The droughte of March hath perced to the roote,	
	And bathed every veine in swich licour,°	*such liquid*
	Of which vertu° engendred is the flowr;	*by whose strength*
5	Whan Zephyrus[2] eek° with his sweete breeth	*also*
	Inspired hath in every holt and heeth°	*wood and field*
	The tendre croppes, and the yonge sonne	
	Hath in the Ram° his halve cours yronne,	*the zodiac sign Aries*
	And smale fowles maken melodye	
10	That sleepen al the night with open yë°—	*eye*
	So priketh hem Nature in hir corages°—	*hearts, spirits*
	Thanne longen folk to goon on pilgrimages,	
	And palmeres[3] for to seeken straunge strondes°	*shores*
	To ferne halwes,° couthe° in sondry londes;	*far-off shrines / known*
15	And specially from every shires ende	
	Of Engelond to Canterbury they wende,°	*go*
	The holy blisful martyr[4] for to seeke	
	That hem hath holpen° whan that they were seke.°	*helped / sick*
	Bifel that in that seson on a day,	
20	In Southwerk[5] at the Tabard as I lay,	
	Redy to wenden on my pilgrimage	
	To Canterbury with ful devout corage,	
	At night was come into that hostelrye	
	Wel nine and twenty in a compaignye	
25	Of sondry folk, by aventure yfalle	
	In felaweshipe, and pilgrimes were they alle	
	That toward Canterbury wolden ride.	
	The chambres° and the stables weren wide,	*guestrooms*
	And wel we weren esed° at the beste.	*accommodated*
30	And shortly, whan the sonne was to reste,	
	So hadde I spoken with hem everichoon	
	That I was of hir felaweshipe anoon,	
	And made forward° erly for to rise,	*agreed*
	To take oure way ther as I you devise.°	*relate*
35	But nathelees, whil I have time and space,°	*opportunity*

---

1. Each page of The General Prologue in Middle English is followed by its modern English translation by David Wright on the facing page. Because the number of verse lines in the modern translation does not always match the Middle English precisely—for example, Wright translates Chaucer's first 36 lines of The General Prologue in 35 lines—no line numbers have been included in Wright's translation.

2. In Roman mythology Zephyrus was the demigod of the west wind, herald of warmer weather.

3. Pilgrims who had traveled to the Holy Land.

4. St. Thomas Becket, murdered in Canterbury Cathedral in 1170.

5. Southwark, a suburb of London south of the Thames and the traditional starting point for the pilgrimage to Canterbury in Kent, was notorious as a center of gambling and prostitution. The Tabard Inn was an actual public house at the time, named for the shape of its sign which resembled the coarse, sleeveless outer garment worn by members of the lower classes, monks, and foot soldiers alike.

The General Prologue

When the sweet showers of April have pierced
The drought of March, and pierced it to the root,
And every vein is bathed in that moisture
Whose quickening force will engender the flower;
And when the west wind too with its sweet breath
Has given life in every wood and field
To tender shoots, and when the stripling sun
Has run his half-course in Aries, the Ram,
And when small birds are making melodies,
That sleep all the night long with open eyes,
(Nature so prompts them, and encourages);
Then people long to go on pilgrimages.
And palmers to take ship for foreign shores,
And distant shrines, famous in different lands;
And most especially, from all the shires
Of England, to Canterbury they come,
The holy blessed martyr there to seek,
Who gave his help to them when they were sick.
   It happened at this season, that one day
In Southwark at the Tabard where I stayed
Ready to set out on my pilgrimage
To Canterbury, and pay devout homage,
There came at nightfall to the hostelry
Some nine-and-twenty in a company,
Folk of all kinds, met in accidental
Companionship, for they were pilgrims all;
It was to Canterbury that they rode.
The bedrooms and the stables were good-sized,
The comforts offered us were of the best.
And by the time the sun had gone to rest
I'd talked with everyone, and soon became
One of their company, and promised them
To rise at dawn next day to take the road
For the journey I am telling you about.
   But, before I go further with this tale,

Er that I ferther in this tale pace,°   *proceed*
Me thinketh it accordant to resoun
To telle you al the condicioun°   *circumstances*
Of eech of hem, so as it seemed me,
40 And whiche they were, and of what degree,°   *social status*
And eek in what array that they were inne:
And at a knight thanne wol I first biginne.
      A Knight ther was, and that a worthy man,
That fro the time that he first bigan
45 To riden out, he loved chivalrye,
Trouthe and honour, freedom and curteisye.[6]
Ful worthy was he in his lordes werre,°   *war*
And therto hadde he riden, no man ferre,°   *farther*
As wel in Cristendom as hethenesse,°   *heathen lands*
50 And evere honoured for his worthinesse.
      At Alisandre[7] he was whan it was wonne;
Ful ofte time he hadde the boord bigonne[8]
Aboven alle nacions in Pruce;
In Lettou had he reised,° and in Ruce,   *campaigned*
55 No Cristen man so ofte of his degree;
In Gernade at the sege eek hadde he be
Of Algezir, and riden in Belmarye;
At Lyeis was he, and at Satalye,
Whan they were wonne; and in the Grete See
60 At many a noble arivee° hadde he be.   *military landing*
      At mortal batailes[9] hadde he been fifteene,
And foughten for oure faith at Tramissene
In listes° thries, and ay° slain his fo.   *duels / always*
      This ilke° worthy Knight hadde been also   *same*
65 Somtime with the lord of Palatye
Again° another hethen in Turkye;   *against*
And everemore he hadde a soverein pris.°   *reputation*
And though that he were worthy, he was wis,
And of his port° as meeke as is a maide.   *bearing*
70 He nevere yit no vilainye° ne saide   *rudeness*
In al his lif unto no manere wight:°   *no kind of man*
He was a verray,° parfit,° gentil° knight.   *true / perfect / noble*
But for to tellen you of his array,°   *equipment*
His hors were goode, but he was nat gay.°   *gaily attired*
75 Of fustian° he wered a gipoun°   *coarse cloth / tunic*
Al bismotered with his haubergeoun,[1]

---

6. Fidelity and good reputation, generosity and courtliness.
7. The place-names Chaucer lists over the next 15 lines were primarily associated with 14th-century Crusades against both Muslims and Eastern Orthodox Christians. Alisandre: Alexandria in Egypt; Pruce: Prussia; Lettou: Lithuania; Ruce: Russia; Gernade and Algezir: Granada and Algeciras in Spain; Belmarye: Ben-Marin near Morocco; Lyeis: Ayash in Turkey; Satalye: Atalia in Turkey; Grete See: Mediterranean; Tramissene: Tlemcen near Morocco; Palatye: Balat in Turkey.
8. Held the place of honor at feasts.
9. Tournaments waged to the death.
1. Rust-stained from his coat of mail.

And while I can, it seems reasonable
That I should let you have a full description
Of each of them, their sort and condition,
At any rate as they appeared to me;
Tell who they were, their status and profession,
What they looked like, what kind of clothes they dressed in;
And with a knight, then, I shall first begin.
   There was a knight, a reputable man,
Who from the moment that he first began
Campaigning, had cherished the profession
Of arms; he also prized trustworthiness,
Liberality, fame, and courteousness.
In the king's service he'd fought valiantly,
And travelled far; no man as far as he
In Christian and in heathen lands as well,
And ever honoured for his ability.
   He was at Alexandria when it fell,
Often he took the highest place at table
Over the other foreign knights in Prussia;
He'd raided in Lithuania and Russia,
No Christian of his rank fought there more often.
Also he'd been in Granada, at the siege
Of Algeciras; forayed in Benmarin;
At Ayas and Adalia he had been
When they were taken; and with the great hosts
Freebooting on the Mediterranean coasts;
   Fought fifteen mortal combats; thrice as champion
In tournaments, he at Tramassene
Fought for our faith, and each time killed his man.
   This worthy knight had also, for a time,
Taken service in Palatia for the Bey,
Against another heathen in Turkey;
And almost beyond price was his prestige.
Though eminent, he was prudent and sage,
And in his bearing mild as any maid.
He'd never been foul-spoken in his life
To any kind of man; he was indeed
The very pattern of a noble knight.
But as for his appearance and outfit,
He had good horses, yet was far from smart.
He wore a tunic made of coarse thick stuff,
Marked by his chainmail, all begrimed with rust,

For he was late come from his viage,°   *expedition*
And wente for to doon his pilgrimage.
   With him ther was his sone, a yong Squier,
80   A lovere and a lusty bacheler,[2]
With lokkes crulle° as they were laid in presse.   *curled*
Of twenty yeer of age he was, I gesse.
Of his stature he was of evene° lengthe,   *average*
And wonderly delivere,° and of greet strengthe.   *agile*
85   And he hadde been som time in chivachye°   *cavalry expedition*
In Flandres, in Artois, and Picardye,[3]
And born him wel as of so litel space,°   *time*
In hope to stonden in his lady grace.°   *lady's favor*
   Embrouded° was he as it were a mede,°   *embroidered / meadow*
90   Al ful of fresshe flowres, white and rede;
Singing he was, or floiting,° al the day: *playing the flute*
He was as fressh as is the month of May.
Short was his gowne, with sleeves longe and wide.
Wel coude he sitte on hors, and faire ride;
95   He coude songes make, and wel endite,°   *compose*
Juste° and eek daunce, and wel portraye° and write.   *joust / draw*
So hote he loved that by nightertale°   *nighttime*
He slepte namore than dooth a nightingale.
Curteis he was, lowely,° and servisable,°   *humble / attentive*
100   And carf° biforn his fader° at the table   *carved / father*
   A Yeman[4] hadde he° and servants namo   *i.e., the Knight*
At that time, for him liste° ride so;   *he liked*
And he was clad in cote and hood of greene.
A sheef of pecok arwes,° bright and keene,   *peacock arrows*
105   Under his belt he bar ful thriftily;
Wel coude he dresse° his takel° yemanly: *arrange / gear*
His arwes drouped nought with fetheres lowe.
And in his hand he bar a mighty bowe.
A not-heed° hadde he with a brown visage.°   *short haircut / face*
110   Of wodecraft° wel coude he al the usage.   *forestry*
Upon his arm he bar a gay bracer,°   *archer's armguard*
And by his side a swerd and a bokeler,°   *small shield*
And on that other side a gay daggere,
Harneised wel and sharp as point of spere;
115   A Cristophre[5] on his brest of silver sheene;
An horn he bar, the baudrik° was of greene.   *shoulder strap*
A forster° was he soothly,° as I gesse.   *gamekeeper / truly*
   Ther was also a Nonne, a Prioresse,
That of hir smiling was ful simple and coy.°   *quiet, shy*

---

2. An unmarried and unpropertied younger knight.
3. Regions in the north of France and in what is now Belgium, where the English and the French were fighting out the Hundred Years' War.

4. A yeoman was a freeborn servant (not a peasant), who looked after the affairs of the gentry. This particular yeoman was a forester and gamekeeper for the Knight.
5. Medal of St. Christopher, patron saint of travelers.

Having just returned from an expedition,
And on his pilgrimage of thanksgiving.
　With him there was his son, a young squire,
A lively knight-apprentice, and a lover,
With hair as curly as if newly waved;
I took him to be twenty years of age.
In stature he was of an average length,
Wonderfully athletic, and of great strength.
He'd taken part in cavalry forays
In Flanders, in Artois, and Picardy,
With credit, though no more than a novice,
Hoping to stand well in his lady's eyes.
　His clothes were all embroidered like a field
Full of the freshest flowers, white and red.
He sang, or played the flute, the livelong day,
And he was fresher than the month of May.
Short was his gown, with sleeves cut long and wide.
He'd a good seat on horseback, and could ride,
Make music too, and songs to go with it;
Could joust and dance, and also draw and write.
So burningly he loved, that come nightfall
He'd sleep no more than any nightingale.
Polite, modest, willing to serve, and able,
He carved before his father at their table.
　The knight had just one servant, a yeoman,
For so he wished to ride, on this occasion.
The man was clad in coat and hood of green.
He carried under his belt, handily,
For he looked to his gear in yeoman fashion,
A sheaf of peacock arrows, sharp and shining,
Not liable to fall short from poor feathering;
And in his hand he bore a mighty bow.
He had a cropped head, and his face was brown;
Of woodcraft he knew all there was to know.
He wore a fancy leather guard, a bracer,
And by his side a sword and a rough buckler,
And on the other side a fancy dagger,
Well-mounted, sharper than the point of spear,
And on his breast a medal: St Christopher,
The woodman's patron saint, in polished silver.
He bore a horn slung from a cord of green,
And my guess is, he was a forester.
　There was also a nun, a prioress,
Whose smile was unaffected and demure;

120	Hir gretteste ooth was but by Sainte Loy!⁶
	And she was cleped° Madame Eglantine.° *called / Brier-rose*
	Ful wel she soong the service divine,
	Entuned in hir nose ful semely;° *becomingly*
	And Frenssh she spak ful faire and fetisly,° *elegantly*
125	After the scole of Stratford at the Bowe⁷
	For Frenssh of Paris was to hire unknowe.
	At mete° wel ytaught was she withalle: *meals*
	She leet no morsel from hir lippes falle,
	Ne wette hir fingres in hir sauce deepe;
130	Wel coude she carye a morsel, and wel keepe° *safeguard*
	That no drope ne fille upon hir brest.
	In curteisye was set ful muchel hir lest.° *her great pleasure*
	Hir over-lippe° wiped she so clene *upper lip*
	That in hir coppe ther was no ferthing⁸ seene
135	Of grece,° whan she dronken hadde hir draughte; *grease*
	Ful semely after hir mete she raughte.° *reached for her food*
	And sikerly° she was of greet disport,° *certainly / good cheer*
	And ful plesant, and amiable of port,
	And pained hire to countrefete cheere° *appearance*
140	Of court, and to been estatlich° of manere, *stately*
	And to been holden digne° of reverence. *worthy*
	But, for to speken of hir conscience,
	She was so charitable and so pitous
	She wolde weepe if that she saw a mous
145	Caught in a trappe, if it were deed or bledde.
	Of smale houndes hadde she that she fedde
	With rosted flessh,° or milk and wastelbreed;⁹ *meat*
	But sore wepte she if oon of hem were deed,
	Or if men smoot° it with a yerde° smerte;° *hit / rod / painfully*
150	And al was conscience and tendre herte.
	Ful semely hir wimpe¹ pinched was,
	Hir nose tretis,° hir yën greye as glas, *shapely*
	Hir mouth ful smal, and therto softe and reed—
	But sikerly she hadde a fair forheed:
155	It was almost a spanne² brood, I trowe,° *believe*
	For hardily,° she was nat undergrowe.° *assuredly / short*
	Ful fetis° was hir cloke, as I was war; *elegant*
	Of smal coral aboute hir arm she bar
	A paire of bedes, gauded al with greene,³
160	And theron heeng a brooch of gold ful sheene,

---

6. St. Eligius, patron saint of metalworkers, believed never to have sworn an oath in his life.
7. From the school (i.e., after the manner) of Stratford, a suburb of London where the prosperous convent of St. Leonard's was located; her French is Anglo-Norman as opposed to the French spoken on the Continent.
8. Spot the size of a farthing.

9. Bread of the finest quality.
1. A pleated headdress covering all but the face, such as nuns and married women wore.
2. A hand's width, 7 to 9 inches.
3. A set of rosary beads, marked off by larger beads (gauds) to indicate where the Paternosters should be said.

Her greatest oath was just, "By St Eloi!"
And she was known as Madame Eglantine.
She sang the divine service prettily,
And through the nose, becomingly intoned;
And she spoke French well and elegantly
As she'd been taught it at Stratford-at-Bow,
For French of Paris was to her unknown.
Good table manners she had learnt as well:
She never let a crumb from her mouth fall;
She never soiled her fingers, dipping deep
Into the sauce; when lifting to her lips
Some morsel, she was careful not to spill
So much as one small drop upon her breast.
Her greatest pleasure was in etiquette.
She used to wipe her upper lip so clean,
No print of grease inside her cup was seen,
Not the least speck, when she had drunk from it.
Most daintily she'd reach for what she ate.
No question, she possessed the greatest charm,
Her demeanour was so pleasant, and so warm;
Though at pains to ape the manners of the court,
And be dignified, in order to be thought
A person well deserving of esteem.
But, speaking of her sensibility,
She was so full of charity and pity
That if she saw a mouse caught in a trap,
And it was dead or bleeding, she would weep.
She kept some little dogs, and these she fed
On roast meat, or on milk and fine white bread.
But how she'd weep if one of them were dead,
Or if somebody took a stick to it!
She was all sensitivity and tender heart.
Her veil was pleated most becomingly;
Her nose well-shaped; eyes blue-grey, of great beauty;
And her mouth tender, very small, and red.
And there's no doubt she had a fine forehead,
Almost a span in breadth, I'd swear it was,
For certainly she was not undersized.
Her cloak, I noticed, was most elegant.
A coral rosary with gauds of green
She carried on her arm; and from it hung
A brooch of shining gold; inscribed thereon

On which ther was first writen a crowned A.[4]
And after, *Amor vincit omnia*.[5]
   Another Nonne with hire hadde she
That was hir chapelaine,° and preestes three.   *secretary*
165   A Monk ther was, a fair for the maistrye,°   *very good-looking*
An outridere[6] that loved venerye,°   *hunting*
A manly° man, to been an abbot able.   *courageous*
Ful many a daintee° hors hadde he in stable,   *fine*
And whan he rood, men mighte his bridel heere
170   Ginglen° in a whistling wind as clere   *jingling*
And eek as loude as dooth the chapel belle
Ther as this lord was kepere of the celle.[7]
The rule of Saint Maure or of Saint Beneit,[8]
By cause that it was old and somdeel strait°—   *somewhat strict*
175   This ilke Monk leet olde thinges pace,
And heeld after the newe world the space.°   *the times (customs)*
He yaf nought of that text° a pulled° hen   *regulation / plucked*
That saith that hunteres been nought holy men,
Ne that a monk, whan he is recchelees,°   *careless*
180   Is likned til a fissh that is waterlees—
This is to sayn, a monk out of his cloistre;
But thilke° text heeld he nat worth an oystre.   *that same*
And I saide his opinion was good:
What sholde he studye and make himselven wood°   *crazy*
185   Upon a book in cloistre alway to poure,
Or swinke° with his handes and laboure,   *work*
As Austin[9] bit?° How shal the world be served?   *orders*
Lat Austin have his swink° to him reserved!   *toil*
Therfore he was a prikasour° aright.   *hunter on horseback*
190   Grehoundes he hadde as swift as fowl in flight.
Of priking and of hunting for the hare
Was al his lust,° for no cost wolde he spare.   *pleasure*
I sawgh his sleeves purfiled° at the hand   *fur-lined*
With gris,° and that the fineste of a land;   *gray fur*
195   And for to festne his hood under his chin
He hadde of gold wrought a ful curious° pin: *elaborate*
A love-knotte[1] in the grettere° ende ther was.   *larger*
His heed was balled,° that shoon as any glas,   *bald*
And eek his face, as he hadde been anoint:
200   He was a lord ful fat and in good point;°   *in good shape*
His yën steepe,° and rolling in his heed,   *bright*

---

4. The letter "A" with a crown on top.
5. Love conquers all (Virgil, *Eclogues*, 10.69). Though pagan and secular in origin, the phrase was often used to refer to divine love as well.
6. A monk who worked outside the confines of the monastery.
7. Supervisor of the outlying cell of the monastery.
8. St. Benedict (Beneit) was the founder of Western monasticism, and his Rule prohibited monks from leaving the grounds of the monastery without special permission. St. Maurus introduced the Benedictine order into France.
9. St. Augustine recommended that monks perform manual labor.
1. An elaborate knot.

Was, first of all, a crowned "A,"
And under, *Amor vincit omnia.*
   With her were three priests, and another nun,
Who was her chaplain and companion.
   There was a monk; a nonpareil was he,
Who rode, as steward of his monastery,
The country round; a lover of good sport,
A manly man, and fit to be an abbot.
He'd plenty of good horses in his stable,
And when he went out riding, you could hear
His bridle jingle in the wind, as clear
And loud as the monastery chapel-bell.
Inasmuch as he was keeper of the cell,
The rule of St Maurus or St Benedict
Being out of date, and also somewhat strict,
This monk I speak of let old precepts slide,
And took the modern practice as his guide.
He didn't give so much as a plucked hen
For the maxim, "Hunters are not pious men,"
Or "A monk who's heedless of his regimen
Is much the same as a fish out of water,"
In other words, a monk out of his cloister.
But that's a text he thought not worth an oyster;
And I remarked his opinion was sound.
What use to study, why go round the bend
With poring over some book in a cloister,
Or drudging with his hands, to toil and labour
As Augustine bids? How shall the world go on?
You can go keep your labour, Augustine!
So he rode hard—no question about that—
Kept greyhounds swifter than a bird in flight.
Hard riding, and the hunting of the hare,
Were what he loved, and opened his purse for.
I noticed that his sleeves were edged and trimmed
With squirrel fur, the finest in the land.
For fastening his hood beneath his chin,
He wore an elaborate golden pin,
Twined with a love-knot at the larger end.
His head was bald and glistening like glass
As if anointed; and likewise his face.
A fine fat patrician, in prime condition,
His bright and restless eyes danced in his head,

That stemed as a furnais of a leed;[2]

His bootes souple,° his hors in greet estat[3]—   *supple*

Now certainly he was a fair prelat.[4]

205 He was nat pale as a forpined° gost: *tormented*

A fat swan loved he best of any rost.

His palfrey° was as brown as is a berye.   *saddle horse*

  A Frere° ther was, a wantoune[5] and a merye,   *Friar*

A limitour,[6] a ful solempne man.

210 In alle the ordres foure[7] is noon that can°   *knows*

So muche of daliaunce° and fair langage: *flirtation*

He hadde maad ful many a mariage

Of yonge wommen at his owene cost;

Unto his ordre he was a noble post.°   *pillar*

215 Ful wel biloved and familier was he

With frankelains[8] over al in his contree,

And with worthy wommen of the town—

For he hadde power of confessioun,

As saide himself, more than a curat,°   *parish priest*

220 For of his ordre he was licenciat.[9]

Ful swetely herde he confessioun,

And plesant was his absolucioun.

He was an esy man to yive penaunce

Ther as he wiste to have a good pitaunce;[1]

225 For unto a poore ordre for to yive

Is signe that a man is wel yshrive;°   *absolved*

For if he yaf, he dorste make avaunt°   *boast*

He wiste that a man was repentaunt;

For many a man so hard is of his herte

230 He may nat weepe though him sore smerte:°   *hurts*

Therfore, in stede of weeping and prayeres,

Men mote yive silver to the poore freres.

  His tipet° was ay farsed° ful of knives   *scarf / packed*

And pinnes, for to yiven faire wives;

235 And certainly he hadde a merye note;

Wel coude he singe and playen on a rote;°   *fiddle*

Of yeddinges° he bar outrely the pris.[2]   *singing ballads*

His nekke whit was as the flowr-de-lis;[3]

Therto he strong was as a champioun.

240 He knew the tavernes wel in every town,

And every hostiler and tappestere,°   *innkeeper and barmaid*

Bet than a lazar or a beggestere.°   *a leper or a beggar*

For unto swich a worthy man as he

---

2. Glowed like a furnace under a cauldron.
3. Excellent condition.
4. Prelate, important churchman.
5. Jovial, pleasure-seeking.
6. Friar licensed by his order to beg for alms within a given district.
7. The four orders of friars were the Carmelites, Augustinians, Dominicans, and Franciscans.
8. Franklins, important property holders.
9. Licensed by the Church to hear confessions.
1. Where he knew he would get a good donation.
2. Utterly took the prize.
3. Lily, emblem of the royal house of France.

And sparkled like the fire beneath a pot;
Boots of soft leather, horse in perfect trim:
No question but he was a fine prelate!
Not pale and wan like some tormented spirit.
A fat roast swan was what he loved the best.
His saddle-horse was brown as any berry.
     There was a begging friar, a genial merry
Limiter and a most imposing person.
In all of the four Orders there was none
So versed in small talk and in flattery:
And many was the marriage in a hurry
He'd had to improvise and even pay for.
He was a noble pillar of his Order,
And was well in and intimate with every
Well-to-do freeman farmer of his area,
And with the well-off women in the town;
For he was qualified to hear confession,
And absolve graver sins than a curate,
Or so he said; he was a licentiate.
How sweetly he would hear confession!
How pleasant was his absolution!
He was an easy man in giving shrift,
When sure of getting a substantial gift:
For, as he used to say, generous giving
To a poor Order is a sign you're shriven;
For if you gave, then he could vouch for it
That you were conscience-stricken and contrite;
For many are so hardened in their hearts
They cannot weep, though burning with remorse.
Therefore, instead of weeping and prayers,
They should give money to the needy friars.
The pockets of his hood were stuffed with knives
And pins to give away to pretty wives.
He had a pleasant singing voice, for sure,
Could sing and play the fiddle beautifully;
He took the biscuit as a ballad-singer,
And though his neck was whiter than a lily,
Yet he was brawny as a prize-fighter.
He knew the taverns well in every town,
And all the barmaids and the innkeepers,
Better than lepers or the street-beggars;
It wouldn't do, for one in his position,

	Accorded nat, as by his facultee,°[4]	*official position*
245	To have with sike° lazars aquaintaunce:	*such*
	It is nat honeste,° it may nought avaunce,°	*dignified / profit*
	For to delen with no swich poraile,°	*poor people*
	But al with riche, and selleres of vitaile;°	*food*
	And over al ther as profit sholde arise,	
250	Curteis he was, and lowely° of servise.	*humble*
	Ther was no man nowher so vertuous:°	*capable*
	He was the beste beggere in his hous.	
	And yaf a certain ferme for the graunt:[5]	
	Noon of his bretheren cam ther in his haunt.°	*territory*
255	For though a widwe hadde nought a sho,	
	So plesant was his *In principio*[6]	
	Yit wolde he have a ferthing er he wente;	
	His purchas° was wel bettre than his rente.°	*income / expense*
	And rage° he coude as it were right a whelpe;°	*flirt / puppy*
260	In love-dayes[7] ther coude he muchel helpe,	
	For ther he was nat lik a cloisterer,	
	With a thredbare cope, as is a poore scoler,	
	But he was lik a maister° or a pope.	*professor*
	Of double worstede was his semicope,°[8]	*short cloak*
265	And rounded as a belle out of the presse.°	*bell-mold*
	Somwhat he lipsed for his wantounesse	
	To make his Englissh sweete upon his tonge;	
	And in his harping, whan that he hadde songe,	
	His yën twinkled in his heed aright	
270	As doon the sterres in the frosty night.	
	This worthy limitour was cleped° Huberd.	*called*
	A Marchant was ther with a forked beerd,	
	In motlee,° and hye on hors he sat,	*multicolored fabric*
	Upon his heed a Flandrissh° bevere hat,	*Flemish*
275	His bootes clasped faire and fetisly.°	*elegantly*
	His resons° he spak ful solempnely,	*opinions*
	Souning° alway th'encrees of his winning.	*announcing*
	He wolde the see were kept for any thing°	*protected at all costs*
	Bitwixen Middelburgh and Orewelle.[9]	
280	Wel coude he in eschaunge sheeldes[1] selle.	
	This worthy man ful wel his wit bisette:°	*employed*
	Ther wiste° no wight° that he was in dette,	*knew / person*
	So estatly° was he of his governaunce,°	*dignified / management*
	With his bargaines, and with his chevissaunce.°	*borrowing*
285	Forsoothe° he was a worthy man withalle;	*in truth*
	But, sooth to sayn, I noot° how men him calle.	*do not know*

4. It was unbecoming to his official post.
5. And gave a certain fee for the license to beg.
6. "In the beginning," the opening line in Genesis and the Gospel of John, popular for devotions.
7. Holidays for settling disputes out of court.

8. His short cloak was made of thick woolen cloth.
9. Middleburgh in the Netherlands and Orwell in Suffolk were major ports for the wool trade.
1. Unit of exchange, a credit instrument for foreign merchants.

One of his ability and distinction,
To hold acquaintance with diseased lepers.
It isn't seemly, and it gets you nowhere,
To have any dealings with that sort of trash,
Stick to provision-merchants and the rich!
And anywhere where profit might arise
He'd crawl with courteous offers of service.
You'd nowhere find an abler man than he,
Or a better beggar in his friary;
He paid a yearly fee for his district,
No brother friar trespassed on his beat.
A widow might not even own a shoe,
But so pleasant was his *In principio*
He'd win her farthing in the end, then go.
He made his biggest profits on the side.
He'd frolic like a puppy. He'd give aid
As arbitrator upon settling-days,
For there he was not like some cloisterer
With threadbare cape, like any poor scholar,
But like a Master of Arts, or the Pope!
Of the best double-worsted was his cloak,
And bulging like a bell that's newly cast.
He lisped a little, from affectation,
To make his English sweet upon his tongue;
And when he harped, as closing to a song,
His eyes would twinkle in his head just like
The stars upon a sharp and frosty night.
This worthy limiter was called Hubert.
   A merchant was there, on a high-saddled horse:
He'd a forked beard, a many-coloured dress,
And on his head a Flanders beaver hat,
Boots with expensive clasps, and buckled neatly.
He gave out his opinions pompously,
Kept talking of the profits that he'd made,
How, at all costs, the sea should be policed
From Middleburg in Holland to Harwich.
At money-changing he was an expert;
He dealt in French gold florins on the quiet.
This worthy citizen could use his head:
No one could tell whether he was in debt,
So impressive and dignified his bearing
As he went about his loans and bargaining.
He was a really estimable man,
But the fact is I never learnt his name.

A Clerk ther was of Oxenforde also
That unto logik hadde longe ygo.°   *gone (studied)*
As lene was his hors as is a rake,
290   And he was nought right fat, I undertake,
But looked holwe,° and therto sobrely.   *emaciated*
Ful thredbare was his overeste courtepy,°   *outer cloak*
For he hadde geten him yit no benefice,°   *church income*
Ne was so worldly for to have office.°   *secular employment*
295   For him was levere° have at his beddes heed   *he preferred*
Twenty bookes, clad in blak or reed,
Of Aristotle and his philosophye,
Than robes riche, or fithele,° or gay sautrye.°   *fiddle / harp*
But al be that he was a philosophre[2]
300   Yit hadde he but litel gold in cofre;
But al that he mighte of his freendes hente,°   *get*
On bookes and on lerning he it spente,
And bisily gan for the soules praye
Of hem that yaf him wherwith to scoleye.°   *study*
305   Of studye took he most cure° and most heede.   *care*
Nought oo° word spak he more than was neede,   *one*
And that was said in forme° and reverence,   *formally*
And short and quik, and ful of height sentence:°   *lofty meaning*
Souning in° moral vertu was his speeche,   *consonant with*
310   And gladly wolde he lerne, and gladly teche.
A Sergeant of the Lawe,[3] war and wis,
That often hadde been at the Parvis[4]
Ther was also, ful riche of excellence.
Discreet he was, and of greet reverence—
315   He seemed swich, his wordes weren so wise.
Justice he was ful often in assise[5]
By patente and by plein commissioun.[6]
For his science° and for his heigh renown   *knowledge*
Of fees and robes hadde he many oon.
320   So greet a purchasour° was nowher noon;   *buyer of land*
Al was fee simple[7] to him in effect—
His purchasing mighte nat been infect.°   *invalidated*
Nowher so bisy a man as he ther nas;
And yit he seemed bisier than he was.
325   In termes hadde he caas and doomes° alle   *lawsuits and judgments*
That from the time of King William[8] were falle.
Therto he coude endite and make a thing,[9]
Ther coude no wight° pinchen° at his writing;   *person / find fault with*
And every statut coude he plein by rote.[1]

---

2. A philosopher could be a scientist or alchemist.
3. A lawyer of the highest rank.
4. The porch of St. Paul's Cathedral, a meeting place for lawyers.
5. He was often judge in the court of assizes (civil court).
6. By letter of appointment from the king and by full

jurisdiction.
7. Owned outright with no legal impediments.
8. Since the introduction of Norman law in England under William the Conqueror.
9. Compose and draw up a deed.
1. He knew entirely from memory.

There was a scholar from Oxford as well,
Not yet an MA, reading Logic still;
The horse he rode was leaner than a rake,
And he himself, believe me, none too fat,
But hollow-cheeked, and grave and serious.
Threadbare indeed was his short overcoat:
A man too unworldly for lay office,
Yet he'd not got himself a benefice.
For he'd much rather have at his bedside
A library, bound in black calf or red,
Of Aristotle and his philosophy,
Than rich apparel, fiddle, or fine psaltery.
And though he was a man of science, yet
He had but little gold in his strongbox;
But upon books and learning he would spend
All he was able to obtain from friends;
He'd pray assiduously for their souls,
Who gave him wherewith to attend the schools.
Learning was all he cared for or would heed.
He never spoke a word more than was need,
And that was said in form and decorum,
And brief and terse, and full of deepest meaning.
Moral virtue was reflected in his speech,
And gladly would he learn, and gladly teach.
    There was a wise and wary sergeant-at-law,
A well-known figure in the portico
Where lawyers meet; one of great excellence,
Judicious, worthy of reverence,
Or so he seemed, his sayings were so wise.
He'd often acted as Judge of Assize
By the king's letters patent, authorized
To hear all cases. And his great renown
And skill had won him many a fee, or gown
Given in lieu of money. There was none
To touch him as a property-buyer; all
He bought was fee-simple, without entail;
You'd never find a flaw in the conveyance.
And nowhere would you find a busier man;
And yet he seemed much busier than he was.
From yearbooks he could quote, chapter and verse,
Each case and judgement since William the First.
And he knew how to draw up and compose
A deed; you couldn't fault a thing he wrote;
And he'd reel all the statutes off by rote.

330 He rood but hoomly° in a medlee° cote, *simply / multicolored*
  Girt with a ceint° of silk, with barres° smale. *belt / stripes*
  Of his array telle I no lenger tale.
   A Frankelain[2] was in his compaignye:
  Whit was his beerd as is the dayesye;° *daisy*
335 Of his complexion he was sanguin.[3]
  Wel loved he by the morwe a sop in win.[4]
  To liven in delit° was evere his wone,° *pleasure / custom*
  For he was Epicurus owene sone,
  That heeld opinion that plein° delit *complete*
340 Was verray felicitee parfit.[5]
  An housholdere and that a greet was he:
  Saint Julian[6] he was in his contree.
  His breed, his ale, was always after oon;° *just as good*
  A bettre envined° man was nevere noon. *stocked with wine*
345 Withouten bake mete was nevere his hous,
  Of fissh and flessh, and that so plentevous° *plentiful*
  It snewed° in his hous of mete and drinke, *snowed*
  Of alle daintees that men coude thinke.
  After the sondry sesons of the yeer
350 So chaunged he his mete and his soper.[7]
  Ful many a fat partrich° hadde he in mewe,° *partridge / cage*
  And many a breem,° and many a luce° in stewe.° *carp / pike / pond*
  Wo was his cook but if his sauce were
  Poinant° and sharp, and redy al his gere. *pungent*
355 His table dormant[8] in his halle alway
  Stood redy covered al the longe day.
  At sessions[9] ther was he lord and sire.
  Ful ofte time he was Knight of the Shire.[1]
  An anlaas° and a gipser° al of silk *dagger / purse*
360 Heeng at his girdel, whit as morne milk.
  A shirreve hadde he been, and countour.[2]
  Was nowher swich a worthy vavasour.[3]
   An Haberdasshere° and a Carpenter, *hat-maker*
  A Webbe, a Dyere, and a Tapicer[4]—
365 And they were clothed alle in oo liveree° *in the same uniform*
  Of a solempne and a greet fraternitee.° *parish guild*
  Ful fresshe and newe hir gere apiked was;[5]
  Hir knives were chaped° nought with bras, *mounted*
  But al with silver; wrought ful clene° and weel *quite nicely made*
370 Hir girdles and hir pouches everydeel.° *entirely*

2. A large landholder, freeborn but not belonging to the nobility.
3. In temperament he was sanguine (optimistic, governed by blood as his chief humor).
4. In the morning a sop of bread soaked in wine.
5. True and perfect happiness.
6. Patron saint of hospitality.
7. For health he changed his diet according to the different seasons.

8. Left standing rather than dismantled between meals.
9. Meetings of the justices of the peace.
1. A representative of the district at Parliament.
2. He had been sheriff and auditor of the county finances.
3. Lower member of the feudal elite.
4. A weaver, dyer, and tapestry-maker, all members of the same commercial guild.
5. Their gear was decorated.

He was dressed simply, in a coloured coat,
Girt by a silk belt with thin metal bands.
I have no more to tell of his appearance.
    A franklin—that's a country gentleman
And freeman landowner—was his companion.
White was his beard, as white as any daisy;
Sanguine his temperament; his face ruddy.
He loved his morning draught of sops-in-wine,
Since living well was ever his custom,
For he was Epicurus' own true son
And held with him that sensuality
Is where the only happiness is found.
And he kept open house so lavishly
He was St Julian to the country round,
The patron saint of hospitality.
His bread and ale were always of the best,
Like his wine-cellar, which was unsurpassed.
Cooked food was never lacking in his house,
Both meat and fish, and that so plenteous
That in his home it snowed with food and drink,
And all the delicacies you could think.
According to the season of the year,
He changed the dishes that were served at dinner.
He'd plenty of fat partridges in coop,
And kept his fishpond full of pike and carp.
His cook would catch it if his sauces weren't
Piquant and sharp, and all his equipment
To hand. And all day in his hall there stood
The great fixed table, with the places laid.
When the justices met, he'd take the chair;
He often served as MP for the shire.
A dagger, and a small purse made of silk,
Hung at his girdle, white as morning milk.
He'd been sheriff, and county auditor:
A model squireen, no man worthier.
    A haberdasher and a carpenter,
A weaver, dyer, tapestry-maker—
And they were in the uniform livery
Of a dignified and rich fraternity,
A parish-guild: their gear all trim and fresh,
Knives silver-mounted, none of your cheap brass;
Their belts and purses neatly stitched as well,
All finely finished to the last detail.

	Wel seemed eech of hem a fair burgeis°	*townsperson*
	To sitten in a yeldehalle° on a dais.	*guildhall*
	Everich, for the wisdom that he can,°	*knows*
	Was shaply° for to been an alderman.°	*fit / mayor*
375	For catel° hadde they ynough and rente,°	*property / income*
	And eek hir wives wolde it wel assente—	
	And elles certain were they to blame:	
	It is ful fair to been ycleped° "Madame,"	*called*
	And goon to vigilies⁶ al bifore,	
380	And have a mantel royalliche ybore.	
	A Cook they hadde with hem for the nones,°	*for the occasion*
	To boile the chiknes with the marybones,°	*marrowbones*
	And powdre-marchant tart and galingale.°	*aromatic spices*
	Wel coude he knowe a draughte of London ale.	
385	He coude roste, and seethe,° and broile, and frye,	*boil*
	Maken mortreux,° and wel bake a pie.	*stews*
	But greet harm was it, as it thoughte me,	
	That on his shine a mormal° hadde he.	*ulcer*
	For blankmanger,° that made he with the beste.	*thick stew*
390	A Shipman was ther, woning° fer by weste—	*dwelling*
	For ought I woot,° he was of Dertemouthe.⁷	*know*
	He rood upon a rouncy° as he couthe,	*nag*
	In a gowne of falding° to the knee.	*coarse brown cloth*
	A daggere hanging on a laas° hadde he	*strap*
395	Aboute his nekke, under his arm adown.	
	The hote somer hadde maad his hewe al brown;	
	And certainly he was a good felawe.	
	Ful many a draughte of win hadde he drawe	
	Fro Burdeuxward, whil that the chapman° sleep:⁸	*merchant*
400	Of nice° conscience took he no keep;°	*scrupulous / care*
	If that he faught and hadde the hyer hand,	
	By water he sente hem hoom to every land.	
	But of his craft, to rekene wel his tides,	
	His stremes° and his daungers° him bisides,	*currents / hazards*
405	His herberwe° and his moone, his lodemenage,°	*harboring / navigation*
	Ther was noon swich from Hulle to Cartage.⁹	
	Hardy he was and wis to undertake;	
	With many a tempest hadde his beerd been shake;	
	He knew alle the havenes as they were	
410	Fro Gotlond to the Cape of Finistere,¹	
	And every crike° in Britaine° and in Spaine.	*inlet / Brittany*
	His barge ycleped was the Maudelaine.	
	With us ther was a Doctour of Physik:°	*Medicine*

---

6. Feasts held the night before a holy day.
7. Dartmouth, a port on the southwestern coast.
8. On the trip back from Bordeaux while the merchant slept.
9. Hull, on the northeastern coast in Yorkshire; Cartage:

Carthage in North Africa or Cartagena on the Mediterranean coast of Spain.
1. Gotland in the Baltic Sea; Finistere: Land's End in western Spain.

Each of them looked indeed like a burgess,
And fit to sit on any guildhall dais.
Each was, in knowledge and ability,
Eligible to be an alderman;
For they'd income enough and property.
What's more, their wives would certainly agree,
Or otherwise they'd surely be to blame
It's very pleasant to be called "Madam"
And to take precedence at church processions,
And have one's mantle carried like a queen's.
    They had a cook with them for the occasion,
To boil the chickens up with marrowbones,
Tart powdered flavouring, spiced with galingale.
No better judge than he of London ale.
And he could roast, and seethe, and boil, and fry,
Make a thick soup, and bake a proper pie;
But to my mind it was the greatest shame
He'd got an open sore upon his shin;
For he made chicken-pudding with the best.
    A sea-captain, whose home was in the west,
Was there—a Dartmouth man, for all I know
He rode a cob as well as he knew how,
And was dressed in a knee-length woollen gown.
From a lanyard round his neck, a dagger hung
Under his arm. Summer had tanned him brown.
As rough a diamond as you'd hope to find,
He'd tapped and lifted many a stoup of wine
From Bordeaux, when the merchant wasn't looking.
He hadn't time for scruples or fine feeling,
For if he fought, and got the upper hand,
He'd send his captives home by sea, not land.
But as for seamanship, and calculation
Of moon, tides, currents, all hazards at sea,
For harbour-lore, and skill in navigation,
From Hull to Carthage there was none to touch him.
He was shrewd adventurer, tough and hardy.
By many a tempest had his beard been shaken.
And he knew all the harbours that there were
Between the Baltic and Cape Finisterre,
And each inlet of Britanny and Spain.
The ship he sailed was called "The Magdalen."
    With us there was a doctor, a physician;

In al this world ne was ther noon him lik
415   To speken of physik and of surgerye.
      For he was grounded in astronomye,°   *astrology*
      He kepte his pacient a ful greet deel
      In houres° by his magik naturel.   *astronomical hours*
      Wel coude he fortunen the ascendent[2]
420   Of his images° for his pacient.   *talismans*
      He knew the cause of every maladye,
      Were it of hoot or cold or moiste or drye,[3]
      And where engendred° and of what humour:[4]   *originated*
      He was a verray parfit praktisour.°   *practitioner*
425   The cause yknowe, and of his harm the roote,
      Anoon he yaf the sike man his boote.°   *remedy*
         Ful redy hadde he his apothecaries
      To senden him drogges and his letuaries,°   *medicines*
      For eech of hem made other for to winne:
430   Hir frendshipe was nought newe to biginne.
      Wel knew he the olde Esculapius,[5]
      And Deiscorides and eek Rufus,
      Olde Ipocras, Hali, and Galien,
      Serapion, Razis, and Avicen,
435   Averrois, Damascien, and Constantin,
      Bernard, and Gatesden, and Gilbertin.
      Of his diete mesurable° was he,   *moderate*
      For it was of no superfluitee,
      But of greet norissing and digestible.
440   His studye was but litel on the Bible.
      In sanguin° and in pers° he clad was al,   *red / Persian blue*
      Lined with taffata and with sendal;°   *silks*
      And yit he was but esy of dispence;°   *thrifty*
      He kepte that he wan in pestilence.
445   For gold in physik is a cordial,°   *tonic*
      Therfore he loved gold in special.
         A good Wif was ther of biside Bathe,
      But she was somdeel deef,° and that was scathe.°   *somewhat deaf / a pity*
      Of cloth-making she hadde swich an haunt,°   *practice*
450   She passed hem of Ypres and of Gaunt.[6]
      In al the parissh wif ne was ther noon
      That to the offring[7] bifore hire sholde goon,
      And if ther dide, certain so wroth° was she   *angry*
      That she was out of alle charitee.

2. Calculate the ascendent (propitious moment).
3. The qualities of the four natural elements, correspond-
ing to the humors of the body and the composition of the
universe, needed to be kept in perfect balance.
4. Bodily fluids, or "humors," thought to govern moods
(blood, phlegm, black bile, yellow bile).
5. The Physician is acquainted with a full range of medical authorities from among the ancient Greeks (Aesculapius, Dioscorides, Rufus, Hippocrates, Galen, and Serapion), the Persians (Hali and Rhazes), the Arabs
(Avicenna and Averroes), the Mediterranean transmit-
ters of Eastern science to the West (John of Damascus,
Constantine the African), and later medical school pro-
fessors (Bernard of Gordon, who taught at Montpellier;
John of Gaddesden, who taught at Merton College; and
Gilbertus Anglicus, an early contemporary of Chaucer's).
6. Centers of Flemish cloth-making.
7. The collection of gifts at the consecration of the Mass.

Nowhere in all the world was one to match him
Where medicine was concerned, or surgery;
Being well grounded in astrology
He'd watch his patient with the utmost care
Until he'd found a favourable hour,
By means of astrology, to give treatment.
Skilled to pick out the astrologic moment
For charms and talismans to aid the patient,
He knew the cause of every malady,
If it were "hot" or "cold" or "moist" or "dry,"
And where it came from, and from which humour.
He was a really fine practitioner.
Knowing the cause, and having found its root,
He'd soon give the sick man an antidote.
Ever at hand he had apothecaries
To send him syrups, drugs, and remedies,
For each put money in the other's pocket—
Theirs was no newly founded partnership.
Well-read was he in Aesculapius,
In Dioscorides, and in Rufus,
Ancient Hippocrates, Hali, and Galen,
Avicenna, Rhazes, and Serapion,
Averroës, Damascenus, Constantine,
Bernard, and Gilbertus, and Gaddesden.
In his own diet he was temperate,
For it was nothing if not moderate,
Though most nutritious and digestible.
He didn't do much reading in the Bible.
He was dressed all in Persian blue and scarlet
Lined with taffeta and fine sarsenet,
And yet was very chary of expense.
He put by all he earned from pestilence;
In medicine gold is the best cordial.
So it was gold that he loved best of all.

     There was a business woman, from near Bath,
But, more's the pity, she was a bit deaf;
So skilled a clothmaker, that she outdistanced
Even the weavers of Ypres and Ghent.
In the whole parish there was not a woman
Who dared precede her at the almsgiving,
And if there did, so furious was she,
That she was put out of all charity.

455   Hir coverchiefs ful fine were of ground[8]—
    I dorste swere they weyeden° ten pound   *weighed*
    That on a Sonday weren upon hir heed.
    Hir hosen° weren of fin scarlet reed,   *stockings*
    Ful straite yteyd,° and shoes ful moiste° and newe.   *tightly laced / supple*
460   Bold was hir face and fair and reed of hewe.
    She was a worthy womman al hir live:
    Housbondes at chirche dore she hadde five,
    Withouten other compaignye in youthe—
    But therof needeth nought to speke as nouthe.°   *for now*
465   And thries hadde she been at Jerusalem;
    She hadde passed many a straunge streem;
    At Rome she hadde been, and at Boloigne,[9]
    In Galice at Saint Jame, and at Coloigne:
    She coude° muchel of wandring by the waye.   *knew*
470   Gat-toothed° was she, soothly for to saye.   *gap-toothed*
    Upon an amblere[1] esily she sat,
    Ywimpled[2] wel, and on hir heed an hat
    As brood as is a bokeler or a targe,°   *small shields*
    A foot-mantel° aboute hir hipes large,   *riding skirt*
475   And on hir feet a paire of spores° sharpe.   *spurs*
    In felaweshipe wel coude she laughe and carpe:
    Of remedies of love she knew parchaunce,[3]
    For she coude of that art the olde daunce.°   *tricks*
      A good man was ther of religioun,
480   And was a poore Person° of a town,   *parson*
    But riche he was of holy thought and werk.
    He was also a lerned man, a clerk,
    That Cristes gospel trewely wolde preche;
    His parisshens° devoutly wolde he teche.   *parishioners*
485   Benigne he was, and wonder diligent,
    And in adversitee ful pacient,
    And swich he was preved ofte sithes.
    Ful loth were him to cursen for his tithes,[4]
    But rather wolde he yiven, out of doute,
490   Unto his poore parisshens aboute
    Of his offring and eek of his substaunce:°   *possessions*
    He coude in litel thing have suffisaunce.
    Wid was his parissh, and houses fer asonder,
    But he ne lafte nought for rain ne thonder,
495   In siknesse nor in meschief, to visite
    The ferreste in his parissh, muche and lite,[5]
    Upon his feet, and in his hand a staf.

8. Her linen kerchiefs were fine in texture.
9. Rome, Boulogne, Santiago Compostela, and Cologne were major European pilgrimage sites.
1. A horse with a gentle pace.
2. Wearing a large headdress that covers all but the face.
3. She knew cures for lovesickness, as it happened.

4. And so was he shown to be many times. / He was most unwilling to curse parishioners (with excommunication) if they failed to pay his tithes (a tenth of their income due to the Church).
5. The furthest away in his parish, great and small.

Her headkerchiefs were of the finest weave,
Ten pounds and more they weighed, I do believe,
Those that she wore on Sundays on her head.
Her stockings were of finest scarlet red,
Very tightly laced; shoes pliable and new.
Bold was her face, and handsome; florid too.
She had been respectable all her life,
And five times married, that's to say in church,
Not counting other loves she'd had in youth,
Of whom, just now, there is no need to speak.
And she had thrice been to Jerusalem;
Had wandered over many a foreign stream;
And she had been at Rome, and at Boulogne,
St James of Compostella, and Cologne;
She knew all about wandering—and straying:
For she was gap-toothed, if you take my meaning.
Comfortably on an ambling horse she sat,
Well-wimpled, wearing on her head a hat
That might have been a shield in size and shape;
A riding-skirt round her enormous hips,
Also a pair of sharp spurs on her feet.
In company, how she could laugh and joke!
No doubt she knew of all the cures for love,
For at that game she was a past mistress.
    And there was a good man, a religious.
He was the needy priest of a village,
But rich enough in saintly thought and work.
And educated, too, for he could read;
Would truly preach the word of Jesus Christ,
Devoutly teach the folk in his parish.
Kind was he, wonderfully diligent;
And in adversity most patient,
As many a time had been put to the test.
For unpaid tithes he'd not excommunicate,
For he would rather give, you may be sure,
From his own pocket to the parish poor;
Few were his needs, so frugally he lived.
Wide was his parish, with houses far asunder,
But he would not neglect, come rain or thunder,
Come sickness or adversity, to call
On the furthest of his parish, great or small;
Going on foot, and in his hand a staff.

This noble ensample° to his sheep he yaf   *example*
That first he wroughte,° and afterward he taughte.   *did*
500   Out of the Gospel he tho° wordes caughte,   *those*
And this figure° he added eek therto: *saying*
That if gold ruste, what shal iren do?
For if a preest be foul, on whom we truste,
No wonder is a lewed° man to ruste.   *uneducated*
505   And shame it is, if a preest take keep,°   *is concerned*
A shiten° shepherde and a clene sheep.   *shit-covered*
Wel oughte a preest ensample for to yive
By his clennesse how that his sheep sholde live.
He sette nought his benefice to hire[6]
510   And leet his sheep encombred in the mire
And ran to London, unto Sainte Poules,
To seeken him a chaunterye for soules,
Or with a bretherhede to been withholde,
But dwelte at hoom and kepte wel his folde,
515   So that the wolf ne made it nought miscarye:
He was a shepherde and nought a mercenarye.
And though he holy were and vertuous,
He was to sinful men nought despitous,°   *scornful*
Ne of his speeche daungerous ne digne,°   *haughty*
520   But in his teching discreet and benigne,
To drawen folk to hevene by fairnesse
By good ensample—this was his bisinesse.
But it were any persone obstinat,
What so he were, of heigh or lowe estat,
525   Him wolde he snibben° sharply for the nones:°   *rebuke / on the spot*
A bettre preest I trowe° ther nowher noon is.   *believe*
He waited after° no pompe and reverence,   *expected*
Ne maked him a spiced° conscience,   *overly critical*
But Cristes lore° and his Apostles twelve   *teaching*
530   He taughte, but first he folwed° it himselve.   *followed*
    With him ther was a Plowman, was his brother,
That hadde ylad of dong ful many a fother.[7]
A trewe swinkere° and a good was he,   *worker*
Living in pees° and parfit° charitee.   *peace / perfect*
535   God loved he best with al his hoole herte
At alle times, though him gamed or smerte,[8]
And thanne his neighebor right as himselve.
He wolde thresshe, and therto dike and delve,°   *make ditches and dig*
For Cristes sake, for every poore wight,°   *person*
540   Withouten hire,° if it laye in his might.   *pay*
His tithes payed he ful faire and wel,

6. The priest did not rent out his parish to another in order to take a more profitable position saying masses for the dead at the chantries of St. Paul's in London or to serve as chaplain to a wealthy guild (bretherhede).
7. That had carried many a cartload of manure.
8. Enjoyed himself or suffered pain.

This was the good example that he set:
He practised first what later he would teach.
Out of the gospel he took that precept;
And what's more, he would cite this saying too:
"If gold can rust, then what will iron do?"
For if a priest be rotten, whom we trust,
No wonder if a layman comes to rust.
It's shame to see (let every priest take note)
A shitten shepherd and a cleanly sheep.
It's the plain duty of a priest to give
Example to his sheep; how they should live.
He never let his benefice for hire
And left his sheep to flounder in the mire
While he ran off to London, to St Paul's
To seek some chantry and sing mass for souls,
Or to be kept as chaplain by a guild;
But stayed at home, and took care of his fold,
So that no wolf might do it injury.
He was a shepherd, not a mercenary.
And although he was saintly and virtuous,
He wasn't haughty or contemptuous
To sinners, speaking to them with disdain,
But in his teaching tactful and humane.
To draw up folk to heaven by goodness
And good example, was his sole business.
But if a person turned out obstinate,
Whoever he was, of high or low estate,
He'd earn a stinging rebuke then and there.
You'll never find a better priest, I'll swear.
He never looked for pomp or deference,
Nor affected an over-nice conscience.
But taught the gospel of Christ and His twelve
Apostles; but first followed it himself.
   With him there was his brother, a ploughman,
Who'd fetched and carried many a load of dung;
A good and faithful labourer was he,
Living in peace and perfect charity.
God he loved best, and that with all his heart,
At all times, good and bad, no matter what;
And next he loved his neighbour as himself.
He'd thresh, and ditch, and also dig and delve,
And for Christ's love would do as much again
If he could manage it, for all poor men,
And ask no hire. He paid his tithes in full,

Bothe of his propre swink⁹ and his catel.°   *possessions*
In a tabard° rood upon a mere.°   *smock / mare*
   Ther was also a Reeve° and a Millere,   *estate manager*
545 A Somnour, and a Pardoner¹ also,
A Manciple,° and myself—ther were namo.   *Steward*
   The Millere was a stout carl° for the nones.   *fellow*
Ful big he was of brawn and eek of bones—
That preved wel, for overal ther he cam
550 At wrastling he wolde have alway the ram.²
He was short-shuldred, brood, a thikke knarre.°   *bully*
Ther was no dore that he nolde heve of harre,°   *push off its hinges*
Or breke it at a renning with his heed.
His beerd as any sowe or fox was reed,
555 And therto brood, as though it were a spade;
Upon the cop° right of his nose he hade   *tip*
A werte, and theron stood a tuft of heres,
Rede as the bristles of a sowes eres;
His nosethirles° blake were and wide.   *nostrils*
560 A swerd and a bokeler° bar° he by his side.   *small shield / carried*
His mouth as greet was as a greet furnais.
He was a janglere and a Goliardais,³
And that was most of sinne and harlotries.°   *obscenities*
Wel coude he stelen corn and tollen thries⁴—
565 And yit he hadde a thombe of gold,⁵ pardee.°   *by God*
A whit cote and a blew hood wered he.
A baggepipe wel coude he blowe and soune,
And therwithal he broughte us out of towne.
   A gentil Manciple was ther of a temple,°   *law school*
570 Of which achatours° mighte take exemple   *buyers*
For to been wise in bying of vitaile;°   *food*
For wheither that he paide or took by taile,°   *on credit*
Algate he waited so in his achat⁶
That he was ay biforn° and in good stat.°   *always ahead / well off*
575   Now is nat that of God a ful fair grace°   *blessing*
That swich a lewed° mannes wit shal pace°   *uneducated / surpass*
The wisdom of an heep of lerned men?
Of maistres° hadde he mo than thries ten   *scholars*
That weren of lawe expert and curious,°   *skillful*
580 Of whiche ther were a dozeine in that house
Worthy to been stiwardes of rente° and lond   *managers of revenues*
Of any lord that is in Engelond,
To make him live by his propre good°   *own wealth*

---

9. Money earned from his own work.
1. A Summoner, a server of summonses for the ecclesias-tical courts; Pardoner: a seller of indulgences.
2. Awarded as a prize for wrestling.
3. He was a teller of dirty stories and a reveller.
4. Collect three times as much tax as was due.

5. It was proverbial that millers were dishonest and that an honest miller was as rare as one who had a golden thumb. The statement is meant ironically.
6. He was always so watchful for his opportunities to pur-chase.

On what he earned and on his goods as well.
He wore a smock, and rode upon a mare.
  There was a reeve as well, also a miller,
A pardon-seller and a summoner,
A manciple, and myself—there were no more.
  The miller was a burly fellow—brawn
And muscle, big of bones as well as strong,
As was well seen—he always won the ram
At wrestling-matches up and down the land.
He was barrel-chested, rugged and thickset,
And would heave off its hinges any door
Or break it, running at it with his head.
His beard was red as any fox or sow,
And wide at that, as though it were a spade.
And on his nose, right on its tip, he had
A wart, upon which stood a tuft of hairs
Red as the bristles are in a sow's ears.
Black were his nostrils; black and squat and wide.
He bore a sword and buckler by his side.
His big mouth was as big as a furnace.
A loudmouth and a teller of blue stories
(Most of them vicious or scurrilous),
Well versed in stealing corn and trebling dues,
He had a golden thumb—by God he had!
A white coat he had on, and a blue hood.
He played the bagpipes well, and blew a tune,
And to its music brought us out of town.
  A worthy manciple of the Middle Temple
Was there; he might have served as an example
To all provision-buyers for his thrift
In making purchase, whether on credit
Or for cash down: he kept an eye on prices,
So always got in first and did good business.
  Now isn't it an instance of God's grace,
Such an unlettered man should so outpace
The wisdom of a pack of learned men?
He'd more than thirty masters over him,
All of them proficient experts in law,
More than a dozen of them with the power
To manage rents and land for any peer
So that—unless the man were off his head—

	In honour dettelees but if he were wood,°	*unless he were crazy*
585	Or live as scarsly° as him list° desire,	*thriftily / pleases*
	And able for to helpen al a shire	
	In any caas° that mighte falle° or happe,	*event / befall*
	And yit this Manciple sette hir aller cappe!°	*made fools of them all*
	The Reeve was a sclendre° colerik° man;	*lean / ill-tempered*
590	His beerd was shave as neigh° as evere he can;	*close*
	His heer was by his eres ful round yshorn;	
	His top was dokked° lik a preest biforn;°	*clipped / in front*
	Ful longe were his legges and ful lene,	
	Ylik° a staf, ther was no calf yseene.°	*like / visible*
595	Wel coude he keepe a gerner° a binne—	*granary*
	Ther was noon auditour coude on him winne.[7]	
	Wel wiste he by the droughte and by the rain	
	The yeelding of his seed and of his grain.	
	His lordes sheep, his neet,° his dayerye,°	*cattle / dairy cattle*
600	His swim, his hors, his stoor,° and his pultrye	*livestock*
	Was hoolly in this Reeves governinge,	
	And by his covenant° yaf the rekeninge,°	*contract / gave account*
	Sin that his lord was twenty yeer of age.	
	Ther coude no man bringe him in arrerage.°	*financial arrears*
605	Ther nas baillif, hierde, nor other hine,[8]	
	That he ne knew his sleighte° and his covine°—	*tricks / plotting*
	They were adrad of him as of the deeth.	
	His woning° was ful faire upon an heeth;°	*dwelling / meadow*
	With greene trees shadwed was his place.	
610	He coude bettre than his lord purchace.°	*buy property*
	Ful riche he was astored prively.°	*stocked in secret*
	His lord wel coude he plesen subtilly,	
	To yive and lene° him of his owene good,°	*lend / possessions*
	And have a thank,° and yit a cote and hood.	*gratitude*
615	In youthe he hadde lerned a good mister:°	*profession*
	He was a wel good wrighte, a carpenter.	
	This Reeve sat upon a ful good stot°	*stallion*
	That was a pomely° grey and highte° Scot.	*dappled / named*
	A long surcote° of pers° upon he hade,	*overcoat / blue*
620	And by his side he bar a rusty blade.	
	Of Northfolk[9] was this Reeve of which I telle,	
	Biside a town men clepen° Baldeswelle.	*call*
	Tukked[1] he was as is a frere aboute,	
	And evere he rood the hindreste° of oure route.°	*hindmost / group*
625	A Somnour was ther with us in that place	
	That hadde a fir-reed° cherubinnes° face,	*fire-red / cherub's*
	For saucefleem° he was, with yën narwe,	*pimply*
	And hoot he was, and lecherous as a sparwe,°	*sparrow*

7. Gain anything (by catching him out).
8. There was no foreman, herdsman, or other farmhand.
9. Norfolk in the north of England. The Reeve is notable for his northern dialect and regionalisms.
1. He wore his clothes tucked up with a cinch as friars did.

He could live honourably, free of debt,
Or sparingly, if that were his desire;
And able to look after a whole shire
In whatever emergency might befall;
And yet this manciple could hoodwink them all.
    There was a reeve, a thin and bilious man;
His beard he shaved as close as a man can;
Around his ears he kept his hair cropped short,
Just like a priest's, docked in front and on top.
His legs were very long, and very lean,
And like a stick; no calf was to be seen.
His granary and bins were ably kept;
There was no auditor could trip him up.
He could foretell, by noting drought and rain,
The likely harvest from his seed and grain.
His master's cattle, dairy, cows, and sheep,
His pigs and horses, poultry and livestock,
Were wholly under this reeve's governance.
And, as was laid down in his covenant,
Of these he'd always rendered an account
Ever since his master reached his twentieth year.
No man could ever catch him in arrears.
He was up to every fiddle, every dodge
Of every herdsman, bailiff, or farm-lad.
All of them feared him as they feared the plague.
His dwelling was well placed upon a heath,
Set with green trees that overshadowed it.
At business he was better than his lord:
He'd got his nest well-feathered, on the side,
For he was cunning enough to get round
His lord by lending him what was his own,
And so earn thanks, besides a coat and hood.
As a young man he'd learned a useful trade
As a skilled artisan, a carpenter.
The reeve rode on a sturdy farmer's cob
That was called Scot: it was a dapple grey.
He had on a long blue-grey overcoat,
And carried by his side a rusty sword.
A Norfolk man was he of whom I tell,
From near a place that they call Bawdeswell.
Tucked round him like a friar's was his coat;
He always rode the hindmost of our troop.
    A summoner was among us at the inn,
Whose face was fire-red, like the cherubim;
All covered with carbuncles; his eyes narrow;
He was as hot and randy as a sparrow.

With scaled° browes blake and piled² beerd: *scabby*
630   Of his visage children were aferd.°   *frightened*
      Ther nas quiksilver, litarge, ne brimstoon,
      Boras, ceruce, ne oile of tartre noon,³
      Ne oinement that wolde clense and bite,
      That him mighte helpen of his whelkes° white,   *blotches*
635   Nor of the knobbes° sitting on his cheekes.   *lumps*
      Wel loved he garlek, oinons, and eek leekes,
      And for to drinke strong win reed as blood.
      Thanne wolde he speke and crye as he were wood;°   *crazy*
      And whan that he wel dronken hadde the win,
640   Thanne wolde he speke no word but Latin:
      A fewe termes hadde he, two or three,
      That he hadde lerned out of som decree;
      No wonder is—he herde it al the day,
      And eek ye knowe wel how that a jay°   *parrot*
645   Can clepen "Watte°" as wel as can the Pope—   *call "Walter"*
      But whoso coude in other thing him grope,°   *examine*
      Thanne hadde he spent all his philosophye;
      Ay *Questio quid juris*⁴ wolde he crye.
         He was a gentil harlot° and a kinde;   *rascal*
650   A bettre felawe sholde men nought finde:
      He wolde suffre,° for a quart of win,   *allow*
      A good felawe to have his concubin°   *mistress*
      A twelfmonth, and excusen him at the fulle;
      Ful prively a finch eek coude he pulle.⁵
655   And if he foond owher° a good felawe   *anywhere*
      He wolde techen him to have noon awe
      In swich caas of the Ercedekenes curs,⁶
      But if a mannes soule were in his purs,°   *wallet*
      For in his purs he sholde ypunisshed be.
660   "Purs is the Ercedekenes helle," saide he.
         But wel I woot° he lied right in deede: *know*
      Of cursing° oughte eech gilty man him drede,°   *excommunication / fear*
      For curs wol slee° right as assoiling° savith—   *will kill / absolving*
      And also war him of a *significavit*.⁷
665   In daunger hadde he at his owene gise⁸
      The yonge girles of the diocise,
      And knew hir conseil,° and was al hir reed.°   *secrets / advice*
      A gerland hadde he set upon his heed
      As greet as it were for an ale-stake;°   *tavern sign*
670   A bokeler hadde he maad him of a cake.°   *loaf of bread*
         With him ther rood a gentil Pardoner
      Of Rouncival,⁹ his freend and his compeer,°   *companion*

---

2. With hair falling out.

3. There was not mercury, lead ointment, or sulphur, / Borax, white lead, nor any oil of tartar that could clean him.

4. "The question as to what point of law (applies)"; often used in ecclesiastical courts.

5. And secretly he also knew how to fool around.

6. In case of excommunication by the archdeacon.

7. Order of transfer from ecclesiastical to secular courts.

8. Under his control he had at his disposal.

9. A hospital at Charing Cross in London.

He'd scabbed black eyebrows, and a scraggy beard,
No wonder if the children were afraid!
There was no mercury, white lead, or sulphur,
No borax, no ceruse, no cream of tartar,
Nor any other salves that cleanse and burn,
Could help with the white pustules on his skin,
Or with the knobbed carbuncles on his cheeks.
He'd a great love of garlic, onions, leeks,
Also for drinking strong wine, red as blood,
When he would roar and gabble as if mad.
And once he had got really drunk on wine,
Then he would speak no language but Latin.
He'd picked up a few tags, some two or three,
Which he'd learned from some edict or decree—
No wonder, for he heard them every day.
Also, as everybody knows, a jay
Can call out "Wat" as well as the Pope can.
But if you tried him further with a question,
You'd find his well of learning had run dry;
"*Questio quid juris*" was all he'd ever say.
    A most engaging rascal, and a kind,
As good a fellow as you'd hope to find:
For he'd allow—given a quart of wine—
A scallywag to keep his concubine
A twelvemonth, and excuse him altogether.
He'd dip his wick, too, very much sub rosa.
And if he found some fellow with a woman,
He'd tell him not to fear excommunication
If he were caught, or the archdeacon's curse,
Unless the fellow's soul was in his purse,
For it's his purse must pay the penalty.
"Your purse is the archdeacon's Hell," said he.
    Take it from me, the man lied in his teeth:
Let sinners fear, for that curse is damnation,
Just as their souls are saved by absolution.
Let them beware, too, of a "*Significavit.*"
    Under his thumb, to deal with as he pleased,
Were the young people of his diocese;
He was their sole adviser and confidant.
Upon his head he sported a garland
As big as any hung outside a pub,
And, for a shield, he'd a round loaf of bread.
    With him there was a peerless pardon-seller
Of Charing Cross, his friend and his confrère,

That straight was comen fro the Court of Rome.
Ful loude he soong, "Com hider, love, to me."[1]
675 This Somnour bar to him a stif burdoun:°   *a strong baritone*
Was nevere trompe° of half so greet a soun.   *trumpet*
      This Pardoner hadde heer as yelow as wex,
But smoothe it heeng as dooth a strike of flex;°   *clump of flax*
By ounces° heenge his lokkes that he hadde,   *thin strands*
680 And therwith he his shuldres overspradde,
But thinne it lay, by colpons,° oon by oon;   *strands*
But hood for jolitee° wered he noon,   *fanciness*
For it was trussed up in his walet:°   *pack*
Him thoughte he rood al of the newe jet.°   *fashion*
685 Dischevelee° save his cappe he rood al bare.   *loose-haired*
Swiche glaring yën hadde he as an hare.
A vernicle[2] hadde he sowed upon his cappe,
His walet biforn him in his lappe,
Bretful of pardon,[3] comen from Rome al hoot.
690 A vois he hadde as smal° as hath a goot;°   *high-pitched / goat*
No beerd hadde he, ne nevere sholde have;
As smoothe it was as it were late yshave:
I trowe he were a gelding or a mare.[4]
But of his craft,° fro Berwik into Ware,[5]   *skill*
695 Ne was ther swich another pardoner;
For in his male° he hadde a pilwe-beer°   *bag / pillowcase*
Which that he saide was Oure Lady veil;
He saide he hadde a gobet° of the sail   *chunk*
That Sainte Peter hadde whan that he wente
700 Upon the see, til Jesu Crist him hente.°   *grabbed*
He hadde a crois of laton,° ful of stones,   *brass cross*
And in a glas he hadde pigges bones,
But with thise relikes whan that he foond
A poore person° dwelling upon lond,   *parson*
705 Upon a day he gat him more moneye
Than that the person gat in monthes twaye;°   *two*
And thus with feined flaterye and japes°   *tricks*
He made the person and the peple his apes.°   *dupes*
But trewely to tellen at the laste,
710 He was in chirche a noble ecclesiaste;
Wel coude he rede a lesson and a storye,°   *liturgical texts*
But alderbest° he soong an offertorye,   *best of all*
For wel he wiste whan that song was songe,
He moste preche and wel affile° his tonge   *sharpen*
715 To winne silver, as he ful wel coude—
Therfore he soong the merierly and loude.
      Now have I told you soothly° in a clause°   *truly / briefly*
Th'estaat, th'array, the nombre, and eek the cause

---

1. A popular ballad.
2. A pilgrim badge, reproducing St. Veronica's veil bearing the imprint of Christ's face.
3. Full to the brim with indulgences.

4. I believe he was a gelding (eunuch) or a mare (perhaps a passive homosexual).
5. Towns north and south of London.

Who'd come straight from the Vatican in Rome.
Loudly he sang, "Come to me, love, come hither!"
The summoner sang the bass, a loud refrain;
No trumpet ever made one half the din.
    This pardon-seller's hair was yellow as wax,
And sleekly hanging, like a hank of flax.
In meagre clusters hung what hair he had;
Over his shoulders a few strands were spread,
But they lay thin, in rat's tails, one by one.
As for a hood, for comfort he wore none,
For it was stowed away in his knapsack.
Save for a cap, he rode with head all bare,
Hair loose; he thought it was the *dernier cri*.
He had big bulging eyes, just like a hare.
He'd sewn a veronica on his cap.
His knapsack lay before him, on his lap,
Chockful of pardons, all come hot from Rome.
His voice was like a goat's, plaintive and thin.
He had no beard, nor was he like to have;
Smooth was his face, as if he had just shaved.
I took him for a gelding or a mare.
As for his trade, from Berwick down to Ware
You'd not find such another pardon-seller.
For in his bag he had a pillowcase
Which had been, so he said, Our Lady's veil;
He said he had a snippet of the sail
St Peter had, that time he walked upon
The sea, and Jesus Christ caught hold of him.
And he'd a brass cross, set with pebble-stones,
And a glass reliquary of pigs' bones.
But with these relics, when he came upon
Some poor up-country priest or backwoods parson,
In just one day he'd pick up far more money
Than any parish priest was like to see
In two whole months. With double-talk and tricks
He made the people and the priest his dupes.
But to speak truth and do the fellow justice,
In church he made a splendid ecclesiastic.
He'd read a lesson, or saint's history,
But best of all he sang the offertory:
For, knowing well that when that hymn was sung.
He'd have to preach and polish smooth his tongue
To raise—as only he knew how—the wind,
The louder and the merrier he would sing.
    And now I've told you truly and concisely
The rank, and dress, and number of us all,

Why that assembled was this compaignye

720 In Southwerk at this gentil hostelrye

That highte the Tabard, faste by the Belle;[6]

But now is time to you for to telle

How that we baren us that like° night   *same*

Whan we were in that hostelrye alight;

725 And after wol I telle of oure viage,°   *trip*

And al the remenant of oure pilgrimage.

But first I praye you of youre curteisye

That ye n'arette° it nought my vilainye°   *consider / rudeness*

Though that I plainly speke in this matere

730 To telle you hir wordes and hir cheere,°   *comportment*

Ne though I speke hir wordes proprely;°   *accurately*

For this ye knowen also wel as I:

Who so shal telle a tale after a man

He moot reherce,° as neigh as evere he can,   *must repeat*

735 Everich a word, if it be in his charge,

Al speke he nevere so rudeliche° and large,°   *crudely / freely*

Or elles he moot telle his tale untrewe,

Or feine° thing, or finde wordes newe;   *invent, falsify*

He may nought spare although he were his brother:

740 He moot as wel saye oo word as another.

Crist spak himself ful brode° in Holy Writ,   *plainly*

And wel ye woot° no vilainye is it;   *know*

Eek Plato saith, who so can him rede,

The wordes mote be cosin° to the deede.   *closely related*

745 Also I praye you to foryive it me

Al° have I nat set folk in hir degree°   *although / rank*

Here in this tale as that they sholde stonde:

My wit is short, ye may wel understonde.

Greet cheere made oure Host us everichoon,

750 And to the soper sette he us anoon.

He served us with vitaile at the beste.

Strong was the win, and wel to drinke us leste.°   *it pleased*

A semely° man oure Hoste was withalle   *apt*

For to been a marchal° in an halle;   *master of ceremonies*

755 A large man he was, with yën steepe;°   *glaring eyes*

A fairer burgeis was ther noon in Chepe°—   *Cheapside (in London)*

Bold of his speeche, and wis, and wel ytaught,

And of manhood him lakkede° right naught.   *he lacked*

Eek therto he was right a merye man,

760 And after soper playen he bigan,

And spak of mirthe amonges othere thinges—

Whan that we hadde maad oure rekeninges°—   *paid the bill*

And saide thus, "Now, lordinges, trewely,

Ye been to me right welcome, hertely.

765 For by my trouthe, if that I shal nat lie,

6. Another tavern in Southwark.

And why we gathered in a company
In Southwark, at that noble hostelry
Known as the Tabard, that's hard by the Bell.
But now the time has come for me to tell
What passed among us, what was said and done
The night of our arrival at the inn;
And afterwards I'll tell you how we journeyed,
And all the remainder of our pilgrimage.
     But first I beg you, not to put it down
To my ill-breeding if my speech be plain
When telling what they looked like, what they said,
Or if I use the exact words they used.
For, as you all must know as well as I,
To tell a tale told by another man
You must repeat as nearly as you can
Each word, if that's the task you've undertaken,
However coarse or broad his language is;
Or, in the telling, you'll have to distort it
Or make things up, or find new words for it.
You can't hold back, even if he's your brother:
Whatever word is used, you must use also.
Christ Himself spoke out plain in Holy Writ,
And well you know there's nothing wrong with that.
Plato, as those who read him know, has said,
"The word must be related to the deed."
     Also I beg you to forgive it me
If I overlooked all standing and degree
As regards the order in which people come
Here in this tally, as I set them down:
My wits are none too bright, as you can see.
     Our host gave each and all a warm welcome,
And set us down to supper there and then.
The eatables he served were of the best;
Strong was the wine; we matched it with our thirst.
A handsome man our host, handsome indeed,
And a fit master of ceremonies.
He was a big man with protruding eyes
—You'll find no better burgess in Cheapside—
Racy in talk, well-schooled and shrewd was he;
Also a proper man in every way.
And moreover he was a right good sort,
And after supper he began to joke,
And, when we had all paid our reckonings,
He spoke of pleasure, among other things:
"Truly," said he, ladies and gentlemen,
Here you are all most heartily welcome.
Upon my word—I'm telling you no lie—

I sawgh nat this yeer so merye a compaignye
At ones in this herberwe° as is now.   *inn*
Fain wolde I doon you mirthe, wiste I how.
And of a mirthe I am right now bithought,
770   To doon you ese, and it shal coste nought.
        Ye goon to Canterbury—God you speede;
The blisful martyr quite° you youre meede.°   *repay / reward*
And wel I woot° as ye goon by the waye   *know*
Ye shapen° you to talen° and to playe,   *intend / tell tales*
775   For trewely, confort ne mirthe is noon
To ride by the waye domb as stoon;
And therfore wol I maken you disport
As I saide erst,° and doon you som confort;   *before*
And if you liketh alle, by oon assent,
780   For to stonden at my juggement,
And for to werken as I shal you saye,
Tomorwe whan ye riden by the waye—
Now by my fader soule that is deed,
But° ye be merye I wol yive you myn heed!   *unless*
785   Holde up youre handes withouten more speeche."
        Oure conseil was nat longe for to seeche;°   *seek*
Us thoughte it was nat worth to make it wis,°   *deliberate*
And graunted him withouten more avis,°   *opinions*
And bade him saye his voirdit° as him leste.   *verdict*
790   "Lordinges," quod he, "now herkneth for the beste;
But taketh it nought, I praye you, in desdain.
This is the point, to speken short and plain,
That eech of you, to shorte with oure waye
In this viage, shal tellen tales twaye°—   *two*
795   To Canterburyward, I mene it so,
And hoomward he shal tellen othere two,
Of aventures that whilom° have bifalle;   *long ago*
And which of you that bereth him best of alle—
That is to sayn, that telleth in this cas
800   Tales of best sentence° and most solas°—   *substance / pleasure*
Shal have a soper at oure aller cost,
Here in this place, sitting by this post,
Whan that we come again fro Canterbury.
And for to make you the more mury
805   I wol myself goodly° with you ride—   *gladly*
Right at myn owene cost—and be youre gide.
And who so wol my juggement withsaye°   *contradict*
Shal paye al that we spende by the waye.
And if ye vouche sauf° that it be so,   *grant*
810   Telle me anoon, withouten wordes mo,
And I wol erly shape° me therfore."   *prepare*
        This thing was graunted and oure othes swore
With ful glad herte, and prayden him also

All year I've seen no jollier company
At one time in this inn, than I have now.
I'd make some fun for you, if I knew how.
And, as it happens, I have just now thought
Of something that will please you, at no cost.
   "You're off to Canterbury—so Godspeed!
The blessed martyr give you your reward!
And I'll be bound, that while you're on your way,
You'll be telling tales, and making holiday;
It makes no sense, and really it's no fun
To ride along the road dumb as a stone.
And therefore I'll devise a game for you,
To give you pleasure, as I said I'd do.
And if with one accord you all consent
To abide by my decision and judgement,
And if you'll do exactly as I say,
Tomorrow, when you're riding on your way,
Then, by my father's soul—for he is dead—
If you don't find it fun, why, here's my head!
Now not another word! Hold up your hands!"
   We were not long in making up our minds.
It seemed not worth deliberating, so
We gave our consent without more ado,
Told him to give us what commands he wished,
   "Ladies and gentlemen," began our host,
"Do yourselves a good turn, and hear me out:
But please don't turn your noses up at it.
I'll put it in a nutshell: here's the nub:
It's that you each, to shorten the long journey,
Shall tell two tales *en route* to Canterbury,
And, coming homeward, tell another two,
Stories of things that happened long ago.
Whoever best acquits himself, and tells
The most amusing and instructive tale,
Shall have a dinner, paid for by us all,
Here in this inn, and under this roof-tree,
When we come back again from Canterbury.
To make it the more fun, I'll gladly ride
With you at my own cost, and be your guide.
And anyone who disputes what I say
Must pay all our expenses on the way!
And if this plan appeals to all of you,
Tell me at once, and with no more ado,
And I'll make my arrangements here and now."
   To this we all agreed, and gladly swore
To keep our promises; and furthermore
We asked him if he would consent to do

That he wolde vouche sauf for to do so,
815   And that he wolde been oure governour,
And of oure tales juge° and reportour,°   *judge / recordkeeper*
And sette a soper at a certain pris,°   *price*
And we wol ruled been at his devis,°   *plan*
In heigh and lowe; and thus by oon assent
820   We been accorded to his juggement.
And therupon the win was fet° anoon;   *fetched*
We dronken and to reste wente eechoon°   *everyone*
Withouten any lenger taryinge.
Amorwe° whan that day bigan to springe   *next morning*
825   Up roos oure Host and was oure aller cok,°   *cock, wake-up call*
And gadred us togidres in a flok,
And forth we riden, a litel more than pas,°   *slow walk*
Unto the watering of Saint Thomas;[7]
And ther oure Host bigan his hors arreste,°   *stop*
830   And saide, "Lordes, herkneth if you leste:°   *it please*
"Ye woot youre forward° and it you recorde:°   *agreement / remember*
If evensong and morwesong accorde,
Lat see now who shal telle the firste tale.
As evere mote I drinken win or ale,
835   Who so be rebel to my juggement
Shal paye for al that by the way is spent.
Now draweth cut° er that we ferrer twinne:°   *lots / separate further*
He which that hath the shorteste shal biginne.
"Sire Knight," quod he, "my maister and my lord,
840   Now draweth cut, for that is myn accord.°   *wish*
Cometh neer," quod he, "my lady Prioresse,
And ye, sire Clerk, lat be youre shamefastnesse°—   *modesty*
Ne studieth nought. Lay hand to, every man!"
Anoon to drawen every wight° bigan,   *person*
845   And shortly for to tellen as it was,
Were it by aventure, or sort, or cas,°   *luck, fate or chance*
The soothe° is this, the cut fil° to the Knight;   *truth / fell*
Of which ful blithe° and glad was every wight,   *happy*
And telle he moste his tale, as was resoun,
850   By forward and by composicioun,°   *agreement*
As ye han herd. What needeth wordes mo?
And whan this goode man sawgh that it was so,
As he that wis was and obedient
To keepe his forward by his free assent,
855   He saide, "Sin I shal biginne the game,
What, welcome be the cut, in Goddes name!
Now lat us ride, and herkneth what I saye."
And with that word we riden forth oure waye,
And he bigan with right a merye cheere°   *expression*
860   His tale anoon, and saide as ye may heere.

7. A brook two miles from London.

As he had said, and come and be our leader,
And judge our tales, and act as arbiter,
Set up our dinner too, at a fixed price;
And we'd obey whatever he might decide
In everything. And so, with one consent,
We bound ourselves to bow to his judgement.
And thereupon wine was at once brought in.
We drank; and not long after, everyone
Went off to bed, and that without delay.
　　Next morning our host rose at break of day:
He was our cockcrow; so we all awoke.
He gathered us together in a flock,
And we rode, at little more than walking-pace
Till we had reached St Thomas' watering-place,
Where our host began reining in his horse.
"Ladies and gentlemen, attention please!"
Said he. "All of you know what we agreed,
And I'm reminding you. If evensong
And matins are in harmony—that's to say,
If you are still of the same mind today—
Let's see who'll tell the first tale, and begin.
And whosoever baulks at my decision
Must pay for all we spend upon the way,
Or may I never touch a drop again!
And now let's draw lots before going on.
The one who draws the short straw must begin.
　　Sir Knight, my lord and master," said our host,
"Now let's draw lots, for such is my request.
Come near," said he, "my lady Prioress,
And, Mister Scholar, lay by bashfulness,
Stop dreaming! Hands to drawing, everyone!"
　　To cut the story short, the draw began,
And, whether it was luck, or chance, or fate,
The truth is this: the lot fell to the knight,
Much to the content of the company.
Now, as was only right and proper, he
Must tell his tale, according to the bargain
Which, as you know, he'd made. What more to say?
And when the good man saw it must be so,
Being sensible, and accustomed to obey
And keep a promise he had freely given,
He said, "Well, since I must begin the game,
Then welcome to the short straw, in God's name!
Now let's ride on, and listen to what I say."
And at these words we rode off on our way,
And he at once began, with cheerful face,
His tale. The way he told it was like this.

THE MILLER'S TALE *The Miller's Tale* both answers and parodies *The Knight's Tale*, a long aristocratic romance about two knights in rivalry for the hand of a lady. While the Miller tells a nearly analogous story of erotic competition, his tale is radically shorter and explicitly sexual. Such brevity and physicality fit his tale's genre—a fabliau, or short comic tale, usually bawdy and often involving a clerk, a wife, and a cuckolded husband. Following the convention (if not the reality) that romances were written by and for the nobility and fabliaux by and for the commons, Chaucer suits *The Miller's Tale* to its teller as aptly as he does the Knight's. Slyly disclaiming responsibility for the tale, he explains its bawdiness by the Miller's class status: "the Millere is a cherle" and like his peer the Reeve who follows and "requites" him, tells "harlotrye."

The drunken Miller's insistence on telling his tale to requite the Knight's tale has been called a "literary peasants' revolt." Although the Miller, a free man, was not actually a peasant, yeomen of his status were active in the Rising of 1381, and millers in particular played a symbolic role in it (see the letters of John Ball, page 475). In fact, this tale is highly literate, with its echoes of the Song of Songs and its parody of the language of courtly love: an actual miller would have had neither the education nor the social sophistication to tell it. Yet a parody implies some degree of attachment to the very model being ridiculed, and *The Miller's Tale* is as much a claim upon the Knight's world as a repudiation of it. The Miller wants to "quiten" the Knight's tale, he says, using a word that can mean to repay or avenge, but also to fulfill. The tale's several plots converge brilliantly upon a single cry: "Water!" The tale's impact derives as well from its plenitude of pleasures (sexual, comic, even religious) after the austere and rigid desires of *The Knight's Tale*.

The Miller's Tale
The Introduction

	Whan that the Knight hadde thus his tale ytold,	
	In al the route° nas ther yong ne old	group
	That he ne saide it was a noble storye,	
	And worthy for to drawen° to memorye,	recall
5	And namely the gentils° everichoon.	upper class
	Oure Hoste lough° and swoor, "So mote I goon,[1]	laughed
	This gooth aright: unbokeled is the male.[2]	
	Lat see now who shal telle another tale.	
	For trewely the game is wel bigonne.	
10	Now telleth ye, sire Monk, if that ye conne,°	know
	Somwhat to quite° with the Knightes tale."	repay
	The Millere, that for dronken was al pale,	
	So that unnethe° upon his hors he sat,	barely
	He nolde avalen° neither hood ne hat,	would not remove
15	Ne abiden no man for his curteisye,	
	But in Pilates[3] vois he gan to crye,	
	And swoor, "By armes and by blood and bones,°	(of Christ)
	I can° a noble tale for the nones,	know
	With which I wol now quite the Knightes tale."	
20	Oure Hoste sawgh that he was dronke of ale,	
	And saide, "Abide,° Robin, leve° brother,	wait / dear

1. Thus I may proceed.
2. The bag is opened (i.e., the games are begun).

3. The role of Pilate was traditionally played in a loud and raucous voice in the mystery plays.

Som bettre man shal telle us first another.
Abide, and lat us werken thriftily."°   *properly*
    "By Goddes soule," quod he, "that wol nat I,
25   For I wol speke or elles go my way."
    Oure Host answerde, "Tel on, a devele way!°   *in the devil's name*
Thou art a fool; thy wit is overcome."
    "Now herkneth," quod the Millere, "alle and some.°   *one and all*
But first I make a protestacioun
30   That I am dronke: I knowe it by my soun.°   *sound*
And therfore if that I mis speke or saye,
Wite it° the ale of Southwerk, I you praye;   *blame it on*
For I wol telle a legende and a lif[4]
Bothe of a carpenter and of his wif,
35   How that a clerk hath set the wrightes cappe."[5]
    The Reeve answerde and saide, "Stint thy clappe!°   *hold your tongue*
Lat be thy lewed° dronken harlotrye.°   *unlearned / obscenity*
It is a sinne and eek a greet folye
To apairen° any man or him defame,   *injure*
40   And eek to bringen wives in swich fame.
Thou maist ynough of othere thinges sayn."
    This dronken Millere spak ful soone again,
And saide, "Leve brother Osewold,
Who hath no wif, he is no cokewold.°   *cuckold*
45   But I saye nat therfore that thou art oon.
Ther ben ful goode wives many oon,
And evere a thousand goode ayains oon badde.°   *against one bad*
That knowestou wel thyself but if thou madde.°   *go insane*
Why artou angry with my tale now?
50   I have a wif, pardee,° as wel as thou,   *by God*
Yet nolde I, for the oxen in my plough,[6]
Take upon me more than ynough
As deemen° of myself that I were oon:°   *judge / one (a cuckold)*
I wol bileve wel that I am noon.
55   An housbonde shal nought been inquisitif
Of Goddes privetee,° nor of his wif.   *secrets*
So he may finde Goddes foison° there,   *plenty*
Of the remenant needeth nought enquere."
    What sholde I more sayn but this Millere
60   He nolde° his wordes for no man forbere,   *would not*
But tolde his cherles° tale in his manere.   *commoner's*
M'athinketh° that I shal reherce° it here,   *I regret / repeat*
And therfore every gentil wight° I praye,   *person*
Deemeth nought, for Goddes love, that I saye
65   Of yvel entente, but for° I moot° reherse   *because / must*
Hir tales alle, be they bet or werse,
Or elles falsen som of my matere.

---

4. The story of a saint's life.
5. Made a fool of the carpenter.

6. Yet I wouldn't, not even (in wager) for the oxen in my
plough.

And therfore, whoso list it nought yheere

Turne over the leef,° and chese° another tale,   *page / choose*

70   For he shal finde ynowe,° grete and smale,   *enough*

Of storial° thing that toucheth gentilesse,°   *historical / nobility*

And eek moralitee and holinesse:

Blameth nought me if that ye chese amis.

The Millere is a cherl, ye knowe wel this,

75   So was the Reeve eek, and othere mo,

And harlotrye they tolden bothe two.

Aviseth you,° and putte me out of blame: *be warned*

And eek men shal nought maken ernest of game.°   *treat jokes seriously*

The Tale

Whilom° ther was dwelling at Oxenforde   *long ago*

80   A riche gnof° that gestes heeld to boorde,°   *fool / took in boarders*

And of his craft he was a carpenter.

With him ther was dwelling a poore scoler,

Hadde lerned art,[7] but al his fantasye°   *fancy*

Was turned for to lere° astrologye,   *learn*

85   And coude a certain of conclusiouns,°   *predictions*

To deemen by interrogaciouns,[8]

If that men axed° him in certain houres   *asked*

Whan that men sholde have droughte or elles showres,

Or if men axed him what shal bifalle

90   Of every thing—I may nat rekene° hem alle.   *count*

This clerk was cleped° hende[9] Nicholas.   *called*

Of derne° love he coude, and of solas,[1]   *secret*

And therto he was sly and ful privee,°   *secretive*

And lik a maide meeke for to see.

95   A chambre hadde he in that hostelrye°   *inn*

Allone, withouten any compaignye,

Ful fetisly ydight with herbes swoote,[2]

And he himself as sweete as is the roote

Of licoris or any setewale.[3]

100 His Almageste[4] and bookes grete and smale,

His astrelabye,[5] longing for° his art,   *belonging to*

His augrim stones,° layen faire apart   *abacus beads*

On shelves couched° at his beddes heed;   *arranged*

His presse° ycovered with a falding° reed;   *dresser / coarse cloth*

105 And al above ther lay a gay sautrye,°   *harp*

On which he made a-nightes melodye

So swetely that al the chambre roong,

And *Angelus ad Virginem*[6] he soong,

---

7. The arts curriculum (trivium).
8. To estimate by consulting (the stars).
9. Handsome, courteous, handy.
1. Pleasure, (sexual) comforts.
2. Elegantly decked out with sweet herbs.

3. Setwall, a gingerlike spice used as a stimulant.
4. An astrological treatise by Ptolemy.
5. Astrolabe, an astrological instrument.
6. A prayer commemorating the Annunciation.

	And after that he soong the *Kinges Note:*[7]	
110	Ful often blessed was his merye throte.	
	And thus this sweete clerk his time spente	
	After his freendes finding and his rente.[8]	
	This carpenter hadde wedded newe a wif	
	Which that he loved more than his lif.	
115	Of eighteteene yeer she was of age;	
	Jalous he was, and heeld hire narwe in cage,	
	For she was wilde and yong, and he was old,	
	And deemed° himself been lik a cokewold.	*supposed*
	He knew nat Caton,[9] for his wit was rude,	
120	That bad men sholde wedde his similitude:°	*equal in age*
	Men sholde wedden after hir estat,°	*station in life*
	For youthe and elde is often at debat.	
	But sith that he was fallen in the snare,	
	He moste endure, as other folk, his care.	
125	Fair was this yonge wif, and therwithal	
	As any wesele hir body gent and smal.[1]	
	A ceint° she wered, barred° al of silk;	*belt / striped*
	A barmcloth° as whit as morne milk	*apron*
	Upon hir lendes,° ful of many a gore;°	*loins / flounce*
130	Whit was hir smok,° and broiden° al bifore	*slip / embroidered*
	And eek bihinde, on hir coler aboute,°	*around her collar*
	Of col-blak silk, withinne and eek withoute;	
	The tapes° of hir white voluper°	*ribbons / cap*
	Were of the same suite° of hir coler;	*pattern*
135	Hir filet° brood° of silk and set ful hye;	*headband / broad*
	And sikerly she hadde a likerous yë;[2]	
	Ful smale ypulled° were hir browes two,	*plucked*
	And tho° were bent, and blake as any slo.°	*they / plum*
	She was ful more blisful on to see	
140	Than is the newe perejonette° tree,	*pear*
	And softer than the wolle is of a wether;°	*ram*
	And by hir girdel° heeng a purs of lether,	*belt*
	Tasseled with silk and perled° with latoun.°	*decorated / brass*
	In al this world, to seeken up and down,	
145	Ther nis no man so wis that coude thenche°	*imagine*
	So gay a popelote° or swich a wenche.[3]	*doll*
	Ful brighter was the shining of hir hewe	
	Than in the Towr the noble° yforged newe.[4]	*gold coin*
	But of hir song, it was as loud and yerne°	*lively*
150	As any swalwe sitting on a berne.	
	Therto she coude skippe and make game	

7. A popular song.
8. According to what his friends gave him and his income.
9. Cato, Latin author of a book of maxims used in elementary education.

1. Her body as delicate and slender as any weasel.
2. And certainly she had a wanton eye.
3. Woman of the working class.
4. Than the new-forged gold coin in the Tower (of London, the royal mint).

As any kide or calf folwing his dame.°   *mother*
Hir mouth was sweete as bragot or the meeth,°   *honey drinks*
Or hoord of apples laid in hay or heeth.°   *heather*
155 Winsing° she was as is a joly° colt,   *skittish / spirited*
Long as a mast, and upright° as a bolt.°   *strait / arrow*
A brooch she bar upon hir lowe coler
As brood as is the boos° of a bokeler;°   *boss / shield*
Hir shoes were laced on hir legges hye.
160 She was a primerole,° a piggesnye,[5]   *primrose*
For any lord to leggen in his bedde,
Or yet for any good yeman to wedde.
     Now sire, and eft° sire, so bifel the cas   *again*
That on a day this hende Nicholas
165 Fil with this yonge wif to rage° and playe,   *sport*
Whil that hir housbonde was at Oseneye°   *Osney, near Oxford*
(As clerkes been ful subtil and ful quainte°),   *clever*
And prively he caughte hire by the queinte,[6]
And saide, "Ywis,° but if ich have my wille,   *certainly*
170 For derne° love of thee, lemman,° I spille,"°   *secret / sweetheart / die*
And heeld hire harde by the haunche-bones,
And saide, "Lemman, love me al atones,°   *at once*
Or I wol dien, also° God me save."   *so*
And she sproong as a colt dooth in a trave,[7]
175 And with hir heed she wried° faste away;   *twisted*
She saide, "I wol nat kisse thee, by my fay.°   *faith*
Why, lat be," quod she, "lat be, Nicholas!
Or I wol crye 'Out, harrow, and allas!'
Do way youre handes, for your curteisye!"
180   This Nicholas gan mercy for to crye,
And spak so faire, and profred him° so faste,   *pressed his case*
That she hir love him graunted atte laste,
And swoor hir ooth by Saint Thomas of Kent
That she wolde been at his comandement,
185 Whan that she may hir leiser° wel espye.   *opportunity*
"Myn housbonde is so ful of jalousye
That but ye waite wel and been privee,[8]
I woot° right wel I nam but deed,"° quod she.   *know / am no more than*
"Ye moste been ful derne° as in this cas."   *secret*
190   "Nay, therof care thee nought," quod Nicholas.
"A clerk hadde litherly biset his while,°   *wasted his time*
But if he coude a carpenter bigile."
And thus they been accorded and ysworn
To waite a time, as I have told biforn.
195 Whan Nicholas hadde doon this everydeel,
And thakked° hire upon the lendes° weel,   *patted / loins*
He kiste hire sweete, and taketh his sautrye,

5. Pig's eye, a flower.   7. A restraint for horses when they are being shod.
6. Literally "dainty part," slang for the female genitals.   8. That unless you're very cautious and discreet.

And playeth faste, and maketh melodye.
　　Thanne fil it thus, that to the parissh chirche,
200　Cristes owene werkes for to wirche,
This goode wif wente on an haliday:°　　　　　　　　　*holy day*
Hir forheed shoon as bright as any day,
So was it wasshen whan she leet° hir werk.　　　　　*left off*
　　Now was ther of that chirche a parissh clerk,
205　The which that was ycleped° Absolon:　　　　　　　*called*
Crul° was his heer, and as the gold it shoon,　　　　*curly*
And strouted as a fanne[9] large and brode;
Ful straight and evene lay his joly shode.°　　　　　*part in his hair*
His rode° was reed, his y'n greye as goos.　　　　　*complexion*
210　With Poules window[1] corven° on his shoos,　　　*carved*
In hoses rede he wente fetisly.°　　　　　　　　　　*elegantly*
Yclad he was ful smale° and proprely,　　　　　　　*fine*
Al in a kirtel° of a light waget°—　　　　　　　　　*tunic / blue*
Ful faire and thikke been the pointes° set—　　　　　*laces*
215　And therupon he hadde a gay surplis,°　　　　　　*clerical robe*
As whit as is the blosme upon the ris.°　　　　　　　*twig*
A merye child° he was, so God me save.　　　　　　　*lad*
Wel coude he laten blood,[2] and clippe,° and shave,　*cut hair*
And maken a chartre of land, or acquitaunce;°　　　　*legal release*
220　In twenty manere coude he trippe and daunce
After the scole of Oxenforde tho,
And with his legges casten° to and fro,　　　　　　　*fling*
And playen songes on a smal rubible;°　　　　　　　*fiddle*
Therto he soong somtime a loud quinible,°　　　　　　*high treble*
225　And as wel coude he playe on a giterne:°　　　　　*guitar*
In al the town nas brewhous ne taverne
That he ne visited with his solas,[3]
Ther any gailard tappestere° was.　　　　　　　　　*saucy barmaid*
But sooth to sayn, he was somdeel squaimous°　　　　*somewhat squeamish*
230　Of farting, and of speeche daungerous.°　　　　　*haughty*
　　This Absolon, that joly was and gay,
Gooth with a cencer° on the haliday,　　　　　　　　*incense bowl*
Cencing the wives of the parissh faste,
And many a lovely look on hem he caste,
235　And namely on this carpenteres wif:
To looke on hire him thoughte a merye lif.
She was so propre and sweete and likerous,°　　　　　*sexy*
I dar wel sayn, if she hadde been a mous,
And he a cat, he wolde hire hente° anoon.　　　　　　*catch*
240　This parissh clerk, this joly Absolon,
Hath in his herte swich a love-longinge
That of no wif ne took he noon offringe—

9. And spread out like a winnowing fan (for separating
wheat from chaff).
1. The windows of St. Paul's Chapel were intricately
patterned.
2. Let blood (a medical treatment performed by barbers).
3. Entertainment (also with sexual connotations).

For curteisye he saide he wolde noon.
The moone, whan it was night, ful brighte shoon,

245   And Absolon his giterne hath ytake—
For paramours he thoughte for to wake[4]—
And forth he gooth, jolif° and amorous,   *pretty*
Til he cam to the carpenteres hous,
A litel after cokkes hadde ycrowe,

250   And dressed° him up by a shot-windowe°   *placed / hinged window*
That was upon the carpenteres wal.
He singeth in his vois gentil and smal,°   *high*
"Now dere lady, if thy wille be,
I praye you that ye wol rewe° on me,"   *take pity*

255   Ful wel accordant° to his giterninge.   *harmonizing*
This carpenter awook and herde him singe,
And spak unto his wif, and saide anoon,
"What, Alison, heerestou nought Absolon
That chaunteth thus under oure bowres° wal?"   *bedroom's*

260   And she answerde hir housbonde therwithal,
"Yis, God woot,° John, I heere it everydeel."°   *knows / every bit*
    This passeth forth. What wol ye bet than weel?[5]
Fro day to day this joly Absolon
So woweth° hire that him is wo-bigoon: *woos*

265   He waketh al the night and al the day;
He kembed° his lokkes brode° and made him gay;   *combed / wide-spreading*
He woweth hire by menes and brocage,[6]
And swoor he wolde been hir owene page;°   *attendant*
He singeth, brokking° as a nightingale;   *trilling*

270   He sente hire piment,° meeth,° and spiced ale,   *spiced wine / mead*
And wafres° piping hoot out of the gleede;°   *pastries / coals*
And for she was of towne, he profred meede°—   *bribes*
For som folk wol be wonnen for richesse,
And som for strokes,° and som for gentilesse.   *by force*

275   Somtime to shewe his lightnesse° and maistrye,°   *agility / skill*
He playeth Herodes[7] upon a scaffold° hye.   *platform*
But what availeth him as in this cas?
She loveth so this hende Nicholas
That Absolon may blowe the bukkes horn;[8]

280   He ne hadde for his labour but a scorn.
And thus she maketh Absolon hir ape,°   *fool*
And al his ernest turneth til a jape.°   *joke*
Ful sooth° is this proverbe, it is no lie;   *true*
Men saith right thus: "Alway the nye slye°   *sly one nearby*

285   Maketh the ferre leve to be loth."[9]
For though that Absolon be wood° or wroth,°   *crazy / angry*

---

4. For the sake of love he thought to keep a vigil.
5. What more would you want?
6. He woos her with go-betweens and mediation.
7. In the English mystery plays, Herod was often portrayed as a bully.
8. Undertake a useless endeavor.
9. Makes the distant beloved seem hateful.

By cause that he fer was from hir sighte,
This nye Nicholas stood in his lighte.°   *in the way*
   Now beer thee wel, thou hende Nicholas,
290 For Absolon may waile and singe allas.
   And so bifel it on a Saterday
This carpenter was goon til Oseney,
And hende Nicholas and Alisoun
Accorded been to this conclusioun,
295 That Nicholas shal shapen hem a wile°   *devise them a trick*
This sely° jalous housbonde to bigile,   *innocent*
And if so be this game wente aright,
She sholden sleepen in his arm al night—
For this was his desir and hire also.
300 And right anoon, withouten wordes mo,
This Nicholas no lenger wolde tarye,
But dooth ful softe unto his chambre carye
Bothe mete and drinke for a day or twaye,
And to hir housbonde bad hire for to saye,
305 If that he axed after Nicholas,
She sholde saye she niste° wher he was—   *did not know*
Of al that day she sawgh him nought with yë:
She trowed° that he was in maladye,   *believed*
For for no cry hir maide coude him calle,
310 He nolde° answere for no thing that mighte falle.°   *would not / happen*
   This passeth forth al thilke° Saterday   *that same*
That Nicholas stille in his chambre lay,
And eet, and sleep, or dide what him leste,°   *he liked*
Til Sonday that the sonne gooth to reste.
315 This sely carpenter hath greet mervaile°   *wonder*
Of Nicholas, or what thing mighte him aile,
And saide, "I am adrad,° by Saint Thomas,   *afraid*
It stondeth nat aright with Nicholas.
God shilde° that he deide sodeinly!   *forbid*
320 This world is now ful tikel,° sikerly:°   *changeable / surely*
I sawgh today a corps yborn to chirche
That now a Monday last I sawgh him wirche.°   *working*
Go up," quod he unto his knave° anoon,   *manservant*
"Clepe° at his dore or knokke with a stoon.   *call*
325 Looke how it is and tel me boldely."
   This knave gooth him up ful sturdily,
And at the chambre dore whil that he stood
He cride and knokked as that he were wood,
"What? How? What do ye, maister Nicholay?
330 How may ye sleepen al the longe day?".
But al for nought: he herde nat a word.
An hole he foond ful lowe upon a boord,
Ther as the cat was wont in for to creepe,
And at that hole he looked in ful deepe,
335 And atte laste he hadde of him a sighte.

	This Nicholas sat evere caping° uprighte	*staring*
	As he hadde kiked° on the newe moone.	*gazed*
	A down he gooth and tolde his maister soone	
	In what array° he saw this ilke° man.	*condition / same*
340	This carpenter to blessen him[1] bigan.	
	And saide, "Help us, Sainte Frideswide![2]	
	A man woot litel what him shal bitide.	
	This man is falle, with his astromye,	
	In som woodnesse° or in som agonye.°	*madness / fit*
345	I thoughte ay° wel how that it sholde be:	*always*
	Men sholde nought knowe of Goddes privetee.	
	Ye, blessed be alway a lewed° man	*unlearned*
	That nought but only his bileve can.°	*knows his creed*
	So ferde° another clerk with astromye:	*fared*
350	He walked in the feeldes for to prye°	*gaze*
	Upon the sterres, what ther sholde bifalle,	
	Til he was in a marle-pit° yfalle—	*clay-pit*
	He saw nat that. But yet, by Saint Thomas,	
	Me reweth sore° for hende Nicholas.	*feel sorry*
355	He shal be rated° of his studying,	*scolded*
	If that I may, by Jesus, hevene king!	
	Get me a staf that I may underspore,°	*pry upward*
	Whil that thou, Robin, hevest up the dore.	
	He shal out of his studying, as I gesse."	
360	And to the chambre dore he gan him dresse.°	*placed himself*
	His knave was a strong carl° for the nones,°	*fellow / purpose*
	And by the haspe° he haaf° it up atones:	*hinge / heaved*
	Into the floor the dore fil anoon.	
	This Nicholas sat ay as stille as stoon,	
365	And evere caped up into the air.	
	This carpenter wende° he were in despair,	*thought*
	And hente° him by the shuldres mightily,	*grabbed*
	And shook him harde, and cride spitously,°	*vigorously*
	"What, Nicholay, what, how! What! Looke adown!	
370	Awaak and thenk on Cristes passioun![3]	
	I crouche° thee from elves and fro wightes."°	*bless / evil spirits*
	Therwith the nightspel° saide he anoonrightes	*charm*
	On foure halves° of the hous aboute,	*sides*
	And on the thresshfold on the dore withoute:	
375	"Jesu Crist and Sainte Benedight,[4]	
	Blesse this hous from every wikked wight!	
	For nightes nerye° the White Pater Noster.[5]	*protect*
	Where wentestou, thou Sainte Petres soster?"°	*sister*
	And at the laste this hende Nicholas	
380	Gan for to sike° sore, and saide, "Allas,	*sigh*

1. Bless himself (with the sign of the cross).
2. A saint venerated for her healing powers.
3. Thinking about Christ's death and resurrection was
supposed to ward off evil spells.
4. St. Benedict, founder of Western monasticism.
5. The Lord's Prayer, used as a charm.

Shal al the world be lost eftsoones° now"?   *immediately*
   This carpenter answerde, "What saistou?
What, thenk on God as we doon, men that swinke."°   *work*
   This Nicholas answerde, "Fecche me drinke,
385   And after wol I speke in privetee
Of certain thing that toucheth me and thee.
I wol telle it noon other man, certain."
   This carpenter gooth down and comth again,
And broughte of mighty ale a large quart,
390   And whan that eech of hem hadde dronke his part,
This Nicholas his dore faste shette,°   *shut*
And down the carpenter by him he sette,
And saide, "John, myn hoste lief° and dere,   *beloved*
Thou shalt upon thy trouthe° swere me here   *word of honor*
395   That to no wight thou shalt this conseil° wraye;°   *advice / disclose*
For it is Cristes conseil that I saye,
And if thou telle it man, thou art forlore,°   *lost*
For this vengeance thou shalt have therfore,
That if thou wraye° me, thou shalt be wood."°   *reveal / mad*
400   "Nay, Crist forbede it, for his holy blood,"
Quod tho this sely man. "I nam no labbe,°   *am no blabbermouth*
And though I saye, I nam nat lief° to gabbe.   *do not like*
Say what thou wilt, I shal it nevere telle
To child ne wif, by him that harwed helle."[6]
405   "Now John," quod Nicholas, "I wol nought lie.
I have yfounde in myn astrologye,
As I have looked in the moone bright,
That now a Monday next, at quarter night,°   *near dawn*
Shal falle a rain, and that so wilde and wood,°   *furious*
410   That half so greet was nevere Noees° flood.   *Noah's*
This world," he saide, "in lasse than an hour
Shal al be dreint,° so hidous is the showr.   *drowned*
Thus shal mankinde drenche° and lese hir lif."°   *drown / lose their lives*
   This carpenter answerde, "Allas, my wif!
415   And shal she drenche? Allas, myn Alisoun!"
For sorwe of this he fil almost adown,
And saide, "Is there no remedye in this cas?"
   "Why yis, for Gode," quod hende Nicholas,
"If thou wolt werken° after lore° and reed°—   *act / learning / advice*
420   Thou maist nought werken after thyn owene heed;
For thus saith Salomon that was ful trewe,
'Werk al by conseil and thou shalt nought rewe.'°   *regret*
And if thou werken wolt by good conseil,
I undertake, withouten mast or sail,
425   Yet shal I save hire and thee and me.
Hastou nat herd how saved was Noee

---

6. Christ, who harrowed hell upon his resurrection, releasing captive souls.

Whan that Oure Lord hadde warned him biforn
That al the world with water sholde be lorn?"°   *lost*
"Yis," quod this carpenter, "ful yore° ago."   *long*
430   "Hastou nat herd," quod Nicholas, "also
The sorwe° of Noee with his felaweshipe?°   *sorrow / companions*
Er that he mighte gete his wif to shipe,
Him hadde levere,° I dar wel undertake,   *would have preferred*
At thilke° time than alle his wetheres blake°   *that / black rams*
435   That she hadde had a ship hirself allone.[7]
And therfore woostou° what is best to doone?   *do you know*
This axeth haste, and of an hastif° thing   *urgent*
Men may nought preche or maken tarying.
Anoon go gete us faste into this in°   *inn*
440   A kneeding trough or elles a kimelin°   *brewing trough*
For eech of us, but looke that they be large,
In whiche we mowen swimme as in a barge,
And han therinne vitaile suffisaunt°   *enough food*
But for a day—fy on the remenaunt!
445   The water shal aslake° and goon away   *recede*
Aboute prime° upon the nexte day.   *6 A.M.*
But Robin may nat wite° of this, thy knave,   *know*
Ne eek thy maide Gille I may nat save.
Axe nought why, for though thou axe me,
450   I wol nought tellen Goddes privetee.
Suffiseth thee, but if thy wittes madde,°   *go mad*
To han° as greet a grace as Noee hadde.   *have*
Thy wif shal I wel saven, out of doute.
Go now thy way, and speed thee heraboute.
455   But whan thou hast for hire and thee and me
Ygeten° us thise kneeding-tubbes three,   *gotten*
Thanne shaltou hangen hem in the roof ful hye,
That no man of oure purveyance° espye.   *preparations*
And whan thou thus hast doon as I have said,
460   And hast oure vitaile faire in hem ylaid,
And eek° an ax to smite° the corde atwo,   *also / cut*
Whan that the water comth that we may go,
And broke an hole an heigh° upon the gable   *on high*
Unto the gardinward,° over the stable,   *toward the garden*
465   That we may freely passen forth oure way,
Whan that the grete showr is goon away,
Thanne shaltou swimme as merye, I undertake,
As dooth the white doke° after hir drake.   *female duck*
Thanne wol I clepe,° 'How, Alison? How, John?   *call out*
470   Be merye, for the flood wol passe anoon.'
And thou wolt sayn, 'Hail, maister Nicholay!
Good morwe, I see thee wel, for it is day!'

---

7. Noah's wife was traditionally portrayed in the mystery plays as a complaining wife who resisted boarding the ark.

And thanne shal we be lordes al oure lif
Of al the world, as Noee and his wif.
475 But of oo thing I warne thee ful right:
Be wel avised on that ilke night
That we been entred into shippes boord
That noon of us ne speke nought a word,
Ne clepe,° ne crye, but been in his prayere,   *call out*
480 For it is Goddes owene heeste° dete.   *commandment*
Thy wif and thou mote° hange fer atwinne,°   *must / apart*
For that bitwixe you shal be no sinne—
Namore in looking than ther shal in deede.
This ordinance is said: go, God thee speede.
485 Tomorwe at night whan men been alle asleepe,
Into oure kneeding-tubbes wol we creepe,
And sitten there, abiding Goddes grace.
Go now thy way, I have no lenger space°   *time*
To make of this no lenger sermoning.
490 Men sayn thus: 'Send the wise and say no thing.'
Thou art so wis it needeth thee nat teche:
Go save oure lif, and that I thee biseeche."
     This sely° carpenter gooth forth his way: *hapless*
Ful ofte he saide allas and wailaway,
495 And to his wif he tolde his privetee,
And she was war,° and knew it bet° than he,   *aware / better*
What al this quainte cast° was for to saye.°   *clever trick / mean*
But nathelees she ferde° as she wolde deye,   *acted*
And saide, "Allas, go forth thy way anoon.
500 Help us to scape,° or we been dede eechoon.   *escape*
I am thy trewe verray wedded wif:
Go, dere spouse, and help to save oure lif."
     Lo, which a greet thing is affeccioun!°   *emotion*
Men may dien,° of imaginacioun,°   *die / fantasy*
505 So deepe may impression be take.
This sely carpenter biginneth quake;
Him thinketh verrailiche° that he may see   *truly*
Noees flood come walwing° as the see   *rolling in*
To drenchen Alison, his hony dere.
510 He weepeth, waileth, maketh sory cheere;°   *expression*
He siketh° with ful many a sory swough,°   *sighs / breath*
And gooth and geteth him a kneeding-trough,
And after a tubbe and a kimelin,
And prively he sente hem to his in,
515 And heeng hem in the roof in privetee;
His owene hand he made laddres three,
To climben by the ronges and the stalkes°   *uprights*
Unto the tubbes hanging in the balkes,°   *rafters*
And hem vitailed, bothe trough and tubbe,
520 With breed and cheese and good ale in a jubbe,°   *jug*
Suffising right ynough as for a day.

But er that he hadde maad al this array,
He sente his knave, and eek his wenche also,
Upon his neede° to London for to go.   *errand*
525 And on the Monday whan it drow to nighte,
He shette his dore withouten candel-lighte,
And dressed° alle thing as it sholde be,   *arranged*
And shortly up they clomben alle three.
They seten stille wel a furlong way.[8]
530   "Now, Pater Noster, clum,"[9] saide Nicholay,
And "Clum" quod John, and "Clum" saide Alisoun.
This carpenter saide his devocioun,
And stille he sit and biddeth his prayere,
Awaiting on the rain, if he it heere.
535   The dede sleep, for wery bisinesse,
Fil on this carpenter right as I gesse
Aboute corfew time,° or litel more.   *dusk*
For travailing of his gost° he groneth sore,   *spirit*
And eft he routeth,° for his heed mislay.   *snores*
540   Down of the laddre stalketh Nicholay,
And Alison ful softe adown she spedde:
Withouten wordes mo they goon to bedde
Ther as the carpenter is wont to lie.
Ther was the revel and the melodye,
545 And thus lith Alison and Nicholas
In bisinesse of mirthe and of solas,
Til that the belle of Laudes[1] gan to ringe,
And freres° in the chauncel° gonne singe.   *friars / chapel*
This parissh clerk, this amorous Absolon,
550 That is for love alway so wo-bigoon,
Upon the Monday was at Oseneye,
With compaignye him to disporte and playe,
And axed upon caas° a cloisterer[2]   *by chance*
Ful prively after John the carpenter;
555 And he drow him apart out of the chirche,
And saide, "I noot:° I sawgh him here nought wirche° *don't know / working*
Sith Saterday. I trowe that he be went
For timber ther oure abbot hath him sent.
For he is wont for timber for to go,
560 And dwellen atte grange° a day or two.   *outlying farm*
Or elles he is at his hous, certain.
Where that he be I can nought soothly° sayn."   *truly*
This Absolon ful jolif was and light,°   *amorous and happy*
And thoughte, "Now is time to wake al night,
565 For sikerly,° I sawgh him nought stiringe   *surely*
Aboute his dore sin° day bigan to springe.°   *since / break*
So mote I thrive,° I shal at cokkes crowe   *may I prosper*

8. The length of time to travel a furlong.   1. Lauds, daily church service before sunrise.
9. Say the Lord's Prayer and hush.   2. Member of the monastery.

	Ful prively knokken at his windowe	
	That stant ful lowe upon his bowres° wal.	*bedroom's*
570	To Alison now wol I tellen al	
	My love-longing, for yet I shal nat misse	
	That at the leeste way I shal hire kisse.	
	Som manere confort shal I have, parfay.°	*indeed*
	My mouth hath icched° al this longe day:	*itched*
575	That is a signe of kissing at the leeste.	
	Al night me mette° eek I was at a feeste.	*dreamed*
	Therfore I wol go sleepe an hour or twaye,	
	And al the night thanne wol I wake and playe."	
	Whan that the firste cok hath crowe, anoon	
580	Up rist this joly lovere Absolon,	
	And him arrayeth gay at point devis.°	*fastidiously*
	But first he cheweth grain³ and licoris,	
	To smellen sweete, er he hadde kembd his heer.	
	Under his tonge a trewe-love⁴ he beer.	
585	For therby wende° he to be gracious.°	*supposed / attractive*
	He rometh to the carpenteres hous,	
	And stille he stant under the shot-windowe—	
	Unto his brest it raughte,° it was so lowe—	*reached*
	And ofte he cougheth with a semisoun.°	*soft noise*
590	"What do ye, hony-comb, sweete Alisoun,	
	My faire brid,° my sweete cinamome?	*bird or bride*
	Awaketh, lemman° myn, and speketh to me.	*sweetheart*
	Wel litel thinken ye upon my wo	
	That for your love I swete° ther I go.	*dissolve*
595	No wonder is though that I swelte° and swete:	*swelter*
	I moorne as dooth a lamb after the tete.	
	Ywis,° lemman, I have swich love-longinge,	*certainly*
	That lik a turtle° trewe is my moorninge:	*turtle-dove*
	I may nat ete namore than a maide."	
600	"Go fro the windowe, Jakke fool," she saide.	
	"As help me God, it wol nat be com-pa-me.°	*come kiss me*
	I love another, and elles I were to blame,	
	Wel bet than thee, by Jesu, Absolon.	
	Go forth thy way or I wol caste a stoon,	
605	And lat me sleepe, a twenty devele way."⁵	
	"Allas," quod Absolon, "and wailaway,	
	That trewe love was evere so yvele biset.°	*badly done to*
	Thanne kis me, sin that it may be no bet,	
	For Jesus love and for the love of me."	
610	"Woltou thanne go thy way therwith?" quod she.	
	"Ye, certes, lemman," quod this Absolon.	
	"Thanne maak thee redy," quod she. "I come anoon."	
	And unto Nicholas she said stille,	

---

3. Grain of paradise, an aromatic spice.
4. Four-leafed herb in the shape of a love knot.

5. In the name of 20 devils.

"Now hust,° and thou shalt laughen al thy fille."   *hush*
615   This Absolon down sette him on his knees,
And saide, "I am a lord at alle degrees,°   *in every way*
For after this I hope ther cometh more.
Lemman, thy grace, and sweete brid, thyn ore!"°   *mercy*
    The windowe she undooth, and that in haste.
620   "Have do," quod she, "com of and speed thee faste,
Lest that oure neighebores thee espye."
    This Absolon gan wipe his mouth ful drye:
Derk was the night as pich or as the cole,
And at the windowe out she putte hir hole.
625   And Absolon, him fil no bet ne wers,
But with his mouth he kiste hir naked ers,
Ful savourly,° er he were war of this.   *enthusiastically*
Abak he sterte, and thoughte it was amis,
For wel he wiste a womman hath no beerd.
630   He felte a thing al rough and longe yherd,°   *haired*
And saide, "Fy, allas, what have I do?"
"Teehee," quod she, and clapte the windowe to.
And Absolon gooth forth a sory pas.°   *with downcast step*
"A beerd, a beerd!" quod hende Nicholas,
635   "By Goddes corpus,° this gooth faire and weel."   *body*
    This sely Absolon herde everydeel,
And on his lippe he gan for anger bite,
And to himself he saide, "I shal thee quite."°   *repay*
    Who rubbeth now, who froteth now his lippes
640   With dust, with sond, with straw, with cloth, with chippes,
But Absolon, that saith ful ofte allas?
"My soule bitake° I unto Satanas,   *hand over*
But me were levere than[6] all this town," quod he,
"Of this despit° awroken° for to be.   *insult / avenged*
645   Allas," quod he, "allas I ne hadde ybleint!"°   *turned aside*
His hote love was cold and al yqueint,°   *quenched*
For fro that time that he hadde kist hir ers
Of paramours he sette nought a kers,[7]
For he was heled of his maladye.
650   Ful ofte paramours he gan defye,°   *renounce*
And weep as dooth a child that is ybete.°   *beaten*
A softe paas he wente over the streete
Until a smith men clepen daun Gervais,°   *call Sir*
That in his forge smithed plough harneis:°   *equipment*
655   He sharpeth shaar° and cultour° bisily.   *plowshare / plough-blade*
This Absolon knokketh al esily,°   *softly*
And saide, "Undo,° Gervais, and that anoon."   *open up*
    "What, who artou?" "It am I, Absolon."
"What, Absolon? What, Cristes sweete tree!

---

6. I would rather than (have).   7. Did not value as much as a piece of cress.

660	Why rise ye so rathe?° Ey, benedicite,°	*early / bless me*
	What aileth you? Som gay girl, God it woot,	
	Hath brought you thus upon the viritoot.°	*on the prowl*
	By Sainte Note,[8] ye woot wel what I mene."	
	This Absolon ne roughte nat a bene°	*did not care a bean*
665	Of al his play. No word again he yaf:°	*gave*
	He hadde more tow on his distaf[9]	
	Than Gervais knew, and saide, "Freend so dere,	
	This hote cultour in the chimenee° here,	*fireplace*
	As lene it me:[1] I have therwith to doone.	
670	I wol bringe it thee again ful soone."	
	Gervais answerde, "Certes, were it gold,	
	Or in a poke nobles alle untold,[2]	
	Thou sholdest have, as I am trewe smith.	
	Ey, Cristes fo,[3] what wol ye do therwith?"	
675	"Therof," quod Absolon, "be as be may.	
	I shal wel telle it thee another day,"	
	And caughte the cultour by the colde stele.°	*handle*
	Ful softe out at the dore he gan to stele,	
	And wente unto the carpenteres wal:	
680	He cougheth first and knokketh therwithal	
	Upon the windowe, right as he dide er.°	*before*
	This Alison answerde, "Who is ther	
	That knokketh so? I warante° it a thief."	*bet*
	"Why, nay," quod he, "God woot, my sweete lief,°	*dear*
685	I am thyn Absolon, my dereling.	
	Of gold," quod he, "I have thee brought a ring—	
	My moder yaf it me, so God me save;	
	Ful fin it is and therto wel ygrave:°	*engraved*
	This wol I yiven thee if thou me kisse."	
690	This Nicholas was risen for to pisse,	
	And thoughte he wolde amenden al the jape:[4]	
	He sholde kisse his ers er that he scape.	
	And up the windowe dide he hastily,	
	And out his ers he putteth prively,	
695	Over the buttok to the haunche-boon.°	*thigh*
	And therwith spak this clerk, this Absolon,	
	"Speek, sweete brid, I noot nought wher thou art."	
	This Nicholas anoon leet flee° a fart	*let fly*
	As greet as it hadde been a thonder-dent°	*thunderbolt*
700	That with the strook he was almost yblent,°	*blinded*
	And he was redy with his iren hoot,	
	And Nicholas amiddle the ers he smoot:	
	Of gooth the skin an hande-brede° aboute;	*hand's width*

8. St. Noet, a ninth-century saint, with possible pun on
Noah.
9. Flax on his distaff (i.e., cares on his mind).
1. Be so good as to lend it to me.

2. Or in a pouch of uncounted gold coins.
3. By Christ's foe (i.e., the Devil).
4. Make the joke even better.

The hote cultour brende so his toute°   backside
705   That for the smert° he wende° for to die;   pain / thought
As he were wood for wo he gan to crye,
"Help! Water! Water! Help, for Goddes herte!"
    This carpenter out of his slomber sterte,
And herde oon cryen "Water!" as he were wood,
710   And thoughte, "Allas, now cometh Noweles° flood!"   Noah's
He sette him up withoute wordes mo,
And with his ax he smoot the corde atwo,
And down gooth al: he foond neither to selle
Ne breed ne ale til he cam to the celle,[5]
715   Upon the floor, and ther aswoune° he lay.   stunned
    Up sterte° hire Alison and Nicholay,   leaped
And criden "Out" and "Harrow" in the streete.
The neighebores, bothe smale and grete,[6]
In ronnen for to gauren° on this man   stare
720   That aswoune lay bothe pale and wan,
For with the fal he brosten° hadde his arm;   broken
But stonde he moste unto his owene harm,
For whan he spak he was anoon bore down°   restrained
With° hende Nicholas and Alisoun: by
725   They tolden every man that he was wood°—   crazy
He was agast° so of Noweles flood,   afraid
Thurgh fantasye, that of his vanitee°   folly
He hadde ybought him kneeding-tubbes three,
And hadde hem hanged in the roof above,
730   And that he prayed hem, for Goddes love,
To sitten in the roof, par compaignye.°   for fellowship
    The folk gan laughen at his fantasye.
Into the roof they kiken° and they cape,°   peer / gape
And turned al his harm unto a jape,
735   For what so that this carpenter answerde,
It was for nought: no man his reson herde;
With othes grete he was so sworn adown,°   refuted by oaths
That he was holden wood in al the town,
For every clerk anoonright heeld with other:
740   They saide, "The man was wood, my leve brother,"
And every wight° gan laughen at this strif.   person
Thus swived° was the carpenteres wif   screwed
For al his keeping and his jalousye,
And Absolon hath kist hir nether° yë,   lower
745   And Nicholas is scalded in the toute:
This tale is doon, and God save al the route!

---

5. He found no time to sell either bread or ale until he reached the floor (i.e., he fell to the ground too quickly to be aware of what was happening).
6. Lower- and upper-class people alike.

THE WIFE OF BATH'S PROLOGUE AND TALE   Dame Alison, the Wife of Bath, is Chaucer's greatest contribution to the stock characters of Western culture. She has a long literary ancestry, most immediately in the Duenna of the thirteenth-century French poem, *The Romance of the Rose,* and stretching back to the Roman poet Ovid. Dame Alison stands out in bold relief, even among the vivid Canterbury pilgrims, partly because Chaucer gives her so rebellious and explicitly self-created a biography. She has outlived five husbands, accumulated wealth from the first three, and made herself rich in the growing textile industry of her time. At once a great companion and greatly unnerving, Alison lives in constant battle with a secular and religious world mostly controlled by men and yet has a keen appetite both for the men and for the battle.

The Wife of Bath's *Prologue* and *Tale* seem only the current installments of a multifaceted struggle in which Dame Alison has long been engaged, at first through her body and social role and now, in the face of advancing years, through the remaining agency of retrospective storytelling. She battles a society in which many young women are almost chattels in a marital market, as was the twelve-year-old version of herself who first was married off to a wealthier, much older man. She battles him and later husbands for power within the marriage, and her ambition to social dominance, as the *General Prologue* reports, extends to life in her urban parish.

By the moment of the Canterbury pilgrimage, though, the Wife's adversaries are more daunting, less easily conquered. The *Wife's Prologue,* for all its autobiographical energy, is primarily a debate with the clergy and with "auctoritee"—the whole armature of learning and literacy by which the clergy (like her clerically educated fifth husband, Jankyn) seeks to silence her.

The Wife's *Tale,* too, can be seen as an angry riposte to the secular fantasies of Arthurian chivalry and genetic nobility. The Wife's well-born Arthurian knight is a common rapist, who finds himself at the mercy of a queen and then in the arms of a crone. The tale turns Arthurian conventions on their head, lays sexual violence in the open, and puts legal and magical power in the hands of women. It is explicitly a fantasy, but a powerful one.

Alison's final enemy, mortality itself, is what makes her both most desperate and most sympathetic. The husbands are gone. Even the fondly recalled Jankyn slips into a rosy glow and the past tense; so does her own best friend and "gossip," the odd mirror-double "Alisoun." The Wife of Bath keeps addressing other "wives" in her *Prologue,* but there are no others on the pilgrimage. Her very argument with the institutionalized church distances her from its comforts, and she is deeply aware that time is stealing her beauty as it has taken away the companions who made up her earlier life. If Alison's *Tale* closes with a delicious fantasy of restored youth, it is only a pendant to the much longer *Prologue* and its cheerful yet poignant acceptance of age.

The Wife of Bath's Prologue

Experience, though noon auctoritee[1]
Were in this world, is right ynough for me
To speke of wo that is in mariage:
For lordinges,° sith I twelf yeer was of age—   *gentlemen*
5   Thanked be God that is eterne on live—
Housbondes at chirche dore I have had five
(If I so ofte mighte han wedded be),
And alle were worthy men in hir° degree.   *their*
But me was told, certain, nat longe agoon is,
10 That sith that Crist ne wente nevere but ones°   *once*

---

1. Even if no authority, textual precedent.

To wedding in the Cane of Galilee,[2]
That by the same ensample taughte he me
That I ne sholde wedded be but ones.
Herke eek, lo, which a sharp word for the nones,° *for the purpose*
15   Biside a welle, Jesus, God and man,
Spak in repreve° of the Samaritan:[3] *reproof*
"Thou hast yhad five housbondes," quod he,
"And that ilke° man that now hath thee *same*
Is nat thyn housbonde." Thus saide he certain.
20   What that he mente therby I can nat sayn,
But that I axe why that the fifthe man
Was noon housbonde to the Samaritan?
How manye mighte she han in mariage?
Yit herde I nevere tellen in myn age
25   Upon this nombre diffinicioun.
Men may divine° and glosen° up and down, *guess / interpret*
But wel I woot,° expres,° withouten lie, *know / manifestly*
God bad us for to wexe° and multiplye: *increase*
That gentil text can I wel understonde.
30   Eek wel I woot he saide that myn housbonde
Sholde lete° fader and moder and take to me, *leave*
But of no nombre mencion made he—
Of bigamye or of octogamye:
Why sholde men thanne speke of it vilainye?° *as churlish*
35   Lo, here the wise king daun° Salomon: *Lord*
I trowe° he hadde wives many oon, *believe*
As wolde God it leveful° were to me *lawful*
To be refresshed half so ofte as he.
Which yifte° of God hadde he for alle his wives! *what a gift*
40   No man hath swich that in this world alive is.
God woot° this noble king, as to my wit,° *knows / understanding*
The firste night hadde many a merye fit
With eech of hem, so wel was him on live.
Blessed be God that I have wedded five,
45   Of whiche I have piked° out the beste, *picked*
Bothe of hir nether purs and of hir cheste.[4]
Diverse° scoles maken parfit° clerkes, *different / accomplished*
And diverse practikes in sondry werkes
Maken the werkman° parfit sikerly:° *craftsman / surely*
50   Of five housbondes scoleying° am I. *studying*
Welcome the sixte whan that evere he shal!
For sith I wol nat keepe me chast in al,
Whan myn housbonde is fro the world agoon,
Som Cristen man shal wedde me anoon.
55   For thanne th'Apostle[5] saith that I am free

2. Cana, where Jesus performed his first miracle at a wedding feast (John 2.1).
3. The story of Jesus and the Samaritan woman is related
in John 4.6 ff.
4. Money chest, with a pun on body parts.
5. St. Paul, in Romans 7.2.

To wedde, a Goddes half,[6] where it liketh° me.   *please*
He said that to be wedded is no sinne:
Bet° is to be wedded than to brinne.°   *better / burn (in hell)*
What rekketh° me though folk saye vilainye   *do I care*
60 Of shrewed° Lamech[7] and his bigamye?   *cursed*
I woot wel Abraham was an holy man,
And Jacob eek, as fer as evere I can,°   *know*
And eech of hem hadde wives mo than two,
And many another holy man also.
65   Where can ye saye in any manere age
That hye God defended° mariage   *prohibited*
By expres word? I praye you, telleth me.
Or where comanded he virginitee?
I woot as wel as ye, it is no drede,°   *doubt*
70 Th'Apostle, whan he speketh of maidenhede,°   *virginity*
He saide that precept° therof hadde he noon: *command*
Men may conseile a womman to be oon,°   *single*
But conseiling nis no comandement.
He putte it in oure owene juggement.
75 For hadde God comanded maidenhede,
Thanne hadde he dampned° wedding with the deede;   *condemned*
And certes, if ther were no seed ysowe,
Virginitee, thanne wherof sholde it growe?
Paul dorste nat comanden at the leeste
80 A thing of which his maister yaf no heeste.°   *commandment*
The dart° is set up for virginitee: *prize*
Cacche whoso may, who renneth° best lat see.   *runs*
But this word is nought take° of every wight,°   *required / person*
But ther as God list° yive it of his might.   *pleases*
85 I woot wel that th'Apostle was a maide,°   *virgin*
But nathelees, though that he wroot or saide
He wolde that every wight were swich as he,
Al nis but° conseil to virginitee;   *it is only*
And for to been a wif he yaf me leve
90 Of indulgence; so nis it no repreve
To wedde me if that my make° die,   *mate*
Withouten excepcion° of bigamye—   *legal objection*
Al were it good no womman for to touche
(He mente as in his bed or in his couche,
95 For peril is bothe fir and tow t'assemble[8]—
Ye knowe what this ensample may resemble).
This al and som,° he heeld virginitee   *all told*
More parfit than wedding in freletee.°   *due to weakness*
(Freletee clepe° I but if° that he and she   *call / except*
100 Wolde leden al hir lif in chastitee).
I graunte it wel, I have noon envye

6. From God's perspective.   8. To bring together fire and flax.
7. The earliest bigamist in the Bible (Genesis 4.19).

Though maidenhede preferre° bigamye: surpasses
It liketh hem to be clene in body and gost.°   soul
Of myn estaat° ne wol I make no boost;   condition
105 For wel ye knowe, a lord in his houshold
Ne hath nat every vessel al of gold:
Some been of tree,° and doon hir lord servise.   wood
God clepeth° folk to him in sondry wise,   calls
And everich hath of God a propre yifte,
110 Som this, som that, as him liketh shifte.⁹
Virginitee is greet perfeccioun,
And continence eek with devocioun,
But Crist, that of perfeccion is welle,°   source
Bad nat every wight° he sholde go selle   person
115 Al that he hadde and yive it to the poore,
And in swich wise folwe° him and his fore:°   follow / footsteps
He spak to hem that wolde live parfitly°—   perfectly
And lordinges, by youre leve, that am nat I.
I wol bistowe the flour of al myn age
120 In th'actes and in fruit of mariage.
          Telle me also, to what conclusioun°   end
Were membres maad of generacioun
And of so parfit wis a wrighte ywrought?¹
Trusteth right wel, they were nat maad for nought.
125 Glose whoso wol, and saye bothe up and down
That they were maked for purgacioun
Of urine, and oure bothe thinges smale
Was eek to knowe a femele from a male,
And for noon other cause—saye ye no?
130 Th'experience woot wel it is nought so.
So that the clerkes be nat with me wrothe,°   angry
I saye this, that they maked been for bothe—
That is to sayn, for office° and for ese°   use / pleasure
Of engendrure,° ther we nat God displese.   procreation
135 Why sholde men elles in hir bookes sette
That man shal yeelde° to his wif hir dette?°   pay / marriage debt
Now wherwith sholde he make his payement
If he ne used his sely° instrument?   innocent
Thanne were they maad upon a creature
140 To purge urine, and eek for engendrure.
          But I saye nought that every wight is holde,°   bound
That hath swich harneis° as I to you tolde,   equipment
To goon and usen hem in engendrure:
Thanne sholde men take of chastitee no cure.°   heed
145 Crist was a maide and shapen as a man,
And many a saint sith that the world bigan,
Yit lived they evere in parfit° chastitee.   perfect

---

9. As it pleases him to provide.   1. And created by so perfectly wise a Creator?

I nil envye no virginitee:
Lat hem be breed° of pured° whete seed,   *bread / refined*
150   And lat us wives hote° barly breed—   *be called*
And yit with barly breed, Mark telle can,
Oure Lord Jesu refresshed many a man.
In swich estaat as God hath cleped° us   *called*
I wol persevere: I nam nat precious.°   *am not fussy*
155   In wifhood wol I use myn instrument
As freely° as my Makere hath it sent.   *generously*
If I be daungerous,° God yive me sorwe:°   *withholding / sorrow*
Myn housbonde shal it han both eve and morwe,°   *morning*
Whan that him list come forth and paye his dette.
160   An housbonde wol I have, I wol nat lette,°   *forgo*
Which shal be bothe my dettour and my thral,°   *slave*
And have his tribulacion withal
Upon his flessh whil that I am his wif.
I have the power during al my lif
165   Upon his propre° body, and nat he: *own*
Right thus th'Apostle tolde it unto me,
And bad oure housbondes for to love us weel.
Al this sentence° me liketh everydeel.   *interpretation*

An Interlude

Up sterte° the Pardoner and that anoon: *started*
170   "Now dame," quod he, "by God and by Saint John,
Ye been a noble prechour° in this cas.   *preacher*
I was aboute to wedde a wif: allas,
What° sholde I bye° it on my flessh so dere?   *why / buy*
Yit hadde I levere° wedde no wif toyere."°   *rather / this year*
175   "Abid," quod she, "my tale is nat bigonne.
Nay, thou shalt drinken of another tonne,°   *barrel*
Er that I go, shal savoure wors than ale.
And whan that I have told thee forth my tale
Of tribulacion in mariage,
180   Of which I am expert in al myn age—
This is to saye, myself hath been the whippe—
Thanne maistou chese° wheither thou wolt sippe   *may you choose*
Of thilke° tonne that I shal abroche:°   *that same / open*
Be war of it, er thou too neigh approche,
185   For I shal telle ensamples mo than ten.
'Whoso that nile° be war by othere men,   *will not*
By him shal othere men corrected be.'
Thise same wordes writeth Ptolomee:[2]
Rede in his Almageste and take it there."
190   "Dame, I wolde praye you if youre wil it were,"
Saide this Pardoner, "as ye bigan,

2. Ptolemy, ancient Greek astronomer and author of the *Almageste*.

Telle forth youre tale; spareth for no man,
And teche us yonge men of youre practike."
     "Gladly," quod she, "sith it may you like;

195   But that I praye to al this compaignye,
If that I speke after my fantasye,°   *fancy*
As taketh nat agrief° of that I saye,   *amiss*
For myn entente nis but° for to playe."   *intent is only*

The Wife Continues

Now sire, thanne wol I telle you forth my tale.

200   As evere mote I drinke win or ale,
I shal saye sooth:° tho° housbondes that I hadde,   *truth / those*
As three of hem were goode, and two were badde.
The three men were goode, and riche, and olde;
Unnethe° mighte they the statut holde   *scarcely*

205   In which they were bounden unto me—
Ye woot wel what I mene of this, pardee.°   *by God*
As help me God, I laughe whan I thinke
How pitously anight I made hem swinke;°   *work*
And by my fay,° I tolde of it no stoor:°   *faith / gave it no heed*

210   They hadde me yiven hir land and hir tresor;°   *wealth*
Me needed nat do lenger diligence
To winne hir love or doon hem reverence.
They loved me so wel, by God above,
That I ne tolde no daintee° of hir love.   *set no value on*

215   A wis womman wol bisye hire evere in oon°   *constantly*
To gete hire love, ye, ther as she hath noon.
But sith I hadde hem hoolly in myn hand,
And sith that they hadde yiven me al hir land,
What sholde I take keep° hem for to plese,   *care*

220   But it were for my profit and myn ese?
I sette hem so awerke, by my fay,°   *faith*
That many a night they songen wailaway.
The bacon was nat fet° for hem, I trowe,   *collected*
That some men han in Essexe at Dunmowe.[3]

225   I governed hem so wel after my lawe
That eech of hem ful blisful was and fawe°   *glad*
To bringe me gaye thinges fro the faire;
They were ful glade whan I spak to hem faire,
For God it woot, I chidde° hem spitously.°   *scolded / cruelly*

230   Now herkneth how I bar me proprely:
Ye wise wives, that conne understonde,
Thus sholde ye speke and bere him wrong on honde°—   *wrongly accuse*
For half so boldely can ther no man
Swere and lie as a woman can.

235   I saye nat this by wives that been wise,

---

3. At Dunmowe, spouses who had spent a year without quarrelling were awarded a side of bacon.

But if it be whan they hem misavise.°   *err*
A wis wif, if that she can hir good,[4]
Shal bere him on hande the cow is wood,[5]
And take witnesse of hir owene maide
240   Of hir assent.° But herkneth how I saide: *as her accomplice*
    "Sire olde cainard,° is this thyn array?   *dotard*
Why is my neighebores wif so gay?
She is honoured overal ther she gooth:
I sitte at hoom; I have no thrifty° cloth.   *decent*
245   What doostou at my neighebores hous?
Is she so fair? Artou so amorous?
What roune° ye with oure maide, benedicite?°   *whisper / bless us*
Sire olde lechour, lat thy japes° be.   *tricks*
And if I have a gossib° or a freend,   *confidante*
250   Withouten gilt ye chiden as a feend,
If that I walke or playe unto his hous.
Thou comest hoom as dronken as a mous,
And prechest on thy bench, with yvel preef.°   *bad luck to you*
Thou saist to me, it is a greet meschief
255   To wedde a poore womman for costage.°   *expense*
And if that she be riche, of heigh parage,°   *breeding*
Thanne saistou that it is a tormentrye
To suffre hir pride and hir malencolye.
And if that she be fair, thou verray knave,
260   Thou saist that every holour° wol hire have: *whoremonger*
She may no while in chastitee abide
That is assailed upon eech a side.
    "Thou saist som folk desiren us for richesse,
Som for oure shap, and som for oure fairnesse,
265   And som for she can outher° singe or daunce,   *either*
And som for gentilesse and daliaunce,°   *conversation*
Som for hir handes and hir armes smale—
Thus gooth al to the devel by thy tale![6]
Thou saist men may nat keepe a castel wal,
270   It may so longe assailed been overal.
And if that she be foul, thou saist that she
Coveiteth° every man that she may see;   *desires*
For as a spaniel she wol on him lepe,
Til that she finde som man hire to chepe.°   *take*
275   Ne noon so grey goos gooth ther in the lake,
As, saistou, wol be withoute make;°   *mate*
And saist it is an hard thing for to weelde°   *control*
A thing that no man wol, his thankes,° heelde.°   *willingly / hold*
Thus saistou, lorel,° whan thou goost to bedde,   *scoundrel*
280   And that no wis man needeth for to wedde,
Ne no man that entendeth° unto hevene—   *expects (to go)*

---

4. Knows what's good for her.
5. Shall convince him the chough is mad. The chough, a
crow-like bird, was fabled to reveal wives' infidelities.
6. According to what you say.

With wilde thonder-dint° and firy levene°   *thunderclap / lightning*
Mote° thy welked° nekke be tobroke!°   *may / withered / broken*
Thou saist that dropping° houses and eek smoke   *leaking*
285   And chiding wives maken men to flee
Out of hir owene houses: a, benedicite,
What aileth swich an old man for to chide?
Thou saist we wives wil oure vices hide
Til we be fast,° and thanne we wol hem shewe—   *bound (in marriage)*
290   Wel may that be a proverbe of a shrewe!°   *scoundrel*
Thou saist that oxen, asses, hors, and houndes,
They been assayed° at diverse stoundes;°   *tested / times*
Bacins,° lavours,° er that men hem bye,   *basins / wash bowls*
Spoones, stooles, and al swich housbondrye,
295   And so be pottes, clothes, and array—
But folk of wives maken noon assay°   *trial*
Til they be wedded—olde dotard shrewe!
And thanne, saistou, we wil oure vices shewe.
Thou saist also that it displeseth me
300   But if° that thou wolt praise my beautee,   *unless*
And but thou poure alway upon my face,
And clepe° me 'Faire Dame' in every place,   *call*
And but thou make a feeste on thilke° day   *that*
That I was born, and make me fressh and gay,
305   And but thou do to my norice° honour,   *nurse*
And to my chamberere° within my bowr,°   *chambermaid / bedroom*
And to my fadres folk, and his allies°—   *kinsmen*
Thus saistou, olde barel-ful of lies.
And yit of our apprentice Janekin,
310   For his crispe heer,° shining as gold so fin,   *curly hair*
And for he squiereth° me bothe up and down,   *chaperones*
Yit hastou caught a fals suspecioun;
I wil° him nat though thou were deed tomorwe.   *desire*
    "But tel me this, why hidestou with sorwe
315   The keyes of thy cheste away fro me?
It is my good as wel as thyn, pardee.°   *by God*
What, weenestou° make an idiot of oure dame?   *do you suppose*
Now by that lord that called is Saint Jame,[7]
Thou shalt nought bothe, though that thou were wood,°   *enraged*
320   Be maister of my body and of my good:
That oon thou shalt forgo, maugree thine yën.[8]
    "What helpeth it of me enquere and spyen?
I trowe thou woldest loke° me in thy cheste.   *lock*
Thou sholdest saye, 'Wif, go wher thee leste.°   *it pleases*
325   Taak youre disport.° I nil leve° no tales: *amusement / believe*
I knowe you for a trewe wif, dame Alis.'
We love no man that taketh keep° or charge   *notice*

7. Santiago de Compostela, whose shrine in Spain the   8. In spite of your eyes (an oath).
Wife of Bath has already made a pilgrimage to visit.

Wher that we goon: we wol been at oure large.°   *liberty*
Of alle men yblessed mote he be
330 The wise astrologen daun Ptolomee,
That saith this proverbe in his Almageste:
'Of alle men his wisdom is the hyeste
That rekketh° nat who hath the world in honde.'   *cares*
By this proverbe thou shalt understonde,
335 Have thou ynough, what thar° thee rekke° or care *need / be concerned*
How merily that othere folkes fare?°   *go about*
For certes, olde dotard, by youre leve,
Ye shal han queinte° right ynough at eve: *sex*
He is too greet a nigard that wil werne°   *refuse*
340 A man to lighte a candle at his lanterne;
He shal han nevere the lasse lighte, pardee.°   *by God*
Have thou ynough, thee thar nat plaine thee.°   *complain*
  "Thou saist also that if we make us gay
With clothing and with precious array,
345 That it is peril of oure chastitee,
And yit with sorwe thou moste enforce thee,[9]
And saye thise wordes in th'Apostles name:
'In habit° maad with chastitee and shame   *clothing*
Ye wommen shal apparaile you,' quod he,
350 'And nat in tressed heer° and gay perree,° *styled hair / jewels*
As perles ne with gold ne clothes riche.'
After thy text, ne after thy rubriche,[1]
I wol nat werke as muchel as a gnat.
Thou saidest this, that I was lik a cat:
355 For whoso wolde senge° a cattes skin,   *singe*
Thanne wolde the cat wel dwellen in his in;°   *inn*
And if the cattes skin be slik° and gay,   *sleek*
She wol nat dwelle in house half a day,
But forth she wol, er any day be dawed,°   *dawned*
360 To shewe her skin and goon a-caterwawed.° *caterwauling*
This is to saye, if I be gay, sire shrewe,
I wol renne out, my borel° for to shewe.   *coarse cloth*
Sire olde fool, what helpeth thee t'espyen?
Though thou praye Argus[2] with his hundred yën
365 To be my wardecors,° as he can best,   *bodyguard*
In faith, he shal nat keepe me but me lest:
Yit coude I make his beerd,[3] so mote I thee.° *so may I prosper*
  "Thou saidest eek that ther been thinges three,
The whiche thinges troublen al this erthe,
370 And that no wight° may endure the ferthe.° *person / fourth*
O leve sire shrewe, Jesu shorte thy lif!
Yit prechestou and saist an hateful wif

---

9. Reinforce (your position).
1. Rubric, interpretive heading on a text.
2. Mythical hundred-eyed monster employed by Juno to guard over Io, one of Jove's many lovers, whom the goddess turned into a cow.
3. Deceive him.

Yrekened° is for oon of thise meschaunces.   *accounted*
Been ther nat none othere resemblaunces
375   That ye may likne youre parables to,
But if a sely° wif be oon of tho?   *innocent*
    "Thou liknest eek wommanes love to helle,
To bareine land ther water may nat dwelle;
Thou liknest it also to wilde fir—
380   The more it brenneth,° the more it hath desir   *burns*
To consumen every thing that brent wol be;
Thou saist right as wormes shende° a tree,   *destroy*
Right so a wif destroyeth hir housbonde—
This knowen they that been to wives bonde."
385   Lordinges, right thus, as ye han understonde,
Bar I stifly° mine olde housbondes on honde°   *firmly / swore*
That thus they saiden in hir dronkenesse—
And al was fals, but that I took witnesse
On Janekin and on my nece° also.   *kinswoman*
390   O Lord, the paine I dide hem and the wo,
Ful giltelees, by Goddes sweete pine!°   *suffering*
For as an hors I coude bite and whine;
I coude plaine and° I was in the gilt,°   *when / wrong*
Or elles often time I hadde been spilt.°   *ruined*
395   Whoso that first to mille comth first grint.°   *grinds*
I plained first: so was oure werre° stint.°   *war / stopped*
They were ful glad to excusen hem ful blive°   *quickly*
Of thing of which they nevere agilte° hir live.   *offended (in)*
Of wenches wolde I beren hem on honde,
400   Whan that for sik they mighte unnethe° stonde,   *barely*
Yit tikled I his herte for that he
Wende° I hadde had of him so greet cheertee.°   *supposed / fondness*
I swoor that al my walking out by nighte
Was for to espye wenches that he dighte.°   *had sex with*
405   Under that colour° hadde I many a mirthe.   *pretense*
For al swich wit is yiven us in oure birthe:
Deceite, weeping, spinning God hath yive
To wommen kindely° whil they may live.   *by nature*
And thus of oo thing I avaunte° me: *boast*
410   At ende I hadde the bet in eech degree,
By sleighte° or force, or by som manere thing,   *deception*
As by continuel murmur° or grucching;°   *complaining / grumbling*
Namely abedde° hadden they meschaunce:°   *in bed / misfortune*
Ther wolde I chide and do hem no plesaunce;
415   I wolde no lenger in the bed abide
If that I felte his arm over my side,
Til he hadde maad his raunson° unto me;   *amends*
Thanne wolde I suffre him do his nicetee.°   *lust*
And therfore every man this tale I telle:
420   Winne whoso may, for al is for to selle;
With empty hand men may no hawkes lure.

	For winning° wolde I al his lust endure,	*profit*
	And make me a feined appetit—	
	And yit in bacon° hadde I nevere delit.	*old meat*
425	That made me that evere I wolde hem chide;	
	For though the Pope hadde seten° hem biside,	*sat*
	I wolde nought spare hem at hir owene boord.°	*table*
	For by my trouthe, I quitte° hem word for word.	*repaid*
	As help me verray God omnipotent,	
430	Though I right now sholde make my testament,	
	I ne owe hem nat a word that it nis quit.°	*is not repaid*
	I broughte it so aboute by my wit	
	That they moste yive it up as for the beste,	
	Or elles hadde we nevere been in reste;	
435	For though he looked as a wood leoun,°	*crazed lion*
	Yit sholde he faile of his conclusion.°	*purpose*
	Thanne wolde I saye, "Goodelief,° taak keep,	*Sweetheart*
	How mekely looketh Wilekin, oure sheep!	
	Com neer my spouse, lat me ba° thy cheeke—	*kiss*
440	Ye sholden be al pacient and meeke,	
	And han a sweete-spiced conscience,	
	Sith ye so preche of Jobes[4] pacience;	
	Suffreth alway, sin ye so wel can preche;	
	And but ye do, certain, we shal you teche	
445	That it is fair to han a wif in pees.	
	Oon of us two moste bowen, doutelees,	
	And sith a man is more resonable	
	Than womman is, ye mosten been suffrable.°	*patient*
	What aileth you to grucche thus and grone?	
450	Is it for ye wolde have my queinte allone?	
	Why, taak it al—lo, have it everydeel.	
	Peter,° I shrewe° you but ye love it weel.	*by St. Peter / curse*
	For if I wolde selle my bele chose,[5]	
	I coude walke as fressh as is a rose;	
455	But I wol keepe it for youre owene tooth.°	*taste*
	Ye be to blame. By God, I saye you sooth!"	
	Swiche manere wordes hadde we on honde.	
	Now wol I speke of my ferthe housbonde.	
	My ferthe housbonde was a revelour—	
460	This is to sayn, he hadde a paramour°—	*lover*
	And I was yong and ful of ragerye,°	*wantonness*
	Stibourne° and strong and joly as a pie:°	*stubborn / magpie*
	How coude I daunce to an harpe smale,°	*gracefully*
	And singe, ywis,° as any nightingale,	*certainly*
465	Whan I hadde dronke a draughte of sweete win.	
	Metellius,[6] the foule cherl,° the swin,	*ruffian*

4. The biblical Job, who suffers patiently the trials imposed by God.
5. "Beautiful thing," a euphemism for female genitals.
6. Egnatius Metellius, whose actions are described in Valerius Maximus's *Facta et dicta memorabilia*, 6.3.

That with a staf birafte his wif hir lif
For she drank win, though I hadde been his wif,
Ne sholde nat han daunted me fro drinke;
470   And after win on Venus moste I thinke,
For also siker° as cold engendreth hail,   *certainly*
A likerous° mouth moste han a likerous° tail: *gluttonous / lecherous*
In womman vinolent° is no defence—   *drunken*
This knowen lechours by experience.
475   But Lord Crist, whan that it remembreth me
Upon my youthe and on my jolitee,
It tikleth me aboute myn herte roote°—   *bottom of my heart*
Unto this day it dooth myn herte boote°   *good*
That I have had my world as in my time.
480   But age, allas, that al wol envenime,°   *poison*
Hath me biraft my beautee and my pith°—   *vigor*
Lat go, farewel, the devel go therwith!
The flour is goon, ther is namore to telle:
The bren° as I best can now moste I selle;   *bran*
485   But yit to be right merye wol I fonde.°   *try*
Now wol I tellen of my ferthe housbonde.
        I saye I hadde in herte greet despit
That he of any other hadde delit,
But he was quit,° by God and by Saint Joce:°   *repaid / St. Judocus*
490   I made him of the same wode a croce°—   *cross*
Nat of my body in no foul manere—
But, certainly, I made folk swich cheere
That in his owene grece° I made him frye,   *grease*
For angre and for verray jalousye.
495   By God, in erthe I was his purgatorye,
For which I hope his soule be in glorye.
For God it woot, he sat ful ofte and soong
Whan that his sho° ful bitterly him wroong.°   *shoe / pinched*
Ther was no wight° save God and he that wiste   *person*
500   In many wise how sore I him twiste.
He deide whan I cam fro Jerusalem,
And lith ygrave° under the roode-beem,°   *buried / crossbeam*
Al is his tombe nought so curious°   *carefully made*
As was the sepulcre of him Darius,[7]
505   Which that Appelles wroughte subtilly:
It nis but wast to burye him preciously.°   *expensively*
Lat him fare wel, God yive his soule reste;
He is now in his grave and in his cheste.
        Now of my fifthe housbonde wol I telle—
510   God lete his soule nevere come in helle—
And yit he was to me the moste shrewe:
That feele I on my ribbes al by rewe,°   *in a row*

---

7. Persian Emperor defeated by Alexander the Great, whose tomb was elaborately designed by the Jewish craftsman Apelles.

And evere shal unto myn ending day.
But in oure bed he was so fressh and gay,

515 And therwithal so wel coude he me glose°   *flatter*
Whan that he wolde han my bele chose,°   *pretty thing*
That though he hadde me bet° on every boon,°   *beaten / bone*
He coude winne again my love anoon.
I trowe I loved him best for that he

520 Was of his love daungerous° to me.   *hard to get*
We wommen han, if that I shal nat lie,
In this matere a quainte fantasye:
Waite° what thing we may nat lightly° have,   *note that / easily*
Therafter wol we crye al day and crave;

525 Forbede us thing, and that desiren we;
Presse on us faste, and thanne wol we flee.
With daunger oute we al oure chaffare:⁸
Greet prees° at market maketh dere ware,°   *crowd / costly goods*
And too greet chepe° is holden at litel pris.   *bargain*

530 This knoweth every womman that is wis.
    My fifthe housbonde—God his soule blesse!—
Which that I took for love and no richesse,
He somtime was a clerk of Oxenforde,
And hadde laft scole° and wente at hoom to boorde   *left school*

535 With my gossib,° dwelling in oure town—   *close friend*
God have hir soule!—hir name was Alisoun;
She knew myn herte and eek my privetee°   *secrets*
Bet than oure parissh preest, as mote I thee.
To hire biwrayed° I my conseil° al,   *revealed / thoughts*

540 For hadde myn housbonde pissed on a wal,
Or doon a thing that sholde han cost his lif,
To hire, and to another worthy wif,
And to my nece which that I loved weel,
I wolde han told his conseil everydeel;

545 And so I dide ful often, God it woot,
That made his face often reed° and hoot°   *red / hot*
For verray shame, and blamed himself for he
Hadde told to me so greet a privetee.
    And so bifel that ones in a Lente—

550 So often times I to my gossib wente,
For evere yit I loved to be gay,
And for to walke in March, Averil, and May,
From hous to hous, to heere sondry tales—
That Janekin clerk and my gossib dame Alis

555 And I myself into the feeldes wente.
Myn housbonde was at London al that Lente:
I hadde the better leiser° for to playe,   *opportunity*
And for to see, and eek for to be seye°   *seen*

8. With coyness we spread out all our merchandise.

	Of lusty° folk—what wiste I wher my grace°	*merry / luck*
560	Was shapen° for to be, or in what place?	*destined*
	Therfore I made my visitaciouns	
	To vigilies⁹ and to processiouns,	
	To preching eek, and to thise pilgrimages,	
	To playes of miracles and to mariages,	
565	And wered upon my gaye scarlet gites°—	*robes*
	Thise wormes ne thise motthes ne thise mites,	
	Upon my peril, frete° hem neveradeel:	*devoured*
	And woostou why? For they were used weel.	
	Now wol I tellen forth what happed me.	
570	I saye that in the feeldes walked we,	
	Til trewely we hadde swich daliaunce,°	*flirtation*
	This clerk and I, that of my purveyaunce°	*providence*
	I spak to him and saide him how that he,	
	If I were widwe, sholde wedde me.	
575	For certainly, I saye for no bobaunce°	*boast*
	Yit was I nevere withouten purveyaunce	
	Of mariage n'of othere thinges eek:	
	I holde a mouses herte nought worth a leek	
	That hath but oon hole for to sterte° to,	*flee*
580	And if that faile thanne is al ydo.	
	I bar him on hand he hadde enchaunted me	
	(My dame taughte me that subtiltee);	
	And eek I saide I mette° of him al night:	*dreamed*
	He wolde han slain me as I lay upright,°	*facing up*
585	And al my bed was ful of verray blood—	
	"But yit I hope that ye shul do me good;	
	For blood bitokeneth gold, as me was taught."	
	And al was fals, I dremed of it right naught,	
	But as I folwed ay° my dames lore°	*always / teaching*
590	As wel of that as of othere thinges more.	
	But now sire—lat me see, what shal I sayn?	
	Aha, by God, I have my tale again.	
	Whan that my ferthe housbonde was on beere,°	*funeral bier*
	I weep algate,° and made sory cheere,	*constantly*
595	As wives moten, for it is usage,°	*custom*
	And with my coverchief covered my visage;	
	But for that I was purveyed° of a make,°	*provided / mate*
	I wepte but smale, and that I undertake.°	*vouch*
	To chirche was myn housbonde born amorwe°	*next morning*
600	With neighebores that for him maden sorwe,	
	And Janekin oure clerk was oon of tho.	
	As help me God, whan that I saw him go	
	After the beere, me thoughte he hadde a paire	
	Of legges and of feet so clene and faire,	

9. Services on the eve of holy days.

605　That al myn herte I yaf unto his hold.°　　　　　　　　*possession*
　　He was, I trowe, twenty winter old,
　　And I was fourty, if I shal saye sooth°—　　　　　　　*truth*
　　But yit I hadde alway a coltes tooth:°　　　　　　　*youthful tastes*
　　Gat-toothed° was I, and that bicam me weel;　　　　*gap-toothed*
610　I hadde the prente° of Sainte Venus seel.°　　*imprint / beauty mark*
　　As help me God, I was a lusty oon,
　　And fair and riche and yong and wel-bigoon,°　　　*well situated*
　　And trewely, as mine housbondes tolde me,
　　I hadde the beste quoniam° mighte be.　　　　　*you-know-what*
615　For certes I am al Venerien[1]
　　In feeling, and myn herte is Marcien:°　　　*governed by Mars*
　　Venus me yaf my lust, my likerousnesse,
　　And Mars yaf me my sturdy hardinesse.
　　Myn ascendent° was Taur° and Mars therinne—　*zodiac sign / Taurus*
620　Allas, allas, that evere love was sinne!
　　I folwed ay my inclinacioun
　　By vertu of my constellacioun;
　　That made me I coude nought withdrawe°　　　　　*withhold*
　　My chambre of Venus from a good felawe.
625　Yit have I Martes° merk upon my face,　　　　　　*Mars's*
　　And also in another privee place.
　　For God so wis° be my savacioun,°　　　　*surely / salvation*
　　I loved nevere by no discrecioun,
　　But evere folwede° myn appetit,　　　　　　　　　*followed*
630　Al were he short or long or blak or whit;
　　I took no keep, so that he liked° me,　　　　　　　*pleased*
　　How poore he was, ne eek of what degree.
　　　　What sholde I saye but at the monthes ende
　　This joly clerk Janekin that was so hende°　　　　*courteous*
635　Hath wedded me with greet solempnitee,
　　And to him yaf I al the land and fee°　　　　　　　*property*
　　That evere was me yiven therbifore—
　　But afterward repented me ful sore:
　　He nolde suffre° no thing of my list.°　　*would allow / pleasure*
640　By God, he smoot° me ones on the list°　　　　*struck / ear*
　　For that I rente° out of his book a leef,°　　　　*tore / page*
　　That of the strook myn ere weex° al deef.　　*grew, became*
　　Stibourne I was as is a leonesse,
　　And of my tonge a verray jangleresse,°　　　　*chatterbox*
645　And walke I wolde, as I hadde doon biforn,
　　From hous to hous, although he hadde it sworn;°　*prohibited*
　　For which he often times wolde preche,
　　And me of olde Romain geestes° teche,　　　　*Latin stories*
　　How he Simplicius Gallus[2] lafte his wif,
650　And hire forsook for terme of al his lif,

---

1. Governed by Venus, the planet.　　　　2. Narrated in Valerius Maximus, *Facta et dicta memora-*
　　　　　　　　　　　　　　　　　　　　　　bilia 6.3.

Nought but for open-heveded° he hire sey°   *bareheaded / saw*
Looking out at his dore upon a day.
   Another Romain[3] tolde he me by name
That, for his wif was at a someres° game   *summer's*
655   Withouten his witing,° he forsook hire eke;   *knowledge*
And thanne wolde he upon his Bible seeke
That ilke proverbe of Ecclesiaste[4]
Where he comandeth and forbedeth faste
Man shal nat suffre his wif go roule° aboute;   *roam*
660   Thanne wolde he saye right thus withouten doute:
"Whoso that buildeth his hous al of salwes,°   *willow branches*
And priketh° his blinde hors over the falwes,°   *rides / open fields*
And suffreth his wif to go seeken halwes,°   *shrines*
Is worthy to be hanged on the galwes."
665   But al for nought—I sette nought an hawe[5]
Of his proverbes n'of his olde sawe;
N'I wolde nat of him corrected be:
I hate him that my vices telleth me,
And so doon mo, God woot, of us than I.
670   This made him with me wood al outrely:°   *utterly*
I nolde nought forbere° him in no cas.   *would not submit*
   Now wol I saye you sooth, by Saint Thomas,
Why that I rente out of his book a leef,
For which he smoot me so that I was deef.
675   He hadde a book that gladly night and day
For his disport° he wolde rede alway.   *amusement*
He cleped° it Valerie and Theofraste,[6]   *called*
At which book he lough° alway ful faste;   *laughed*
And eek ther was somtime a clerk at Rome,
680   A cardinal, that highte Saint Jerome,
That made a book again Jovinian;
In which book eek ther was Tertulan,
Crysippus, Trotula, and Helouis,
That was abbesse nat fer fro Paris;
685   And eek the Parables of Salomon,
Ovides Art, and bookes many oon—
And alle thise were bounden in oo volume.
And every night and day was his custume,°   *custom*
Whan he hadde leiser and vacacioun
690   From other worldly occupacioun,
To reden in this book of wikked wives.

---

3. P. Sempronius Sophus, as related in Valerius Maximus, *Facta* 6.3.
4. Ecclesiasticus 25.25.
5. Hawthorn berry (i.e., little value).
6. Janekin's book is a collection of different works, nearly all of which are directed against women: Walter Map's fictitious letter entitled *Valerius's Dissuasion of Rufinus from Marrying* (Valerius); Theophrastus's *Golden Book on Marriage* (Theofraste); Saint Jerome's *Against Jovinian*;

Tertullian's misogynist tracts on sexual continence (Tertulan); Crysippus's writings, mentioned by Jerome but otherwise unknown; *The Sufferings of Women*, an 11th-century book on gynecology by Trotula di Ruggiero, a female physician from Sicily (Trotula); the letters of the abbess Heloise to her lover Abelard (Helouis); the biblical Book of Proverbs (Parables of Salomon), and Ovid's *Art of Love*.

He knew of hem mo legendes and lives
Than been of goode wives in the Bible.
For trusteth wel, it is an impossible°   *impossibility*
695 That any clerk wol speke good of wives,
But if it be of holy saintes lives,
N'of noon other womman nevere the mo—
Who painted the leon, tel me who?[7]
By God, if wommen hadden writen stories,
700 As clerkes han within hir oratories,
They wolde han writen of men more wikkednesse
Than al the merk of° Adam may redresse.   *mark, sex*
The children of Mercurye and Venus[8]
Been in hir werking° ful contrarious:°   *deeds / contradictory*
705 Mercurye loveth wisdom and science,
And Venus loveth riot° and dispence;°   *celebration / expense*
And for hir diverse disposicioun
Each falleth in otheres exaltacioun,[9]
And thus, God woot, Mercurye is desolat°   *powerless*
710 In Pisces wher Venus is exaltat,
And Venus falleth ther Mercurye is raised:
Therfore no womman of no clerk is praised.
The clerk, whan he is old and may nought do
Of Venus werkes worth his olde sho,°   *shoe*
715 Thanne sit he down and writ in his dotage
That wommen can nat keepe hir mariage.
  But now to purpos why I tolde thee
That I was beten for a book, pardee:°   *by God*
Upon a night Janekin, that was oure sire,°   *master of our house*
720 Redde on his book as he sat by the fire
Of Eva[1] first, that for hir wikkednesse
Was al mankinde brought to wrecchednesse,
For which that Jesu Crist himself was slain
That boughte° us with his herte blood again—   *redeemed*
725 Lo, heer expres of wommen may ye finde
That womman was the los° of al mankinde.   *ruin*
  Tho° redde he me how Sampson loste his heres:° *then / hair*
Sleeping his lemman° kitte° it with hir sheres,   *lover / cut*
Thurgh which treson loste he both his yën.
730 Tho redde he me, if that I shal nat lien,
Of Ercules and of his Dianire,[2]
That caused him to sette himself afire.
No thing forgat he the sorwe and wo

---

7. In one of Aesop's fables, a lion asked this question when confronted by a painting of a man killing a lion, indicating that if a lion had painted the picture, the scene would have been very different.
8. Followers of Mercury, the god of rhetoric (scholars, poets, orators); followers of Venus (lovers).
9. Astrologically, one planet diminishes in influence as the other ascends.

1. Eve's temptation by the serpent was blamed for humanity's fall from grace and thus required Christ's incarnation to redeem the world.
2. Deianira gave her husband, Hercules, a robe which she believed was charmed with a love potion, but once he put it on, it burned his flesh so badly that he died.

That Socrates hadde with his wives two—
735 How Xantippa[3] caste pisse upon his heed:
This sely man sat stille as he were deed;
He wiped his heed, namore dorste he sayn
But "Er° that thonder stinte,° comth a rain."   *before / stops*
     Of Phasipha[4] that was the queene of Crete—
740 For shrewednesse° him thoughte the tale sweete—   *wickedness*
Fy, speek namore, it is a grisly thing
Of hir horrible lust and hir liking.
     Of Clytermistra[5] for hir lecherye
That falsly made hir housbonde for to die,
745 He redde it with ful good devocioun.
     He tolde me eek for what occasioun
Amphiorax[6] at Thebes loste his lif:
Myn housbonde hadde a legende of his wif
Eriphylem, that for an ouche° of gold   *trinket*
750 Hath prively unto the Greekes told
Wher that hir housbonde hidde him in a place,
For which he hadde at Thebes sory grace.
     Of Livia[7] tolde he me and of Lucie:
They bothe made hir housbondes for to die,
755 That oon for love, that other was for hate;
Livia hir housbonde on an even late
Empoisoned hath for that she was his fo;
Lucia likerous loved hir housbonde so
That for he sholde alway upon hire thinke,
760 She yaf him swich a manere love-drinke
That he was deed er it were by the morwe.
And thus algates° housbondes han sorwe.   *continually*
     Thanne tolde he me how oon Latumius
Complained unto his felawe Arrius
765 That in his gardin growed swich a tree,
On which he saide how that his wives three
Hanged hemself for herte despitous.°   *cruel*
     "O leve brother," quod this Arrius,
"Yif° me a plante of thilke° blessed tree,   *give / that same*
770 And in my gardin planted shal it be."
     Of latter date of wives hath he red
That some han slain hir housbondes in hir bed
And lete hir lechour dighte° hire al the night,   *screw*
Whan that the cors° lay in the floor upright;°   *corpse / face up*
775 And some han driven nailes in hir brain
Whil that they sleepe, and thus they han hem slain;

3. Xanthippe was famous for nagging her husband, the philosopher Socrates.
4. Pasiphae, wife of Minos, became enamored of a bull, engendering the Minotaur.
5. Clytemnestra, queen of Mycenae, slew her husband Agamemnon when he returned from the Trojan War.
6. Amphiaraus died at the Siege of Thebes after listening to the advice of his wife, Eriphyle.
7. Livia poisoned her husband, Drusus, to satisfy her lover Sejanus; Lucia unwittingly poisoned her husband, the poet Lucretius, with a potion meant to keep him faithful.

Some han hem yiven poison in hir drinke.

He spak more harm than herte may bithinke,

And therwithal he knew of mo proverbes

780   Than in this world ther growen gras or herbes:

"Bet is," quod he, "thyn habitacioun

Be with a leon or a foul dragoun

Than with a wommman using° for to chide."   *accustomed*

"Bet is," quod he, "hye in the roof abide

785   Than with an angry wif down in the hous:

They been so wikked and contrarious,

They haten that hir housbondes loveth ay."°   *always*

He saide, "A womman cast hir shame away

Whan she cast of hir smok,"° and ferthermo,   *slip*

790   "A fair womman, but she be chast also,

Is lik a gold ring in a sowes nose."

Who wolde weene, or who wolde suppose

The wo that in myn herte was and pine?

      And whan I sawgh he wolde nevere fine°   *end*

795   To reden on this cursed book al night,

Al sodeinly three leves have I plight°   *plucked*

Out of his book right as he redde, and eke

I with my fist so took° him on the cheeke   *struck*

That in oure fir he fil bakward adown.

800   And up he sterte as dooth a wood° leoun,   *enraged*

And with his fist he smoot me on the heed

That in the floor I lay as I were deed.

And whan he sawgh how stille that I lay,

He was agast,° and wolde have fled his way,   *afraid*

805   Til atte laste out of my swough° I braide:°   *faint / arose*

"O hastou slain me, false thief?" I saide,

"And for my land thus hastou mordred me?

Er I be deed yit wol I kisse thee."

      And neer he cam and kneeled faire adown,

810   And saide, "Dere suster Alisoun,

As help me God, I shal thee nevere smite.

That I have doon, it is thyself to wite.°   *blame*

Foryif it me, and that I thee biseeke."

And yit eftsoones° I hitte him on the cheeke,   *immediately*

815   And saide, "Thief, thus muchel am I wreke.°   *avenged*

Now wol I die: I may no lenger speke."

      But at the laste with muchel care and wo

We fille accorded by us selven two.

He yaf me al the bridel° in myn hand,   *bridle, control*

820   To han the governance of hous and land,

And of his tonge and his hand also;

And made him brenne his book anoonright tho.

And whan that I hadde geten unto me

By maistrye° al the sovereinetee,°   *skill / dominance*

825   And that he saide, "Myn owene trewe wif,

Do as thee lust° the terme of al thy lif,   *please*
Keep thyn honour, and keep eek myn estat,"
After that day we hadde nevere debat.
God help me so, I was to him as kinde
830 As any wif from Denmark unto Inde,
And also trewe, and so was he to me.
I praye to God that sit in majestee,
So blesse his soule for his mercy dere.
Now wol I saye my tale if ye wol heere.

Another Interruption

835 The Frere lough whan he hadde herd al this:
"Now dame," quod he, "so have I joye or blis,
This is a long preamble of a tale."
And whan the Somnour herde the Frere gale,°   *exclaim*
"Lo," quod the Somnour, "Goddes armes two,
840 A frere wol entremette him° everemo!   *interfere*
Lo, goode men, a flye and eek a frere
Wol falle in every dissh and eek matere.
What spekestou of preambulacioun?
What, amble or trotte or pisse or go sitte down!
845 Thou lettest° oure disport in this manere."   *hinder*
    "Ye, woltou so, sire Somnour?" quod the Frere.
"Now by my faith, I shal er that I go
Telle of a somnour swich a tale or two
That al the folk shal laughen in this place."
850   "Now elles, Frere, I wol bishrewe thy face,"
Quod this Somnour, "and I bishrewe me,
But if I telle tales two or three
Of freres, er I come to Sidingborne,[8]
That I shal make thyn herte for to moorne—
855 For wel I woot thy pacience is goon."
    Oure Hoste cride, "Pees, and that anoon!"
And saide, "Lat the womman telle hir tale:
Ye fare° as folk that dronken been of ale.   *behave*
Do, dame, tel forth youre tale, and that is best."
860   "Al redy, sire," quod she, "right as you lest°—   *it pleases*
If I have licence of this worthy Frere."
"Yis, dame," quod he, "tel forth and I wol heere."

The Wife of Bath's Tale

In th'olde dayes of the King Arthour,
Of which that Britouns° speken greet honour,   *Bretons*
865 Al was this land fulfild° of faïrye: *filled*
The elf-queene° with hir joly compaignye   *fairy queen*

8. Sittingbourne, a town about 40 miles from London.

Daunced ful ofte in many a greene mede°—   *meadow*
This was the olde opinion as I rede;
I speke of many hundred yeres ago.
870   But now can no man see none elves mo,
For now the grete charitee and prayeres
Of limitours,[1] and othere holy freres,
That serchen every land and every streem,
As thikke as motes° in the sonne-beem,   *dust particles*
875   Blessing halles, chambres, kichenes, bowres,°   *bedrooms*
Citees, burghes,° castels, hye towres,   *boroughs*
Thropes,° bernes,° shipnes,° dayeries—   *villages / barns / stables*
This maketh that ther been no faïries.
For ther as wont° to walken was an elf   *where there used*
880   Ther walketh now the limitour himself,
In undermeles° and in morweninges,°   *afternoons / mornings*
And saith his Matins° and his holy thinges,   *morning prayers*
As he gooth in his limitacioun.°   *prescribed district*
Wommen may go saufly° up and down: *safely*
885   In every bussh or under every tree
Ther is noon other incubus[2] but he,
And he ne wol doon hem but dishonour.
       And so bifel it that this King Arthour
Hadde in his hous a lusty bacheler,°   *young knight*
890   That on a day cam riding fro river,°   *hunting waterfowl*
And happed that, allone as he was born,
He sawgh a maide walking him biforn;
Of which maide anoon, maugree hir heed,°   *against her will*
By verray force he rafte° hir maidenheed;   *stole*
895   For which oppression was swich clamour,
And swich pursuite° unto the King Arthour,   *petitioning*
That dampned° was this knight for to be deed   *condemned*
By cours of lawe, and sholde han lost his heed—
Paraventure° swich was the statut tho°—   *as it happens / then*
900   But that the queene and othere ladies mo
So longe prayeden the king of grace,
Til he his lif him graunted in the place,
And yaf him to the queene, al at hir wille,
To chese° wheither she wolde him save or spille.°   *decide / destroy*
905   The queene thanked the king with al hir might,
And after this thus spak she to the knight,
Whan that she saw hir time upon a day:
"Thou standest yit," quod she, "in swich array°   *situation*
That of thy lif yit hastou no suretee.°   *guarantee*
910   I graunte thee lif if thou canst tellen me
What thing it is that wommen most desiren:
Be war and keep thy nekke boon° from iren.°   *bone / iron*

---

1. Friars licensed to beg within set districts.   2. Demon who fornicates with women.

And if thou canst nat tellen me anoon,
Yit wol I yive thee leve for to goon
915　A twelfmonth and a day to seeche° and lere°　　　　　　　　seek out / learn
An answere suffisant° in this matere,　　　　　　　　　　　　satisfactory
And suretee° wol I han er that thou pace,°　　　　　　　　　pledge / pass
Thy body for to yeelden° in this place."　　　　　　　　　　surrender
　　Wo was this knight, and sorwefully he siketh.°　　　　　　sighs
920　But what, he may nat doon al as him liketh,
And atte laste he chees him° for to wende,°　　　　　　decided / travel
And come again right at the yeres ende,
With swich answere as God wolde him purveye,°　　　　　　　provide
And taketh his leve and wendeth forth his waye.
925　He seeketh every hous and every place
Wher as he hopeth for to finde grace,
To lerne what thing wommen love most.
But he ne coude arriven in no coost°　　　　　　　　　　　　country
Wher as he mighte finde in this matere
930　Two creatures according in fere.°　　　　　　　　　agreeing together
　　Some saiden wommen loven best richesse;
Some saide honour, some saide jolinesse;°　　　　　　　　　pleasure
Some riche array, some saiden lust abedde,
And ofte time to be widwe and wedde.
935　Some saide that oure herte is most esed
Whan that we been yflatered and yplesed—
He gooth ful neigh the soothe,° I wol nat lie:　　　　　　near the truth
A man shal winne us best with flaterye,
And with attendance and with bisinesse°　　　　　　　attentive service
940　Been we ylimed,° bothe more and lesse.　　　　　　　　　　ensnared
　　And some sayen that we loven best
For to be free, and do right as us lest,°　　　　　　　　　pleases
And that no man repreve° us of oure vice,　　　　　　　　　scold
But saye that we be wise and no thing nice.°　　　　　　　foolish
945　For trewely, ther is noon of us alle,
If any wight wol clawe us on the galle,°　　　　　　　　rub a sore spot
That we nil kike° for he saith us sooth:°　　　　　　kick / the truth
Assaye° and he shal finde it that so dooth.　　　　　　　　　try
For be we nevere so vicious withinne,
950　We wol be holden° wise and clene of sinne.　　　　　　　considered
　　And some sayn that greet delit han we
For to be holden stable° and eek secree,°　　　　　　constant / discreet
And in oo purpos stedefastly to dwelle,
And nat biwraye° thing that men us telle—　　　　　　　　　reveal
955　But that tale is nat worth a rake-stele.°　　　　　　　　rake handle
Pardee,° we wommen conne no thing hele:°　　　　by God / conceal
Witnesse on Mida.³ Wol ye heere the tale?
　　Ovide, amonges othere thinges smale,

---

3. Midas's story is recounted in Ovid's *Metamorphoses* 9.

Saide Mida hadde under his longe heres,
960   Growing upon his heed, two asses eres,
      The whiche vice° he hidde as he best mighte   *fault*
      Ful subtilly from every mannes sighte,
      That save his wif ther wiste of it namo.°   *no one else know*
      He loved hire most and trusted hire also.
965   He prayed hire that to no creature
      She sholde tellen of his disfigure.°   *deformity*
         She swoor him nay, for al this world to winne,
      She nolde° do that vilainye or sinne   *would not*
      To make hir housbonde han so foul a name:
970   She nolde nat telle it for hir owene shame.
      But nathelees, hir thoughte that she dyde°   *would die*
      That she so longe sholde a conseil° hide;   *secret*
      Hire thoughte it swal so sore aboute hir herte
      That nedely° som word hire moste asterte,°   *surely / come out*
975   And sith she dorste nat telle it to no man,
      Down to a mareis° faste° by she ran—   *marsh / close*
      Til she cam there hir herte was afire—
      And as a bitore° bombleth° in the mire,   *heron / squawks*
      She laide hir mouth unto the water down:
980   "Biwray° me nat, thou water, with thy soun,"°   *betray / sound*
      Quod she. "To thee I telle it and namo:
      Myn housbonde hath longe asses eres two.
      Now is myn herte al hool, now is it oute.
      I mighte no lenger keepe it, out of doute."
985   Here may ye see, though we a time abide,
      Yit oute it moot:° we can no conseil hide.   *must*
      The remenant of the tale if ye wol heere,
      Redeth Ovide, and ther ye may it lere.°   *learn*
         This knight of which my tale is specially,
990   Whan that he sawgh he mighte nat come therby—
      This is to saye what wommen loven most—
      Within his brest ful sorweful was his gost,°   *spirit*
      But hoom he gooth, he mighte nat sojurne:°   *linger*
      The day was come that hoomward moste he turne.
995   And in his way it happed him to ride
      In al this care under a forest side,
      Wher as he sawgh upon a daunce go
      Of ladies foure and twenty and yit mo;
      Toward the whiche daunce he drow° ful yerne,°   *drew / gladly*
1000 In hope that som wisdom sholde he lerne.
      But certainly, er he cam fully there,
      Vanisshed was this daunce, he niste° where.   *did not know*
      No creature sawgh he that bar lif,
      Save on the greene he sawgh sitting a wif—
1005 A fouler wight° ther may no man devise.°   *creature / imagine*
      Again the knight this olde wif gan rise,
      And saide, "Sire knight, heer forth lith no way.°   *road*

Telle me what ye seeken, by youre fay.°   *faith*
Paraventure it may the better be:
1010   Thise olde folk conne° muchel thing," quod she.   *know*
     "My leve moder,"° quod this knight, "certain,   *dear mother*
I nam but° deed but if that I can sayn   *am no more than*
What thing it is that wommen most desire.
Coude ye me wisse,° I wolde wel quite youre hire."°   *inform / repay you*
1015   "Plight° me thy trouthe° here in myn hand," quod she,   *pledge / promise*
"The nexte thing that I require thee,
Thou shalt it do, if it lie in thy might,
And I wol telle it you er it be night."
     "Have heer my trouthe," quod the knight. "I graunte."
1020   "Thanne," quod she, "I dar me wel avaunte°   *brag*
Thy lif is sauf, for I wol stande therby.
Upon my lif the queene wol saye as I.
Lat see which is the pruddeste° of hem alle   *proudest*
That wereth on a coverchief or a calle°   *headdress*
1025   That dar saye nay of that I shal thee teche.
Lat us go forth withouten lenger speeche."
Tho rouned° she a pistel° in his ere,   *whispered / message*
And bad him to be glad and have no fere.
     Whan they be comen to the court, this knight
1030   Saide he hadde holde his day as he hadde hight,°   *promised*
And redy was his answere, as he saide.
Ful many a noble wif, and many a maide,
And many a widwe—for that they been wise—
The queene hirself sitting as justise,°   *judge*
1035   Assembled been this answere for to heere,
And afterward this knight was bode appere.
To every wight comanded was silence,
And that the knight sholde telle in audience
What thing that worldly wommen loven best.
1040   This knight ne stood nat stille° as dooth a best,°   *silent / beast*
But to his question anoon answerde
With manly vois that al the court it herde.
     "My lige° lady, generally," quod he,   *liege*
"Wommen desire to have sovereinetee
1045   As wel over hir housbonde as hir love,
And for to been in maistrye him above.
This is youre moste desir though ye me kille.
Dooth as you list: I am here at youre wille."
     In al the court ne was ther wif ne maide
1050   Ne widwe that contraried that he saide,
But saiden he was worthy han his lif.
     And with that word up sterte that olde wif,
Which that the knight sawgh sitting on the greene;
"Mercy," quod she, "my soverein lady queene,
1055   Er that youre court departe, do me right.
I taughte this answere unto the knight,

For which he plighte me his trouthe there
The firste thing I wolde him requere
He wolde it do, if it laye in his might.
1060 Bifore the court thanne praye I thee, sire knight,"
Quod she, "that thou me take unto thy wif,
For wel thou woost° that I have kept° thy lif.   know / saved
If I saye fals, say nay, upon thy fay."
     This knight answerde, "Allas and wailaway,
1065 I woot° right wel that swich was my biheeste.°   know / promise
For Goddes love, as chees° a newe requeste: choose
Taak al my good and lat my body go."
     "Nay thanne," quod she, "I shrewe° us bothe two.   curse
For though that I be foul and old and poore,
1070 I nolde° for al the metal ne for ore   would not wish
That under erthe is grave° or lith above,   buried
But if thy wif I were and eek thy love."
     "My love," quod he. "Nay, my dampnacioun!
Allas, that any of my nacioun°   lineage
1075 Sholde evere so foule disparaged° be."   degraded
But al for nought, th'ende is this, that he
Constrained was: he needes moste hire wedde,
And taketh his olde wif and gooth to bedde.
     Now wolden some men saye, paraventure,
1080 That for my necligence I do no cure
To tellen you the joy and al th'array
That at the feeste was that ilke day.
To which thing shortly answere I shal:
I saye ther nas no joye ne feeste at al;
1085 Ther nas but hevinesse and muche sorwe.
For prively he wedded hire on morwe,°   in the morning
And al day after hidde him as an owle,
So wo was him, his wif looked so foule.
     Greet was the wo the knight hadde in his thought:
1090 Whan he was with his wif abedde brought,
He walweth° and he turneth to and fro.   rolls over
His olde wif lay smiling everemo,
And saide, "O dere housbonde, benedicite,°   bless us
Fareth° every knight thus with his wif as ye?   behaves
1095 Is this the lawe of King Arthures hous?
Is every knight of his thus daungerous?°   reserved
I am youre owene love and youre wif;
I am she which that saved hath youre lif;
And certes yit ne dide I you nevere unright.°   injustice
1100 Why fare° ye thus with me this firste night?   behave
Ye faren like a man hadde lost his wit.
What is my gilt? For Goddes love, telle it,
And it shal been amended if I may."
     "Amended!" quod this knight. "Allas, nay, nay,
1105 It wol nat been amended neveremo.

Thou art so lothly° and so old also,   *loathsome*
And therto comen of so lowe a kinde,°   *breeding*
That litel wonder is though I walwe and winde.°   *turn*
So wolde God myn herte wolde breste!"°   *burst*
1110   "Is this," quod she, "the cause of youre unreste?"
"Ye, certainly," quod he. "No wonder is."
"Now sire," quod she, "I coude amende al this,
If that me liste,° er it were dayes three,   *it pleased me*
So° wel ye mighte bere you° unto me.   *provided that / behave*
1115   "But for ye speken of swich gentilesse°   *nobility*
As is descended out of old richesse—
That therfore sholden ye be gentilmen—
Swich arrogance is nat worth an hen.
Looke who that is most vertuous alway,
1120   Privee and apert,° and most entendeth ay   *privately and publicly*
To do the gentil deedes that he can,
Taak him for the gretteste gentilman.
Crist wol° we claime of him oure gentilesse,   *wishes*
Nat of oure eldres for hir 'old richesse.'
1125   For though they yive us al hir heritage,
For which we claime to been of heigh parage,°   *noble lineage*
Yit may they nat biquethe for no thing
To noon of us hir vertuous living,
That made hem gentilmen ycalled be,
1130   And bad us folwen° hem in swich degree.   *to follow*
"Wel can the wise poete of Florence,
That highte° Dant,[4] speken in this sentence;°   *was called / opinion*
Lo, in swich manere rym is Dantes tale:
'Ful selde° up riseth by his braunches[5] smale   *seldom*
1135   Prowesse° of man, for God of his prowesse   *excellence*
Wol that of him we claime oure gentilesse.'
For of oure eldres may we no thing claime
But temporel thing that man may hurte and maime.
Eek every wight woot° this as wel as I,   *person knows*
1140   If gentilesse were planted natureelly
Unto a certain linage down the line,
Privee and apert, thanne wolde they nevere fine°   *end*
To doon of gentilesse the faire office°—   *duty*
They mighte do no vilainye or vice.
1145   "Taak fir and beer° it in the derkeste hous   *bring*
Bitwixe this and the Mount of Caucasus,
And lat men shette° the dores and go thenne,°   *shut / thence*
Yit wol the fir as faire lie and brenne
As twenty thousand men mighte it biholde:
1150   His° office natureel ay° wol it holde,   *its / always*
Up peril of my lif, til that it die.

---

4. Dante Alighieri, the 13th-century Italian poet, expressed   5. Branches (of his family tree).
similar views in his *Convivio*.

Heer may ye see wel how that genterye°   *gentility*
Is nat annexed° to possessioun,   *connected*
Sith° folk ne doon hir operacioun°   *since / their work*
1155   Alway, as dooth the fir, lo, in his kinde.°   *nature*
For God it woot, men may wel often finde
A lordes sone do shame and vilainye;
And he that wol han pris° of his gentrye,°   *esteem / noble birth*
For he was boren of a gentil hous,
1160   And hadde his eldres noble and vertuous,
And nil° himselven do no gentil deedes,   *will not*
Ne folwen his gentil auncestre that deed is,
He nis nat gentil, be he duc or erl—
For vilaines sinful deedes maken a cherl.°   *ruffian*
1165   Thy gentilesse nis but renomee°   *reputation*
Of thine auncestres for hir heigh bountee,°   *generosity*
Which is a straunge° thing for thy persone.   *foreign*
For gentilesse cometh fro God allone.
Thanne comth oure verray gentilesse of grace:
1170   It was no thing biquethe us with oure place.
Thenketh how noble, as saith Valerius,[6]
Was thilke° Tullius Hostilius[7]   *that*
That out of poverte roos to heigh noblesse.
Redeth Senek,[8] and redeth eek Boece:
1175   Ther shul ye seen expres that no drede° is   *doubt*
That he is gentil that dooth gentil deedes.
And therfore, leve housbonde, I thus conclude:
Al were it that mine auncestres weren rude,°   *lowborn*
Yit may the hye God—and so hope I—
1180   Graunte me grace to liven vertuously.
Thanne am I gentil whan that I biginne
To liven vertuously and waive° sinne.   *avoid*
     "And ther as ye of poverte me repreve,
The hye God, on whom that we bileve,
1185   In wilful poverte chees to live his lif;
And certes every man, maiden, or wif
May understonde that Jesus, hevene king,
Ne wolde nat chese a vicious living.
Glad poverte is an honeste° thing, certain;   *honorable*
1190   This wol Senek and othere clerkes sayn.
Whoso that halt him paid of his poverte,[9]
I holde him riche al° hadde he nat a sherte.°   *although / shirt*
He that coveiteth is a poore wight,
For he wolde han that is nat in his might;
1195   But he that nought hath, ne coveiteth have,
Is riche, although we holde him but a knave.°   *servant*

6. The Roman historian Valerius Maximus, in his *Facta et dicta memorabilia* 3.4.
7. The legendary third king of Rome who started as a shepherd.
8. Seneca, the Stoic author, in his *Epistle* 44; Boece: Boethius in his *Consolation of Philosophy*.
9. Whoever is satisfied with poverty.

Verray poverte it singeth proprely.
Juvenal[1] saith of poverte, 'Merily
The poore man, whan he gooth by the waye,
1200   Biforn the theves he may singe and playe.'
Poverte is hateful good, and as I gesse,
A ful greet bringere out of bisinesse;°   *worldly cares*
A greet amendere eek of sapience°   *wisdom*
To him that taketh it in pacience;
1205   Poverte is thing, although it seeme elenge,°   *miserable*
Possession that no wight wol chalenge;
Poverte ful often, whan a man is lowe,
Maketh his God and eek himself to knowe;
Poverte a spectacle° is, as thinketh me,   *eyeglass*
1210   Thurgh which he may his verray freendes see.
And therfore, sire, sin that I nought you greve,
Of my poverte namore ye me repreve.
        "Now sire, of elde° ye repreve me: *old age*
And certes sire, though noon auctoritee
1215   Were in no book, ye gentils of honour
Sayn that men sholde an old wight° doon favour,   *person*
And clepe° him fader for youre gentilesse—   *call*
And auctours° shal I finden, as I gesse.   *authorities*
        "Now ther ye saye that I am foul and old:
1220   Thanne drede you nought to been a cokewold,°   *cuckold*
For filthe and elde, also mote I thee,
Been grete wardeins° upon chastitee.   *guardians*
But nathelees, sin I knowe your delit,
I shal fulfille youre worldly appetit.
1225   "Chees° now," quod she, "oon of thise thinges twaye: *choose*
To han me foul and old til that I deye
And be to you a trewe humble wif,
And nevere you displese in al my lif,
Or elles ye wol han me yong and fair,
1230   And take youre aventure° of the repair°   *chances / visits*
That shal be to youre hous by cause of me—
Or in som other place, wel may be.
Now chees youreselven wheither° that you liketh."   *whichever*
        This knight aviseth him° and sore siketh;°   *considers / sighs*
1235   But atte laste he saide in this manere:
"My lady and my love, and wif so dere,
I putte me in youre wise governaunce:
Cheseth youreself which may be most plesaunce
And most honour to you and me also.
1240   I do no fors° the wheither of the two,   *do not care*
For as you liketh it suffiseth° me."   *satisfies*
        "Thanne have I gete of you° maistrye," quod she,   *won from you*
"Sin I may chese and governe as me lest?"°   *it pleases*

---

1. The misogynist Roman poet in his *Satires* 10.21, 22.

"Ye, certes, wif," quod he. "I holde it best."

1245 "Kisse me," quod she. "We be no lenger wrothe.°   *opposed*
For by my trouthe, I wol be to you bothe—
This is to sayn, ye, bothe fair and good.
I praye to God that I mote sterven wood,°   *die mad*
But I to you be al so good and trewe

1250 As evere was wif sin that the world was newe.
And but I be tomorn° as fair to seene   *in the morning*
As any lady, emperisse, or queene,
That is bitwixe the eest and eek the west,
Do with my lif and deeth right as you lest:

1255 Caste up the curtin, looke how that it is."
    And whan the knight sawgh verraily al this,
That she so fair was and so yong therto,
For joye he hente° hire in his armes two;   *seized*
His herte bathed in a bath of blisse;

1260 A thousand time arewe° he gan hire kisse,   *in a row*
And she obeyed him in every thing
That mighte do him plesance or liking.
And thus they live unto hir lives ende
In parfit° joye. And Jesu Crist us sende   *perfect*

1265 Housbondes meeke, yonge, and fresshe abedde—
And grace t'overbide° hem that we wedde.   *outlive*
And eek I praye Jesu shorte hir lives
That nought wol be governed by hir wives,
And olde and angry nigardes of dispence°—   *misers in spending*

1270 God sende hem soone a verray pestilence!

THE PARDONER'S PROLOGUE AND TALE   There is something in Chaucer's Pardoner to unnerve practically everyone. The Pardoner's physiology blurs gender itself, his apparent homosexuality challenges the dominant heterosexual ordering of medieval society, his *Prologue* subverts the notion that the intent and effect of words are connected, and his willingness to convert religious discourse into cash undermines the very bases of faith. He initiates a sequence of moments in the later tales that threaten to puncture or tear the social fabric of the Canterbury company.

The Pardoner and "his freend and his compeer," the Summoner, are the last two pilgrims described in *The General Prologue*, reflecting the distaste with which such marginal clergy were often regarded in the period. Summoners were the policing branch of the ecclesiastical courts, paid to bring in transgressors against the canon law. Pardoners had the job, criticized even within the church, of exchanging indulgences for cash. The sufferings of Christ and saintly martyrs, it was thought, had left the church with a legacy of goodness. This could be transferred to sinners, freeing them from a period in Purgatory, if they proved their penitence (among other ways) by gifts to support good works such as the hospital for which the Pardoner worked.

The Pardoner has turned this part of the structure of penitence into a profit center. In his own *Prologue*, the Pardoner is boastfully explicit about this:

> For myn entente is nat but for to winne,
> And no thing for correccion of sinne . . .

This merciless equation of his verbal power with cash profit deeply subverts the logic of Christian language and the priestly role in salvation. These are replaced by language working in a strange self-consuming circle: the Pardoner brilliantly achieves the very sin his sermon most vituperates.

The Pardoner's physiology—he has either lost his testicles or never had them—may emblematize this exploitation of language emptied of spiritual intention. His uncertain or incomplete gender, though, also challenges the fundamental distinctions of the body within the medieval social economy, as does his apparent homosexuality. The Pardoner's theatrical self-presentation, abetted by rhetorical techniques he lovingly describes, draws the fascinated if queasy attention of his audience and seems to provide him a monstrous though (as it turns out) fragile power.

The Pardoner's tale of three rioters and their encounter with death is actually folded into his Prologue as an exemplum, an illustrative story, in the sermon against cupidity he proposes to offer as a sample of his skills. Yet the Pardoner's obsession with bodies in extremity, seeking or denying death, skeletal or gorged, pulls against his tale as a parable of greed. The tale draws toward its close in a scene of rage, exposure, and angry silence, which threatens to undo the pilgrim society, rather as the Pardoner and his discourse have threatened so much of the broader social contract. The Knight steps in, though, and almost bullies the Host and the Pardoner into a kiss of peace. This ritual gesture, nearly as empty of real goodwill as any of the Pardoner's most cynical words, does allow the shaken group to continue on their way, even as it hints at the emptiness that may hide in other, less openly challenged systems of value in the tales and their world.

The Pardoner's Prologue
The Introduction

	Oure Hoste gan to swere as he were wood;°	*mad*
	"Harrow," quod he, "by nailes[1] and by blood,	
	This was a fals cherl° and a fals justice.°[2]	*villain / judge*
	As shameful deeth as herte may devise	
5	Come to thise juges and hir advocats.°	*lawyers*
	Algate° this sely° maide is slain, allas!	*anyway / innocent*
	Allas, too dere boughte she beautee!	
	Wherfore I saye alday° that men may see	*always*
	The yiftes of Fortune and of Nature	
10	Been cause of deeth to many a creature.	
	As bothe yiftes° that I speke of now,	*gifts*
	Men han ful ofte more for harm than prow.°	*profit*
	"But trewely, myn owene maister dere,	
	This is a pitous tale for to heere.	
15	But nathelees, passe over, is no fors:°	*concern*
	I praye to God so save thy gentil° cors,°	*noble / body*
	And eek thine urinals[3] and thy jurdones,°	*chamber pots*
	Thyn ipocras and eek thy galiones,[4]	
	And every boiste° ful of thy letuarye°—	*box / medicine*
20	God blesse hem, and oure lady Sainte Marye.	
	So mote I theen,° thou art a propre man,	*so may I prosper*

1. Nails (of Christ's cross).
2. Harry Bailey, the host, is responding to *The Physician's Tale* and the story of a young woman named Virginia whose father kills her rather than surrender her to a wicked judge and his accomplice.
3. Physician's vessels for analyzing urine samples.
4. Medicines named after the ancient Greek physicians Hippocrates and Galen.

And lik a prelat,° by Saint Ronian![5] *Church officer*
Saide I nat wel? I can nat speke in terme.° *jargon*
But wel I woot,° thou doost myn herte to erme° *know / grieve*
That I almost have caught a cardinacle.° *heart condition*
By corpus bones,[6] but if I have triacle,° *medicine*
Or elles a draughte of moiste° and corny° ale, *fresh / malted*
Or but I heere anoon a merye tale,
Myn herte is lost for pitee of this maide.
"Thou bel ami,[7] thou Pardoner," he saide,
"Tel us som mirthe or japes° right anoon." *joke*
"It shal be doon," quod he, "by Saint Ronian.
But first," quod he, "here at this ale-stake° *tavern marker*
I wol bothe drinke and eten of a cake."° *loaf of bread*
And right anoon thise gentils gan to crye,
"Nay, lat him telle us of no ribaudye.° *obscenity*
Tel us som moral thing that we may lere,° *learn*
Som wit, and thanne wol we gladly heere."
"I graunte, ywis,"° quod he, "but I moot° thinke *certainly / must*
Upon som honeste° thing whil that I drinke." *honorable*

The Prologue

Lordinges—quod he—in chirches whan I preche,
I paine me to han an hautein° speeche, *loud*
And ringe it out as round as gooth a belle,
For I can al by rote° that I telle. *know it all by heart*
My theme is alway oon,° and evere was: *the same*
Radix malorum est cupiditas.[8]
First I pronounce whennes that I come,
And thanne my bulles° shewe I alle and some: *indulgences*
Oure lige lordes seel[9] on my patente,° *license*
That shewe I first, my body to warente,° *safeguard*
That no man be so bold, ne preest ne clerk,
Me to destourbe of Cristes holy werk.
And after that thanne telle I forth my tales—
Bulles of popes and of cardinales,
Of patriarkes and bisshopes I shewe,
And in Latin I speke a wordes fewe,
To saffron° with my predicacioun,° *season / preaching*
And for to stire hem to devocioun.
Thanne shewe I forth my longe crystal stones,° *jars*
Ycrammed ful of cloutes° and of bones— *rags*
Relikes been they, as weenen they eechoon.° *they all suppose*
Thanne have I in laton° a shulder-boon *brazened*
Which that was of an holy Jewes sheep.

5. St. Ronan, a Scottish saint, with a possible pun on "runnions," the male sexual organs.
6. A confused oath mixing God's body and God's bones.
7. Fair friend (French, affected).
8. Greed is the root of all evil.
9. Seal of our liege lord (i.e., the Pope).

"Goode men," I saye, "take of my wordes keep:°   notice
65   If that this boon be wasshe in any welle,
     If cow, or calf, or sheep, or oxe swelle,
     That any worm° hath ete or worm ystonge,   snake
     Take water of that welle and wassh his tonge,
     And it is hool° anoon. And ferthermoor,   healthy
70   Of pokkes° and of scabbe and every soor   pox
     Shal every sheep be hool that of this welle
     Drinketh a draughte. Take keep eek that I telle:
     If that the goode man that the beestes oweth°   owns
     Wol every wike,° er that the cok him croweth,   week
75   Fasting drinken of this welle a draughte—
     As thilke° holy Jew oure eldres taughte—   that
     His beestes and his stoor° shal multiplye.   stock
          "And sire, also it heleth jalousye:
     For though a man be falle in jalous rage
80   Lat maken with this water his potage,°   soup
     And nevere shal he more his wif mistriste,
     Though he the soothe° of hir defaute wiste,°   truth / offense knows
     Al hadde she taken preestes two or three.
          "Here is a mitein° eek that ye may see: mitten
85   He that his hand wol putte in this mitein
     He shal have multiplying of his grain,
     Whan he hath sowen, be it whete or otes—
     So that he offre pens° or elles grotes.°   pennies / silver coins
          "Goode men and wommen, oo thing warne I you:
90   If any wight° be in this chirche now   person
     That hath doon sinne horrible, that he
     Dar nat for shame of it yshriven° be,   confessed
     Or any womman, be she yong or old,
     That hath ymaked hir housbonde cokewold,°   cuckold
95   Swich folk shal have no power ne no grace
     To offren to my relikes in this place;
     And whoso findeth him out of swich blame,
     He wol come up and offre in Goddes name,
     And I assoile° him by the auctoritee   absolve
100 Which that by bulle ygraunted was to me."
          By this gaude° have I wonne, yeer by yeer,   trick
     An hundred mark[1] sith I was pardoner.
     I stonde lik a clerk in my pulpet,
     And whan the lewed° peple is down yset,   ignorant
105 I preche so as ye han herd bifore,
     And telle an hundred false japes° more.   tricks
     Thanne paine I me to strecche forth the nekke,
     And eest and west upon the peple I bekke°   nod
     As dooth a douve,° sitting on a berne;°   dove / barn

---

1. About 66 pounds.

110	Mine handes and my tonge goon so yerne°	*fast*
	That it is joye to see my bisinesse.	
	Of avarice and of swich cursednesse	
	Is al my preching, for to make hem free°	*generous*
	To yiven hir pens, and namely unto me,	
115	For myn entente is nat but for to winne,°	*profit*
	And no thing for correccion of sinne:	
	I rekke° nevere whan that they been beried°	*care / buried*
	Though that hir soules goon a-blakeberied.[2]	
	For certes, many a predicacioun	
120	Comth ofte time of yvel entencioun:	
	Som for plesance of folk and flaterye,	
	To been avaunced by ypocrisye,	
	And som for vaine glorye, and som for hate;	
	For whan I dar noon otherways debate,	
125	Thanne wol I stinge him with my tonge smerte°	*hurting*
	In preching, so that he shal nat asterte°	*escape*
	To been defamed falsly, if that he	
	Hath trespassed to my bretheren or to me.	
	For though I telle nought his propre name,	
130	Men shal wel knowe that it is the same	
	By signes and by othere circumstaunces.	
	Thus quite° I folk that doon us displesaunces;°	*repay / trouble*
	Thus spete I out my venim under hewe°	*color*
	Of holinesse, to seeme holy and trewe.	
135	But shortly myn entente I wol devise:°	*describe*
	I preche of no thing but for coveitise;°	*greed*
	Therfore my theme is yit and evere was	
	Radix malorum est cupiditas.	
	Thus can I preche again that same vice	
140	Which that I use, and that is avarice.	
	But though myself be gilty in that sinne,	
	Yit can I make other folk to twinne°	*separate*
	From avarice, and sore to repente—	
	But that is nat my principal entente:	
145	I preche no thing but for coveitise.	
	Of this matere it oughte ynough suffise.	
	Thanne telle I hem ensamples° many oon	*exemplary tales*
	Of olde stories longe time agoon,	
	For lewed peple loven tales olde—	
150	Swiche thinges can they wel reporte° and holde.°	*repeat / remember*
	What, trowe° ye that whiles I may preche,	*believe*
	And winne gold and silver for I teche,	
	That I wol live in poverte wilfully?	
	Nay, nay, I thoughte it nevere, trewely,	
155	For I wol preche and begge in sondry landes;	

2. Looking for blackberries.

I wol nat do no labour with mine handes,
Ne make baskettes and live therby,
By cause I wol nat beggen idelly.°   *in vain*
I wol none of the Apostles countrefete:°   *imitate*
160 I wol have moneye, wolle,° cheese, and whete,   *wool*
Al were it yiven of the pooreste page,°   *servant*
Or of the pooreste widwe in a village—
Al sholde hir children sterve° for famine.   *die*
Nay, I wol drinke licour of the vine
165 And have a joly wenche in every town.
But herkneth, lordinges, in conclusioun,
Youre liking is that I shal telle a tale:
Now have I dronke a draughte of corny ale,
By God, I hope I shal you telle a thing
170 That shal by reson been at youre liking;
For though myself be a ful vicious man,
A moral tale yit I you telle can,
Which I am wont to preche for to winne.
Now holde youre pees, my tale I wol biginne.

The Pardoner's Tale

175 In Flandres whilom° was a compaignye   *once*
Of yonge folk that haunteden° folye—   *practiced*
As riot, hasard, stewes,[1] and tavernes,
Wher as with harpes, lutes, and giternes°   *guitars*
They daunce and playen at dees° bothe day and night,   *dice*
180 And ete also and drinke over hir might,
Thurgh which they doon the devel sacrifise
Withinne that develes temple in cursed wise
By superfluitee° abhominable.   *overindulgence*
Hir othes been so grete and so dampnable
185 That it is grisly for to heere hem swere:
Oure blessed Lordes body they totere°—   *rip apart*
Hem thoughte that Jewes rente° him nought ynough.   *tore*
And eech of hem at otheres sinne lough.°   *laughed*
And right anoon thanne comen tombesteres,°   *dancing girls*
190 Fetis° and smale,° and yonge frutesteres,[2]   *elegant / slender*
Singeres with harpes, bawdes,° wafereres°—   *pimps / cake sellers*
Whiche been the verray develes officeres,
To kindle and blowe the fir of lecherye
That is annexed° unto glotonye:°   *connected / gluttony*
195 The Holy Writ take I to my witnesse
That luxure° is in win and dronkenesse.   *lechery*
Lo, how that dronken Lot[3] unkindely°   *against nature*
Lay by his doughtres two unwitingly:

---

1. Such as carousing, gambling, brothels.
2. Girls selling fruit.
3. Lot, the nephew of Abraham, whose story is told in Genesis 19.30–38.

Detail from a carved chest, c. 1410. This large wooden panel is the surviving half of the front of a massive chest. It presents scenes from *The Pardoner's Tale:* at left, the youngest rioter buys wine; in the center, his two companions stab him to death; at right, they die from the wine their companion had poisoned. The composition and carving have much of the energy and economical narrative style of the tale itself. Produced about a decade after Chaucer's death, the panel reflects the impact of his tales in settings very different from those that supported such grand aristocratic productions as the Ellesmere manuscript, created around the same time (see Color Plate 9 and page 314).

	So dronke he was he niste what he wroughte.°	*knew not what he did*
200	Herodes,[4] who so wel the stories soughte,	
	Whan he of win was repleet at his feeste,	
	Right at his owene table he yaf his heeste°	*command*
	To sleen° the Baptist John, ful giltelees.	*slay*
	Senek[5] saith a good word douteles:	
205	He saith he can no difference finde	
	Bitwixe a man that is out of his minde	
	And a man which that is dronkelewe,°	*drunk*
	But that woodnesse, yfallen in a shrewe,[6]	
	Persevereth lenger than dooth dronkenesse.	
210	O glotonye, ful of cursednesse!	
	O cause first of oure confusioun!°	*ruin*
	O original of oure dampnacioun,	
	Til Crist hadde bought° us with his blood again!	*redeemed*
	Lo, how dere, shortly for to sayn,	
215	Abought was thilke° cursed vilainye;	*that*
	Corrupt was al this world for glotonye:	
	Adam oure fader and his wif also	
	Fro Paradis to labour and to wo	

4. King Herod, who was enticed by Salome into bringing her the head of John the Baptist (Mark 6.17–29, Matthew 14.1–12).

5. The stoic author Seneca in his *Epistle* 83.18.493–97.
6. Madness, occurring in a wicked person.

Were driven for that vice, it is no drede.° — doubt
220　For whil that Adam fasted, as I rede,
He was in Paradis; and whan that he
Eet of the fruit defended° on a tree, — forbidden
Anoon he was out cast to wo and paine.
O glotonye, on thee wel oughte us plaine!° — lament
225　　O, wiste a man how manye maladies
Folwen of° excess and of glotonies, — result from
He wolde been the more mesurable° — moderate
Of his diete, sitting at his table.
Allas, the shorte throte, the tendre mouth,
230　Maketh that eest and west and north and south,
In erthe, in air, in water, men to swinke,° — labor
To gete a gloton daintee mete and drinke.
Of this matere, O Paul, wel canstou trete:° — discuss
"Mete unto wombe, and wombe° eek unto mete, — belly
235　Shal God destroyen bothe," as Paulus saith.[7]
Allas, a foul thing is it, by my faith,
To saye this word, and fouler is the deede
Whan man so drinketh of the white and rede° — white and red wines
That of his throte he maketh his privee° — toilet
240　Thurgh thilke cursed superfluitee.
　　The Apostle[8] weeping saith ful pitously,
"Ther walken manye of which you told have I—
saye it now weeping with pitous vois—
They been enemies of Cristes crois,° — cross
245　Of whiche the ende is deeth—wombe is hir god!"
O wombe, O bely, O stinking cod,° — bag
Fulfilled of dong° and of corrupcioun! — dung
At either ende of thee foul is the soun.° — sound
How greet labour and cost is thee to finde!° — provide for
250　Thise cookes, how they stampe and straine and grinde,
And turnen substance into accident[9]
To fulfillen al thy likerous talent!° — greedy desire
Out of the harde bones knokke they
The mary,° for they caste nought away — marrow
255　That may go thurgh the golet° softe and soote.° — gullet / sweet
Of spicerye of leef and bark and roote
Shal been his sauce ymaked by delit,
To make him yit a newer appetit.
But certes, he that haunteth swiche delices° — delicacies
260　Is deed whil that he liveth in tho° vices. — those
　　A lecherous thing is win, and dronkenesse
Is ful of striving° and of wrecchednesse. — quarreling
O dronke man, disfigured is thy face!

---

7. St. Paul in 1 Corinthians 6.13.
8. St. Paul, in Philippians 3.18–19.
9. A learned joke about the Eucharist where, in Catholic doctrine, the essence ("substance") of bread and wine is transformed into the body and blood of Christ, though their form ("accident") remains unchanged.

	Sour is thy breeth, foul artou to embrace!	
265	And thurgh thy dronke nose seemeth the soun	
	As though thou saidest ay° "Sampsoun, Sampsoun."	*always*
	And yit, God woot,° Sampson drank nevere win.	*knows*
	Thou fallest as it were a stiked swin;°	*stuck pig*
	Thy tonge is lost, and al thyn honeste cure,°	*care for honor*
270	For dronkenesse is verray sepulture°	*grave*
	Of mannes wit and his discrecioun.	
	In whom that drinke hath dominacioun	
	He can no conseil keepe, it is no drede.	
	Now keepe you fro the white and fro the rede—	
275	And namely fro the white win of Lepe[1]	
	That is to selle in Fisshstreete or in Chepe:[2]	
	The win of Spaine creepeth subtilly[3]	
	In othere wines growing faste° by,	*close*
	Of which ther riseth swich fumositee°	*vapors*
280	That whan a man hath dronken draughtes three	
	And weeneth that he be at hoom in Chepe,	
	He is in Spaine, right at the town of Lepe,	
	Nat at The Rochele ne at Burdeux town;	
	And thanne wol he sayn "Sampsoun, Sampsoun."	
285	But herkneth, lordinges, oo word I you praye,	
	That alle the soverein actes,° dar I saye,	*excellent deeds*
	Of victories in the Olde Testament,	
	Thurgh verray God that is omnipotent,	
	Were doon in abstinence and in prayere:	
290	Looketh the Bible and ther ye may it lere.°	*learn*
	Looke Attilla, the grete conquerour,[4]	
	Deide in his sleep with shame and dishonour,	
	Bleeding at his nose in dronkenesse:	
	A capitain sholde live in sobrenesse.	
295	And overal this, aviseth you right wel	
	What was comanded unto Lamuel[5]—	
	Nat Samuel, but Lamuel, saye I—	
	Redeth the Bible and finde it expresly,	
	Of win-yiving° to hem that han° justise:	*wine-serving / dispense*
300	Namore of this, for it may wel suffise.	
	And now that I have spoken of glotonye,	
	Now wol I you defende hasardrye:°	*gambling*
	Hasard is verray moder of lesinges,°	*lies*
	And of deceite and cursed forsweringes,	
305	Blaspheme of Crist, manslaughtre, and wast° also	*waste*
	Of catel° and of time; and ferthermo,	*property*

---

1. Wine-growing region in Spain.
2. Commercial districts in London.
3. Chaucer is referring to the illegal practice of using cheap wine (here, Spanish wine from Lepe) to dilute more expensive wines (from the neighboring French provinces of

La Rochelle and Bordeaux).
4. Attila the Hun died on his wedding night from excessive drinking.
5. Biblical king of Massa, warned against drinking in Proverbs 31.4.

It is repreve° and contrarye of honour   *reprobate*
For to been holden a commune hasardour,
And evere the hyer he is of estat
310   The more is he holden desolat.°   *dissolute*
If that a prince useth hasardrye,
In alle governance and policye
He is, as by commune opinioun,
Yholde the lasse in reputacioun.
315   Stilbon,⁶ that was a wis embassadour,
Was sent to Corinthe in ful greet honour
Fro Lacedomye° to make hir alliaunce,   *Sparta*
And whan he cam him happede parchaunce
That alle the gretteste that were of that lond
320   Playing at the hasard he hem foond,
For which as soone as it mighte be
He stal him hoom again to his contree,
And saide, "Ther wol I nat lese° my name,   *lose*
N'I wol nat take on me so greet defame
325   You to allye unto none hasardours:
Sendeth othere wise embassadours,
For by my trouthe, me were levere° die   *I would rather*
Than I you sholde to hasardours allye.
For ye that been so glorious in honours
330   Shal nat allye you with hasardours
As by my wil, ne as by my tretee."
This wise philosophre, thus saide he.
        Looke eek that to the king Demetrius
The King of Parthes,⁷ as the book saith us,
335   Sente him a paire of dees of gold in scorn,
For he hadde used hasard therbiforn,
For which he heeld his glorye or his renown
At no value or reputacioun.
Lordes may finden other manere play
340   Honeste ynough to drive the day away.
        Now wol I speke of othes false and grete
A word or two, as olde bookes trete:
        Greet swering is a thing abhominable,
And fals swering is yit more reprevable.°   *reprehensible*
345   The hye God forbad swering at al—
Witnesse on Mathew. But in special
Of swering saith the holy Jeremie,⁸
"Thou shalt swere sooth° thine othes and nat lie,   *truly*
And swere in doom° and eek in rightwisnesse,   *judgment*
350   But idel swering is a cursednesse."
        Biholde and see that in the firste Table°   *tablet*
Of hye Goddes heestes° honorable   *commandments*

---

6. Possibly referring to the Greek philosopher Stilbo or   7. Parthia in northern Persia.
Chilon.   8. The prophet Jeremiah (4.2).

How that the seconde heeste of him is this:
"Take nat my name in idel or amis."
355 Lo, rather° he forbedeth swich swering   *sooner*
Than homicide, or many a cursed thing.
I saye that as by ordre thus it stondeth—
This knoweth that° his heestes understondeth   *he who*
How that the seconde heeste of God is that.
360 And fertherover, I wol thee telle al plat°   *flatly*
That vengeance shal nat parten from his hous
That of his othes is too outrageous.
"By Goddes precious herte!" and "By his nailes!"
And "By the blood of Crist that is in Hailes,[9]
365 Sevene is my chaunce, and thyn is cink and traye!"° *five and three*
"By Goddes armes, if thou falsly playe
This daggere shal thurghout thyn herte go!"
This fruit cometh of the bicche bones° two—   *cursed dice*
Forswering, ire, falsnesse, homicide.
370 Now for the love of Crist that for us dyde,
Lete° youre othes bothe grete and smale.   *leave off*
But sires, now wol I telle forth my tale.
  Thise riotoures° three of whiche I telle,   *revelers*
Longe erst er° prime° ronge of any belle,   *before / 6 A.M.*
375 Were set hem in a taverne to drinke,
And as they sat they herde a belle clinke
Biforn a cors° was caried to his grave.   *corpse*
That oon of hem gan callen to his knave:°   *servant*
"Go bet,"° quod he, "and axe redily   *quickly*
380 What cors is this that passeth heer forby,
And looke that thou reporte his name weel."
  "Sire," quod this boy, "it needeth neveradeel:[1]
It was me told er ye cam heer two houres.
He was, pardee,° an old felawe of youres,   *by God*
385 And sodeinly he was yslain tonight,
Fordronke° as he sat on his bench upright;   *very drunk*
Ther cam a privee° thief men clepeth° Deeth,   *stealthy / call*
That in this contree al the peple sleeth,°   *slays*
And with his spere he smoot his herte atwo,
390 And wente his way withouten wordes mo.
He hath a thousand slain this pestilence.°   *during this plague*
And maister, er ye come in his presence,
Me thinketh that it were necessarye
For to be war of swich an adversarye;
395 Beeth redy for to meete him everemore:
Thus taughte me my dame.° I saye namore."   *mother*
  "By Sainte Marye," saide this taverner,
"The child saith sooth,° for he hath slain this yeer, *truth*

---

9. Hales Abbey in Gloucestershire owned a relic of 1. Is not necessary in the least.
Christ's blood.

	Henne° over a mile, within a greet village,	*from here*
400	Bothe man and womman, child and hine° and page.°	*farmhand / servant*
	I trowe his habitacion be there.	
	To been avised° greet wisdom it were	*warned*
	Er that he dide a man a dishonour."	
	"Ye, Goddes armes," quod this riotour,	
405	"Is it swich peril with him for to meete?	
	I shal him seeke by way and eek by streete,	
	I make avow to Goddes digne° bones.	*worthy*
	Herkneth, felawes, we three been alle ones:	
	Lat eech of us holde up his hand to other	
410	And eech of us bicome otheres brother,	
	And we wol sleen this false traitour Deeth.	
	He shal be slain, he that so manye sleeth,	
	By Goddess dignitee, er it be night."	
	Togidres han thise three hir trouthes° plight°	*words of honor / pledged*
415	To live and dien eech of hem with other,	
	As though he were his owene ybore° brother.	*born*
	And up they sterte, al dronken in this rage,	
	And forth they goon towardes that village	
	Of which the taverner hadde spoke biforn.	
420	And many a grisly ooth thanne han they sworn,	
	And Cristes blessed body they torente:°	*tore apart*
	Deeth shal be deed if that they may him hente.°	*capture*
	Whan they han goon nat fully, half a mile,	
	Right as they wolde han treden° over a stile,	*stepped*
425	An old man and a poore with hem mette;	
	This olde man ful mekely hem grette,°	*greeted*
	And saide thus, "Now lordes, God you see."°	*look after*
	The pruddeste° of thise riotoures three	*proudest*
	Answerde again, "What, carl with sory grace,°	*unlucky fellow*
430	Why artou al forwrapped° save thy face?	*bundled up*
	Why livestou so longe in so greet age?"	
	This olde man gan looke in his visage,	
	And saide thus, "For I ne can nat finde	
	A man, though that I walked into Inde,	
435	Neither in citee ne in no village,	
	That wolde chaunge his youthe for myn age;	
	And therfore moot I han° myn age stille,	*I must have*
	As longe time as it is Goddes wille.	
	"Ne Deeth, allas, ne wol nat have my lif.	
440	Thus walke I lik a restelees caitif,°	*wretch*
	And on the ground which is my modres° gate	*mother's*
	I knokke with my staf bothe erly and late,	
	And saye, 'Leve° moder, leet me in:	*dear*
	Lo, how I vanisshe, flessh and blood and skin.	
445	Allas, whan shal my bones been at reste?	
	Moder, with you wolde I chaunge° my cheste°	*exchange / strongbox*
	That in my chambre longe time hath be,	

Ye, for an haire-clout° to wrappe me.'   *winding sheet*
But yit to me she wol nat do that grace,
450 For which ful pale and welked° is my face.   *withered*
But sires, to you it is no curteisye
To speken to an old man vilainye,°   *discourtesy*
But he trespasse in word or elles in deede.
In Holy Writ ye may yourself wel rede,
455 'Agains an old man, hoor° upon his heed,   *grey*
Ye shal arise.' Wherfore I yive you reed,°   *advice*
Ne dooth unto an old man noon harm now,
Namore than that ye wolde men dide to you
In age, if that ye so longe abide.
460 And God be with you wher ye go or ride:
I moot go thider as I have to go."
      "Nay, olde cherl, by God thou shalt nat so,"
Saide this other hasardour anoon.
"Thou partest nat so lightly,° by Saint John!   *easily*
465 Thou speke right now of thilke traitour Deeth,
That in this contree alle oure freendes sleeth:
Have here my trouthe, as thou art his espye,
Tel wher he is, or thou shalt it abye,°   *pay for*
By God and by the holy sacrament!
470 For soothly thou art oon of his assent°   *in league with him*
To sleen us yonge folk, thou false thief."
      "Now sires," quod he, "if that ye be so lief°   *eager*
To finde Deeth, turne up this crooked way,
For in that grove I lafte him, by my fay,
475 Under a tree, and ther he wol abide:
Nat for youre boost he wol him no thing hide.
See ye that ook?° Right ther ye shal him finde.   *oak*
God save you, that boughte again° mankinde,   *redeemed*
And you amende." Thus saide this olde man.
480   And everich of thise riotoures ran
Til he cam to that tree, and ther they founde
Of florins° fine of gold ycoined rounde   *gold coins*
Wel neigh an eighte busshels as hem thoughte—
Ne lenger thanne after Deeth they soughte,
485 But eech of hem so glad was of the sighte,
For that the florins been so faire and brighte,
That down they sette hem by this precious hoord.
The worste of hem he spak the firste word:
      "Bretheren," quod he, "take keep what that I saye:
490 My wit is greet though that I bourde° and playe.   *joke*
This tresor hath Fortune unto us yiven
In mirthe and jolitee oure lif to liven,
And lightly as it cometh so wol we spende.
Ey, Goddes precious dignitee, who wende°   *would suppose*
495 Today that we sholde han so fair a grace?
But mighte this gold be caried fro this place

Hoom to myn hous—or elles unto youres—
For wel ye woot that al this gold is oures—
Thanne were we in heigh felicitee.°   *happiness*
500   But trewely, by daye it mighte nat be:
Men wolde sayn that we were theves stronge,°   *flagrant*
And for oure owene tresor doon us honge.°   *have us hanged*
This tresor moste ycaried be by nighte,
As wisely and as slyly as it mighte.
505   Therfore I rede° that cut° amonges us alle   *advise / lots*
Be drawe, and lat see wher the cut wol falle;
And he that hath the cut with herte blithe°   *happy*
Shal renne to the town, and that ful swithe,°   *swiftly*
And bringe us breed and win ful prively;
510   And two of us shal keepen subtilly
This tresor wel, and if he wol nat tarye,
Whan it is night we wol this tresor carye
By oon assent wher as us thinketh best."
That oon of hem the cut broughte in his fest°   *fist*
515   And bad hem drawe and looke wher it wol falle;
And it fil on the yongeste of hem alle,
And forth toward the town he wente anoon.
And also soone as that he was agoon,
That oon of hem spak thus unto that other:
520   "Thou knowest wel thou art my sworen brother;
Thy profit wol I telle thee anoon:
Thou woost wel that oure felawe is agoon,
And here is gold, and that ful greet plentee,
That shal departed° been among us three.   *divided*
525   But nathelelees, if I can shape° it so   *arrange*
That it departed were among us two,
Hadde I nat doon a freendes turn to thee?"
        That other answerde, "I noot° how that may be: *do not know*
He woot° that the gold is with us twaye.   *knows*
530   What shal we doon? What shal we to him saye?"
        "Shal it be conseil°?" saide the firste shrewe.°   *secret / villain*
"And I shal telle in a wordes fewe
What we shul doon, and bringe it wel aboute."
        "I graunte," quod that other, "out of doute,
535   That by my trouthe I wol thee nat biwraye."°   *betray*
        "Now," quod the firste, "thou woost wel we be twaye,
And two of us shal strenger be than oon:
Looke whan that he is set that right anoon
Aris as though thou woldest with him playe,
540   And I shal rive° him thurgh the sides twaye,   *stab*
Whil that thou strugelest with him as in game,
And with thy daggere looke thou do the same;
And thanne shal al this gold departed be,
My dere freend, bitwixe thee and me.
545   Thanne we may bothe oure lustes° al fulfille,   *desires*

And playe at dees right at oure owene wille."
And thus accorded been thise shrewes twaye
To sleen the thridde, as ye han herd me saye.
    This yongeste, which that wente to the town,
550 Ful ofte in herte he rolleth up and down
The beautee of thise florins newe and brighte.
"O Lord," quod he, "if so were that I mighte
Have al this tresor to myself allone,
Ther is no man that liveth under the trone°   *throne*
555 Of God that sholde live so merye as I."
And at the laste the feend oure enemy
Putte in his thought that he sholde poison beye,°   *buy*
With which he mighte sleen his felawes twaye—
Forwhy° the feend foond him in swich livinge   *wherefore*
560 That he hadde leve° him to sorwe° bringe: *permission / sorrow*
For this was outrely his fulle entente,
To sleen hem bothe, and nevere to repente.
    And forth he gooth—no lenger wolde he tarye—
Into the town unto a pothecarye,°   *druggist*
565 And prayed him that he him wolde selle
Som poison that he mighte his rattes quelle,°   *kill*
And eek ther was a polcat° in his hawe°   *weasel / yard*
That, as he saide, his capons° hadde yslawe,°   *chickens / slain*
And fain° he wolde wreke° him if he mighte   *gladly / avenge*
570 On vermin that destroyed him by nighte.
    The pothecarye answerde, "And thou shalt have
A thing that, also° God my soule save,   *so*
In al this world ther is no creature
That ete or dronke hath of this confiture°—   *concoction*
575 Nat but the mountance° of a corn° of whete—   *amount / grain*
That he ne shal his lif anoon forlete.°   *lose*
Ye, sterve° he shal, and that in lasse while   *die*
Than thou wolt goon a paas° nat but a mile,   *walking*
The poison is so strong and violent."
580 This cursed man hath in his hand yhent°   *taken*
This poison in a box and sith he ran
Into the nexte streete unto a man
And borwed of him large botels three,
And in the two his poison poured he—
585 The thridde he kepte clene for his drinke,
For al the night he shoop° him for to swinke°   *prepared / work*
In carying of the gold out of that place.
And whan this riotour with sory grace
Hadde filled with win his grete botels three,
590 To his felawes again repaireth he.
    What needeth it to sermone of it more?
For right as they had cast° his deeth bifore,   *planned*
Right so they han him slain, and that anoon.
And whan that this was doon, thus spak that oon:

595   "Now lat us sitte and drinke and make us merye,
    And afterward we wol his body berye."
    And with that word it happed him par cas°   *by chance*
    To take the botel ther the poison was,
    And drank, and yaf his felawe drinke also,
600   For which anoon they storven bothe two.
        But certes I suppose that Avicen[2]
    Wroot nevere in no canon ne in no *fen*
    Mo wonder signes of empoisoning
    Than hadde thise wrecches two er hir ending:
605   Thus ended been thise homicides two,
    And eek the false empoisonere also.
        O cursed sinne of alle cursednesse!
    O traitours homicide, O wikkednesse!
    O glotonye, luxure,° and hasardrye!   *lechery*
610   Thou balsphemour of Crist with vilainye
    And othes grete of usage° and of pride!   *habit*
    Allas, mankinde, how may it bitide
    That to thy Creatour which that thee wroughte,
    And with his precious herte blood thee boughte,
615   Thou art so fals and so unkinde,° allas?   *unnatural*
        Now goode men, God foryive you youre trespas,
    And ware° you fro the sinne of avarice: *guard*
    Myn holy pardon may you alle warice°—   *save*
    So that ye offre nobles or sterlinges,°   *gold or silver coins*
620   Or elles silver brooches, spoones, ringes.
    Boweth your heed under this holy bulle!
    Cometh up, ye wives, offreth of youre wolle!°   *wool*
    Youre name I entre here in my rolle: anoon
    Into the blisse of hevene shul ye goon.
625   I you assoile° by myn heigh power—   *absolve*
    Ye that wol offre—as clene and eek as cleer°   *pure*
    As ye were born.—And lo, sires, thus I preche.
    And Jesu Crist that is oure soules leeche°   *physician*
    So graunte you his pardon to receive,
630   For that is best—I wol you nat deceive.

The Epilogue

    "But sires, oo word forgat I in my tale:
    I have relikes and pardon in my male°   *bag*
    As faire as any man in Engelond,
    Whiche were me yiven by the Popes hond.
635   If any of you wol of devocioun
    Offren and han myn absolucioun,

---

2. The 12th-century Arab philosopher Avicenna composed a *Canon of Medicine*, divided into sections called "fens."

Come forth anoon, and kneeleth here adown,
And mekely receiveth my pardoun,
Or elles taketh pardon as ye wende,°   *travel*
640 Al newe and fressh at every miles ende—
So that ye offre alway newe and newe°   *over and over*
Nobles or pens whiche that be goode and trewe.
It is an honour to everich that is heer
That ye mowe have a suffisant° pardoner   *competent*
645 T'assoile you in contrees as ye ride,
For aventures whiche that may bitide:
Paraventure ther may falle oon or two
Down of his hors and breke his nekke atwo;
Looke which a suretee° is it to you alle   *safeguard*
650 That I am in youre felaweshipe yfalle
That may assoile you, bothe more and lasse,
Whan that the soule shal fro the body passe.
I rede° that oure Hoste shal biginne,   *advise*
For he is most envoluped in sinne.
655 Com forth, sire Host, and offre first anoon,
And thou shalt kisse the relikes everichoon,
Ye, for a grote:° unbokele anoon thy purs."   *fourpence coin*
     "Nay, nay," quod he, "thanne have I Cristes curs!
Lat be," quod he, "it shal nat be, so theech!°   *may I prosper*
660 Thou woldest make me kisse thyn olde breech
And swere it were a relik of a saint,
Though it were with thy fundament° depeint.°   *bowels / stained*
But, by the crois° which that Sainte Elaine[3] foond,   *cross*
I wolde I hadde thy coilons° in myn hond,   *testicles*
665 In stede of relikes or of saintuarye.°   *container of relics*
Lat cutte hem of: I wol thee helpe hem carye.
They shal be shrined in an hogges tord."°   *turd*
     This Pardoner answerde nat a word:
So wroth° he was no word ne wolde he saye.   *angry*
670   "Now," quod oure Host, "I wol no lenger playe
With thee, ne with noon other angry man."
     But right anoon the worthy Knight bigan,
Whan that he sawgh that al the peple lough,
"Namore of this, for it is right ynough.
675 Sire Pardoner, be glad and merye of cheere,
And ye, sire Host that been to me so dere,
I praye you that ye kisse the Pardoner,
And Pardoner, I praye thee, draw thee neer,
And as we diden lat us laughe and playe."
680 Anoon they kiste and riden forth hir waye.

---

3. St. Helen, who was said to have found the True Cross on which Jesus was crucified.

THE NUN'S PRIEST'S TALE   Of all his varied and ambitious output, *The Nun's Priest's Tale* may be Chaucer's most impressive tour de force. At its core is a wonderful animal fable, free of the conventionality and sometimes easy moralities this ancient form had taken on by the fourteenth century. The fable of Chauntecleer and Pertelote achieves quite extraordinary density, further, because of the multiple frames—structural and thematic—that surround it.

As part of the Canterbury tale-telling competition, the priest's fable plays a role in that broadest contest of classes and literary genres. More locally, it is one of many moments in which the Host, Harry Bailey, demands a tale from a male pilgrim in a style that also suggests a sexual challenge, and then adjusts his estimate of the teller's virility (even his social position) to suit. The fable itself is surrounded by an intimate portrait of Chauntecleer's peasant owner and her simple life, content with "hertes suffisaunce," a marked contrast to courtly values.

The central story of Chauntecleer's dream, danger, and escape works within a subtle and funny exploration of relations between the sexes. This is conditioned by courtly love conventions, literacy and education, and even the vocabulary of Pertelote's mostly Anglo-Saxon diction and Chauntecleer's love of French. This linguistic competition has its high point when Chauntecleer condescendingly mistranslates a misogynist Latin tag. Linguistic vanity, though, is exactly what puts Chauntecleer most in jeopardy. It is not the destiny Chauntecleer thinks he glimpses in his dream that almost costs his life, but rather another verbal competition, and an almost Oedipal challenge to his father.

Much of the story's energy, however, derives not from its frames but from the explosion of those frames—literary, spatial, even social—enacted and recalled at the heart of the tale. The chickens are simultaneously, and hilariously, both courtly lovers and very realistic fowl. When Chauntecleer is carried off, the whole world of the tale—widow, daughters, dogs, even bees—bursts outward in pursuit. In the midst of mock-epic and mock-romance comparisons to this joyful disorder, Chaucer even inserts one of his very few direct references to the greatest disorder of his time, the Rising of 1381 (see page 468).

The Nun's Priest's Tale is a comedy as well as a fable, reversing a lugubrious series of tragedies in the preceding *Monk's Tale*. In the end, it is a story of canniness, acquired self-knowledge, and self-salvation. Woven into the priest's humor are a gentle satire and a quiet assertion that free will is the final resource of any agent, avian or human.

The Nun's Priest's Tale
The Introduction

	"Ho!" quod the Knight, "good sire, namore of this:	
	That ye han said is right ynough, ywis,°	*indeed*
	And muchel more, for litel hevinesse	
	Is right ynough to muche folk° I gesse:[1]	*for most folks*
5	I saye for me it is a greet disese,	
	Wher as men han been in greet welthe and ese,	
	To heeren of hir sodein° fal, allas;	*sudden*
	And the contrarye is joye and greet solas,°	*comfort*
	As whan a man hath been in poore estat,	
10	And climbeth up and wexeth° fortunat,	*becomes*
	And there abideth in prosperitee:	
	Swich thing is gladsom, as it thinketh° me,	*seems to*
	And of swich thing were goodly for to telle."	
	"Ye," quod oure Host, "by Sainte Poules° belle,	*Paul's*
15	Ye saye right sooth:° this Monk he clappeth° loude.	*truly / chatters*

1. The Monk has just told a series of stark and repetitive "tragedies"—the falls of men both ancient and modern.

He spak how Fortune covered with a cloude—
I noot nevere what.° And als of a tragedye   *I don't know what*
Right now ye herde, and pardee,° no remedye   *by God*
It is for to biwaile ne complaine
20   That that is doon, and als° it is a paine,   *also*
As ye han said, to heere of hevinesse.
      "Sire Monk, namore of this, so God you blesse:
Youre tale anoyeth al this compaignye;
Swich talking is nat worth a boterflye,
25   For therinne is ther no disport ne game.
Wherfore, sire Monk, or daun° Piers by youre name,   *Master*
I praye you hertely telle us somwhat elles:
For sikerly, nere clinking of youre belles,[2]
That on youre bridel hange on every side,
30   By hevene king that for us alle dyde,
I sholde er this have fallen down for sleep,
Although the slough° hadde nevere been so deep.   *mud*
Thanne hadde youre tale al be told in vain;
For certainly, as that thise clerkes sayn,
35   Wher as a man may have noon audience,
Nought helpeth it to tellen his sentence;°   *statement*
And wel I woot° the substance is in me,   *know*
If any thing shal wel reported be.
Sire, saye somwhat of hunting, I you praye."
40   "Nay," quod this Monk, "I have no lust° to playe.   *wish*
Now lat another telle, as I have told."
      Thanne spak oure Host with rude speeche and bold,
And saide unto the Nonnes Preest anoon,
"Com neer, thou Preest,[3] com hider, thou sire John:
45   Tel us swich thing as may oure hertes glade.°   *gladden our hearts*
Be blithe,° though thou ride upon a jade!°   *happy / nag*
What though thyn hors be bothe foul and lene?°   *thin*
If he wol serve thee, rekke nat a bene.°   *don't care a bean*
Looke that thyn herte be merye everemo."
50   "Yis, sire," quod he, "yis, Host, so mote I go,
But I be merye, ywis, I wol be blamed."
And right anoon his tale he hath attamed,°   *begun*
And thus he saide unto us everichoon,
This sweete Preest, this goodly man sire John.

The Tale

55   A poore widwe somdeel stape° in age   *well along*
Was whilom° dwelling in a narwe cotage,   *once upon a time*
Biside a grove, stonding in a dale:
This widwe of which I telle you my tale,
Sin° thilke° day that she was last a wif,   *since / that*

---

2. For truly, were it not for the jingling of your bells.

3. The Host uses the familiar, somewhat condescending "thou," then contemptuously calls the priest "Sir John."

60	In pacience ladde a ful simple lif.	
	For litel was hir catel° and hir rente,°	*property / income*
	By housbondrye° of swich as God hire sente	*management*
	She foond° hirself and eek hir doughtren two.	*provided for*
	Three large sowes hadde she and namo,	
65	Three kin,° and eek a sheep that highte° Malle.	*cows / was named*
	Ful sooty was hir bowr° and eek hir halle,	*bedroom*
	In which she eet ful many a sclendre meel;	
	Of poinant° sauce hire needed neveradeel:	*pungent*
	No daintee morsel passed thurgh hir throte—	
70	Hir diete was accordant to hir cote.°	*cottage*
	Repleccioun° ne made hire nevere sik:	*gluttony*
	Attempre° diete was al hir physik,	*moderate*
	And exercise and hertes suffisaunce.	
	The goute lette hire nothing for to daunce,[4]	
75	N'apoplexye shente° nat hir heed.	*hurt*
	No win ne drank she, neither whit ne reed:	
	Hir boord° was served most with whit and blak,	*table*
	Milk and brown breed, in which she foond no lak;°	*fault*
	Seind° bacon, and somtime an ey° or twaye,°	*singed / egg / two*
80	For she was as it were a manere daye.°	*dairy maid*
	A yeerd° she hadde, enclosed al withoute	*yard*
	With stikkes, and a drye dich aboute,	
	In which she hadde a cok heet° Chauntecleer:	*called*
	In al the land of crowing nas his peer.	
85	His vois was merier than the merye orgon	
	On massedayes that in the chirche goon;°	*is played*
	Wel sikerer° was his crowing in his logge°	*surer / dwelling*
	Than is a clok or an abbeye orlogge;°	*timepiece*
	By nature he knew eech ascensioun	
90	Of th'equinoxial[5] in thilke town:	
	For whan degrees fifteene were ascended,	
	Thanne crew he that it mighte nat been amended.°	*surpassed*
	His comb was redder than the fin coral,	
	And batailed° as it were a castel wal;	*crenellated*
95	His bile° was blak, and as the jeet° it shoon;	*beak / jet*
	Like asure° were his legges and his toon;°	*azure / toes*
	His nailes whitter than the lilye flowr,	
	And lik the burned° gold was his colour.	*burnished*
	This gentil cok hadde in his governaunce	
100	Sevene hennes for to doon al his plesaunce,	
	Whiche were his sustres and his paramours,°	*lovers*
	And wonder like to him as of colours;	
	Of whiche the faireste hewed° on hir throte	*colored*
	Was cleped° faire damoisele Pertelote:	*called*
105	Curteis she was, discreet, and debonaire,°	*gracious*

---

4. Did not keep her from dancing.   5. The points marking the celestial hours.

And compaignable,° and bar hirself so faire,   *sociable*
Sin thilke° day that she was seven night old,   *that*
That trewely she hath the herte in hold
Of Chauntecleer, loken in every lith.[6]
110   He loved hire so that wel was him therwith.
But swich a joye was it to heere hem singe,
Whan that the brighte sonne gan to springe,
In sweete accord "My Lief is Faren in Londe"[7]—
For thilke time, as I have understonde,
115   Beestes and briddes° couden speke and singe.   *birds*
   And so bifel that in a daweninge,
As Chauntecleer among his wives alle
Sat on his perche that was in the halle,
And next him sat this faire Pertelote,
120   This Chauntecleer gan gronen in his throte,
As man that in his dreem is drecched° sore.   *disturbed*
   And whan that Pertelote thus herde him rore,
She was agast, and saide, "Herte dere,
What aileth you to grone in this manere?
125   Ye been a verray° slepere, fy, for shame!"   *true*
   And he answerde and saide thus, "Madame,
I praye you that ye take it nat agrief.°   *amiss*
By God, me mette° I was in swich meschief   *I dreamed*
Right now, that yit myn herte is sore afright.
130   Now God," quod he, "my swevene recche aright,[8]
And keepe my body out of foul prisoun!
Me mette how that I romed up and down
Within oure yeerd, wher as I sawgh a beest,
Was lik an hound and wolde han maad arrest°   *taken captive*
135   Upon my body, and han had me deed.
His colour was bitwixe yelow and reed,
And tipped was his tail and bothe his eres
With blak, unlik the remenant of his heres;°   *the rest of his hair*
His snoute smal, with glowing yën twaye.
140   Yit of his look for fere almost I deye:
This caused me my groning, doutelees."
   "Avoi,"° quod she, "fy on you, hertelees!°   *Have done! / coward*
Allas," quod she, "for by that God above,
Now han ye lost myn herte and al my love!
145   I can nat love a coward, by my faith.
For certes, what so any womman saith,
We alle desiren, if it mighte be,
To han housbondes hardy, wise, and free,°   *generous*
And secree,° and no nigard, ne no fool,   *discreet*
150   Ne him that is agast° of every tool,°   *afraid / weapon*
Ne noon avauntour.° By that God above,   *braggart*

---

6. Locked in every limb (i.e., thoroughly).   (see page 554).
7. A popular ballad, "My Lefe Is Faren in a Lond"   8. Intepret my dream correctly.

How dorste ye sayn for shame unto youre love
That any thing mighte make you aferd?
Have ye no mannes herte and han a beerd?
155   Allas, and conne ye been agast of swevenes?
No thing, God woot,° but vanitee° in swevene is!   *knows / illusion*
Swevenes engendren of replexiouns,°   *surfeits*
And ofte of fume° and of complexiouns,°   *gas / bodily humors*
Whan humours been too habundant in a wight.°   *creature*
160   Certes, this dreem which ye han met tonight
Comth of the grete superfluitee
Of youre rede colera,⁹ pardee,°   *by God*
Which causeth folk to dreden in hir dremes
Of arwes,° and of fir with rede lemes,°   *arrows / flames*
165   Of rede beestes, that they wol hem bite,
Of contek,° and of whelpes° grete and lite—   *strife / dogs*
Right as the humour of malencolye¹
Causeth ful many a man in sleep to crye
For fere of blake beres or boles° blake,   *bulls*
170   Or elles blake develes wol hem take.
Of othere humours coude I telle also
That werken many a man in sleep ful wo,
But I wol passe as lightly as I can.
Lo, Caton,² which that was so wis a man,
175   Saide he nat thus? 'Ne do no fors° of dremes.'   *pay no attention to*
Now, sire," quod she, "whan we flee° fro the bemes,°   *fly / rafters*
For Goddes love, as take som laxatif.
Up° peril of my soule and of my lif,   *upon*
I conseile you the beste, I wol nat lie,
180   That bothe of colere and of malencolye
Ye purge you; and for ye shal nat tarye,
Though in this town is noon apothecarye,
I shal myself to herbes techen you,
That shal been for youre hele° and for youre prow,°   *health / profit*
185   And in oure yeerd tho° herbes shal I finde,   *then*
The whiche han of hir propretee by kinde°   *nature*
To purge you binethe and eek above.
Foryet nat this, for Goddes owene love.
Ye been ful colerik of complexioun;
190   Ware° the sonne in his ascencioun   *beware lest*
Ne finde you nat repleet° of humours hote;°   *full / hot*
And if it do, I dar wel laye³ a grote°   *fourpence*
That ye shul have a fevere terciane,⁴
Or an agu° that may be youre bane.°   *fever / death*
195   A day or two ye shul han digestives
Of wormes, er ye take youre laxatives

---

9. Choleric bile, thought to overheat the body.
1. Black bile, thought to produce dark thoughts.
2. Marcus Porcius Cato, ancient author of a book of

proverbs used by schoolchildren.
3. Bet (with a pun on egg-laying).
4. Recurring fever.

Of lauriol, centaure, and fumetere,[5]
Or elles of ellebor that groweth there,
Of catapuce, or of gaitres beries,
200 Of herbe-ive growing in oure yeerd ther merye is.°   *where it is pleasant*
Pekke hem right up as they growe and ete hem in.
Be merye, housbonde, for youre fader kin!
Dredeth no dreem: I can saye you namore."
    "Madame," quod he, "graunt mercy of youre lore.°   *learning*
205 But nathelees, as touching daun Catoun,
That hath of wisdom swich a greet renown,
Though that he bad no dremes for to drede,
By God, men may in olde bookes rede
Of many a man more of auctoritee
210 Than evere Caton was, so mote I thee,°   *so may I prosper*
That al the revers sayn of his sentence,°   *opinion*
And han wel founden by experience
That dremes been significaciouns
As wel of joye as tribulaciouns
215 That folk enduren in this lif present.
Ther needeth make of this noon argument:
The verray preve° sheweth it in deede.   *proof*
    "Oon of the gretteste auctour that men rede
Saith thus, that whilom two felawes wente
220 On pilgrimage in a ful good entente,
And happed so they comen in a town,
Wher as ther was swich congregacioun
Of peple, and eek so strait of herbergage,°   *short of lodging*
That they ne founde as muche as oo° cotage   *one*
225 In which they bothe mighte ylogged be;
Wherfore they mosten of necessitee
As for that night departe compaignye.
And eech of hem gooth to his hostelrye,
And took his logging as it wolde falle.
230 That oon of hem was logged in a stalle,
Fer in a yeerd, with oxen of the plough;
That other man was logged wel ynough,
As was his aventure or his fortune,
That us governeth alle as in commune.
235 And so bifel that longe er it were day,
This man mette in his bed, ther as he lay,
How that his felawe gan upon him calle,
And saide, 'Allas, for in an oxes stalle
This night I shal be mordred° ther I lie!   *murdered*
240 Now help me, dere brother, or I die!
In alle haste com to me,' he saide.
    "This man out of his sleep for fere abraide,°   *bolted up*

5. These and the following are bitter herbs that produce hot and dry sensations and lead to purging.

But whan that he was wakened of his sleep,
He turned him and took of this no keep:°   *heed*
245   Him thoughte his dreem nas° but a vanitee.   *was not*
Thus twies in his sleeping dremed he,
And atte thridde time yit his felawe
Cam, as him thoughte, and saide, 'I am now slawe:°   *slain*
Bihold my bloody woundes deepe and wide.
250   Aris up erly in the morwe tide°   *morning time*
And atte west gate of the town,' quod he,
A carte ful of dong° ther shaltou see,   *dung*
In which my body is hid ful prively:
Do thilke° carte arresten° boldely.   *that / have seized*
255   My gold caused my mordre, sooth° to sayn'—   *truth*
And tolde him every point how he was slain,
With a ful pitous face, pale of hewe.
And truste wel, his dreem he foond ful trewe,
For on the morwe as soone as it was day,
260   To his felawes in he took the way,
And whan that he cam to this oxes stalle,
After his felawe he bigan to calle.
      "The hostiler° answerde him anoon,   *innkeeper*
And saide, 'Sire, youre felawe is agoon:
265   As soone as day he wente out of the town.'
      "This man gan fallen in suspicioun,
Remembring on his dremes that he mette;
And forth he gooth, no lenger wolde he lette,°   *delay*
Unto the west gate of the town, and foond
270   A dong carte, wente as it were to donge° lond,   *spread manure on*
That was arrayed in that same wise
As ye han herd the dede man devise;
And with an hardy herte he gan to crye,
'Vengeance and justice of this felonye!
275   My felawe mordred is this same night,
And in this carte he lith gaping upright!°   *facing up*
I crye out on the ministres,'° quod he,   *magistrates*
'That sholde keepe and rulen this citee.
Harrow, allas, here lith my felawe slain!'
280   What sholde I more unto this tale sayn?
The peple up sterte and caste the carte to grounde,
And in the middel of the dong they founde
The dede man that mordred was al newe.°   *just recently*
      "O blisful God that art so just and trewe,
285   Lo, how that thou biwrayest° mordre alway!   *reveal*
Mordre wol out, that see we day by day:
Mordre is so wlatsom° and abhominable   *loathsome*
To God that is so just and resonable,
That he ne wol nat suffre it heled° be,   *concealed*
290   Though it abide a yeer or two or three.
Mordre wol out: this my conclusioun.

And right anoon ministres of that town
Han hent° the cartere and so sore him pined,°   *seized / tortured*
And eek the hostiler so sore engined,
295   That they biknewe° hir wikkednesse anoon,   *confessed*
And were anhanged by the nekke boon.
Here may men seen that dremes been to drede.
"And certes, in the same book I rede—
Right in the nexte chapitre after this—
300   I gabbe° nat, so have I joye or blis—   *lie*
Two men that wolde han passed over see
For certain cause into a fer contree,
If that the wind ne hadde been contrarye
That made hem in a citee for to tarye,
305   That stood ful merye upon an haven° side—   *harbor*
But on a day again° the even tide   *toward*
The wind gan chaunge, and blewe right as hem leste:°   *they wanted*
Jolif° and glad they wenten unto reste,   *merry*
And casten hem° ful erly for to saile.   *decided*
310   "But to that oo man fil a greet mervaile;
That oon of hem, in sleeping as he lay,
Him mette a wonder dreem again the day:
Him thoughte a man stood by his beddes side,
And him comanded that he sholde abide,
315   And saide him thus, 'If thou tomorwe wende,°   *travel*
Thou shalt be dreint:° my tale is at an ende.'   *drowned*
"He wook and tolde his felawe what he mette,
And prayed him his viage to lette;°   *put off his journey*
As for that day he prayed him to bide.
320   His felawe that lay by his beddes side
Gan for to laughe, and scorned him ful faste.
'No dreem,' quod he, 'may so myn herte agaste
That I wol lette for to do my thinges.°   *business*
I sette nat a straw by thy dreminges,
325   For swevenes been but vanitees and japes:°   *tricks*
Men dreme alday° of owles or of apes,   *constantly*
And of many a maze° therwithal—   *delusion*
Men dreme of thing that nevere was ne shal.
But sith° I see that thou wolt here abide,   *since*
330   And thus forsleuthen° wilfully thy tide,   *waste due to sloth*
Good woot, it reweth me; and have good day.'
And thus he took his leve and wente his way.
But er that he hadde half his cours ysailed—
Noot° I nat why ne what meschaunce it ailed°—   *know / went wrong*
335   But casuelly° the shippes botme rente,°   *by accident / split apart*
And ship and man under the water wente,
In sighte of othere shippes it biside,
That with hem sailed at the same tide.
And therfore, faire Pertelote so dere,
340   By swiche ensamples olde maistou lere°   *may you learn*

That no man sholde been too recchelees°   *careless*
Of dremes, for I saye thee doutelees
That many a dreem ful sore is for to drede.
     "Lo, in the lif of Saint Kenelm[6] I rede—
345 That was Kenulphus sone, the noble king
Of Mercenrike—how Kenelm mette a thing
A lite° er he was mordred on a day.   *little while*
His mordre in his avision° he sey.°   *dream / saw*
His norice° him expounded everydeel   *nurse*
350 His swevene, and bad him for to keepe him° weel   *guard against*
For traison, but he nas but seven yeer old,
And therfore litel tale hath he told°   *he cared little for*
Of any dreem, so holy was his herte.
By God, I hadde levere than my sherte°   *would give my shirt*
355 That ye hadde rad his legende as have I.
     "Dame Pertelote, I saye you trewely,
Macrobeus,[7] that writ the Avisioun
In Affrike of the worthy Scipioun,
Affermeth° dremes, and saith that they been   *confirms*
360 Warning of thinges that men after seen.
     "And ferthermore, I praye you looketh wel
In the Olde Testament of Daniel,
If he heeld dremes any vanitee.[8]
     "Rede eek of Joseph and ther shul ye see
365 Wher° dremes be somtime—I saye nat alle—   *whether*
Warning of thinges that shul after falle.
     "Looke of Egypte the king daun Pharao,
His bakere and his botelere° also,   *butler*
Wher they ne felte noon effect in dremes.[9]
370 Whoso wol seeke actes of sondry remes°   *various kingdoms*
May rede of dremes many a wonder thing.
     "Lo Cresus, which that was of Lyde° king,   *Lydia*
Mette he nat that he sat upon a tree,
Which signified he sholde anhanged be?
375   "Lo here Andromacha, Ectores° wif,   *Hector of Troy*
That day that Ector sholde lese° his lif,   *lose*
She dremed on the same night biforn
How that the lif of Ector sholde be lorn,
If thilke day he wente into bataile;
380 She warned him, but it mighte nat availe:
He wente for to fighte nathelees,
But he was slain anoon of Achilles.
But thilke tale is al too long to telle,
And eek it is neigh day, I may nat dwelle.

---

6. St. Cenhelm, son of Cenwulf, a 9th-century child-king
in Mercia who was murdered at his sister's orders.
7. Macrobius, a 4th-century author, wrote an extensive
commentary on Cicero's Dream of Scipio.

8. Daniel interprets the pagan King Nebuchadnezzar's
dream, which foretells his downfall (Daniel 4).
9. Joseph interpreted dreams for the pharaoh's chief baker
and butler (Genesis 40–41).

385 Shortly I saye, as for conclusioun,
    That I shal han of this avisioun
    Adversitee, and I saye ferthermoor
    That I ne telle of laxatives no stoor,°   *hold no regard for*
    For they been venimes,° I woot° it weel: *poisons / know*
390 I hem defye, I love hem neveradeel.
        "Now lat us speke of mirthe and stinte° al this.   *stop*
    Madame Pertelote, so have I blis,
    Of oo thing God hath sente me large grace:
    For whan I see the beautee of youre face—
395 Ye been so scarlet reed aboute youre yën—
    It maketh al my drede for to dien.
    For also siker° as *In principio*,[1]   *certain*
    Mulier est hominis confusio.[2]
    Madame, the sentence° of this Latin is,   *meaning*
400 'Womman is mannes joye and al his blis.'
    For whan I feele anight youre softe side—
    Al be it that I may nat on you ride,
    For that oure perche is maad so narwe, allas—
    I am so ful of joye and of solas°   *delight*
405 That I defye bothe swevene and dreem."
    And with that word he fleigh down fro the beem,
    For it was day, and eek° his hennes alle,   *also*
    And with a "chuk" he gan hem for to calle,
    For he hadde founde a corn lay in the yeerd.
410 Real° he was, he was namore aferd:°   *regal / afraid*
    He fethered Pertelote twenty time,
    And trad° hire as ofte er it was prime.[3]   *mounted*
    He looketh as it were a grim leoun,°   *lion*
    And on his toes he rometh up and down:
415 Him deined nat to sette his foot to grounde.
    He chukketh whan he hath a corn yfounde,
    And to him rennen thanne his wives alle.
    Thus royal, as a prince is in his halle,
    Leve I this Chauntecleer in his pasture,
420 And after wol I telle his aventure.
        Whan that the month in which the world bigan,
    That highte March, whan God first maked man,
    Was compleet, and passed were also,
    Sin March biran,° thritty days and two,[4]   *finished*
425 Bifel that Chauntecleer in al his pride,
    His sevene wives walking him biside,
    Caste up his yën to the brighte sonne,
    That in the signe of Taurus hadde yronne
    Twenty degrees and oon and somwhat more,

---

1. "In the beginning," the opening verse of the Book of   3. First hour of the day.
Genesis and the Gospel of John.   4. The date is thus May 3.
2. "Woman is the ruination of mankind."

430	And knew by kinde,° and by noon other lore,	*nature*
	That it was prime, and crew with blisful stevene.°	*voice*
	"The sonne," he saide, "is clomben up on hevene	
	Fourty degrees and oon and more, ywis.°	*indeed*
	Madame Pertelote, my worldes blis,	
435	Herkneth thise blisful briddes° how they singe,	*birds*
	And see the fresshe flowres how they springe:	
	Ful is myn herte of revel and solas."	
	But sodeinly him fil a sorweful cas,°	*event*
	For evere the latter ende of joye is wo—	
440	God woot that worldly joye is soone ago,	
	And if a rethor° coude faire endite,°	*rhetorician / compose*
	He in a cronicle saufly° mighte it write,	*safely*
	As for a soverein notabilitee.	
	Now every wis man lat him herkne me:	
445	This storye is also° trewe, I undertake,	*as*
	As is the book of Launcelot de Lake,[5]	
	That wommen holde in ful greet reverence.	
	Now wol I turne again to my sentence.°	*topic*
	A colfox° ful of sly iniquitee,	*black fox*
450	That in the grove° hadde woned° yeres three,	*woods / lived*
	By heigh imaginacion forncast,[6]	
	The same night thurghout the hegges brast°	*burst*
	Into the yeerd ther Chauntecleer the faire	
	Was wont, and eek his wives, to repaire;	
455	And in a bed of wortes° stille he lay	*cabbages*
	Til it was passed undren° of the day,	*midmorning*
	Waiting his time on Chauntecleer to falle,	
	As gladly doon thise homicides alle,	
	That in await liggen to mordre men.	
460	O false mordrour, lurking in thy den!	
	O newe Scariot! Newe Geniloun![7]	
	False dissimilour!° O Greek Sinoun,[8]	*dissembler*
	That broughtest Troye al outrely° to sorwe!	*entirely*
	O Chauntecleer, accursed be that morwe	
465	That thou into the yeerd flaugh fro the bemes!	
	Thou were ful wel ywarned by thy dremes	
	That thilke day was perilous to thee;	
	But what that God forwoot moot° needes be,	*foreknew must*
	After the opinion of certain clerkes:	
470	Witnesse on him that any parfit° clerk is	*accomplished*
	That in scole is greet altercacioun	
	In this matere, and greet disputisoun,	
	And hath been of an hundred thousand men.	

---

5. The adventures of the Arthurian knight.
6. Predicted (in Chauntecleer's dream).
7. Judas Iscariot, who handed Jesus over to the Roman authorities for execution; Ganelon, a medieval traitor who betrayed the hero Roland to his Saracen enemies.
8. The Greek who tricked the Trojans into accepting the Trojan horse behind the city walls.

But I ne can nat bulte it to the bren,[9]
475 As can the holy doctour Augustin,
Or Boece, or the bisshop Bradwardin[1]—
Wheither that Goddes worthy forwiting°   foreknowledge
Straineth° me nedely for to doon a thing   compels
("Nedely" clepe I simple necessitee),
480 Or elles if free chois be graunted me
To do that same thing or do it nought,
Though God forwoot it er that I was wrought;°   made
Or if his witing straineth neveradeel,
But by necessitee condicionel[2]—
485 I wol nat han to do of swich matere:
My tale is of a cok, as ye may heere,
That took his conseil of his wif with sorwe,
To walken in the yeerd upon that morwe
That he hadde met the dreem that I you tolde.
490 Wommenes conseils been ful ofte colde,°   disastrous
Wommanes conseil broughte us first to wo,
And made Adam fro Paradis to go,
Ther as he was ful merye and wel at ese.
But for I noot° to whom it mighte displese   do not know
495 If I conseil of wommen wolde blame,
Passe over, for I saide it in my game—
Rede auctours° where they trete of swich matere,   authors
And what they sayn of wommen ye may heere—
Thise been the cokkes wordes and nat mine:
500 I can noon harm of no womman divine.°   guess at
       Faire in the sond° to bathe hire merily   sand
Lith° Pertelote, and alle hir sustres by,   lies
Again the sonne, and Chauntecleer so free
Soong merier than the mermaide in the see—
505 For Physiologus[3] saith sikerly
How that they singen wel and merily.
       And so bifel that as he caste his yë
Among the wortes on a boterflye,°   butterfly
He was war of this fox that lay ful lowe.
510 No thing ne liste him° thanne for to crowe,   he wanted
But cride anoon "Cok cok!" and up he sterte,
As man that was affrayed in his herte—
For naturelly a beest desireth flee
Fro his contrarye° if he may it see,   natural enemy
515 Though he nevere erst° hadde seen it with his yë.   before
This Chauntecleer, whan he gan him espye,
He wolde han fled, but that the fox anoon

---

9. Sift it from the husks (i.e., discriminate).
1. St. Augustine, the ancient writer Boethius, and the 14th-century Archbishop of Canterbury Thomas Bradwardine attempted to explain how God's predestination of events still allowed for humans to have free will.
2. Boethius argued only for conditional necessity, which still permitted for much exercise of free will.
3. Said to have written a bestiary.

Saide, "Gentil sire, allas, wher wol ye goon?
Be ye afraid of me that am youre freend?
520 Now certes, I were worse than a feend°   devil
If I to you wolde harm or vilainye.
I am nat come youre conseil for t'espye,
But trewely the cause of my cominge
Was only for to herkne how that ye singe:
525 For trewely, ye han as merye a stevene°   voice
As any angel hath that is in hevene.
Therwith ye han in musik more feelinge
Than hadde Boece,[4] or any that can singe.
My lord your fader—God his soule blesse!—
530 And eek youre moder, of hir gentilesse,°   gentility
Han in myn hous ybeen, to my grete ese.
And certes sire, ful fain° wolde I you plese.   gladly
But for men speke of singing, I wol saye,
So mote I brouke° wel mine yën twaye,   use
535 Save ye, I herde nevere man so singe
As dide youre fader in the morweninge.
Certes, it was of herte° al that he soong.   heartfelt
And for to make his vois the more strong,
He wolde so paine him that with bothe his yën
540 He moste winke,° so loude wolde he cryen;   shut his eyes
And stonden on his tiptoon therwithal,
And strecche forth his nekke long and smal;
And eek he was of swich discrecioun
That ther nas no man in no regioun
545 That him in song or wisdom mighte passe.°   surpass
I have wel rad in Daun Burnel the Asse.[5]
Among his vers how that ther was a cok,
For° a preestes sone yaf him a knok   because
Upon his leg whil he was yong and nice,°   foolish
550 He made him for to lese his benefice.[6]
But certain, ther nis no comparisoun
Bitwixe the wisdom and discrecioun
Of youre fader and of his subtiltee.
Now singeth, sire, for sainte° charitee!   holy
555 Lat see, conne ye youre fader countrefete?"°   imitate
This Chauntecleer his winges gan to bete,
As man that coude his traison nat espye,
So was he ravisshed with his flaterye.
Allas, ye lordes, many a fals flatour
560 Is in youre court, and many a losengeour,°   deceiver
That plesen you wel more, by my faith,
Than he that soothfastnesse° unto you saith!   truth

---

4. In addition to theology, Boethius also wrote a music textbook.
5. The hero of a 12th-century satirical poem, *Speculum*

Stultorum, by Nigel Wirecker, Brunellus was a donkey who traveled around Europe trying to educate himself.
6. Lose his commission (because he overslept).

Redeth Ecclesiaste[7] of flaterye.
Beeth war, ye lordes, of hir trecherye.
565   This Chauntecleer stood hye upon his toos,
Strecching his nekke, and heeld his yën cloos,
And gan to crowe loude for the nones;°   *for the purpose*
And daun Russel the fox sterte up atones,°   *at once*
And by the gargat° hente° Chauntecleer,   *throat / seized*
570 And on his bak toward the wode him beer,
For yit ne was ther no man that him sued.
    O destinee that maist nat been eschued!°   *avoided*
Allas that Chauntecleer fleigh fro the bemes!
Allas his wif ne roughte° nat of dremes!   *cared*
575 And on a Friday[8] fil al this meschaunce!
    O Venus that art goddesse of plesaunce,
Sin that thy servant was this Chauntecleer,
And in thy service dide al his power—
More for delit than world° to multiplye—   *population*
580 Why woldestou suffre him on thy day to die?
    O Gaufred,[9] dere maister soverein,
That, whan thy worthy king Richard was slain
With shot,° complainedest his deeth so sore,   *(of an arrow)*
Why ne hadde I now thy sentence and thy lore,
585 The Friday for to chide as diden ye?
For on a Friday soothly° slain was he.   *truly*
Thanne wolde I shewe you how that I coude plaine°   *lament*
For Chauntecleres drede and for his paine.
    Certes, swich cry ne lamentacioun
590 Was nevere of ladies maad whan Ilioun°   *Troy*
Was wonne, and Pyrrus[1] with his straite° swerd,   *drawn*
Whan he hadde hent King Priam by the beerd
And slain him, as saith us Eneidos,°   *Virgil's* Aeneid
As maden alle the hennes in the cloos,°   *yard*
595 Whan they hadde seen of Chauntecleer the sighte.
But sovereinly Dame Pertelote shrighte°   *shrieked*
Ful louder than dide Hasdrubales wif[2]
Whan that hir housbonde hadde lost his lif,
And that the Romains hadden brend Cartage:
600 She was so ful of torment and of rage
That wilfully unto the fir she sterte,
And brende hirselven with a stedefast herte.
    O woful hennes, right so criden ye
As, whan that Nero[3] brende the citee
605 Of Rome, criden senatoures wives

---

7. The Book of Ecclesiasticus.
8. Venus's day, but also an ominous day of the week.
9. Geoffrey of Vinsauf, who wrote a poem when King Richard the Lion-Hearted died, cursing the day of the week on which he died, a Friday.
1. Pyrrhus, the son of Achilles, who slew Troy's King

Priam.
2. Hasdrubal was King of Carthage when it was defeated by the Romans during the Punic Wars.
3. The Emperor Nero set fire to Rome, killing many of his senators.

For that hir housbondes losten alle hir lives:
Withouten gilt this Nero hath hem slain.
Now wol I turne to my tale again.
        The sely° widwe and eek hir doughtres two   *innocent*
610 Herden thise hennes crye and maken wo,
And out at dores sterten they anoon,
And sien° the fox toward the grove goon,   *saw*
And bar upon his bak the cok away,
And criden, "Out, harrow, and wailaway,
615 Ha, ha, the fox," and after him they ran,
And eek with staves many another man;
Ran Colle oure dogge, and Talbot and Gerland,[4]
And Malkin with a distaf in hir hand,
Ran cow and calf, and eek the verray hogges,
620 Sore aferd for berking of the dogges
And shouting of the men and wommen eke.
They ronne so hem thoughte hir herte breke;
They yelleden as feendes doon in helle;
The dokes° criden as men wolde hem quelle;°   *ducks / kill*
625 The gees for fere flowen over the trees;
Out of the hive cam the swarm of bees;
So hidous was the noise a, benedicite,
Certes, he Jakke Straw[5] and his meinee
Ne made nevere shoutes half so shrille
630 Whan that they wolden any Fleming kille,
As thilke day was maad upon the fox:
Of bras they broughten bemes° and of box,°   *trumpets / boxwood*
Of horn, of boon, in whiche they blewe and pouped,°   *puffed*
And therwithal they skriked and they houped—
635 It seemed as that hevene sholde falle.
        Now goode men, I praye you herkneth alle:
Lo, how Fortune turneth sodeinly
The hope and pride eek of hir enemy.
This cok that lay upon the foxes bak,
640 In al his drede unto the fox he spak,
And saide, "Sire, if that I were as ye,
Yit sholde I sayn, as wis° God helpe me,   *certainly*
'Turneth ayain, ye proude cherles° alle!   *ruffians*
A verray pestilence upon you falle!
645 Now am I come unto this wodes side,
Maugree° your heed,° the cok shal here abide.   *despite / planning*
I wol him ete, in faith, and that anoon.'"
        The fox answerde, "In faith, it shal be doon."
And as he spak that word, al sodeinly
650 The cok brak from his mouth deliverly,°   *nimbly*
And hye upon a tree he fleigh anoon.

---

4. Common names for dogs.
5. Jack Straw was one of the leaders of the Peasants'

Revolt of 1381, which was directed in part against the
Flemish traders in London.

And whan the fox sawgh that he was agoon,
"Allas," quod he, "O Chauntecleer, allas!
I have to you," quod he, "ydoon trespas,
655 In as muche as I maked you aferd
Whan I you hente and broughte out of the yeerd.
But sire, I dide it in no wikke° entente: *wicked*
Come down, and I shal telle you what I mente.
I shal saye sooth to you, God help me so."
660   "Nay thanne," quod he, "I shrewe° us bothe two: *curse*
But first I shrewe myself, bothe blood and bones,
If thou bigile me ofter than ones;
Thou shalt namore thurgh thy flaterye
Do° me to singe and winken with myn yë.°   *make*
665 For he that winketh whan he sholde see,
Al wilfully, God lat him nevere thee."°   *prosper*
         "Nay," quod the fox, "but God yive him meschaunce
That is so undiscreet of governaunce
That jangleth° whan he sholde holde his pees."   *chatters*
670   Lo, swich it is for to be recchelees°   *careless*
And necligent and truste on flaterye.
But ye that holden this tale a folye
As of a fox, or of a cok and hen,
Taketh the moralitee, goode men.
675 For Saint Paul saith that al that writen is
To oure doctrine° it is ywrit, ywis:°   *instruction / indeed*
Taketh the fruit, and lat the chaf be stille.
Now goode God, if that it be thy wille,
As saith my lord, so make us alle goode men,
680 And bringe us to his hye blisse. Amen.

The Epilogue

"Sire Nonnes Preest," oure Hoste saide anoon,
"Yblessed be thy breech° and every stoon:°   *buttocks / testicle*
This was a merye tale of Chauntecleer.
But by my trouthe, if thou were seculer°   *a layman*
685 Thou woldest been a tredefowl° aright: *a cock*
For if thou have corage° as thou hast might   *desire*
Thee were neede of hennes, as I weene,°   *suppose*
Ye, mo than sevene times seventeene.
See whiche brawnes° hath this gentil preest—   *muscles*
690 So greet a nekke and swich a large breest.
He looketh as a sperhawk° with his yën;   *sparrowhawk*
Him needeth nat his colour for to dyen
With brasil ne with grain of Portingale.⁶
Now sire, faire falle you for youre tale."
695 And after that he with ful merye cheere
Saide unto another as ye shul heere.

6. Two types of red dye, the latter from Portugal.

THE PARSON'S TALE   Although *The Canterbury Tales* remain unfinished and even the order of the tales is unclear, we know that Chaucer's plan was to end them with *The Parson's Tale*, just as it was to begin them with the pilgrimage to Canterbury in *The General Prologue*. Thus, when the Parson responds to the Host's request for a final tale by praying Jesus to show the way to the "glorious pilgrimage" called "Jerusalem celestial," there is a sense of closure in his return to an idea that has been obscured during the tale-telling. His shift of the destination from Canterbury to the heavenly city, however, gives us pause. The view that life on earth is a pilgrimage to heaven was a Christian commonplace, but was it Chaucer's view? The three parts of *The Parson's Tale* included here raise questions about how Chaucer's religious beliefs relate to his art. What is his final judgment of the artful, but often sinful, tales he has been telling?

In the introduction, the Parson rejects the idea of poetry entirely, scornfully refusing to tell a "fable" or to adorn his tale with alliteration or rhyme; instead, he will tell what he refers to as a "merye tale in prose," which turns out to be a forty-page treatise on penitence. Thus Chaucer specifically attributes to him an ascetic view of art which is hard to reconcile with his own extraordinary poetry. Does the Parson speak for Chaucer? Although he has a measure of authority as the only exemplary member of the clergy on the pilgrimage, he is nevertheless a fictional character. Since, however, Chaucer is thought to have written the introduction to this tale as well as the *Retraction* at the same time at the end of his life, perhaps he could have come to share the Parson's aesthetic views.

The Parson begins his tale proper with a second reference to celestial Jerusalem, stating that the route to it is through penitence. The tale, which Chaucer had translated at an earlier period, belongs to a common type of manual of confession for either clergy or laity. Included in it is an analysis of the seven deadly sins—pride, envy, anger, sloth, avarice, gluttony, and lechery—in an order that suggests that Chaucer, like Dante, considered the last to be the least serious, although still worthy of damnation. The passage on lechery excerpted here offers an opportunity to measure *The Parson's Tale* against the tales that have gone before, particularly such "sinful" works as *The Miller's Tale* and *The Wife of Bath's Prologue*.

Whatever conclusion we draw about the relevance of *The Parson's Tale* to the tales preceding, the *Retraction* appended to it is troubling yet intriguing. In it Chaucer repudiates much of the work for which he is most loved and admired, such "worldly vanitees" as *Troilus and Criseyde*, *The Parliament of Fowls*, and those of the *Canterbury Tales* that "sounen [lead] into sinne." On the other hand, he thanks God for his works of "moralitee," including his translation of Boethius and his saints' legends, works that are seldom read today. He himself is engaged in penance—repentance, confession, and satisfaction—thus connecting his own spiritual experience with the manual he has translated. However disappointing it is to read this rejection of his most artistically satisfying tales, we must remember that a concept of art for art's sake would have been historically unavailable to him. Perhaps his last tale was indeed his last word.

from **The Parson's Tale**
The Introduction

By that° the Manciple hadde his tale al ended,	*by that time*
The sonne fro the south line[1] was descended	
So lowe, that he nas nat to my sighte	
Degrees nine and twenty as in highte.	
5 Four of the clokke it was, so as I gesse,	
For elevene foot,° or litel more or lesse,	*feet*

---

1. Astronomical marking parallel to the celestial equator.

My shadwe was at thilke° time as there,   *that*
Of swich feet as my lengthe parted were
In sixe feet equal of proporcioun.

10   Therwith the moones exaltacioun°—   *dominant influence*
I mene Libra²—alway gan ascende,
As we were entring at a thropes ende.°   *village boundary*
For which oure Host, as he was wont to gie°   *lead*
As in this caas oure joly compaignye,
15   Saide in this wise, "Lordinges everichoon,
Now lakketh us no tales mo than oon:
Fulfild is my sentence° and my decree;   *design*
I trowe° that we han herd of eech degree;   *believe*
Almost fulfild is al myn ordinaunce.
20   I praye to God, so yive him right good chaunce
That telleth this tale to us lustily.
Sire preest," quod he, "artou a vicary,°   *vicar*
Or arte a Person?° Say sooth, by thy fay.°   *parish priest / faith*
Be what thou be, ne breek thou nat oure play,
25   For every man save thou hath told his tale.
Unbokele and shew us what is in thy male!°   *bag*
For trewely, me thinketh by thy cheere°   *expression*
Thou sholdest knitte up wel a greet matere.
Tel us a fable anoon, for cokkes bones!"³
30   This Person answerde al atones,
"Thou getest fable noon ytold for me,
For Paul, that writeth unto Timothee,⁴
Repreveth hem that waiven soothfastnesse,°   *truth*
And tellen fables and swich wrecchednesse.
35   Why sholde I sowen draf° out of my fest,°   *chaff / fist*
Whan I may sowen whete if that me lest?°   *it pleases*
For which I saye that if you list to heere
Moralitee and vertuous matere,
And thanne that ye wol yive me audience,
40   I wol ful fain,° at Cristes reverence,   *gladly*
Do you plesance leveful° as I can.   *lawfully*
But trusteth wel, I am a southren man:⁵
I can nat geeste° Rum-Ram-Ruf by lettre—   *tell stories*
Ne, God woot,° rym holde° I but litel bettre.   *knows / appreciate*
45   And therfore, if you list, I wol nat glose;°   *adorn my speech*
I wol you telle a merye tale in prose,
To knitte up al this feeste and make an ende.
And Jesu for his grace wit me sende
To shewe you the way in this viage°   *journey*
50   Of thilke parfit° glorious pilgrimage   *that perfect*

---

2. Seventh sign in the Zodiac, the Scales.
3. Cock's bones, a euphemism for God's bones.
4. St. Paul's Epistle to Timothy.
5. The parson, like Chaucer himself, comes from the south
of England and so is not accustomed to telling stories in
the alliterative meter used traditionally in the north. Rum-
Ram-Ruf is an example of alliteration.

That highte Jerusalem celestial.
And if ye vouche-sauf,° anoon I shal   *agree*
Biginne upon my tale, for which I praye
Telle youre avis:° I can no bettre saye.   *opinion*
55   But nathelees, this meditacioun
I putte it ay° under correccioun   *always*
Of clerkes, for I am nat textuel:°   *a literalist*
I take but the sentence,° trusteth wel.   *sense*
Therfore I make protestacioun
60   That I wol stonde to correccioun."
        Upon this word we han assented soone,
For, as it seemed, it was for to doone
To enden in som vertuous sentence,°   *topic*
And for to yive him space° and audience;   *time*
65   And bede oure Host he sholde to him saye
That alle we to telle his tale him praye.
        Oure Hoste hadde the wordes for us alle:
"Sire preest," quod he, "now faire you bifalle:
Telleth," quod he, "youre meditacioun.
70   But hasteth you, the sonne wol adown.
Beeth fructuous, and that in litel space,
And to do wel God sende you his grace.
Saye what you list, and we wol gladly heere."
And with that word he saide in this manere.

from *The Tale*

Oure sweete Lord God of Hevene, that no man wol perisse[1] but wol
that we comen alle to the knowliche of him and to the blisful lif that
is perdurable,° amonesteth° us by the prophete Jeremie[2] that saith in   *enduring / warns*
this wise: "Stondeth upon the wayes and seeth and axeth of olde
pathes (that is to sayn, of olde sentences°) which is the goode way,   *opinions*
and walketh in that way, and ye shul finde refresshing for youre
soules."

Manye been the wayes espirituels that leden folk to oure Lord
Jesu Crist and to the regne of glorye: of whiche wayes ther is a ful
noble way and a ful covenable° which may nat faile to man ne to   *suitable*
womman that thurgh sinne hath misgoon fro the righte way of
Jerusalem celestial; and this way is cleped° Penitence. * * *   *called*

THE REMEDY FOR THE SIN OF LECHERY

Now cometh the remedye agains Lecherye, and that is generally
Chastitee and Continence that restraineth alle the desordainee
mevinges° that comen of flesshly talents.° And evere the gretter   *impulses / desires*
merite shal he han that most restraineth the wikkede eschaufinges°   *inflammations*
of the ardure of this sinne. And this is in two maneres: that is to
sayn, chastitee in mariage and chastitee of widwehood.

---

1. Who wishes no man to perish.   2. Jeremiah 6.16.

Now shaltou understonde that matrimoine is leeful° assembling *lawful*
of man and of womman that receiven by vertu of the sacrement the
bond thurgh which they may nat be departed in al hir life—that is
to sayn, whil that they liven bothe. This, as saith the book, is a ful
greet sacrement: God maked it, as I have said, in Paradis, and wolde
himself be born in mariage. And for to halwen° mariage, he was at a *bless*
wedding where as he turned water into win, which was the firste
miracle that he wroughte in erthe biforn his disciples. Trewe effect
of mariage clenseth fornicacion and replenisseth Holy Chirche of
good linage° (for that is the ende of mariage), and it chaungeth *offspring*
deedly sinne[3] into venial sinne bitwixe hem that been ywedded,
and maketh the hertes al oon° of hem that been ywedded, as wel as *united*
the bodies.

This is verray mariage that was establissed by God er that sinne
bigan, whan naturel lawe was in his right point° in Paradis; and it *order*
was ordained that oo man sholde have but oo womman, and oo
womman but oo man (as saith Saint Augustine) by manye resons:
First, for mariage is figured° bitwixe Crist and Holy Chirche; and *represented*
that other is for a man is heved° of a womman—algate,° by ordi- *head / at least*
nance it sholde be so. For if a womman hadde mo men than oon,
thanne sholde she have mo hevedes than oon, and that were an
horrible thing biforn God; and eek a womman ne mighte nat plese
to many folk at ones. And also ther ne sholde nevere be pees ne
reste amonges hem, for everich wolde axen his owene thing. And
fortherover, no man sholde knowe his owene engendrure,° ne who *offspring*
sholde have his heritage, and the womman sholde been the lesse
biloved fro the time that she were conjoint to manye men.

Now cometh how that a man sholde bere him with his wif, and
namely in two thinges, that is to sayn, in suffrance° and in rever- *obedience*
ence, as shewed Crist whan he made first womman. For he ne made
hire nat of the heved of Adam for she sholde nat claime too greet
lorshipe: for ther as womman hath the maistrye she maketh too greet
desray° (ther needen none ensamples of this: the experience of day *disorder*
by day oughte suffise). Also, certes, God ne made nat womman of
the foot of Adam, for she ne sholde nat be holden too lowe, for she
can nat paciently suffre. But God made womman of the rib of Adam
for womman sholde be felawe unto man. Man sholde bere him to his
wif in faith, in trouthe, and in love, as saith Sainte Paul, that a man
sholde loven his wif as Crist loved Holy Chirche, that loved it so wel
that he deide for it. So sholde a man for his wif, if it were neede.

Now how that a womman sholde be subjet to hir housbonde,
that telleth Sainte Peter: First, in obedience. And eek, as saith the
decree, a womman that is a wif, as longe as she is a wif, she hath
noon auctoritee° to swere ne to bere witnesse withoute leve of hir *power*
housbonde that is hir lord—algate, he sholde be so by reson. She
sholde eek serven him in alle honestee, and been attempree° of hir *moderate*
array; I woot wel that they sholde setten hir entente° to plesen hir *purpose*

---

3. Sex remains a minor sin even within marriage, but it is a more serious sin outside of marriage.

housbondes, but nat by hir quaintise of array:° Saint Jerome saith *flamboyant attire*
that wives that been apparailed in silk and in precious purpre ne
mowe nat clothen hem in Jesu Crist. What saith Saint John eek in
this matere? Saint Gregorye eek saith that no wight° seeketh pre- *person*
cious array but only for vaine glorye to been honoured the more
biforn the peple. It is a greet folye a womman to have a fair array
outward and in hireself be foul inward. A wif sholde eek be
mesurable° in looking and in bering and in laughing, and discreet in *modest*
alle hir wordes and hir deedes. And aboven alle worldly thinges she
sholde loven hir housbonde with al hir herte, and to him be trewe
of hir body (so sholde an housbonde eek be to his wif): for sith that° *since*
al the body is the housbondes, so sholde hir herte been, or elles ther
is bitwixe hem two as in that no parfit mariage.

Thanne shul men understonde that for three thinges a man and
his wif flesshly mowen° assemble. The firste is in entente of engen- *may*
drure of children to the service of God: for certes, that is the cause
final of matrimoine. Another cause is to yeelden everich° of hem to *each*
other the dette of hir bodies, for neither of hem hath power of his
owene body. The thridde is for to eschewe lecherye and vilainye.
The ferthe is, for soothe, deedly sinne. As to the firste, it is merito-
rye; the seconde also, for, as saith the decree, that she hath merite
of chastitee that yeeldeth to hir housbonde the dette of hir body, ye,
though it be again hir liking and the lust of hir herte. The thridde
manere is venial sinne—and, trewely, scarsly may any of thise be
withoute venial sinne, for the corrupcion and for the delit. The ferthe manere is for to understonde if they assemble only for amorous
love and for noon of the forsaide causes, but for to accomplice
thilke brenning delit—they rekke° nevere how ofte—soothly, it is *care*
deedly sinne. And yit with sorwe some folk wol painen hem° more *trouble themselves*
to doon than to hir appetit suffiseth. * * *

Another remedye agains lecherye is specially to withdrawen
swiche thinges as yive occasion to thilke vilainye, as ese,° eting, and *leisure*
drinking: for certes, whan the pot boileth strongly, the beste remedye
is to withdrawe the fir. Sleeping longe in greet quiete is eek a greet
norice° to lecherye. Another remedye agains lecherye is that a man *nurse*
or a womman eschewe the compaignye of hem by whiche he
douteth° to be tempted: for al be it so that the deede be withston- *suspects*
den, yit is ther greet temptacion. Soothly, a whit wal,° although it ne *wall*
brenne nought fully by stiking of a candele, yit is the wal blak of the
leit.° Ful ofte time I rede that no man truste in his owene perfeccion *from the flame*
but he be stronger than Sampson, holier than David, and wiser than
Salomon.

Chaucer's Retraction

Here Taketh the Makere of This Book His Leve

Now praye I to hem alle that herkne this litel tretis° or rede,° that if *treatise / advice*
ther be any thing in it that liketh° hem, that therof they thanken *pleases*
oure Lord Jesu Crist, of whom proceedeth al wit and al goodnesse.

And if ther be any thing that displese hem, I praye hem also that they arrette° it to the defaute of myn unconning,° and nat to my wil, *attribute / inability* that wolde ful fain° have said bettre if I hadde had conning. For oure *gladly* book saith, "Al that is writen is writen for oure doctrine," and that is myn entente. Wherfore I biseeke you mekely, for the mercy of God, that ye praye for me that Crist have mercy on me and foryive me my giltes,° and namely of my translacions and enditinges° of worldly *sins / writings* vanitees, the whiche I revoke in my retraccions:[4] as is the book of Troilus; the book also of Fame; the book of the five and twenty Ladies; the book of the Duchesse; the book of Saint Valentines Day of the Parlement of Briddes; the tales of Canterbury, thilke that sounen° into sinne; the book of the Leon; and many another book, if *lead* they were in my remembrance, and many a song and many a lecch-erous lay: that Crist for his grete mercy foryive me the sinne. But of the translacion of Boece *de Consolatione*, and othere bookes of legen-des of saintes, and omelies, and moralitee, and devocion, that thanke I oure Lord Jesu Crist and his blisful Moder and alle the saintes of hevene, biseeking hem that they from hennes forth unto my lives ende sende me grace to biwaile° my giltes and to studye to *repent* the salvacion of my soule, and graunte me grace of verray penitence, confession, and satisfaccion to doon in this present lif, thurgh the benigne grace of him that is king of kinges and preest over alle preestes, that boughte° us with the precious blood of his herte, so *redeemed* that I may been oon of hem at the day of doom° that shulle be saved. *judgment* *Qui cum patre et Spiritu Sancto vivis et regnas Deus per omnia saecula. Amen.*[5]

To His Scribe Adam[1]

Adam scrivain,° if evere it thee bifalle *copyist*
Boece[2] or Troilus for to writen newe,
Under thy longe lokkes thou moste have° the scalle,° *may you get / mange*
But after my making thou write more trewe,[3]
5   So ofte a day I moot° thy werk renewe, *must*
It to correcte, and eek to rubbe and scrape:
And al is thurgh thy necligence and rape.° *haste*

---

4. Here Chaucer repents having written most of his major works: *Troilus and Criseyde, The Book* (or *House) of Fame, The Legend of Good Women, The Book of the Duchess, The Parliament of Fowls,* and various of *The Canterbury Tales. The Book of the Lion* has not been preserved. Chaucer's translation of Boethius's *Consolation of Philosophy* is ex-cepted.
5. You who live with the Father and the Holy Spirit and reign as God through all the centuries. Amen.
1. Given his position at court, Chaucer was asked to write many lyrics and occasional poems, such as this poem and the one that follows. In both, he wittily bemoans the conditions of authorship under which he was forced to work, depending on scribes to reproduce his poetry and on patrons to support it. In *To His Scribe Adam,* he strikes a pose of affectionate raillery toward his scribe, whose oc-cupation writers widely scorned. Perhaps he sees it as fit-ting to curse Adam with a skin disease which will make him scratch his scalp, just as Chaucer has had to scratch out the errors from his manuscripts. However, the poem has a serious undertone too. In fearing that Adam will miscopy his great romance, *Troilus and Criseyde,* he echoes a concern for the accurate reproduction of his work, which he voiced at the end of *Troilus* itself: he prays God that, in view of the great dialectal "diversitee / in Englissh," and in writing of oure tonge," no one "mis-write" his book (5.1793–94).
2. Chaucer's translation of Boethius's *Consolation of Phi-losophy.*
3. Unless you make a more reliable copy of what I have composed.

Complaint to His Purse[1]

To you, my purs, and to noon other wight,°　　　　　　　　*creature*
Complaine I, for ye be my lady dere
I am so sory, now that ye be light,°　　　　　　*empty, wanton*
For certes, but if° ye make me hevy cheere,[2]　　　　　*unless*
5　　Me were as lief° be laid upon my beere;°　　*I would prefer / bier*
For which unto youre mercy thus I crye:
Beeth hevy again, or elles moot° I die.　　　　　　　　*must*

Now voucheth sauf° this day er it be night　　　　　　*grant*
That I of you the blisful soun may heere,
10　　Or see youre colour, lik the sonne bright,
That of yelownesse hadde nevere peere.
Ye be my lif, ye be myn hertes steere,°　　　　　　　　*guide*
Queene of confort and of good compaignye:
Beeth hevy again, or elles moot I die.

15　　Ye purs, that been to me my lives light
And saviour, as in this world down here,
Out of this tonne° helpe me thurgh your might,　　*dark situation*
Sith that ye wol nat be my tresorere;
For I am shave as neigh° as any frere.[3]　　　　　　　*close*
20　　But yit I praye unto youre curteisye:
Beeth hevy again, or elles moot I die.

Envoy to Henry IV[4]

O conquerour of Brutus Albioun,[5]
Which that by line° and free eleccioun　　　　　　*inheritance*
Been verray king, this song to you I sende:
25　　And ye, that mowen° alle oure harmes amende,　　　*may*
Have minde upon my supplicacioun.

—✦✦✦—

William Langland
c. 1330–1387

Little is known of William Langland. On the basis of internal evidence in *Piers Plowman*, he is thought to have been a clerk in minor orders whose career in the church was curtailed by his marriage. He may have come from the Malvern Hills in the west of England, but he spent

---

1. This is a traditional "begging" poem, based on French models. The request for money is presented humorously, as a parody of a courtly love complaint to a cruel mistress. The parallel takes on ironic force when one recalls Chaucer's presentation of himself, in such early poems as *The Parliament of Fowls*, as a failed lover. This is one of Chaucer's last poems, written a year before his death. It was addressed to Henry IV when he took the throne in 1399, to request a renewal of the annuity Chaucer had received from the deposed Richard II. The flattering "envoy" to Henry at the end alludes to the tradition dating

from Geoffrey of Monmouth that Britain was founded by Brutus, the grandson of Aeneas, the exiled prince of Troy and founder of Rome.
2. Serious expression (in a person); full weight (in a purse).
3. Friar (with a bald tonsure).
4. The "envoy" is the traditional close of a ballad, usually directed to its addressee.
5. According to legend, Brutus conquered the kingdom of Albion and renamed it "Britain," after himself.

much of his professional life in London. He was clearly learned, using many Latin quotations from the Bible (given below primarily in English translation, designated by italics and unnumbered), and the style of his poem in many ways resembles sermon rhetoric.

Piers Plowman is an ambitious and multilayered allegory, an attempt to combine Christian history, social satire, and an account of the individual soul's quest for salvation. It is presented as a dream vision whose hero is a humble plowman, and whose narrator, the naive dreamer named Will, may be only a convenient fiction. Even its first audience sometimes reacted to this mysterious poem in surprising ways. *Piers Plowman* was so inspiring to the leaders of the Rising of 1381 that they saw Piers not as a fictional character but as an actual seditious person, as can be seen in the letter of radical priest John Ball in the readings following this poem (pages 475–77). This interpretation of the poem is remarkable given Langland's profound conservatism; despite his scathing social satire, he offers no program for social change. In fact, he supports the traditional model of the three estates, whereby the king and knights protect the body politic, the clergy prays for it, and the commons provide its food. Although he was sympathetic toward the poor and scornful of the rich and powerful, he felt that what ailed society was that *none* of the three estates was performing its proper role.

Piers Plowman survives in many manuscripts, a fact that suggests a large audience, which most likely included secular readers in the government and law as well as the clergy. Most of John Ball's followers would have been unable to read it. The poem exists in three versions—known as the A-, B-, and C-texts—and their history throws light on the poem's role in the Rising of 1381. The short A-text was expanded into the B-text some time between 1377 and 1381, when John Ball and other rebel leaders referred to it, while the C-text (which is translated in the excerpts below) is generally agreed to reflect Langland's attempt to distance himself from the radical beliefs of the rebels. Nevertheless, the poem remained popular for the next two centuries as a document of social protest and was ultimately regarded as a prophecy of the English Reformation. Langland's social criticism, however, is only part of his project, for he considered individual salvation to be equally important. A strictly political reading of *Piers Plowman*—whether in the fourteenth century or the twenty-first—misses a great deal of its originality and its power.

Piers Plowman is a challenge to read: it is almost surrealistic in its rapid and unexplained transitions, its many dreams, and its complex use of allegory. It is as confusing to people reading it in its entirety as to those reading it in excerpts, as here. Nevertheless, the poem does have a kind of unity, of a thematic rather than a narrative sort. It is held together by the dreamer's vision of the corruption of society and his personal quest to save his own soul. This quest is loosely structured by the metaphor of the journey, which is reflected in the poem's subdivision into parts called *passūs*—Latin for "steps." The poem is further unified by the allegorical character of Piers the plowman: a literal fourteenth-century English farmer when we first meet him, in the course of the poem he becomes a figural representation of Saint Peter, the first pope and founder of the church, and of Christ himself.

The five passages included here suggest the connection between the social and spiritual aspects of the poem. In the *Prologue*, the dreamer has a vision of a tower on a hill (later explained as the seat of Truth, i.e., God), a hellish dungeon beneath, and between them, a "field full of folk," representing various professions from the three estates, who are later said to be more concerned with their material than their spiritual welfare.

Passus 2 is the first of three on the marriage of Lady Meed, an ambiguous allegorical figure whose name can mean "just reward," "bribery," or the profit motive generally, the last being a cause for anxiety as England moved from a barter economy to one based on money. The dreamer is invited by Lady Holy Church to Meed's marriage to "False Fickle Tongue." Members of all three estates attend this event, a sign of corruption on every social level.

Langland sees greed as a sin of the poor as well as the rich, and in a comic passage of personification allegory represents the seven deadly sins as members of the commons. Included here from *Passus 6* is the vividly realized portrait of Glutton, who revels in his sin as he confesses it. Langland discusses the issues of poverty and work most directly in *Passus 8*, where Piers Plowman insists that the assembled people help him plow his half-acre before he will agree to lead them on a pilgrimage to Truth. Piers supports the traditional division of labor, explicitly exempting the knight from producing food, as long as he protects the commons and clergy from "wasters"—lazy shirkers. He insists, however, that the knight treat peasants well—in part because roles may be reversed in heaven, and earthly underlings can become heavenly masters. Yet Langland is not simply taking the workers' side. The knight turns out to be too courteous to control wasters, and Hunger must be called in to offer an incentive to work. When Piers takes pity on the poor and sends Hunger away, Waster refuses to work and the laborers demand more money, cursing the king for the statutes that have instituted wage freezes.

The spiritual climax of the poem takes place in *Passus 20*, which depicts Christ's crucifixion, harrowing of hell (release of the souls of Adam and other Old Testament figures), and resurrection. After many *passūs* of theological debate about his own salvation, the dreamer falls asleep on Palm Sunday and dreams of a man entering Jerusalem on a donkey. The dreamer thinks the man looks like Piers the Plowman, until he recognizes him as Jesus. This man is presented as a young knight going to be dubbed: he will joust against the devil in Piers's armor ("human nature") for the "fruit of Piers the Plowman" (human souls).

Before Christ can release the souls from hell, a lively debate takes place among the "four daughters of God"—Mercy and Truth, Righteousness and Peace—homely "wenches" who embody the words of Psalm 84.11: "Mercy and Truth have met together, Righteousness and Peace have kissed each other." They concede that forgiveness can take precedence over retribution, whereupon Jesus, having "jousted well," leads out the patriarchs and prophets in victory. As church bells ring to signal the resurrection, the dreamer awakes and calls his wife and daughter to church to celebrate Easter with him, thus connecting the grand scheme of salvation history to his personal experience.

The remainder of the poem, *Passūs 21–22*, which are not included here, recount the foundation of the church (by Piers as Saint Peter), and offer an apocalyptic vision of its subsequent corruption by the friars and its attack by Antichrist. There are no answers: the poem ends inconclusively with the allegorical figure of Conscience setting out on a pilgrimage in search of Piers Plowman.

Langland did not write French-inspired rhymed poetry, which was fashionable in London and used by Chaucer, but rather he composed old-fashioned alliterative poetry, which survived from Old English. The so-called Alliterative Revival was divided into two traditions, one based in the north of England and featuring romances in the alliterative "high" style, such as *Sir Gawain and the Green Knight*, and the other based in the south and west, and tending to social protest poems in a plain style. Langland's subject matter and style link him to the latter tradition, which includes satirical poems such as *Richard the Redeless*, *Mum and the Sothsegger*, and *Jack Upland*. In Middle English alliterative poetry, each line contains at least four major stressed syllables, with the first three usually beginning with the same sound. The translations of alliterative poems in this anthology—including *Beowulf* and *Sir Gawain*, as well as *Piers Plowman*—all sufficiently retain the alliteration to convey its flavor in modern English. The following passage from *Piers Plowman* in Middle English, the description of Lady Meed in her gaudy clothes, makes the point more clearly. The dreamer, with naive admiration, reports that he

> . . . was war of a womman wonderliche yclothed,
> Purfiled with Pelure, the pureste on erthe,
> Ycorouned in a coroune, the kyng hath noon bettre.
> Fetisliche hire fyngres were fretted with gold wyr
> And theron riche Rubyes as rede as any gleede,
> And Diamaundes of derrest pris and double manere saphires,
> Orientals and Ewages enuenymes to destroye.

> Hire Robe ful riche, of reed scarlet engreyned,
> With Ribanes of reed gold and of riche stones.
> Hire array me rauysshed; swich richesse saugh I neuere.

Although Langland generally uses the plainer alliterative style of southern protest poetry, here he uses the high style of northern alliterative romances, for satirical purposes. Meed's dress recalls that of Bercilak's lady in *Sir Gawain*, in "rich red rayled" (line 952), as well as the elegant clothing of the Green Knight, "with pelure pured apert, the pane ful clene" (154). In contrast to the clothing of Lady Holy Church, whom Langland introduces in *Passus* 1 simply as "a lady lovely of look, clothed in linen," the robes of lady Meed seem dangerously seductive, thus underscoring a sexual metaphor for bribery which Langland consistently develops. Thus, in a more subtle fashion than some of his followers, such as the Wycliffite author of *Pierce the Ploughman's Crede*, Langland was able to use the specialized language of alliterative poetry in the service of social criticism.

from **Piers Plowman**[1]
Prologue

> In a summer season when the sun shone softly
> I wrapped myself in woolens as if I were a sheep;
> In a hermit's habit, unholy in his works,
> I went out into the world to hear wonders
> 5 And to see many strange and seldom-known things.
> But on a May morning in the Malvern Hills[2]
> I happened to fall asleep, worn out from walking;
> And in a meadow as I lay sleeping,
> I dreamed most marvelously, as I recall.
> 10 All the world's wealth and all of its woe,
> Dozing though I was, I certainly saw;
> Truth and treachery, treason and guile,
> Sleeping I saw them all, as I shall record.
>   I looked to the East toward the rising sun
> 15 And saw a tower—I took it Truth was inside.
> To the West then I looked after a while
> And saw a deep dale—Death, as I believe,
> Dwelled in that place, along with wicked spirits.
> Between them I found a fair field full of folk
> 20 Of all manner men, the common and the poor,
> Working and wandering as this world asks us.
>   Some put themselves to the plow, and seldom played,
> To work hard as they can at planting and sowing
> And won what these wasters through gluttony destroy.
> 25 And some put themselves in pride's ways and apparel
> Themselves accordingly in clothes of all kinds.
> Many put themselves to prayers and penances,
> All for love of our lord they live so severely
> In hope of good ending and heaven-kingdom's bliss;

---

1. Translated by George Economou.   2. These hills in the west of England were probably Langland's original home.

30 As anchorites and hermits[3] that keep to their cells,
 With no great desire to cruise the countryside
 Seeking carnal pleasures and luxurious lives.
  And some turned to trade—they made out better,
 As it always seems to us that such men thrive;
35 And some know as minstrels how to make mirth,
 Will neither work nor sweat, but swear out loud,
 Invent sleazy stories and make fools of themselves
 Though it's in their power to work if they want.
 What Paul preached about them I surely can prove;
40 *Qui turpiloquium loquitur*[4] is Lucifer's man.
  Beggars and moochers moved about quickly
 Till their bags and their bellies were crammed to the top,
 Faking it for food and fighting over ale.
 In gluttony those freeloaders go off to bed
45 And rise to rob and run off at the mouth.
 Sleep and sloth are their steady companions.
  Pilgrims and palmers[5] pledged to travel together
 To seek Saint James[6] and the saints of Rome,
 Went on their way with many wise tales
50 And took leave to lie about it for a lifetime.
 A heap of hermits with their hooked staves
 Went to Our Lady of Walsingham,[7] with wenches in tow;
 Great deadbeats that hated a good day's work
 Clothed themselves in hooded cloaks to stand apart
55 And proclaimed themselves hermits, for the easy life.
  I found there friars from all four orders,[8]
 Preaching to people to profit their gut,
 And glossing the gospel to their own good liking;
 Coveting fine copes,° some of these doctors° contradicted   *monk's capes /*
  authorities.   *of divinity*
60 Many of these masterful mendicant° friars   *begging*
 Bind their love of money to their proper business.
 And since charity's become a broker and chief agent for lords'
  confessions[9]
 Many strange things have happened these last years;
 Unless Holy Church and charity clear away such confessors
65 The world's worst misfortune mounts up fast.
  A pardoner[1] preached there as if he were a priest
 And brought forth a bull° with the bishops' seals,   *papal license*
 Said that he himself could absolve them all

---

3. Both were vowed to a religious life of solitude, hermits in the wilderness and anchorites walled in a tiny dwelling.
4. Who speaks filthy language; not Paul, though (cf. Ephesians 5.3–4).
5. "Professional" pilgrims who took advantage of the hospitality offered them in order to travel.
6. That is, his shrine at Compostela, in Spain.
7. English town, site of a famous shrine to the Virgin Mary.

8. The four orders of friars—Franciscans, Dominicans, Carmelites, and Augustinians. In 14th-century England they were much satirized for their corruption (cf. the friar in the *General Prologue* to Chaucer's *Canterbury Tales*).
9. Confession and the remission of sins is cynically sold by the friars.
1. An official empowered to pass on from the Pope absolution for the sins of people who had given money to charity.

Of phony fasts and of broken vows.

70 Illiterates believed him and liked what they heard
And came up and kneeled to kiss his pardons;
He bonked them with his bulls and bleared their eyes
And with this rigmarole raked in their brooches and rings.
Thus you give your gold to help out gluttons

75 And lose it for good to full-time lechers.
If the bishop were true and kept his ear to the ground
He'd not consign his seal to deceit of the people.
But it's not through the bishop that this guy preaches,
For the parish priest and pardoner split the silver

80 That, if not for them, the parishoners would have.

* * *

Still I kept dreaming about poor and rich,

220 Like barons and burgesses and village bondmen,[2]
All I saw sleeping as you shall hear next:
Bakers and brewers, butchers and others,
Weavers and websters, men that work with their hands,
Like tailors and tanners and tillers of earth,

225 Like dike and ditch diggers that do their work badly
And drive out their days with "*Dew vous saue, dame Emme.*"[3]
Cooks and their helpers cried, "Get your hot pies!
Good geese and pig meat! Come on up and eat!"
And taverners touted in much the same way:

230 "White wine of Alsace and wine from Gascony,
Wash down your roast with La Reole and La Rochelle!"
All this, and seven times more, I saw in my sleep.

Passus 2
[The Marriage of Lady Mead]

And then I kneeled before her[1] and cried to her for grace,
"Mercy, madame, for the love of Mary in heaven
That bore the blessed child that bought us on the cross,
Teach me the way to recognize Falsehood."

5 "Look to your left and see where he stands.
Falsehood and Fave[2] and fickle-tongued Liar
And many more men and women like them."
I looked to my left as the lady said
And saw a woman wonderfully clothed.

10 She was trimmed all in fur, the world's finest,
And crowned with a coronet as good as the king's;
On all five fingers were the richest rings
Set with red rubies and other precious gems.

---

2. Barons were members of the higher aristocracy; burgesses were town-dwellers with full rights as citizens; and bondmen were peasants who held their land from a lord in return for services or rent.

3. Presumably a popular song.
1. Lady Holy Church.
2. "Lying"; the name of characters representing deceit in Old French literature.

Her robes were richer than I can describe,
15   To talk of her attire I don't have time;
Her raiment and riches ravished my heart.
Whose wife she was and her name I wanted to know,
"Dear lady," I then asked, "conceal nothing from me."
    "That is the maid Meed[3] who has hurt me many times
20   And lied against my beloved who is called Loyalty
And slanders him to the lords that keep all our laws,
In the king's court and the commons' she contradicts my teaching,
In the pope's palace is privy as I,
But Truth would she weren't for she's a bastard.
25   Favel was her father who has a fickle tongue
And seldom speaks truth unless it's a trick,
And Meed takes after him, as men remark on kin:
    Like father, like daughter.
For never shall a briar put forth berries
Nor on a rough, crooked thorn a real fig grow:
    A good tree bringeth forth good fruit.[4]
30   I should be higher, for I come from better stock;
He that fathered me *filius dei*° is named,   son of God
Who never lied or laughed in his entire life,
And I am his dear daughter, duchess of heaven,
The man that loves me and follows my will
35   Shall have grace a-plenty and a good end,
And the man that loves Meed, I'll bet my life,
Will lose for her love a morsel of charity.
What is man's most help to heaven Meed will most hinder—
I base this on King David, whose book[5] does not lie:
    Lord, who shall dwell in thy tabernacle.[6]
40   And David himself explains, as his mute book shows:
    And not taken bribes against the innocent.[7]
    Tomorrow Meed marries a miserable wretch,
One False Faithless of the Fiend's lineage.
With flattery Favel's fouly enchanted Meed
And Liar's made all the arrangements for the match.
45   Be patient and you will see those that are pleased
By Meed's marriage, tomorrow you'll view it.
Get to know them if you can and avoid all those
Who love her lordship, both the high and the low.
Don't fault them but let them be till Loyalty's judge
50   And has power to punish them, then do your pleading.
Now I commend you to Christ and his pure mother,
And never load your conscience with coveting meed."
    Thus the lady left me lying asleep

---

3. A richly ambiguous word referring to a wide variety of "reward," both positive and negative, including just reward, heavenly salvation, recompense, the profit motive, graft, and bribery.

4. Matthew 7.17.
5. The book of Psalms.
6. Psalms 14.1.
7. Psalms 14.5.

And still dreaming I saw Meed's marriage.
55   All the rich retinue rooted in false living
Were bid to the bridal from the entire country,
All kinds of men that were Meed's kin,
Knights, clerics, and other common people,
Like jurors, summoners, sheriffs and their clerks,
60   Beadles, bailiffs, businessmen, and agents,
Purveyors, victualers, advocates of the Arches,[8]
I can't keep count of the crowd that ran with Meed.
But Simony and Civil[9] and his jurymen
Were tightest with Meed it seemed of all men.
65   But Favel was first to fetch her out of chamber
And like a broker brought her to be joined with False.

from Passus 6
[THE CONFESSION OF GLUTTON]

350   Now Glutton heads for confession
And moves towards the Church, his *mea culpa*[1] to say.
Fasting on a Friday he made forth his way
By the house of Betty Brewer, who bid him good morning
And where was he going that brew-wife asked.
355   "To Holy Church," he said, "to hear mass,
And then sit and be shriven and sin no more."
   "I have good ale, Glutton, old buddy, want to give it a try?"
   "Do you have," he asked, "any hot spices?"
   "I have pepper, peony, and a pound of garlic,
360   A farthing-worth of fennel seed[2] for fasting days I bought it."
   Then in goes Glutton and great oaths after.
Cissy the shoemaker sat on the bench,
Wat the game warden and his drunken wife,
Tim the tinker and two of his workmen,
365   Hick the hackney-man and Hugh the needler,
Clarice of Cock's Lane[3] and the clerk of the church,
Sir Piers of Pridie and Purnel of Flanders,
A hayward, a hermit, the hangman of Tyburn,
Daw the ditchdigger and a dozen rascals
370   In the form of porters and pickpockets and bald tooth-pullers,
A fiddler, a rat-catcher, a street-sweeper and his helper,
A rope-maker, a road-runner, and Rose the dish-seller,
Godfrey the garlic-man and Griffith the Welshman,
And a heap of secondhand salesmen, early in the morning
375   Stood Glutton with glad cheers to his first round of ale.

---

8. The officials in this and the two preceding lines had jobs that made them particularly open to bribery.
9. Simony is the buying and selling of church offices or spiritual functions; Civil is civil as opposed to criminal law (especially noted for its bribery and corruption).

1. By my own fault; formula used in Christian prayers and confession.
2. An herb thought to be good for someone drinking on an empty stomach.
3. Clarice and Purnel (of the next line) are prostitutes.

Clement the cobbler took off his cloak
And put it up for a game of New Fair[4]
Hick the hackney-man saw with his hood
And asked Bart the butcher to be on his side.
380 Tradesmen were chosen to appraise this bargain,
That whoso had the hood should not have the cloak,
And that the better thing, according to the arbiters, compensate the
     worse.
They got up quickly and whispered together
And appraised these items apart in private,
385 And there was a load of swearing, for one had to get the worse.
They could not in conscience truthfully accord
Till Robin the rope-maker they asked to arise
And named him umpire so that all arguing would stop.
     Hick the hostler got the cloak
390 On condition that Clement should fill the cup
And have Hick the hostler's hood and rest content;
And whoever took it back first had to get right up
And greet Sir Glutton with a gallon of ale.
     There was laughing and louring and "please pass the cup!"
395 Bargaining and drinking they kept starting up
And sat so till evensong[5] and sang from time to time,
Until Glutton had gobbled down a gallon and a gill°   1/4 pint
His guts began to rumble like two greedy sows;
He pissed half a gallon in the time of a *pater noster*,[6]
400 He blew his round bugle at his backbone's bottom,
So that all who heard that horn had to hold their noses
And wished it had been well plugged with a wisp of briars.
He could neither step nor stand unless he held a staff,
And then he moved like a minstrel's performing dog,
405 Sometimes sideways and sometimes backwards,
Like some one laying lines in order to trap birds.
     And when he reached the door, then his eyes dimmed,
And he stumbled on the threshold and fell to the ground,
And Clement the cobbler grabbed him by the waist
410 And in order to lift him up set him on his knees.
But Glutton was a huge boor and troubled in the lifting
And barfed up a mess into Clement's lap;
There is no hound so hungry in Hertfordshire
That he'd dare lap up that leaving, so unlovely it smacked.°   tasted
415   With all the woe in this world his wife and his daughter
Bore him to his bed and put him in it,
And after all this excess he had a bout of sloth;
He slept through Saturday and Sunday till sundown.
Then he awoke pale and wan and wanted a drink;

4. An elaborate game involving the exchange of clothing.
5. Vespers, the evening prayer service said just before
sunset.

6. The time it takes to say the Paternoster, the Lord's
Prayer.

420 The first thing he said was "Who's got the bowl?"
His wife and his conscience reproached him for his sin;
He became ashamed, that scoundrel, and made quick confession
To Repentance like this: "Have pity on me," he said,
"Lord who are aloft and shape all that lives!
425   To you God, I, Glutton, acknowledge my guilt
Of how I've trespassed with tongue, how often I can't tell,
Sworn 'God's soul and his sides!' and 'So help me God, Almighty!'
There was no need for it so many times falsely;
And overate at supper and sometime at noon
430 More than my system could naturally handle,
And like a dog that eats grass I began to throw up
And wasted what I might have saved—I can't speak for my shame
Of the depravity of my foul mouth and maw—
And on fasting days before noon I fed myself ale
435 Beyond all reason, among dirty jokesters, their dirty jokes to hear.
    For this, good God, grant me forgiveness
For my worthless living during my entire lifetime.
For I swear by the true God, despite any hunger or thirst,
Never shall on Friday a piece of fish digest in my stomach
440 Till my aunt Abstinence has given me leave—
And yet I've hated her all my lifetime."

from *Passus 8*
[PIERS PLOWING THE HALF-ACRE]

Perkin[1] the plowman said, "By Saint Peter of Rome!
I have a half-acre to plow by the highway;
Had I plowed this half-acre and afterwards sown it
I'd go along with you and teach you the way."
5   "That would be a long delay," said a lady in a veil,
"What should we women work on meanwhile?"
    "I appeal to you for your profit," said Piers to the ladies,
"That some sew the sack to keep the wheat from spilling,
And you worthy women with your long fingers
10 That you have silk and sandal[2] to sew when you've time
Chasubles° for chaplains to the church's honor.   *robes*
Wives and widows spin wool and flax;
Conscience counsels you to make cloth
To benefit the poor and for your own pleasure.
15 For I shall see to their sustenance, unless the land fail,
As long as I live, for love of the Lord of heaven.
And all manner of men who live off the land
Help him work well who obtains your food."
    "By Christ," said a knight then, "he teaches us the best;
20 But truly on the plow theme I was never taught.
I wish I knew how," said the knight, "by Christ and his mother;

---

1. A nickname for Piers, or Peter.   2. A thin, rich form of silk.

Plowmen, from the *Luttrell Psalter*, early 14th century.

I'd try it sometime for fun as it were."
    Certainly, sir knight," said Piers then,
"I shall toil and sweat and sow for us both
25   And labor for those you love all my lifetime,
On condition you protect Holy Church and me
From wasters and wicked men who spoil the world,
And go hunt hardily for hares and foxes,
Boars and bucks that break down my hedges,
30   And train your falcons to kill the wild birds
Because they come to my croft° and defile my corn."°   *field / grain*
    Courteously the knight then commenced with these words:
"By my power, Piers, I pledge you my truth
To defend you faithfully, though I should fight."
35   "And still one point," said Piers, "I ask of you further:
Try not to trouble any tenant unless Truth agrees
And when you fine any man let Mercy be assessor
And Meekness your master, despite Meed's moves.
And though poor men offer you presents and gifts
40   Don't take them on the chance you're not deserving,
For it may be you'll have to return them or pay for them dearly.
Don't hurt your bondman, you'll be better off;
Though he's your underling here, it may happen in heaven
He'll be sooner received and more honorably seated.
    Friend, go up higher[3]
45   At church in the charnel[4] it's hard to discern churls
Or between knight and knave or a queen on a corner[5] and one on the
       throne.
It becomes you, knight, to be courteous and gracious,
True of tongue and loth to hear tales
Unless they're about goodness, battles, or good faith.

3. Luke 14.10.   5. I.e., "queen," a prostitute.
4. Crypt for dead bodies.

50   Don't keep company with crude-mouths or listen to their stories,
And especially at your meals avoid such men
For they are the Devil's entertainers and draw men to sin.
And do not oppose Conscience or the rights of Holy Church."
"I assent, by Saint Giles," said the knight then,
55   "To work by your wisdom and my wife, too."
"And I shall dress myself," said Perkin, "in pilgrims' fashion
And go with all those who wish to live in Truth."

* * *

Now Perkin and these pilgrims go to their plowing;
Many helped him to turn over the half-acre.
Ditchers and diggers dug up the strip-ridges;
115   All this pleased Perkin and he paid them good wages.
Other workmen were there who worked very hard,
Each man in his way made himself useful
And some to please Perkin picked weeds in the field.
At high prime, about nine[6] Piers let the plow stand
120   And oversaw them himself; whoever worked best
Would later be hired when harvest time comes.
And then, some sat down and sang at ale
And helped plow this half-acre with a "hey trolliloly![7]
Said Piers the plowman in a pure anger:
125   "If you don't get up quickly and rush back to work
No grain that grows here will cheer you in need,
And though you die of grief, the devil take him who cares."
Then the phonies were frightened and pretended to be blind
And twisted their legs backwards as such losers know how
130   And moaned to Piers about how they couldn't work:
"And we pray for you Piers and for your plow, too,
That God for his grace multiply your grain
And reward you for the alms you give us here.
We may neither sweat nor strain, such sickness ails us,
135   Nor have we limbs to labor with, the Lord God we thank."
"Your prayers," said Piers, "if you were upright,
Might help, as I hope, but high Truth would
That no fakery were found in people that go begging.
You're wasters, I know well, and waste and devour
140   What true land-tilling men loyally work for.
But Truth shall teach you to drive his team
Or you'll eat barley bread and drink from the brook,
Unless he's blind or broken-legged or braced with iron—
Such poor," said Piers, "shall share in my goods,
145   Both of my corn and my cloth to keep them from want.
But anchorites and hermits who eat only at noon
And friars who don't flatter and poor sick people,
Hey! I and mine will provide for their needs."

---

6. Nine in the morning, after a substantial amount of   7. Probably the refrain of a popular song.
work has been done.

     Then Waster got angry and wanted to fight
150 And pressed Piers the plowman to "put 'em up!"
And told him to go piss with his plow, pigheaded creep!
A Breton came bragging and threatened Piers also:
"Whether you like it or not," he said, "we'll have our way,
And take your flour and meat whenever we like
155 And make merry with it, despite any grumbling."
     Piers the plowman then complained to the knight
To keep him and his property as they had agreed:
"Avenge me on these wasters who bring harm to the world;
Excommunication they take no account of nor fear Holy Church.
160 There will be no plenty," said Piers, "if the plow stands still."
     Then the knight, as was his nature, courteously
Warned Waster and advised him to improve:
"Or I'll beat you according to the law and put you in the stocks."
     "I'm not used to working," said Waster, "and I won't start now!"
165 And made light of the law and less of the knight
And sized up Piers as a pea to complain wherever he would.
     "Now by Christ," said Piers the plowman, "I'll punish you all,"
And whooped after Hunger who heard right away.
"I pray you," Piers said then, "Sir Hunger, *pour charite*[8]
170 Avenge me on these wasters, for the knight will not."
     Hunger in haste then grabbed Waster around the belly
And hugged him so tight that his eyes watered.
He battered the Breton about the cheeks
So that he looked like a lantern the rest of his life,
175 And he so beat both of them up he nearly busted their guts
Had not Piers with a peas-load[9] called him off.
"Have mercy on them, Hunger," said Piers, "and let me give them
    beans,
And what was baked for Bayard[1] may come to their relief."
     Then the fakers were frightened and flew into Piers' barns.
180 And flapped with flails from morning till evening,
So that Hunger was less intent on looking upon them.
For a potful of pottage that Piers' wife had made
A heap of hermits took up spades,
Dug and spread dung to despite Hunger.
185 They cut up their capes and made them short coats
And went as workmen to weeding and mowing
All for fear of death, so hard did Hunger hit.
The blind and broken-legged he bettered by the thousand
And lame men he healed with animal entrails.
190 Priests and other people drew towards Piers
And friars from all five orders,[2] all for fear of Hunger.
For what was baked for Bayard relieved many hungry,

8. For charity's sake.
9. Cheapest kind of bread, standard fare for the poor.
1. A generic name for a horse; a bread made of beans and bran was fed to horses.

2. See Prologue, n.8 (line 56) on the four orders. The fifth order referred to here may be the Crutched Friars, a minor order.

Dross and dregs were drink for many beggars.
There was no lad living that wouldn't bow to Piers
195 To be his faithful servant though he had no more
Than food for his labor and his gift at noon.
    Then Piers was proud and put them all to work
At daubing and digging, at dung bearing afield,
At threshing, at thatching, at whittling pins,
200 At every kind of true craft that man can devise.
There was no beggar so bold, unless he were blind,
Dared oppose what Piers said for fear of Sir Hunger.
And Piers was proud of that and put them all to work
And gave them food and money according to their deserts.
205   Then Piers had pity for all poor people
And bade Hunger hurry up out of the country
Back home to his own yard and stay there forever.

* * *

    "I promise you," said Hunger, "I won't go away
Before I have this day both dined and drunk."
    "I've no penny," said Piers, "with which to buy pullets,
Nor goose or pork but two green cheeses
305 And a few curds and cream and an oat cake
And bean and pea bread for my kids.
And still I say, by my soul, I've no salt bacon
Nor any egg, by Christ, to fry up together.
But I have leeks, parsley and scallions,
310 Chives and chervil and half-ripe cherries,
And a cow with a calf and a cart-mare
To draw my dung afield during dry spells.
And we must live by this means of life till Lammas time[3]
And by then I hope to have harvest in my fields;
315 Then may I make dinner just as I like."
    All the poor people then fetched peascods;
Beans and baked apples they brought by the lapful,
And offered Piers this present with which to please Hunger.
Hunger ate it all in haste and asked for more.
320 For fear then poor folk fed Hunger quickly
With cream and curds, with cress and other herbs.
By then harvest drew near and new corn came to market
And people were happy and fed Hunger deliciously,
And then Glutton with good ale put Hunger to sleep.
325   And then Waster refused to work and wandered around,
Nor'd any beggar eat bread in which there were beans,
But the finest white breads and of pure wheat,
Nor no way would they drink half-penny ale
But the best and brownest that brewsters sell.
330 Laborers with no land to live on but their own hands

---

3. The harvest festival, August 1, when a loaf made from the first wheat of the season was offered at mass.

Wouldn't deign to dine today on last night's veggies;
No penny-ale or piece of bacon pleased them
But it had to be fresh meat or fish, fried or baked,
And that *chaud* or *plus chaud*[4] against a chilled stomach.
335 And unless he's hired for high pay he'll otherwise argue
And curse the time he was made a workman.
He begins to grumble against Cato's counsel:
Paupertatis onus pacienter ferre memento.[5]
And then he curses the king and all his justices
340 For teaching such laws that grieve workingmen[6]
But as long as Hunger was master none of them would bitch,
Nor strive against his statute, he looked so stern.
      I warn you workmen, get ahead while you can,
For Hunger's hurrying this way fast as he can.
345 He shall awake through water, wasters to punish,
And before a few years finish famine shall arise,
And so says Saturn[7] and sends us warning.
Through floods and foul weather fruits shall fail;
Pride and pestilence shall take out many people.
350 Three ships and a sheaf with an 8 following
Shall bring bane and battle under both halves of the moon.
And then death shall withdraw and dearth be the judge
And Dave the ditcher° die of hunger   *ditch-digger*
Unless God of his goodness grant us a truce.

Passus 20
[THE CRUCIFIXION AND THE HARROWING OF HELL]

Wool-shirted and wet-shoed I went forth after
Like a careless man who takes no care of sorrow,
And tramped forth like a vagrant all my lifetime
Till I grew weary of the world and wanted to sleep again
5 And lay down till Lent and slept a long time.
      I dreamed a great deal of children and of *gloria laus*[1]
And how to instruments elder folks sang osanna.°   *Hosanna*
One who resembled the Samaritan and Piers the plowman
      somewhat
Barefoot came riding bootless on an ass's back
10 Without spurs or spear—sprightly he looked,
As is natural for a knight who came to be dubbed,
To get his gilt spurs and cut-away shoes.
And then Faith was in a window and cried, "A, *filii Dauid*"[2]

---

4. Hot or very hot.
5. Remember to bear your burden of poverty patiently. From Cato's *Distichs*, a collection of phrases used to teach Latin to beginning students.
6. A reference to the Statutes of Laborers, passed after 1351, when the Black Death depopulated the countryside and a labor shortage ensued. They were intended to control the mobility and the wages of laborers.

7. Planet thought to influence the weather, generally perceived to be hostile.
1. "Glory, praise [and honor]": the first words of an anthem sung by children on Palm Sunday. This part of the poem reflects the biblical account of Christ's entry into Jerusalem.
2. On the first Palm Sunday, crowds greeted Christ crying "Hosanna [line 7] to the son of David."

As a herald of arms does when adventurous knights come to jousts.
15   Old Jews of Jerusalem sang for joy,
     Blessed is he that cometh in the name of the Lord.[3]
   Then I asked Faith what all this activity meant,
And who should joust in Jerusalem? "Jesus," he said,
"And fetch what the Fiend claims, the fruit of Piers the plowman."
"Is Piers in this place?" I said, and he looked at me knowingly:
20   "*Liberum-dei-arbitrium*"[4] has for love undertaken
That this Jesus for his gentility will joust in Piers' armor,
In his helmet and in his mail, *humana natura;*[5]
So that Christ not be known as *consummatus deus,*[6]
In the plate-armor of Piers the plowman this cavalier will ride,
25   For no dent will damage him as *in deitate patris.*"[7]
    "Who will joust with Jesus," I said, "Jews or scribes?"[8]
    "No," Faith said, "but the Fiend and False-doom-to-die.
Death says he will undo and bring down
All that live or look on land or in water.
30   Life says he lies and lays his life as pledge,
That for all Death can do, within three days, he'll walk
And fetch from the Fiend the fruit of Piers the plowman,
And lay it wherever he likes and Lucifer bind
And beat down death and bring death to death forever.
    O death, I will be thy death, thy bite!"[9]
35   Then came Pilate with many people, *sedens pro tribunali,*[1]
To see how doughtily Death would do and to judge both their
     rights.
The Jews and the justices were against Jesus,
And all the court cried "*Crucifige*"[2] loud.
Then a prosecutor appeared before Pilate and said.
40   "This Jesus made jokes and despised our Jewish Temple,
To demolish it in one day, and in three days after
Rebuild it anew—here he stands who said it—
And still make it as sizable in all ways,
Both as long and as large, aloft and on ground,
45   And as broad as it was ever; this we all heard."
"*Crucifige*" said a court officer, "he practices witchcraft."
"*Tolle, Tolle!*"[3] said another, and took sharp thorns
And began to make of green thorns a garland
And set it roughly on his head, and then hatefully said,
50   "*Aue, raby,*[4] that scoundrel said, and poked reeds at his eyes;
And they nailed him with three nails naked upon a cross

3. Matthew 21.9.
4. The Free Will of God.
5. In the Incarnation Christ assumed human nature, to suffer humankind.
6. The perfect (triune) God.
7. In the godhead of the Father: as God Christ could not suffer, but as man he could.
8. Scribes were persons who made a strict literal interpretation of the Old Law and hence rejected Christ's teaching of the New.
9. Hosea 13.14.
1. Sitting as a judge (Matthew 27.19).
2. Crucify! (John 19.6).
3. "Away with him! Away with him!" (John 19.15).
4. "Hail, Rabbi [i.e., Master]" (Matthew 26.49): the words Judas spoke when he kissed Christ to identify him to the arresting officers.

And with a pole put poison up to his lips
And bade him drink, to delay his death and lengthen his days,
And said, "If he's subtle, he'll help himself now;"
55   And "If you're Christ—and Christ, God's Son—
Come down from this cross and then we'll believe!
That Life loves you and won't let you die."
     "*Consummatum est*,"[5] said Christ and started to swoon.
Piteously and pale, like a dying prisoner,
60   The Lord of Life and Light then laid his eyes together.
For dread the day withdrew and dark became the sun;
The wall of the Temple split apart all to pieces,
The hard rock completely riven, and darkest night it seemed.
The earth shivered and shook as if it were alive
65   And dead men for that din came out of deep graves
And told why the storm had lasted so long:
"For a bitter battle," the dead body said;
"Life and Death in this darkness destroy one another,
And no man will know for sure who shall have the mastery
70   Before Sunday, around sunrise," and sank with that to earth.
Some said he was God's Son who died so fairly,
     Indeed this was the Son of God,[6]
And some said, "He's a sorcerer; good that we test
Whether he's dead or not dead before he's taken down."
     At that time two thieves suffered death
75   Upon crosses beside Christ, such was the common law.
A court officer came and cracked their legs in two
And the arms after of each of those thieves.
But there was no punk so bold as to touch God's body;
Because he was a knight and a king's son, Kind[7] fully granted that time
80   That no punk had nerve enough to touch him in dying.
     But a blind knight with a sharply honed spear came forth,
Named Longinus,[8] as the record shows, and he had long lost his sight;
Before Pilate and the other people in the place he waited in readiness.
Over his protests he was forced at that time
85   To joust with Jesus, this blind Jew Longinus;
For they were all gutless who hovered or stood there
To touch him or contact him or take him down and bury him,
Except this blind bachelor, who pierced him through the heart.
The blood sprang down the spear and spread open the knight's eyes.
90   Then the knight fell straight on his knees and cried Jesus mercy—
"It was against my will," he said, "that I was made to wound you."
And sighed and said, "Sorely I repent it,
For the deed that I've done I put myself in your grace.
Both my land and my body take at your pleasure,
95   And have mercy on me, rightful Jesus!" and right with that he wept.

---

5. "It is finished" (John 19.30).
6. Matthew 27.54.
7. Nature (an aspect of God).

8. Longinus appears in the apocryphal Gospel of Nicodemus, which was the principal source of this account of Christ's harrowing of hell.

Then Faith began fiercely to upbraid the false Jews[9]
Called them low-down no-goods, accursed forever:
"For this was a vile villainy; may vengeance befall you
Who made the blind beat the dead—this was a punk's doing!
100   Cursed low-downs! It was never knighthood
To beat a bound body with any bright weapon.
Yet he's taken the prize for all his great wounds,
For your champion rider, chief knight of you all,
Surrendered crying out defeat, right at the will of Jesus.
105   When this darkness passes, Death shall be vanquished,
And you clowns have lost, for Life shall have mastery,
And your unstinted freedom fall into servitude,
And all your children, churls, will never achieve prosperity,
Nor have lordship over land or any land to till,
110   And as barren be, and live by usury,
Which is a life that our Lord forbids in all laws.
Now your good times are over, as Daniel told you,
When Christ through the cross overcame, your kingdom will fall apart.
      When the holy of holies comes, it ceases, etc."[1]
      What for fear of wonder and of the false Jews
115   I withdrew in that darkness to *descendit ad inferna,*[2]
And there I surely saw, *secundum scripturas,*[3]
Out of the west, as it were, a young woman, as I thought,
Came walking on the way, hellward she looked.
Mercy that maid was named, a mild thing as well
120   And a very good-willed maiden and modest of speech.
Her sister, as it seemed, came walking softly
Squarely out of the east, and westward she was headed,
A comely and pure creature, Truth was her name.
Because of the virtue that followed her, she was never afraid.
125   When these maidens met, Mercy and Truth,
They asked each other about this great wonder,
About the din and the darkness and how the day dawned,
And what a light and a shining lay before hell.
      "I'm astonished by this business, in faith," said Truth,
130   "And I'm coming to discover what this wonder means."
      "Don't marvel at it," said Mercy, "joy is its meaning.
A maid called Mary, and mother without contact
With any kind of creature, conceived through speech
And grace of the Holy Ghost, grew great with child,
135   Without womanly spot brought him into this world;
And that my tale is true I take God to witness.
Since this baby was born thirty winters have passed,
Died and suffered death this day about midday;
And that is the cause of this eclipse that now shuts out the sun,

---

9. This and the next 18 lines are an example of late
medieval antisemitism.
1. Compare with Daniel 9.24.

2. He descended into hell (from the Apostles' Creed)
3. According to the Scriptures.

140 In meaning that man shall be drawn out of murkiness
While this light and this beam will blind Lucifer.
For patriarchs and prophets have preached of this often,
That what was lost through a tree, a tree shall win back,[4]
And what death brought down, death shall raise up."

145   "What you're saying," said Truth, "Is nothing but hot air!
For Adam and Eve and Abraham with other
Patriarchs and prophets who lie in pain,
Never believe that yonder light will lift them up
Or have them out of hell—hold your tongue, Mercy!

150 What you're saying is just a trifle; I, Truth, know the truth,
That a thing that's once in hell never comes out.
Job the perfect patriarch discredits your sayings:
    Because there is no redemption in hell."[5]
    Then Mercy most mildly mouthed these words:
"From experience," she said, "I hope they'll be saved;

155 For venom undoes venom, from which I fetch proof
That Adam and Eve shall have remedy.
Of all devouring venoms the vilest is the scorpion's;
No medicine may amend the place where it stings
Until it's dead and applied thereto, and then it destroys

160 The first poisoning through its own virtue.
And so this death shall undo, I'll bet my life,
All that Death and the Devil first did to Eve.
And just as the deceiver through deceit deceived men first,
So shall grace, which began all, make a good end

165 And deceive the deceiver, and that's a good deception:
    It takes a trick to undo a trick."[6]
    "Now let's just hold it," said Truth; "it seems to me I see
Out of the nip° of the north, not very far from here,   *chill*
Righteousness come running. Let's take it easy,
For she knows more than we—she was before we both were."

170   "That's true," said Mercy, "and I see here to the south
Where Peace, clothed in patience, comes ready to play;
Love has desired her long—I believe none other
But Love has sent her some letter about what this light means
That hovers over hell thus; she'll tell us."

175   When Peace, clothed in patience, approached them both,
Righteousness reverenced Peace in her rich clothing
And prayed Peace tell her to what place she was going
And whom she meant to gladden in her gay garments.
    "My wish is to go," said Peace, "and welcome them all

180 Who for many a day I could not see for murkiness of sin,
Adam and Eve and many others in hell.
Moses and many more will sing merrily

---

4. The first tree bore the fruit that Adam and Eve ate, thereby damaging humankind; the second tree is the cross on which Christ was crucified, thereby redeeming humankind.
5. Compare with Job 7.9.
6. From a hymn sung on Palm Sunday.

And I'll dance to their tune—do the same, sister!
For Jesus jousted well, joy begins to dawn.
   In the evening weeping shall have place, and in the morning gladness.[7]
185   Love, who is my lover, sent me such letters
That my sister Mercy and I shall save mankind,
And that God has forgiven and granted to all mankind
Mercy, my sister, and me to bail them all out;
And that Christ has converted the nature of righteousness
190   Into peace and pity out of his pure grace.
Look, here's the letter patent![8] said Peace, *"in pace in idipsum—*
And that this deed shall endure—*dormiam et requiescam."*[9]
   "Do you rave?" said Righteousness, "or are you just drunk!
Do you believe that yonder light might unlock hell
195   And save man's soul? Sister, never believe it!
At the world's beginning, God gave the judgment himself
That Adam and Eve and all their issue
Should downright die and dwell in pain forever
If they touched that tree and ate of its fruit.
200   Afterwards Adam against his prohibition
Ate of the fruit and forsook, as it were,
The love of our Lord and his teachings, too,
And followed what the Fiend taught and his flesh's will,
Against reason; I, Righteousness, record this with Truth
205   That their pain is perpetual—no prayer can help them.
Therefore let them chew as they chose and let's not fight about it,
     sisters,
For it is care past cure, the bite that they ate."
   "And I shall prove," said Peace, "their pain must end,
And finally their woe must turn into well-being.
210   For had they known no woe, they'd not know well-being;
For no one knows well-being who never suffered woe,
Nor what hot hunger is who never was famished.
Who could naturally describe with color
If all the world were white or all things swan-white?
215   If there were no night, I believe no man
Should really know what day means;
Or had God suffered at the hands of some one other than himself,
He'd never have known for sure whether death is sour or sweet.
For never would a very rich man, who lives in rest and health,
220   Know what woe is if there were no natural death.
So God, who began all, of his good will
Became man of a maiden, to save mankind,
And suffered to be sold to see the sorrow of dying,
Which unknits all care and is the beginning of rest.
225   For until plague meets with us, I give you assurance,
Nobody knows, as I see it, the meaning of enough.

---

7. Psalms 29.6.
8. Document conferring authority.

9. In peace in the self-same: . . . I will find rest (Psalms 4.9).

Therefore, God of his goodness the first man Adam
Set up in first solace and in sovereign joy;
And then suffered him to sin, in order to feel sorrow,
230   To know thereby what well-being was, to understand it naturally.
And afterward, God ventured himself and took Adam's nature
To know what he had suffered in three different places,
Both in heaven and on earth—and now to hell he heads,
To know what all woe is, he who knew all joy.
     But prove all things; hold fast that which is good.[1]
235   So it shall go for these folk: their folly and their sin
Shall teach them what love is and bliss without end.
For nobody knows what war is where peace rules
Nor what is real well-being till he's taught by woe-is-me."
     Then there was a person with two broad eyes;[2]
240   Book that good father was named, a bold man of speech.
"By God's body," said this Book, "I will bear witness,
That when this baby was born a star blazed
So that all the wise men in the world fully agreed
That such a baby was born in Bethlehem city
245   Who should save man's soul and destroy sin.
And all the elements," said the Book, "bear witness of this.
That he was God that made everything the sky showed first:
Those in heaven took *stella comata*[3]
And tended it like a torch to reverence his birth;
250   The light followed the Lord into the low earth.
The water witnessed that he was God, for he walked on it dry:
Peter the Apostle perceived his passage
And as he went on the water knew him well, and said,
     '*Lord, bid me come to thee.*'[4]
And oh, how the sun locked up her light in herself
255   When she saw him suffer, who made the sun and sea!
Oh, how the earth for heaviness that he would suffer
Quaked as if alive and the rocks cracked also!
Oh no, hell might not hold, but opened when God suffered
And let out Simeon's sons[5] to see him hang on cross.
     He should not see death.[6]
260   And now shall Lucifer believe it, loath though he be;
For Jesus comes yonder as a giant with an engine[7]
To break and beat down all that oppose him
And to have out of hell all those he pleases.
And yet I, Book, will be burnt if he not arise to life
265   And comfort all his kin and bring them out of care
And all joy of the Jews dissolve and despise,

1. 1 Thessalonians 5.21.
2. Book's two broad eyes suggest the Old and New Testaments.
3. Hairy star (i.e., comet).
4. Matthew 14.28.
5. According to the apocryphal Gospel of Nicodemus,
Simeon's sons were raised from the dead at the time of Christ's crucifixion.
6. Luke 2.26, which continues, "before he had seen the Christ the Lord."
7. A military device, perhaps like a giant slingshot.

And unless they revere this resurrection and honor the cross
And believe in a new law, be lost body and soul."
  "Quiet," said Truth: "I both hear and see

270 A spirit speaks to hell and bids the gates be opened."
  Lift up your gates.[8]
  A loud voice within that light said to Lucifer:
"*Princepes*° of this place, quickly undo these gates,   *Princes*
For he comes here with crown, the king of all glory!"
  Then Satan[9] sighed and said to Hell,

275 "Such a light against our leave fetched away Lazarus;[1]
Care and encumbrance is come to us all.
If this king comes in, he'll fetch mankind
And lead it where Lazarus is and bind me easily.
Patriarchs and prophets have long talked of this

280 That such a lord and light shall lead them all hence.
But rise up, Ragamuffin, and hand over all the bars
That Belial your grandfather beat with your mother,
And I shall block this lord and stop his light.
Before we're blinded by this brightness, let's go bar the gates.

285 Let's check and chain and stop every chink
So that no light leaps in through louver or loophole.
Ashtaroth, call out, and have out our boys,
Colting and his kin to save the castle.
Boiling brimstone pour it out burning

290 All hot on their heads who come near the walls.
Set high tension cross bows and brazen guns
And shoot out enough shot to blind his squadron.
Set Mahmet[2] at the siege-engine and throw out millstones
And with hooks and caltrops[3] let's block them all!"

295 "Listen," said Lucifer, "for I know this lord;
Both this lord and this light, I knew him long ago.
No death may hurt this lord, nor devil's cunning,
And where he wills is his way—but let him beware the dangers:
If he deprives me of my rights, he robs me by a power play.

300 For by right and reason the crowd that is here
Belongs to me body and soul, both good and evil.
For he himself said it, who is Sire of heaven,
That Adam and Eve and all their issue
Should grievously die and dwell here forever

305 If they touched a tree or took an apple from it.
Thus this lord of light made such a law,
And since he is a loyal lord I can't believe
He'll deprive us of our rights, since reason damned them.
And since we've possessed them seven thousand winters

---

8. The first words from Psalms 23.9, which reads in the Latin Bible, "Lift up your gates, O princes, and be ye lifted up, ye everlasting doors, and the King of Glory shall come in."
9. Langland pictures hell as populated by a number of devils: Satan, Lucifer, Goblin, Belial, and Ashtaroth.
1. Compare with John 11.
2. Mohammed.
3. Iron balls with spikes meant to impede the progress of enemy cavalry.

310   Without any objections, and if now he begins,
    Then his word is deceitful, who is truth's witness."
        "That's true," said Satan, "but I sorely fear,
    For you got them with guile and broke into his garden;
    Against his love and his leave went into his land,
315   Not in a fiend's form but in form of an adder
    And enticed Eve to eat on her own—
      Woe to him that is alone![4]—
    And promised her and him then to know
    As two gods, with God, both good and evil.
    Thus with treason and treachery you bewitched them both
320   And made them break their obedience through false promises,
    And so you had them out and in here at the end."
        "It's not duly got where guile is the root,
    And God will not be duped," said Goblin, "or taken in.
    We have no true title to them, for your treason caused it.
325   I'm afraid, therefore," the Devil said, "lest Truth fetch them out.
    For as you beguiled God's image by going as an adder,
    So has God beguiled us all by going as a man.
    For God has gone," said Goblin, "in man's likeness
    These thirty winters, I believe, and went around preaching.
330   I've assailed him with sin, and sometimes asked
    Whether he was God or God's son? His answer was short.
    Thus he's rolled on like a proper man these thirty-two winters;
    And when I saw it was so, I contrived how I might
    Slow down those who loved him not, lest they martyr him.
335   I would have lengthened his life, for I believed, if he died,
    That if his soul came here it would destroy us all.
    For the body, while its bones walked, was ever about
    To teach men to be loyal and to love one another;
    Which life and law, should it be long in use,
340   It will undo us devils and bring us all down."
        "And now I see where his soul comes sailing this way
    With glory and great light—it's God, I know it.
    I advise we flee," said the Fiend, "straightaway from here,
    For it were better not to be than to abide in his sight.
345   Because of your lies, Lucifer, we first lost our joy,
    And your pride made us fall here out of heaven;
    Because we believed in your lies, we had to lose our bliss.
    And now, for a later lie you told Eve,
    We've lost our lordship on land and in hell.
      Now shall the prince of this world, etc."[5]
350   After Satan so rudely berated
    Lucifer for his lying, I believe none other
    But our Lord in the end rebuked liars here
    And blamed on them all the misery that is made here on earth.

---

4. Ecclesiastes 4.10.

5. John 12.31, continues "be cast out"; "prince of this world" is a title of the devil.

Take note, you wise clerks and you smart lawyers,
355   That you not mislead unlettered men, for David in the end
Witnesses in his writing what is the reward of liars:
  Thou hatest all workers of iniquity: thou wilt destroy all that speak a lie.[6]
(I've digressed a bit for the sake of lies,
To call them as I saw them, pursuing my theme!)
  For again that light commanded them unlock, and Lucifer
    answered.
360   "What lord are you?" asked Lucifer. A voice said aloud:
"The lord of might and main, that made all things.
Dukes of this dim place, undo these gates now
That Christ may come in, the son of heaven's king."
  And with that breath hell with all of Belial's bars broke;
365   Despite all prevention, the gates were wide open.
Patriarchs and prophets, *populus in tenebris*,[7]
Sang with Saint John, *"Ecce agnus dei!"*[8]
Lucifer could not look, so blinded him had the light,
And those whom our Lord loved with that light flowed forth.
370   "Now hear this," said our Lord, "both body and soul,
To live up to both our rights to all sinful souls.
Mine they were and of me; I may the better claim them.
Though reason recorded, and right of myself,
That if they ate the apple all should die,
375   I consigned them not here to hell forever.
For the deadly sin they did was caused by your deceit;
You got them with guile against all reason.
For in my palace, paradise, in an adder's person
You falsely fetched there those I happened to watch over,
380   Sweet-talked and deceived them and broke into my garden
Against my love and my leave. The Old Law teaches
That deceivers be deceived and fall in their guile,
And whoever knocks out a man's eye or else his front teeth
Or any manner member maims or hurts,
385   The same injury he'll have who strikes another so.
  Tooth for tooth and eye for eye.[9]
So a life shall lose life where a life has life destroyed,
So that life pays for life—the Old Law demands it;
Ergo,[1] soul shall pay for soul and sin counter sin,
And all that men did wrong, I became man to amend;
390   And that death my death destroys to relieve
And both revive and requite what was quenched through sin,
And guile be beguiled through grace in the end.
  It takes a trick to undo a trick.
  So do not believe it, Lucifer, that against the law I fetch
From here any sinful soul by a pure power play,

---

6. Psalms 5.7.
7. People in darkness (Matthew 4.16, citing Isaiah 9.2).
8. Behold the Lamb of God (John 1.36).

9. Matthew 5.38, citing Exodus 21.14.
1. "Therefore," a central term in scholastic argument, used to introduce the logical conclusion to an argument.

395   But through right and reason ransom here my servants.
       I am not come to destroy the law, but to fulfill it.[2]
      So what was gotten with guile, is now through grace won back.
      And as Adam and all through a tree died
      Adam and all through a tree shall return to life.
      And now your guile begins to turn back on you
400   And my grace to grow wider and wider.
      The bitterness you've brewed, enjoy it now yourself;
      You who are doctor of death, drink what you've mixed!
       For I who am Lord of life, love is my drink,
      And for that drink I died today, as it seemed.
405   But I will drink from no deep dish of learning
      But from the common cups of all Christian souls;
      But your drink becomes death and deep hell your bowl.
      I fought so, I thirst even more for the sake of man's soul.
       I thirst.[3]
      May no sweet wine or cider or precious drink
410   Fully wet my whistle or my thirst slake
      Till grape harvest time fall in the vale of Jehosaphat,[4]
      And I drink fully ripe new wine, *resureccio mortuorum.*[5]
      And then I shall come as king, with crown and with angels,
      And have out of hell all men's souls.
415   Fiends and fiendkins shall stand before me
      And be at my bidding, of bliss or of pain.
      But to be merciful to man then my nature demands,
      For we are brothers of one blood, but not all in baptism.
      But all that are my full brothers in blood and in baptism
420   Shall never come to hell again, once they are out.
       To thee only have I sinned, and have done evil before thee[6]
      It's not the practice on earth to hang any felons
      More often than once, though they were traitors.
      And if the king of the kingdom come in the time
      When a thief should suffer death or other sentence,
425   The law requires he grant him a reprieve if he sees him.
      And I who am King of Kings shall come at such time
      When doom damns to death all the wicked,
      And if law wills I look on them it lies within my grace
      Whether they die or die not, did they never so ill.
430   Be it to any extent paid for, the boldness of their sin,
      I may do mercy out of my righteousness and all my true words.
       For holy writ wills that I take satisfaction from those who did ill,
      As *nullum malum impunitum, et nullum bonum irremuneratum.*[7]
      And so on all the wicked I will take vengeance here.
435   And yet my kind nature in my keen anger shall constrain my will—

2. Matthew 5.17.
3. John 19.28.
4. On the evidence of Joel 3.2, 12, the Last Judgment was to take place at the Vale of Jehosaphat.
5. The resurrection of the dead (from the Nicene Creed).

6. Psalms 50.6.
7. [He is a just judge who leaves] no evil unpunished [and no good unrewarded] (from Pope Innocent III's tract *Of Contempt for the World*; see 4.143–44).

Rebuke me not, O Lord, in thy indignation[8]—
To be merciful to many of my half-brothers.
For blood may see blood both thirsty and cold
But blood may not see blood bleed without taking pity.
I heard secret words, which it is not granted to man to utter.[9]
But my righteousness and right shall reign in hell,
440   And mercy over all mankind before me in heaven.
For I'd be an unkind king unless I help my kin,
And namely in such need that needs to ask for help.
Enter not into judgment with thy servant.[1]
Thus by law," said our Lord, "I will lead out of here
The people I love and who believe in my coming.
445   But for the lies that you lied, Lucifer, to Eve
You shall bitterly abide," God said, and bound him with chains.
Ashtoreth and company hid in nooks and crannies,
They dared not look on our Lord, the least of them all,
But let him lead forth those he liked and leave behind whomever he
pleased.
450   Many hundreds of angels then harped and sang,
Flesh sins, flesh clears, flesh of God reigns as God.[2]
Then Peace piped a note of poetry:
After darkest clouds, the sun will shine bright;
And love shine brighter after every fight.[3]
455   "After sharpest showers," said Peace, "brightest is the sun;
There is no warmer weather than after watery clouds,
Nor any love dearer, nor dearer friends,
Than after war and wreckage when love and peace are masters.
There was never a war in this world nor wickeder envy
460   That Love, if he wanted to, could not turn it to laughter,
And Peace through patience stop all perils."
"Truce," said Truth, "You tell us the truth, by Jesus!
Let us kiss each other and clutch in covenant!"
"And let no people," said Peace, "perceive that we squabbled,
465   For nothing's impossible to him who is almighty."
"That's the truth," said Righteousness and kissed Peace
reverently,
And Peace her, *per secula seculorum.*[4]
Mercy and truth have met each other; justice and peace have kissed.[5]
Truth trumpeted then and sang *Te deum laudamus,*[6]
And then Love strummed a loud note on the lute,
Behold how good and how pleasant it is, etc.[7]
470   Till dawn the next day these damoiselles caroled
On which men rang bells for the resurrection, and right with that I
awoke

8. Psalms 37.2.
9. In 2 Corinthians 12.4, St. Paul tells of how in a mystical vision he was caught up to heaven, where he saw
things that cannot be repeated.
1. Psalms 142.2.
2. From a medieval Latin hymn.

3. From Alain de Lille, a 12th-century poet and philosopher.
4. Forever and ever (the liturgical formula).
5. Psalms 84.11.
6. We praise thee, God (a celebrated Latin hymn).
7. Psalms 132.1.

And called Kit my wife and my daughter Calote:
"Arise, and go reverence God's resurrection,
And creep on your knees to the cross and kiss it as a jewel
475   And most rightfully as a relic, none richer on earth.
For it bore God's blessed body for our good,
And it terrified the Fiend, for such is its might
No grisly ghost may glide in its shadow!"

❦ "PIERS PLOWMAN" AND ITS TIME ❦
The Rising of 1381

The event previously known as the "Peasants' Revolt" is generally referred to by today's historians as the "Rising of 1381," since it is now recognized that it included many members of the
commons who were not peasants but rather middle-class landholders, artisans, and so forth.
William Langland had a rather ambiguous relation to the rising, for while deploring the conditions that caused it, he refused to endorse its radical social program. When the rebels
invoked his character Piers as a cultural hero, he revised *Piers Plowman* for a second time (the
so-called C-text), thus disassociating himself from them. This section brings together a number of documents that record the events of the rising, and more importantly, reveal the sub-
jective responses of contemporary writers to it.

The causes of the rising were varied. Among them was the "Statute of Laborers" enacted
by Parliament in 1351 to freeze wages and restrict laborers' mobility, both of which had been
increasing as a result of the depopulation caused by the Black Death. The more immediate
catalyst, however, was a flat poll tax enacted in 1380, which hurt the poor disproportionately
and which the government collected in a particularly ruthless way.

The rising itself was astonishingly brief, beginning at the end of May 1381 and col-
lapsing by the end of July. From the prosperous southern counties of Essex and Kent the
rebels marched to London, swearing loyalty to one another and to Richard II. Their hostility was directed against the church hierarchy and the feudal lords rather than against the
monarchy. In London they burned the Savoy Palace, the local residence of the powerful
John of Gaunt, Duke of Lancaster and uncle of King Richard. The king, then only fourteen years old, found his advisers ineffectual, and so retreated with them to the Tower of
London.

Having agreed to meet the Essex contingent outside the city, at Mile End, the king
acceded to their demands of an end to villeinage (serfdom), and ordered his office of chancery
to make multiple copies of charters to that effect. During this meeting, some rebels broke into
the Tower of London and beheaded two of the most hated men in the kingdom, Simon
Sudbury (the king's chancellor and Archbishop of Canterbury) and Robert Hales (his treasurer).
Afterward, they displayed their heads on London Bridge, as a sign that they were traitors to
the commons.

The next day the king met with the Kentish rebels, again outside the city, at Smithfield.
Here their captain Wat Tyler demanded not only the abolition of villeinage but fixed rents,
partial disendowment of the church and dispersal of its goods to the poor, and punishment of
all "traitors" held to be responsible for the poll tax. In the course of a scuffle, the Lord Mayor
of London, William Walworth, stabbed Tyler and mortally wounded him; thereupon, the
king rode before the rebels and declared himself their new captain, successfully leading them
off the field.

Adam and Eve, detail of a misericord, c. 1379. Misericords were shallow seats in the choir stalls of medieval churches, on which worshipers could rest, still standing, during the long celebrations of the Mass and Daily Office. Their undersides were often carved with animal grotesques and scenes of common life, both seen in this depiction of Adam and Eve from a misericord in Worcester Cathedral. Eve spins and Adam digs, in a moment reminiscent of the couplet from John Ball's sermon: "Whan Adam dalf and Eve span, / who was thanne a gentilman?"

Tyler's death broke the will of the rebels, and the king promptly revoked the charters freeing the serfs. In a series of trials, he prosecuted the instigators, among them John Ball, the priest who had shortly before preached to the rebels at Blackheath the famous sermon challenging the division of society into three estates: "Whan Adam dalf and Eve span, / who was thanne a gentilman?" Ball was found guilty of treason, and drawn, hanged, and quartered. Aside from such punishments, there were few apparent effects of the rising, although the nobles and the clergy relented in their treatment of the commons, and in the long run, the institution of villeinage declined. For the ruling class itself, the rising caused intense anxiety. John Gower, in his allegorized account, *The Voice of One Crying*, reports hiding in the woods to escape the peasants. Like him, the monastic chroniclers like Thomas of Walsingham generally present the rebels as mad beasts.

What is perhaps most significant about the written reception of the rising is the languages—Latin, French, and English—in which it occurs. Like Gower's *Voice of One Crying*, the chronicles are generally written in Latin, although the *Anonimalle Chronicle*, from which a passage is included here, is in French. Langland and Chaucer wrote in English, while the short poem below, *The Course of Revolt*, is macaronic, alternating English lines with Latin ones. Although there is little written evidence in the voice of the rebels themselves (who were generally illiterate), there are two tantalizing scraps identified as John Ball's letters, written in English although embedded in hostile Latin chronicle accounts of Ball's trial and execution. It has been suggested recently that the most important fact about the rebel speeches and writings is their "vernacularity"—the fact that they appear in a language that the common people could understand.

from *The Anonimalle Chronicle*[1]
[*Wat Tyler's Demands to Richard II, and His Death*]

At this time a great body of the commons[2] went to the Tower of London to speak with the king. As they could not get a hearing from him, they laid siege to the Tower from the side of Saint Katherine's, towards the south. Another group of the commons, who were within the city, went to the Hospital of Saint John, Clerkenwell, and on their way they burned the place and houses of Roger Legett, questmonger,[3] who had been beheaded in Cheapside, as well as all the rented property and tenements of the Hospital of Saint John they could find. Afterwards they came to the beautiful priory of the said hospital, and set on fire several fine and pleasant buildings within it—a great and horrible piece of damage to the priory for all time to come. They then returned to London to rest or to do more mischief.

At this time the king was in a turret of the great Tower of London, and saw the manor of the Savoy[4] and the Hospital of Clerkenwell, and the houses of Simon Hosteler near Newgate, and John Butterwick's place, all in flames. He called all the lords about him into a chamber, and asked their counsel as to what should be done in such a crisis. But none of them could or would give him any counsel; and so the young king said that he would order the mayor of the city to command the sheriffs and aldermen to have it cried within their wards that everyone between the age of fifteen and sixty, on pain of life and limb, should go next morning (which was Friday) to Mile End, and meet him there at seven of the bell. He did this in order that all the commons who were stationed around the Tower would be persuaded to abandon the siege, and come to Mile End to see him and hear him, so that those who were in the Tower could leave safely at their will and save themselves as they wished. But it came to nothing, for some of them did not have the good fortune to be saved.

Later that Thursday, the said feast of Corpus Christi, the king, remaining anxiously and sadly in the Tower, climbed on to a little turret facing Saint Katherine's, where a large number of the commons were lying. He had it proclaimed to them that they should all go peaceably to their homes, and he would pardon them all their different offenses. But all cried with one voice that they would not go before they had captured the traitors within the Tower, and obtained charters to free them from all manner of serfdom, and certain other points which they wished to demand. The king benevolently granted their requests and made a clerk write a bill in their presence in these terms: "Richard, king of England and France, gives great thanks to his good commons, for that they have so great a desire to see and maintain their king; and he grants them pardon for all manner of trespasses and misprisions and felonies done up to this hour, and wills and commands that every one should now quickly return to his own home: He wills and commands that everyone should put his grievances in writing, and have them sent to him; and he will provide, with the aid of his loyal lords and his good council, such remedy as shall be profitable both to him and to them, and to the kingdom." He put his signet seal to this document in their presence and then sent the said bill by the hands of two of his knights to the

---

1. This gripping account describes the rebel Wat (Walter) Tyler's confrontation with the King. Written in French rather than Latin, *The Anonimalle Chronicle* is considered to be more contemporary and more balanced than judgmental Latin accounts like that of Thomas of Walsingham. Translated by R. B. Dobson.

2. The common people as opposed to the nobility or the clergy; the third estate.

3. One who made a business of conducting inquests.

4. The beautiful palace of John of Gaunt, the King's powerful uncle.

people around Saint Katherine's. And he caused it to be read to them, the man who read it standing up on an old chair above the others so that all could hear. All this time the king remained in the Tower in great distress of mind. And when the commons had heard the bill, they said that it was nothing but a trifle and mockery. Therefore they returned to London and had it cried around the city that all lawyers, all the men of the Chancery and the Exchequer and everyone who could write a writ or a letter should be beheaded,[5] wherever they could be found. At this time they burnt several more houses within the city. The king himself ascended to a high garret of the Tower to watch the fires; then he came down again, and sent for the lords to have their counsel. But they did not know how to advise him, and were surprisingly abashed.

On the next day, Friday, the commons of the country and the commons of London assembled in fearful strength, to the number of a hundred thousand or more, besides some four score who remained on Tower Hill to watch those who were within the Tower. Some went to Mile End, on the way to Brentwood, to wait for the king's arrival, because of the proclamation that he had made. But others came to Tower Hill, and when the king knew that they were there, he sent them orders by a messenger to join their companions at Mile End, saying that he would come to them very soon. And at this time of the morning he advised the archbishop of Canterbury and the others who were in the Tower, to go down to the little water-gate, and take a boat and save themselves. And the archbishop proceeded to do this; but a wicked woman raised a cry against him, and he had to turn back to the Tower, to his own confusion.

And by seven of the bell the king himself came to Mile End, and with him his mother in a carriage, and also the earls of Buckingham, Kent, Warwick and Oxford, as well as Sir Thomas Percy, Sir Robert Knolles, the mayor of London and many knights and squires; and Sir Aubrey de Vere carried the royal sword. And when the king arrived and the commons saw him, they knelt down to him, saying "Welcome our Lord King Richard, if it pleases you, and we will not have any other king but you." And Wat Tyghler, their master and leader, prayed on behalf of the commons that the king would suffer them to take and deal with all the traitors against him and the law. The king granted that they should freely seize all who were traitors and could be proved to be such by process of law. The said Walter and the commons were carrying two banners as well as pennons and pennoncels[6] while they made their petition to the king. And they required that henceforward no man should be a serf nor make homage or any type of service to any lord, but should give four pence for an acre of land. They asked also that no one should serve any man except at his own will and by means of regular covenant. And at this time the king had the commons arrayed in two lines, and had it proclaimed before them that he would confirm and grant that they should be free, and generally should have their will; and that they could go through all the realm of England and catch all traitors and bring them to him in safety, and then he would deal with them as the law demanded.

Because of this grant Wat Tyghler and the commons took their way to the Tower, to seize the archbishop and the others while the king remained at Mile End. Meanwhile the archbishop had sung his mass devoutly in the Tower, and confessed

5. Chancery held the archives of public record and the Exchequer dealt with the collection of revenue. The Latin chroniclers saw the rising as a threat to writing itself; Thomas of Walsingham, for example, reports that the rebels gleefully burned records they saw as guaranteeing the lords' legal power over them.
6. Small flags and streamers borne on a lance.

the prior of the Hospital of Clerkenwell and others; and then he heard two or three masses and chanted the *Commendatio,* and the *Placebo* and *Dirige,* and the Seven Psalms, and the Litany; and when he was at the words "*Omnes sancti orate pro nobis*" [All saints pray for us], the commons entered and dragged him out of the chapel of the Tower, and struck and hustled him roughly, as they did also the others who were with him, and led them to Tower Hill. There they cut off the heads of Master Simon of Sudbury, archbishop of Canterbury, of Sir Robert Hales,[7] High Prior of the Hospital of Saint John's of Clerkenwell, Treasurer of England, of Brother William of Appleton, a great physician and surgeon, and one who had much influence with the king and the duke of Lancaster. And some time after they beheaded John Legge, the king's serjeant-at-arms, and with him a certain juror. At the same time the commons had it proclaimed that whoever could catch any Fleming[8] or other aliens of any nation, might cut off their heads; and so they did accordingly. Then they took the heads of the archbishop and of the others and put them on wooden poles, and carried them before them in procession through all the city as far as the shrine of Westminster Abbey, to the contempt of themselves, of God and of Holy Church: for which reason vengeance descended on them shortly afterwards. Then they returned to London Bridge and set the head of the archbishop above the gate, with the heads of eight others they had executed, so that all who passed over the bridge could see them. This done, they went to the church of Saint Martin's in the Vintry, and found therein thirty-five Flemings, whom they dragged outside and beheaded in the street. On that day there were beheaded 140 or 160 persons. Then they took their way to the places of Lombards and other aliens, and broke into their houses, and robbed them of all their goods that they could discover. So it went on for all that day and the night following with hideous cries and horrible tumult.

At this time, because the Chancellor had been beheaded, the king made the earl of Arundel Chancellor for the day, and entrusted him with the Great Seal; and all that day he caused various clerks to write out charters, patents, and letters of protection, granted to the commons in consequence of the matters before mentioned, without taking any fines for the sealing or transcription.

On the next day, Saturday, great numbers of the commons came into Westminster Abbey at the hour of Tierce,[9] and there they found John Imworth, Marshal of the Marshalsea and warden of the prisoners, a tormentor without pity; he was near the shrine of Saint Edward, embracing a marble pillar, hoping for aid and succor from the saint to preserve him from his enemies. But the commons wrenched his arms away from the pillar of the shrine, and dragged him into Cheap, and there beheaded him. And at the same time they took from Bread Street a valet named John of Greenfield, merely because he had spoken well of Brother William Appleton and the other murdered persons; and they brought him into Cheap and beheaded him. All this time the king was having it cried through the city that every one should go peaceably to his own country and his own house, without doing more mischief; but to this the commons would not agree.

And on this same day, at three hours after noon, the king came to Westminster Abbey and about two hundred persons with him. The abbot and convent of the said

---

7. Sudbury and Hales were especially hated by the rebels—the former, as chancellor of England, for instituting the poll tax, and the latter, as treasurer, for collecting it.
8. Immigrants from Flanders, who had become wealthy in the London wool trade; they were particular targets of the rebels (see Chaucer, *The Nun's Priest's Tale,* line 576).
9. The third of seven canonical "hours" around which clerics organized their day; usually, the third hour after sunrise.

abbey, and the canons and vicars of Saint Stephen's Chapel, came to meet him in procession, clothed in their copes and their feet bare, halfway to Charing Cross; and they brought him to the abbey, and then to the high altar of the church. The king made his prayers devoutly, and left an offering for the altar and the relics. Afterwards he spoke with the anchorite,[1] and confessed to him, and remained with him some time. Then the king caused a proclamation to be made that all the commons of the country who were still within the city should come to Smithfield[2] to meet him there; and so they did.

And when the king with his retinue arrived there, he turned to the east, in a place before Saint Bartholomew's a house of canons: and the commons arrayed themselves in bands of great size on the west side. At this moment the mayor of London, William of Walworth, came up, and the king ordered him to approach the commons, and make their chieftain come to him. And when he was called by the mayor, this chieftain, Wat Tyghler of Maidstone by name, approached the king with great confidence, mounted on a little horse so that the commons might see him. And he dismounted, holding in his hand a dagger which he had taken from another man; and when he had dismounted he half bent his knee and took the king by the hand, shaking his arm forcefully and roughly, saying to him, "Brother, be of good comfort and joyful, for you shall have, in the fortnight that is to come, forty thousand more commons than you have at present, and we shall be good companions." And the king said to Walter, "Why will you not go back to your own country?" But the other answered, with a great oath, that neither he nor his fellows would leave until they had got their charter as they wished to have it with the inclusion of certain points which they wished to demand. Tyghler threatened that the lords of the realm would rue it bitterly if these points were not settled at the commons' will. Then the king asked him what were the points which he wished to have considered, and he should have them freely and without contradiction, written out and sealed. Thereupon the said Wat rehearsed the points which were to be demanded; and he asked that there should be no law except for the law of Winchester[3] and that henceforward there should be no outlawry[4] in any process of law, and that no lord should have lordship in future, but it should be divided among all men, except for the king's own lordship. He also asked that the goods of Holy Church should not remain in the hands of the religious, nor of parsons and vicars, and other churchmen; but that clergy already in possession should have a sufficient sustenance and the rest of their goods should be divided among the people of the parish. And he demanded that there should be only one bishop in England and only one prelate, and all the lands and tenements of the possessioners should be taken from them and divided among the commons, only reserving for them a reasonable sustenance. And he demanded that there should be no more villeins[5] in England, and no serfdom nor villeinage but that all men should be free and of one condition. To this the king gave an easy answer, and said that Wat should have all that he could fairly grant, reserving only for himself the regality of his crown. And then he ordered him to go back to his own home, without causing further delay.

During all the time that the king was speaking, no lord or counselor dared or wished to give answer to the commons in any place except for the king himself. Presently Wat Tyghler, in the presence of the king, sent for a jug of water to rinse his mouth, because of the great heat that he felt; and as soon as the water was

---

1. A religious recluse who lived enclosed in a tiny dwelling.
2. An area outside the walls of the city of London.
3. The reference is unclear; it may refer to a claim by the rebels to the rights of tenants on royal lands.
4. Condition of being outside traditional legal protection.
5. Serfs tied to the land; bondmen.

brought he rinsed out his mouth in a very rude and villainous manner before the king. And then he made them bring him a jug of ale, and drank a great draught, and then, in the presence of the king, climbed on his horse again. At that time a certain valet from Kent, who was among the king's retinue, asked to see the said Wat, chieftain of the commons. And when he saw him, he said aloud that he was the greatest thief and robber in all Kent. Wat heard these words, and commanded the valet to come out to him, shaking his head at him as a sign of malice; but Wat himself refused to go to him for fear that he had of the others there. But at last the lords made the valet go out to Wat, to see what the latter would do before the king. And when Wat saw him he ordered one of his followers, who was mounted on horseback and carrying a banner displayed, to dismount and behead the said valet. But the valet answered that he had done nothing worthy of death, for what he had said was true, and he would not deny it, although he could not lawfully debate the issue in the presence of his liege lord, without leave, except in his own defense: but that he could do without reproof, for whoever struck him would be struck in return. For these words Wat wanted to strike the valet with his dagger, and would have slain him in the king's presence; but because he tried to do so, the mayor of London, William of Walworth, reasoned with the said Wat for his violent behavior and contempt, done in the king's presence, and arrested him. And because he arrested him, the said Wat stabbed the mayor with his dagger in the body in great anger. But, as it pleased God, the mayor was wearing armor and took no harm, but like a hardy and vigorous man drew his dagger and struck back at the said Wat, giving him a deep cut in the neck, and then a great blow on the head. And during this scuffle a valet of the king's household drew his sword, and ran Wat two or three times through the body, mortally wounding him. Wat spurred his horse, crying to the commons to avenge him, and the horse carried him some four score paces, and then he fell to the ground half dead. And when the commons saw him fall, and did not know for certain how it happened, they began to bend their bows and to shoot. Therefore the king himself spurred his horse, and rode out to them, commanding them that they should all come to him at the field of Saint John of Clerkenwell.

Meanwhile the mayor of London rode as hastily as he could back to the city, and commanded those who were in charge of the twenty-four wards to have it cried round their wards, that every man should arm himself as quickly as he could, and come to the king's aid in Saint John's Fields, where the commons were, for he was in great trouble and necessity. But at this time almost all of the knights and squires of the king's household, and many others, were so frightened of the affray that they left their liege lord and went each his own way.

Afterwards, when the king had reached the open fields, he made the commons array themselves on the west side. And presently the aldermen came to him in a body, bringing with them the keepers of the wards arrayed in several bands, a fine company of well-armed men in great strength. And they enveloped the commons like sheep within a pen. Meanwhile, after the mayor had sent the keepers of the town on their way to the king, he returned with a good company of lances to Smithfield in order to make an end of the captain of the commons. And when he came to Smithfield he failed to find there the said captain Wat Tyghler, at which he marveled much, and asked what had become of the traitor. And he was told that Wat had been carried by a group of the commons to the hospital for the poor near Saint Bartholomew's, and put to bed in the chamber of the master of the hospital. The mayor went there and found him, and had him carried out to the middle of Smithfield, in the presence of his companions, and had him beheaded. And so ended his wretched life. But the mayor had his head set on a pole and carried before him to the king, who still remained in the field. And when the king saw the head he had it brought near him to subdue the commons, and thanked the mayor greatly for what he had done. And when the commons saw that their chieftain, Wat Tyghler, was dead in such a manner, they fell to the ground there among the corn, like beaten men, imploring the king for mercy for their misdeeds. And the king benevolently granted them mercy, and most of them took to flight.

Three Poems on the Rising of 1381
John Ball's First Letter[1]

John Ball Saint Mary Priest, greeteth well all manner of men, and biddeth them in name of the Trinitie, Father, Sonne, & holy Ghost, stand manlike together in truth, & helpe truth, and truth shall helpe you:

> now raygneth pride in price,
> couetise° is holden° wise   *greed / held*
> lechery without shame,
> gluttonie without blame,
> enuye raygneth° with reason,   *reigns*
> and sloath is taken in great season,
> God doe boote° for nowe is time. Amen.   *make amends*

John Ball's Second Letter[2]

LITTERA IOHANNIS BALLE MISSA COMMUNIBUS ESTSEXIE
[THE LETTER OF JOHN BALL TO THE ESSEX COMMONS]

Iohan schep, som-tyme seynte marie prest of york, and now of colchestre, Greteth wel Iohan nameles & Iohn the mullere and Iohon cartere, and biddeth hem thei bee war of gyle [treachery] in borugh, and stondeth to-gidere in godes name, and biddeth Pers ploughman / go to his werk and chastise wel hobbe the robbere; and taketh with yow Iohan Trewman and alle hijs felawes and no mo, and loke schappe you to on heued[3] and no mo.

> Iohan the mullere hath y-grounde smal, smal, smal.
> The kynges sone of heuene schal paye for al.
> be war or the be wo.°   *beware or be sorry*
> knoweth your freend fro your foo.

1. This and the piece following can only provisionally be called "poems," despite their rhymed couplets and sporadic alliteration. The court that tried and convicted Ball regarded them as actual directions to his followers, and modern scholarship has tended to concur. If so they are directions in code, for they are, in the words of one chronicler, "full of enigmas." In this poem the complaint about the seven deadly sins running rampant is conventional, but the conclusion, "God do bote for now is time" (God make amends, for now is the time) is highly unusual in its call to action. Significantly, the sin of anger is absent from the list.
2. According to the chronicle from which this "letter" was taken, Ball sent it to "the leaders of the commons in Essex . . . in order to urge them to finish what they had begun," and it was "afterwards found in the sleeve of a man about to be hanged for disturbing the peace." It appears

in Thomas Walsingham's Latin *Historia Anglicana*, where it is included as evidence of the treason for which Ball was hanged. In the prose introduction to the poem, John the "shep," priest of Colchester, is the assumed name of John Ball (as "pastor"), while John Carter and John the Miller are both generic occupational names often ascribed to the leaders of the rebels. The reference to "Pers Ploughman" in the poem's introduction indicates that the rebels interpreted Langland's conservative poem for their own purposes. It presents Piers not as Langland's patient laborer, but as one who should get to his "work" of punishing "robbers," perhaps "Hobbe" (Robert) Hales, the treasurer of the king, beheaded by the rebels for his role in collecting the poll tax.
3. Take one head for yourself; possibly a reference to the rebels' loyalty to Richard II as opposed to the nobles.

haueth y-now & seith hoo!
and do wel and bettre and fleth° synne,   *flee*
and seketh pees and hold yow ther-inne.
and so biddeth Iohan trewaman and alle his felawes.

Hanc litteram Idem Iohannes balle confessus est scripisse, et communibus transmisisse, et plura alia fatebatur et fecit; propter-que, ut diximus, traitus, suspensus, et decollatus apud sanctum albanum Idibus Iulij, presente rege, et cadauer eius quadripertitum quatuor regni cuntatibus missum est. [John Ball confessed that he wrote this letter and sent it to the commons, and said and did many other things. For which reason, as we have said, he was drawn, hanged, and beheaded before the king at Saint Albans, on the ides of July; and his body was quartered and sent to four cities in the kingdom.]

The Course of Revolt[4]

The taxe hath tened° vs alle,		*harmed*
probat hoc mors tot validorum;°		*this death tests so many of the strong[?]*
The Kyng therof had small,		
ffuit in manibus cupidorum°[5]		*it was in the hands of the greedy ones*
5 yt had ful hard hansell,°		*bad omen*
dans causam fine dolorum;°		*giving cause to an end of sorrows*
vengeaunce nedes most° fall,		*must*
propter peccata malorum.°		*on account of the sins of the wicked*
In Kent care° be-gan,[6]		*troubles*
10 *mox infestando potentes;*°		*soon attacking the rulers*
On rowtes° tho Rebawdes° they ran,		*crowds / rascals*
Sua turpida arma ferentes.°		*bearing their shameful weapons*
ffoles° they dred no man,		*fools*
Regni Regem, neque gentes;°		*neither king of the realm, nor the people*
15 laddes° they were there Cheveteyns,°		*churls / captains*
Sine iure fere superantes.°		*lawlessly rising above their station*
laddes° lowde they lowght,°		*churls / laughed*
Clamantes voce sonora,°		*shouting in a loud voice*
The bischop[7] wan they slowght,°		*slew*
20 *Et corpora plura decora.*°		*and many handsome people*
Maners down they drowght,°		*they threw down manor houses*
In regno non meliora;°		*there were none better in the kingdom*
Harmes they dyde y-nowght;°		*enough*
habuerunt libera lora.°		*they had free rein*
25 Iak strawe[8] made yt stowte°		*swaggered*
Cum profusa comitiua,°		*with a captain's munificence*
And seyd al schuld hem lowte,°		*bow down to them*

4. Unlike the two preceding letters, there is no doubt that this piece is a poem: it is written in six- or eight-line stanzas of English alternating with Latin, with a rhyme scheme *ababab (ab)*. The masculine rhymes of the English (*alle, small,* etc.) contrast with the feminine rhymes of the Latin (*validorum, cupidorum,* etc.) to give it a lilting quality. The poem laments the violence of the rising, although it opens with a recognition of the rebels' grievances: the poll tax of 1377, 1379, and 1380–1381 "hath

tened [harmed] vs alle."
5. Much of the tax revenue was diverted to collectors rather than returned to the king.
6. The rising actually began in Essex and spread to Kent.
7. Simon Sudbury, Archbishop of Canterbury.
8. Jack Straw was a fictional character believed to have been a leader of the rising; see Chaucer, *Nun's Priest's Tale,* lines 628–31.

Anglorum corpora viua.°	the living community of Englishmen
Sadly° can they schowte,°	vigorously / shouted
30 *pulsant pietatis oliua,*°	they beat the olive branch of pity
The wycche were wont to lowte,°	those who used to skulk
aratrum traducere stiua.°	disgrace the plough and plough handle
Hales,[9] that dowghty° knyght,	brave
quo splenduit Anglia tota,°	in whom all England shone
35 dolefully° he was dyght,°	pitiably / cut down
Cum stultis pace remota.°	when removed from peace by fools
There he myght not fyght,	
nec Christo soluere vota.°	nor say his prayers to Christ
Savoy[1] semely set°	beautifully built
40 *heu! funditus igne cadebat.*°	alas, it was given over to the fire
Arcan don there they bett,[2]	
Et eos virtute premebat.°	and threatened them with force
deth was ther dewe dett,	
qui captum quisque ferebat.°	whoever carried off stolen goods
45 Oure kyng myght have no rest,	
Alii latuere cauerna;°	others hid in caves
To ride he was ful prest,	
recolendo gesta paterna.°	remembering his father's deeds
Iak straw dovn they cast[3]	
50 *Smethefeld virtute superna.*°	at Smithfield with superior strength
god, as thou may best,	
Regem defende, guberna.°	defend the kingdom and govern it

John Gower
from *The Voice of One Crying*[1]
from PROLOGUE

In the beginning of this work, the author intends to describe how the lowly peasants violently revolted against the freemen and nobles of the realm. And since an event of this kind was as loathsome and horrible as a monster, he reports that in a dream

9. Sir Robert Hales, treasurer of England and therefore closely associated with the collection of the poll tax. He was beheaded at the Tower of London during the rising.

1. John of Gaunt's London residence.

2. A reference to Achan (Joshua 7), who transgressed the law of God by stealing valuables from Jericho. Several chronicles mention the rebels' restraint in not looting the houses of the nobles.

3. It was not (the fictional) Jack Straw, but Wat Tyler who was mortally wounded at Smithfield.

1. Gower grew up in Kent (one of the counties where the Rising of 1381 started), in a well-connected family, and both Richard II and Henry IV were his patrons. He was a friend of Chaucer, who refers to him as "moral Gower." The immorality of contemporary society, particularly the refusal of the three estates to work together, is in fact the unifying theme of Gower's work. Of his three long poems (written in the three languages of the period, English, Anglo-Norman, and Latin), the Middle English *Lover's Confession* (*Confessio amantis*), though primarily a dream vision exploring the frustrations and folly of human

divine love, is set a framing complaint about the three estates, and the Anglo-Norman *Mirror of Man* (*Mirour de l'Omme*) is based on such a complaint.

Gower's Latin *Voice of One Crying* (*Vox Clamantis*) laments the failure of the three estates in a more prophetic way: the speaker identifies himself with John the Baptist, crying in the wilderness of 14th-century England. Like *Piers Plowman*, the poem takes the form of an allegorical dream vision. Like Langland, Gower revised his work in response to the revolt. He had written Books 2-7 by 1378 as a general complaint about the three estates, though he blamed the peasants in particular. Their refusal to produce food "by the sweat of their brow" as God decreed shows their laziness, and their demand of higher wages shows their wickedness and greed (bk. 5.9). After the Rising of 1381 occurred, he composed what is now Book 1 to decry the violence, which he saw as led by the devil; in it, he casts the peasants as beasts lacking reason, and their leader, Wat Tyler, as a rabble-rousing jackdaw, or jay (bk. 1.9). Translated by Eric W. Stockton.

he saw different throngs of the rabble transformed into different kinds of domestic animals. He says, moreover, that those domestic animals deviated from their true nature and took on the barbarousness of wild beasts. In accordance with the separate divisions of this book, which is divided into seven parts (as will appear more clearly below in its headings), he treats furthermore of the causes for such outrages taking place among men. * * *

[Wat Tyler as a Jackdaw Inciting the Peasants to Riot][2]

Here he says that in his dream he saw that when all the aforementioned madmen stood herded together, a certain Jackdaw (in English a Jay, which is commonly called Wat) assumed the rank of command over the others. And to tell the truth of the matter, this Wat was their leader.

When this great multitude of monsters like wild beasts stood united, a multitude like the sands of the sea, there appeared a Jackdaw, well instructed in the art of speaking, which no cage could keep at home. While all were looking on, this bird spread his wings and claimed to have top rank, although he was unworthy. Just as the Devil was placed in command over the army of the lower world, so this scoundrel was in charge of the wicked mob. A harsh voice, a fierce expression, a very faithful likeness to a death's head—these things gave token of his appearance. He checked the murmuring and all kept silent so that the sound from his mouth might be better heard. He ascended to the top of a tree, and with the voice from his open mouth he uttered such words as these to his compeers:

"O you low sort of wretches, which the world has subjugated for a long time by its law, look, now the day has come when the peasantry will triumph and will force the freemen to get off their lands. Let all honor come to an end, let justice perish, and let no virtue that once existed endure further in the world. Let the law give over which used to hold us in check with its justice, and from here on let our court rule."

The whole mob was silent and took note of the speaker's words, and they liked every command he delivered from his mouth. The rabble lent a deluded ear to his fickle talk, and it saw none of the future things that would result. For when he had been honored in this way by the people, he quickly grabbed all the land for himself. Indeed, when the people had unadvisedly given themselves into servitude, he called the populace together and gave orders. Just as a billow usually grows calm after a stiff breeze, and just as a wave swells by the blast of a whirlwind, so the Jackdaw stirred up all the others with his outrageous shouting, and he drew the people's minds toward war. The stupid portion of the people did not know what its "court" might be, but he ordered them to adopt the laws of force. He said, "Strike," and one man struck. He said, "Kill," and another killed. He said, "Commit crime"; everyone committed it, and did not oppose his will. Everyone he called to in his madness listened with ears pricked up, and once aroused to his voice, pursued the [prescribed] course. Thus many an unfortunate man, driven by his persuasive raving, stuck his hand into the fire again and again. All proclaimed in a loud voice, "So be it," so that the sound was like the din of the sea. Stunned by the great noise of their voice, I now could scarcely lift my trembling feet. Yet from a distance I

2. From Book 1.

observed how they made their mutual arrangements by clasping their hands. For they said this, that the mob from the country would destroy whatever was left of the noble class in the world.

With these words, they all marched together in the same fashion, and the wicked ruler of hell led the way. A black cloud mingled with the furies of hell approached, and every wickedness poured into their hearts rained down. The earth was so thoroughly soaked with the dew of hell that no virtue could flourish from that time forth. But every vice that a worthy man abhors flourished and filled men's hearts from that time on. Then at midday the Devil attacked and his hard-shot arrow flew during that painful day. Satan himself was freed and on hand, together with all the sinful band of servile hell. Behold, the untutored heart's sense of shame was lost, and it no longer feared the terrors of crime or punishment. And so when I saw the leaders of hell ruling the world, the rights of heaven were worth nothing. The more I saw them, the more I judged I ought to be afraid of them, not knowing what sort of end would be bound to come.

[THE LAZINESS AND GREED OF PLOUGHMEN][3]

Now that he has spoken of those of knightly rank who ought to keep the state unharmed, it is necessary to speak of those who are under obligation to enter into the labors of agriculture, which are necessary for obtaining food and drink for the sustenance of the human race.

Now you have heard what knighthood is, and I shall speak in addition of what the guiding principle for other men ought to be. For after knighthood there remains only the peasant rank; the rustics in it cultivate the grains and vineyards. They are the men who seek food for us by the sweat of their heavy toil, as God Himself has decreed. The guiding principle of our first father Adam, which he received from the mouth of God on high, is rightly theirs. For God said to him, when he fell from the glories of Paradise, "O sinner, the sweat and toil of the world be thine; in them shalt thou eat thy bread."[4] So if God's peasant pays attention to the plowshare as it goes along, and if he thus carries on the work of cultivation with his hand, then the fruit which in due course the fertile field will bear and the grape will stand abundant in their due seasons. Now, however, scarcely a farmer wishes to do such work; instead, he wickedly loafs everywhere.

An evil disposition is widespread among the common people, and I suspect that the servants of the plow are often responsible for it. For they are sluggish, they are scarce, and they are grasping. For the very little they do they demand the highest pay. Now that this practice has come about, see how one peasant insists upon more than two demanded in days gone by. Yet a short time ago one performed more service than three do now, as those maintain who are well acquainted with the facts. For just as the fox seeks his hole and enters it while the woods are echoing on every side of the hole, so does the servant of the plow, contrary to the law of the land, seek to make a fool of the land. They desire the leisures of great men, but they have nothing to feed themselves with, nor will they be servants. God and Nature have ordained that they shall serve, but neither knows how to keep them within bounds. Everyone owning land complains in his turn about these people;

3. From Book 5.   4. Genesis 3.19.

each stands in need of them and none has control over them. The peasants of old did not scorn God with impunity or usurp a noble worldly rank. Rather, God imposed servile work upon them, so that the peasantry might subdue its proud feelings; and liberty, which remained secure for freemen, ruled over the serfs and subjected them to its law.

The experience of yesterday makes us better informed as to what perfidy the unruly serf possesses. As the teasel[5] harmfully thins out the standing crops if it is not thinned out itself, so does the unruly peasant weigh heavily upon the well-behaved ones. The peasant strikes at the subservient and soothes the troublesome, yet the principle which the old order of things teaches is not wrong: let the law accordingly cut down the harmful teasels of rabble, lest they uproot the nobler grain with their stinging. Unless it is struck down first, the peasant race strikes against freemen, no matter what nobility or worth they possess. Its actions outwardly show that the peasantry is base, and it esteems the nobles the less because of their very virtues. Just as lopsided ships begin to sink without the right load, so does the wild peasantry, unless it is held in check.

God and our toil confer and bestow everything upon us. Without toil, man's advantages are nothing. The peasant should therefore put his limbs to work, as is proper for him to do. Just as a barren field cultivated by the plowshare fails the granaries and brings home no crop in autumn, so does the worthless churl, the more he is cherished by your love, fail you and bring on your ruin. The serfs perform none of their servile duties voluntarily and have no respect for the law. Whatever the serf's body suffers patiently under compulsion, inwardly his mind ever turns toward utter wickedness. Miracles happen only contrary to nature; only the divinity of nature can go against its own powers. It is not for man's estate that anyone from the class of serfs should try to set things right.

END OF "PIERS PLOWMAN" AND ITS TIME

MYSTICAL WRITINGS

Throughout the Middle Ages, religious belief was communally expressed in the great public liturgies: the mass and the Divine Office—those prayers, hymns, and readings performed, especially by monastic communities, at the eight liturgical "hours" from dawn until dark. Private devotion, however, also had a continuous place in medieval Christianity. The British Isles enjoyed a particularly rich and ancient tradition of lives led in holy solitude and of texts and collections intended for private devotion by both clergy and laity. Such early works were enriched in the late eleventh century by the influential *Prayers or Meditations* of Anselm, Archbishop of Canterbury.

Anselm's prayers and related works were collected into portable books. Beginning in the thirteenth century, England also produced distinguished, sometimes elaborately decorated psalters—collections of psalms and other prayers—that were often privately owned. Toward the middle of the thirteenth century, an Oxford workshop produced the earliest of the decorated

---

5. A bristly plant like a thistle.

Books of Hours, a form that was to prove enormously popular across Europe for the rest of the Middle Ages.

Books of Hours typically contained the "Little Hours of the Virgin," an abbreviated version of the Divine Office that allowed for private commemoration of the holy hours, as well as other prayers, extracts from the gospels, and the "seven penitential psalms." Psalters and Books of Hours both featured texts devoted to the Virgin Mary, only one manifestation of a widespread English tradition. Many were explicitly intended for use by women, both lay and clerical, and emphasize female readership in their illustrations, as in the scene of women reading from the Bedford Hours (see Color Plate 10). Psalters and especially Books of Hours played a key role in the growth of lay literacy during the later Middle Ages.

By the fourteenth century, then, England had an ancient tradition of private religious devotion and varied books created especially for that purpose as well as a growing readership, lay and clerical. Two further, related elements added to the growth in that century of works that have been grouped, largely retrospectively, as "mystical." First, across Europe there was a renewed expression of "affective spirituality," the emotionally, even physically empathetic contemplation of the crises of salvation, especially the crucifixion of Christ and the sufferings of the Virgin Mary. This is reflected in the vision of the crucifixion in *Passus* 18 of Langland's *Piers Plowman*, and in many lyrics, as well as in sculpture and drawings like that on page 530. Second, widespread dissatisfaction with the established church—or a more diffuse sense of spiritual needs left unfulfilled there—led a growing number of Christians to explore more immediate and often private avenues of religious experience. The quest for a mystical union with Christ or God the Father is a particularly ambitious aspect of such exploration.

This search was often exercised, particularly in the lay community and among religious women, in the recently invigorated vernacular, which (whether French or English) had long had a place along with Latin in Books of Hours. Among these expressions were the "Wycliffite" translations of the Bible into Middle English, as well as texts intended for religious recluses and for people seeking mystical experience even as they remained active in the mundane world. These emergent religious aspirations, as well as some of their accompanying fears and tensions, are expressed below in Julian of Norwich's *Book of Showings* and the Companion Readings that follow it.*

Julian of Norwich
1342–c. 1420

Dame Julian of Norwich was an anchoress, a woman dedicated to prayer and contemplation who lived separate from the world, literally enclosed in a modest residence and symbolically "dead" to the secular world. Yet Julian also lived in the midst of the world. Her anchorhold at the church of Saint Julian—hence her name—was in a busy market neighborhood of Norwich. Dame Julian's lifelong stability as an anchoress, and her persistent rhetoric of humility (she most often speaks of herself only as a "creature"), may have masked or softened the daring of her theology. This she developed from decades of meditation on a sequence of sixteen visions of the Crucifixion—"showings"—that she received in extreme illness at age thirty.

The urban space and domestic arrangements of Julian's anchorhold serve as an emblem for her theology and her place in the spiritual world. She had a maidservant, and received and

*The editors express their gratitude to Professor Nicholas Watson for his advice on this section.

spoke to guests. Some of those encounters were reported, as for example by Margery Kempe from nearby Lynn, whose own work appears later in this anthology (page 529). Julian brought eminence to the churches of Norwich without threatening their hierarchy; she lived under the direction of a priestly confessor, made no claim to worldly power, and insisted upon her orthodoxy. Yet a visitor like Margery Kempe could use Julian's approval as a defense for her own more mobile and subversive quest for holiness.

Dame Julian used her own background of household and family as images to create a complex and subtle domestic theology of the trinity and especially of the sacrifice of Christ. Julian's metaphors for the divine are not exclusively intimate or domestic, however. She repeatedly speaks of God in socially conservative terms, as a great secular lord whose grace is a form of public "courtesy." Her revelation of the soul as a great citadel (ch. 68) features Jesus as its bishop, king, and lord.

Julian probably dictated the two versions of her *Book of Showings*, although it is clear that she was deeply versed in the Bible and liturgy, and in the writings of English and Continental mystics. The earlier version is largely focused on the visions themselves, while the very much longer version (selections from which follow) reflects the ensuing decades of theological speculations to which Julian's visions led her. She will often expound a statement by Christ in one of her visions with all the nuance that contemporary theologians would apply to a line from the Bible. In an extraordinary series of reflections, Julian at once meditates upon key moments in her initial visions, and explores the role of Christ in mankind and in the Trinity through the multifaceted image of the Lord as mother. Julian exploits all the moments of motherhood—conception, labor, breast-feeding, nurture, and upbringing—to articulate the place of Christ in the scheme of salvation and the necessity of sin. At the same time, other aspects of motherhood also serve Julian to explore the other persons of the Trinity, God the Father and the Holy Spirit, as well as the sufferings and joys of the Virgin Mary.

Even more than Richard Rolle or the *Cloud of Unknowing* (selections from which follow in the Companion Readings), Julian is explicitly concerned with the love and salvation of all the faithful, not just private communion with the divine. She addresses herself, more broadly than her predecessors, to the entire community of the faithful. She explicitly does not privilege herself above those of simple belief, and again uses the imagery of a nurturing mother to urge the sinful soul's recourse to the Holy Church.

from A Book of Showings[1]
[Three Graces. Illness. The First Revelation]

Chapter 2

This revelation was made to a simple, unlettered creature, living in this mortal flesh, the year of our Lord one thousand, three hundred and seventy-three, on the thirteenth day of May;[2] and before this the creature had desired three graces by the gift of God. The first was recollection of the Passion. The second was bodily sickness. The third was to have, of God's gift, three wounds. As to the first, it seemed to me that I had some feeling for the Passion of Christ, but still I desired to have more by the grace of God. I thought that I wished that I had been at that time with Magdalen and with the others who were Christ's lovers, so that I might have seen with my own eyes the Passion which our Lord suffered for me, so that I might have suffered with him as others did who loved him. Therefore I desired a bodily sight, in which I might have more knowledge of our savior's bodily pains, and of the compassion of our Lady and of all his true lovers who were living at that time and saw his pains, for I would have been one of them and have

---

1. Translated by Edmund Colledge and James Walsh.
2. Julian provides the biographical setting of her visions in this chapter. By "unlettered" she may mean that she was not formally schooled; it is clear that she was literate.

suffered with them. I never desired any other sight of God or revelation, until my soul would be separated from the body, for I believed that I should be saved by the mercy of God. This was my intention, because I wished afterwards, because of that revelation, to have truer recollection of Christ's Passion. As to the second grace, there came into my mind with contrition—a free gift which I did not seek—a desire of my will to have by God's gift a bodily sickness. I wished that sickness to be so severe that it might seem mortal, so that I might in it receive all the rites which Holy Church has to give me, whilst I myself should think that I was dying, and everyone who saw me would think the same; for I wanted no comfort from any human, earthly life in that sickness. I wanted to have every kind of pain, bodily and spiritual, which I should have if I had died, every fear and temptation from devils, and every other kind of pain except the departure of the spirit. I intended this because I wanted to be purged by God's mercy, and afterwards live more to his glory because of that sickness; because I hoped that this would be to my reward when I should die, because I desired soon to be with my God and my Creator.

These two desires about the Passion and the sickness which I desired from him were with a condition, for it seemed to me that this was not the ordinary practice of prayer; therefore I said: Lord, you know what I want, if it be your will that I have it, and if it be not your will, good Lord, do not be displeased, for I want nothing which you do not want. When I was young I desired to have this sickness when I would be thirty years old. As to the third, by the grace of God and the teaching of Holy Church I conceived a great desire to receive three wounds in my life, that is, the wound of true contrition, the wound of loving compassion, and the wound of longing with my will for God. Just as I asked for the other two conditionally, so I asked urgently for this third without any condition. The two desires which I mentioned first passed from my mind, and the third remained there continually.

CHAPTER 3

And when I was thirty and a half years old, God sent me a bodily sickness in which I lay for three days and three nights, and on the third night I received all the rites of Holy Church, and did not expect to live until day. And after this I lay for two days and two nights, and on the third night I often thought that I was on the point of death, and those who were with me often thought so. And yet in this I felt a great reluctance to die, not that there was anything on earth which it pleased me to live for, or any pain of which I was afraid, for I trusted in the mercy of God. But it was because I wanted to live to love God better and longer, so that I might through the grace of that living have more knowledge and love of God in the bliss of heaven. Because it seemed to me that all the time that I had lived here was very little and short in comparison with the bliss which is everlasting, I thought: Good Lord, can my living no longer be to your glory? And I understood by my reason and the sensation of my pains that I should die; and with all the will of my heart I assented to be wholly as was God's will.

So I lasted until day, and by then my body was dead from the middle downwards, as it felt to me. Then I was helped to sit upright and supported, so that my heart might be more free to be at God's will, and so that I could think of him whilst my life would last. My curate was sent for to be present at my end; and before he came my eyes were fixed upwards, and I could not speak. He set the cross before my face, and said: I have brought the image of your savior; look at it and take comfort from it. It seemed to me that I was well, for my eyes were set upwards towards heaven, where I trusted that I by God's mercy was going; but nevertheless I agreed to fix my eyes on the face of the crucifix if I could, and so I did, for it seemed to me that I would hold out longer with my eyes set in front of me rather than upwards. After this my sight began to fail. It grew as dark around me in the room as if it had been night, except that there was ordinary light trained upon the image of the cross, I did not know how. Everything around the cross was ugly and terrifying to me, as if it were occupied by a great crowd of devils.

After this the upper part of my body began to die, until I could scarcely feel anything. My greatest pain was my shortness of breath and the ebbing of my life. Then truly I believed that I was at the point of death. And suddenly at that moment all my pain was taken from me, and I was as sound, particularly in the upper part of my body, as ever I was before. I was astonished by this sudden change, for it seemed to me that it was by God's secret doing and not natural; and even so, in this ease which I felt, I had no more confidence that I should live, nor was the ease I felt complete for me, for I thought that I would rather have been delivered of this world, because that was what my heart longed for.

Then suddenly it came into my mind that I ought to wish for the second wound as a gift and a grace from our Lord, that my body might be filled full of recollection and feeling of his blessed Passion, as I had prayed before, for I wished that his pains might be my pains, with compassion which would lead to longing for God. So it seemed to me that I might with his grace have the wounds which I had before desired; but in this I never wanted any bodily vision or any kind of revelation from God, but the compassion which I thought a loving soul could have for our Lord Jesus, who for love was willing to become a mortal man. I desired to suffer with him, living in my mortal body, as God would give me grace.

Chapter 4

And at this, suddenly I saw the red blood running down from under the crown, hot and flowing freely and copiously, a living stream, just as it was at the time when the crown of thorns was pressed on his blessed head.[3] I perceived, truly and powerfully, that it was he who just so, both God and man, himself suffered for me, who showed it to me without any intermediary.

And in the same revelation, suddenly the Trinity filled my heart full of the greatest joy, and I understood that it will be so in heaven without end to all who will come there. For the Trinity is God, God is the Trinity. The Trinity is our maker, the Trinity is our protector, the Trinity is our everlasting lover, the Trinity is our endless joy and our bliss, by our Lord Jesus Christ and in our Lord Jesus Christ. And this was revealed in the first vision and in them all, for where Jesus appears the blessed Trinity is understood, as I see it. And I said: Blessed be the Lord! This I said with a reverent intention and in a loud voice, and I was greatly astonished by this wonder and marvel, that he who is so to be revered and feared would be so familiar with a sinful creature living in this wretched flesh.

I accepted it that at that time our Lord Jesus wanted, out of his courteous love, to show me comfort before my temptations began; for it seemed to me that I might well be tempted by devils, by God's permission and with his protection, before I would die. With this sight of his blessed Passion, with the divinity which I saw in my understanding, I knew well that this was strength enough for me, yes, and for all living creatures who were to be saved, against all the devils of hell and against all their spiritual enemies.

---

3. This begins the first of Julian's 16 revelations.

In this he brought our Lady Saint Mary to my understanding. I saw her spiritually in her bodily likeness, a simple, humble maiden, young in years, grown a little taller than a child, of the stature which she had when she conceived.[4] Also God showed me part of the wisdom and the truth of her soul, and in this I understood the reverent contemplation with which she beheld her God, who is her Creator, marveling with great reverence that he was willing to be born of her who was a simple creature created by him. And this wisdom and truth, this knowledge of her Creator's greatness and of her own created littleness, made her say very meekly to Gabriel: Behold me here, God's handmaiden. In this sight I understood truly that she is greater, more worthy and more fulfilled, than everything else which God has created, and which is inferior to her. Above her is no created thing, except the blessed humanity of Christ, as I saw.

CHAPTER 5

At the same time as I saw this sight of the head bleeding, our good Lord showed a spiritual sight of his familiar love. I saw that he is to us everything which is good and comforting for our help. He is our clothing, who wraps and enfolds us for love, embraces us and shelters us, surrounds us for his love, which is so tender that he may never desert us. And so in this sight I saw that he is everything which is good, as I understand.

And in this he showed me something small, no bigger than a hazelnut, lying in the palm of my hand, as it seemed to me, and it was as round as a ball. I looked at it with the eye of my understanding and thought: What can this be? I was amazed that it could last, for I thought that because of its littleness it would suddenly have fallen into nothing. And I was answered in my understanding: It lasts and always will, because God loves it; and thus everything has being through the love of God.

In this little thing I saw three properties. The first is that God made it, the second is that God loves it, the third is that God preserves it. But what did I see in it? It is that God is the Creator and the protector and the lover. For until I am substantially united to him, I can never have perfect rest or true happiness, until, that is, I am so attached to him that there can be no created thing between my God and me.

This little thing which is created seemed to me as if it could have fallen into nothing because of its littleness. We need to have knowledge of this, so that we may delight in despising as nothing everything created, so as to love and have uncreated God. For this is the reason why our hearts and souls are not in perfect ease, because here we seek rest in this thing which is so little, in which there is no rest, and we do not know our God who is almighty, all wise and all good, for he is true rest. God wishes to be known, and it pleases him that we should rest in him; for everything which is beneath him is not sufficient for us. And this is the reason why no soul is at rest until it has despised as nothing all things which are created. When it by its will has become nothing for love, to have him who is everything, then is it able to receive spiritual rest.

And also our good Lord revealed that it is very greatly pleasing to him that a simple soul should come naked, openly and familiarly. For this is the loving yearning of the soul through the touch of the Holy Spirit, from the understanding which I have in this revelation: God, of your goodness give me yourself, for you are enough for me, and I can ask for nothing which is less which can pay you full

---

4. Julian will have two further visions of the Virgin Mary in different manifestations: as mother mourning at the Crucifixion and as ascended saint.

worship. And if I ask anything which is less, always I am in want; but only in you do I have everything.

And these words of the goodness of God are very dear to the soul, and very close to touching our Lord's will, for his goodness fills all his creatures and all his blessed works full, and endlessly overflows in them. For he is everlastingness, and he made us only for himself, and restored us by his precious Passion and always preserves us in his blessed love; and all this is of his goodness.

CHAPTER 9

I am not good because of the revelations, but only if I love God better; and inasmuch as you love God better, it is more to you than to me. I do not say this to those who are wise, because they know it well. But I say it to you who are simple, to give you comfort and strength; for we are all one in love, for truly it was not revealed to me that God loves me better than the humblest soul who is in a state of grace. For I am sure that there are many who never had revelations or visions, but only the common teaching of Holy Church, who love God better than I. If I pay special attention to myself, I am nothing at all; but in general I am, I hope, in the unity of love with all my fellow Christians. For it is in this unity that the life of all men consists who will be saved. For God is everything that is good, as I see; and God has made everything that is made, and God loves everything that he has made. And he who has general love for all his fellow Christians in God has love towards everything that is. For in mankind which will be saved is comprehended all, that is to say all that is made and the maker of all. For God is in man and in God is all. And he who loves thus loves all. And I hope by the grace of God that he who may see it so will be taught the truth and greatly comforted, if he has need of comfort.

I speak of those who will be saved, for at this time God showed me no one else. But in everything I believe as Holy Church preaches and teaches. For the faith of Holy Church, which I had before I had understanding, and which, as I hope by the grace of God, I intend to preserve whole and to practice, was always in my sight, and I wished and intended never to accept anything which might be contrary to it. And to this end and with this intention I contemplated the revelation with all diligence, for throughout this blessed revelation I contemplated it as God intended.

All this was shown in three parts,[5] that is to say, by bodily vision and by words formed in my understanding and by spiritual vision. But I may not and cannot show the spiritual visions as plainly and fully as I should wish. But I trust in our Lord God almighty that he will, out of his goodness and for love of you, make you accept it more spiritually and more sweetly than I can or may tell it.

[LAUGHING AT THE DEVIL]

CHAPTER 13[6]

And after this, before God revealed any words, he allowed me to contemplate him for a fitting length of time, and all that I had seen, and all the significance that was contained in it, as well as my soul's simplicity could accept it. And then he, without voice and without opening of lips, formed in my soul this saying: With this the fiend is overcome. Our Lord said this to me with reference to his blessed Passion, as he had shown it before. In this he showed a part of the fiend's malice, and all of his impotence,

---

5. Or three ways of perception.   6. The fifth revelation.

because he showed that his Passion is the overcoming of the fiend. God showed me that the fiend has now the same malice as he had before the Incarnation, and he works as hard, and he sees as constantly as he did before that all souls who will be saved escape him to God's glory by the power of our Lord's precious Passion. And that is the devil's sorrow, and he is put to terrible shame, for everything which God permits him to do turns to joy for us and to pain and shame for him. And he has as much sorrow when God permits him to work as when he is not working. And that is because he can never do as much evil as he would wish, for his power is all locked in God's hands. But in God there can be no anger, as I see it, and it is with power and justice, to the profit of all who will be saved, that he opposes the damned, who in malice and malignity work to frustrate and oppose God's will.

Also I saw our Lord scorn his malice and despise him as nothing, and he wants us to do so. Because of this sight I laughed greatly, and that made those around me to laugh as well; and their laughter was pleasing to me. I thought that I wished that all my fellow Christians had seen what I saw. Then they would all have laughed with me; but I did not see Christ laughing, but I know well that it was the vision he showed me which made me laugh, for I understood that we may laugh, to comfort ourselves and rejoice in God, because the devil is overcome. And when I saw our Lord scorn his malice, that was through the fixing of my understanding on him, that is, that this was an interior revelation of his truth, in which his demeanour did not change. For as I see it, this is an attribute of God which must be honoured, and which lasts forever.

And after this I became serious again, and said: I see three things: sport and scorn and seriousness. I see sport, that the devil is overcome; and I see scorn, that God scorns him and he will be scorned; and I see seriousness, that he is overcome by the blessed Passion and death of our Lord Jesus Christ, which was accomplished in great earnest and with heavy labour. And when I said that he is scorned, I meant that God scorns him, that is, because he sees him now as he will forever. For in this God revealed that the devil is damned. And I meant this when I said that he ought to be scorned; for I saw that on Judgment Day he will be generally scorned by all who will be saved, of whose salvation he has had great envy. For then he will see that all the woe and tribulation which he has caused them will be changed into the increase of their eternal joy. And all the pain and the sorrow that he wanted to bring them into will go forever with him to hell.

[CHRIST DRAWS JULIAN IN THROUGH HIS WOUND]

CHAPTER 24[7]

With a kindly countenance our good Lord looked into his side, and he gazed with joy, and with his sweet regard he drew his creature's understanding into his side by the same wound;[8] and there he revealed a fair and delectable place, large enough for all mankind that will be saved and will rest in peace and in love. And with that he brought to mind the dear and precious blood and water which he suffered to be shed for love. And in this sweet sight he showed his blessed heart split in two, and as he rejoiced he showed to my understanding a part of his blessed divinity, as much as was his will at that time, strengthening my poor soul to understand what can be said, that is the endless love which was without beginning and is and always shall be.

---

7. This chapter recounts Julian's tenth revelation.   8. The spear wound in Christ's side.

And with this our good Lord said most joyfully: See how I love you, as if he had said, my darling, behold and see your Lord, your God, who is your Creator and your endless joy; see your own brother, your savior; my child, behold and see what delight and bliss I have in your salvation, and for my love rejoice with me.

And for my greater understanding, these blessed words were said: See how I love you, as if he had said, behold and see that I loved you so much, before I died for you, that I wanted to die for you. And now I have died for you, and willingly suffered what I could. And now all my bitter pain and my hard labor is turned into everlasting joy and bliss for me and for you. How could it now be that you would pray to me for anything pleasing to me which I would not very gladly grant to you? For my delight is in your holiness and in your endless joy and bliss in me.

This is the understanding, as simply as I can say it, of these blessed words: See how I loved you. Our Lord revealed this to make us glad and joyful.

CHAPTER 25[9]

And with this same appearance of mirth and joy our good Lord looked down on his right, and brought to my mind where our Lady stood at the time of his Passion, and he said: Do you wish to see her? And these sweet words were as if he had said, I know well that you wish to see my blessed mother, for after myself she is the greatest joy that I could show you, and the greatest delight and honor to me, and she is what all my blessed creatures most desire to see. And because of the wonderful, exalted and singular love that he has for this sweet maiden, his blessed mother, our Lady Saint Mary, he reveals her bliss and joy through the sense of these sweet words, as if he said, do you wish to see how I love her, so that you could rejoice with me in the love which I have in her and she has in me?

And for greater understanding of these sweet words our good Lord speaks in love to all mankind who will be saved, addressing them all as one person, as if he said, do you wish to see in her how you are loved? It is for love of you that I have made her so exalted, so noble, so honorable; and this delights me. And I wish it to delight you. For next to him, she is the most blissful to be seen. But in this matter I was not taught to long to see her bodily presence whilst I am here, but the virtues of her blessed soul, her truth, her wisdom, her love, through which I am taught to know myself and reverently to fear my God.

And when our good Lord had revealed this, and said these words: Do you wish to see her? I answered and said: Yes, good Lord, great thanks, yes, good Lord, if it be your will. Often times I had prayed for this, and I had expected to see her in a bodily likeness; but I did not see her so. And Jesus, saying this, showed me a spiritual vision of her. Just as before I had seen her small and simple, now he showed her high and noble and glorious and more pleasing to him than all creatures. And so he wishes it to be known that all who take delight in him should take delight in her, and in the delight that he has in her and she in him.

And for greater understanding he showed this example, as if, when a man loves some creature particularly, more than all other creatures, he will make all other creatures to love and delight in that creature whom he loves so much. And in these words which Jesus said: Do you wish to see her? it seemed to me that these were the most delectable words which he could give me in this spiritual vision of her which he gave me. For our Lord showed me no particular person except our Lady Saint

---

9. The eleventh revelation.

Mary, and he showed her on three occasions. The first was as she conceived, the second was as she had been under the Cross, and the third was as she is now, in delight, honor and joy.

Chapter 26[1]

And after this our Lord showed himself to me, and he appeared to me more glorified than I had seen him before, in which I was taught that our soul will never have rest till it comes into him, acknowledging that he is full of joy, familiar and courteous and blissful and true life. Again and again our Lord said: I am he, I am he, I am he who is highest. I am he whom you love. I am he in whom you delight. I am he whom you serve. I am he for whom you long. I am he whom you desire. I am he whom you intend. I am he who is all. I am he whom Holy Church preaches and teaches to you. I am he who showed himself before to you. The number of the words surpasses my intelligence and my understanding and all my powers, for they were the most exalted, as I see it, for in them is comprehended I cannot tell what; but the joy which I saw when they were revealed surpasses all that the heart can think or the soul may desire. And therefore these words are not explained here, but let every man accept them as our Lord intended them, according to the grace God gives him in understanding and love.

[The Necessity of Sin, and of Hating Sin]

Chapter 27[2]

And after this our Lord brought to my mind the longing that I had for him before, and I saw that nothing hindered me but sin, and I saw that this is true of us all in general, and it seemed to me that if there had been no sin, we should all have been pure and as like our Lord as he created us. And so in my folly before this time I often wondered why, through the great prescient wisdom of God, the beginning of sin was not prevented. For then it seemed to me that all would have been well.

The impulse to think this was greatly to be shunned; and nevertheless I mourned and sorrowed on this account, unreasonably, lacking discretion. But Jesus, who in this vision informed me about everything needful to me, answered with these words and said: Sin is necessary, but all will be well, and all will be well, and every kind of thing will be well. In this naked word "sin," our Lord brought generally to my mind all which is not good, and the shameful contempt and the direst tribulation which he endured for us in this life, and his death and all his pains, and the passions, spiritual and bodily, of all his creatures. For we are all in part troubled, and we shall be troubled, following our master Jesus until we are fully purged of our mortal flesh and all our inward affections which are not very good.

And with the beholding of this, with all the pains that ever were or ever will be, I understood Christ's Passion for the greatest and surpassing pain. And yet this was shown to me in an instant, and it quickly turned into consolation. For our good Lord would not have the soul frightened by this ugly sight. But I did not see sin, for I believe that it has no kind of substance, no share in being, nor can it be recognized except by the pain caused by it. And it seems to me that this pain is something for a time, for it purges and makes us know ourselves and ask for mercy; for the Passion of our Lord is comfort to us against all this, and that is his blessed will. And because of the tender love which our good Lord has for all who will be saved, he comforts readily

---

1. The twelfth revelation.   2. The thirteenth revelation.

and sweetly, meaning this: It is true that sin is the cause of all this pain, but all will be well, and every kind of thing will be well.

These works were revealed most tenderly, showing no kind of blame to me or to anyone who will be saved. So it would be most unkind of me to blame God or marvel at him on account of my sins, since he does not blame me for sin.

And in these same words I saw hidden in God an exalted and wonderful mystery, which he will make plain and we shall know in heaven. In this knowledge we shall truly see the cause why he allowed sin to come, and in this sight we shall rejoice forever.

CHAPTER 40

And this is a supreme friendship of our courteous Lord, that he protects us so tenderly whilst we are in our sins; and furthermore he touches us most secretly, and shows us our sins by the sweet light of mercy and grace. But when we see ourselves so foul, then we believe that God may be angry with us because of our sins. Then we are moved by the Holy Spirit through contrition to prayer, and we desire with all our might an amendment of ourselves to appease God's anger, until the time that we find rest of soul and ease of conscience. And then we hope that God has forgiven us our sin; and this is true. And then our courteous Lord shows himself to the soul, happily and with the gladdest countenance, welcoming it as a friend, as if it had been in pain and in prison, saying: My dear darling, I am glad that you have come to me in all your woe. I have always been with you, and now you see me loving, and we are made one in bliss.

So sins are forgiven by grace and mercy, and our soul is honorably received in joy, as it will be when it comes into heaven, as often as it comes by the operation of grace of the Holy Spirit and the power of Christ's Passion.

Here I truly understood that every kind of thing is made available to us by God's great goodness, so much so that when we ourselves are at peace and in charity we are truly safe. But because we cannot have this completely whilst we are here, therefore it is fitting for us to live always in sweet prayer and in loving longing with our Lord Jesus. For he always longs to bring us to the fullness of joy, as has been said before, where he reveals his spiritual thirst. But now, because of all this spiritual consolation which has been described, if any man or woman be moved by folly to say or to think "If this be true, then it would be well to sin so as to have the greater reward, or else to think sin less important," beware of this impulse, for truly, should it come, it is untrue and from the fiend.

For the same true love which touches us all by its blessed strength, that same blessed love teaches us that we must hate sin only because of love. And I am sure by what I feel that the more that each loving soul sees this in the courteous love of our Lord God, the greater is his hatred of sinning and the more he is ashamed. For if it were laid in front of us, all the pain there is in hell and in purgatory and on earth, death and all the rest, we should choose all that pain rather than sin. For sin is so vile and so much to be hated that it can be compared with no pain which is not itself sin. And no more cruel hell than sin was revealed to me, for a loving soul hates no pain but sin; for everything is good except sin, and nothing is evil except sin. And when by the operation of mercy and grace we set our intention on mercy and grace, we are made all fair and spotless.

And God is as willing as he is powerful and wise to save man. And Christ himself is the foundation of all the laws of Christian men, and he taught us to do good in return for evil. Here we may see that he is himself this love, and does to us as he teaches us to do; for he wishes us to be like him in undiminished, everlasting love towards ourselves and our fellow Christians. No more than his love towards us is withdrawn because of our sin does he wish our love to be withdrawn from ourselves or from our fellow Christians; but we must unreservedly hate sin and endlessly love the soul as God loves it. Then we should hate sin just as God hates it, and love the soul as God loves it. For these words which God said are an endless strength: I protect you most truly.

[GOD AS FATHER, MOTHER, HUSBAND]

CHAPTER 58

God the blessed Trinity, who is everlasting being, just as he is eternal from without beginning, just so was it in his eternal purpose to create human nature, which fair nature was first prepared for his own Son, the second person; and when he wished, by full agreement of the whole Trinity he created us all once. And in our creating he joined and united us to himself, and through this union we are kept as pure and as noble as we were created. By the power of that same precious union we love our Creator and delight in him, praise him and thank him and endlessly rejoice in him. And this is the work which is constantly performed in every soul which will be saved, and this is the godly will mentioned before.

And so in our making, God almighty is our loving Father, and God all wisdom is our loving Mother,[3] with the love and the goodness of the Holy Spirit, which is all one God, one Lord. And in the joining and the union he is our very true spouse and we his beloved wife and his fair maiden, with which wife he was never displeased; for he says: I love you and you love me, and our love will never divide in two.

I contemplated the work of all the blessed Trinity, in which contemplation I saw and understood these three properties: the property of the fatherhood, and the property of the motherhood, and the property of the lordship in one God. In our almighty Father we have our protection and our bliss, as regards our natural substance, which is ours by our creation from without beginning; and in the second person, in knowledge and wisdom we have our perfection, as regards our sensuality, our restoration and our salvation, for he is our Mother, brother and savior; and in our good Lord the Holy Spirit we have our reward and our gift for our living and our labor, endlessly surpassing all that we desire in his marvelous courtesy, out of his great plentiful grace. For all our life consists of three: In the first we have our being, and in the second we have our increasing, and in the third we have our fulfillment. The first is nature, the second is mercy, the third is grace.

As to the first, I saw and understood that the high might of the Trinity is our Father, and the deep wisdom of the Trinity is our Mother, and the great love of the Trinity is our Lord; and all these we have in nature and in our substantial creation. And furthermore I saw that the second person, who is our Mother, substantially the same beloved person, has now become our mother sensually, because we are double by God's creating, that is to say substantial and sensual. Our substance is the higher part, which we have in our Father, God almighty; and the second person of the Trinity is our Mother in nature in our substantial creation, in whom we are founded

---

3. The image of God as a wise woman draws from an ancient tradition of the female Sophia, Holy Wisdom, who figures in the apocryphal book of Ecclesiasticus (ch. 24).

and rooted, and he is our Mother of mercy in taking our sensuality. And so our Mother is working on us in various ways, in whom our parts are kept undivided; for in our Mother Christ we profit and increase, and in mercy he reforms and restores us, and by the power of his Passion, his death and his Resurrection, he unites us to our substance. So our Mother works in mercy on all his beloved children who are docile and obedient to him, and grace works with mercy, and especially in two properties, as it was shown, which working belongs to the third person, the Holy Spirit. He works, rewarding and giving. Rewarding is a gift for our confidence which the Lord makes to those who have labored; and giving is a courteous act which he does freely, by grace, fulfilling and surpassing all that creatures deserve.

Thus in our Father, God almighty, we have our being, and in our Mother of mercy we have our reforming and our restoring, in whom our parts are united and all made perfect man, and through the rewards and the gifts of grace of the Holy Spirit we are fulfilled. And our substance is in our Father, God almighty, and our substance is in our Mother, God all wisdom, and our substance is in our Lord God, the Holy Spirit, all goodness, for our substance is whole in each person of the Trinity, who is one God. And our sensuality is only in the second person, Christ Jesus, in whom is the Father and the Holy Spirit; and in him and by him we are powerfully taken out of hell and out of the wretchedness on earth, and gloriously brought up into heaven, and blessedly united to our substance, increased in riches and nobility by all the power of Christ and by the grace and operation of the Holy Spirit.

CHAPTER 59

And we have all this bliss by mercy and grace, and this kind of bliss we never could have had and known, unless that property of goodness which is in God had been opposed, through which we have this bliss. For wickedness has been suffered to rise in opposition to that goodness; and the goodness of mercy and grace opposed that wickedness, and turned everything to goodness and honor for all who will be saved. For this is that property in God which opposes good to evil. So Jesus Christ, who opposes good to evil, is our true Mother. We have our being from him, where the foundation of motherhood begins, with all the sweet protection of love which endlessly follows.

As truly as God is our Father, so truly is God our Mother, and he revealed that in everything, and especially in these sweet words where he says: I am he; that is to say: I am he, the power and goodness of fatherhood; I am he, the wisdom and the lovingness of motherhood; I am he, the light and the grace which is all blessed love; I am he, the Trinity; I am he, the unity; I am he, the great supreme goodness of every kind of thing; I am he who makes you to love; I am he who makes you to long; I am he, the endless fulfilling of all true desires. For where the soul is highest, noblest, most honorable, still it is lowest, meekest and mildest.

And from this foundation in substance we have all the powers of our sensuality by the gift of nature, and by the help and the furthering of mercy and grace, without which we cannot profit. Our great Father, almighty God, who is being, knows us and loved us before time began. Out of this knowledge, in his most wonderful deep love, by the prescient eternal counsel of all the blessed Trinity, he wanted the second person to become our Mother, our brother and our savior. From this it follows that as truly as God is our Father, so truly is God our Mother. Our Father wills, our Mother works, our good Lord the Holy Spirit confirms. And therefore it is our part to love our God in whom we have our being, reverently thanking and praising him for our creation, mightily praying to our Mother for mercy and pity, and to our Lord the Holy Spirit for help and grace. For in these three is all our life: nature, mercy and grace, of which we have mildness, patience and pity, and hatred of sin and wickedness; for the virtues must of themselves hate sin and wickedness.

And so Jesus is our true Mother in nature by our first creation, and he is our true Mother in grace by his taking our created nature. All the lovely works and all the sweet loving offices of beloved motherhood are appropriated to the second person, for in him we have this godly will, whole and safe forever, both in nature and in grace, from his own goodness proper to him.

I understand three ways of contemplating motherhood in God. The first is the foundation of our nature's creation; the second is his taking of our nature, where the motherhood of grace begins; the third is the motherhood at work. And in that, by the same grace, everything is penetrated, in length and in breadth, in height and in depth without end; and it is all one love.

CHAPTER 60

But now I should say a little more about this penetration, as I understood our Lord to mean: How we are brought back by the motherhood of mercy and grace into our natural place, in which we were created by the motherhood of love, a mother's love which never leaves us.

Our Mother in nature, our Mother in grace, because he wanted altogether to become our Mother in all things, made the foundation of his work most humbly and most mildly in the maiden's womb. And he revealed that in the first revelation, when he brought that meek maiden before the eye of my understanding in the simple stature which she had when she conceived; that is to say that our great God, the supreme wisdom of all things, arrayed and prepared himself in this humble place, all ready in our poor flesh, himself to do the service and the office of motherhood in everything. The mother's service is nearest, readiest and surest: nearest because it is most natural, readiest because it is most loving, and surest because it is truest. No one ever might or could perform this office fully, except only him. We know that all our mothers bear us for pain and for death. O, what is that? But our true Mother Jesus, he alone bears us for joy and for endless life, blessed may he be. So he carries us within him in love and travail, until the full time when he wanted to suffer the sharpest thorns and cruel pains that ever were or will be, and at the last he died. And when he had finished, and had borne us so for bliss, still all this could not satisfy his wonderful love. And he revealed this in these great surpassing words of love: If I could suffer more, I would suffer more. He could not die any more, but he did not want to cease working; therefore he must needs nourish us, for the precious love of motherhood has made him our debtor.

The mother can give her child to suck of her milk, but our precious Mother Jesus can feed us with himself, and does, most courteously and most tenderly, with the blessed sacrament, which is the precious food of true life; and with all the sweet sacraments he sustains us most mercifully and graciously, and so he meant in these blessed words, where he said: I am he whom Holy Church preaches and teaches to you. That is to say: All the health and the life of the sacraments, all the power and the grace of my word, all the goodness which is ordained in Holy Church for you, I am he.

The mother can lay her child tenderly to her breast, but our tender Mother Jesus can lead us easily into his blessed breast through his sweet open side, and show us there a part of the godhead and of the joys of heaven, with inner certainty of end-less bliss. And that he revealed in the tenth revelation, giving us the same under-standing in these sweet words which he says: See, how I love you, looking into his blessed side, rejoicing.

This fair lovely word "mother" is so sweet and so kind in itself that it cannot truly be said of anyone or to anyone except of him and to him who is the true Mother of life and of all things. To the property of motherhood belong nature, love, wisdom and knowledge, and this is God. For though it may be so that our bodily bringing to birth is only little, humble and simple in comparison with our spiritual bringing to birth, still it is he who does it in the creatures by whom it is done. The kind, loving mother who knows and sees the need of her child guards it very tenderly, as the nature and condition of motherhood will have. And always as the child grows in age and in stature, she acts differently, but she does not change her love. And when it is even older, she allows it to be chastised to destroy its faults, so as to make the child receive virtues and grace. This work, with every-thing which is lovely and good, our Lord performs in those by whom it is done. So he is our Mother in nature by the operation of grace in the lower part, for love of the higher part. And he wants us to know it, for he wants to have all our love attached to him; and in this I saw that every debt which we owe by God's com-mand to fatherhood and motherhood is fulfilled in truly loving God, which blessed love Christ works in us. And this was revealed in everything, and especially in the great bounteous words when he says: I am he whom you love.

CHAPTER 61

And in our spiritual bringing to birth he uses more tenderness, without any comparison, in protecting us. By so much as our soul is more precious in his sight, he kindles our understanding, he prepares our ways, he eases our conscience, he comforts our soul, he illumines our heart and gives us partial knowledge and love of his blessed divinity, with gracious memory of his sweet humanity and his blessed Passion, with courteous wonder over his great surpassing goodness, and makes us to love everything which he loves for love of him, and to be well satisfied with him and with all his works. And when we fall, quickly he raises us up with his loving embrace and his gracious touch. And when we are strengthened by his sweet working, then we willingly choose him by his grace, that we shall be his servants and his lovers, constantly and forever.

And yet after this he allows some of us to fall more heavily and more grievously than ever we did before, as it seems to us. And then we who are not all wise think that everything which we have undertaken was all nothing. But it is not so, for we need to fall, and we need to see it; for if we did not fall, we should not know how feeble and how wretched we are in ourselves, nor, too, should we know so completely the wonderful love of our Creator.

For we shall truly see in heaven without end that we have sinned grievously in this life; and notwithstanding this, we shall truly see that we were never hurt in his love, nor were we ever of less value in his sight. And by the experience of this falling we shall have a great and marvelous knowledge of love in God without end; for enduring and marvelous is that love which cannot and will not be broken because of offenses.

And this was one profitable understanding; another is the humility and meek-ness which we shall obtain by the sight of our fall, for by that we shall be raised high in heaven, to which raising we might never have come without that meekness. And therefore we need to see it; and if we do not see it, though we fell, that would not profit us. And commonly we first fall and then see it; and both are from the mercy of God.

The mother may sometimes suffer the child to fall and to be distressed in various ways, for its own benefit, but she can never suffer any kind of peril to come to her child, because of her love. And though our earthly mother may suffer her child to perish, our heavenly Mother Jesus may never suffer us who are his children to perish, for he is almighty, all wisdom and all love, and so is none but he, blessed may he be.

But often when our falling and our wretchedness are shown to us, we are so much afraid and so greatly ashamed of ourselves that we scarcely know where we can put ourselves. But then our courteous Mother does not wish us to flee away, for nothing would be less pleasing to him; but he then wants us to behave like a child. For when it is distressed and frightened, it runs quickly to its mother; and if it can do no more, it calls to the mother for help with all its might. So he wants us to act as a meek child, saying: My kind Mother, my gracious Mother, my beloved Mother, have mercy on me. I have made myself filthy and unlike you, and I may not and cannot make it right except with your help and grace.

And if we do not then feel ourselves eased, let us at once be sure that he is behaving as a wise Mother. For if he sees that it is profitable to us to mourn and to weep, with compassion and pity he suffers that until the right time has come, out of his love. And then he wants us to show a child's characteristics, which always naturally trusts in its mother's love in well-being and in woe. And he wants us to commit ourselves fervently to the faith of Holy Church, and find there our beloved Mother in consolation and true understanding, with all the company of the blessed. For one single person may often be broken, as it seems to him, but the entire body of Holy Church was never broken, nor ever will be without end. And therefore it is a certain thing, and good and gracious to will, meekly and fervently, to be fastened and united to our mother Holy Church, who is Christ Jesus. For the flood of mercy which is his dear blood and precious water is plentiful to make us fair and clean. The blessed wounds of our savior are open and rejoice to heal us. The sweet gracious hands of our Mother are ready and diligent about us; for he in all this work exercises the true office of a kind nurse, who has nothing else to do but attend to the safety of her child.

It is his office to save us, it is his glory to do it, and it is his will that we know it; for he wants us to love him sweetly and trust in him meekly and greatly. And he revealed this in these gracious words: I protect you very safely.

[THE SOUL AS CHRIST'S CITADEL]

CHAPTER 68

And then our good Lord opened my spiritual eye, and showed me my soul in the midst of my heart. I saw the soul as wide as if it were an endless citadel, and also as if it were a blessed kingdom, and from the state which I saw in it, I understood that it is a fine city. In the midst of that city sits our Lord Jesus, true God and true man, a handsome person and tall, highest bishop, most awesome king, most honourable lord. And I saw him splendidly clad in honours. He sits erect there in the soul, in peace and rest, and he rules and guards heaven and earth and everything that is. The humanity and the divinity sit at rest, the divinity rules and guards, without instrument or effort. And the soul is wholly occupied by the blessed divinity, sovereign power, sovereign wisdom and sovereign goodness.

The place which Jesus takes in our soul he will nevermore vacate, for in us is his home of homes and his everlasting dwelling. And in this he revealed the delight that he has in the creation of man's soul; for as well as the Father could create a creature and as well as the Son could create a creature, so well did the Holy Spirit want man's spirit to be created, and so it was done. And therefore the blessed Trinity rejoices without end in the creation of man's soul, for it saw without beginning what would delight it without end.

Everything which God has made shows his dominion, as understanding was given at the same time by the example of a creature who is led to see the great nobility and the rulership which is fitting to a lord, and when it had seen all the nobility beneath, then in wonder it was moved to seek up above for that high place where the lord dwells, knowing by reason that his dwelling is in the most honourable place. And thus I understood truly that our soul may never have rest in anything which is beneath itself. And when it comes above all creatures into itself, still it cannot remain contemplating itself; but all its contemplation is blessedly set in God, who is the Creator, dwelling there, for in man's soul is his true dwelling.

And the greatest light and the brightest shining in the city is the glorious love of our Lord God, as I see it. And what can make us to rejoice more in God than to see in him that in us, of all his greatest works, he has joy? For I saw in the same revelation that if the blessed Trinity could have created man's soul any better, any fairer, any nobler than it was created, the Trinity would not have been fully pleased with the creation of man's soul. But because it made man's soul as beautiful, as good, as precious a creature as it could make, therefore the blessed Trinity is fully pleased without end in the creation of man's soul. And it wants our hearts to be powerfully lifted above the depths of the earth and all empty sorrows, and to rejoice in it.

This was a delectable sight and a restful showing, which is without end, and to contemplate it while we are here is most pleasing to God and very great profit to us. And this makes the soul which so contemplates like to him who is contemplated, and unites it in rest and peace. And it was a singular joy and bliss to me that I saw him sitting, for the truth of sitting revealed to me endless dwelling; and he gave me true knowledge that it was he who had revealed everything to me before. And when I had contemplated this with attention, our Lord very humbly revealed words to me, without voice and without opening of lips, just as he had done before, and said very sweetly: Know it well, it was no hallucination which you saw today, but accept and believe it and hold firmly to it, and comfort yourself with it and trust in it, and you will not be overcome.

These last words were said to me to teach me perfect certainty that it is our Lord Jesus who revealed everything to me; and just as in the first words which our good Lord revealed, alluding to his blessed Passion: With this the fiend is overcome, just so he said in the last words, with perfect fidelity, alluding to us all: You will not be overcome. And all this teaching and this true strengthening apply generally to all my fellow Christians, as is said before, and so is the will of God.

And these words: You will not be overcome, were said very insistently and strongly, for certainty and strength against every tribulation which may come. He did not say: You will not be troubled, you will not be belaboured, you will not be disquieted; but he said: You will not be overcome. God wants us to pay attention to these words, and always to be strong in faithful trust, in well-being and in woe, for he loves us and delights in us, and so he wishes us to love him and delight in him and trust greatly in him, and all will be well.

And soon all was hidden, and I saw no more after this.

[THE MEANING OF THE VISIONS IS LOVE]

CHAPTER 86

This book is begun by God's gift and his grace, but it is not yet performed, as I see it. For charity, let us all join with God's working in prayer, thanking, trusting, rejoicing, for so will our good Lord be entreated, by the understanding which I took in all his own intention, and in the sweet words where he says most happily: I am the foundation of your beseeching. For truly I saw and understood in our Lord's meaning that he revealed it because he wants to have it better known than it is. In which knowledge he wants to give us grace to love him and to cleave to him, for he beholds his heavenly treasure with so great love on earth that he will give us more light and solace in heavenly joy, by drawing our hearts from the sorrow and the darkness which we are in.

And from the time that it was revealed, I desired many times to know in what was our Lord's meaning. And fifteen years after and more, I was answered in spiritual understanding, and it was said: What, do you wish to know your Lord's meaning in this thing? Know it well, love was his meaning. Who reveals it to you? Love. What did he reveal to you? Love. Why does he reveal it to you? For love. Remain in this, and you will know more of the same. But you will never know different, without end.

So I was taught that love is our Lord's meaning. And I saw very certainly in this and in everything that before God made us he loved us, which love was never abated and never will be. And in this love he has done all his works, and in this love he has made all things profitable to us, and in this love our life is everlasting. In our creation we had beginning, but the love in which he created us was in him from without beginning. In this love we have our beginning, and all this shall we see in God without end.

Thanks be to God. Here ends the book of revelations of Julian the anchorite of Norwich, on whose soul may God have mercy.[4]

May Jesus grant us this. Amen. So ends the revelation of love of the blessed Trinity, shown by our savior Jesus Christ for our endless comfort and solace, and also that we may rejoice in him in the passing journey of this life. Amen. Jesus. Amen. I pray almighty God that this book may not come except into the hands of those who wish to be his faithful lovers, and those who will submit themselves to the faith of Holy Church and obey the wholesome understanding and teaching of men who are of virtuous life, settled age and profound learning; for this revelation is exalted divinity and wisdom, and therefore it cannot remain with him who is a slave to sin and to the devil. And beware that you do not accept one thing which is according to your pleasure and liking, and reject another, for that is the disposition of heretics. But accept it all together, and understand it truly; it all agrees with Holy Scripture, and is founded upon it, and Jesus, our true love and light and truth, will show this to all pure souls who meekly and perseveringly ask this wisdom from him. And you to whom this book will come, give our savior Christ Jesus great and hearty thanks that he made these showings and revelations for you and to you out of his endless love, mercy and goodness, for a safe guide and conduct for you and us to everlasting bliss, which may Jesus grant us. Amen. Here end the sublime and wonderful revelations of the unutterable love of God, in Jesus Christ vouchsafed to a dear lover of his, and in her to all his dear friends and lovers whose hearts like hers do flame in the love of our dearest Jesus.

---

4. What follows is a lengthy version of the traditional "colophon" in which the author takes leave of the work and its audience; expressions of inadequacy and appeals to God are common elements.

◈

COMPANION READINGS
Richard Rolle: from The Fire of Love[1]

It is obvious to those who are in love that no one attains the heights of devotion at once, or is ravished with contemplative sweetness. In fact it is only very occasionally—and then only momentarily—that they are allowed to experience heavenly things; their progress to spiritual strength is a gradual one. When they have attained the gravity of behavior so necessary and have achieved a certain stability of mind—as much as changing circumstances permit—a certain perfection is acquired after great labor. It is then that they can feel some joy in loving God.

Notwithstanding, it appears that all those who are mighty performers in virtue immediately and genuinely experience the warmth of uncreated or created charity, melt in the immense fire of love, and sing within their hearts the song of divine praise. For this mystery is hidden from the many, and is revealed to the few, and those the most special. So the more sublime such a level is, the fewer—in this world—are those who find it. Rarely in fact have we found a man who is so holy or even perfect in this earthly life endowed with love so great as to be raised up to contemplation to the level of jubilant song. This would mean that he would receive within himself the sound that is sung in heaven, and that he would echo back the praises of God as it were in harmony, pouring forth sweet notes of music and composing spiritual songs as he offers his heavenly praises, and that he would truly experience in his heart the genuine fire of the love of God. It would be surprising if anyone without such experience should claim the name of contemplative when the psalmist, speaking in character as the typical contemplative, exclaims, *I will go into the house of the Lord, with the voice of praise and thanksgiving.*[2] The praise, of course, is the praise offered by the banqueter, one who is feeding on heavenly sweetness.

Further, perfect souls who have been caught up into this friendship—surpassing, abundant, and eternal!—discover that life is suffused with imperishable sweetness from the glittering chalice of sweet charity. In holy happy wisdom they inhale joyful heat into their souls, and as a result are much cheered by the indescribable comfort of God's healing medicine. Here at all events is refreshment for those who love their high and eternal heritage, even though in their earthly exile distress befell them. However they think it not unfitting to endure a few years' hardship in order to be raised to heavenly thrones, and never leave them. They have been selected out of all mankind to be the beloved of their Maker and to be crowned with glory, since, like the seraphim in highest heaven, they have been inflamed with the same love. Physically they may have sat in solitary state, but in mind they have companied with angels, and have yearned for their Beloved. Now they sing most sweetly a prayer of love everlasting as they rejoice in Jesus:

---

1. Richard Rolle (c. 1300–1349) studied at Oxford and then spent part of his life as a hermit, but he also acted as spiritual director for women engaged in solitary contemplation. In seeking to express and draw his readers toward the ineffable experience of the divine, Rolle made particularly intensive use of the imagery of bodily sensation and action—warmth, sweetness, and song. Well-known biblical texts such as the Song of Songs provided both a precedent and a language for Rolle's explorations. Unlike more rigorous mystics, he presents at least the earlier stages of the mystical ascent as an almost spontaneous, if also conflict-ridden, rising of the soul like a spark toward God. Rolle wrote a number of English lyrics and meditations; *The Fire of Love* is his most famous treatise in Latin. The passage here, taken from ch. 2, is translated by Clifton Wolters.

2. Psalms 42.4.

O honeyed flame, sweeter than all sweet, delightful beyond all creation!
My God, my Love, surge over me, pierce me by your love, wound me with
    your beauty.
Surge over me, I say, who am longing for your comfort.
Reveal your healing medicine to your poor lover.
See, my one desire is for you; it is you my heart is seeking.
My soul pants for you; my whole being is athirst for you.
    Yet you will not show yourself to me; you look away;
    you bar the door, shun me, pass me over;
You even laugh at my innocent sufferings.
And yet you snatch your lovers away from all earthly things.
You lift them above every desire for worldly matters.
You make them capable of loving you—
    and love you they do indeed.
So they offer you their praise in spiritual song
    which bursts out from that inner fire;
    they know in truth the sweetness of the dart of love.
Ah, eternal and most lovable of all joys,
    you raise us from the very depths,
    and entrance us with the sight of divine majesty so often!
Come into me, Beloved!
All ever I had I have given up for you;
    I have spurned all that was to be mine,
    that you might make your home in my heart,
    and I your comfort.
Do not forsake me now, smitten with such great longing,
    whose consuming desire is to be amongst those who love you.
Grant me to love you, to rest in you, that in your kingdom I may be worthy
    to appear before you world without end.

from *The Cloud of Unknowing*[1]

CHAPTER 3

Lift up your heart to God with humble love: and mean God himself, and not what
you get out of him. Indeed, hate to think of anything but God himself, so that nothing occupies your mind or will but only God. Try to forget all created things that he
ever made, and the purpose behind them, so that your thought and longing do not
turn or reach out to them either in general or in particular. Let them go, and pay no
attention to them. It is the work of the soul that pleases God most. All saints and
angels rejoice over it, and hasten to help it on with all their might. All the fiends,
however, are furious at what you are doing, and try to defeat it in every conceivable

1. Written toward the end of the 14th century, *The Cloud of Unknowing* draws upon an influential tradition of Neoplatonic Christianity. One strand of this tradition extolled the *via negativa*: the approach to union with God by emptying the
mind of worldly consciousness, and entering instead a dark place of uncertainty, a "cloud of unknowing." Though informed by a very private notion of disciplined spiritual quest, the *Cloud* nevertheless insists that the mystic's work serves
the salvation of all the faithful. At the same time, the text also betrays considerable anxiety about, even hostility to, the
spread of an undirected and body-oriented spirituality in its time. It particularly warns against the danger of demonic influence in those seeking too eagerly some bodily sign of the divine. It mentions the sensation of heat and other enthusiastic bodily manifestations, which may recall the affective imagery of Rolle. The translation here is by Clifton Wolters.

way. Moreover, the whole of mankind is wonderfully helped by what you are doing, in ways you do not understand. Yes, the very souls in purgatory find their pain eased by virtue of your work. And in no better way can you yourself be made clean or virtuous than by attending to this. Yet it is the easiest work of all when the soul is helped by grace and has a conscious longing. And it can be achieved very quickly. Otherwise it is hard and beyond your powers.

Do not give up then, but work away at it till you have this longing. When you first begin, you find only darkness, and as it were a cloud of unknowing. You don't know what this means except that in your will you feel a simple steadfast intention reaching out towards God. Do what you will, this darkness and this cloud remain between you and God, and stop you both from seeing him in the clear light of rational understanding, and from experiencing his loving sweetness in your affection. Reconcile yourself to wait in this darkness as long as is necessary, but still go on longing after him whom you love. For if you are to feel him or to see him in this life, it must always be in this cloud, in this darkness. And if you will work hard at what I tell you, I believe that through God's mercy you will achieve this very thing.

from CHAPTER 4

So that you may make no mistake, or go wrong in this matter, let me tell you a little more about it as I see it. This work does not need a long time for its completion. Indeed, it is the shortest work that can be imagined! It is no longer, no shorter, than one atom, which as a philosopher of astronomy will tell you is the smallest division of time. It is so small that it cannot be analyzed: it is almost beyond our grasp. Yet it is as long as the time of which it has been written, "All the time that is given to thee, it shall be asked of thee how thou hast spent it." And it is quite right that you should have to give account of it. It is neither shorter nor longer than a single impulse of your will, the chief part of your soul. * * *

So pay great attention to this marvelous work of grace within your soul. It is always a sudden impulse and comes without warning, springing up to God like some spark from the fire. An incredible number of such impulses arise in one brief hour in the soul who has a will to this work! In one such flash the soul may completely forget the created world outside. Yet almost as quickly it may relapse back to thoughts and memories of things done and undone—all because of our fallen nature. And as fast again it may rekindle.

This then, in brief, is how it works. It is obviously not make-believe, nor wrong thinking, nor fanciful opinion. These would not be the product of a devout and humble love, but the outcome of the pride and inventiveness of the imagination. If this work of grace is to be truly and genuinely understood, all such proud imaginings must ruthlessly be stamped out!

For whoever hears or reads about all this, and thinks that it is fundamentally an activity of the mind, and proceeds then to work it all out along these lines, is on quite the wrong track. He manufactures an experience that is neither spiritual nor physical. He is dangerously misled and in real peril. So much so, that unless God in his great goodness intervenes with a miracle of mercy and makes him stop and submit to the advice of those who really know, he will go mad, or suffer some other dreadful form of spiritual mischief and devilish deceit. Indeed, almost casually as it were, he may be lost eternally, body and soul. So for the love of God be careful, and do not attempt to achieve this experience intellectually. I tell you truly it cannot come this way. So leave it alone.

Do not think that because I call it a "darkness" or a "cloud" it is the sort of cloud you see in the sky, or the kind of darkness you know at home when the light is out. That kind of darkness or cloud you can picture in your mind's eye in the height of summer, just as in the depth of a winter's night you can picture a clear and shining light. I do not mean this at all. By "darkness" I mean "a lack of knowing"—just as anything that you do not know or may have forgotten may be said to be "dark" to you, for you cannot see it with your inward eye. For this reason it is called "a cloud," not of the sky, of course, but "of unknowing," a cloud of unknowing between you and your God.

CHAPTER 52

The madness I speak of is effected like this: they read and hear it said that they should stop the "exterior" working with their mind, and work interiorly. And because they do not know what this "interior" work means, they do it wrong. For they turn their actual physical minds inwards to their bodies, which is an unnatural thing, and they strain as if to see spiritually with their physical eyes, and to hear within with their outward ears, and to smell and taste and feel and so on inwardly in the same way. So they pervert the natural order, and with this false ingenuity they put their minds to such unnecessary strains that ultimately their brains are turned. And at once the devil is able to deceive them with false lights and sounds, sweet odors and wonderful tastes, glowing and burning in their hearts or stomachs, backs or loins or limbs.

In all this make-believe they imagine they are peacefully contemplating their God, unhindered by vain thoughts. So they are, in a fashion, for they are so stuffed with falsehood that a little extra vanity cannot disturb them. Why? Because it is the same devil that is working on them now as would be tempting them if they were on the right road. You know very well that he will not get in his own way. He does not remove all thought of God from them, lest they should become suspicious.

◦❦◦

[END OF MYSTICAL WRITINGS]

MEDIEVAL BIBLICAL DRAMA

Medieval biblical drama entertains with both comedy and pathos, but it was meant to instruct as well. It developed not from classical drama, which was little imitated in the Middle Ages, but from church liturgies, especially those associated with Easter and the feast of Corpus Christi, a holiday celebrating Christ's presence among the faithful through the Eucharist. Although biblical dramas originated on the Continent, in Latin and then the vernacular languages, they also had a great flowering in England from the late fourteenth to the late sixteenth centuries. Two surviving play collections, from Chester and York, were conceived as complete cycles of sacred history from Creation to the Last Judgment, including such events as the fall of Lucifer, Noah's flood, the nativity of Christ, and Christ's crucifixion and resurrection. The York plays were performed, across a single vastly ambitious day, around the feast of Corpus Christi in midsummer. The huge arc of biblical narrative gains coherence in these plays (as in other medieval treatments) by a pattern of typology whereby Old Testament events are understood to be fulfilled in the New Testament. Hence Satan's deception and Adam's fall are redeemed by Christ's sacrifice. At a level of analogy, Old Testament events and characters predict and are fulfilled by New Testament ones—Isaac and Moses, for instance, are seen as "types" of Christ, while Cain and Pharaoh are types of Satan.

Other surviving groups of plays, some individually much longer and more ambitious than those from York and Chester, may have been collected together in play-books without being conceived or performed as a cycle. These include the plays now known only as "N-Town" and the Townley plays. Some of the Townley plays are linked to the town of Wakefield, not far from York. These Middle English biblical plays represent a wide range of styles, staging techniques, and sponsors. The York plays were financed by craft guilds (also called "mysteries," which led to the cycles being called mystery plays); the Townley plays may have been produced individually under parish sponsorship. The York plays were enacted on large carts that rolled from one public space to another, each play performed repeatedly; some Townley plays (like the *Second Play of the Shepherds*) require a central acting area surrounded by several more specific scenes, perhaps on scaffolds. What the plays have in common is their largely outdoor production, their association with prosperous towns and cities, many (not all) in the north, and their connection with a newly prosperous mercantile class. Often guilds sponsored plays specifically linked to their craft; at York, the Shipwrights produced the play of Noah's Ark, and the Fishers and Mariners the play of the Flood.

The popularity of these dramas—as well as their function as a surrogate Bible for the poor—can be seen in Chaucer's *Miller's Tale*. The Miller himself insists on telling his tale out of order, and does so in "Pilate's voice," the ranting manner of Pontius Pilate in the Passion plays, and in the tale, the foppish Absolon woos his beloved Alison by playing the role of the tyrant Herod on a scaffold. Indeed, Chaucer's tale may be our first solid reference to Middle English biblical drama, and the locales both of the Miller's performance (between London and Canterbury) and of Absolon's (Oxford, where the tale is set) suggest the geographical range of these plays, many of which must have been lost when they were discouraged during the Reformation.

The Second Play of the Shepherds

Nowhere are the sacred and the profane paired as brilliantly as in the Nativity play known as the *Second Play of the Shepherds*, one of the Townley collection of plays probably performed at the prosperous Yorkshire town of Wakefield. The play was written or revised by an artist of dramatic imagination and poetic skill, often called the Wakefield Master. His great achievement is his ability to make biblical stories relevant to fifteenth-century England in such a way that daily life takes on typological significance. The key example of this, at once moving and funny, is the parallel between Mak's stolen sheep, hidden in swaddling clothes in a cradle, and the newborn Christ child whom the shepherds visit at the end of the play. The mercy that the shepherds show to Mak by tossing him in a blanket rather than delivering him to be hanged prefigures the mercy that Christ will bring into the world.

No matter how neatly the typological scheme works, however, the author does not present the birth of Christ as nullifying the complaints of the play's characters. With his guileful assault on the sheepfold and his concealment of the "horned lad" swaddled in a cradle, Mak may be a type of the devil, but his complaints of poverty are real: he steals the sheep to feed a hungry family. Just as real are the complaints of the shepherds, to which the first 180 lines of the play are devoted. The shepherds grumble about taxes, lords and their condescending servants, and their own nagging, prolific wives.

The plight of the shepherds reflects the impact of the wool and cloth trade; it enriched England in the fourteenth and fifteenth centuries, but it also impoverished peasant farmers when landlords enclosed tracts of land for conversion to lucrative sheep farming. These complaints cannot simply be dismissed as the "moan" of fallen men who fail to understand their need for divine grace. Nor can the complaints of Mak's wife Gill against women's work be seen as simply setting her up as a contrast with the patient Virgin Mary at the end of the play. Nonetheless, the social and musical harmony exhibited as the play closes does suggest the transformation these shepherds undergo, and into which the play invites its believing audience.

The Second Play of the Shepherds

[Scene: Field near Bethlehem.]

I PASTOR: Lord, what these weathers are cold!   And I am ill happed.[1]

    I am near hand dold,°   so long have I napped;   *almost numb*

    My legs they fold,   my fingers are chapped.

    It is not as I would,   for I am all lapped°   *tied up*

5   In sorrow.

    In storms and tempest,

    Now in the east, now in the west,

    Woe is him has never rest

    Mid-day nor morrow!

10   But we sely° shepherds   that walks on the moor,   *poor*

    In faith we are near hands   out of the door.

    No wonder, as it stands,   if we be poor,

    For the tilthe of our lands   lies fallow as the floor,

    As ye ken.°   *know*

15   We are so hamed,°   *hamstrung*

    For-taxed° and ramed,°   *overburdened / oppressed*

    We are made hand tamed

    With these gentlery men.°   *gentry, aristocrats*

    Thus they reave° us our rest,   our Lady them wary!°   *rob / curse*

20   These men that are lord-fest,[2]   they cause the plow tarry.

    That men say is for the best,   we find it contrary.

    Thus are husbandys° opprest,   in point to miscarry   *farmhands*

    On live.

    Thus hold they us hunder;°   *under*

25   Thus they bring us in blonder;°   *trouble*

    It were great wonder

    And ever should we thrive.

    For may he get a paint slefe°   or a broche now on days,   *painted sleeve*

    Woe is him that him grefe°   or once again says!   *troubles*

30   Dare noman him reprefe,°   what mastry° he mays,   *reprove / power*

    And yet may noman lefe°   one word that he says,   *believe*

    No letter.

    He can make purveance°   *provision*

    With boast and bragance,

35   And all is through maintenance

    Of men that are greater.

---

1. Clothed.   2. Bound to their lords.

There shall come a swane as proud as a po,[3]
He must borrow my wane,° my plow also,   *wagon*
Then I am full fane° to grant or he go.   *pleased*
40 Thus live we in pain, anger, and woe,
By night and day.
He must have if he langed,°   *desired*
If I should forgang° it;   *forgo*
I were better be hanged
45 Then once say him nay.

It does me good, as I walk thus by mine one,
Of this world for to talk in manner of moan.
To my sheep will I stalk, and hearken anone,° *awhile*
There abide on a balk,° or sit on a stone, *ridge*
50 Full soon.
For I trowe,° perde,°   *believe / by God*
True men if they be,
We get more company
Or° it be noon.   *before*

[*The Second Shepherd enters without noticing the First.*]
II PASTOR: Benste and Dominus![4] What may this bemean?
Why fares this world thus? Oft have we not seen?
Lord, these weathers are spytus,° and the winds full keen, *spiteful*
And the frosts so hideous they water my eyes—
No lie.
60 Now in dry, now in wete,
Now in snow, now in sleet;
When my shoen° freeze to my feet,   *shoes*
It is not all easy.

But as far as I ken, or yet as I go,
65 We sely wedmen dre mekyll woe;[5]
We have sorrow then and then: it falls oft so.
Sely Copple,[6] our hen, both to and fro
She cackles;
But begin she to croak,
70 To groan or to cluck,
Woe is him is of our cock,
For he is in the shackels.

These men that are wed have not all their will;
When they are full hard sted,° they sigh full still; *placed*
75 God wayte° they are led full hard and full ill; *knows*
In bower° nor in bed they say nought there till,° *bedroom / thereto*
This tide.°   *time*
My part have I fun;°   *found*

---

3. A servant as proud as a peacock.
4. Corruption of a Latin blessing, *Benedicite ad Dominum.*
5. We poor, innocent married men suffer much.
6. A copple is the crest on a bird's head.

I know my lesson.

80 Woe is him that is bun,°   *bound in marriage*

For he must abide.

But now late in our lives a marvel to me,

That I think my heart rives°   such wonders to see.   *breaks*

What that destiny drives   it should so be;

85 Some men will have two wives   and some men three,

In store;

Some are woe that has any,

But so far can I,

Woe is him that has many,

90 For he felys° sore.   *suffers*

But young men of a-wooing,   for God that you bought,°   *redeemed*

Be well ware of wedding,   and think in your thought,

"Had I wist"° is a thing   it serves of nought;   *known*

Mekyll° still° mourning   has wedding home brought,   *much / constant*

95 And griefs,

With many a sharp shower;

For thou may catch in an hour

That shall savour fulle sour

As long as thou lives.

100 For, as ever read I pistill[7]   I have one to my fere,°   *mate*

As sharp as a thistle,   as rough as a brere;

She is browed like a bristle   with a sour-loten cheer;[8]

Had she once wet her whistle   she could sing full clear

Her *Paternoster*.°   *Lord's Prayer*

105 She is as great as a whale;

She has a gallon of gall.

By him that died for us all,

I would I had run to°   I had lost her.   *until*

I PASTOR: God look over the raw![9]   Full deafly ye stand.

II PASTOR: Yea, the devil in thy maw,°   so tariand.°   *mouth / slow*

Saw thou awre° of Daw?[1]   *anywhere*

I PASTOR: Yea, on a ley land°   *fallow ground*

Hard I him blaw.[2]   He comes here at hand,

Not far.

Stand still.

II PASTOR: Why?

I PASTOR: For he comes, hope I.

II PASTOR: He will make us both a lie

But if° we beware.   *unless*

7. [St. Paul's] Epistle.   attend me.
8. Sour-looking face.   1. The Third Shepherd.
9. Let God pay attention to his audience (row), i.e., God   2. I just blew by him.

[*Enter Third Shepherd.*]

III PASTOR: Christ's cross me speed,   and Saint Nicholas!
    There of had I need;   it is worse than it was.
120   Whoso could take heed   and let the world pass,
    It is ever in dread   and brekill° as glass,   *brittle*
    And slithes.°   *slides away*
    This world fowre° never so,   *fared*
    With marvels mo and mo,
125   Now in weal, now in woe,
    And all thing writhes.°   *turns about*

    Was never sin° Noah's flood   such floods seen;   *since*
    Winds and rains so rude,   and storms so keen;
    Some stammerd, some stood   in doubt,° as I ween;   *fear*
130   Now God turn all to good!   I say as I mean,
    For° ponder.   *to*
    These floods so they drown,
    Both fields and in town,
    And bears all down,
135   And that is a wonder.

    We that walk on the nights,   our cattle to keep,
    We see sudden sights   when other men sleep.
    Yet me think my heart lights;   I see shrews peep;[3]
    Ye are two ill wights.   I will give my sheep
140   A turn.
    But full ill have I meant;
    As I walk on this bent,
    I may lightly repent,
    My toes if I spurn.

145   Ah, sir, God you save,   and master mine!
    A drink fain would I have,   and somewhat to dine
I PASTOR: Christ's curse, my knave,   thou art a leder hine!°   *lazy servant*
II PASTOR: What, the boy list rave!   Abide unto sine;[4]
    We have made it.[5]
150   Ill thrift on thy pate!
    Though the shrew came late,
    Yet is he in state
    To dine, if he had it.

III PASTOR: Such servants as I,   that sweats and swinks,°   *works*
155   Eats our bread full dry,   and that me forthinks;°   *upsets*
    We are oft wet and weary   when master-men winks;°   *sleeps*
    Yet comes full lately   both diners and drinks,
    But nately.°   *thoroughly*
    Both our dame and our sire,
160   When we have run in the mire,
    They can nip° at our hire,°   *trim / wages*

3. I see villains peeping out.   5. We have already eaten.
4. The boy is crazy; wait a while.

And pay us full lately.

But here my troth, master: for the fare that ye make,
I shall do therafter,   work as I take;
165   I shall do a little, sir,   and emang ever lake,[6]
For yet lay my supper   never on my stomach
In fields.
Whereto should I threpe?°   *wrangle*
With my staff can I leap,
170   And men say "Light cheap°   *little cost*
Letherly for-yields."°   *poorly yields*

I PASTOR: Thou were an ill lad   to ride a-wooing
With a man that had   but little of spending.
II PASTOR: Peace, boy, I bade.   No more jangling,°   *chattering*
175   Or I shall make there full rad,°   by the heavens king!   *quickly*
With thy gauds°—   *tricks*
Where are our sheep, boy?—we scorn.°   *despise*
III PASTOR: Sir, this same day at morn
I them left in the corn,
180   When they rang lauds.[7]

They have pasture good,   they cannot go wrong.
I PASTOR: That is right, by the roode![8]   these nights are long,
Yet I would, or we yode,°   one gave us a song.   *went*
II PASTOR: So I thought as I stood,   to mirth us among.
III PASTOR: I grant.
I PASTOR: Let me sing the tenory.
II PASTOR: And I treble so hee.
III PASTOR: Then the meyne° falls to me: *middle*
Let see how ye chant.
[*They sing.*]
Tunc intrat Mak in clamide se super togam vestitus.[9]

MAK: Now, Lord, for thy names vii,[1]   that made both moon and starns°   *stars*
Well mo then can I neven°   thy will, Lord, of me tharns;[2]   *say*
I am all uneven,   that moves oft my harness.
Now would God I were in heaven,   for there weep no barnes°   *babies*
So still.
I PASTOR: Who is that pipes so poor?
MAK: Would God ye wist how I foor!°   *fared*
Lo, a man that walks on the moor,
And has not all his will!

II PASTOR: Mak, where has thou gone?   Tell us tiding.
III PASTOR: Is he comme? Then ylkon°   take heed to his thing.   *everyone*

---

6. Keep playing besides.
7. The first church service of the day.
8. Cross; the humor here, as with the other oaths, is based
on the anachronism that Jesus has not yet been born,

much less crucified.
9. Then Mak enters, wearing a cloak over his garment.
1. Seven (written by the copyist as the roman numeral).
2. Is lacking.

Et accipit clamidem ab ipso.[3]

MAK: What! Ich be a yoman,[4]   I tell you, of the king;
    The self and the same,   sond° from a great lording,   *messenger*
    And sich.°   *such like*
    Fy on you! Goeth hence
205   Out of my presence!
    I must have reverence;
    Why, who be ich?

I PASTOR: Why make ye it so quaint?[5]   Mak, ye do wrang.
II PASTOR: But, Mak, list ye saint?   I trow that ye lang.[6]
III PASTOR: I trow the shrew can paint,   the devill might him hang!
MAK: Ich shall make complaint, and make you all to thwang[7]
    At a word,
    And tell even how ye doth.
I PASTOR: But, Mak, is that sooth?
215   Now take out that southren tooth,°   *accent*
    And set in a turd!

II PASTOR: Mak, the devil in your eye!   A stroke would I lean° you.   *lend*
III PASTOR: Mak, know ye not me?   By God, I could teen° you.   *rage at*
MAK: God look you all three!   Me thought I had seen you;
220   Ye are a fair company.
I PASTOR: Can ye now mean you?
II PASTOR: Shrew, pepe![8]
    Thus late as thou goes,
    What will men suppose?
    And thou has an ill nose°   *reputation*
225   Of steeling of sheep.

MAK: And I am true as steel,   all men waytt,°   *know*
    But a sickness I feel   that holds me full haytt;°   *hot*
    My belly fares not weel;   it is out of estate.
III PASTOR: Seldom lies the devil   dead by the gate.[9]
MAK: Therfore
    Full sore am I and ill,
    If I stand stone still;
    I eat not an nedill°   *scrap*
    This month and more.

I PASTOR: How fares thy wife? By my hood,   how fares sho?°   *she*
MAK: Lies waltering,° by the rood,   by the fire, lo!   *collapsed*
    And a house full of brood.°   She drinks well, too;   *children*
    Ill spede° other good   that she will do!   *success*
    But sho
240   Eats as fast as she can,

---

3. And he takes his cloak from him.
4. Freeborn property-holder.
5. Why act so elegant?
6. Do you want to be a saint? I think you long to be.
7. Be beaten.
8. Villain, look around!
9. Proverbial: The devil seldom lies dead by the wayside; i.e., the devil is not often an innocent victim.

And ilk° year that comes to man   *each*
She brings forth a lakan,°   *baby*
And some years two.
But were I not more gracious   and richer by far;
245   I were eaten out of house   and of harbar;°   *home*
Yet is she a foul dowse,°   if ye come nar;   *wench*
There is none that trowse°   nor knows a war°   *imagines / worse*
Than ken I.
Now will ye see what I proffer,
250   To give all in my coffer
To morn at next to offer
Her hed mas-penny.[1]

II PASTOR: I wote so forwaked°   is none in this shire: *sleepless*
     I would sleep if I taked   less to my hire.
III PASTOR: I am cold and naked,   and would have a fire.
I PASTOR: I am weary, for-rakyd,°   and run in the mire.   *exhausted*
     Wake thou!
II PASTOR: Nay, I will lyg° down by,   *lie*
     For I must sleep truly.
III PASTOR: As good a man's son was I
     As any of you.

     But, Mak, come hither! Between   shall thou lyg down.
     [*Mak lies down with the Shepherds.*]
MAK: Then might I let you bedene   of that ye would rowne,[2]
     No drede.
265   From my top to my toe,
     Manus was commendo,
     Poncio Pilato,[3]
     Christ cross me speed!
   Tunc surgit, pastoribus dormientibus, et dicit[4]

     Now were time for a man that   lacks what he would
270   To stalk privily than   unto a fold,
     And nimbly to work than,   and be not too bold,
     For he might aby the bargain,   if it were told
     At the ending.
     Now were time for to reyll;°   *revel*
275   But he needs good counsel
     That fain would fare well,
     And has but little spending.

     But about you a circle,   as round as a moon,
     Too I have done that I will,   till° that it be noon,[5]   *until*

1. Penny offering for a mass for the dead.
2. That way I can readily prevent you from whispering together.
3. An amusing corruption of two Bible verses: "Into your hands I commend my soul" and "I wash my hands of this man."
4. Then Mak arises, while the shepherds are sleeping, and speaks.
5. Mak is casting a spell on the shepherds in the form of a fairy circle to keep them from waking.

280   That ye lyg stone still   to that I have done,
    And I shall say theretill   of good words a foyne.°   *a few*
    "On hight
    Over your heads my hand I lift;
    Out go your eyes! Fordo° your sight!"   *ruin*
285   But yet I must make better shift,
    And it be right.

    Lord, what they sleep hard!   That may ye all here;
    Was I never a shepherd,   but now will I lere.°   *learn*
    If the flock be scared,   yet shall I nip near.
290   How, drawes° hitherward!   Now mends our cheer   *come*
    From sorrow:
    A fat sheep, I dare say,
    A good fleece, dare I lay,
    Eft-whyte when I may,[6]
295   But this will I borrow.
    [Mak goes home to his wife.]

    How, Gill, art thou in?   Get us some light.
UXOR EIUS:[7] Who makes such din   this time of the night?
    I am set for to spin;   I hope not[8] I might
    Rise a penny to win,°   I shrew° them on height!   *gain / curse*
300   So fares
    A housewife that has been
    To be raised° thus between: *disturbed*
    Here may no note° be seen   *scrap*
    For such small chares.°   *chores*

MAK: Good wife, open the hek!°   Sees thou not what I bring?   *inner door*
UXOR: I may thole the dray the snek.[9]   Ah, come in, my sweeting!
MAK: Yea, thou thar not rek°   of my long standing.   *care*
UXOR: By the naked neck   art thou like for to hing.
MAK: Do way:
310   I am worthy my meat,°   *supper*
    For in a strait° can I get   *tight spot*
    More than they that swink° and sweat   *work*
    All the long day.

    Thus it fell to my lot,   Gill, I had such grace.
UXOR: It were a foul blot   to be hanged for the case.
MAK: I have skaped, Jelot,[1]   oft as hard a glase.°   *blow*
UXOR: But so long goes the pot   to the water, men says,
    At last
    Comes it home broken.
MAK: Well know I the token,

---

6. I will pay it back when I can.
7. His wife.
8. I don't expect that.

9. I will let you draw the latch.
1. Affectionate nickname for "Gill."

        But let it never be spoken;
        But come and help fast.
        I would he were flayn;°   I lyst° well eat: *skinned / wish*
        This twelvemonth was I not   so fain of one sheep mete.
UXOR: Come they or° he be slain,   and hear the sheep bleat—   *before*
MAK: Then might I be tane.°   That were a cold sweat!   *taken*
        Go spar°   *lock*
        The gate-door.
UXOR: Yes, Mak,
        For and° they come at thy back—   *if*
MAK: Then might I buy, for all the pack,[2]
        The devil of the war.

UXOR: A good bowrde° have I spied,   sin thou can none.   *trick*
        Here shall we him hide   to° they be gone;   *until*
335   In my cradle abide.   Let me alone,
        And I shall lyg beside   in childbed, and groan.
MAK: Thou red;°   *get ready*
        And I shall say thou was light°   *delivered*
        Of a knave child this night.
UXOR: Now well is me day bright,
340   That ever was I bred.

        This is a good gise°   and a far cast;   *way*
        Yet a woman avise   helps at the last.
        I wote° never who spies,   agane° go thou fast.   *know / back*
MAK: But I come or they rise, else blows a cold blast!
345   I will go sleep.
    [*Mak returns to the Shepherds and lies down.*]
        Yet sleeps all this meneye,°   *household*
        And I shall go stalk privily
        As it had never been I
        That carried there sheep.

I PASTOR: *Resurrex a mortruis!*[3]   Have hold my hand.
        Iudas carnas dominus![4]   I may not well stand:
        My foot sleeps, by Jesus,   and I water fastand.[5]
        I thought that we had laid us   full near England.
II PASTOR: Ah ye!
355   Lord, what I have slept well;
        As fresh as an eel,
        As light I me feel
        As leaf on a tree.

III PASTOR: Benste° be here in!   So my heart quakes,   *a blessing*
360   My heart is out of skin,°   what so it makes.   *(body)*

---

2. Then I may have the worse, for there are such a pack of them.
3. Corruption from the Latin Bible of "He rose from the dead."
4. A corruption into Latin gibberish, "Judas lord of the flesh."
5. Stagger from lack of food.

Who makes all this din?   So my brows blakes°   *darkens*
To the door will I win.   Hark, fellows, wakes!
We were four:
See ye awre° of Mak now?   *anywhere*

I PASTOR: We were up or thou.
II PASTOR: Man, I give God a vow,
Yet yede° he nawre.°   *went / nowhere*

III PASTOR: Me thought he was lapt,°   in a wolf skin.   *clothed*
I PASTOR: So are many hapt°   now namely within.   *covered*
II PASTOR: When we had long napped,   me thought with a gyn°   *trap*
A fat sheep he trapped,   but he made no din.
III PASTOR: Be still:
Thy dream makes thee woode:°   *mad*
It is but phantom, by the roode.°   *cross*
I PASTOR: Now God turn all to good,
If it be his will.

II PASTOR: Rise, Mak, for shame!   Thou lies right long.
MAK: Now Christ's holy name   be us among!
What is this? For Saint Jame,   I may not well gang!
380   I trow I be the same.   Ah, my neck has lain wrong
Enough.
Mekill,° thanks syn° yister even,   *many / since*
Now, by Saint Steven,
I was flayd° with a sweven,°   *frightened /dream*
385   My heart out of slough.°   *skin*

I thought Gill began to croak   and travail° full sad,   *struggle*
Welner° at the first cock,   of a young lad   *nearly*
For to mend our flock.   Then be I never glad;
I have tow° on my rock°   more then ever I had.   *flax / distaff*
390   Ah, my head!
A house full of young tharms;°   *children*
The devil knock out their harns!°   *brains*
Woe is him has many barns,
And thereto little bread!

395   I must go home, by your leave,   to Gill, as I thought.
I pray you looke,° my sleeve   that I steal nought: *inspect*
I am loath you to grieve, or from you take ought.
III PASTOR: Go forth, ill might thou chefe!° Now would I we sought,   *fare*
This morn,
400   That we had all our store.
I PASTOR: But I will go before;
Let us meet.
II PASTOR: Whore?
III PASTOR: At the crooked thorn.
[*The Shepherds leave. Mak knocks at his door.*]

MAK: Undo this door! Who is here?   How long shall I stand?

UXOR EIUS: Who makes such a bere?°   Now walk in the wenyand.[6]   *noise*
MAK: Ah Gill, what cheer?   It is I, Mak, your husband.
UXOR: Then may we be here   the devil in a band,
    Sir Gyle:[7]
    Lo, he comes with a lote°   *noise*
410   As he were holden° in the throat.   *held*
    I may not sit at my note,°   *work*
    A hand-lang° while.   *little*

MAK: Will ye hear what fare she makes   to get her a glose?[8]
    And does nought but lakes°   and claws her toes.   *plays*
UXOR: Why, who wanders, who wakes?   Who commes, who goes?
    Who brews, who bakes?   What makes me thus hose?°   *hoarse*
    And than,
    It is rewthe° to behold,   *pitiful*
    Now in hot, now in cold,
420   Full woeful is the household
    That wants a woman.

    But what end has thou made   with the herds, Mak?
MAK: The last word that thay said   when I turned my back,
    They would look that they had   their sheep, all the pack.
425   I hope[9] they will not be well paid   when they their sheep lack,
    Perde!
    But how so the game goes,
    To me they will suppose,
    And make a foul noise,
430   And cry out upon me.

    But thou must do as thou hight.°   *said*
UXOR: I accord me there till.
    I shall swaddle him right   in my cradle;
    If it were a greater sleight,°   yet could I help till.   *trick*
    I will lyg down straight.   Come hap me.
MAK: I will.
UXOR: Behind!
    Come Coll[1] and his maroo,°   *mate*
    They will nyp° us full naroo.°   *pinch / hard*
MAK: But I may cry out "Haroo!"
    The sheep if they find.

UXOR: Harken ay when they call;   they will come onone.°   *soon*
    Come and make ready all   and sing by thine one;
    Sing "lullay" thou shall,   for I must groan,
    And cry out by the wall   on Mary and John,
    For sore.

6. Waning hour, unlucky time.   9. Expect.
7. Mister Deceiver (the Devil).   1. The First Shepherd.
8. Make up an excuse.

445   Sing "lullay" on fast
           When thou hears at the last;
           And but I play a false cast,°   trick
           Trust me no more.

      [*At the crooked thorn.*]
III PASTOR: Ah, Coll, good morn.   Why sleeps thou not?
I PASTOR: Alas, that ever was I born!   We have a foul blot.
           A fat wether° have we lorne.°   ram / lost
III PASTOR: Mary, God's forbot!
II PASTOR: Who should do us that scorn?°   That were a foul spot.   harm
I PASTOR: Some shrewe.°   villain
           I have sought with my dogs
455   All Horbury² shrogs,°   hedges
           And of xv° hogs   fifteen
           Found I but one ewe.

III PASTOR: Now trow me, if ye will,   by Saint Thomas of Kent,
           Either Mak or Gill   was at that assent.°   affair
I PASTOR: Peace, man, be still!   I saw when he went;
           Thou slanders him ill;   thou ought to repent,
           Good speed.
II PASTOR: Now as ever might I the,°   thrive
           If I should even here die,
465   I would say it were he,
           That did that same deed.

III PASTOR: Go we thither, I read,   and run on our feet.
           Shall I never eat bread   the sothe to I wytt.³
I PASTOR: Nor drink in my head   with him till I meet.
II PASTOR: I will rest in no stead   till that I him greet,
           My brother.
           One I will hight:°   promise
           Till I see him in sight
           Shall I never sleep one night
475   There I do another.

      [*They approach Mak's house.*]
III PASTOR: Will ye hear how they hack?⁴   Our sire list croon.
I PASTOR: Heard I never none crack   so clear out of toon;
           Call on him.
II PASTOR: Mak,   undo your door soon.
MAK: Who is that spake,   as it were noon
480   On loft?
           Who is that, I say?

---

2. A town south of Wakefield.   4. Sing (badly).
3. Until I know the truth.

III PASTOR: Good felows, were it day.

MAK: As far as ye may,
Good, speaks soft,

485   Over a sick woman's head   that is at malaise;
I had lever° be dead   or she had any disease.   *rather*

UXOR: Go to another stead!   I may not well qweasse.°   *breathe*
Each foot that ye tread   goes through my nese,°   *nose*
So hee!°   *loudly*

I PASTOR: Tell us, Mak, if ye may,
How fare ye, I say?

MAK: But are ye in this town to-day?
Now how fare ye?

Ye have run in the mire,   and are wet yit:
495   I shall make you a fire,   if you will sit.
A nurse would I hire.   Think ye on yit,
Well quit is my hire[5]—   my dream this is it—
A season.
I have barns, if ye knew,
500   Well mo then enewe,
But we must drink as we brew,
And that is but reason.

I would ye dined or ye yode.[6]   Me think that ye sweat.

II PASTOR: Nay, neither mends our mood   drink nor meat.

MAK: Why, sir, ails you ought but good?

III PASTOR: Yea, our sheep that we get,
Are stolen as they yode.   Our loss is great.

MAK: Sirs, drinks!
Had I been there,
Some should have bought it full sore.

I PASTOR: Mary, some men trowes° that ye wore,   *believes*
And that us forthinks.°   *disturbs*

II PASTOR: Mak, some men trowys   that it should be ye.

III PASTOR: Either ye or your spouse,   so say we.

MAK: Now if ye have suspowse°   to Gill or to me,   *suspicion*
515   Come and ripe° our house,   and then may ye see   *search*
Who had her;
If I any sheep fot,°   *took*
Either cow or stot;°   *heifer*
And Gill, my wife, rose not
520   Here sin she laid her.

As I am true and leal,°   to God here I pray,   *loyal*
That this be the first meal   that I shall eat this day.

I PASTOR: Mak, as have I ceyll,°   advise thee, I say;   *heaven*

---

5. My wages are paid; i.e., his dream has been fulfilled.   6. I would like you to eat before you go.

He learned timely to steal   that could not say nay.
UXOR: I swelt!°   *die*
Out, thieves, from my wonys!°   *home*
Ye come to rob us for the nonys.°   *for the purpose*
MAK: Here ye not how she groans?
Your hearts should melt.

UXOR: Out, thieves, from my barn!   Nigh him not thor!°   *there*
MAK: Wist ye how she had farn,°   your hearts would be sore.   *fared*
Ye do wrong, I you warn,   that thus comes before
To a woman that has farn—   but I say no more.
UXOR: Ah, my medill!°   *middle*
535   I pray to God so mild,
If ever I you beguiled,
That I eat this child
That lies in this cradle.

MAK: Peace, woman, for God's pain,   and cry not so:
540   Thou spills thy brain,   and makes me full woe.
II PASTOR: I trow our sheep be slain.   What find ye two?
III PASTOR: All work we in vain;   as well may we go.
But hatters,°   *(an oath)*
I can find no flesh,
545   Hard nor nesh,°   *soft*
Salt nor fresh,
But two tome° platters.   *empty*

Whik° cattle but this,   tame nor wild,   *living*
None, as have I bliss,   as loud as he smiled.°   *smelled*
UXOR: No, so God me bliss,   and give me joy of my child!
I PASTOR: We have marked amiss;   I hold us beguiled.
II PASTOR: Sir, don,°   *it is done*
Sir, our Lady him save,
Is your child a knave?[7]
MAK: Any lord might him have
This child to his son.

When he wakens he kips,°   that joy is to see.   *snatches*
III PASTOR: In good time to his hips,   and in cele.°   *heaven*
But who was his gossips,°   so soon rede?°   *godparents / ready*
MAK: So fair fall their lips!
I PASTOR: Hark now, a le.°   *lie*
MAK: So God them thank,
Parkin, and Gibon Waller I say,
And gentle John Horne,[8] in good fay,
He made all the garray,°   *noise*

---

7. Boy-child (of the serving-class).
8. Parkin, Gibon Waller, and John Horne are the names
of the shepherds in the First Play of the Shepherds, possibly referring to actual townspeople.

565   With the great shank.°   *leg*

II PASTOR: Mak, friends will we be,   for we are all one.
MAK: We? Now I hold for me,   for mends° get I none.   *profit*
        Farewell all three!   All glad were ye gone.
    [*The Shepherds depart.*]
III PASTOR: Fair words may there be,   but love is there none
570   This year.
I PASTOR: Gave ye the child anything?
II PASTOR: I trow not one farthing.
III PASTOR: Fast again will I fling,°   *hurry*
        Abide ye me there.
    [*Returns to the house.*]

575   Mak, take it to no grief   if I come to thy barn.°   *baby*
MAK: Nay, thou does me great reproof,   and foul has thou farn.°   *done*
III PASTOR: The child will it not grief,   that little daystarn.⁹
        Mak, with your leaf,   let me give your barn
        But vi° pence.   *six*
MAK: Nay, do way: he sleeps.
III PASTOR: Me think he peeps.
MAK: When he wakens he weeps.
        I pray you go hence.
    [*The other Shepherds return.*]

III PASTOR: Give me leave him to kiss,   and lift up the clout.°   *cloth*
585   What the devil is this?   He has a long snout.
I PASTOR: He is marked amiss.   We wat° ill about.   *watch*
II PASTOR: Ill-spun weft, iwys,   ay comes foul out.¹
        Aye, so!
        He is like to our sheep!
III PASTOR: How, Gyb,° may I peep?   *the Second Shepherd*
I PASTOR: I trow kind° will creep   *Nature*
        Where it may not go.°   *walk*

II PASTOR: This was a quaint gawde,°   and a far cast.   *clever trick*
        It was a high fraud.

III PASTOR: Yea, sirs, was't.
595   Let bren° this bawd,   and bind her fast.   *burn*
        A false skawd°   hang at the last;   *scold*
        So shall thou.
        Will ye see how they swaddle
        His four feet in the middle?
600   Saw I never in a cradle
        A horned lad² or° now.   *before*

MAK: Peace bid I. What,   let be youre fare;

---

9. Little day star; a term also used for the Christ child
later in the play, indicating a parallel with Mak's baby.

1. Badly spun thread always makes poor cloth.
2. A horned child (devil).

I am he that him gat,°   and yond woman him bare.   *begat*
I PASTOR: What devil shall he hat,°   Mak? Lo, God, Mak's heir.   *be called*
II PASTOR: Let be all that.   Now God give him care,
    I sagh.°   *saw*
UXOR: A pretty child is he
    As sits on a woman's knee;
    A dillydown,° perde,   *darling*
610   To gar° a man laugh.   *make*

III PASTOR: I know him by the earn mark: that is a good token.
MAK: I tell you, sirs, hark!—   his nose was broken.
    Sithen° told me a clerk   that he was forspoken.°   *since / bewitched*
I PASTOR: This is a false work;   I would fain be wroken.°   *avenged*
615   Get wepyn.
UXOR: He was taken with° an elf;   *by*
    I saw it myself.
    When the clock struck twelve
    Was he forshapen.°   *changed*

II PASTOR: Ye two are well feft°   sam° in a stead.   *endowed / together*
III PASTOR: Sin they maintain their theft,   let do them to dead.
MAK: If I trespass eft,°   gird° off my head.   *again / cut*
    With you will I be left.
I PASTOR: Sirs, do my read.°   *advice*
    For this trespass,
625   We will neither ban ne flite,°   *curse nor quarrel*
    Fight nor chite,°   *chide*
    But have done as tite,°   *quickly*
    And cast him in canvas.
    [*They toss Mak in a sheet.*]

    Lord, what I am sore, in point for to brist.
630   In faith I may no more; therefore will I rist.
II PASTOR: As a sheep of vii score[3]   he weighed in my fist.
    For to sleep ay-whore° me think that I list.   *anywhere*
III PASTOR: Now I pray you,
    Lyg down on this green.
I PASTOR: On these thieves yet I mene.°   *speak*
III PASTOR: Whereto should ye tene?°   *be angry*
    Do as I say you.
    [*The Shepherds sleep.*]
    Angelus cantat "Gloria in excelsis"; postea dicat[4]

ANGELUS: Rise, herd-men heynd!° For now is he born   *virtuous*
    That shall take fro the fiend   that Adam had lorn;°   *lost*
640   That warloo° to shend,°   this night is he born.   *devil / destroy*
    God is made your friend   now at this morn.

---

3. Seven score pounds (140 lbs).   4. The Angel sings "Glory to God in the highest," and afterward says.

He behestys°   *orders*
At Bedlem° go see: *Bethlehem*
There lies that fre°   *lord*
645   In a crib full poorly,
Betwyx two bestys.

I PASTOR: This was a quaint steven°   that ever yet I heard.   *voice*
It is a marvel to neven,°   thus to be scared.   *mention*
II PASTOR: Of God's son of heaven   he spake upward.°   *on high*
650   All the wood on a leven   me thought that he gard
Appear.[5]
III PASTOR: He spake of a barn
In Bedlem, I you warn.
I PASTOR: That betokens yond starn.°   *star*
655   Let us seek him there.

II PASTOR: Say, what was his song?   Heard ye not how he cracked° it?   *roared*
Three breves to a long.[6]
III PASTOR: Yea, marry, he hakt° it.   *sang*
Was no crochett° wrong,   nor nothing that lacked it.   *note*
I PASTOR: For to sing us among   right as he knacked° it,   *sang*
660   I can.
II PASTOR: Let se how ye croon.
Can ye bark at the moon?
III PASTOR: Hold your tongues, have done!
I PASTOR: Hark after than.
     [*Sings.*]

II PASTOR: To Bedlem he bade   that we should gang:
I am full fard°   that we tarry too lang.   *afraid*
III PASTOR: Be merry and not sad;   of mirth is our sang;
Ever-lasting glad   to mede° may we fang,°   *reward / get*
Without noise.
I PASTOR: Hie we thither for-thy;°   *therefore*
If we be wet and weary,
To that child and that lady,
We have it not to lose.

II PASTOR: We find by the prophecy—   let be your din—
675   Of David and Isay,[7]   and mo than I min,
They prophesied by clergy   that in a virgin
Should he light and lie,   to sloken° our sin   *remove*
And slake it,
Our kynd° from woe;   *humankind*
680   For Isay said so,
Ecce virgo

---

5. I thought he lit up the woods like lightning.   7. The prophet Isaiah.
6. Three short notes to one long.

Concipiet[8] a child that is naked.

III PASTOR: Full glad may we be,   and abide that day
        That lovely to see,   that all mights may.
685   Lord, well were me,   for once and for ay,
        Might I kneel on my knee,   some word for to say
        To that child.
        But the angel said
        In a crib was he laid;
690   He was poorly arrayed,
        Both mener° and milde.   *poor*

I PASTOR: Patriarchs that has been,   and prophets beforn,
        They desired to have seen   this child that is born.
        They are gone full clean,°   that have they lorn.°   *entirely / lost*
695   We shall see him, I ween,   or it be morn,
        To token.°   *as proof*
        When I see him and feel,
        Then wot I full weel
        It is true as steel
700   That prophets have spoken:

        To so poore as we are   that he would appear,
        First find, and declare   by his messenger.
II PASTOR: Go we now, let us fare;   the place is us near.
III PASTOR: I am ready and yare;°   go we in fere°   *prepared / together*
705   To that bright.
        Lord, if thy wills be,
        We are lewde° all three,   *unschooled*
        Thou grant us somkyns glee°   *some kind of joy*
        To comfort thy wight.°   *creature*
    [*They enter the stable.*]

I PASTOR: Hail, comely and clean!   Hail, young child!
        Hail, maker, as I mean,   of a maiden so mild!
        Thou has waryd,° I ween,   the warlo° so wild;   *cursed / devil*
        The false gyler° of teen°   now goes he beguiled.   *deceiver / anger*
        Lo, he merries!
715   Lo, he laughs, my sweeting!
        A well fair meeting!
        I have holden my heting;°   *kept my promise*
        Have a bob° of cherries.   *bunch*

II PASTOR: Hail, sovereign saviour,   for thou has us sought!
720   Hail, freely food and flour,[9]   that all thing has wrought!
        Hail, full of favour,   that made all of nought!
        Hail! I kneel and I cower.   A bird have I brought
        To my barn.

8. Behold, a virgin conceives (Isaiah 7.14).   9. Noble child and flower.

	Hail, little tyne mop!°	*tiny baby*
725	Of our creed thou art crop:°	*fruit, fulfillment*
	I would drink on thy cop,°	*cup*
	Little day starn.°	*star*

III PASTOR: Hail, darling dear,   full of Godhede!
    I pray thee be near   when that I have need.
730   Hail, sweet is thy cheer!   My heart would bleed
    To see thee sit here   in so poor weed,°   *clothing*
    With no pennies.
    Hail, put forth thy dall!°   *hand*
    I bring thee but a ball:
735   Have and play thee with all,
    And go to the tenys.°   *tennis*

MARIA: The Father of heaven,   God omnipotent,
    That set all on seven,[1]   his son has he sent.
    My name could he neven,°   and light or he went.   *name*
740   I conceived him full even   through might, as he ment,°   *intended*
    And now is he born.
    He keep you from woe!
    I shall pray him so.
    Tell forth as ye go,
745   And myn° on this morn.   *remember*

I PASTOR: Farewell, lady,   so fair to behold,
    With thy child on thy knee.
II PASTOR: But he lies full cold.
    Lord, well is me!   Now we go, thou behold.
III PASTOR: Forsooth already   it seems to be told
750   Full oft.
I PASTOR: What grace we have fun!°   *found*
II PASTOR: Come forth: now are we won.
III PASTOR: To sing are we bun:°   *bound*
    Let take on loft![2]
    [*They go out singing.*]

Explicit pagina Pastorum.[3]

—⊨◊⊒—

The York Play of the Crucifixion

The York *Crucifixion* serves as a counterpoint to the *Second Play of the Shepherds*, focusing not on the beginning of Christ's earthly life but on its end. Like the Townley play, it was shaped by an anonymous playwright of great literary skill, a master of concrete detail, colloquial speech,

---

1. Made everything in seven days.   3. The play of the Shepherds is finished.
2. Let us sing on high.

and sometimes grotesque humor. This writer is often called the "York Realist" by historians of drama, but such a title raises more issues than it answers. Why do we need a name for an unknown reviser (or series of revisers)? What kind of "realism" characterizes a moment so fraught with uncanny implications as is the Crucifixion?

Like many of the cycle plays, the York *Crucifixion* was produced by a guild whose business bore some relation to the subject at hand. In this case, it is the pinners—the makers of wooden pegs—whose craft provides a certain grim irony. The soldiers carrying out the Crucifixion joke about their task, at once boasting about their skills yet repeatedly unable to accomplish them. Their frustrated patter provides a powerful counter-rhythm and counter-tone to the overwhelming moment they help enact.

In striking contrast to the busy buffoonery of the soldiers is the dignified demeanor and physical stability of Christ. He speaks only twice, first to accept the sacrifice of his life, and second to beg God's forgiveness for his torturers. His portrayal reflects a balance of two conflicting images: the heroic Christ who defeats Satan and the human Christ who suffers. The former, militant image can be seen in poems as early as the Old English *Dream of the Rood* and as late as Passus 18 of *Piers Plowman*. The latter, "gothic" image is widespread in religious lyrics and mystical writings of the later Middle Ages, whose purpose was to inspire the laity to meditation by focusing on Christ's wounds. Both in the agitated shouting of the soldiers and the silent agony of Christ, theatrical enactment of grim realities serves a profound and symbolic purpose.

The York Play of the Crucifixion

SOLDIER 1: Sir knights, take heed hither in hie,°		*in haste*
This deed on dreigh we may not draw.[1]		
Ye wot° yourselves as well as I		*know*
How lords and leaders of our law		
5 Have given doom° that this dote° shall die.		*judgment / fool*
SOLDIER 2: Sir, all their counsel well we know.		
Since we are come to Calvary		
Let ilk° man help now as him owe.°		*each / ought*
SOLDIER 3: We are all ready, lo,		
10 That foreward° to fulfil.		*undertaking*
SOLDIER 4: Let hear how we shall do,		
And go we tite theretill.°		*quickly thereto*
SOLDIER 1: It may not help here for to hone°		*delay*
If we shall any worship° win.		*honor*
SOLDIER 2: He must be dead needlings° by noon.		*necessarily*
SOLDIER 3: Then is good time that we begin.		
SOLDIER 4: Let ding° him down, then is he done—		*knock*
He shall not dere° us with his din.		*harm*
SOLDIER 1: He shall be set and learned soon,[2]		
20 With care° to him and all his kin.		*sorrow*
SOLDIER 2: The foulest death of all		
Shall he die for his deeds.		
SOLDIER 3: That means cross° him we shall.		*crucify*
SOLDIER 4: Behold, so right he redes.°		*he advises well*

---

1. We may not draw this task out too long.   2. He shall be put in his place and taught a lesson.

SOLDIER 1: Then to this work us must take heed,
    So that our working be not wrong.
SOLDIER 2: None other note° to neven° is need,   *matter / mention*
    But let us haste him for to hang.°   *crucify*
SOLDIER 3: And I have gone for gear good speed,°   *with haste*
30   Both hammers and nails large and long.
SOLDIER 4: Then may we boldly do this deed.
    Come on, let kill this traitor strong.
SOLDIER 1: Fair might ye fall in fere[3]
    That has wrought on this wise.
SOLDIER 2: Us needs not for to lere[4]
    Such faitours° to chastise.   *traitors*

SOLDIER 3: Since ilka° thing is right arrayed,°   *every / prepared*
    The wiselier° now work may we.   *more wisely*
SOLDIER 4: The cross on ground is goodly graid°   *prepared*
40   And bored° even as it ought to be.   *drilled*
SOLDIER 1: Look° that the lad on length be laid   *see to it*
    And made me° then unto this tree.°   *fastened / cross*
SOLDIER 2: For all his fare° he shall be flayed,°   *deeds / tortured*
    That on assay° soon shall ye see.   *by trial*
SOLDIER 3: Come forth, thou cursed knave,
    Thy comfort soon shall keel.°   *turn cold*
SOLDIER 4: Thine hire° here shall thou have.   *reward*
SOLDIER 1: Walk on—now work we well.

JESUS: Almighty God, my Father free,°   *gracious*
50   Let these matters be made in mind:
    Thou bade° that I should buxom° be,   *commanded / willing*
    For Adam's plight for to be pined.°   *tormented*
    Here to death I oblige me,°   *pledge myself*
    For that sin for to save mankind,
55   And sovereignly beseech I thee
    That they for me may favour find.
    And from the fiend° them fend,°   *devil / defend*
    So that their souls be safe
    In wealth° without end—   *joy*
60   I keep° nought else to crave.°   *care / ask for*

SOLDIER 1: We, hark sir knights, for Mahound's° blood, *Muhammad's*
    Of Adam's kind° is all his thought.   *offspring*
SOLDIER 2: The warlock waxes war than wood;[5]
    This doleful° death ne dreadeth° he nought. *terrible / fears*
SOLDIER 3: Thou should have mind,° with main° and mood, *recall / might*
    Of wicked works that thou hast wrought.
SOLDIER 4: I hope° that he had been as good   *think*
    Have ceased of saws° that he upsought.° *sayings / thought up*
SOLDIER 1: Tho saws shall rue him° sore,   *words he will regret*

---

3. Good fortune to all of you.   5. The sorcerer grows worse than mad.
4. We do not need to be taught.

70   For all his sauntering,° soon.   *babbling*
SOLDIER 2: Ill speed them° that him spare   *bad luck (to) them*
       Till he to death be done.

SOLDIER 3: Have done belive, boy, and make thee boun,[6]
       And bend thy back unto this tree.
SOLDIER 4: Behold, himself has laid him down
       In length and breadth as he should be.
SOLDIER 1: This traitor here tainted° of treason,   *convicted*
       Go fast and fetter him then ye three;
       And since he claimeth kingdom with crown,
80   Even as a king here hang shall he.
SOLDIER 2: Now, certes,° I shall not fine°   *indeed / stop*
       Ere° his right hand be fast.°   *before / tightly tied*
SOLDIER 3: The left hand then is mine—
       Let see who bears him best.

SOLDIER 4: His limbs on length then shall I lead,°   *stretch*
       And even unto the bore° them bring.   *bored holes*
SOLDIER 1: Unto his head I shall take heed,
       And with mine hand help him to hang.
SOLDIER 2: Now since we four shall do this deed
90   And meddle with this unthrifty° thing,   *unprofitable*
       Let no man spare for° special speed   *refrain from (using)*
       Till that we have made ending.
SOLDIER 3: This foreward° may not fail;   *deed*
       Now are we right arrayed.°   *prepared*
SOLDIER 4: This boy° here in our bail°   *rascal / custody*
       Shall bide° full bitter braid.°   *suffer / torment*

SOLDIER 1: Sir knights, say, how work we now?
SOLDIER 2: Yes, certes,° I hope° I hold this hand,   *indeed / think*
       And to the bore° I have it brought   *bored holes*
100   Full buxomly° without band.°   *obediently / ropes*
SOLDIER 1: Strike on then hard, for him thee bought.°   *redeemed*
SOLDIER 2: Yes, here is a stub° will stiffly stand,   *thick nail*
       Through bones and sinews it shall be sought°—   *found*
       This work is well, I will warrand.°   *warrant*
SOLDIER 1: Say sir, how do we there?
       This bargain° may not blin.°   *business / cease*
SOLDIER 3: It fails a foot and more,°   *i.e., is too short*
       The sinews are so gone in.°   *shrunken*

SOLDIER 4: I hope that mark amiss° be bored.°   *wrongly / drilled*
SOLDIER 2: Then must he bide° in bitter bale.°   *suffer / torment*
SOLDIER 3: In faith, it was over-scantily scored,°   *marked too short*
       That makes it foully° for to fail.   *badly*
SOLDIER 1: Why carp° ye so? Fast on° a cord   *speak / fasten*

6. Be done quickly, wretch, and make yourself ready.

And tug° him to, by top and tail.° · *stretch / head and feet*
SOLDIER 3: Yah, thou commands lightly° as a lord; · *effortlessly*
   Come help to haul, with ill hail.° · *bad luck to you*
SOLDIER 1: Now certes that shall I do—
   Full snelly° as a snail. · *quickly*
SOLDIER 3: And I shall tache° him to,° · *attach / to (the cross)*
120   Full nimbly with a nail.

This work will hold, that dare I hete,° · *promise*
   For now are fest° fast both his hend.° · *fastened / hands*
SOLDIER 4: Go we all four then to his feet,
   So shall our space° be speedily spend.° · *time / usefully spent*
SOLDIER 2: Let see what bourd his bale might beet,[7]
   Thereto my back now would I bend.
SOLDIER 4: Oh, this work is all unmeet°— · *out of place*
   This boring must all be amend.° · *corrected*
SOLDIER 1: Ah, peace man, for Mahound,° · *by Muhammad*
130   Let no man wot° that wonder,° · *know about / miracle*
   A rope shall rug° him down · *yank*
   If° all his sinews go asunder. · *even if*

SOLDIER 2: That cord full kindly° can I knit,° · *fittingly / fasten*
   The comfort of this carl° to keel.° · *churl / cool, lessen*
SOLDIER 1: Fast° on then fast, that all be fit,° · *fasten / ready*
   It is no force° how fell° he feel. · *matter / terrible*
SOLDIER 2: Lug° on ye both a little yet. · *pull*
SOLDIER 3: I shall not cease, as I have sele.° · *joy*
SOLDIER 4: And I shall fond° him for to hit. · *try*
SOLDIER 2: Oh, hale!° · *haul*
SOLDIER 4:   Whoa, now, I hold it well.
SOLDIER 1: Have done, drive in that nail,
   So that no fault be found.
SOLDIER 4: This working would not fail
   If four bulls here were bound.

SOLDIER 1: These cords have evil° increased his pains, · *sorely*
   Ere he were to the borings° brought. · *bored holes*
SOLDIER 2: Yea, asunder are both sinews and veins
   On ilka° side, so have we° sought. · *each / as we have*
SOLDIER 3: Now all his gauds nothing him gains,[8]
150   His sauntering shall with bale be bought.[9]
SOLDIER 4: I will go say to our sovereigns
   Of all these works how we have wrought.
SOLDIER 1: Nay sirs, another thing
   Falls first to you and me,
155   They bade we should him hang
   On high, that men might see.

7. Let us see what joke might lighten his sorrow.   9. His babbling shall be paid for with pain.
8. Now all his tricks gain him nothing.

SOLDIER 2: We wot° well so° their words were, *know / what*
  But sir, that deed will do us dere.° *harm*
SOLDIER 1: It may not mend° for to moot° more, *help / argue*
160 This harlot° must be hanged here. *rascal*
SOLDIER 2: The mortice° is made fit° therefore. *slot / ready*
SOLDIER 3: Fast° on your fingers then, in fere.° *fasten / together*
SOLDIER 4: I ween° it will never come° there— *believe / rise*
  We four raise° it not right to-year.° *will raise / this year*
SOLDIER 1: Say man, why carps° thou so? *talk*
  Thy lifting was but light.° *weak*
SOLDIER 2: He means there must be more
  To heave him up on height.

SOLDIER 3: Now certes, I hope it shall not need° *be necessary*
170 To call to us more company.° *help*
  Methink we four should do this deed
  And bear him to yon hill on high.
SOLDIER 1: It must be done, without dread.° *doubt*
  No more, but look ye be ready,
175 And this part° shall I lift and lead; *(the head)*
  On length he shall no longer lie.
  Therefore now make you boun,° *ready*
  Let bear him to yon hill.
SOLDIER 4: Then will I bear here down,
180 And tent his toes until.° *attend to his toes*

SOLDIER 2: We two shall see to either side,
  For else this work will wry° all wrong. *go awry*
SOLDIER 3: We are ready.
SOLDIER 4:   Good sirs, abide,
  And let me first his feet up fang.° *take up*
SOLDIER 2: Why tent ye so to tales this tide?[1]
SOLDIER 1: Lift up!
SOLDIER 4:   Let see!
SOLDIER 2:   Oh, lift along.
SOLDIER 3: From all this harm he should him hide° *protect himself*
  And° he were God. *if*
SOLDIER 4:   The devil him hang!
SOLDIER 1: For-great harm have I hent,° *received*
190 My shoulder is in sunder.° *asunder*
SOLDIER 2: And certes, I am near shent,° *ruined*
  So long have I borne under.° *lifted up*

SOLDIER 3: This cross and I in two must twin,° *separate*
  Else breaks my back in sunder° soon. *asunder*
SOLDIER 4: Lay down again and leave° your din,° *stop / noise*
  This deed for us will never be done.
SOLDIER 1: Assay,° sirs, let see if any gin° *try / device*
  May help him up without hone,° *delay*
  For here should wight men worship win,

1. Why are you paying so much attention to talk at this time (i.e., instead of working)?

200	And not with gauds° all day to gone.°	tricks / spend
	SOLDIER 2: More wighter° men than we	stronger
	Full few I hope° ye find.	expect
	SOLDIER 3: This bargain° will not be,°	job / (ever) be done
	For certes, me wants wind.°	I am winded
	SOLDIER 4: So will° of work never we were—	bewildered
	I hope this carl some cautels cast.[2]	
	SOLDIER 2: My burden sat° me wonder sore,	distressed
	Unto the hill I might not last.	
	SOLDIER 1: Lift up, and soon he shall be there,	
210	Therefore fast on° your fingers fast.	fasten
	SOLDIER 3: Oh, lift!	
	SOLDIER 1: We, lo!	
	SOLDIER 4: A little more.	
	SOLDIER 2: Hold then!	
	SOLDIER 1: How now?	
	SOLDIER 2: The worst is past.	
	SOLDIER 3: He weighs a wicked weight.	
	SOLDIER 2: So may we all four say,	
215	Ere he was heaved on height°	aloft
	And raised in this array.°	fashion
	SOLDIER 4: He made us stand as° any stones,	as (still) as
	So boistous° was he for to bear.	awkward
	SOLDIER 1: Now raise him nimbly for the nonce	
220	And set him by this mortice° here,	slot
	And let him fall in all at once,	
	For certes, that pain shall have no peer.	
	SOLDIER 3: Heave up!	
	SOLDIER 4: Let down, so all his bones	
	Are asunder now on sides sere.°	in many places
	SOLDIER 1: This falling was more fell°	cruel
	Than all the harms he had.	
	Now may a man well tell°	easily count
	The least lith° of this lad.	smallest limbs
	SOLDIER 3: Methinketh this cross will not abide°	hold firm
230	Ne stand still in this mortice° yet.	slot
	SOLDIER 4: At the first time was it made over-wide;	
	That makes it wave,° thou may well wit.°	wobble / know
	SOLDIER 1: It shall be set on ilka° side	each
	So that it shall no further flit.°	move
235	Good wedges shall we take this tide°	time
	And fast the foot,° then is all fit.	fasten the base
	SOLDIER 2: Here are wedges arrayed°	ready
	For that, both great and small.	
	SOLDIER 3: Where are our hammers laid	
240	That we should work withal?°	with

2. I think this churl has cast some spells.

SOLDIER 4: We have them even here at our hand.
SOLDIER 2: Give me this wedge, I shall it in drive.
SOLDIER 4: Here is another yet ordained.°   *ready*
SOLDIER 3: Do take it me hither belive.°   *to me quickly*
SOLDIER 1: Lay on then fast.
SOLDIER 2:   Yes, I warrand.°   *warrant*
     I thring them sam, so mote I thrive.[3]
     Now will this cross full stably° stand,   *firmly*
     All if° he rave they will not rive.°   *even if / split*
SOLDIER 1: Say sir, how likes you now,
250   This work that we have wrought?
SOLDIER 4: We pray you say° us how   *tell*
     Ye feel, or faint ye aught.°   *if you feel faint at all*

JESUS: All men that walk by way or street,
     Take tent ye shall no travail tine.[4]
255   Behold mine head, mine hands, and my feet,
     And fully feel now, ere ye fine,°   *before you finish*
     If any mourning may be meet,°   *matched with*
     Or mischief measured° unto mine.   *misfortune compared*
     My father, that all bales° may beet,°   *sorrows / remedy*
260   Forgive these men that do me pine.°   *pain*
     What they work,° wot° they not;   *do / know*
     Therefore, my father, I crave,
     Let never their sins be sought,°   *examined*
     But see° their souls to save.   *see that*

SOLDIER 1: We, hark, he jangles° like a jay.   *chatters*
SOLDIER 2: Methink he patters like a pie.°   *magpie*
SOLDIER 3: He has been doing all this day,
     And made great moving of° mercy.   *reference to*
SOLDIER 4: Is this the same that gan us say°   *is said to us*
270   That he was God's son almighty?
SOLDIER 1: Therefore he feels full fell affray,°   *cruel assault*
     And deemed° this day for to die.   *was judged*
SOLDIER 2: *Vath, qui destruis templum!*[5]
SOLDIER 3: His saws° were so, certain.   *words*
SOLDIER 4: And sirs, he said to some
     He might raise it again.

SOLDIER 1: To muster° that he had no might,   *manifest*
     For all the cautels° that he could cast.   *spells*
     All if he were in word so wight,[6]
280   For all his force now is he fast.°   *bound*
     As Pilate deemed is done and dight,°   *dealt with*
     Therefore I rede° that we go rest.   *advise*
SOLDIER 2: This race° mun be rehearsed° right,   *action / reported*

---

3. I'll thrust them together, so I may prosper.
4. Take heed that you miss none of my suffering.
5. Ah! thou who destroyeth the temple! (Mark 14:58, John 2:19).
6. Even though his words were so bold.

Through the world both east and west.
SOLDIER 3: Yea, let him hang there still
And make mows on° the moon.   *faces at*
SOLDIER 4: Then may we wend at will.°   *go when we please*
SOLDIER 1: Nay, good sirs, not so soon.

For certes us needs another note:°   *we have other business*
290   This kirtle° would I of you crave.   *garment*
SOLDIER 2: Nay, nay, sir, we will look by lot°   *draw lots*
Which of us four falls it to° have.   *it falls to*
SOLDIER 3: I rede° we draw cut° for this coat—   *advise / straws*
Lo, see how soon—all sides to save.°   *to satisfy all parties*
SOLDIER 4: The short cut shall win, that well ye wot,°   *know*
Whether it fall to knight or knave.
SOLDIER 1: Fellows, ye tharf° not flite,°   *need / quarrel*
For this mantle is mine.
SOLDIER 2: Go we then hence tite,°   *quickly*
300   This travail° here we tine.°   *effort / waste*

[END OF MEDIEVAL BIBLICAL DRAMA]

━━◆━━

Margery Kempe
c. 1373–after 1439

Margery Kempe's religious life—its temptations, visions, ecstasies, and pilgrimages—was unusual in intensity, but not in kind, for her time. She was very much in the mainstream of later medieval affective piety. What gained Margery both admiration and contempt, to the extent of endangering her life, was her drive to express these experiences publicly and have them acknowledged within an official hierarchy that had very little place for her. *The Book of Margery Kempe* is only one aspect of a lifetime of religious performance—from "holy conversation" and the vexed dictation of her book, through the kinds of bodily gestures, weeping, and roaring that Margery knew to be almost theatrical in their impact.

The daughter of a mayor in the prosperous market town of Lynn, Margery began her adult life quite traditionally, married to the burger John Kempe. The mental and religious crisis following the birth of her first child inspired her to pursue a holier form of life. To create this mixed life of secular marriage and sacred quest, Margery Kempe had to struggle and negotiate with a hierarchy of male authority. By canon law, her husband could demand the rights of the marriage bed, and did so for many years. She approached her local confessors for permission to undertake pilgrimages. Only a bishop could allow the weekly Eucharist for which Margery yearned, or officially approve her wearing white clothes. Hostile officials and clerics at all levels repeatedly attempted to misrepresent or silence her. She depended on male readers for her knowledge of other mystics, and on a sequence of recalcitrant male amanuenses for the very writing of her book.

Kempe's activities enraged political and ecclesiastical authorities, alienated her fellow pilgrims, and angered people at home. Yet those same activities gained her many admirers, increasingly among common laypeople. Her weeping and noisy mourning for the sufferings of Christ intruded upon daily life and often interrupted religious ceremonies. Just as daringly in the anxious and repressive religious climate of her day, Kempe spoke about her experiences

Crucifixion Scene, from a manuscript of Michael de Massa's *On the Passion of Our Lord,* 1405. This illumination is found at the beginning of a narrative of the Passion written in Latin and Middle English. Delicate yet emotive, it evokes much of the "affective spirituality" of its era. The drawing is in pale brown ink and wash, which only renders more emphatic and disturbing the bright red of Christ's elaborately detailed wounds. The weeping Virgin Mary sways, nearly fainting, while Mary Magdalene kneels and clutches Christ's legs. Even the angels look down in sorrow, though the men at right are more restrained. Late-medieval worshipers were encouraged to imagine themselves as if present at such scenes of high pathos. Here, the author of the text, Michael de Massa, is depicted among the witnesses of Christ's suffering; the scroll hanging from his desk contains the first words of his book: *Angeli pacis. . . .*

without clerical mediation, and defended herself effectively before the highest clerics in England, including the Archbishop of York. She did not even hesitate to criticize them. She was repeatedly accused and taken into custody as a Lollard heretic, although she was doctrinally quite conservative (almost radically orthodox), as she ably and repeatedly proved under hostile examination.

Along with this pattern of negotiation and striving with a largely male ecclesiastical establishment, Kempe engaged more quietly with a network of female religious. She knew she had predecessors among married women who experienced visions and moved into a holy life while still living in the secular world. She specifically mentions "Saint Bride"—Bridget of Sweden (c. 1303–1373), who like Margery had many children and took up the holy life (once widowed), traveled to Rome and Jerusalem, and engaged in prophecy. Margery may also have known about the Blessed Angela of Foligno (1248–1309), whose temptations, weeping, and conversations with Christ are similar to Margery's own. She records a visit and long conversation with the mystic and anchoress Julian of Norwich. During her arrest by agents of the Duke of Bedford, local women sympathize with Margery, bring her wine, and listen to her religious discourse. Indeed, it seems that the Duke had Margery arrested because he suspected her of having encouraged a woman cousin to leave her own husband and pursue a religious life.

It is possible, though, to exaggerate Kempe's struggle with male power, secular and ecclesiastical. She was warmly supported by a number of holy men including the bishop of Lincoln. She met the Archbishop of Canterbury and gained at least his qualified approval. For all the conflicts within her marriage, Margery often expressed a wry and affectionate sense of John Kempe's indulgence, and sympathy for his weakness. Indeed, when John became ill and senile in later years, Margery suspended her life of prayer and returned to their home to care for him. Much of the domestic imagery of the *Book* derives from this fractious but loving relationship with her husband.

Perhaps the most appealing aspects of Kempe's religious imagery derive in fact from urban and domestic life. Money is a constant hindrance to her ambitions, and figures in her conversations with Christ. Her understanding of mystical language is often highly literal. If Jesus becomes her mystic lover, he does so very much as a husband, inviting her embraces; and when Kempe has a vision of Christ's birth she bustles about like a midwife. Her concentration on the Eucharist is continuous with her experience of meals (and fasting) within the family and in society. Indeed, a long negotiation with her husband, crucial to Margery's pursuit of chastity, centers upon the heat and thirst of travel, a cake and a bottle of beer. The humble meal that caps their agreement has clear eucharistic implications. Whatever the spectacle of her religious expression, and the struggle to maintain and record it, Margery Kempe's religion and sense of her own limits are grounded in the very life she was eager to abjure.

from The Book of Margery Kempe[1]
The Preface

A short treatise of a creature set in great pomp and pride of the world, who later was drawn to our Lord by great poverty, sickness, shame, and great reproofs in many diverse countries and places, of which tribulations some shall be shown hereafter, not in the order in which they befell, but as the creature could remember them when they were written.

For it was twenty years and more from the time when this creature had forsaken the world and busily cleaved to our Lord before this book was written, notwithstanding that this creature had much advice to have her tribulations and her feelings

---

1. Translated by B. A. Windeatt.

written down, and a White Friar[2] freely offered to write for her if she wished. And she was warned in her spirit that she should not write so soon. And many years later she was bidden in her spirit to write.

And then it was written first by a man who could neither write English nor German well, so that it could not be read except by special grace alone, for there was so much obloquy and slander of this creature that few men would believe her.

And so at last a priest was greatly moved to write this treatise, and he could not read it for four years together. And afterwards, at the request of this creature, and compelled by his own conscience, he tried again to read it, and it was much easier than it was before. And so he began to write in the year of our Lord 1436, on the next day after Mary Magdalene,[3] after the information of this creature.

[EARLY LIFE AND TEMPTATIONS, REVELATION, DESIRE FOR FOREIGN PILGRIMAGE]

CHAPTER 1

When this creature was twenty years of age, or somewhat more, she was married to a worshipful burgess and was with child within a short time, as nature would have it. And after she had conceived, she was troubled with severe attacks of sickness until the child was born. And then, what with the labor-pains she had in childbirth and the sickness that had gone before, she despaired of her life, believing she might not live. Then she sent for her confessor, for she had a thing on her conscience which she had never revealed before that time in all her life. For she was continually hindered by her enemy—the devil—always saying to her while she was in good health that she didn't need to confess but to do penance by herself alone, and all should be forgiven, for God is merciful enough. And therefore this creature often did great penance in fasting on bread and water, and performed other acts of charity with devout prayers, but she would not reveal that one thing in confession.

And when she was at any time sick or troubled, the devil said in her mind that she should be damned, for she was not shriven of that fault.[4] Therefore, after her child was born, and not believing she would live, she sent for her confessor, as said before, fully wishing to be shriven of her whole lifetime, as near as she could. And when she came to the point of saying that thing which she had so long concealed, her confessor was a little too hasty and began sharply to reprove her before she had fully said what she meant, and so she would say no more in spite of anything he might do. And soon after, because of the dread she had of damnation on the one hand, and his sharp reproving of her on the other, this creature went out of her mind and was amazingly disturbed and tormented with spirits for half a year, eight weeks and odd days.

And in this time she saw, as she thought, devils opening their mouths all alight with burning flames of fire, as if they would have swallowed her in, sometimes pawing at her, sometimes threatening her, sometimes pulling her and hauling her about both night and day during the said time. And also the devils called out to her with great threats, and bade her that she should forsake her Christian faith and belief, and deny her God, his mother, and all the saints in heaven, her good works and all good virtues, her father, her mother, and all her friends. And so she did. She slandered her husband, her friends, and her own self. She spoke many sharp and reproving words; she recognized no virtue nor goodness; she desired all wickedness; just as

---

2. Alan of Lynne, a Carmelite.
3. July 23.
4. Margery had not completed the stages of penance: con-
trition, confession, restitution (or other act of repentance), absolution. She never says openly what her unconfessed sin was.

the spirits tempted her to say and do, so she said and did. She would have killed herself many a time as they stirred her to, and would have been damned with them in hell,[5] and in witness of this she bit her own hand so violently that the mark could be seen for the rest of her life. And also she pitilessly tore the skin on her body near her heart with her nails, for she had no other implement, and she would have done something worse, except that she was tied up and forcibly restrained both day and night so that she could not do as she wanted.

And when she had long been troubled by these and many other temptations, so that people thought she should never have escaped from them alive, then one time as she lay by herself and her keepers were not with her, our merciful Lord Christ Jesus—ever to be trusted, worshiped be his name, never forsaking his servant in time of need—appeared to his creature who had forsaken him, in the likeness of a man, the most seemly, most beauteous, and most amiable that ever might be seen with man's eye, clad in a mantle of purple silk, sitting upon her bedside, looking upon her with so blessed a countenance that she was strengthened in all her spirits, and he said to her these words: "Daughter, why have you forsaken me, and I never forsook you?"

And as soon as he had said these words, she saw truly how the air opened as bright as any lightning, and he ascended up into the air, not hastily and quickly, but beautifully and gradually, so that she could clearly behold him in the air until it closed up again.

And presently the creature grew as calm in her wits and her reason as she ever was before, and asked her husband, as soon as he came to her, if she could have the keys of the buttery to get her food and drink as she had done before. Her maids and her keepers advised him that he should not deliver up any keys to her, for they said she would only give away such goods as there were, because she did not know what she was saying, as they believed.

Nevertheless, her husband, who always had tenderness and compassion for her, ordered that they should give her the keys. And she took food and drink as her bodily strength would allow her, and she once again recognized her friends and her household, and everybody else who came to her in order to see how our Lord Jesus Christ had worked his grace in her—blessed may he be, who is ever near in tribulation. When people think he is far away from them he is very near through his grace. Afterwards this creature performed all her responsibilities wisely and soberly enough, except that she did not truly know our Lord's power to draw us to him.

Chapter 2

And when this creature had thus through grace come again to her right mind, she thought she was bound to God and that she would be his servant. Nevertheless, she would not leave her pride or her showy manner of dressing, which she had previously been used to, either for her husband, or for any other person's advice. And yet she knew full well that people made many adverse comments about her, because she wore gold pipes on her head,[6] and her hoods with the tippets were fashionably slashed. Her cloaks were also modishly slashed and underlaid with various colors between the slashes, so that she would be all the more stared at, and all the more esteemed.

---

5. Suicide was considered a mortal sin.

6. Margery wore the fashionable *crespine*, a horned headdress of wire, often in gold or silver.

And when her husband used to try and speak to her, to urge her to leave her proud ways, she answered sharply and shortly, and said that she was come of worthy kindred—he should never have married her—for her father was sometime mayor of the town of N., and afterwards he was alderman of the High Guild of the Trinity in N.[7] And therefore she would keep up the honor of her kindred, whatever anyone said.

She was enormously envious of her neighbors if they were dressed as well as she was. Her whole desire was to be respected by people. She would not learn her lesson from a single chastening experience, nor be content with the worldly goods that God had sent her—as her husband was—but always craved more and more.

And then, out of pure covetousness, and in order to maintain her pride, she took up brewing, and was one of the greatest brewers in the town of N. for three or four years until she lost a great deal of money, for she had never had any experience in that business. For however good her servants were and however knowledgeable in brewing, things would never go successfully for them. For when the ale had as fine a head of froth on it as anyone might see, suddenly the froth would go flat, and all the ale was lost in one brewing after another, so that her servants were ashamed and would not stay with her. Then this creature thought how God had punished her before—and she could not take heed—and now again by the loss of her goods; and then she left off and did no more brewing.

And then she asked her husband's pardon because she would not follow his advice previously, and she said that her pride and sin were the cause of all her punishing, and that she would willingly put right all her wrongdoing. But yet she did not entirely give up the world, for she now thought up a new enterprise for herself. She had a horse-mill. She got herself two good horses and a man to grind people's corn, and thus she was confident of making her living. This business venture did not last long, for shortly afterwards, on the eve of Corpus Christi,[8] the following marvel happened. The man was in good health, and his two horses were strong and in good condition and had drawn well in the mill previously, but now, when he took one of those horses and put him in the mill as he had done before, this horse would not pull in the mill in spite of anything the man might do. The man was sorry, and tried everything he could think of to make his horse pull. Sometimes he led him by the head, sometimes he beat him, and sometimes he made a fuss of him, but nothing did any good, for the horse would rather go backwards than forwards. Then this man set a pair of sharp spurs on his heels and rode on the horse's back to make him pull, but it was no better. When this man saw it was no use, he put the horse back in his stable, and gave him food, and the horse ate well and freshly. And afterwards he took the other horse and put him in the mill. And just as his fellow had done so did he, for he would not pull for anything the man might do. And then this man gave up his job and would not stay any longer with the said creature.[9]

Then it was noised about in the town of N. that neither man nor beast would serve the said creature, and some said she was accursed; some said God openly took vengeance on her; some said one thing and some said another. And some wise men, whose minds were more grounded in the love of our Lord, said it was the high mercy of our Lord Jesus Christ that called her from the pride and vanity of this wretched world.

---

7. Margery here uses an initial for her town; later she openly calls it Lynn.

8. A feast day toward midsummer commemorating the Eucharist; marked by the performance of mystery plays in major mercantile towns such as York.

9. Popular superstition can be glimpsed behind the failure in brewing and milling, and the servants' refusal to stay with Margery thereafter.

And then this creature, seeing all these adversities coming on every side, thought they were the scourges of our Lord that would chastise her for her sin. Then she asked God for mercy, and forsook her pride, her covetousness, and the desire that she had for worldly dignity, and did great bodily penance, and began to enter the way of everlasting life as shall be told hereafter.

CHAPTER 3

One night, as this creature lay in bed with her husband, she heard a melodious sound so sweet and delectable that she thought she had been in paradise.[1] And immediately she jumped out of bed and said, "Alas that ever I sinned! It is full merry in heaven." This melody was so sweet that it surpassed all the melody that might be heard in this world, without any comparison, and it caused this creature when she afterwards heard any mirth or melody to shed very plentiful and abundant tears of high devotion, with great sobbings and sighings for the bliss of heaven, not fearing the shames and contempt of this wretched world. And ever after her being drawn towards God in this way, she kept in mind the joy and the melody that there was in heaven, so much so that she could not very well restrain herself from speaking of it. For when she was in company with any people she would often say, "It is full merry in heaven!"

And those who knew of her behavior previously and now heard her talk so much of the bliss of heaven said to her, "Why do you talk so of the joy that is in heaven? You don't know it, and you haven't been there any more than we have." And they were angry with her because she would not hear or talk of worldly things as they did, and as she did previously.

And after this time she never had any desire to have sexual intercourse with her husband, for paying the debt of matrimony was so abominable to her that she would rather, she thought, have eaten and drunk the ooze and muck in the gutter than consent to intercourse, except out of obedience.

And so she said to her husband, "I may not deny you my body, but all the love and affection of my heart is withdrawn from all earthly creatures and set on God alone." But he would have his will with her, and she obeyed with much weeping and sorrowing because she could not live in chastity. And often this creature advised her husband to live chaste and said that they had often (she well knew) displeased God by their inordinate love, and the great delight that each of them had in using the other's body, and now it would be a good thing if by mutual consent they punished and chastised themselves by abstaining from the lust of their bodies. Her husband said it was good to do so, but he might not yet—he would do so when God willed. And so he used her as he had done before, he would not desist. And all the time she prayed to God that she might live chaste, and three or four years afterwards, when it pleased our Lord, her husband made a vow of chastity, as shall be written afterwards, by Jesus's leave.

And also, after this creature heard this heavenly melody, she did great bodily penance. She was sometimes shriven two or three times on the same day, especially of that sin which she had so long concealed and covered up, as is written at the beginning of this book. She gave herself up to much fasting and keeping of vigils; she rose at two or three of the clock and went to church, and was there at her prayers until midday and also the whole afternoon. And then she was slandered and reproved by many people because she led so strict a life. She got herself a hair-cloth from a kiln—the sort that malt is dried on—and put it inside her gown as discreetly

---

1. Compare Richard Rolle's discussion of heavenly music, pages 498–99.

and secretly as she could, so that her husband should not notice it. And nor did he, although she lay beside him every night in bed and wore the hair-shirt every day, and bore him children during that time.

Then she had three years of great difficulty with temptations, which she bore as meekly as she could, thanking our Lord for all his gifts, and she was as merry when she was reproved, scorned or ridiculed for our Lord's love, and much more merry than she was before amongst the dignities of this world. For she knew very well that she had sinned greatly against God and that she deserved far more shame and sorrow than any man could cause her, and contempt in this world was the right way heaven-wards, for Christ himself chose that way. All his apostles, martyrs, confessors and virgins, and all those who ever came to heaven, passed by the way of tribulation, and she desired nothing as much as heaven. Then she was glad in her conscience when she believed that she was entering upon the way which would lead her to the place that she most desired.

And this creature had contrition and great compunction, with plentiful tears and much loud and violent sobbing, for her sins and for her unkindness towards her maker. She reflected on her unkindness since her childhood, as our Lord would put it into her mind, very many times. And then when she contemplated her own wickedness, she could only sorrow and weep and ever pray for mercy and forgive-ness. Her weeping was so plentiful and so continual that many people thought that she could weep and leave off when she wanted, and therefore many people said she was a false hypocrite, and wept when in company for advantage and profit. And then very many people who loved her before while she was in the world abandoned her and would not know her, and all the while she thanked God for everything, desiring nothing but mercy and forgiveness of sin.

CHAPTER 5

Then on a Friday before Christmas Day, as this creature was kneeling in a chapel of Saint John, within a church of Saint Margaret in N., weeping a very great deal and asking mercy and forgiveness for her sins and her trespasses, our merciful Lord Christ Jesus—blessed may he be—ravished her spirit and said to her, "Daughter, why are you weeping so sorely? I have come to you, Jesus Christ, who died on the cross suf-fering bitter pains and passion for you. I, the same God, forgive you your sins to the uttermost point. And you shall never come into hell nor into purgatory, but when you pass out of this world, within the twinkling of an eye, you shall have the bliss of heaven, for I am the same God who has brought your sins to your mind and caused you to be shriven of them. And I grant you contrition until your life's end.

"Therefore, I command you, boldly call me Jesus, your love, for I am your love and shall be your love without end. And, daughter, you have a hair-shirt on your back. I want you to leave off wearing it, and I shall give you a hair-shirt in your heart which shall please me much more than all the hair-shirts in the world. But also, my beloved daughter, you must give up that which you love best in this world, and that is the eating of meat. And instead of meat you shall eat my flesh and my blood, that is the true body of Christ in the sacrament of the altar. This is my will, daughter, that you receive my body every Sunday, and I shall cause so much grace to flow into you that everyone shall marvel at it.[2]

---

2. Weekly communion was uncommon, and required special ecclesiastical permission. Margery may have known that an admired predecessor, St. Bridget of Sweden, took weekly communion.

"You shall be eaten and gnawed by the people of the world just as any rat gnaws the stockfish.[3] Don't be afraid, daughter, for you shall be victorious over all your enemies. I shall give you grace enough to answer every cleric in the love of God. I swear to you by my majesty that I shall never forsake you whether in happiness or in sorrow. I shall help you and protect you, so that no devil in hell shall ever part you from me, nor angel in heaven, nor man on earth—for devils in hell may not, nor angels in heaven will not, nor man on earth shall not.

"And daughter, I want you to give up your praying of many beads, and think such thoughts as I shall put into your mind. I shall give you leave to pray until six o'clock to say what you wish. Then you shall lie still and speak to me in thought, and I shall give you high meditation and true contemplation.[4] And I command you to go to the anchorite at the Preaching Friars and tell him my confidences and counsels which I reveal to you, and do as he advises, for my spirit shall speak in him to you."

Then this creature went off to see the anchorite as she was commanded, and revealed to him the revelations that had been shown to her. Then the anchorite, with great reverence and weeping, thanking God, said, "Daughter, you are sucking even at Christ's breast, and you have received a pledge of paradise.[5] I charge you to receive such thoughts—when God will give them—as meekly and devoutly as you can, and then come and tell me what they are, and I shall, by the leave of our Lord Jesus Christ, tell you whether they are from the Holy Ghost or else from your enemy the devil."

CHAPTER 11

It happened one Friday, Midsummer Eve,[6] in very hot weather—as this creature was coming from York carrying a bottle of beer in her hand, and her husband a cake tucked inside his clothes against his chest—that her husband asked his wife this question: "Margery, if there came a man with a sword who would strike off my head unless I made love with you as I used to do before, tell me on your conscience—for you say you will not lie—whether you would allow my head to be cut off, or else allow me to make love with you again, as I did at one time?"

"Alas, sir," she said, "why are you raising this matter, when we have been chaste for these past eight weeks?"

"Because I want to know the truth of your heart."

And then she said with great sorrow, "Truly, I would rather see you being killed, than that we should turn back to our uncleanness."

And he replied, "You are no good wife."

And then she asked her husband what was the reason that he had not made love to her for the last eight weeks, since she lay with him every night in his bed. And he said that he was made so afraid when he would have touched her, that he dared do no more.

"Now, good sir, mend your ways and ask God's mercy, for I told you nearly three years ago that your desire would suddenly be slain—and this is now the third year, and I hope yet that I shall have my wish. Good sir, I pray you to grant what I shall ask, and I shall pray for you to be saved through the mercy of our Lord Jesus Christ, and you shall have more reward in heaven than if you wore a hair-shirt or wore a coat of

---

3. Dried cod.
4. Christ thus promises Margery the mystic way, without the ecclesiastical mediation of set prayers.
5. The image of Christ as mother particularly recalls Julian of Norwich, whom Margery later visits.

6. Probably 23 June 1413. The feast of Corpus Christi fell on the previous day, and it is likely that Margery and her husband had seen the great cycle of biblical plays traditionally performed in York on that day.

mail as a penance. I pray you, allow me to make a vow of chastity at whichever bishop's hand that God wills."

"No," he said, "I won't allow you to do that, because now I can make love to you without mortal sin, and then I wouldn't be able to."

Then she replied, "If it be the will of the Holy Ghost to fulfill what I have said, I pray God that you may consent to this; and if it be not the will of the Holy Ghost, I pray God that you never consent."

Then they went on towards Bridlington[7] and the weather was extremely hot, this creature all the time having great sorrow and great fear for her chastity. And as they came by a cross her husband sat down under the cross, calling his wife to him and saying these words to her: "Margery, grant me my desire, and I shall grant you your desire. My first desire is that we shall still lie together in one bed as we have done before; the second, that you shall pay my debts before you go to Jerusalem; and the third, that you shall eat and drink with me on Fridays as you used to do."

"No, sir," she said, "I will never agree to break my Friday fast as long as I live."

"Well," he said, "then I'm going to have sex with you again."

She begged him to allow her to say her prayers, and he kindly allowed it. Then she knelt down beside a cross in the field and prayed in this way, with a great abundance of tears: "Lord God, you know all things. You know what sorrow I have had to be chaste for you in my body all these three years, and now I might have my will and I dare not, for love of you. For if I were to break that custom of fasting from meat and drink on Fridays which you commanded me, I should now have my desire. But, blessed Lord, you know I will not go against your will, and great is my sorrow now unless I find comfort in you. Now, blessed Jesus, make your will known to my unworthy self, so that I may afterwards follow and fulfill it with all my might."

And then our Lord Jesus Christ with great sweetness spoke to this creature, commanding her to go again to her husband and pray him to grant her what she desired: "And he shall have what he desires. For, my beloved daughter, this was the reason why I ordered you to fast, so that you should the sooner obtain your desire, and now it is granted to you. I no longer wish you to fast, and therefore I command you in the name of Jesus to eat and drink as your husband does."

Then this creature thanked our Lord Jesus Christ for his grace and his goodness, and afterwards got up and went to her husband, saying to him, "Sir, if you please, you shall grant me my desire, and you shall have your desire. Grant me that you will not come into my bed, and I grant you that I will pay your debts before I go to Jerusalem. And make my body free to God, so that you never make any claim on me requesting any conjugal debt after this day as long as you live—and I shall eat and drink on Fridays at your bidding."[8]

Then her husband replied to her, "May your body be as freely available to God as it has been to me."

This creature thanked God greatly, rejoicing that she had her desire, praying her husband that they should say three paternosters in worship of the Trinity for the great grace that had been granted them. And so they did, kneeling under a cross, and afterwards they ate and drank together in great gladness of spirit. This was on a Friday, on Midsummer's Eve.

Then they went on to Bridlington and also to many other places, and spoke with God's servants, both anchorites and recluses, and many other of our Lord's

---

7. On the coast, east of York.
8. Margery may have received an inheritance from her fa-
ther by now, giving her the financial leverage to strike a deal, in effect, for her chastity.

lovers, with many worthy clerics, doctors and bachelors of divinity as well, in many different places. And to various people amongst them this creature revealed her feelings and her contemplations, as she was commanded to do, to find out if there were any deception in her feelings.

[MEETING WITH BISHOP OF LINCOLN AND ARCHBISHOP OF CANTERBURY]
CHAPTER 15

This creature, when our Lord had forgiven her her sin (as has been written before), had a desire to see those places where he was born, and where he suffered his Passion and where he died, together with other holy places where he was during his life, and also after his resurrection.

While she was feeling these desires, our Lord commanded her in her mind—two years before she went[9]—that she should go to Rome, to Jerusalem, and to Santiago de Compostela, and she would gladly have gone, but she had no money to go with.

And then she said to our Lord, "Where shall I get the money to go to these holy places with?"

Our Lord replied to her, "I shall send you enough friends in different parts of England to help you. And, daughter, I shall go with you in every country and provide for you. I shall lead you there and bring you back again in safety, and no Englishman shall die in the ship that you are in. I shall keep you from all wicked men's power. And, daughter, I say to you that I want you to wear white clothes and no other color, for you shall dress according to my will."[1]

"Ah, dear Lord, if I go around dressed differently from how other chaste women dress, I fear people will slander me. They will say I am a hypocrite and ridicule me."

"Yes, daughter, the more ridicule that you have for love of me, the more you please me."

Then this creature dared not do otherwise than as she was commanded in her soul. And so she set off on her travels with her husband, for he was always a good and easygoing man with her. Although he sometimes—out of groundless fear—left her on her own for a while, yet he always came back to her again, and felt sorry for her, and spoke up for her as much as he dared for fear of other people. But all others that went along with her forsook her, and they most falsely accused her—through temptation of the devil—of things that she was never guilty of.

And so did one man in whom she greatly trusted, and who offered to travel with her, at which she was very pleased, believing he would give her support and help her when she needed it, for he had been staying a long time with an anchorite, a doctor of divinity and a holy man, and that anchorite was this woman's confessor.

And so his servant—at his own inward stirring—took his leave to travel with this creature; and her own maidservant went with her too, for as long as things went well with them and nobody said anything against them.

But as soon as people—through the enticing of our spiritual enemy, and by permission of our Lord—spoke against this creature because she wept so grievously, and said she was a false hypocrite and deceived people, and threatened her with burning, then this man, who was held to be so holy, and in whom she trusted so much, rebuked her with the utmost force and scorned her most foully, and would not go any further with her. Her maidservant, seeing discomfort on every side, grew obstreperous

9. Probably 1411.   1. White dress implied special holiness or virginity.

with her mistress. She would not do as she was told, or follow her mistress's advice. She let her mistress go alone into many fine towns and would not go with her.

And always, her husband was ready when everybody else let her down, and he went with her where our Lord would send her, always believing that all was for the best, and would end well when God willed.

And at this time, he took her to speak with the Bishop of Lincoln, who was called Philip,[2] and they stayed for three weeks before they could speak to him, for he was not at home at his palace. When the Bishop came home, and heard tell of how such a woman had waited so long to speak to him, he then sent for her in great haste to find out what she wanted. And then she came into his presence and greeted him, and he warmly welcomed her and said he had long wanted to speak with her, and he was very glad she had come. And so she asked him if she might speak with him in private and confide in him the secrets of her soul, and he appointed a convenient time for this.

When the time came, she told him all about her meditations and high contemplations, and other secret things, both of the living and the dead, as our Lord revealed to her soul.[3] He was very glad to hear them, and graciously allowed her to say what she pleased, and greatly commended her feelings and her contemplations, saying they were high matters and most devout matters, and inspired by the Holy Ghost, advising her seriously that her feelings should be written down.

And she said that it was not God's will that they should be written so soon, nor were they written for twenty years afterwards and more.

And then she said furthermore, "My Lord, if it please you, I am commanded in my soul that you shall give me the mantle and the ring, and clothe me all in white clothes. And if you clothe me on earth, our Lord Jesus Christ shall clothe you in heaven, as I understand through revelation."[4]

Then the Bishop said to her, "I will fulfill your desire if your husband will consent to it."

Then she said to the Bishop, "I pray you, let my husband come into your presence, and you shall hear what he will say."

And so her husband came before the Bishop, and the Bishop asked him, "John, is it your will that your wife shall take the mantle and the ring and that you live chaste, the two of you?"

"Yes, my lord," he said, "and in token that we both vow to live chaste I here offer my hands into yours," and he put his hands between the Bishop's hands.

And the Bishop did no more with us on that day, except that he treated us very warmly and said we were most welcome.[5] * * *

CHAPTER 16

Then this creature went on to London with her husband, to Lambeth,[6] where the Archbishop was in residence at that time. And as they came into the hall in the afternoon, there were many of the Archbishop's clerks about and other heedless men, both squires and yeomen, who swore many great oaths and spoke many

2. Philip Repyngdon, Bishop of Lincoln 1405–1419. This journey occurred after their private agreement of chastity in June 1413.
3. Margery had some prophetic visions, though on a smaller scale than those of her predecessor St. Bridget of Sweden.
4. By clothing her, the bishop would acknowledge Margery and John's vow of chastity. In the Book of Reve-

lation, the saints in heaven are clothed in white robes.
5. The Bishop instructs Margery to approach the Archbishop of Canterbury, England's highest prelate, and obtain his permission to receive the mantle and ring. She agrees to go but says she will not ask the archbishop for that particular gift.
6. Lambeth Palace was (and is) the Archbishop's home nearest London.

thoughtless words, and this creature boldly rebuked them, and said they would be damned unless they left off their swearing and the other sins they practised.[7]

And with that there came forward a woman of that town dressed in a pilch[8] who reviled this creature, cursed her, and said very maliciously to her in this way: "I wish you were in Smithfield,[9] and I would bring a bundle of sticks to burn you with—it is a pity that you are alive."

This creature stood still and did not answer, and her husband endured it with great pain and was very sorry to hear his wife so rebuked.

Then the Archbishop sent for this creature to come to him in his garden.[1] When she came into his presence she made her obeisances to him as best she could, praying him, out of his gracious lordship, to grant her authority to choose her confessor and to receive communion every Sunday—if God would dispose her to this—under his letter and his seal throughout all his province. And he granted her with great kindness her whole desire without any silver or gold, nor would he let his clerks take anything for the writing or sealing of the letter.

When this creature found this grace in his sight, she was much comforted and strengthened in her soul, and so she told this worshipful lord about her manner of life, and such grace as God wrought in her mind and in her soul, in order to discover what he would say about it, and if he found any fault with either her contemplation or her weeping.

And she also told him the cause of her weeping, and the manner in which our Lord conversed with her soul. And he did not find fault at all, but approved her manner of life, and was very glad that our merciful Lord Christ Jesus showed such grace in our times—blessed may he be.

Then this creature spoke to him boldly about the correction of his household, saying with reverence, "My lord, our Lord of all, Almighty God, has not given you your benefice and great worldly wealth in order to maintain those who are traitors to him, and those who slay him every day by the swearing of great oaths. You shall answer for them, unless you correct them or else put them out of your service."

In the most meek and kindly way he allowed her to say what was on her mind and gave her a handsome answer, she supposing that things would then be better. And so their conversation continued until stars appeared in the sky. Then she took her leave, and her husband too.

Afterwards they went back to London, and many worthy men wanted to hear her converse, for her conversation was so much to do with the love of God that those who heard it were often moved to weep very sadly.

And so she had a very warm welcome there—and her husband because of her— for as long as they wished to stay in the city. Afterwards they returned to Lynn, and then this creature went to the anchorite at the Preaching Friars in Lynn and told him how she had been received, and how she had got on while she was travelling round the country. And he was very pleased at her homecoming and held it to be a great miracle, her coming and going to and fro.

And he said to her: "I have heard much evil talk of you since you went away, and I have been strongly advised to leave you and not to associate with you any more, and great friendships are promised me on condition that I give you up. And I

7. Margery frequently reproaches people for swearing.
8. A garment of animal skin with the hair still on it.
9. This is not an idle threat. Lollard heretics were put to death in Margery's lifetime, beginning in 1401 when

William Sawtry (formerly a priest at Lynn) was burned at Smithfield outside London.
1. Thomas Arundel (Archbishop of Canterbury 1396–1414) was a vigorous opponent of Lollards.

answered for you in this way: 'If you were still the same as you were when we parted, I certainly dared say you were a good woman, a lover of God, and highly inspired with the Holy Ghost. I will not forsake her for any lady in this realm, if speaking with the lady means leaving her, for I would rather leave the lady and speak with Margery, if I might not do both, than do the contrary.'" (Read first the twenty-first chapter and then this chapter after that.)

[VISIT WITH JULIAN OF NORWICH]
CHAPTER 17

One day long before this time, while this creature was bearing children and was newly delivered of a child, our Lord Christ Jesus said to her that she should bear no more children, and therefore he commanded her to go to Norwich. * * *

CHAPTER 18

This creature was charged and commanded in her soul that she should go to a White Friar in the same city of Norwich, who was called William Southfield, a good man who lived a holy life, to reveal to him the grace that God had wrought in her, as she had done to the good Vicar before. She did as she was commanded and came to the friar one morning, and was with him in a chapel for a long time, and told him her meditations and what God had wrought in her soul, in order to know if she were deceived by any delusions or not.[2]

This good man, the White Friar, all the time that she told him of her feelings, held up his hands and said, "Jesus, mercy, and thanks be to Jesus."

"Sister," he said, "have no fear about your manner of life, for it is the Holy Ghost plentifully working his grace in your soul. Thank him highly of his goodness, for we are all bound to thank him for you, who now in our times inspires you with his grace, to the help and comfort of all of us who are supported by your prayers and by others such as you. And we are preserved from many misfortunes and troubles which we should deservedly suffer for our trespasses, were there not such good creatures among us. Blessed be Almighty God for his goodness.

"And therefore, sister, I advise you to dispose yourself to receive the gifts of God as lowly and meekly as you can, and put up no obstacle or objections against the goodness of the Holy Ghost, for he may give his gifts where he will, and the unworthy he makes worthy, the sinful he makes righteous. His mercy is always ready for us unless the fault be in ourselves, for he does not dwell in a body subject to sin. He flies from all false pretense and falsehood; he asks of us a low, a meek, and a contrite heart, with a good will.[3] Our Lord says himself, 'My spirit shall rest upon a meek man, a contrite man, and one who fears my words.'[4]

"Sister, I trust to our Lord that you have these conditions either in your will or in your affections or else in both, and I do not consider that our Lord allows to be endlessly deceived those who place their trust in him, and seek and desire nothing but him only, as I hope you do. And therefore believe fully that our Lord loves you and is working his grace in you. I pray God increase it and continue it to his everlasting worship, for his mercy."

2. Southfield was a Carmelite friar who received visions of the Virgin Mary. Many mystical texts warn against the possibility that visions may be of demonic origin; see selections from *The Cloud of Unknowing*, pages 499–501.
3. Psalm 51.17.
4. Isaiah 66.2.

The said creature was much comforted both in body and in soul by this good man's words, and greatly strengthened in her faith.

And then she was commanded by our Lord to go to an anchoress in the same city who was called Dame Julian.[5] And so she did, and told her about the grace, that God had put into her soul, of compunction, contrition, sweetness and devotion, compassion with holy meditation and high contemplation, and very many holy speeches and converse that our Lord spoke to her soul, and also many wonderful revelations, which she described to the anchoress to find out if there were any deception in them, for the anchoress was expert in such things and could give good advice.

The anchoress, hearing the marvelous goodness of our Lord, highly thanked God with all her heart for his visitation, advising this creature to be obedient to the will of our Lord and fulfill with all her might whatever he put into her soul, if it were not against the worship of God and the profit of her fellow Christians.[6] For if it were, then it were not the influence of a good spirit, but rather of an evil spirit. "The Holy Ghost never urges a thing against charity, and if he did, he would be contrary to his own self, for he is all charity. Also he moves a soul to all chasteness, for chaste livers are called the temple of the Holy Ghost,[7] and the Holy Ghost makes a soul stable and steadfast in the right faith and the right belief.

"And a double man in soul is always unstable and unsteadfast in all his ways.[8] He that is forever doubting is like the wave of the sea which is moved and borne about with the wind, and that man is not likely to receive the gifts of God.[9]

"Any creature that has these tokens may steadfastly believe that the Holy Ghost dwells in his soul. And much more, when God visits a creature with tears of contrition, devotion or compassion, he may and ought to believe that the Holy Ghost is in his soul. Saint Paul says that the Holy Ghost asks for us with mourning and weeping unspeakable;[1] that is to say, he causes us to ask and pray with mourning and weeping so plentifully that the tears may not be numbered. No evil spirit may give these tokens, for Saint Jerome says that tears torment the devil more than do the pains of hell. God and the devil are always at odds, and they shall never dwell together in one place, and the devil has no power in a man's soul.

"Holy Writ says that the soul of a righteous man is the seat of God,[2] and so I trust, sister, that you are. I pray God grant you perseverance. Set all your trust in God and do not fear the talk of the world, for the more contempt, shame and reproof that you have in this world, the more is your merit in the sight of God.[3] Patience is necessary for you, for in that shall you keep your soul."[4]

Great was the holy conversation that the anchoress and this creature had through talking of the love of our Lord Jesus Christ for the many days that they were together.

This creature revealed her manner of life to many a worthy clerk, to honored doctors of divinity, both religious men and others of secular habit, and they said that God wrought great grace in her and bade her not to be afraid—there was no delusion

5. Julian of Norwich; see selections from her *Book of Showings*, pages 481–97.
6. This concern with the whole community of the faithful, a new note in Kempe's book, is highly characteristic of Julian's spirituality.
7. 1 Corinthians 6.19. The density of biblical reference in this passage suggests not only Dame Julian's learning but also Kempe's powerful memory for Scripture and theol-

ogy. It is important that such biblical justification comes to Kempe through another holy woman.
8. James 1.8.
9. James 1.6–7.
1. Romans 8.26.
2. 2 Corinthians 6.16, Revelation 21.3.
3. Luke 6.22–23.
4. Luke 21.19.

in her manner of living. They counseled her to be persevering, for their greatest fear was that she would turn aside and not keep her perfection. She had so many enemies and so much slander, that it seemed to them that she might not bear it without great grace and a mighty faith. * * *

[PILGRIMAGE TO JERUSALEM]

CHAPTER 28[5]

* * * And so they went on into the Holy Land until they could see Jerusalem. And when this creature saw Jerusalem—she was riding on an ass—she thanked God with all her heart, praying him for his mercy that, just as he had brought her to see this earthly city of Jerusalem, he would grant her grace to see the blissful city of Jerusalem above, the city of heaven. Our Lord Jesus Christ, answering her thought, granted her her desire.

Then for the joy that she had and the sweetness that she felt in the conversation of our Lord, she was on the point of falling off her ass, for she could not bear the sweetness and grace that God wrought in her soul. Then two German pilgrims went up to her and kept her from falling—one of them was a priest, and he put spices in her mouth to comfort her, thinking she was ill. And so they helped her onwards to Jerusalem, and when she arrived there she said, "Sirs, I beg you, don't be annoyed though I weep bitterly in this holy place where our Lord Jesus Christ lived and died."

Then they went to the Church of the Holy Sepulchre in Jerusalem, and they were let in on the one day at evensong time, and remained until evensong time on the next day. Then the friars lifted up a cross and led the pilgrims about from one place to another where our Lord had suffered his pains and his Passion, every man and woman carrying a wax candle in one hand.[6] And the friars always, as they went about, told them what our Lord suffered in every place. And this creature wept and sobbed as plenteously as though she had seen our Lord with her bodily eyes suffering his Passion at that time. Before her in her soul she saw him in truth by contemplation, and that caused her to have compassion. And when they came up on to the Mount of Calvary, she fell down because she could not stand or kneel, but writhed and wrestled with her body, spreading her arms out wide, and cried with a loud voice as though her heart would have burst apart, for in the city of her soul she saw truly and freshly how our Lord was crucified. Before her face she heard and saw in her spiritual sight the mourning of our Lady, of Saint John and Mary Magdalene, and of many others that loved our Lord.

And she had such great compassion and such great pain to see our Lord's pain, that she could not keep herself from crying and roaring though she should have died for it. And this was the first crying that she ever cried in any contemplation. And this kind of crying lasted for many years after this time, despite anything that anyone might do, and she suffered much contempt and much reproof for it. The crying was so loud and so amazing that it astounded people, unless they had heard it before, or else knew the reason for the cryings. And she had them so often that they made her very weak in her bodily strength, and specially if she heard of our Lord's Passion.

---

5. In autumn 1413, Margery sets out to the Holy Land. Her party of pilgrims repudiates Margery, and she is helped by the Papal legate at Constance, an English friar. She continues her travel toward Italy with an elderly Englishman. She rejoins the English pilgrims at Bologna, but continues to suffer their hostility because of her austere diet and dramatic displays of religious emotion. 6. Although Jerusalem was under Islamic control, Franciscan friars had negotiated permission to keep a convent next to the Church of the Holy Sepulchre and to guide pilgrims around a number of holy sites.

And sometimes, when she saw the crucifix, or if she saw a man had a wound, or a beast, whichever it were, or if a man beat a child before her or hit a horse or other beast with a whip, if she saw or heard it, she thought she saw our Lord being beaten or wounded, just as she saw it in the man or in the beast, either in the fields or in the town, and alone by herself as well as among people.

When she first had her cryings at Jerusalem, she had them often, and in Rome also. And when she first came home to England her cryings came but seldom, perhaps once a month, then once a week, afterwards daily, and once she had fourteen in one day, and another day she had seven, just as God would visit her with them, sometimes in church, sometimes in the street, sometimes in her chamber, sometimes in the fields, when God would send them, for she never knew the time nor hour when they would come. And they never came without surpassingly great sweetness of devotion and high contemplation.

And as soon as she perceived that she was going to cry, she would hold it in as much as she could, so that people would not hear it and get annoyed. For some said it was a wicked spirit tormented her; some said it was an illness; some said she had drunk too much wine; some cursed her; some wished she was in the harbor; some wished she was on the sea in a bottomless boat; and so each man as he thought. Other, spiritually inclined men loved her and esteemed her all the more. Some great clerks said our Lady never cried so, nor any saint in heaven, but they knew very little what she felt, nor would they believe that she could not stop herself from crying if she wanted.

And therefore, when she knew that she was going to cry, she held it in as long as she could, and did all that she could to withstand it or else to suppress it, until she turned the color of lead, and all the time it would be seething more and more in her mind until such time as it burst out. And when the body might no longer endure the spiritual effort, but was overcome with the unspeakable love that worked so fervently in her soul, then she fell down and cried astonishingly loud. And the more that she labored to keep it in or to suppress it, so much the more would she cry, and the louder.

And thus she did on the Mount of Calvary, as it is written before: she had as true contemplation in the sight of her soul as if Christ had hung before her bodily eye in his manhood.[7] And when through dispensation of the high mercy of our sovereign savior, Christ Jesus, it was granted to this creature to behold so truly his precious tender body, all rent and torn with scourges, more full of wounds than a dovecote ever was of holes, hanging upon the cross with the crown of thorns upon his head, his blessed hands, his tender feet nailed to the hard wood, the rivers of blood flowing out plenteously from every limb, the grisly and grievous wound in his precious side shedding out blood and water for her love and her salvation, then she fell down and cried with a loud voice, twisting and turning her body amazingly on every side, spreading her arms out wide as if she would have died, and could not keep herself from crying and these physical movements, because of the fire of love that burned so fervently in her soul with pure pity and compassion.[8]

---

7. The detailed rendering of Christ's suffering corresponds to Julian of Norwich's visions and to depictions of the Crucifixion in later medieval art. Margery's gestures reinforce the pattern of imitation of Christ seen throughout her book.

8. Margery's images of the dovecote and the fire of love echo Richard Rolle.

[ARREST BY DUKE OF BEDFORD'S MEN; MEETING WITH ARCHBISHOP OF YORK]
CHAPTER 53[9]

Afterwards that good man who was her escort brought her out of the town, and they went on to Bridlington to her confessor, who was called Sleytham, and spoke with him and with many other good men who had encouraged her previously and done much for her. Then she would not stay there, but took her leave to walk on upon her journey. And then her confessor asked her if she dared not stay because of the Archbishop of York, and she said, "No, truly."

Then the good man gave her silver, begging her to pray for him. And so she went on to Hull. And there, on one occasion, as they went in procession, a great woman treated her with utter contempt, and she said not a word in reply. Many other people said that she ought to be put in prison and made great threats. And notwithstanding all their malice, a good man still came and asked her to a meal, and made her very welcome. Then the malicious people who had despised her before came to this good man, and told him that he ought not do her any kindness, for they considered that she was not a good woman. On the next day, in the morning, her host escorted her out to the edge of town, for he dared not keep her with him any longer.

And so she went to Hessle and would have crossed over the Humber.[1] Then she happened to find there two Preaching Friars, and two yeomen of the Duke of Bedford's.[2] The friars told the yeomen which woman she was, and the yeomen arrested her as she was about to board her boat, and also arrested a man who travelled with her.

"For our lord," they said, "the Duke of Bedford, has sent for you, and you are held to be the greatest Lollard in all this part of the country, or around London either. We have sought you in many a part of the land, and we shall have a hundred pounds for bringing you before our lord."

She said to them, "With a good will, sirs, I shall go with you wherever you will lead me."

Then they brought her back to Hessle, and there men called her Lollard, and women came running out of their houses with their distaffs, crying to the people, "Burn this false heretic."

So as she went on towards Beverley with the said yeomen and friars, they many times met with men of that district who said to her, "Woman, give up this life that you lead, and go and spin, and card wool, as other women do, and do not suffer so much shame and so much unhappiness. We would not suffer so much for any money on earth."

Then she said to them, "I do not suffer as much sorrow as I would do for our Lord's love, for I only suffer cutting words, and our merciful Lord Christ Jesus— worshipped be his name—suffered hard strokes, bitter scourgings, and shameful death at the last, for me and for all mankind, blessed may he be. And therefore, it is truly nothing that I suffer, in comparison to what he suffered."

And so, as she went along with the said men, she told them good stories, until one of the Duke's men who had arrested her said to her, "I rather regret that I met with you, for it seems to me that you speak very good words."

9. Margery returns from pilgrimage to Santiago de Compostela. Traveling from Bristol to York, she has twice been detained by civil and clerical authorities, and questioned as a suspected Lollard. Each time she establishes her orthodoxy, most recently to the Archbishop of York, who nevertheless has her escorted from his archdiocese.

1. By crossing the Humber, Margery would have passed beyond the authority of the Archbishop of York, and closer to the Bishop of Lincoln, who had been sympathetic to her.
2. John, third son of King Henry IV, first Duke of Bedford, 1389–1435; at this time he was Lieutenant of the kingdom. (See the Book of Hours made for him, Color Plate 10.)

Then she said to him, "Sir, do not regret nor repent that you met with me. Do your lord's will, and I trust that all shall be for the best, for I am very well pleased that you met with me."

He replied, "If ever you're a saint in heaven, lady, pray for me."

She answered, saying to him, "Sir, I hope you will be a saint yourself, and every man that shall come to heaven."

So they went on till they came into Beverley, where lived the wife of one of the men who had arrested her. And they escorted her there and took away from her her purse and her ring. They provided her with a nice room and a decent bed in it, with all the necessaries, locking the door with a key, and bearing the key away with them. * * *

* * * Then she stood looking out at a window, telling many edifying tales to those who would hear her, so much so that women wept bitterly, and said with great heaviness of heart, "Alas, woman, why should you be burned?"

Then she begged the good wife of the house to give her a drink, for she was terribly thirsty. And the good wife said her husband had taken away the key, because of which she could not come in to her, nor give her a drink. And then the women took a ladder and set it up against the window, and gave her a pint of wine in a pot, and also a cup, begging her to conceal the pot and cup, so that when the good man came back he might not notice it.

Chapter 54

The said creature, lying in her bed on the following night, heard with her bodily ears a loud voice calling, "Margery." With that voice she awoke, greatly frightened, and, lying still in silence, she said her prayers as devoutly as she could at that time. And soon our merciful Lord, everywhere present, comforting his unworthy servant, said to her, "Daughter, it is more pleasing to me that you suffer scorn and humiliation, shame and rebukes, wrongs and distress, than if your head were struck off three times a day every day for seven years. And therefore, daughter, do not fear what any man can say to you. But in my goodness, and in your sorrows that you have suffered, you have great cause to rejoice, for when you come home to heaven, then shall every sorrow be turned into joy for you."

On the next day she was brought into the Chapterhouse of Beverley,[3] and there was the Archbishop of York, and many great clerics with him, priests, canons, and secular men. Then the Archbishop said to this creature, "What, woman, have you come back again? I would gladly be rid of you."

And then a priest brought her before him, and the Archbishop said, in the hearing of all present, "Sirs, I had this woman before me at Cawood, and there I with my clerics examined her in her faith and found no fault in her. Furthermore, sirs, I have since that time spoken with good men who hold her to be a perfect woman and a good woman. Notwithstanding all this, I gave one of my men five shillings to lead her out of this part of the country, in order to quieten the people down. And as they were going on their journey they were taken and arrested, my man put in prison because of her; also her gold and her silver was taken away from her, together with her beads and her ring, and she is brought before me again here. Is there any man here who can say anything against her?"

---

3. Just north of the Humber.

Then other men said, "Here is a friar who knows many things against her."

The friar came forward and said that she disparaged all men of Holy Church—and he uttered much evil talk about her that time. He also said that she would have been burnt at Lynn, had his order—that was the Preaching Friars—not been there. "And, sir, she says that she may weep and have contrition when she will."

Then came the two men who had arrested her, saying with the friar that she was Cobham's daughter, and was sent to carry letters about the country.[4] And they said she had not been to Jerusalem, nor in the Holy Land, nor on other pilgrimage, as she had been in truth. They denied all truth, and maintained what was wrong, as many others had done before. When they had said enough for a long while, they held their peace.

Then the Archbishop said to her, "Woman, what do you say to all this?"

She said, "My lord, saving your reverence, all the words that they say are lies."

Then the Archbishop said to the friar, "Friar, the words are not heresy; they are slanderous words and erroneous."

"My lord," said the friar, "she knows her faith well enough. Nevertheless, my lord of Bedford is angry with her, and he will have her."[5] * * *

A short time afterwards the Archbishop sent for her, and she was led into his chamber, and even up to his bedside. Then she, bowing, thanked him for his gracious favour that he had shown her before.

"Yes, yes," said the Archbishop, "I am told worse things of you than I ever was before."

She said, "My lord, if you care to examine me, I shall avow the truth, and if I be found guilty, I will be obedient to your correction."

Then a Preaching Friar came forward, who was Suffragan[6] to the Archbishop, to whom the Archbishop said, "Now, sir, as you said to me when she was not present, say now while she is present."

"Shall I do so?" said the Suffragan.

"Yes," said the Archbishop.

Then the Suffragan said to this creature, "Woman, you were at my Lady Westmorland's."[7]

"When, sir?" said she.

"At Easter," said the Suffragan.

She, not replying, said, "Well, sir?"

Then he said, "My Lady herself was well pleased with you and liked your talk, but you advised my Lady Greystoke to leave her husband,[8] and she is a baron's wife, and daughter to my Lady of Westmorland. And now you have said enough to be burned for." And so he multiplied many sharp words in front of the Archbishop—it is not fitting to repeat them.

At last she said to the Archbishop, "My lord, if it be your will, I have not seen my Lady Westmorland these two years and more. Sir, she sent for me before I went to Jerusalem[9] and, if you like, I will go to her again for a testimonial that I prompted no such matter."

4. Sir John Oldcastle, Lord Cobham, a leading Lollard, had mounted an unsuccessful rising against Henry V. He was executed, in the presence of the Duke of Bedford, 14 December 1417.

5. Margery becomes part of a potential dispute over jurisdiction between clergy and laity.

6. A subsidiary bishop, usually assisting a bishop or archbishop in local matters.

7. Joan de Beaufort (d. 1440), daughter of John of Gaunt and at this time wife of Ralph Neville, first Earl of Westmorland. She was the Duke of Bedford's aunt.

8. Elizabeth, Lady Greystoke, daughter of Joan de Beaufort, hence a relative of the Duke of Bedford. Margery had already been accused of encouraging the wives of urban commoners to leave their husbands.

9. At least four years earlier.

"No," said those who stood round about, "let her be put in prison, and we will send a letter to the noble lady, and, if it be the truth that she is saying, let her go free, without any grudging."

And she said she was quite satisfied that it should be so.

Then a great cleric who stood a little to one side of the Archbishop said, "Put her in prison forty days, and she will love God the better for the rest of her life."

The Archbishop asked her what tale it was that she told the Lady of Westmorland when she spoke with her.

She said, "I told her a good tale of a lady who was damned because she would not love her enemies, and of a bailiff who was saved because he loved his enemies and forgave them their trespasses against him, and yet he was held to be an evil man."

The Archbishop said it was a good tale. Then his steward said, and many others with him, crying with a loud voice to the Archbishop, "My lord, we pray you, let her go from here this time, and if she ever comes back again, we will burn her ourselves."

The Archbishop said, "I believe there was never woman in England so treated as she is, and has been."

Then he said to this creature, "I do not know what I shall do with you."

She said, "My lord, I pray you, let me have your letter and your seal as a record that I have vindicated myself against my enemies, and that nothing admissible is charged against me, neither error nor heresy that may be proved against me, our Lord be thanked. And let me have John, your man, again to bring me over the water."

And the Archbishop very kindly granted her all she desired—our Lord grant him his reward—and delivered to her her purse with her ring and beads, which the Duke of Bedford's men had taken from her before. The Archbishop was amazed at where she got the money to travel about the country with, and she said good men gave it her so that she would pray for them.

Then she, kneeling down, received his blessing and took her leave with a very glad heart, going out of his chamber. And the Archbishop's household asked her to pray for them, but the Steward was angry because she laughed and was so cheerful, saying to her, "Holy folk should not laugh."

She said, "Sir, I have great cause to laugh, for the more shame and scorn I suffer, the merrier I may be in our Lord Jesus Christ."

Then she came down into the hall, and there stood the Preaching Friar who had caused her all that unhappiness. And so she passed on with a man of the Archbishop's, bearing the letter which the Archbishop had granted her for a record, and he brought her to the River Humber, and there he took his leave of her, returning to his lord and bearing the said letter with him again, and so she was left alone, without any knowledge of the people.[1]

All the aforesaid trouble befell her on a Friday, God be thanked for everything.[2]

CHAPTER 55

When she had crossed the River Humber, she was immediately arrested as a Lollard and led towards prison. There happened to be a person there who had seen her before the Archbishop of York, and he got her leave to go where she wanted, and excused her to the bailiff, and undertook for her that she was no Lollard. And so she escaped away in the name of Jesus. * * *

1. At the southern edge of the archbishop's territory, Margery is again left alone and without the document that would guarantee her orthodoxy.

2. Margery's greatest trials often occur on a Friday, connecting her sufferings to events of the Crucifixion.

⊷　⊱✦⊰　⊶

Middle English Lyrics

Although many Middle English lyrics have a beguilingly fresh and unselfconscious tone, they owe much to learned and sophisticated continental sources—the medieval Latin lyrics of the "Goliard poets" and the Provençal and French lyrics of the Troubadours and Trouvères. Most authors were clerics, aware of the similarities between earthly and divine love, and fond of punning in Latin or English.

The anonymity of the Middle English lyrics prevents us from seeing them as part of a single poet's *oeuvre*, as we can, for instance, with the poems of Chaucer, Dunbar, and Dafydd ap Gwilym. Rather, we must rely on more general contexts, such as genre, to establish relationships among poems. One of the most popular genres among the secular lyrics was the *reverdie*, a poem celebrating the return of spring. The early thirteenth-century *Cuckoo Song* ("Sumer is icumen in") joyfully invokes the bird's song, and revels in the blossoming of the countryside and the calls of the animals to their young. More typical examples of the *reverdie* are *Alisoun* and *Spring,* whose male speakers ruefully contrast the burgeoning of nature with the stinginess of their beloveds; in *Spring,* flowers bloom, birds sing, animals mate—but one woman remains unmoved. In the genre of the love complaint, *My Lefe Is Faren in a Lond* and *Fowls in the Frith* express erotic loss and frustration with great succinctness.

Frustration was not the only attitude in Middle English love lyrics, however. A stance more boasting than adoring or despairing is taken in the witty lyric *I Have a Noble Cock.* Furthermore, clerical misogyny is expressed in *Abuse of Women,* which ostensibly praises women by absolving them of the vices—gossip, infidelity, shrewishness—typically attributed to them in satires against women; yet the refrain first praises women as the best of creatures but then undercuts this claim in Latin, which few women would have been able to understand.

Although most of the Middle English lyrics are in the male voice, there are a few "women's songs"—most likely written by men—which convey female experience. Occasionally these songs are invitations (for instance, the enigmatic *Irish Dancer*), but more often they are laments by an abandoned, and often pregnant, woman. *A Forsaken Maiden's Lament* is punctuated by the regretful refrain: "Were it undo that is ido, / I wolde bewar." Two of the women's songs, while concluding with laments about pregnancy, stress the cleverness and charm of the clerical seducers, perhaps suggesting that churchmen were their audience as well as their authors. *The Wily Clerk* attributes a young man's skill at deception to his scholarly training, as does *Jolly Jankin,* whose clerk engages in multilingual wordplay, turning the "Kyrie Eleison" into a request for mercy from the woman herself, "Alison."

The majority of Middle English lyrics were not secular but religious. Songs in praise of the Virgin Mary or Christ, however, employ the same erotic language as the secular lyrics, often in conjunction with typological figures linking events in the Old Testament to those in the New. In *Adam Lay Ibounden,* for instance, the poet follows a statement of the "fortunate Fall"—that Adam's sin was necessary to permit Christ's redemption—with a courtly compliment to the Virgin Mary. Similarly, *I Sing of a Maiden* draws on the typological significance of Gideon's fleece in Judges 6 (the soaking of the fleece by dew figuring Mary's impregnation by the Holy Spirit) while also employing the courtly imagery of a poet "singing of a maiden" who "chooses" Christ as her son, as if he were a lover. In a much longer poem in praise of the Virgin, the poet—casting himself as Mary's "knight" caught in the bonds of love—begs her mercy and also compliments her by contrasting her with her antitype, Eve.

Occasionally the Middle English religious lyric uses secular motifs and genres in a way that approaches parody. For instance, the second stanza of the Nativity poem *Mary Is with Child* resembles a pregnancy lament by a young girl. Mary, however, explains that her condition will be a source of joy rather than shame, when she will sing a lullaby to her "darling."

This Middle English poet, far from blaspheming, was trying to humanize the mystery of the Nativity and relate it to daily life.

Other religious poems either celebrate Christ or reject the world. The poems to Christ, in their tenderness and immediacy, resemble those to Mary. In only four lines, *Now Goeth Sun Under Wood* evokes nature's oneness with Christ (the setting sun figuring the crucifixion) and the poet's empathy with the Virgin mother. Poets used erotic language in poems to Christ as well as those to Mary, as in *Sweet Jesus, King of Bliss* and *Jesus, My Sweet Lover*. Finally, in a different vein, the *Contempt of the World* questions the values of courtly life, with the "*ubi sunt*" ("where are") motif. "Where beth they biforen us weren?" it asks, evoking the lovely women who enjoyed their paradise on earth and now suffer the eternal fires of hell.

The Cuckoo Song

Sumer is icumen in,°	*spring has come in*
Lhude° sing, cuccu!°	*loudly / cuckoo*
Groweth sed° and bloweth° med°	*seed / blooms / meadow*
And springth° the wude° nu.°	*grows / forest / now*
5 Sing, cuccu!	
Awe° bleteth after lomb,	*ewe*
Lhouth° after calve° cu,°	*lows / calf / cow*
Bulluc sterteth,° bucke ferteth.°	*leaps / farts*
Murie° sing, cuccu!	*merrily*
10 Cuccu, cuccu,	
Wel singes thu, cuccu.	
Ne swik° thu naver° nu!	*cease / never*
Sing cuccu nu, sing cuccu!	
Sing cuccu, sing cuccu nu!	

Spring

Lenten° is come with love to toune,°	*spring / town*
With blosmen° and with briddes° roune,°	*flowers / birds' / song*
That all this blisse bringeth.	
Dayeseyes° in this° dales,	*daisies / these*
5 Notes swete of nightegales—	
Uch° foul° song singeth.	*each / bird*
The threstelcok him threteth o;[1]	
Away is here° winter wo	*their*
When woderove° springeth.°	*woodruff / grows*
10 This foules° singeth ferly fele,°	*birds / wonderfully much*
And wliteth on here winne wele,[2]	
That all the wode ringeth.	
The rose raileth hire rode,°	*puts on her rosy hue*
The leves on the lighte° wode	*bright*
15 Waxen° all with wille.°	*grow / pleasure*
The mone mandeth hire bleo,[3]	

1. The song thrush contends always.   3. The moon sends forth her light.
2. And chirp their wealth of joys.

This page contains the words and music to one of the earliest and best loved of Middle English lyrics, *The Cuckoo Song* ("Sumer is icumen in"). The lyric is a *reverdie*, or spring song, but its joyful description of nature's rebirth is given a more sober allegorical interpretation by the interlinear Latin gloss, apparently to be sung to the same tune. The gloss parallels the lyric's celebration of the reawakening landscape with an account of the "heavenly farmer" (*celicus agricola*) whom "rot on the vine" (*vitis vicio*) leads to sacrifice his Son. The fact that the manuscript was copied at a monastery reminds us that this song, like much other early English secular poetry, survives only because it was seen to have religious relevance.

	The lilie is lossom° to seo,°	*lovely / see*
	The fenil° and the fille.°	*fennel / chervil*
	Wowes° this° wilde drakes;	*woo / these*
20	Miles murgeth here makes,[4]	
	Ase strem that striketh° stille.°	*flows / softly*
	Mody meneth, so doth mo;[5]	
	Ichot° ich° am one of tho,°	*I know / I / those*
	For love that likes° ille.	*pleases*
25	The mone mandeth hire light;	
	So doth the semly° sonne bright,	*lovely*
	When briddes singeth breme.°	*loudly*
	Deawes donketh the dounes;[6]	
	Deores with here derne rounes,[7]	
30	Domes for to deme;[8]	
	Wormes woweth under cloude,°	*the soil*
	Wimmen waxeth° wounder° proude,	*become / wondrously*

4. Beasts gladden their mates.
5. The high-spirited man mourns, so do others.
6. Dew moistens the downs (hills).
7. Animals with their secret whispers.
8. Speak their opinions.

So well it wol hem° seme.°   *to them / appear*
If me shall wonte wille of on,[9]
35 This wunne weole° I wole forgon   *wealth of joys*
And wight° in wode be fleme.°   *quickly / exile*

Alisoun

Bitwene Mersh° and Averil°   *March / April*
When spray° biginneth to springe,°   *twig / grow*
The lutel° fowl° hath hire° will   *little / bird / her*
On° hire lud° to singe.   *in / language*
5   Ich° libbe° in love-longinge   *I / live*
For semlokest° of alle thinge: *fairest*
He° may me blisse bringe;   *she*
Ich° am in hire baundoun.°   *I / power*
    An hendy hap ich habbe ihent![1]
10   *Ichot°from hevene it is me sent;*   *I know*
    From alle wimmen my love is lent,°   *taken away*
    And light°on Alisoun.[2]   *settled*

On hew° hire her° is fair inogh,   *color / hair*
Hire browe browne, hire eye blake;
15 With lossum chere he on me logh,[3]
With middel° small and well imake.°   *waist / made*
Bote° he me wolle° to hire take   *unless / will*
For to ben hire° owen° make,°   *her / own / mate*
Longe to liven ichulle° forsake,°   *I will / refuse*
20 And feye° fallen adoun.   *doomed*
    An hendy hap ich habbe ihent!
    Ichot from hevene it is me sent;
    From alle wimmen my love is lent,
    And light on Alisoun.

25 Nightes° when I wende° and wake—   *at night / turn*
Forthy min wonges waxeth won[4]—
Levedy,° all for thine sake   *lady*
Longinge is ilent° me on.   *come*
In world nis non so witer° mon   *wise*
30 That all hire° bounte° telle con: *her / excellence*
Hire swire° is whittore° then the swon,   *neck / whiter*
And feirest may° in toune.   *maiden*
    An hendy hap ich habbe ihent!
    Ichot from hevene it is me sent;

---

9. If I shall lack the pleasure of one.   3. With lovely manner she laughed at me.
1. A fair destiny I have received.   4. Therefore my cheeks become pale.
2. Alison is a stock name for a country woman, shared by
the wife in Chaucer's *Miller's Tale* and by his Wife of
Bath.

35   *From alle wimmen my love is lent,*
      And light on Alisoun.

Ich am for wowing all forwake,[5]
Wery so water in wore[6]
Lest eny reve° me my make°   *steal / mate*
40 Ich habbe iyerned yore.[7]
Betere is tholien while sore[8]
Then mournen evermore.
Geynest° under gore,°   *kindest / petticoat*
Herkne to my roun!°   *song*
45   *An hendy hap ich habbe ihent!*
    Ichot from hevene it is me sent;
    From alle wimmen my love is lent,
      And light on Alisoun.

I Have a Noble Cock

I have a gentil° cok,   *noble*
    Croweth° me day;   *who crows*
He doth° me risen erly,   *makes*
    My matins for to say.

5   I have a gentil cok,
      Comen he is of gret;°   *a great family*
    His comb is of red corel,
      His tayel is of jet.

    I have a gentil cok,
10   Comen he is of kinde;°   *good lineage*
    His comb is of red corel,
      His tail is of inde.°   *indigo*

    His legges ben of asor,°   *azure*
      So gentil and so smale;
15   His spores° arn of silver white,   *spurs*
      Into the worte-wale.°   *root of cock's spur*

    His eynen° arn of cristal,   *eyes*
      Loken° all in aumber;   *set*
    And every night he percheth him
20   In min ladyes chaumber.

My Lefe Is Faren in a Lond[1]

My lefe is faren in a lond[2]—
    Alas! why is she so?
    And I am so sore bound

---

5. I am for wooing all sleepless.
6. Weary as water in a troubled pool.
7. (For whom) I have long yearned.
8. It is better to suffer sorely for a time.

1. Chaucer alludes to this poem in *The Nun's Priest's Tale*, line 113.
2. My beloved has gone away.

I may nat com her to.
She hath my hert in hold,°   *imprisoned*
Where-ever she ride or go,
With trew love a thousandfold.

5

Fowls in the Frith

Foweles° in the frith,°   *birds / wood*
The fisses° in the flod,°   *fishes / river*
And I mon° waxe° wod.°   *must / become / mad*
Mulch° sorw° I walke with   *much / sorrow*
For beste[1] of bon° and blod.°   *bone / blood*

Abuse of Women

Of all creatures women be best:
Cuius contrarium verum est.[1]

In every place ye may well see
That women be trewe as tirtil° on tree,   *turtledove*
Not liberal° in langage, but ever in secree,°   *licentious / secrecy*
And gret joye amonge them is for to be.

5

Of all creatures women be best:
Cuius contrarium verum est.

The stedfastnes of women will never be don,
So jentil, so curtes they be everychon,[2]
Meke as a lambe, still as a stone,
Croked° nor crabbed find ye none!   *perverse*

10

Of all creatures women be best:
Cuius contrarium verum est.

Men be more cumbers° a thousand fold,   *troublesome*
And I mervail how they dare be so bold
Against women for to hold,
Seeing them so pacient, softe, and cold.

15

Of all creatures women be best:
Cuius contrarium verum est.

20

For tell a woman all your counsaile,
And she can kepe it wonderly well;
She had lever go quik° to hell,   *alive*
Than to her neighbour she wold it tell!

Of all creatures women be best:
Cuius contrarium verum est.

25

---

1. Either "beast" or "best."   2. So well-bred, so courteous is each one.
1. Latin for "The opposite of this is true."

For by women men be reconsiled,
For by women was never man begiled,
For they be of the condicion of curtes Grisell,[3]
30   For they be so meke and milde.

    Of all creatures women be best:
    Cuius contrarium verum est.

Now say well by° women or elles be still,   *about*
For they never displesed man by ther will;
35   To be angry or wroth they can° no skill,   *have*
For I dare say they think non ill.

    Of all creatures women be best:
    Cuius contrarium verum est.

Trow° ye that women list° to smater,°   *think / like / chatter*
40   Or against ther husbondes for to clater?
Nay, they had lever° fast bred and water,   *rather*
Then for to dele in suche a mater.

    Of all creatures women be best:
    Cuius contrarium verum est.

45 Though all the paciens in the world were drownd,
And non were lefte here on the ground,
Again in a woman it might be found,
Suche vertu in them dothe abound!

    Of all creatures women be best:
50   *Cuius contrarium verum est.*

To the tavern they will not go,
Nor to the alehous never the mo,°   *more*
For, God wot,° ther hartes wold be wo, knows   *knows*
To spende ther husbondes money so.

55   *Of all creatures women be best:*
    Cuius contrarium verum est.

If here were a woman or a maid,
That list for to go freshely arayed,
Or with fine kirchers° to go displayed,   *kerchiefs*
60   Ye wold say, "They be proude": it is ill said.

    Of all creatures women be best:
    Cuius contrarium verum est.

The Irish Dancer

Ich° am of Irlaunde,   *I*
And of the holy londe
Of Irlande.
Gode° sire, pray ich thee,   *good*

---

3. Griselda, the long-suffering wife of Chaucer's *Clerk's Tale*; the tale ends with the observation that there are no more Griseldas left.

5 For of sainte° charitee,°   *holy / charity*
   Come and daunce wit me
   In Irlaunde.

A Forsaken Maiden's Lament

Were it undo° that is ido,°   *undone / done*
  I wolde bewar.

I lovede a child° of this cuntree,   *young man*
And so I wende° he had do me;   *thought*
5 Now myself the sothe° I see,   *truth*
    That he is far.

Were it undo that is ido,
I wolde bewar.

He seide to me he wolde be trewe,
10 And change me for non other newe;
    Now I sikke° and am pale of hewe,   *sigh*
      For he is far.

Were it undo that is ido,
I wolde bewar.

15 He seide his sawes° he wolde fulfille: *promises*
    Therfore I lat him have all his wille;
    Now I sikke and morne stille,°   *quietly*
      For he is far.

Were it undo that is ido,
20 *I wolde bewar.*

The Wily Clerk

A, dere God, what I am fayn,
For I am madyn now gane![1]

This enther° day I mete a clerke,°   *other / cleric*
And he was wily in his werke;
5 He prayd me with° him to herke,°   *to / listen*
    And his counsel all for to layne.°   *conceal*

A, dere God, what I am fayn,
For I am madyn now gane!

I trow° he coud° of gramery;[2]   *believe / knew*
10 I shall now telle a good skill° why: *reason*
    For what I hade siccurly,°   *certainly*
      To warne° his will had I no mayn.°   *resist / strength*

---

1. Ah, dear God, how worthless I am, / For I am no longer
a virgin.

2. Latin learning, or magic—indicates the magical power
which the speaker attributes to the clergy, who could
read Latin.

A, *dere God, what I am fayn,*
For I am madyn now gane!

15 Whan he and me brout° un° us the schete,°   brought / on / sheet
    Of all his will I him lete;°   permitted
    Now will not my girdil met°—   meet
        A, *dere God, what shall I sayn?*

    A, *dere God, what I am fayn,*
20 *For I am madyn now gane!*

    I shall sey to man and page°   youth
    That I have bene of pilgrimage.
    Now will I not lete° for no rage°   permit / lust
        With me a clerk for to pleyn.°   play

25 A, *dere God, what I am fayn,*
    For I am madyn now gane!

Jolly Jankin[1]

    "Kyrie,"°so "Kyrie,"   Lord
    Jankin singeth merie,°   merrily
    With "aleison."[2]

    As I went on Yol° Day in our procession,   Yule (Christmas)
5   Knew I joly Jankin be° his mery ton.°   by / tone
        Kyrieleison.

    "Kyrie," so "Kyrie,"
    Jankin singeth merie,
    With "aleison."

10 Jankin began the offis° on the Yol Day,   church service
    And yet me thinketh[3] it dos me good, so merie gan he say
        Kyrieleison.

    "Kyrie," so "Kyrie,"
    Jankin singeth merie,
15 *With "aleison."*

    Jankin red the pistil° full fair and full well,   Epistle
    And yet me thinketh it dos me good, as evere have I sell.°   luck
        Kyrieleison.

    "Kyrie," so "Kyrie,"
20 *Jankin singeth merie,*
    With "aleison."

    Jankin at the *Sanctus* craked° a merie note,   uttered
    And yet me thinketh it dos me good—I payed for his cote.
        Kyrieleison.

---

1. "Johnny," a stock name. Also the name of Chaucer's
Wife of Bath's fifth husband, who was a clerk.
2. *"Kyrie eleison,"* Greek for "Lord have mercy upon us"

(an early part of the Mass). The poem puns on "Alison,"
supposedly the speaker's name (a stock female name).
3. It seems to me.

25 "Kyrie," so "Kyrie,"
Jankin singeth merie,
With "aleison."

Jankin craked notes an hundered on a knot,°   *at once*
And yet he hakked hem smaller than wortes⁴ to the pot.
30   Kyrieleison.

"Kyrie," so "Kyrie,"
Jankin singeth merie,
With "aleison."

Jankin at the *Angnus* bered the *pax-brede*;⁵
35 He twinkeled, but said nout, and on min fot he trede.⁶
      Kyrieleison.

"Kyrie," so "Kyrie,"
Jankin singeth merie,
With "aleison."

40 *Benedicamus Domino*,⁷ Crist fro° schame me schilde.°   *from / shield*
Deo gracias,⁸ therto—alas, I go with childe!
      Kyrieleison.

"Kyrie," so "Kyrie,"
Jankin singeth merie,
45 With "aleison."

Adam Lay Ibounden

Adam lay ibounden,°   *bound*
Bounden in a bond;
Foure thousand winter
Thowt° he not too long.   *thought*
5 And all was for an appil,
An appil that he took,
As clerkes finden wreten
In here° book.   *their*
Ne hadde° the appil take° ben,   *had not / taken*
10 The appil taken ben,
Ne° hadde never our lady   *not*
A ben hevene quen.¹
Blissed be the time
That appil take was!
15 Therfore we moun° singen   *may*
"Deo gracias!"°   *Thanks be to God!*

---

4. Vegetables.
5. At the *Agnus Dei* (at the later part of the Mass), Jankin carried the *pax-brede*, an article signalling the exchanging of the kiss of peace.

6. He winked, but said nothing, and on my foot he stepped.
7. Let us bless the Lord.
8. Thanks be to God.
1. Have been heaven's queen.

I Sing of a Maiden

I sing of a maiden
That is makeles,[1]
King of alle kinges
To° here° sone she ches.°   *for / her / chose*

5   He cam also° stille°   *as / quietly*
Ther° his moder was   *where*
As dew in Aprille
That falleth on the gras.

He cam also stille
10   To his moderes bowr
As dew in Aprille
That falleth on the flour.

He cam also stille
Ther his moder lay
15   As dew in Aprille
That falleth on the spray.°   *twigs*

Moder and maiden
Was never non but she:
Well may swich° a lady   *such*
20   Godes moder be.

In Praise of Mary

Edi° be thu, Hevene Quene,   *blessed*
Folkes froure° and engles° blis,   *comfort / angels'*
Moder unwemmed° and maiden clene,   *unspotted*
Swich° in world non other nis.°   *such / is*
5   On thee it is well eth° sene°   *easily / seen*
Of alle wimmen thu havest that pris.°   *prize*
My swete Levedy,° her my bene,°   *Lady / prayer*
And rew° of me yif° thy wille is.   *take pity / if*

Thu asteye° so° the dais-rewe°   *climb / as / dawn's ray*
10   The° deleth° from the derke night;   *that / separates*
Of thee sprong a leme° newe   *light*
That all this world haveth ilight.°   *illuminated*
Nis non maide of thine hewe
So fair, so shene,° so rudy, so bright.   *beautiful*
15   Swete Levedy, of me thu rewe,
And have mercy of thine knight.

Sprunge° blostme° of one rote,°   *sprung / blossom / root*
The Holy Ghost thee reste upon;
That wes for monkunnes° bote,°   *mankind's / healing*

---

1. Spotless, matchless, and mateless.

20 And here° soule to alesen° for on.	*their / deliver*
Levedy milde, softe and swote,°	*sweet*
Ic° crye thee mercy: ic am thy mon,°	*I / man*
Bothe to honde and to fote,	
On alle wise° that ic con.°	*way / can*
25 Thu ert° erthe° to° gode sede;	*art / earth / for*
On thee lighte° the Hevene° dews;	*came down / of heaven*
Of thee sprong the edi° blede°—	*blessed / fruit*
The Holy Ghost hire on thee sews.°	*sowed it*
Thu bring us ut of care, of drede,°	*fear*
30 That Eve bitterliche us brews.	
Thu shalt us into Hevene lede—	
Welle° swete is the ilke° dews.	*most / same*
Moder, full of thewes° hende,°	*virtues / gracious*
Maide, dreigh° and well itaught,°	*patient / taught*
35 Ic em in thine lovebende,°	*bonds of love*
And to thee is all my draught.°	*leaning*
Thu me shilde° from the Fende,°	*shield / Fiend*
Ase thu ert fre,° and wilt° and maught:°	*noble / will / can*
Help me to my lives ende,	
40 And make me with thine sone isaught.°	*reconciled*
Thu ert icumen° of heghe° cunne,°	*come / high / lineage*
Of David the riche king.	
Nis non maiden under sunne	
The° mey be thine evening,°	*that / equal*
45 Ne that so derne° loviye cunne,°	*secretly / can*
Ne non so trewe of alle thing.	
Thy love us broughte eche° wunne:°	*eternal / bliss*
Ihered° ibe° thu, swete thing!	*praised / be*
Selcudliche ure Louerd it dighte[1]	
50 That thu, maide, withute were,°	*mate*
That all this world bicluppe ne mighte,°	*could not encompass*
Thu sholdest of thine boseme° bere.°	*womb / bear*
Thee ne stighte,° ne thee ne prighte,°	*stabbed / pricked*
In side, in lende° ne elleswhere:°	*loins / elsewhere*
55 That wes° with full muchel° righte,	*was / much*
For thu bere° thine Helere.°	*bore / Savior*
Tho° Godes sune alighte wolde°	*when / wished*
On erthe, all for ure° sake,	*our*
Herre° teyen° he him nolde	*higher / servant*
60 Thene° that maide to ben° his make:°	*than / be / mate*
Betere ne mighte he, thaigh° he wolde,	*though*
Ne swetture thing on erthe take.	

1. Marvellously our Lord arranged it.

Levedy,° bring us to thine bolde°   *Lady / abode*
And shild° us from helle wrake.°   *shield / vengeance*
Amen.

Mary Is with Child

Nowel! nowel! nowel!
Sing we with mirth!
Christ is come well
With us to dwell,
5   *By his most noble birth.*
Under a tree
In sporting me,
Alone by a wod-side,°   *side of a wood*
I hard° a maid[1]   *heard*
10   That swetly said,
"I am with child this tide.°   *time*

"Graciously
Conceived have I
The Son of God so swete:
15   His gracious will
I put me till,
As moder° him to kepe.   *mother*

"Both night and day
I will him pray,
20   And her° his lawes taught,   *hear*
And every dell°   *in every way*
His trewe gospell
In his apostles fraught.°   *carried*

"This ghostly° case°   *spiritual / act*
25   Doth me embrace,
Without despite or mock;
With my derling,
'Lullay,'° to sing,   *lullabye*
And lovely him to rock.

30   "Without distress
In grete lightness
I am both night and day.
This hevenly fod°   *child*
In his childhod
35   Shall daily with me play.

"Soone must I sing
With rejoicing,
For the time is all ronne°   *run out*

---

1. A poem that opens with the speaker in the countryside overhearing a woman's lament raises expectations that we will hear a *chanson d'aventure*, with erotic connotations.

give birth to

40   That I shall child,°
        All undefil'd,
        The King of Heven's Sonne."

Sweet Jesus, King of Bliss

Swete Jesu, king of blisse,
Min herte° love, min herte lisse,°   *heart's / joy*
Thou art swete mid iwisse.°   *certainly*
Wo is him that thee shall misse!

5   Swete Jesu, min herte light,
    Thou art day withoute night,
    Thou geve° me streinthe and eke° might   *may you give / also*
    For to lovien thee aright.

    Swete Jesu, min herte bote,°   *remedy*
10   In min herte thou sete° a rote°   *may you set / root*
    Of thy love, that is so swote,°   *sweet*
    And leve° that it springe mote.°   *grant / may grow*

    Swete Jesu, min herte gleem,°   *light*
    Brightore then the sonnebeem,
15   Ibore° thou were in Bedleheem;   *born*
    Thou make me here thy swete dreem.[1]

    Swete Jesu, thy love is swete;
    Wo is him that thee shall lete!°   *abandon*
    Gif me grace for to grete°   *cry*
20   For my sinnes teres° wete.°   *with tears / wet*

    Swete Jesu, king of londe,
    Thou make me fer° understonde   *to*
    That min herte mote° fonde°   *may / experience*
    How swete beth° thy love-bonde.   *is*

25   Swete Jesu, Louerd° min,   *Lord*
    My lif, min herte, all is thin;°   *yours*
    Undo° min herte and light° therin,   *open / alight*
    And wite° me from fendes° engin.°   *guard / the Devil's / trick*

    Swete Jesu, my soule° fode,   *soul's*
30   Thin werkes beth° bo° swete and gode;   *are / both*
    Thou boghtest° me upon the rode;°   *redeemed / cross*
    For me thou sheddest thy blode.

    Swete Jesu, me reoweth° sore   *I regret*
    Gultes that I ha wroght yore;[2]
35   Tharefore I bidde° thin milse° and ore;°   *beg / mercy / grace*
    Mercy, Lord, I nul° namore.   *will not*

---

1. May thou make me hear thy sweet melody.   2. The sins that I have committed in the past.

Swete Jesu, Louerd God,
Thou me boghtest with thy blod;
Out of thin herte orn° the flod;   *ran*
40   Thy moder° it segh° that thee by stod.   *mother / saw*

Swete Jesu, bright and shene,°   *beautiful*
I preye thee thou here my bene°   *prayer*
Thourgh ernding° of the hevene quene,   *intercession*
That thy love on me be sene.°   *seen*

45   Swete Jesu, berne° best,   *of men*
With thee ich hope habbe° rest;   *to have*
Whether I be south other° west,   *or*
The help of thee be me nest.°   *nearest*

Swete Jesu, well may him be
50   That thee may in blisse see.
With love-cordes drawe thou me
That I may comen and wone° with thee.   *dwell*

Swete Jesu, hevene king,
Feir and best of alle thing,
55   Thou bring me of° this longing   *out of*
To come to thee at min ending.

Swete Jesu, all folkes reed,°   *counsel*
Graunte us er we buen° ded   *are*
Thee underfonge° in fourme of bred,   *to receive*
60   And sethe° to heovene thou us led.°   *later / may lead*

Now Goeth Sun under Wood

Now goth° sonne under wod:°   *goes / forest*
Me reweth,[1] Marye, thy faire rode.°   *face*
Now goth sonne under tree:
Me reweth, Marye, thy sone and thee.

Jesus, My Sweet Lover

Jesu Christ, my lemmon° swete,   *lover*
That diyedest on the Rode Tree,°   *Cross*
With all my might I thee beseche,
For thy woundes two and three,
5   That also° faste mot° thy love   *as / may*
Into mine herte fitched° be   *fixed*
As was the spere into thine herte,
Whon thou soffredest deth for me.

1. I feel pity for.

Contempt of the World

Where beth° they biforen us weren? *are*
Houndes ladden° and hawkes beren,° *led / bore*
And hadden feld and wode;
The riche levedies° in here° bour,° *ladies / their / bower*
5   That wereden° gold in here tressour,° *wore / head-dress*
With here° brighte rode:° *their / face*

Eten and drounken and maden hem° glad; *themselves*
Here lif was all with gamen° ilad.° *sport / spent*
Men keneleden° hem° biforen; *kneeled / them*
10   They beren hem well swithe° heye°— *very / high*
And in a twinkling of an eye
Here soules weren forloren.° *lost*

Where is that laughing and that song,
That trailing¹ and that proude gong,° *gait*
15   Tho° hawkes and tho houndes? *those*
All that joye is went away,
That wele° is comen to weylaway,° *prosperity / woe*
To manye harde stoundes.° *times*

Here° paradis hy° nomen° here, *their / they / took*
20   And now they lien° in helle ifere;° *lie / together*
The fuir° it brennes° evere. *fire / burns*
Long is "ah!" and long is "oh!"
Long is "wy!" and long is "wo!"
Thennes° ne cometh they nevere. *thence*

25   Drey° here, man, thenne, if thou wilt, *suffer*
A litel pine that me thee bit;²
Withdraw thine eyses° ofte. *comforts*
They° thy pine° be unrede,° *though / pain / severe*
And° thou thenke° on thy mede,° *if / think / reward*
30   It shall thee thinken° softe. *seem*

If that fend,° that foule thing, *the Devil*
Thorou wikke roun, thorou fals egging,° *counsel*
Nethere° thee haveth icast, *down*
Up and be good chaunpioun!
35   Stond, ne fall namore adoun
For a litel blast.

Thou tak the rode° to° thy staf, *cross / as*
And thenk on him that thereonne gaf° *gave*
His lif that wes so lef.° *dear*
40   He it gaf for thee; thou yelde° it him, *give back*
Agein° his of that staf thou nim° *against / take*
And wrek° him of that thef.° *avenge / thief*

---

1. Walking with trailing garments.   2. A little pain that one enjoins.

Of righte bileve° thou nim that sheld,   *belief*
The whiles that thou best° in that feld,   *are*
45   Thin hond to strengthen fonde;°   *try*
And kep thy of with° staves° ord,°   *at / staff's / point*
And do° that traitre seyen that word.   *make*
Biget° that murie° londe.   *win/ happy*

Thereinne is day withouten night,
50   Withouten ende strengthe and might,
And wreche° of everich fo;   *punishment*
Mid° God himselven eche° lif,   *with / eternal*
And pes° and rest withoute strif,   *peace*
Wele° withouten wo.   *happiness*

55   Maiden moder,° hevene° quene,   *mother / heaven's*
Thou might and const and owest to bene[3]
Oure sheld agein the fende;°   *Devil*
Help us sunne° for to flen,°   *sin / flee*
That we moten° thy sone° iseen°   *may / Son / see*
60   In joye withouten ende.

Dafydd ap Gwilym

Widely regarded as the greatest Welsh poet, Dafydd ap Gwilym flourished in the fourteenth century, during a period of relative peace between two failed rebellions—that of Llywelyn, the last native prince of Wales, in 1282, and that of Owain Glyn Dwr (Owen Glendower), in 1400. A member of an upper-class family whose ancestors had served the English king, he wrote for a sophisticated audience of poets and patrons.

Dafydd drew inspiration from both continental and Welsh poetry but not, significantly, from English. (Influence, if any, went the other way, for the Middle English Harley lyrics, composed near the Welsh border, may owe their intricate rhyme scheme and ornamental alliteration to Welsh poetry; see *Spring and Alisoun*, pages 551–54). Among continental poets, the Roman Ovid is the greatest influence, whether directly or through twelfth-century Latin adaptations. He is the only foreign poet whom Dafydd mentions by name (*One Saving Place*, line 39). Dafydd is also indebted to medieval French and Provençal lyric genres—the *aubade* (dawn song), and the *reverdie* (spring song)—as well as to the *fabliau*.

Much of Dafydd's charm comes from his undercutting and transforming inherited poetic conventions through his personal revelations. His most endearing device, the self-deprecating persona, has been compared to that of his younger contemporary, Geoffrey Chaucer. There is an important difference, however, for while Chaucer in early love poems like *The Parliament of Fowls* presents himself as a failed lover, Dafydd often boasts of his success. Although he gives comic accounts of romantic failures in such anecdotal poems as the *Tale of a Wayside Inn* (in which a tryst ends in disaster when he goes to the wrong room), these are as often due to external obstacles as to his own inadequacy. In fact, Dafydd's persona is much more akin to Ovid's than to Chaucer's. In *The Ruin*, Dafydd gives an erotic twist to the ascetic Christian motif of the impermanence of worldly pleasures (as in the Old English *Wanderer*, page 172,

---

3. You may and can and ought to be.

and the Middle English *Contempt of the World,* page 565) by recalling that he once made love in a cottage that is now abandoned. He concludes his complaint *The Winter* with the observation that he would not venture out in such snowy weather for the sake of any girl.

Dafydd's poetry owes an equal debt to the rich poetic tradition of Wales. He shows familiarity with characters from the Arthurian tradition, which was originally Celtic although transformed by French adaptations by the time it reached him. In the poems included here, he often emphasizes the local Welsh setting. In *One Saving Place,* for instance, he lists all the locales where he sought his beloved Morvith, or she refused him—places with names like Meirch, Eleirch, Rhiw, and Cwcwll hollow. In *The Winter,* it is specifically in north Wales that he is assailed by snow. Finally, part of the humor in the *Tale of a Wayside Inn* derives from Dafydd's self-presentation as a "Welshman" whose accidental presence in their bedroom is discovered by three coarse Englishmen.

Dafydd's work is also distinguished by the poetic techniques of Welsh poetry, which are extraordinarily complex. His *cywyddau* (lyric poems) are written in the traditional lines of seven syllables, which rhyme in couplets, with the rhyming syllables alternately stressed and unstressed. He applies further ornamentation with a technique called *cynghanned*—internal alliteration or rhyme, which he sometimes extends over many lines. Although such an intricate style is impossible to capture in English, Rolfe Humphries has tried to approximate it in the translations given here. Easier to reproduce are Daffyd's *dyfalu*—strings of fanciful comparisons, such as the metaphors for snow used in *The Winter:*

> The snowflakes wander,
> A swarm of white bees.
> Over the woods
> A cold veil lies.
> A load of chalk
> Bows down the trees.
>
>   * * *
>
> Will someone tell me
> What angels lift
> Planks in the flour-loft
> Floor of heaven
> Shaking down dust?
> An angel's cloak
> Is cold quicksilver.

In extending the virtuoso techniques of the native tradition, Dafydd set the standard for Welsh poets for the next two centuries.

Aubade[1]

> It seemed as if we did not sleep
> One wink that night; I was sighing deep.
> The cruellest judge in the costliest court
> Could not condemn a night so short.
> 5   We had the light out, but I know,
> Each time I turned, a radiant glow
> Suffused the room, and shining snow

---

1. The *aubade* or dawn song is a genre of love lyric with a long European tradition, in which two lovers lament the necessity of parting at dawn. Chaucer uses the aubade, as later do Shakespeare (in *Romeo and Juliet*) and John Donne in *The Sun Rising.*

A lit from Heaven's candle-fires
Illuminated our desires.

10   But the last time I held her, strong,
Excited, closest, very long,
Something started going wrong.
The edge of dawn's despotic veil
Showed at the eastern window-pale
15   And there it was,—the morning light!
Gwen[2] was seized with a fearful fright,
Became an apparition, cried,
"Get up, go now with God, go hide!

"Love is a salt, a gall, a rue,
20   A vinegar-vintage. *Dos y Ddw,*
Vaya con Dios,[3] quickly, too!"
"Ah, not yet, never yet, my love;
The stars and moon still shine above."
"Then why do the raucous ravens talk
25   With such a loud insistent squawk?"
"Crows always cry like that, when fleas
Nibble their ankles, nip their knees."

"And why do the dogs yip, yammer, yell?"
"They think they've caught a fox's smell."
30   "Poet, the wisdom of a fool
Offers poor counsel as a rule.
Open the door, open it wide
As fast as you can, and leap outside.
The dogs are fierce when they get untied."
35   "The woods are only a bound from here,
And I can outjump a deer, my dear!"

"But tell me, best beloved of men,
Will you come again? Will you come again?"
"Gwen, you know I'm your nightingale,
40   And I'll be with you, without fail,
When the cloud is cloak, and the dark is sky,
And when the night comes, so will I."

One Saving Place

What wooer ever walked through frost and snow,
Through rain and wind, as I in sorrow?
My two feet took me to a tryst in Meirch[1]
No luck; I swam and waded the Eleirch,
5   No golden loveliness, no glimpse of her;

2. Along with Morvith and Dovekie, a woman's name
which recurs in many of Dafydd's love poems.
3. "Go with God"; this Spanish phrase represents license,
on the part of the translator, in the spirit of Dafydd's

playfulness.
1. This and other Welsh place names are listed by Dafydd
in his account of his search for his beloved, Morvith.

Night or day, I came no nearer
Except in Bleddyn's arbors, where I sighed
When she refused me, as she did beside
Maesalga's murmuring water-tide.
10   I crossed the river, Bergul, and went on
Beyond its threatening voices; I have gone
Through the mountain-pass of Meibion,
Came to Camallt, dark in my despair,
For one vision of her golden hair.
15   All for nothing. I've looked down from Rhiw,
All for nothing but a valley view,
Kept on going, on my journey through
Cyfylfaen's gorge, with rock and boulder,
Where I had thought to ermine-cloak her shoulder.
20   Never; not here, there, thither, thence,
Could I ever find her presence.
Eagerly on summer days I'd go
Brushing my way through Cwcwll hollow,
Never stopped, continued, skirting
25   Gastell Gwrgan and its ring
Where the red-winged blackbirds sing,
Tramped across fields where goslings feed
Below the cat-tail and the reed.
I have limped my way, a weary hound,
30   In shadow of the walls that bound
Adail Heilyn's broken ground.
I have hidden, like a friar,
In Ifor's Court, among the choir,
Sought to seek my sweet one there,
35   But there was no sign of her.
On both sides of Nant-y-glo
There's no vale, no valley, no
Stick or stump where I failed to go,
Only Gwynn of the Mist for guide,
40   Without Ovid[2] at my side.

Gwenn-y-Talwrn!—there I found
My hand close on hers, on ground
Where no grass was ever green,
Where not even a shrub was seen,
45   There at last I made the bed
For my Morvith,[3] my moon-maid,
Underneath the dark leaf-cloak
Woven by saplings of an oak.
Bitter, if a man must move
50   On his journeys without love.

---

2. See introduction to Dafydd for Dafydd's indebtedness to the Roman love poet.

3. The lady most frequently mentioned in Dafydd's love poems, apparently married.

Bitter, if soul's pilgrimage
Must be like the body's rage,
Must go down the desolate road
Midway through the darkling wood.

Tale of a Wayside Inn

With one servant, I went down
To a sportive sort of town
Where a Welshman might secure
Comely welcome, and pleasure.
5   There we found the book to sign
In the inn, and ordered wine.

But whatever did I see
But the loveliest lady
Blooming beautiful and bright,
10   Blossom stemming from sunlight,
Graceful as the gossamer.
I said, "Let me banquet her!"
Feasting's a fine way, it seems,
For fulfilling young men's dreams.

15   So, unshy, she took her seat
At my side, and we did eat,
Sipped our wine, and smiled and dallied
Like a man and maid, new-married.
Bold I was, but whispering,
20   And the others heard nothing.

Troth and tryst we pledged, to keep
When the others were asleep.
I should find my way, and come
Through the darkness to her room.
25   Love would haul my steps aright
Down the hallways of the night;
Love would steer my steps,—alas,

This was not what came to pass.
For, by some outrageous miss,
30   What I got was not a kiss,
But a stubble-whiskered cheek
And a triple whiskey-reek,
Not one Englishman, but three,
(What a Holy Trinity!)
35   Diccon, 'Enry, Jerk-off Jack,
Each one pillowed on his pack.

One of them let out a yell,
"What's that thing I think I smell?
There's a Welshman must have hid

40 In the closet or under t' bed,
 Come to cut our throats with knives,
 Guard your wallets and your lives,
 They're all thieves, beyond all doubt,
 Throw the bloody bugger out!"

45 None too nimble for my need,
 First I found how shins will bleed
 When you bark them in your haste
 On a stool that's been misplaced
 By some ostler-stupid fool,
50 Then the sawney of a stool
 Squealed its pig-stuck tattle-tale
 After my departing trail.

 By good luck, I never got
 Wet-foot from the chamber-pot.
55 That was all I saved myself,
 Knocked my noggin on a shelf,
 Overturned the table-trestles,
 Down came all the pans and kettles.
 As I dove to outer dark,
60 All the dogs began to bark.

 Asses bray, and scullions rouse
 Every sleeper in the house.
 I could hear the hunt come round me,
 Scowl-faced scoundrels, till they found me.
65 I could feel their stones and sticks,
 So I clasped my crucifix,
 Jesu, Jesu, Jesu dear,
 Don't let people catch me here!

 Since my prayer was strong, I came
70 Through the mercy of His name
 Safely to my room at last,
 All my perils over-passed.
 No girl's love to ease my plight,
 Only God's that dreadful night,
75 To the saints be brought the praise,
 And the Good Lord mend my wicked ways.

The Winter

 Across North Wales
 The snowflakes wander,
 A swarm of white bees.
 Over the woods
5 A cold veil lies.
 A load of chalk
 Bows down the trees.

No undergrowth
Without its wool,
10   No field unsheeted;
No path is left
Through any field;
On every stump
White flour is milled.

15   Will someone tell me
What angels lift
Planks in the flour-loft
Floor of heaven
Shaking down dust?
20   An angel's cloak
Is cold quicksilver.

And here below
The big drifts blow,
Blow and billow
25   Across the heather
Like swollen bellies.
The frozen foam
Falls in fleeces.

Out of my house
30   I will not stir
For any girl
To have my coat
Look like a miller's
Or stuck with feathers
35   Of eider down.
What a great fall
Lies on my country!
A wide wall, stretching
One sea to the other,
40   Greater and graver
Than the sea's graveyard.
When will rain come?

The Ruin

Nothing but a hovel now
Between moorland and meadow,
Once the owners saw in you
A comely cottage, bright, new,
5   Now roof, rafters, ridge-pole, all
Broken down by a broken wall.

A day of delight was once there
For me, long ago, no care
When I had a glimpse of her

10   Fair in an ingle-corner.
      Beside each other we lay
      In the delight of that day.

      Her forearm, snowflake-lovely,
      Softly white, pillowing me,
15   proferred a pleasant pattern
      For me to give in my turn,
      And that was our blessing for
      The new-cut lintel and door.

      "Now the wild wind, wailing by,
20   Crashes with curse and with cry
      Against my stones, a tempest
      Born and bred in the East,
      Or south ram-batterers break
      The shelter that folk forsake."

25   Life is illusion and grief;
      A tile whirls off, as a leaf
      Or a lath goes sailing, high
      In the keening of kite-kill cry.
      Could it be, our couch once stood
30   Sturdily under that wood?

      "Pillar and post, it would seem
      Now you are less than a dream.
      Are you that, or only the lost
      Wreck of a riddle, rune-ghost?"

35   "Dafydd, the cross on their graves
      Marks what little it saves,
      Says, *They did well in their lives.*"

MIDDLE SCOTS POETS

In the late fifteenth and early sixteenth centuries, Scotland enjoyed a brief flowering of poetry centered in a sophisticated court society. Relations with England were fraught with irony, marked, on the one hand, by royal alliance (James IV married Margaret Tudor, daughter of England's Henry VII in 1503) and on the other by disastrous warfare (James IV also, in alliance with France, invaded England and perished with most of the Scottish nobility at the Battle of Flodden in 1513). The poets of this period have been variously known as the "Scottish Chaucerians," the "Middle Scots Poets," and the "Makars"—each term privileging a significant, though only partial, aspect of their work. The first conveys the debt that William Dunbar, Robert Henryson, and Gavin Douglas (to name the three most famous) owed to Chaucer's subject matter, rhetorical style, and techniques of parody. The second suggests their equal debt to a native Scottish tradition, which includes such overtly nationalist works as Barbour's *Bruce* and Blind Harry's *Wallace*. The best term to describe these poets is perhaps the one used by Dunbar himself—"Makars" (makers)—for it suggests their powerful and self-conscious artistry.

William Dunbar

Of all the Makars, Dunbar is the greatest virtuoso, intoxicated with language, whether it be the elevated vocabulary borrowed from Latin, or the Germanic diction of alliterative poetry, whose tradition was kept alive in Scotland a century after it had died out in England. He was versatile in his choice of genres, writing occasional poems (such as an allegory in celebration of the marriage of James IV and Princess Margaret), divine poems, and parodies such as *The Treatise of the Two Married Women and the Widow*, a bawdy satire on the morals of court ladies written in the traditional alliterative long line. Included here are a meditation on death (*Lament for the Makars*), an Easter hymn (*Done Is a Battell*) and a parody of the courtly genre of the *chanson d'aventure* (*In Secreit Place This Hyndir Nycht*).

Lament for the Makars[1]

	I that in heill° wes° and gladnes	*health / was*
	Am trublit now with gret seiknes	
	And feblit with infermite:	
	Timor mortis conturbat me.[2]	
5	Our plesance heir is all vane glory,	
	This fals warld is bot transitory,	
	The flesche is brukle,° the Fend° is sle:°	*frail / Devil / sly*
	Timor mortis conturbat me.	
	The stait of man dois change and vary,	
10	Now sound, now seik, now blith, now sary,	
	Now dansand mery, now like to dee:°	*die*
	Timor mortis conturbat me.	
	No stait in erd° heir standis sickir;°	*on earth / secure*
	As with the wynd wavis the wickir,	
15	Wavis this warldis vanite:	
	Timor mortis conturbat me.	
	On to the ded gois all estatis,	
	Princis, prelotis,° and potestatis,°	*prelates / rulers*
	Baith riche and pur of al degre:	
20	*Timor mortis conturbat me.*	
	He takis the knychtis° in to feild,°	*knights / the field*
	Anarmit° under helme and scheild;	*armed*
	Victour he is at all mellie:°	*battles*
	Timor mortis conturbat me.	

1. This poem reflects the late medieval fascination with death. The speaker wistfully observes that beautiful ladies, brave knights, and wise clerks have had their lives cut short but gives most of his attention to poets. He lists 23 of these—three English (Chaucer, Gower, and Lydgate) and 20 Scots, only half of whom modern scholars can identify. Since Death has taken all his "brothers," he regards himself as next and resolves to prepare himself for the next world. The poem was printed in 1508 by Walter Chepman and Andrew Myllar, who introduced the printing press to Scotland.

2. Fear of death shakes me (from the liturgical Office of the Dead).

25   That strang unmercifull tyrand
      Takis, on the moderis° breist sowkand,°   *mother's | sucking*
      The bab full of benignite:
          Timor mortis conturbat me.

      He takis the campion° in the stour,°   *champion | conflict*
30   The capitane closit in the tour,
      The lady in bour° full of bewte: *bower*
          Timor mortis conturbat me.

      He sparis no lord for his piscence,°   *power*
      Na clerk for his intelligence;
35   His awfull strak° may no man fle: *stroke*
          Timor mortis conturbat me.

      Art magicianis and astrologgis,
      Rethoris,° logicianis and theologgis,   *rhetoricians*
      Thame helpis no conclusionis sle:°   *clever*
40   *Timor mortis conturbat me.*

      In medicyne the most practicianis,
      Lechis,° surrigianis,° and phisicianis,   *doctors | surgeons*
      Thame self fra ded° may not supple:°   *death | deliver*
          Timor mortis conturbat me.

45   I se that makaris° amang the laif°   *poets | remainder*
      Playis heir ther pageant, syne gois to graif;°   *grave*
      Sparit° is nocht ther faculte: *spared*
          Timor mortis conturbat me.

      He hes done petuously devour
50   The noble Chaucer of makaris flour,°   *flower of poets*
      The Monk of Bery,[3] and Gower, all thre:
          Timor mortis conturbat me.

      The gude Syr Hew of Eglintoun,[4]
      And eik Heryot, and Wyntoun,[5]
55   He hes tane out of this cuntre:
          Timor mortis conturbat me.

      That scorpion fell° hes done infek°   *fierce | infect*
      Maister Johne Clerk and James Afflek[6]
      Fra ballat making and tragidie:
60   *Timor mortis conturbat me.*

      Holland and Barbour[7] he hes berevit;
      Allace,° that he nocht with us levit   *alas*

---

3. John Lydgate, monk of Bury St. Edmunds, a minor poet who was an imitator of Chaucer. He also used the *"timor mortis"* refrain in a poem on the same subject.
4. Brother-in-law of Robert II and not otherwise known as a poet.
5. Andrew of Wyntoun, author of the *Oryginale Chronykil of Scotland.*

6. These two are unknown, as are the other poets in this list not identified.
7. Sir Richard Holland, author of the allegorical *Buke of the Howlat* (c. 1450), and John Barbour, author of the patriotic *Actes and Life . . . of Robert Bruce* (1376).

Schir Mungo Lokert of the Le:[8]
Timor mortis conturbat me.

65   Clerk of Tranent eik he hes tane,
That maid the Anteris° of Gawane;   *adventures*
Schir Gilbert Hay endit hes he:[9]
Timor mortis conturbat me.

He hes Blind Hary and Sandy Traill
70   Slaine with his schour° of mortall haill,   *shower*
Quhilk Patrik Johnestoun[1] myght nocht fle:
Timor mortis conturbat me.

He hes reft° Merseir his endite°   *taken from / talent*
That did in luf so lifly° write,   *in a lively manner*
75   So schort, so quyk, of sentence hie:
Timor mortis conturbat me.

He hes tane Roull of Aberdene
And gentill Roull of Corstorphin;
Two bettir fallowis did no man se:
80   *Timor mortis conturbat me.*

In Dunfermelyne he hes done roune°   *held conversation*
With Maister Robert Henrisoun.[2]
Schir Johne the Ros enbrast° hes he: *embraced*
Timor mortis conturbat me.

85   And he hes now tane last of aw
Gud gentill Stobo and Quintyne Schaw,[3]
Of quham all wichtis hes pete:[4]
Timor mortis conturbat me.

Gud Maister Walter Kennedy[5]
90   In° poynt of dede° lyis veraly;°   *on / death / truly*
Gret reuth° it wer that so suld be: *pity*
Timor mortis conturbat me.

Sen he hes all my brether tane
He will nocht lat me lif alane;
95   On forse° I man his nyxt pray be: *of necessity*
Timor mortis conturbat me.

Sen for the deid remeid° is none,   *remedy*
Best is that we for dede dispone°   *prepare*
Eftir our deid that lif may we:
100   *Timor mortis conturbat me.*

---

8. This Scotsman (d. 1489?) is not otherwise known as a poet.
9. The "clerk of Tranent" is unknown, but Arthurian romances focusing on Gawain were popular in Scotland; Sir Gilbert Hay (d. 1456) translated the poem *The Buik of Alexander* from French.
1. Blind Hary is credited with writing the Scots epic *Wallace* (c. 1475); Patrick Johnstoune was a producer of stage entertainments at court in the late 1400s.
2. Henryson was a major Middle Scots poet; see his *Robene and Makyne*, page 580.
3. John Reid, known as Stobo, was priest and secretary to James II, James III, and James IV; Schaw was a minor Scots poet.
4. On whom all people have pity.
5. Known for his *Flyting* (poem of ritual insult) with Dunbar.

Done Is a Battell[1]

Done is a battell on° the dragon blak,   *with*
Our campioun° Chryst confountet hes his force;   *champion*
The yettis° of hell ar brokin with a crak,   *gates*
The signe triumphall rasit is of the croce,°   *cross*
5   The divillis trymmillis° with hiddous voce,   *trembles*
The saulis° ar borrowit° and to the blis can go,   *souls / redeemed*
Chryst with his blud our ransonis dois indoce:°   *endorse*
Surrexit dominus de sepulchro.[2]

Dungin° is the deidly dragon Lucifer,   *beaten*
10   The crewall° serpent with the mortall stang,°   *cruel / sting*
The auld kene tegir with his teith on char°   *ajar*
Quhilk° in a wait hes lyne° for us so lang,   *which / lain*
Thinking to grip us in his clowis strang:
The mercifull lord wald° nocht that it wer so,   *would*
15   He maid him for to felye° of that fang:°   *fail / booty*
Surrexit dominus de sepulchro.

He for our saik that sufferit to be slane
And lyk a lamb in sacrifice wes dicht,°   *prepared*
Is lyk a lyone° rissin up agane,   *lion*
20   And as a gyane raxit him on hicht.[3]
Sprungin° is Aurora radius° and bricht,   *arisen / radiant*
On loft° is gone the glorius Appollo,[4]   *aloft*
The blisfull day depairtit° fro the nycht: *separated*
Surrexit dominus de sepulchro.

25   The grit victour agane is rissin on hicht
That for our querrell to the deth wes woundit;
The sone that wox° all paill now schynis bricht,   *became*
And, dirknes clerit, our fayth is now refoundit:°   *reestablished*
The knell of mercy fra the hevin is soundit,[5]
30   The Cristin ar deliverit of thair wo,
The Jowis° and thair errour ar confoundit: *Jews*
Surrexit dominus de sepulchro.

The fo is chasit, the battell is done ceis,°   *ceased*
The presone brokin, the jevellouris fleit and flemit,[6]
35   The weir° is gon, confermit is the peis,°   *war / peace*
The fetteris lowsit° and the dungeoun temit,°   *loosed / emptied*
The ransoun maid, the presoneris° redemit,°   *prisoners / redeemed*

---

1. This Easter hymn heroically portrays Christ's Resurrection as a battle with the devil, drawing on the account of the harrowing of hell in the apocryphal Gospel of Nicodemus, in which Christ journeys to hell to release worthy souls who had been born before his coming. It gains much of its power from the juxtaposition of alliterative diction from the Scots tradition with Latinate vocabulary. As in the *Lament for the Makars,* the Latin refrain fits within the overall English rhyme scheme.
2. The Lord is risen from the tomb. From the opening of the service for matins on Easter Sunday.

3. And like a giant stretched himself on high. A reference to Samson, who in bearing off the gates of Gaza was seen as a type of Christ breaking the gates of hell.
4. Christ, the sun (and Son) of righteousness, is identified with Apollo, the sun god, which explains the reference to Aurora, goddess of the dawn.
5. An allusion to the ringing of the bells on Easter morning.
6. The prison broken, the jailers fled and banished.

The feild is win°, ourcummin° is the fo,   *won / overcome*
Dispulit° of the tresur that he yemit:°   *despoiled / kept*
40 Surrexit dominus de sepulchro.

In Secreit Place This Hyndir Nycht[1]

In secreit place this hyndir° nycht   *last*
I hard ane beyrne° say till ane bricht,°   *man / fair lady*
"My huny, my hart, my hoip, my heill,[2]
I have bene lang° your luifar° leill°   *long / lover / loyal*
5 And can of yow get confort nane:°   *none*
How lang will ye with danger deill?[3]
Ye brek my hart, my bony ane."°   *pretty one*

His bony beird was kemmit and croppit,[4]
Bot all with cale° it was bedroppit,°   *soup / smeared*
10 And he wes townysche, peirt and gukit.[5]
He clappit fast, he kist and chukkit[6]
As with the glaikis° he wer ouirgane;°   *lust / overcome*
Yit be his feirris° he wald have fukkit: *manner*
"Ye brek my hart, my bony ane."

15 Quod he, "My hairt, sweit° as the hunye,   *sweet*
Sen that I borne wes of my mynnye°   *mother*
I never wowit° weycht° bot yow;   *wooed / creature*
My wambe° is of your luif sa fow°   *belly / full*
That as ane gaist° I glour° and grane,°   *ghost / glower / groan*
20 I trymble° sa, ye will not trow:°   *tremble / believe*
Ye brek my hart, my bony ane."

"Tehe,"° quod scho, and gaif ane gawfe;°   *Teehee / guffaw*
"Be still my tuchan[7] and my calfe,
My new spanit howffing fra the sowk,[8]
25 And all the blythnes° of my bowk;°   *joy / body*
My sweit swanking,° saif yow allane   *fine fellow*
Na leid° I luiffit° all this owk:°   *no man / loved / week*
Full leifis° me° your graceles gane."°   *dear / to me / face*

Quod he, "My claver° and my curldodie,°   *clover / a plant*
30 My huny soppis, my sweit possodie,°   *sheep's head broth*
Be not oure bosteous° to your billie,°   *rough / sweetheart*
Be warme hairtit° and not evill willie;°   *hearted / ill-willed*
Your heylis quhyt as quhalis bane,[9]

---

1. This comic account of the wooing of a kitchen maid by a boorish man parodies the *chanson d'aventure*, a genre in which the speaker overhears a dialogue between two lovers. Dunbar undercuts the poem's courtly language, which he has used seriously elsewhere, with overtly sexual references. In addition to words familiar to modern readers, the poem features terms of endearment from colloquial Scots which have long since been lost.
2. My honey, my heart, my hope, my salvation.
3. Ladies were expected to be "dangerous" (reluctant) in a courtship situation.

4. His handsome beard was combed and trimmed.
5. And he was townish (uncourtly), pert, and foolish.
6. He fondled fast, kissed, and chucked her under the chin.
7. Calf skin stuffed with straw, to encourage a cow to give milk.
8. My clumsy fellow newly weaned from nursing.
9. Your neck white as whale's bone; a common alliterative phrase in the conventional love poetry.

Garris ryis° on loft my quhillelillie:°   *makes rise / penis*
35   Ye brek my hart, my bony ane.”

Quod scho, “My clype, my unspaynit gyane[1]
With moderis° mylk yit in your mychane,°   *mother's / mouth*
My belly huddrun,° my swete hurle bawsy,[2]   *big-bellied glutton*
My huny gukkis,° my slawsy gawsy,   *sweet fool*
40   Your musing waild perse° ane hart of stane: *would pierce*
Tak gud confort, my grit heidit° slawsy,   *great-headed*
Full leifis me your graceles gane.”

Quod he, “My kid, my capirculyoun,°   *woodgrouse*
My bony baib° with the ruch° brylyoun,   *babe / rough*
45   My tendir gyrle, my wallie gowdye,°   *pretty goldfinch*
My tyrlie myrlie, my crowdie mowdie,°   *milky porridge*
Quhone° that oure mouthis dois meit° at ane   *when / do meet*
My stang dois storkyn with your towdie:[3]
Ye brek my hairt, my bony ane.”

50   Quod scho, “Now tak me be the hand,
Welcum, my golk° of Marie° land,   *cuckoo / fairy*
My chirrie and my maikles munyoun,[4]
My sowklar° sweit as ony unyoun,°   *suckling / any onion*
My strumill stirk yit new to spane,[5]
55   I am applyit° to your opunyoun:°   *inclined / opinion*
I luif rycht weill° your graceles gane.”   *love right well*

He gaiff to hir ane apill rubye;°   *apple red*
Quod scho, “Gramercye,° my sweit cowhubye.”°   *thanks / fool*
And thai tway to ane play began
60   Quhilk° men dois call the dery dan,[6]   *which*
Quhill° that thair myrthis° met baythe in ane: *while / pleasure*
“Wo is me,” quod scho, “Quhair will ye,° man?   *where will you go*
Best now I luif° that graceles gane.”   *love*

Robert Henryson

We know little about Robert Henryson, although he is said to have been a schoolmaster at the town of Dumferline, and Dunbar implies that he was dead by 1506, when he mentions him in the *Lament for the Makars*. Unlike Dunbar, he wrote not for the Scottish court but for the literate middle class, which gives his poetry a more moralistic and less witty tone. Henryson is a “Scottish Chaucerian” with a somber cast, for his major work, the *Testament of Crisseid*, picks up where Chaucer's great romance, *Troilus and Criseide*, leaves off, depicting the faithless heroine as punished with leprosy, achieving a kind of redemption, and writing her will. *Robene and Makyne*, however, is a much more lighthearted poem. Like Dunbar's *In*

1. Said she, “My big soft fellow, my unweaned giant.”
2. An obscure term of endearment, as are several other phrases in the following lines.
3. My pole does stiffen by your thing.

4. My cherry and my matchless darling.
5. My stumbling bullock still newly weaned.
6. A dance (i.e., copulation).

Secreit Place, it is a *chanson d'aventure* which parodies the language of courtly love, though its shepherd and shepherdess are far more appealing than Dunbar's grimy lovers. The roles are comically reversed, with the shepherdess Makyne, offering to instruct the shepherd Robene in the "ABCs" of love's lore, while he, in his ignorance, resists. After Robene dutifully departs with his sheep, he has regrets and returns, only to have Makyne tell him that he has delayed too long. She states the poem's moral, *carpe diem:*

> The man that will nocht quhen he may
> Sall haif nocht quhen he wald.

Robyn is thus left to repeat in vain courtly love sentiments that he learned from her.

Robene and Makyne[1]

	Robene sat on gud grene hill	
	Kepand° a flok of fe;°	keeping / sheep
	Mirry Makyne said him till:°	to
	"Robene, thow rew° on me!	have pity
5	I haif the luvit lowd and still[2]	
	Thir yeiris° two or thre;	these years
	My dule in dern bot gif thow dill,[3]	
	Dowtless but dreid° I de."	surely
	Robene ansuerit: "Be the Rude,°	by the Cross
10	Nathing of lufe I knaw,	
	Bot keipis my scheip under yone° wude—	yonder
	Lo quhair thay raik on raw![4]	
	Quhat° hes marrit° the in thy mude,°	what / harmed / mind
	Makyne, to me thow schaw:°	declare
15	Or quhat is lufe, or to be lude?°	loved
	Fane° wald I leir° that law."	gladly / learn
	"At luvis lair gife thow will leir,[5]	
	Tak thair ane ABC:	
	Be heynd, courtas and fair of feir,[6]	
20	Wyse, hardy° and fre;°	brave / generous
	So that no denger° do the deir,°	disdain / do harm
	Quhat dule in dern thow dre,[7]	
	Preiss° the with pane at all poweir°—	strive / effort
	Be patient and previe."°	discreet
25	Robene anserit hir agane:	
	"I wait° nocht quhat is luve,	know
	Bot I haif mervell° in certane	wonder
	Quhat makis the this wanrufe;°	restless
	The weddir is fair and I am fane,°	happy

1. In Scots, as in Middle English poetry, Makyn (or Malkin) was a conventional name for a rustic girl, as Robin was for a boy.
2. I have loved thee openly and secretly.
3. Unless you relieve my secret pain.
4. See how they wander afield!

5. Of love's learning if you would learn.
6. Be gentle, courteous, and fair of manners (these and the qualities that follow are conventional attributes of the courtly lover; cf. Chaucer's *Nun's Priest's Tale,* page 420).
7. What sorrow in secret you suffer.

disport / valley

30 My scheip gois haill aboif;[8]
    And we wald play° us in this plane°   *disport / valley*
    Thay wald us bayth reproif."

    "Robene, tak tent° unto my taill,°   *heed / advice*
    And wirk° all as I reid°,   *do / advise*
35 And thow sall haif my hairt all haill,°   *entirely*
    Eik° and my madinheid: *also*
    Sen God sendis bute° for baill°   *cure / pain*
    And for murnyng° remeid,°   *sorrow / remedy*
    I dern with the bot gif I daill,[9]
40 Dowtles I am bot deid.[1]

    "Makyne, tomorne this ilka° tyde,°   *same / time*
    And° ye will meit me heir,   *if*
    Peraventure my scheip ma gang besyd°   *fend for themselves*
    Quhill we haif liggit full neir[2]—
45 Bot mawgre haif I and I byd,[3]
    Fra° thay begin to steir;°   *when / stray*
    Quhat lyis on hairt° I will nocht hyd;°   *lies in my heart / not*
    Makyn, than mak gud cheir."
    "Robene, thow reivis° me roif° and rest—   *rob / tranquility*
50 I luve bot the allone."
    "Makyne, adew; the sone gois west,
    The day is neir-hand gone."
    "Robene, in dule° I am so drest°   *to pain / resigned*
    That lufe wil be my bone."°   *bane*
55 "Ga lufe, Makyne, quhairever thow list,[4]
    For lemman° I lue° none."   *lover / love*

    "Robene, I stand in sic a styll;°   *such a plight*
    I sicht°—and that full sair."°   *sigh / painfully*
    "Makyne, I haif bene heir this quhyle;°   *while*
60 At hame God gif I wair![5]
    "My huny Robene, talk ane quhill,°   *a while*
    Gif thow will do na mair."
    "Makyne, sum uthir man begyle,[6]
    For hamewart° I will fair."°   *homeward / go*

65 Robene on his wayis went
    Als licht as leif of tre;[7]
    Mawkin murnit° in hir intent   *mourned*
    And trowd° him nevir to se;°   *expected / see*
    Robene brayd attour the bent;[8]

---

8. Are all around me on this hill.
9. Unless in secret I deal (i.e., have sex) with you.
1. Conventionally, the courtly lover threatens to die unless his lady takes pity on him.
2. While we have lain nearby.
3. But yet I am uneasy if I wait.

4. Go love, Makyn, wherever you wish.
5. I wish to God I were at home!
6. Seduce some other man.
7. As light as a leaf on a tree.
8. Bounded across the field.

70   Than Mawkyne cryit on hie:°   *loudly*
      "Now ma thow sing, for I am schent!°   *ruined*
      Quhat alis° lufe at me?"   *ails*

      Mawkyne went hame withowttin faill;
      Full wery eftir cowth weip:[9]
75   Than Robene in a ful fair daill°   *very neat order*
      Assemblit all his scheip.
      Be that, sum pairte of Mawkynis aill°   *pain*
      Outthrow his hairt cowd creip;[1]
      He fallowit fast thair till assaill,[2]
80   And till hir tuke gude keip.°   *paid good heed*

      "Abyd, abyd, thow fair Makyne!
      A word for ony thing!
      For all my luve it sal be thyne,
      Withowttin depairting.°   *wholly*
85   All haill° thy harte for till haif myne   *whole*
      Is all my cuvating;
      My scheip tomorne quhill houris nyne°   *until nine o'clock*
      Will neid of no keiping."

      "Robene, thow hes hard° soung and say   *hast heard*
90   In gestis° and storeis auld,   *legends*
      The man that will nocht quhen° he may   *when*
      Sall haif nocht quhen he wald.°   *would*
      I pray to Jesu every day
      Mot eik thair cairis cauld[3]
95   That first preiss° with the to play   *strives*
      Be firth,° forrest or fawld."°   *wood / sheepfold*

      "Makyne, the nicht° is soft and dry,   *night*
      The wedder° is warme and fair,   *weather*
      And the grene woid° rycht° neir us by *wood / right*
100   To walk attour° allquhair;°   *across / everywhere*
      Thair ma na janglour[4] us espy,
      That is to lufe contrair;
      Thairin, Makyne, bath ye and I
      Unsene we ma repair."

105   "Robene, that warld is all away
      And quyt° brocht° till ane end,   *entirely / brought*
      And nevir agane thairto perfay,°   *by my faith*
      Sall it be as thow wend:°   *think*
      For of my pane thow maid it play,[5]
110   And all in vane I spend:°   *made an effort*
      As thow hes done, sa sall I say:
      Murne° on! I think to mend."   *grieve*

9. Wearily afterward wept.
1. Entered his heart.
2. He went back to accost her there.
3. That he might make them too suffer.

4. Gossip; "janglours" were a stock threat to courtly lovers.
5. For you made fun of my pain.

	"Mawkyne, the howp° of all my heill,°6	hope / salvation
	My hairt on the° is sett,	thee
115	And evirmair to the be leill,°	loyal
	Quhill I may leif but lett;7	
	Nevir to faill—as utheris feill—	
	Quhat grace° that evir I gett."	favor
	"Robene, with the I will nocht deill;8	
120	Adew!° For thus we mett."	adieu
	Malkyne went hame blyth annewche°	blithe enough
	Attour the holttis hair,°9	
	Robene murnit, and Malkyne lewche,°	laughed
	Scho sang,° he sichit sair°—	sang / sighed sorely
125	And so left him bayth wo° and wrewche,°	sad / troubled
	In dolour° and in cair,	sorrow
	Kepand his hird under a huche,°	hovel
	Amangis° the holtis hair.	among

[END OF MIDDLE SCOTS POETS]

LATE MEDIEVAL ALLEGORY

The end of the Middle Ages saw an extraordinary flowering of allegory, a literary mode that at its simplest is a narrative in which a symbolic meaning runs parallel to a literal one, but remains distinct from it. Gone, for the most part, was the elaborate multileved allegory based on biblical exegesis that had held sway in earlier centuries, to be replaced by the more transparent personification allegory, which embodies an abstract quality in a person or a thing, often used to convey an erotic or spiritual quest, or a psychological crisis.

This volume includes passages from the greatest English allegory of the fourteenth century, William Langland's *Piers Plowman,* which uses personification as well as other types of allegory to convey the quest of its hero and its critique of society. The poem's dreamer/narrator "Will" stands for the errant human will, as well as the author's nickname, and the flamboyant Lady Meed stands for monetary reward, whether just or unjust. Borrowing techniques from contemporary sermons, Langland makes many of his personifications grotesquely realistic. When Gluttony goes to confess his sin to Repentance, for instance, he is portrayed as a fourteenth-century churl who is lured into a tavern, then eats and drinks so much that he vomits, and has to be carried home to bed.

By the fifteenth century, when the examples of allegory included in this section were written, personification allegory was even more prominent. Charles d'Orléans imagines himself as a lover in conflict with Fortune and Disdain. The hero of *Mankind* finds himself caught between Mercy and three personifications of novelty—Nowadays, Newguise, and Nought—until he chooses the path of redemption. Christine de Pizan's protagonist, dismayed by the force of misogynist tradition, receives comfort from three allegorical ladies: Reason, Rectitude, and Justice. Two of these writers use the common allegorical image of the building to clarify their points, Charles d'Orléans portraying his own heart as a castle under siege, and Christine constructing a fortified city to honor women.

6. Robene uses the religious metaphors of courtly love.
7. Unceasingly, while I live.
8. Robene, I will not have dealings (i.e., sex) with you.

9. Across the woods gray (a traditional alliterative phrase).

Allegory, with its tendency to abstraction, has often been seen as supporting the status quo. Christine's *City of Ladies* and *Mankind*, however, use allegory in more complex and sometimes subversive ways, as had *Piers Plowman* when criticizing the corruption of the clergy. Christine's protagonist learns to take pride in the achievements of women; her city offers a systematic reinterpretation of women's stories. And while Mankind finally rejects the temptations of Nowadays, Newguise, and Nought, these exuberant figures threaten to steal the show. However one chooses to read these particular texts, personification allegory as a mode proved flexible enough to respond to the social changes of the later Middle Ages and to persist into the Renaissance and Reformation. Its influence can be seen in Butler's *Pilgrim's Progress*, Spenser's *Faerie Queene*, and Shakespeare's plays—most memorably in his villains.

Charles d'Orléans
1394–1465

No other writer of medieval England even approaches the glamour, wealth, and culture that Charles, Duke of Orléans experienced for much of his life. A prince of the French royal house, Charles d'Orléans was superbly educated but also trained in the chivalric arts of battle. Practicing these, Charles was captured at the Battle of Agincourt in 1415 and spent the next twenty-five years of his life as both an aristocratic guest and an enemy prisoner of a series of English nobles, as his ransom and release were painfully negotiated. In these years, he acquired very good but never fully colloquial English; and he certainly read works by Chaucer and other English writers, in addition to his wide reading in Latin, French, and Italian. He finally returned home in 1440, remarried, and rebuilt his fortunes.

In his long exile, Charles cast himself as a prisoner of Fortune, an allegorical figure he inherited from Boethius's late-classical *Consolation of Philosophy*. He adapted the figure of Fortune in lyrics that sometimes hint at his own life, yet equally play on conventions of courtly love, such as the allegorical conceit of the heart as a besieged fortress assailed by the fire of love, or the idea of losing his lady in a game of chess. Charles wrote his fine poems both in English and French, using traditional set forms, especially the ballade and roundel. They circle around love, but reach in many further directions. His frequent theme of separation from a beloved but unidentified lady resonates with other kinds of isolation—political, national, economic, even linguistic—that also affected Charles's life. And like much poetry in established forms, Charles's lyrics invite the reader to delight in their playful wit and technical mastery as well as their message.

Ballade 26[1]

Brennyng Desire to see my fayre maystres°   *mistress*
Hath newe assaylid the nakid, pore loggyng°   *lodging*
Of my faynt hert, which drepith° in distres,   *languishes*
That in eche where within his fyre brennyng
5   Hath he so sett that in a gret feryng
Stande y,[2] God wot, lest hit woll not ben queynt°   *quenched*
Without thi grace. "O God of Love," y cry,

---

1. The medieval ballade is a variable form. Here, typically, it repeats a rhyme scheme across its three main stanzas. A fourth, shorter stanza, often called an "envoy," repeats the final rhymes of the earlier stanzas, and marks a turn from earlier themes, or sends the poem off to its addressee. All the stanzas are linked by a common refrain line.
2. So that everywhere inside [my heart] He has so set his fire burning that I stand in great fear.

"Helpe now myn hert, that many helpe hast sent!"
—Thus calle y for yowre socoure° pitously.   *aid*

10   I have asayd with Teeris of Larges°   *plentiful tears*
This forto quenche, but all to my felyng,
The werse is hit! This fyre, hit will not cesse
Without elliswhere y have sum relevyng.[3]
I brenne, y brenne! O frendis, come rennyng
15   And helpe! Alas, this fyre were fro me rent!°   *removed from me*
For if thorugh fawt in slouthe of yow y dey,[4]
Ye are in synne and blame, to myn entent!°   *opinion*
Thus calle y for yowre socoure pitously.

But what if so y spille° thorugh yowre lacches?°   *die / negligence*
20   I yow biseche but this unsely° thyng: *serious*
That eche of yow do synge for me a messe,°   *mass*
And sone in Paradice have y trustyng
Among lovers to se myn hert sittyng
As a gret seynt and martir, for turment
25   Hath he evene for his trouth and al onewhi,[5]
For which as now in this grevous talent°   *state of mind*
Thus calle y for yowre socoure pitously.

What nede y spende more enke° or parchement,   *ink*
That fele the crampe of deth myn hert so nyghe°   *near*
30   As thorugh this rageous° fyre which hath me hent?°   *fierce / seized*
Thus calle y for yowre socoure pitously.

Ballade 61[1]

Toforne Love[2] have y pleyd at the chesse
To passe the tyme with cursid false Daungere°   *disdain*
And kepte eche poynt bi good avysynes[3]
Withouten losse, to that° (as wol ye here)   *until*
5   That Fortune came to strengthyn his matere.
O woo worthe she° that my game[4] ovyrthrew!   *a curse on her*
For tane° she hath my lady, welaway!   *taken*
That y am matt,[5] this may y se and say,
Without° so be y make[6] a lady newe.   *unless*

10   In my lady lay all my sikirnes,°   *security*
For ay at nede hir socoure was me nere[7]
To helpe me in eche trobill or distres,

---

3. Unless I have help from somewhere else.
4. For if I die through your sin of sloth.
5. For he suffers torment for his loyalty and that entirely unjustly.
1. This ballade, full of dense wordplay, exploits both the figure of Fortune and an allegorical game of chess. The game is played against "Daungere," a courtly-love person-ification of the lady's distance or disdain. But the game is undone, the board perhaps literally overthrown, when Fortune takes away the Queen piece: the beloved lady herself. The identity of the lady is unknown, and perhaps irrelevant. Charles's first wife died before he turned 15;

his second wife died some years before his return to France; and he seems to have had at least ritual love af-fairs during his English imprisonment.
2. In the presence of (the god of) Love.
3. And held on to each piece with great skill.
4. "Game" here may be both the game of chess and the alternate sense of joy or pleasure.
5. Checkmated, or destroyed.
6. A pawn is made queen if it reaches the far end of the board. "Make" can also mean to choose as a mate.
7. For always in time of need her help was near me.

For all my warde that kepte my lady dere[8]
More then knyght, that is of more powere,
15   Or Afyn,° pown, or rook (this fynde y trewe)   *bishop*
For all my game y lost it have and pley
And all my good, god wot, that on it lay,°   *was wagered*
Without so be y make a lady newe.

Not kan y skyfte me° from the sotilnes   *escape*
20   Of seytfull° Fortune, with hir dowbil chere,[9]   *deceitful*
That doth eche game so torne and ovyrdresse
That where to drawe not wot y,[1] there or here.
She cometh on me in a so sodeyne gere°   *caprice*
That y may not myn harmes lo eschewe.
25   Mi game is all forcast in suche aray[2]
That in no wise y hit amenden° may,   *rectify*
Without so be y make a lady newe.
Fare wel, princesse! yowre losse sore doth me rewe
And evir shall unto myn endyng day,
30   For shulde y thenke rekewre[3] me now? Nay, nay,
Without so be y make a lady newe!

Roundel 94[1]

Sum tyme y was a poore serviture°   *servant*
In Lovys court and had a governaunce,
To crewel Fortune, ful of disseyvaunce,
Dischargid me of my good aventure,[2]

5   And the ricches that y had undir cure°   *in my custody*
Bitook it hoole° to Dethis ordinaunce,°—   *wholly / juddment*
      Sum tyme y was a poore serviture
      In Loveys court and had a governaunce.—

And bad me walke, an ofcast° creature,   *outcast*
10   On the wilde desert of Desperaunce,°   *despair*
Where now y dwelle in turment and penaunce
And must unto y dey,° this am y sewre.   *until I die*

      Svm tyme y was a poore serviture
      In Loueys court and had a governaunce,
15   To crewel Fortune, ful of disseyvaunce,
      Dischargid me of my good aventure.

8. For my dear lady (i.e., the queen) kept up my primary defense.
9. Fortune is often depicted smiling on one side of her face, and scowling on the other.
1. Who so twists and reverses each game / That I don't know where to make my move.
2. Put in such utter disarray.
3. To recover myself, to win back the game.
1. The roundel (or rondel) can vary in length, but typically uses only two rhyme sounds, features at least two lines used as a refrain within the poem (see lines 7–8 here), and usually an entire stanza of four lines as a refrain at the end (lines 13–16). The repetition of lines and sounds resists much development of ideas, but helps intensity of expression and, as here, pathos.
2. Was under (Love's) control, / Until cruel Fortune, full of deceit, / Deprived me of my good luck.

Mankind

c. 1464–1479

Mankind is an allegorical drama about the temptation and salvation of a generalized man—at once a laborer with a shovel and a writer with pen and ink. This double figure, named "Mankind," wavers between attachment to a beneficent Mercy and an inclination to figures of vice like Mischief and three personifications of novelty—Nowadays, Newguise (trendy behavior), and Nought. It has been called a "morality play," and grouped with other late-medieval and Tudor dramas like *Everyman* and *The Castle of Perseverance*. While each is quite different, these works do create allegories that explore the inner conflict of one life at a moment of crisis.

Far from the abstract work we might expect from the play's personified characters, *Mankind* is raucous, funny, and often obscene. The play moves between measured descriptions of divine grace, mostly by Mercy, and the blasphemy and disorder of Mischief and his henchmen. Shifting from harmony to carnival and back, *Mankind* mocks a whole range of ideas and institutions (like the church and its message of redemption), yet finally affirms them. Other aspects of the established social order—pomposity, empty learning, legal ritual—are left hilariously shredded. The play works as well as it does exactly because the vices are so funny and attractive, even if Mercy, and Mankind's faith, ultimately triumph over them.

Quite specific local references in *Mankind* suggest that the play, surviving in only one manuscript, was performed between 1464 and 1479, for an audience that would recognize names from around Cambridge and King's Lynn, in the district called East Anglia. References to local

Mankynde: A Postmodern Medieval Musical was adapted by Julie Crosby for the Off-Off-Broadway New York International Fringe Festival, the largest multi-arts festival in North America, in 2004. Here Mischief (Christine Rea) tries to subdue Mercy (Andy Paris), as part of a broadly comic staging of the struggle for the soul of Mankind.

characters, ranging from a Member of Parliament to a tradesman, also contribute a kind of intimacy, and perhaps specific comedy, that would have further engaged the original audience. The ambitious pacing, long speeches, and sometimes swift comic patter of *Mankind* probably required professional players of some sort, though it is unclear whether they were an organized troupe or who paid them. (One moment in the play does involve the collection of money; see lines 457–72.)

Even if he is an allegorical figure, Mankind shows complexity and conflict. He moves from an easy piety to petulance, anger, a frivolity that merges swiftly into despair, and finally contrition. Mercy is more complicated still. Always dignified, in the play's opening scenes, he can also seem long-winded, a bit of a stiff. Mercy's complicated syntax and Latin-derived "aureate" diction invite parody by Newguise and his friends, and presumably aroused complicit laughter by the audience. But we can laugh at things that we still ultimately respect. As a pedantic, sometimes awkward man, Mercy can be funny; as an allegory of one aspect of a Christian God, he can be simultaneously very serious indeed. Mercy's grave dignity is finally what saves Mankind. Some of his speeches have real rhetorical impact, and toward the end of the play they take on the added authority of repeated biblical quotations. Mankind himself moves in and out of such diction (he even writes down a bit of Latin), partly as a measure of whether he's under the influence of Mercy or the vices.

Mankind's faith and agricultural labor are closely linked in the play. This draws on traditional connections of religious virtue and hard work, seen for instance in the episode of Piers sowing his half-acre in *Piers Plowman* (page 451), yet it also recalls the hard work Adam drew on all men as a result of the fall. At the same time, Mankind's easy adoption of urban dress and more urban pleasures reflects the attraction of the cities for common people facing a life of harsh rural labor, especially in areas like East Anglia, where some cities were growing rich from the cloth industry and other trade.

Unlike the biblical plays, allegorical dramas continued to flourish into the Early Modern period. *Mankind* in particular can be seen as part of the background to Early Modern drama, as the play's characters combine allegorical elements with psychological complexity, and its plot veers between low humor and great gravity. A character like the demon Titivillus, and the mortal temptations he offers, echo (though not directly) in Shakespearean villains like Iago in *Othello*, while the more benign personifications of novelty suggest the exuberant and unrepentant Falstaff in *Henry IV, Part I*. The continuing appeal of the play, too, is suggested by a recent New York City production from which we offer an illustration.

The text used here is an "acting edition" by Peter Meredith. It modernizes spellings but retains the original vocabulary.

Mankind

Dramatis Personae

Mercy	Mischief
Newguise	Nowadays
Nought	Mankind
Titivillus	

MERCY The very founder and beginner of our first creation,
　　　　Among us sinful wretches he oweth° to be magnified,°　　　*ought / praised*
　　　　That for our disobedience he had none indignation
　　　　To send his own son to be torn and crucified.
5　　　Our obsequious service to him should be applied;
　　　　Where° he, was° Lord of all and made all thing of nought,　*since / (who) was*
　　　　For the sinful sinner to had° him revived,　　　　　　　　　*have*
　　　　And for his redemption, set his own son at nought.

It may be said and verified, mankind was dear bought.

10 By the piteous death of Jesu he had his remedy.

He was purged of his default, that wretchedly had wrought,

By his glorious passion, that blessed lavatory.°   *cleansing*

O sovereigns, I beseech you your conditions to rectify,

And with humility and reverence to have a remotion°   *turn*

15 To this blessed prince that our nature doth glorify,

That ye may be participable of his retribution.[1]

I have be° the very mean for your restitution.   *been*

Mercy is my name that mourneth for your offence.

Divert not yourself in time of temptation,

20 That ye may be acceptable to God at your going hence.

The great mercy of God, that is of most pre-eminence,

By [mediation] of our Lady, that is ever abundant

To the sinful creature that will repent his negligence.

I pray God, at your most need, that mercy be your defendant.[2]

25 In good works I advise you, sovereigns, to be perseverant,°   *persevering*

To purify your souls that they be not corrupt,

For your ghostly° enemy will make his avaunt,°   *spiritual / boast*

Your good conditions° if he may interrupt.   *habits*

O ye sovereigns that sit and ye brethren that stand right up,[3]

30 Prick° not your felicities in things transitory!   *place*

Behold not the earth, but lift your eye up!

See how the head the members daily do magnify.

Who is the head? Forsooth, I shall you certify;

I mean our Saviour, that was likened to a lamb.

35 And his saints be the members° that daily he doth satisfy   *limbs*

With the precious river that runneth from his womb.°   *side*

There is none such food, by water nor by land,

So precious, so glorious, so needful to our intent;

For it hath dissolved mankind from the bitter bond

40 Of the mortal enemy, that venomous serpent—

From the which God preserve you all at the Last Judgment!

For, sickerly,° there shall be a strait° examination   *truly / strict*

The corn shall be saved, the chaff shall be brent;°[4]   *burnt*

I beseech you heartily, have this premeditation.°   *bear this in mind*

MISCHIEF I beseech you heartily, leave your calcination,°   *burning*

Leave your chaff, leave your corn, leave your dalliation;°   *idle talk*

Your wit is little, your head is mickle;° ye are full of   *big*

    predication.°   *preaching*

    But, sir, I pray, this question to clarify:

    Mish-mash, driff-draff;[5]

---

1. That you may share in his reward (i.e., salvation).
2. That mercy will protect you.
3. I.e., the audience. *Sovereigns that sit* are rich masters with seats, while *brethren that stand* are those of lower status who are standing.

4. A common agricultural metaphor, drawn from the Book of Isaiah in the Bible, for the separation of the saved from the damned on the Day of Judgment.
5. Nonsense verse.

50   Some was corn and some was chaff;
        My dame said my name was Raff,
            Unshut your lock and take an ha'penny!

MERCY Why come ye hither, brother? Ye were not desired.
MISCHIEF For a winter corn-thresher, sir, I have hired.
55   And ye said the corn should be saved and the chaff
            should be fired,
        And he proveth nay, as it sheweth by this verse:

        "Corn *servit bredibus*, chaff *horsibus*, straw *firibusque*."[6]

        This is as much to say to your lewd° understanding   *ignorant*
        As: the corn shall serve to° bread at the next baking.   *to make*
60   "Chaff *horsibus, et reliqua*:"[7]
        The chaff to horse shall be good provent;°   *food*
        When a man is for cold° the straw may be brent;°   *very cold / burnt*
            And so forth, *et cetera*.

MERCY Avoid,° good brother; ye ben culpable   *be gone*
65   To interrupt thus my talking delectable.
MISCHIEF Sir, I have neither horse nor saddle;
            Therefore I may not ride.
MERCY Hie you forth° on foot, brother, in God's name!   *go away*
MISCHIEF I say, sir, I am come hither to make you game.°   *sport*
70   Yet bade ye me not to go out in the devil's name,
            And I will abide.
MERCY
        [*At this point, an entire leaf has disappeared from the manuscript. When the text resumes,
        Mischief has gone, leaving Newguise, Nowadays, and Nought to harass Mercy. Musicians
        are also present. Newguise and Nowadays are urging Nought to dance.*]

NOWADAYS And how, minstrels, play the common trace!°   *dance*
        Lay on with thy baleis° till his belly brest!°   *stick / burst*

NOUGHT I put case° I break my neck; how then?   *suppose*
NEWGUISE I give no force, by St Anne![8]
NOWADAYS Leap about lively! Thou art a wight° man.   *nimble*
        Let us be merry while we be here.
NOUGHT Shall I break my neck to show you sport?
NOWADAYS Therefore ever beware of thy report.[9]
NOUGHT I beshrew° ye all! Here is a shrewd sort.[1]   *curse*
        Have thereat, then, with a merry cheer!

        Here they dance. MERCY *saith:*

MERCY Do way!° Do way this rule,° sirs, do way!   *give up / behavior*
NOWADAYS Do way, good Adam, do way?
        This is no part of thy play.
NOUGHT Yes, marry,° I pray you, for I love not this revelling!   *indeed*
        Come forth, good father, I you pray;

6. Corn serves for bread; chaff serves for horses; straw   9. Be careful of your reputation (or, Be careful of what
serves for fires.   you say).
7. Chaff for horses, and the rest.   1. Rascally company.
8. Mother of the Virgin Mary.

By a little ye may assay.°   *try it*
Anon, off with your clothes, if ye will, pray!
Go to, for I have had a pretty scuttling!°   *prancing about*

MERCY Nay, brother, I will not dance.
NEWGUISE If ye will, sir, my brother will make you to prance.
NOWADAYS With all my heart, sir, if I may you advance!
       Ye may assay by a little trace.°   *dance*
NOUGHT Yea, sir, will ye do well?
95   Trace not with them, by my counsel,
       For I have traced somewhat too fell.°   *violently*

       I tell it is a narrow space!

But, sir, I trow° of us three I heard you speak.   *think*
NEWGUISE Christ's curse had° therefore, for I was in sleep.   *(you) had*
NOWADAYS And I had the cup ready in my hand, ready to go to meat;°   *dinner*
       Therefore, sir, curtly, greet you well.
MERCY Few words, few and well set!
NEWGUISE Sir, it is the new guise and the new jet:°   *fashion*
       Many words, and shortly set;
105   This is the new guise, every dell.°   *bit*

MERCY Lady,[2] help! How wretches delight in their simple ways!
NOWADAYS Say nought again the new guise nowadays;
       Thou shall find us shrews° at all assays   *rascals*
       Beware, ye may soon lick a buffet!°   *take a knock*
MERCY He was well occupied that brought you, brether!°   *brothers*
NOUGHT I heard you call Newguise, Nowadays, Nought—all these
       three together.
       If ye say that I lie, I shall make you to slither.
       Lo, take you here a trippet!°   *trip*

MERCY Say me your names. I know you not.
NEWGUISE Newguise, I.
NOWADAYS   I, Nowadays.
NOUGHT   I, Nought.
MERCY By Jesu Christ, that me dear bought,[3]
       Ye betray many men!
NEWGUISE Betray? Nay, nay, sir, nay, nay!
       We make them both fresh and gay.
120   But of your name, sir I you pray,
       That we may you ken.°   *know*

MERCY Mercy is my name and my denomination.°   *title*
       I conceive ye have but a little favour in my communication.

NEWGUISE Ey, ey, your body is full of English Latin,[4]
125   I am afeard it will brest.°   *burst*
       "*Pravo te*"[5] quod° the butcher unto me   *said*

---

2. The Virgin Mary.
3. Redeemed me (a reference to Christ's death on the
cross to redeem mankind's sins).

4. Newguise makes fun of Mercy's use of "aureate" terms
coined from Latin, such as "denomination."
5. I curse you.

When I stole a leg o'mutton.
Ye are a strong cunning clerk.[6]

NOWADAYS I pray you heartily, worshipful clerk,
130   To have this English made in Latin:
          "I have eaten a dishful of curds,
          And I have shitten your mouth full of turds."
          Now, open your satchel with Latin words,
              And say me this in clerical manner.
135   Also, I have a wife (her name is Rachel)
          Betwix her and me was a great battle,
          And fain° of you I would hear tell   gladly
              Who was the most master.

NOUGHT Thy wife Rachel, I dare lay twenty lice!
NOWADAYS Who spake to thee, fool? Thou art not wise!
          Go and do that longeth° to thine office: belongs
              Osculare fundamentum![7]
NOUGHT Lo, master, lo, here is a pardon belly-met,[8]
          It is granted of Pope Pocket:
145   If ye will put your nose in his wife's socket[9]
              Ye shall have forty days of pardon.

MERCY This idle language ye shall repent.
          Out of this place I would ye went.
NEWGUISE Go we hence all three, with one assent.
150   My father is irk° of our eloquence!   annoyed by
          Therefore, I will no longer tarry.°   delay
          God bring you, master, and blessed Mary,
          To the number of the demonical friary![1]

NOWADAYS Come wind, come rain,
155   Though I come never again,
          The devil put out both your een!°   eyes
          Fellows, go we hence tite.°   quickly
NOUGHT Go we hence, a devil way!
          Here is the door, here is the way.
160   Farewell, gentle Geoffrey,
              I pray God give you good night!

          Exeant simul. Cantent[2]

MERCY Thanked be God we have a fair deliverance
          Of these three unthrifty° guests!   profligate
          They know full little what is their ordinance.°   proper place
165   I prove by reason they be worse than beasts:
          A beast doth after his natural institution.[3]

---

6. You are a very clever scholar.
7. Kiss my ass.
8. Here is a gut-sized (i.e., very full) pardon. Pardons were official documents of the church, sanctioned by the Pope, granting "indulgences" for sins committed in return for

cash payment.
9. Hole, with a pun on vagina.
1. I.e., to hell.
2. Let them go out together. Let them sing.
3. Instinctive nature.

Ye may conceive by their disport° and behaviour,   *conduct*
Their joy and delight is in derision
Of their own Christ, to his dishonour.

170   This condition of living, it is prejudicial,
Beware thereof! It is worse than any felony or treason.
How may it be excused before the Justice of all,
When for every idle word we must yield a reason?

They have great ease, therefore they will take no thought.
175   But, how then, when the angel of heaven shall blow the trump°   *trumpet*
And say to the transgressors that wickedly hath wrought:
"Come forth unto your judge, and yield your account?"

Then shall I, Mercy, begin sore to weep.
Neither comfort nor counsel there shall none be had,
180   But such as they have sown, such shall they reap.[4]
They be wanton° now, but then shall they be sad.   *carefree*

The good new guise nowadays I will not disallow,
I discommend the vicious guise. I pray have me excused;
I need not to speak of it; your reason will tell it you.
185   Take that is to be taken, and leave that is to be refused.

MANKIND Of the earth and of the clay we have our propagation,
By the providence of God thus be we derivate;°   *derived*
To whose mercy I recommend this whole congregation.
I hope unto his bliss ye be all predestinate.°   *predestined*
190   Every man, for his degree, I trust shall be participate,[5]
If we will mortify° our carnal condition   *suppress*
And our voluntary desires that ever be perversionate,°   *perverted*
To renounce them and yield us under God's provision.

My name is Mankind. I have my composition
195   Of a body and of a soul, of condition contrary.
Betwix them twain° is a great division;   *two*
He[6] that should be subject, now he hath the victory.
This is to me a lamentable story,
To see my flesh of my soul to have governance.
200   Where the good-wife° is master the good-man may be sorry.   *woman*
I may both sigh and sob; this is a piteous remembrance!

O thou, my soul, so subtle° in thy substance,   *pure*
Alas! what was thy fortune and thy chance
To be associate with my flesh, that stinking dunghill?

205   Lady,° help! Sovereigns, it doth my soul much ill   *Virgin Mary*
To see the flesh prosperous and the soul trodden under foot.
I shall go to yonder man and assay° him I will;   *test*
I trust of ghostly° solace he will be my boot.°   *spiritual / help*

---

4. See Job 4.8 and Galatians 6.8.
5. Every man, according to his place, I believe will
partake.
6. I.e., the body.

	All hail, seemly° father! Ye be welcome to this house.	worthy
210	Of the very° wisdom ye have participation.°	true / access
	My body with my soul is ever quarrellous;	
	I pray you, for saint° charity, of your supportation.°	holy / support

	I beseech you heartily of your ghostly comfort.	
	I am unsteadfast in living, my name is Mankind.	
215	My ghostly enemy, the devil, will have a great disport,°	delight
	In simple guiding if he may see me end.[7]	

MERCY Christ send you good comfort! Ye be welcome, my friend.
  Stand up on your feet, I pray you, arise!
  My name is Mercy; ye be to me full hend.°   *very dear*
220 To eschew vice I will you advise.

MANKIND O Mercy, of all grace and virtue ye are the well!
  I have heard tell, of right worshipful clerks,
  Ye be approximate to° God and near of his counsel.   *next to*
  He hath institute° you above all his works.   *established*

225 O your lovely words to my soul are sweeter than honey!
MERCY The temptation of the flesh ye must resist like a man,
  For there is ever a battle betwix the soul and the body:
  Vita hominis est militia super terram.[8]

  Oppress your ghostly enemy, and be Christ's own knight;
230 Be never a coward again° your adversary.   *against*
  If ye will be crowned, ye must needs fight.
  Intend well, and God will be you adjutory.[9]

  Remember, my friend, the time of continuance,
  So help me God, it is but a cherry-time;[1]
235 Spend it well! Serve God with heart's affiance.°   *loyalty*
  Distemper° not your brain with good ale nor with wine;   *sicken*

  "Measure is treasure." I forbid you not the use.
  Measure yourself ever, beware of excess.
  The superfluous guise I will that ye refuse;
240 When nature is sufficed, anon that ye cease.

  If a man have an horse, and keep him not too high,
  He may then rule him at his own desire.
  If he be fed over-well, he will disobey,
  And, in hap,° cast his master in the mire.   *perhaps*

NEWGUISE Ye say true, sir, ye are no faitour.°   *liar*
  I have fed my wife so well till she is my master.
  I have a great wound on my head, lo, and thereon lieth a
      plaster°   *poultice*
  And another there° I piss, my peson.°   *where / penis*

---

7. If he may see me end (i.e., die) in foolish living.
8. The life of man is warfare upon the earth (Job 7.1).
9. And God will help you.

1. I.e., brief (like the short period of time when cherries may be harvested).

An my wife were your horse, she would you all to-ban.°   *curse*
250   Ye feed your horse in measure, ye are a wise man;
        I trow an° ye were the king's palfreyman,°   *think if / groom*
            A good horse should be geason.°   *rare*

MANKIND Where speaks this fellow? Will he not come near?
MERCY All too soon, my brother, I fear me, for you.
255   He was here right now (by him that bought me dear)[2]
        With other of his fellows—they can much sorrow![3]

        They will be here right soon if I out depart.
        Think on my doctrine; it shall be your defence.
        Learn while I am here, set my words in heart,
260   Within a short space I must needs° hence.   *must go*

NOWADAYS The sooner the liefer, an° it be even anon!   *better, if*
        I trow your name is Do-little, ye be so long fro home.
        If ye would go hence, we shall come everychone,°   *every one*
            Mo° than a good sort.°   *more / company*

265   Ye have leave,° I dare well say;   *permission*
        When ye will, go forth your way.
        Men have little dainty° of your play,   *pleasure in*
            Because ye make no sport.

NOUGHT Your pottage° shall be for-cold, sir, when will ye go dine?   *porridge*
270   I have seen a man lost twenty nobles[4] in as little time—
        Yet it was not I, by St Quentin!
            For I was never worth a potful of worts° sithen I was born.   *cabbages*
        My name is Nought; I love well to make merry.
        I have be sithen° with the common tapster of Bury;   *been just now*
275   A° played so long the fool that I am even very weary.   *He (or She)*
            Yet shall I be there again tomorn.°   *tomorrow*

MERCY I have much care for you, my own friend,
        Your enemies will be here anon; they make their avaunt.°   *boast*
        Think well in your heart: your name is Mankind,
280   Be not unkind° to God, I pray you, be his servant.   *unnatural*
        Be steadfast in condition, see ye be not variant.
        Lose not through folly that is bought so dear.[5]
        God will prove° you soon, and, if that ye be constant,   *test*
        Of his bliss perpetual ye shall be partner.

285   Ye may not have your intent at your first desire.
        See the great patience of Job[6] in tribulation;
        Like as the smith trieth° iron in the fire,   *tests*
        So was he tried by God's visitation.

---

2. I.e., Christ.
3. Know much sorrow / are acquainted with causing trouble.
4. Coins worth 80 pence, or one-third of a pound.

Twenty nobles would have been an enormous sum.
5. That which is bought at such cost (i.e., salvation).
6. The biblical Job, who suffers patiently the trials imposed by God.

He was of your nature and of your fragility.
290   Follow the steps of him, my own sweet son,
And say, as he said, in your trouble and adversity:
Dominus dedit, Dominus abstulit; sicut sibi placuit, ita
      factum est. Sit nomen Domini benedictum.[7]

Moreover, in special, I give you in charge,
Beware of Newguise, Nowadays, and Nought.
295   Nice° in their array, in language they be large;   *fashionable*
To pervert your conditions° all their means shall be sought.   *behavior*

Good son, intromit° not yourself in their company.   *mix*
They heard not a mass this twelvemonth, I dare well say.
Give them none audience; they will tell you many a lie.
300   Do truly your labour, and keep your holy day.
Beware of Titivillus,[8] for he loseth no way,
That goeth invisible and will not be seen.
He will roun° in your ear, and cast a net before your eye.   *whisper*
He is worst of them all, God let him never theen!°   *prosper*

305   If ye displease God, ask mercy anon,
Else Mischief will be ready to brace° you in his bridle.   *fasten*
Kiss me now, my dear darling. God shield you from your fon!°   *foes*
Do truly your labour, and be never idle.

The blessing of God be with you, and with all these worshipful men![9]
MANKIND Amen, for saint° charity, amen!   *holy*

Now blessed be Jesu, my soul is well satiate°   *satisfied*
With the mellifluous° doctrine of this worshipful man.   *sweet*
The rebellion of my flesh now it is superate.°   *overcome*
Thanking be God of the cunning that I can.[1]

315   Here will I sit, and title° in this paper   *write*
The incomparable estate of my promition.°   *promised place*
Worshipful sovereigns, I have written here
The glorious remembrance of my noble condition

To° have remorse and memory of myself. Thus written it is   *in order to*
320   To defend me from all supersititious charms:
"*Memento, homo, quod cinis es et in cinerem reverteris.*"[2]
Lo, I bear on my breast the badge of mine arms.[3]

NEWGUISE The weather is cold; God send us good fires!
Cum sancto sanctus eris, et cum perverso perverteris.
325   "*Ecce quam bonum et quam jocundum,*" quod the devil to the friars,

---

7. The Lord gave and the Lord has taken away; as it has
pleased him, so it is done. Blessed be the name of the
Lord (Job 1.21).
8. A demon. Literally, "all vile things."
9. I.e., the audience.
1. What wisdom I have.

2. Remember, man, you are dust and to dust you will return. (Genesis 3.19; see also Job 34.15.) This verse is
strongly associated with Christian burial services.
3. Behold, I carry on my breast the sign of my nature.
(Also a play on heraldic devices, such as coats-of-arms,
associated with the aristocracy.)

"*Habitare fratres in unum.*"⁴

MANKIND I hear a fellow speak. With him I will not mell.°   *meddle*
This earth with my spade I shall assay to delve.
To eschew idleness, I do it mine own self.
330   I pray God send it his foison!°   *plenty*

NOWADAYS Make room, sirs, for we have be° long!   *been*
We will come give you a Christmas song.

NOUGHT Now I pray all the yeomanry⁵ that is here,
To sing with us with a merry cheer.

335   It is written with a coal, it is written with a coal
NEWGUISE & NOWADAYS It is written with a coal, it is written *cetera*
NOUGHT He that shitteth with his hole, he that shitteth with his hole.
NEWGUISE & NOWADAYS He that shitteth with his hole, *cetera.*

NOUGHT But he wipe his arse clean, but he *cetera*
NEWGUISE & NOWADAYS But he wipe his arse clean, but he *cetera*

NOUGHT On his breech it shall be seen, on his breech *cetera*
NEWGUISE & NOWADAYS On his breech it shall be seen, on his *cetera*

Cantant omnes.⁶
Holyke, holyke, holyke, holyke, holyke, holyke.⁷

NEWGUISE Ey, Mankind, God speed you with your spade!
345   I shall tell you of a marriage:
I would your mouth and his arse, that this made,⁸
Were married junctly° together!   *jointly*
MANKIND Hie you hence, fellows, with braiding!°   *scolding*
Leave your derision and your japing!°   *horseplay*
350   I must needs labour; it is my living.
NOWADAYS What, sir, we came but late hither!

Shall all this corn° grow here   *grain*
That ye shall have the next year?
If it be so, corn had need be dear,⁹
355   Else ye shall have a poor life.
NOUGHT Alas, good father, this labour fretteth° you to the bone.   *wears*
But for your crop I take great moan;¹
Ye shall never spend it alone,
I shall assay to get you a wife.

360   How many acres suppose ye here by estimation?
NEWGUISE Ey, how ye turn the earth up and down!
I have be in my days in many good town,
Yet saw I never such another tilling!
MANKIND Why stand ye idle? It is pity that ye were born!

4. With the holy you will be holy, and with the perverse perverted. (Psalms 18.26.) Behold how good and how pleasant it is for brothers to dwell together in unity. (Psalms 133.1.)
5. A class of small freeholders who cultivated their own land.
6. Let them all sing.
7. A play on "holy" and "hole lick."
8. Meaning unclear, perhaps "that made this song" or "that made this stain."
9. Will have to be expensive.
1. I am very sad.

NOWADAYS We shall bargain with you, and neither mock nor scorn:
　　　　Take a good cart in harvest, and load it with your corn
　　　　　And what shall we give you for the leaving?°　　　　　　　　　*what is left*

NOUGHT He is a good stark° labourer, he would fain° do well.　　　*strong / wants to*
　　　He hath met with the good-man Mercy, in a shrewd sell.[2]
370　　For all this he may have many a hungry meal.
　　　　　Yet, will ye see, he is politic?°　　　　　　　　　　　　　*prudent*
　　　Here shall be good corn, he may not miss it;
　　　If he will have rain, he may over-piss it.

　　　And if he will have compost, he may over-bless it
375　　　A little with his arse, like . . .

MANKIND Go and do your labour! God let you never thee!°　　　　*prosper*
　　　Or with my spade I shall you ding, by the holy Trinity.
　　　Have ye none other man to mock, but ever me?
　　　　Ye would have me of your set.°　　　　　　　　　　　　　*gang*
380　　Hie you forth lively, for hence I will you drive!
NEWGUISE Alas, my jewels!° I shall be shent of my wife![3]　　　*testicles*
NOWADAYS Alas, and I am like never for to thrive,
　　　I have such a buffet!°　　　　　　　　　　　　　　　　　　*blow*

MANKIND Hence, I say, Newguise, Nowadays, and Nought!
385　　It was said beforn, all the means shall be sought
　　　To pervert my conditions and bring me to nought.
　　　　Hence, thieves! Ye have made many a leasing!°　　　　　*lie*
NOUGHT Marred° I was for cold, but now am I warm!　　　　　*troubled*
　　　Ye are evil-advised, sir, for ye have done harm.
390　　By Cock's body sackered,[4] I have such a pain in my arm
　　　I may not change a man a farthing![5]

MANKIND Now I thank God kneeling on my knee;
　　　Blessed be his name! He is of high degree.
　　　By the subsidy° of his grace that he hath sent me,　　　　　*help*
395　　　Three of mine enemies I have put to flight.

　　　Yet this instrument, sovereigns, is not made to defend;

　　　David saith: "*Nec in hasta, nec in gladio, salvat Dominus.*"[6]
NOUGHT No, marry, I beshrew you, it is *in spadibus*![7]
　　　Therefore Christ's curse come on your head*ibus*
400　　　To send you less might!

　　　Exeant.[8]

MANKIND I promit° you these fellows will no more come here.　　*promise*
　　　For some of them, certainly, were somewhat too near!

---

2. At a bad time.
3. I will be in disgrace with my wife (because I'm impotent).
4. God's sacred body.
5. I can't buy or sell from men worth a farthing

(quarter-penny); i.e., I'm incapacitated.
6. Neither with spear, nor with sword, does the Lord save (Kings 17.47).
7. With spades.
8. Let them go out.

My father, Mercy, advised me to be of a good cheer,
And again° my enemies manly for to fight.   *against*

405 I shall convict° them, I hope, everychone.   *overcome*
Yet I say amiss; I do it not alone.
With the help of the grace of God I resist my fon°   *foes*
And their malicious heart.
With my spade I will depart, my worshipful sovereigns,

410 And live ever with labour, to correct my insolence.
I shall go fetch corn for my land. I pray you of patience;
Right soon I shall revert.°   *return*

MISCHIEF Alas, alas, that ever I was wrought!°   *made*
Alas the while, I am worse than nought!°   *nothing*

415 Sithen° I was here, by him that me bought,   *since*
I am utterly undone!
I, Mischief, was here at the beginning of the game,
And argued with Mercy, God give him shame!
He hath taught Mankind, while I have be wane,⁹

420 To fight manly again his fon.°   *foes*

For, with his spade that was his weapon,
Newguise, Nowadays, Nought he hath all to-beaten.
I have great pity to see them weepen.
Will ye list?° I hear them cry.   *listen*

        *Clamant.*¹

425 Alas, alas, come hither! I shall be your borrow.°   *protection*
Alack, alack, *ven, ven!*² Come hither, with sorrow!
Peace, fair babes! Ye shall have an apple, tomorrow.
Why greet° ye so, why?   *cry*

NEWGUISE Alas, master, alas! My privity!°   *private parts*
MISCHIEF Ah, where? Alack, fair babe, ba me!°   *kiss me*
Abide! Too soon I shall it see.
NOWADAYS Here, here, see my head, good master!
MISCHIEF Lady, help! Seely° darling, *ven, ven!*   *poor*
I shall help thee of thy pain;

435 I shall smite off thy head and set it on again!
NOUGHT By our Lady, sir, a fair plaster!³

Will ye off with his head? It is a shrewd charm!⁴
As for me, I have none harm.
I were loath to forbear° mine arm!   *do without*

440 Ye play: *In nomine patris,*⁵ chop!
NEWGUISE Ye shall not chop my jewels,° an I may!⁶   *testicles*
NOWADAYS Yea, Christ's cross! Will ye smite my head away?

---

9. While I have been away.
1. They cry out.
2. Come, come.
3. Fine poultice.
4. Dangerous cure.

5. In the name of the father. The opening words of the Catholic mass and the first words spoken when making the sign of the cross.
6. If I can help it.

There. Where? One and° one. Out, ye shall not assay!°   *by* / *try it*
I might well be called a fop.°   *fool*

MISCHIEF I can chop it off and make it again.
NEWGUISE I had a shrewd *recumbentibus*,[7] but I feel no pain.
NOWADAYS And my head is all safe and whole again.
          Now, touching° the matter of Mankind,   *regarding*
          Let us have an interlection° sithen ye be come hither.   *conference*
450   It were good to have an end.[8]
MISCHIEF How, how, a minstrel! Know ye any ought?°   *at all*
NOUGHT I can pipe in a Walsingham whistle,[9] I, Nought, Nought.
MISCHIEF Blow apace!° and thou shall bring him in with a flute.   *quickly*
TITIVILLUS I come with my legs under me!
MISCHIEF How Newguise, Nowadays! hark, ere I go;
          When our heads were together I spake of *si dedero*.[1]
NEWGUISE Yea, go thy way! We shall gather money unto,°   *for it*
          Else there shall no man him[2] see.

          Now ghostly to our purpose, worshipful sovereigns,
460   We intend to gather money, if it please your negligence,[3]
          For a man with a head that is of great omnipotence.
NOWADAYS Keep your tale,[4] in goodness I pray you, good brother!
          He is a worshipful man, sirs, saving your reverence,[5]
          He loveth no groats, nor pence of tuppence.
465   Give us red royals,[6] if ye will see his abominable presence.
NEWGUISE Not so! Ye that mow° not pay the ton,° pay the tother.   *may* / *the one*

          At the good-man° of this house first we will assay.   *master*
          God bless you, master! Ye say as ill,[7] yet ye will not say nay.
          Let us go by and by, and do them pay.[8]
470   Ye pay all alike, well mote ye fare![9]
NOUGHT I say, Newguise, Nowadays, *estis vos pecuniatus?*[1]
          I have cried a fair while, I beshrew° your pates!°   *curse* / *heads*
NOWADAYS *Ita vere, magister*, come forth now your gates.[2]
          He is a goodly man, sirs. Make space, and beware!

TITIVILLUS *Ego sum dominantium dominus*,[3] and my name is Titivillus.
          Ye that have good horse, to you I say *caveatis*![4]
          Here is an able fellowship to trice° 'em out at your gates!   *trick*

---

7. A rough knock-down.
8. I.e., it were good to bring the matter of Mankind's temptation to completion.
9. Whistle associated with pilgrimage to Walsingham, where there was a shrine commemorating the Virgin Mary's appearance to Lady Richeldis of the manor of Walsingham. This might suggest disruptive behavior, as there are records of complaints about pilgrims' whistling.
1. Lit., "if I shall have given." They are collecting money from the audience in order to bring Titivillus into the play.
2. I.e., Titivillus.
3. Play on "your reverence."
4. Both "stick to your story" and "keep your tally (of money collected)."

5. He (Titivillus) is a worshipful man, sirs, begging your pardon.
6. Groats were four-penny pieces, pence of tuppence were two-penny pieces, and red royals were gold coins worth ten shillings each (each shilling is worth 12 pence).
7. You can say disparaging things.
8. Get them to pay.
9. May you have good luck.
1. Are you monied?
2. Yes indeed, master, now make your entrance.
3. I am lord of lords. "Lord of lords" is one of the titles for God in the Bible; Titivillus's use of it is therefore blasphemous.
4. Beware.

Ego probo sic:[5]
    Loquitur ad NEWGUISE[6]
        Sir Newguise, lend me a penny.
NEWGUISE I have a great purse, sir, but I have no money.
480   By the mass, I fail two farthings of an ha'penny.
    Yet had I ten pound this night that was.[7]
    Loquitur ad NOWADAYS
TITIVILLUS What is in thy purse? Thou art a stout felon.°   *great rogue*
NOWADAYS The devil a whit! I am a clean gentleman![8]
    I pray God I be never worse stored° than I am.   *provided*
485   It shall be otherwise, I hope, ere this night pass.

    Loquitur ad NOUGHT
TITIVILLUS Hark now, I say thou hast many a penny!
NOUGHT *Non nobis, Domine, non nobis,*[9] by St Denny![1]
    The devil may dance in my purse for any penny—
    It is as clean as a bird's arse!

TITIVILLUS Now I say yet again, *caveatis*![2]
    Here is an able fellowship to trice° 'em out of your gates!   *trick*

    Now I say, Newguise, Nowadays, and Nought,
    Go and search the country—anon it be sought—
    Some here, some there, what if ye may catch ought.[3]

495   If ye fail of horse, take what ye may else.
NEWGUISE Then speak to Mankind for the *recumbentibus* of my jewels![4]
NOWADAYS Remember my broken head, in the worship of the five vowels![5]
NOUGHT Yea, good sir, and the sciatica in my arm!
TITIVILLUS I know full well what Mankind did to you.
500   Mischief hath informed of all the matter through.
    I shall venge your quarrel, I make God avow!°   *vow to god*
    Forth, and espy where ye may do harm!

    Take William Fide,[6] if ye will have any mo.°   *more*
    I say, Newguise, whither art thou avised° to go?   *intending*

NEWGUISE First I shall begin at Master Huntington of Sawston.
    Fro thence I shall go to William Thurlay of Hauxton,
    And so forth to Pichard of Trumpington;
    I will keep me to these three.
NOWADAYS I shall go to William Baker of Walton,
510   To Richard Bollman of Gayton.
    I shall spare Master Wood of Fulbourn,
    He is a *noli me tangere*![7]

5. I prove (their cleverness) thus.
6. He speaks to Newguise.
7. Last night.
8. The devil a bit! I am a pure gentleman (i.e., I lack money).
9. Not unto us, O Lord, not unto us (Psalms 115.1).
1. Saint Denis, patron saint of Paris.
2. Beware.
3. If you can steal anything.

4. For the hitting of my testicles.
5. A play on the five wounds of Christ.
6. This and the following names almost certainly made topical references to the play's original audience in Cambridgeshire and Norfolk, near Cambridge and Lynn, where all the towns mentioned are located.
7. Touch me not (John 20.17). Jesus's words to Mary Magdalene after the resurrection.

NOUGHT I shall go to William Patrick of Massingham;
       I shall spare Master Allington of Bottisham
515   And Hammond of Swaffham
         For dread of *In manus tuas*,[8] queck![9]
       Fellows, come forth, and go we hence together.
NEWGUISE Sith we shall go, let us be well ware and wither.[1]
       If we may be take,° we come no more hither.   *taken*
520   Let us con well our neck-verse that we have not a check.[2]

TITIVILLUS Go your way, a devil way, go your way all!
       I bless you with my left hand; foul you befall![3]
       Come again, I warn, as soon as I you call,
         And bring your advantage° into this place.   *profits*
525   To speak with Mankind I will tarry here this tide,°   *while*
       And assay his good purpose for to set aside.
       The good-man Mercy shall no longer be his guide;
         I shall make him to dance another trace!°   *step*

       Ever I go invisible, it is my jet;°   *fashion*
530   And before his eye thus I will hang my net,
       To blench° his sight. I hope to have his foot met.°   *confuse / measure*
         To irk him of his labour I shall make a frame.°   *plan*
       This board shall be hid under the earth, privily.°   *secretly*
       His spade shall enter, I hope, unreadily!
535   By then° he hath assayed, he shall be very angry,   *by the time*
         And lose his patience, pain° of shame.   *on penalty*
       I shall meng his corn with drawk and with darnel;[4]
       It shall not be like° to sow nor to sell.   *fit*
       Yonder he cometh! I pray of counsel.[5]
540   He shall ween° grace were wane.°   *think / lacking*

MANKIND Now God of his mercy send us of his sand!°   *grace*
       I have brought seed here to sow with my land.
       While I over-delve it,° here it shall stand.   *dig it over*
        In nomine Patris, et Filii, et Spiritus Sancti,[6] now I will begin.
545   This land is so hard it maketh me unlusty° and irk!°   *tired / annoyed*
       I shall sow my corn at venture,° and let God work.   *randomly*
       Alas, my corn is lost! Here is a foul work.
        I see well by tilling little shall I win.

       Here I give up my spade for now and for ever!

---

8. Into your hands (I commend my spirit) (Luke 23.46).
The last words Jesus speaks before dying, and therefore
commonly spoken by those on their deathbed.
9. A choking sound.
1. Let us be very watchful and bold.
2. Let us learn our neck-verse well so that we don't have a
disaster. The neck-verse was the first verse of the fifty-
first psalm, the recitation of which in court allowed a
defendant to claim benefit of clergy and so avoid the
death penalty.
3. May ill fortune befall you.
4. I will mix his grain with weeds.
5. I ask you (i.e., the audience) to say nothing.
6. "In the name of the Father, and of the Son, and of the
Holy Spirit." Opening words of the mass and the words
spoken when making the sign of the cross.

Here Titivillus goeth out with the spade.

550   To occupy my body I will not put me in dever.°   *make the effort*
   I will hear my evensong[7] here, ere I dissever.°   *depart*
     This place I assign as for my kirk.°   *church*
   Here in my kirk I kneel on my knees.
   Pater noster, qui es in celis . . .[8]
TITIVILLUS I promise you I have no lead on my heels![9]
   I am here again to make this fellow irk.
   Whist!° Peace! I shall go to his ear and tittle° therein: *hush / whisper*
   A short prayer thirleth° heaven. Of thy prayer blin.°   *pierces / cease*
   Thou art holier than ever was any of thy kin.
560   Arise and avent thee!° Nature compels.   *relieve yourself*
MANKIND I will° into the yard, sovereigns, and come again soon.   *will go*
   For dread of the colic and eek° of the stone,   *also*
   I will go do that needs must be done.
     My beads° shall be here for whosomever will else.   *prayer beads*

Exeat.[1]

TITIVILLUS Mankind was busy in his prayer, yet I did° him arise.   *made*
   He is conveyed,° by Christ, from his divine service.   *removed*
   Whither is he, trow° ye? Iwis° I am wonder wise,   *think / indeed*
     I have sent him forth to shit leasings.°   *lies*
   If ye have any silver, in hap° pure brass,   *perhaps*
570   Take a little powder-of-Paris,[2] and cast over his° face,   *its (the coin's)*
   And even in the owl-flight[3] let him° pass.   *it*
     Titivillus can learn° you many pretty things.   *teach*

   I trow Mankind will come again soon,
   Or else, I fear me, evensong will be done.
575   His beads shall be triced aside,° and that anon.   *removed*
     Ye shall° a good sport if ye will abide.   *will have*
   Mankind cometh again. Well fare he!
   I shall answer him *ad omnia "quare?"*.[4]
   There shall be set abroach° a clerical matter;   *started*
580   I hope of his purpose to set him aside.

MANKIND Evensong hath be in the saying, I trow, a fair while.
   I am irk° of it; it is too long by one mile.   *tired*
   Do way![5] I will no more so oft over the church stile;
     Be as be may, I shall do another.°   *something else*
585   Of labour and prayer, I am near irk of both.
   I will no more of it, though Mercy be wrath.°   *angry*
   My head is very heavy, I tell you, forsooth.°   *truly*
   I shall sleep full my belly an° he were my brother.   *even if*

---

7. Also called Vespers, the sixth of the seven canonical hours into which the Catholic church divided each day.
8. "Our Father, who art in heaven. . . ." The opening words of the Lord's Prayer.
9. I.e., I'm not slow.
1. Let him go out.

2. Exact meaning uncertain, probably a white powder.
3. I.e., twilight or night.
4. At every "why" (i.e., on every point).
5. Enough! I will no longer go so often over the steps in the churchyard wall.

TITIVILLUS An ever ye did,[6] for me keep now your silence!
590   Not a word, I charge you, pain° of forty pence!   *on penalty*
    A pretty game shall be showed you, ere ye go hence.
        Ye may hear him snore. He is sad° asleep.   *deeply*
    Whist!° Peace! The devil is dead. I shall go roun° in his ear.   *hush / whisper*
    Alas, Mankind, alas! Mercy hath stolen a mare.
595   He is run away fro his master, there wot° no man where.   *knows*
        Moreover he stole both a horse and a neat.°   *cow*

    But yet I heard say he brake° his neck as he rode in France.   *broke*
    But I think he rideth on the gallows to learn for to dance.[7]
    Because of his theft, that is his governance.
600   Trust no more on him, he is a marred° man.   *ruined*
    Mickle° sorrow with thy spade beforn° thou hast wrought.   *much / before*
    Arise, and ask mercy of Newguise, Nowadays, and Nought.
    They can advise thee for the best; let their good will be sought.
        And thy own wife brethel,° and take thee a lemman.°   *deceive / lover*

605   Farewell, everychone, for I have done my game,
    For I have brought Mankind to mischief and to shame!

MANKIND Whoop ho! Mercy hath broken his neckercher, a vows;° *neck, they say*
    Or he hangeth by the neck high upon the gallows.
    Adieu,[8] fair masters! I will haste me to the ale-house,
610   And speak with Newguise, Nowadays, and Nought,
    And get me a lemman with a smattering face![9]
NEWGUISE Make space, for Cock's body sackered,[1] make space!
    Aha, well over-run! God give him[2] evil grace!
    We were near St Patrick's way,[3] by him that me bought.

615   I was twitched by the neck; the game was begun;
    And grace was the halter brast° asunder—*Ecce signum*![4]   *burst*
    The half is about my neck. We had a near run.
        "Beware," quod the good-wife, when she smote off her
           husband's head, "Beware!"
    Mischief is a convict, for he could° his neck-verse.[5]   *knew*
620   My body gave a swing when I hung upon the cross.[6]
    Alas, he will hang such a likely° man and a fierce   *promising*
        For stealing of an horse! I pray God give him care!

    Do way this halter! What devil doth Mankind here, with sorrow?[7]
    Alas, how my neck is sore, I make avow!°   *I swear*
MANKIND Ye be welcome, Newguise, sir. What cheer with you?
NEWGUISE Well, sir; I have no cause to mourn.
MANKIND What was that about your neck, so God you amend?

---

6. If ever you did.   3. St. Patrick is the patron saint of Ireland.
7. I.e., to swing at the end of a noose.   4. Behold the sign.
8. Good-bye (French).   5. See note at line 520.
9. Meaning unclear, perhaps "kissable" or "wanton."   6. Gallows, with a play on Christ's cross.
1. God's sacred body.   7. I curse it.
2. The hangman.

NEWGUISE In faith, St Audrey's holy band.[8]
>I have a little disease, as it please God to send,
630   With a running ringworm.

NOWADAYS Stand a-room,° I pray thee, brother mine,   *make way*
>I have laboured all this night. When shall we go dine?
>A church herebeside° shall pay for ale, bread, and wine—   *near here*
>   Lo, here is stuff will serve!
NEWGUISE Now, by the holy Mary, thou art better merchant than I!
NOUGHT Avaunt,° knaves, let me go by!   *out of the way*
>I cannot get an° I should starve!   *even if*

MISCHIEF Here cometh a man of arms! Why stand ye so still?
>Of murder and manslaughter I have my belly-fill!
NOWADAYS What, Mischief, have ye been in prison, an it be your will?[9]
>Meseemeth ye have scoured° a pair of fetters!   *rubbed clean*
MISCHIEF I was chained by the arms. Lo! I have them here.
>The chains I brast° asunder and killed the jailer.   *burst*
>Yea, and his fair wife halsed° in a corner.   *embraced*
645   Ah, how sweetly I kissed the sweet mouth of hers.

>When I had do,° I was mine own butler;   *finished*
>I brought away with me both dish and doubler.°   *platter*
>Here is enow° for me! Be of good cheer.   *enough*
>   Yet well fare the new chesance![1]
MANKIND I ask mercy of Newguise, Nowadays, and Nought.
>Once with my spade I remember that I fought.
>I will make you amends if I hurt you ought°   *at all*
>   Or did any grievance.

NEWGUISE What a° devil liketh thee to be of this disposition?   *the*
MANKIND I dreamt Mercy was hang, this was my vision,
>And that to you three I should have recourse and remotion.°   *inclination*
>   Now I pray you heartily of your good will;
>I cry° you mercy of all that I did amiss.   *ask*
NOWADAYS I say, Newguise, Nought; Titivillus made all this;
660   As sicker° as God is in heaven, so it is.   *surely*
NOUGHT Stand up on your feet. Why stand ye so still?

NEWGUISE Master Mischief, we will you exhort
>Mankind's name in your book for to report.
MISCHIEF I will not so: I will set a court,
665   And do it *sub forma juris*,[2] dastard!°   *fool*

>Nowadays, make proclamation!

NOWADAYS Oyez, oyez, oyez!° All manner of men and common women   *hear ye*
>To the court of Mischief either come or send.
>Mankind shall return; he is one of our men.

8. A neckband blessed at the shrine of the Anglo-Saxon
St. Audrey, in Ely, a town in eastern England.
9. If you don't mind my asking.
1. Good luck to our new venture.

2. "In a legal manner." Mischief has decided that the ap-
prenticeship needs the legal and ritual sanction of a
manor-court session.

MISCHIEF Nought, come forth, thou shall be steward.[3]

NEWGUISE Master Mischief, his side-gown° may be sold.   long coat
      He may have a jacket thereof, and money told.[4]

MANKIND I will do for the best, so I have no cold.
      Hold, I pray you, and take it with you,
675   And let me have it again in any wise.

NOUGHT scribit.[5]

NEWGUISE I promit you a fresh jacket after the new guise.

MANKIND Go and do that longeth° to your office,   what belongs
      And spare that ye mow.°   what you can

NOUGHT Hold, Master Mischief, and read this.

MISCHIEF Here is 'Blottibus in blottis
      Blottorum blottibus istis'.[6]
      I beshrew° your ears, a fair hand!   curse

NOWADAYS Yea, it is a good running fist;°   cursive hand
      Such an hand may not be missed.

NOUGHT I should have done better, had I wist.°   known how

MISCHIEF Take heed, sirs, it stand you on hand.[7]

      "Curia tenta generalis,
      In a place there good ale is,
      Anno regni regitalis
690   Edwardi nullateni.[8]
      On yestern day in February"—the year passeth fully,
      As Nought hath written (here is our Tully!)[9]—
      "Anno regni regis nulli."[1]

NOWADAYS What, ho, Newguise, thou makest much tarrying°   delay
695   That jacket shall be worth a farthing.

NEWGUISE Out of my way, sirs, for dread of fighting!
      Lo, here is a feat tail, light to leap about.[2]

NOUGHT It is not shapen worth a morsel of bread;
      There is too much cloth; it weighs as any lead!
700   I shall go and mend it, else I will lose my head.
      Make space, sirs, let me go out!

MISCHIEF Mankind, come hither, God send you the gout!
      Ye shall go to all the good fellows in the country about,
      Unto the good-wife when the good-man is out;
705   "I will," say ye.

MANKIND   I will, sir.

NEWGUISE There arn° but six deadly sins, lechery is none;   are

---

3. The man who presided over a manor-court session.
4. Money left over.
5. Nought writes.
6. Nonsense Latin; literally, "To the blots in blots / With these blots of blots."
7. It affects you.
8. "A general court having been held . . . / In the year of

the reign of kingly / Edward the Nothing." This is a play on the usual heading for a record of manor-court proceedings.
9. Marcus Tullius Cicero, a Roman orator and statesman, renowned in the Middle Ages as a Latin prose stylist.
1. In the regnal year of no king.
2. Look, here is a becoming style, easy to move about in.

As it may be verified by us brethels° everychone.   *rogues*
Ye shall go rob, steal, and kill, as fast as ye may gone;
    "I will," say ye.

MANKIND   I will, sir.

NOWADAYS On Sundays, on the morrow early betime,°   *very early*
Ye shall with us to the ale-house early to go dine,
And forbear mass and matins, hours and prime;[3]
    "I will," say ye.

MANKIND   I will, sir.

MISCHIEF Ye must have by your side a long *da-pacem*,[4]

715   As true men ride by the way for to unbrace them,°   *carve them up*
Take their money, cut their throats, thus over-face them;
    "I will," say ye.

MANKIND   I will, sir.

NOUGHT Here is a jolly jacket! How say ye?

NEWGUISE It is a good jack-of-fence° for a man's body.   *protective jacket*

720   Hey, dog, hey! Whoop ho! Go your way lightly!
Ye are well made for to run.

MISCHIEF Tidings, tidings! I have espied one!°   *someone*
Hence with your stuff! Fast we were° gone!   *let us be*
I beshrew the last shall come to his home!

    Dicant omnes.[5]

725   Amen!

MERCY What ho, Mankind, flee that fellowship, I you pray!

MANKIND I shall speak with thee another time, tomorn or the next day.
    We shall go forth together, to keep my father's year-day.°   *death anniversary*
    A tapster,° a tapster! Stow, stot,° stow!   *barmaid / where, slut*

MISCHIEF A mischief go with thee, here I have a foul fall!
Hence, away fro me, or I shall beshit you all!

NEWGUISE What ho! Ostler,° ostler, lend us a football!   *innkeeper*
Whoop, ho! Anow, anow, anow, anow!

MERCY My mind is dispersed, my body trembleth as the aspen leaf.

735   The tears should trickle down by my cheeks, were not your
        reverence.[6]
It were to me solace, the cruel visitation of death.
Without rude behaviour I can not express this inconvenience.°   *misfortune*
Weeping, sighing, and sobbing were my sufficience;°   *sustenance*
All natural nutriment to me as carrion is odible.°   *hateful*

740   My inward affliction yieldeth° me tedious unto your presence.   *makes*
I cannot bear it evenly that Mankind is so flexible.

Man, unkind wherever thou be, for all this world was not
    apprehensible°   *sufficient*
To discharge thine original offence, thraldom, and captivity,
Till God's own well-beloved son was obedient and passible.°   *willing to suffer*

---

3. I.e., all church services. Matins and prime are two of the seven canonical hours into which the Catholic church divides each day.

4. Lit. "give peace," i.e., a dagger.
5. Let them all say.
6. Were you revered people (i.e., the audience) not here.

745   Every drop of his blood was shed to purge thine iniquity.
      I discommend and disallow this often mutability.
      To every creature thou art dispectuous° and odible.   *contemptible*
      Why art thou so uncourteous, so inconsiderate? Alas, woe is
          me,
      As the vane° that turneth with the wind, so thou art
          convertible.   *weather vane*

750   In trust is treason; thy promise is not credible.
      This perversious° ingratitude I cannot rehearse.   *perverse*
      To God and to all the holy court of heaven thou art
          despectible,°   *despicable*

      As a noble versifier maketh mention in this verse:

      "Lex et natura, Cristus et omnia jura
755   *Damnant ingratum; lugent eum fore natum."*[7]

      O good Lady and Mother of Mercy, have pity and compassion
      Of the wretchedness of mankind, that is so wanton and so
          frail!
      Let mercy exceed justice! Dear Mother, admit this
          supplication:
      Equity to be laid on party,° and mercy to prevail.   *aside*

760   Too sensual living is reprovable that is nowadays,
      As by the comprehence° of this matter it may be specified.   *understanding*
      Newguise, Nowadays, Nought, with their allectuous° ways,   *alluring*
      They have perverted Mankind, my sweet son, I have well
          espied.

      Ah, with these cursed caitiffs, an° I may, he shall not long   *wretches, if*
          endure!
765   I, Mercy, his father ghostly, will proceed forth and do my
          property.°   *task*
      Lady, help! This manner of living is a detestable pleasure.
      Vanitas vanitatum[8] all is but a vanity!

      Mercy shall never be convict° of his uncourteous condition.   *conquered by*
      With weeping tears, by night and by day, I will go and never
          cease.
770   Shall I not find him? Yes, I hope. Now God be my protection!
      My predilect° son, where be ye? Mankind, *ubi es?*°[9]   *dearest*

MISCHIEF My prepotent father, when ye sup, sup out your mess!
      Ye are all to-gloried in your terms; ye make many a lease.
      Will ye hear? He crieth ever: 'Mankind, *ubi es?*'.
NEWGUISE *Hic, hic, hic, hic, hic, hic, hic, hic!*[1]
      That is to say: 'Here, here, here', nigh dead in the creek!
      If ye will have him, go and seek, seek, seek!
      Seek not overlong, for losing of your mind.

7. Law and nature, Christ and all justice condemn the in-   8. Vanity of vanities (Ecclesiastes 1.2).
grate; they lament that he was born. (The source is   9. Where are you?
unidentified.)   1. Here.

NOWADAYS If ye will have Mankind, ho, *Domine, Domine, Dominus!*[2]
780   Ye must speak to the shrive° for a *cape corpus,*[3]   *sheriff*
      Else ye must be fain to return with *non est inventus.*[4]
      How say ye, sir? My bolt° is shot.   *arrow*
NOUGHT I am doing of my needings.[5] Beware how ye shoot!
      Fie, fie, fie! I have foul arrayed° my foot!   *foully soiled*
785   Be wise for shooting with your tackles,° for, God wot,°   *weapons / knows*
      My foot is fully overshot!

MISCHIEF A parliament, a parliament! Come forth, Nought, behind!
      A council, belive.° I am afeard Mercy will him find.   *quickly*
      How say ye? And what say ye? How shall we do with
         Mankind?
NEWGUISE Tish, a fly's wing![6] Will ye do well?
      He weeneth° Mercy were hung for stealing of a mare;   *thinks*
      Mischief, go say to him that Mercy seeketh everywhere;
      He will hang himself, I undertake, for fear.
MISCHIEF I assent thereto; it is wittily said and well.

NOWADAYS Whip° it in thy coat, anon it were done!   *put*
      Now, St Gabriel's mother[7] save the clouts° of thy shoon!° *patches / shoes*
      All the books in the world, if they had be undone,°   *been opened*
      Could not a° counselled us bet.   *have*

     Hic exit Mischief.[8]

MISCHIEF How, Mankind, come and speak with Mercy. He is here fast by.
MANKIND A rope, a rope, a rope, I am not worthy!
MISCHIEF Anon, anon, anon, I have it here ready!
      With a tree also, that I have get.

      Hold the tree, Nowadays! Nought, take heed, and be wise!
NEWGUISE Lo, Mankind, do as I do. This is thy new guise.
805   Give the rope just to [thy] neck. This is mine advice.
MISCHIEF Help thyself, Nought! Lo, Mercy is here!
      He scareth us with a baleis;° we may no longer tarry!   *rod*
NEWGUISE Queck![9] queck! queck! Alas, my throat! I beshrew you, marry!
      Ah, Mercy, Christ's copped° curse go with you, and St Davy![1] *greatest*
810   Alas, my weasand!° Ye were somewhat too near!   *windpipe*

     Exeant.[2]

MERCY Arise, my precious redempt° son, ye be to me full dear.   *saved*
      He is so timorous, meseemeth his vital spirit doth expire.
MANKIND Alas! I have be so bestially disposed I dare not appear;
      To see your solacious° face I am not worthy to desire.   *comforting*

---

2. O Lord, O Lord, Lord.
3. Lit., "take the body," a writ of arrest.
4. Lit., "he is not found," a sheriff's certificate that a prisoner cannot be found.
5. I am moving my bowels.
6. I.e., no problem.

7. A hyperbolic oath, since St. Gabriel is, typically, the archangel Gabriel, who has no mother.
8. Here Mischief goes out.
9. A choking sound.
1. St. David, patron saint of Wales.
2. Let them go out.

MERCY Your criminous complaint° woundeth my heart as a lance.   *guilty lament*
    Dispose yourself meekly to ask mercy, and I will assent.
    Yield me neither gold nor treasure, but your humble obeisance,°   *obedience*
    The voluntary subjection of your heart, and I am content.

MANKIND What? Ask mercy yet once again? Alas, it were a vile petition!
820   Ever to offend and ever to ask mercy, it is a puerility.°   *childish act*
    It is so abominable to rehearse my iterate° transgression;   *repeated*
    I am not worthy to have mercy, by no possibility.

MERCY O Mankind, my singular solace, this is a lamentable excuse!
    The dolorous tears of my heart, how they begin to amount!°   *build up*
825   O pierced Jesu, help thou this sinful sinner to reduce!°   *lead back*
    Nam haec est mutatio dexterae Excelsi; vertit impios, et non
                           sunt.[3]

    Arise, and ask mercy, Mankind, and be associate to° me.   *linked with*
    Thy death shall be my heaviness. Alas, 'tis pity it should be
                         thus!

    Thy obstinacy will exclude thee fro the glorious perpetuity.
830   Yet, for my love, ope° thy lips, and say: "*Miserere mei, Deus!*"[4]   *open*

MANKIND The egal° justice of God will not permit such a sinful wretch   *impartial*
    To be revived and restored again. It were impossible.
MERCY The justice of God will as I will, as himself doth preach:
    Nolo mortem peccatoris, inquit[5] if he will be reducible.°   *repentant*

MANKIND Then, Mercy, good Mercy, what is a man without mercy?
    Little is our part of paradise where mercy ne were.[6]
    Good Mercy, excuse the inevitable objection of my ghostly
        enemy.
    The proverb saith: "The truth trieth the self." Alas, I have much
        care!
MERCY God will not make you privy unto[7] his Last judgment.
840   Justice and equity shall be fortified, I will not deny.
    But Truth may not so cruelly proceed in his strait° argument   *strict*
    But that Mercy shall rule the matter without controversy.

    Arise now, and go with me in this deambulatory.°   *walking area*
    Incline your capacity;[8] my doctrine is convenient.°   *appropriate*
845   Sin not in hope of mercy,[9] that is a crime notary;°   *notorious*
    To trust overmuch in a prince, it is not expedient.

    In hope, when ye sin, ye think to have mercy, beware of that
        adventure.
    The good Lord said to the lecherous woman of Canaané

---

3. For this is the change of the right hand of the Most High: he overthrows the wicked, and they are no more. (A mixture of Psalms 77.10 and Proverbs 12.7.)
4. "Have mercy on me, O God!" (Psalms 51.1). Also called the Miserere, it is the most famous of the penitential psalms.

5. I do not want the death of a sinner, he said (see Ezekiel 33.11).
6. If mercy were lacking.
7. Share with you the secrets of.
8. Submit your understanding.
9. See Ecclesiastes 5.4–7.

The holy Gospel is the authority, as we read in scripture:
850   *"Vade, et iam amplius noli peccare!"*[1]

Christ preserved this sinful woman taken in adultery.
He said to her these words: 'Go, and sin no more!'
So to you: 'Go, and sin no more!'. Beware of vain confidence
    of mercy.
Offend not a prince on trust of his favour, as I said before.

855   If ye feel yourself trapped in the snare of your ghostly enemy,
Ask mercy anon. Beware of the continuance.
While a wound is fresh, it is proved curable by surgery,
That, if it proceed overlong, it is cause of great grievance.

MANKIND To ask mercy and to have, this is a liberal° possession.   *generous*
860   Shall this expeditious° petition ever be allowed, as ye have   *urgent*
    insight?
MERCY In this present life mercy is plenty, till death maketh his
    division.
But when ye be go,° *usque ad minimum quadrantem*[2] ye shall   *are gone (dead)*
    reckon your right.

Ask mercy and have, while the body with the soul hath
    his annexion;°   *is joined*
If ye tarry till your decease, ye may hap° of your desire to miss.   *chance*
865   Be repentant here; trust not the hour of death. Think on this
    lesson:
"Ecce nunc tempus acceptabile, ecce nunc dies salutis."[3]
All the virtue in the world if ye might comprehend,°   *contain*
Your merits were not premiable to° the bliss above,   *worthy to (gain)*
Not to the least joy of heaven of your proper effort to ascend.
870   With mercy ye may; I tell you no fable, scripture doth prove.

MANKIND O Mercy, my suavious° solace and singular recreatory,°   *sweet / comfort*
My predilect° special, ye are worthy to have my love!   *dearest*
For, without desert and means supplicatory,[4]
Ye be compatient to my inexcusable reprove.°   *shame*

875   Ah, it sweameth° my heart to think how unwisely I have   *grieves*
    wrought!
Titivillus, that goeth invisible, hung his net before my eye,
And by his fantastical visions, seditiously sought,
To Newguise, Nowadays, Nought caused me to obey.

MERCY Mankind, ye were oblivious of my doctrine monitory.°   *warning*
880   I said before, Titivillus would assay you a brunt.[5]
Beware fro henceforth of his fables delusory.°   *deceitful*
The proverb saith: *Jacula praestita minus laedunt.*[6]

---

1. "Go and sin no more" (John 8.11). In the gospel story, Jesus stops people from stoning to death a woman taken in adultery by suggesting that someone who was without sin should cast the first stone. Since no one was without sin, the woman was spared. He then sends her away with this phrase.

2. To the uttermost farthing. (See Matthew 5.26.)
3. Behold now is the acceptable time, behold now is the day of salvation (2 Corinthians 6.2).
4. Undeserving and unable to plead.
5. Have a go at you.
6. Prepared-for darts wound less.

Ye have three adversaries, and he is master of them all,
That is to say, the Devil, the World, the Flesh and the fell.°   *skin*
885   The Newguise, Nowadays, Nought, the World we may them
        call,
And properly Titivillus signifieth the Fiend of hell;

The Flesh, that is the unclean concupiscence of your body.
These be your three ghostly enemies, in whom ye have put your
        confidence.
They brought you to mischief, to conclude° your temporal°   *end / earthly*
        glory,
890   As it hath be showed before this worshipful audience.

Remember how ready I was to help you? Fro such I was not
        dangerous.
Wherefore, good son, abstain fro sin evermore after this.
Ye may both save and spill° your soul, that is so precious.   *destroy*
Libere velle, libere nolle,[7] God may not deny, iwis.°   *indeed*

895   Beware of Titivillus with his net, and of all envious will,
Of your sinful delectation° that grieveth your ghostly substance.[8]   *pleasure*
Your body is your enemy; let him° not have his° will.   *it / its*
Take your leave when ye will. God send you good
        perseverance!

MANKIND Sith° I shall depart, bless me, father, ere then I go.   *since*
900   God send us all plenty of his great mercy!
MERCY *Dominus custodit te ab omni malo*[9]
      In nomine Patris, et Filii, et Spiritus Sancti.[1]
      Amen.

            Hic exit Mankind.[2]

Worshipful sovereigns, I have do my property:°   *done my part*
905   Mankind is delivered by my favoural patrociny.°   *kind protection*
God preserve him fro all wicked captivity,
And send him grace his sensual conditions to mortify!

Now for his love that for us received his humanity,[3]
Search your conditions with due examination.
910   Think and remember the world is but a vanity,
As it is proved daily by diverse transmutation.°   *changes*

Mankind is wretched; he hath sufficient proof;
Therefore God grant you all, *per suam misericordiam,*[4]
That ye may be play-feres° with the angels above,   *play-fellows*
915   And have to your portion *vitam aeternam.*[5]
      Amen!

                  Finis[6]

---

7. "Freely accept, freely reject." A reference to man's free will.
8. I.e., the soul.
9. (May) the Lord preserve you from all evil (Psalms 121.7).
1. In the name of the Father, and of the Son, and of the Holy Spirit (see note at line 544).

2. Here Mankind goes out.
3. I.e., Christ.
4. Through his mercy.
5. Eternal life.
6. The end.

Christine de Pizan
c. 1364–c. 1430

Christine de Pizan is an epochal figure in the history of European literature, not only for the quality and influence of her many works, but equally because she was Europe's first professional woman of letters. There were many important women writers in the Middles Ages, several of them represented in this anthology, but Christine—widowed in 1389 with three children and no family money—was the first to make writing the sole source of her income. She was well aware of this and wove her unique perspective, as a woman engaged with a largely male (and often misogynist) intellectual tradition, into much of her writing.

Like many late medieval writers, Christine de Pizan spent a good part of her energies translating, adapting, and consolidating earlier works on a wide range of topics. She wrote love poetry in traditional forms such as the ballade, but innovated by writing lyrics on widowhood as well. Like other writers of her time, too, Christine frames many of her books as dream-visions populated by allegorical figures, especially teachers or guides, such as the three ladies (Reason, Rectitude, and Justice) whom she encounters in the *Book of the City of Ladies*. Also like her contemporaries, Christine had to seek patronage in the noble and royal courts of France (where she spent most of her life) and Burgundy, as well as England. She was an innovator here as well, though, carefully supervising the scribes and painters who produced splendid manuscripts of her works for presentation to her patrons.

Christine innovated most of all, however, by persistently reacting to her cultural inheritance from the perspective of women. At the turn of the fifteenth century, she was a major voice in the debate surrounding the famous but often misogynist *Romance of the Rose*. Classical and medieval Latin had an even greater store of works hostile to women. With the *Book of the City of Ladies,* though, Christine offers a systematic response to the depiction of women in biblical and classical texts. The three allegorical ladies who appear to her as the book opens instruct Christine to build a walled city of and for the virtuous women of her cultural past. In doing so, Christine radically reinterprets women's histories as they have been recorded by men, and imagines a symbolic space from which a female literary tradition might emanate.

The works of Christine de Pizan were widely known in England in her own lifetime and well into the early modern period. Splendid manuscripts of her French works came into the hands of English kings and nobles. Her elder son was raised for three years in the household of the Duke of Salisbury, an influential member of the court of Richard II. Christine's *Letter of Othea* was translated three times in the fifteenth century; and Thomas Hoccleve, a late contemporary of Chaucer, adapted her *Letter of the God of Love*—a feminist response to courtly love—as the *Letter of Cupid.* England's first printer, William Caxton, translated and published yet other of her works (some by royal commission) in the 1480s, as did early sixteenth-century printers like Henry Pepwell, who published Brian Anslay's 1521 translation of the *Book of the City of Ladies.*

Her role in England places Christine de Pizan within several key transitions there. The ongoing translations of her works reflect the importation of Continental texts into an increasingly English-language literary and political culture under the Lancastrian and Yorkist kings. The numerous early printings of these translations is part of a massive dissemination of late medieval texts made possible by the rise of print. And in turn, this widespread access to later medieval literary modes carried their influences—not least, that of allegory—into early modern culture in England. Works like the *Book of the City of Ladies* lie behind the allegorized, often female-controlled cities and castles of early modern works like Spenser's *Faerie Queene.* The translation used here is by Earl Jeffrey Richards.

Woodblock from Brian Anslay's English translation of *Book of the City of Ladies*, 1521.

from *Book of the City of Ladies*

[In the first chapter Christine presents herself surrounded by books in her study, and is dismayed to read philosophers and poets all claiming that women are full of vice. While such a view is contrary to her perception of herself and of other women she has known, she concludes that so many famous men cannot be wrong. She is so over-whelmed by sorrow that she asks God why he created women, if they are so vile, and why he did not make her a man, so that she might serve him better.]

[PART I, CHAPTER 2]

[Here Christine Describes how three ladies appeared to her and how the one who was in front spoke first and comforted her in her pain.]

So occupied with these painful thoughts, my head bowed in shame, my eyes filled with tears, leaning on the pommel of my chair's armrest, I suddenly saw a ray of light fall on my lap, as though it were the sun. I shuddered then, as if wakened from sleep, for I was sitting in a shadow where the sun could not have shone at that hour. And as I lifted my head to see where this light was coming from, I saw three crowned ladies standing before me, and the splendor of their bright faces shone on me and throughout the entire room. Now no one would ask whether I was surprised, for my doors were shut and they had still entered. Fearing that some phantom had come to tempt me and filled with great fright, I made the Sign of the Cross on my forehead.

Then she who was the first of the three smiled and began to speak, "Dear daughter, do not be afraid, for we have not come here to harm or trouble you but to console you, for we have taken pity on your distress, and we have come to bring you out of the ignorance which so blinds your own intellect that you shun what you know for a certainty and believe what you do not know or see or recognize except by virtue of many strange opinions. You resemble the fool in the prank who was dressed in women's clothes while he slept; because those who were making fun of him repeatedly told him he was a woman, he believed their false testimony more readily than the certainty of his own identity. Fair daughter, have you lost all sense? Have you forgotten that when fine gold is tested in the furnace, it does not change or vary in strength but becomes purer the more it is hammered and handled in different ways? Do you not know that the best things are the most debated and the most discussed? If you wish to consider the question of the highest form of reality, which consists in ideas or celestial substances, consider whether the greatest philosophers who have lived and whom you support against your own sex have ever resolved whether ideas are false and contrary to the truth. Notice how these same philosophers contradict and criticize one another, just as you have seen in the *Metaphysics* where Aristotle takes their opinions to task and speaks similarly of Plato and other philosophers. And note, moreover, how even Saint Augustine and the Doctors of the Church have criticized Aristotle in certain passages, although he is known as the prince of philosophers in whom both natural and moral philosophy attained their highest level. It also seems that you think that all the words of the philosophers are articles of faith, that they could never be wrong. As far as the poets of whom you speak are concerned, do you not know that they spoke on many subjects in a fictional way and that often they mean the contrary of what their words openly say? One can interpret them according to the grammatical figure of *antiphrasis,* which means, as you know, that if you call something bad, in fact, it is good, and also vice versa. Thus I advise you to profit from their works and to interpret them in the manner in which they are intended in those passages where they attack women. Perhaps this man, who called himself Mathéolus in his own book, intended it in such a way, for there are many things which, if taken literally, would be pure heresy.[1] As for the attack against the estate of marriage—which is a holy estate, worthy and ordained by God—made not only by Mathéolus but also by others and even by the *Romance of the Rose* where greater credibility is averred because of the authority of its author, it is evident and proven by experience that the contrary of the evil which they posit and claim to be found in this estate through the obligation and fault of women is true. For where has the husband ever been found who would allow his wife to have authority to abuse and insult him as a matter of course, as these authorities maintain? I believe that, regardless of what you might have read, you will never see such a husband with your own eyes, so badly colored are these lies. Thus, in conclusion, I tell you, dear friend, that simplemindedness has prompted you to hold such an opinion. Come back to yourself, recover your senses, and do not trouble yourself anymore over such absurdities. For you know that any evil spoken of women so generally only hurts those who say it, not women themselves."

---

1. *The Book of the Lamentations of Matheolus,* the misogynist work that most troubled Christine in her study.

[PART I, CHAPTER 3]

[Here Christine tells how the lady who had said this showed her who she was and what her character and function were and told her how she would construct a city with the help of these same three ladies.]

The famous lady spoke these words to me, in whose presence I do not know which one of my senses was more overwhelmed: my hearing from having listened to such worthy words or my sight from having seen her radiant beauty, her attire, her reverent comportment, and her most honored countenance. The same was true of the others, so that I did not know which one to look at, for the three ladies resembled each other so much that they could be told apart only with difficulty, except for the last one, for although she was of no less authority than the others, she had so fierce a visage that whoever, no matter how daring, looked in her eyes would be afraid to commit a crime; for it seemed that she threatened criminals unceasingly. Having stood up out of respect, I looked at them without saying a word, like someone too overwhelmed to utter a syllable. Reflecting on who these beings could be, I felt much admiration in my heart and, if I could have dared, I would have immediately asked their names and identities and what was the meaning of the different scepters which each one carried in her right hand, which were of fabulous richness, and why they had come here. But since I considered myself unworthy to address these questions to such high ladies as they appeared to me, I did not dare to, but continued to keep my gaze fixed on them, half-afraid and half-reassured by the words which I had heard, which had made me reject my first impression. But the most wise lady who had spoken to me and who knew in her mind what I was thinking, as one who has insight into everything, addressed my reflections, saying:

"Dear daughter, know that God's providence, which leaves nothing void or empty, has ordained that we, though celestial beings, remain and circulate among the people of the world here below, in order to bring order and maintain in balance those institutions we created according to the will of God in the fulfillment of various offices, that God whose daughters we three all are and from whom we were born. Thus it is my duty to straighten out men and women when they go astray and to put them back on the right path. And when they stray, if they have enough understanding to see me, I come to them quietly in spirit and preach to them, showing them their error and how they have failed, I assign them the causes, and then I teach them what to do and what to avoid. Since I serve to demonstrate clearly and to show both in thought and deed to each man and woman his or her own special qualities and faults, you see me holding this shiny mirror which I carry in my right hand in place of a scepter. I would thus have you know truly that no one can look into this mirror, no matter what kind of creature, without achieving clear self-knowledge. My mirror has such great dignity that not without reason is it surrounded by rich and precious gems, so that you see, thanks to this mirror, the essences, qualities, proportions, and measures of all things are known, nor can anything be done well without it. And because, similarly, you wish to know what are the offices of my other sisters whom you see here, each will reply in her own person about her name and character, and this way our testimony will be all the more certain to you. But now I myself will declare the reason for our coming. I must assure you, as we do nothing without good cause, that our appearance here is not at all in vain. For, although we are not common to many places and our knowledge does not come to all people, nevertheless you, for your great love of investigating the truth through long and continual study, for which you come here, solitary and separated from the world, you have deserved and deserve, our devoted friend, to be visited and consoled by us in your agitation and sadness, so that you might also see clearly, in the midst of the darkness of your thoughts, those things which taint and trouble your heart.

"There is another greater and even more special reason for our coming which you will learn from our speeches: in fact we have come to vanquish from the world the same error into which you had fallen, so that from now on, ladies and all valiant women may have a refuge and defense against the various assailants, those ladies who have been abandoned for so long, exposed like a field without a surrounding hedge, without finding a champion to afford them an adequate defense, notwithstanding those noble men who are required by order of law to protect them, who by negligence and apathy have allowed them to be mistreated. It is no wonder then that their jealous enemies, those outrageous villains who have assailed them with various weapons, have been victorious in a war in which women have had no defense. Where is there a city so strong which could not be taken immediately if no resistance were forthcoming, or the law case, no matter how unjust, which was not won through the obstinance of someone pleading without opposition? And the simple, noble ladies, following the example of suffering which God commands, have cheerfully suffered the great attacks which, both in the spoken and the written word, have been wrongfully and sinfully perpetrated against women by men who all the while appealed to God for the right to do so. Now it is time for their just cause to be taken from Pharaoh's hands, and for this reason, we three ladies whom you see here, moved by pity, have come to you to announce a particular edifice built like a city wall, strongly constructed and well founded, which has been predestined and established by our aid and counsel for you to build, where no one will reside except all ladies of fame and women worthy of praise, for the walls of the city will be closed to those women who lack virtue."

[PART I, CHAPTER 4]

[Here the lady explains to Christine the city which she has been commissioned to build and how she was charged to help Christine build the wall and enclosure, and then gives her name.]

"Thus, fair daughter, the prerogative among women has been bestowed on you to establish and build the City of Ladies. For the foundation and completion of this City you will draw fresh waters from us as from clear fountains, and we will bring you sufficient building stone, stronger and more durable than any marble with cement could be. Thus your City will be extremely beautiful, without equal, and of perpetual duration in the world.

"Have you not read that King Tros founded the great city of Troy with the aid of Apollo, Minerva, and Neptune, whom the people of that time considered gods, and also how Cadmus founded the city of Thebes with the admonition of the gods? And yet over time these cities fell and have fallen into ruin. But I prophesy to you, as a true sybil, that this City, which you will found with our help, will never be destroyed, nor will it ever fall, but will remain prosperous forever, regardless of all its jealous enemies. Although it will be stormed by numerous assaults, it will never be taken or conquered.

"Long ago the Amazon kingdom was begun through the arrangement and enterprise of several ladies of great courage who despised servitude, just as history books have testified. For a long time afterward they maintained it under the rule of several queens, very noble ladies whom they elected themselves, who governed them well and maintained their dominion with great strength. Yet, although they were strong and powerful and had conquered a large part of the entire Orient in the course of their rule and terrified all the neighboring lands (even the Greeks, who were then the flower of all countries in the world, feared them), nevertheless, after a time, the power of this kingdom declined, so that as with all earthly kingdoms, nothing but its name has survived to the present. But the edifice erected by you in this City which you must construct will be far stronger, and for its founding I was commissioned, in the course of our common deliberation, to supply you with durable and pure mortar to lay the sturdy foundations and to raise the lofty walls all around, high and thick, with mighty towers and strong bastions, surrounded by moats with firm blockhouses, just as is fitting for a city with a strong and lasting defense. Following our plan, you will set the foundations deep to last all the longer, and then you will raise the walls so high that they will not fear anyone. Daughter, now that I have told you the reason for our coming and so that you will more certainly believe my words, I want you to learn my name, by whose sound alone you will be able to learn and know that, if you wish to follow my commands, you have in me an administrator so that you may do your work flawlessly. I am called Lady Reason; you see that you are in good hands. For the time being then, I will say no more."

[In the following chapters, the other two ladies identify themselves as Rectitude and Justice. Just as Lady Reason had carried a mirror signifying self-knowledge, Rectitude carries a ruler signifying the distinction of right from wrong, and offers to help Christine measure her City of Ladies with it. Lady Justice carries a gold flask from which she portions out justice to all, and promises to help Christine populate her city. The remainder of the book describes Christine's questions to the three ladies about the achievements of women. Countering charges of physical weakness and cowardice, Lady Reason cites the bravery of the Amazons Hippolyta and Penthesilea. As examples of women's intelligence and learning, she offers the wisdom of Sappho and (more problematically) the cleverness of Medea and Circe. Lady Rectitude absolves women of the charge of lustfulness with the biblical examples of Susannah, Sarah, and Rebecca, and the Greek example of Penelope. After praising Christine's construction work, Lady Justice welcomes the Virgin Mary into the City of Ladies, to rule as queen. In the final chapter, Christine offers advice to women of all marital conditions and social stations on how to bear their lot.]

[PART 3, CHAPTER 19]

THE END OF THE BOOK: CHRISTINE ADDRESSES THE LADIES.

My most honored ladies, may God be praised, for now our City is entirely finished and completed, where all of you who love glory, virtue, and praise may be lodged in great honor, ladies from the past as well as from the present and future, for it has been built and established for every honorable lady. And my most dear ladies, it is natural for the human heart to rejoice when it finds itself victorious in any enterprise and its enemies confounded. Therefore you are right, my ladies, to rejoice greatly in God and in honest mores upon seeing this new City completed, which can be not only the refuge for you all, that is, for virtuous women, but also the defense and guard against your enemies and assailants, if you guard it well. For you can see that the substance with which it is made is entirely of virtue, so resplendent that you may see yourselves mirrored in it, especially in the roofs built in the last part as well as in the other parts which concern you. And my dear ladies, do not misuse this new inheritance like the arrogant who turn proud when their prosperity grows and their wealth multiplies, but rather follow the example of your Queen, the sovereign Virgin, who, after the extraordinary honor of being chosen Mother of the Son of God was announced to her humbled herself all the more by calling herself the handmaiden of God. Thus, my ladies, just as it is true that a creature's humility and kindness wax with the increase of its virtues, may this City be an occasion for you to conduct yourselves honestly and with integrity and to be all the more virtuous and humble.

And you ladies who are married, do not scorn being subject to your husbands, for sometimes it is not the best thing for a creature to be independent. This is attested by what the angel said to Ezra: Those, he said, who take advantage of their free will can fall into sin and despise our Lord and deceive the just, and for this they perish. Those women with peaceful, good, and discreet husbands who are devoted to them, praise God for this boon, which is not inconsiderable, for a greater boon in the world could not be given them. And may they be diligent in serving, loving, and cherishing their husbands in the loyalty of their heart, as they should, keeping their peace and praying to God to uphold and save them. And those women who have husbands neither completely good nor completely bad should still praise God for not having the worst and should strive to moderate their vices and pacify them, according to their conditions. And those women who have husbands who are cruel, mean, and savage should strive to endure them while trying to overcome their vices and lead them back, if they can, to a reasonable and seemly life. And if they are so obstinate that their wives are unable to do anything, at least they will acquire great merit for their souls through the virtue of patience. And everyone will bless them and support them.

So, my ladies, be humble and patient, and God's grace will grow in you, and praise will be given to you as well as the Kingdom of Heaven. For Saint Gregory has said that patience is the entrance to Paradise and the way of Jesus Christ. And may none of you be forced into holding frivolous opinions nor be hardened in them, lacking all basis in reason, nor be jealous or disturbed in mind, nor haughty in speech, nor outrageous in your acts, for these things disturb the mind and lead to madness. Such behavior is unbecoming and unfitting for women.

And you, virgin maidens, be pure, simple, and serene, without vagueness, for the snares of evil men are set for you. Keep your eyes lowered, with few words in your mouths, and act respectfully. Be armed with the strength of virtue against the tricks of the deceptive and avoid their company.

And widows, may there be integrity in your dress, conduct, and speech; piety in your deeds and way of life; prudence in your bearing; patience (so necessary!), strength, and resistance in tribulations and difficult affairs; humility in your heart, countenance, and speech; and charity in your works.

In brief, all women—whether noble, bourgeois, or lower-class—be well-informed in all things and cautious in defending your honor and chastity against your enemies! My ladies, see how these men accuse you of so many vices in everything. Make liars of them all by showing forth your virtue, and prove their attacks false by acting well, so that you can say with the Psalmist, "the vices of the evil will fall on their heads." Repel the deceptive flatterers who, using different charms, seek with various tricks to steal that which you must consummately guard, that is, your honor and the beauty of your praise. Oh my ladies, flee, flee the foolish love they urge on you! Flee it, for God's sake, flee! For no good can come to you from it.

Rather, rest assured that however deceptive their lures, their end is always to your detriment. And do not believe the contrary, for it cannot be otherwise. Remember, dear ladies, how these men call you frail, unserious, and easily influenced but yet try hard, using all kinds of strange and deceptive tricks, to catch you, just as one lays traps for wild animals. Flee, flee, my ladies, and avoid their company—under these smiles are hidden deadly and painful poisons. And so may it please you, my most respected ladies, to cultivate virtue, to flee vice, to increase and multiply our City, and to rejoice and act well. And may I, your servant, commend myself to you, praying to God who by His grace has granted me to live in this world and to persevere in His holy service. May He in the end have mercy on my great sins and grant to me the joy which lasts forever, which I may, by His grace, afford to you. Amen.

HERE ENDS THE THIRD AND LAST PART OF THE BOOK OF THE CITY OF LADIES.

[END OF LATE MEDIEVAL ALLEGORY]

CREDITS

TEXT CREDITS

Aldhelm. From *The Riddles of Aldhelm*, translated by James Hall Pitman. Yale University Press, 1925. Reprinted by permission of Yale University Press.

Excerpt from *Amazons, Savages, and Machiavels travel and colonial writing in English, 1550–1630: an anthology* edited by Andrew Hadfield. Copyright © 2001. Reprinted by permission of Oxford University Press.

"The Anonimalle Chronicle." From *The Peasants' Revolt of 1381*, ed. by R.B. Dobson (1970). London: Macmillan. Reproduced with permission of Palgrave Macmillan.

Bede. From *Ecclesiastical History of the English People* by Bede, edited by Bertram Colgrave and R.A.B. Mynors (1969). By permission of Oxford University Press.

Beowulf. This translation first published by Penguin 1973. Copyright © Michael Alexander 1973. Reprinted by permission.

Boland, Eavan. "From the Irish of Pangur Ban" from *An Origin Like Water: Collected Poems 1967–1987* by Eavan Boland. Copyright © 1996 by Eavan Boland. Used by permission of W.W. Norton & Company, Inc.

Bradley, Marion Zimmer. Excerpt from Prologue to *The Mists of Avalon*. Copyright © 1982 by Marion Zimmer Bradley. Reprinted by permission of the author and the author's agents, Scovil Chichak Galen Literary Agency, Inc.

Charles D'Orleans. Excerpted from *Fortunes Stabilnes: Charles of Orleans's English Book of Love* by Mary-Jo Arn. Medieval & Renaissance Texts & Studies Volume, (Binghamton, NY, 1994), pp. 172–73, 211–12, 299. © Arizona Board of Regents for Arizona State University. Reprinted by permission.

Chaucer, Geoffrey. "General Prologue" from Chaucer's *The Canterbury Tales* is reproduced from the modern-verse translation by David Wright. Copyright © Estate of David Wright, 1985. By permission of PFD on behalf of the Estate of David Wright. From *Chaucer's Poetry: An Anthology for the Modern Reader*, 2nd ed., edited by E.Talbot Donaldson. Copyright © 1958, 1975 by Judith Anderson and Deirdre Donaldson. Used by permission of W.W. Norton & Company, Inc.

Christine de Pizan. From *The Book of the City of Ladies* by Christine de Pizan, translated by Earl Jeffrey Richards. Translation copyright © 1982, 1998 by Persea Books, Inc. Reprinted by permission of Persea Books, Inc. (New York).

From *The Cloud of Unknowing* translated by Clifton Wolters. (Penguin Classics, 1961). Copyright © Clifton Wolters, 1961. Reprinted by permission of Penguin Books Ltd.

Dafydd ap Gwilym. "Aubade," "One Saving Place," "Tales of a Wayside Inn," "The Winter," and "The Ruin" from *Nine Thorny Thickets: Selected Poems by Dafydd Ap Gwilym*, arrangements by Rolfe Humphries. Copyright © 1969 Rolfe Humphries. Reprinted by permission of Kent State University Press.

"De Heretico Comburendo" 1401. From *English Historical Documents, Volume IV, 1327–1485*, edited by A.R. Myers (1969). Published by Routledge. Reprinted by permission of Taylor & Francis Group.

"The Dream of the Rood," "The Wanderer," "Wulf and Eadwacer," "The Wife's Lament" from *The Exeter Book of Riddles*, translated by Kevin Crossley Holland. Copyright © Kevin Crossley Holland, 1993. By kind permission of the author c/o Rogers, Coleridge & White Ltd., 20 Powis Mews, London W11 1JN.

Dunbar, William. From *A Midsummer Eve's Dream: Variations on a Theme by William Dunbar* by A.D. Hope. Copyright © 1970 by Alec Derwent Hope. Used by permission of Viking Penguin, a division of Penguin Group (USA) Inc.

Edward I. From *Anglo-Scottish Relations 1174–1328*, edited and translated by E.L.G. Stones (1970) © 1965. By permission of Oxford University Press.

Gardner, John. From *Grendel* by John Gardner. Copyright © 1971 by John Gardner. Used by permission of Alfred A. Knopf, a division of Random House, Inc.

Geoffrey of Monmouth. From *History of Kings of Britain* by Geoffrey of Monmouth, translated by Lewis Thorpe. (Penguin Classics, 1966). Translation copyright © Lewis Thorpe, 1966. Reprinted by permission of Penguin Books Ltd.

Gower, John. From "The Voice of Crying" by John Gower from *The Major Works of John Gower*, edited by Eric W. Stockton. Copyright © 1962 by the University of Washington Press. Reprinted by permission.

"The Holi Prophete David Seith" from *The Idea of the Vernacular* edited by Jocelyn Wogan-Browne, Nicholas Watson, Andrew Taylor, and Ruth Evans, pp. 151–53. University Park, PA: Pennsylvania State University Press, 1990. Copyright © 1990 by The Pennsylvania State University. Reproduced by permission of the publisher.

"Judith." From *Anglo-Saxon Poetry: An Anthology of Old English Poems*, translated by S.A.J. Bradley. Copyright © 1982 by David Campbell Publishers Ltd. Reprinted by permission of David Campbell Publishers Ltd.

Kempe, Margery. From *The Book of Margery Kempe*, translated by B.A. Windeatt. (Penguin Classics, 1965). Copyright © B.A. Windeatt, 1965. Reprinted by permission of Penguin Books Ltd.

INDEX